... One of them created our
Dominican H. Upmann, so you
could forget Havana.
That's One-Upmannship.

CIGAR
Aficionado's

BUYING GUIDE

3RD EDITION

RATINGS & PRICES FOR
MORE THAN 1000 CIGARS

M. SHANKEN COMMUNICATIONS, INC.
NEW YORK

CIGAR AFICIONADO'S
BUYING GUIDE TO PREMIUM CIGARS
THIRD EDITION

Editor & Publisher . . . . Marvin R. Shanken

Executive Editor . . . . Michael Moaba
Managing Editor . . . . Gordon Mott
Editorial Director, Books . . . . Ann Berkhausen
Assistant Editors . . . . Amy Lyons, Tara Collins,
Shandana Durrani
Editorial Assistant . . . . Alan Richtmyer

Creative Director . . . . Martin Leeds
Art Director. . . . . Kathy McGilvery

Director of Business Development . . George Brightman
Marketing Manager . . . . Connie McGilvray
Advertising Director, Luxury Goods. . James J. Archambault Jr.
Associate, Business Development . . . Britta Jensen

Director of Advertising Services . . . . Elizabeth Ferrero
Advertising Services Manager . . . . . . Virginia Juliano

Director of Retail Sales. . . . . Christine Carroll
Director of Circulation . . . . Laura Zandi

PUBLISHED BY M. SHANKEN COMMUNICATIONS, INC.
387 Park Avenue South, New York, NY 10016
Telephone: 212-684-4224

Distributed by Running Press Book Publishers
125 South 22nd Street, Philadelphia, PA 19103
Telephone: 215-567-5080

ISBN: 1-881659-43-7

Manufactured in the United States of America

THE BOMBAY SAPPHIRE MARTINI. AS EXPLORED BY RICHARD JOLLEY.

POUR SOMETHING PRICELESS.

HENNESSY
Martini

Discover this classic. Combine 2 oz. of Hennessy V.S and a squeeze of lemon over ice.
Stir gently, don't shake. Strain into a chilled martini glass. Or ask your bartender.

Foreword

Welcome to the third edition of *Cigar Aficionado*'s Buying Guide. This year our guide contains ratings for over 1,000 cigars. The main listings, organized by score within size categories, includes complete tasting notes. There are also listings by size and country, and by brand. Preceding this is some general information which will help you to purchase, understand and enjoy your cigars.

In addition, we have compiled a list of over 3,000 leading tobacconists around the world where *Cigar Aficionado* is sold. That list includes virtually every major cigar retailer across the United States, and in the major foreign capitals.

The guide to cigar-friendly restaurants focuses on places that have responded to our questionnaires; the list includes over 1,350 dining establishments, bars, nightclubs, coffee bars and more. We ask that you please let us know immediately if a restaurant's cigar policy has changed. Also, we have provided a postcard that we invite you to fill out and drop in the mail if your favorite cigar-friendly restaurant was not included in this book.

Finally, *Cigar Aficionado* invites you to visit us on the World Wide Web—at **http://www.cigaraficionado.com**—where you will find additional information about cigar-friendly restaurants and current information about cigars, business, sports, travel and much more.

We hope this guide enhances your smoking pleasure. Enjoy.

Marvin R. Shanken

Marvin R. Shanken
Editor & Publisher

Table of

Contents

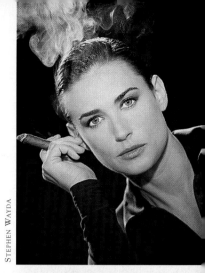

STEPHEN WAYDA

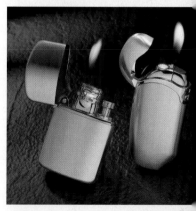

JEFF HARRIS

Shape, Size and Color

Today's cigar smokers are educated consumers. They are aware that there is an enormous selection of cigars available on the market today, and they want to know what they are buying. While most cigar smokers will always have their absolute favorite cigar, they want to experience all the different cigar sizes and tobacco fillers and be able to converse knowledgeably on the subject. It can be very confusing at times, but fortunately, there is an accepted vocabulary and certain basic criteria that apply to all hand-rolled cigars.

The criteria are fairly simple: brand, wrapper, color, and size and shape. Of course, country of manufacture is important too, but today tobacco is a global commodity and cigars made in the Dominican Republic may contain tobacco from Cameroon, Mexico and Nicaragua. Therefore, it may be important to you to understand the origins of tobacco in your

cigar because a particular type may create a certain flavor that you like.

Let's start with the brand name. The brand is the designation given by the manufacturer to a particular line of cigars. Punch, Partagas, Macanudo, Montecristo and Davidoff are just a few well-known names. You'll find these names on the cigar band, which is generally wrapped around the "head," or the closed end, of the cigar.

However, depending on which country you're in, even these well-known names can be a source of confusion. Some brands were first produced in Cuba; after Castro's revolution in 1959, many cigar manufacturers fled, believing they could take their brand names with them. The Cubans argued the brands belonged to the country. So today, you have a

Double Claro

Claro

Colorado Claro or Natural

Punch made in Cuba and one made in Honduras; a Partagas in Cuba and a Partagas in the Dominican Republic. The dual origin problem also affects Romeo y Julieta, La Gloria Cubana, Fonseca, H. Upmann, El Rey del Mundo, Cohiba and Montecristo. You can usually determine which is which by a small Habano or Havana inscribed on the band.

Color refers to the shade of the outer wrapper leaf. In the past, manufacturers used dozens of terms for the wrapper leaves which were grown in Cuba, Sumatra, Brazil and the United States; U.S. cigar makers often described eight to ten different shades. Today, there are six major color grades in use. And wrapper leaf is grown today not only in the countries mentioned above, but in Ecuador, Nicaragua, Honduras and Cameroon as well.

Here are the six basic shades:

• **Double Claro**: Light green, and often called candela. The leaves are cured with heat to fix the chlorophyll in the leaf. They often taste slightly sweet. At at one time a majority of American market cigars came with a light-green wrapper, but claro

claro is not as popular today.

• **Claro:** A light tan color, usually grown under shade tents. Claro is prized for its neutral flavor qualities.

• **Colorado Claro** or **Natural:** Light brown to brown. It is most often sun-grown.

• **Colorado - Colorado Maduro**: Brown to reddish brown. It is also usually shade-grown and has rich flavor and a subtle aroma.

• **Maduro:** From the Spanish word for "ripe," it refers to the extra length of time needed to produce a rich, dark-brown wrapper. A maduro should be silky and oily, with a rich strong flavor and mild aroma. There are several processes used to create maduro: one involves "cooking" the leaves in a pressure chamber; the other uses long, hotter-than-normal fermentation in huge bulks. A maduro wrapper usually produces a slightly sweet taste.

• **Oscuro:** Meaning dark, it is also called *negro* or black in tobacco-producing countries. It usually is left on the plant the longest, and it is matured or sweated the longest.

You've seen the brand you're looking for, you've spotted the color

| Colorado | Colorado Maduro | Maduro | Oscuro |

Parejos
(straight-sided cigars)

CIGARS SHOWN ACTUAL SIZE

Corona

Corona Gorda

Churchill

Double Corona (81/2")

12

Robusto

Petit Corona

Panatela

Lonsdale

Figurados

CIGARS SHOWN ACTUAL SIZE

Pyramid

Belicoso

Perfecto

Diademas (9")

Culebra

wrapper you like to smoke, now it's time to get down to choosing a size and shape. In Spanish, the word *vitola* conveniently covers both concepts, but in English we're left describing both size (girth and length) and shape. Most cigars come in boxes with a front mark that tells you the shape of the cigar such as Punch Double Corona or H. Upmann Lonsdale. As you come to know shapes, you also can make some assumptions about size, such as knowing that a double corona is not a short, thin cigar.

It's unfortunate that there is so much confusion about size and shape when there needn't be. But after several generations of every manufacturer independently deciding which size name went with which length and girth, there is no simple logic to the definitions. In fact, haphazard naming conventions have resulted in the same word, such as Churchill, being used by different manufacturers for cigars of different sizes. If any single statement can be made about the standards of different countries, it is that Cuban standards tend to be more uniform. That's because there is one body governing the state-owned tobacco company in Cuba, and it oversees the entire industry there.

The basic measurement standard, however, is the same. The only variations are whether it is expressed in metric or U.S. customary systems. Length, therefore, is listed in inches or centimeters and thickness or diameter, or ring gauge as it commonly known, is in 64ths of an inch or millimeters. A classic corona size, for example, is 6 by 42, which means it is six inches long and 42/64ths of an inch thick.

If you're searching for common denominators to use as a starting point for shape, it helps to know that all cigars can be divided into two categories: parejos, or straight cigars, and figurados, or irregular shapes.

Simply put, parejos are straight-sided cigars, the kind with which most smokers are familiar. There are three basic groups in this category: coronas, panatelas and lonsdales.

Listed below are some standard size names with their standard sizes in parentheses.

• **Coronas** (6 inches by 42 or 44 ring gauge) have traditionally been the manufacturer's benchmark against which all other cigars are measured. Coronas have an open "foot" (the end you light) and a closed "head" (the end you smoke); the head is most often rounded. A Churchill normally measures 7 by 47. A robusto is 5 by 50. A double corona is 7 1/2 by 49. In other words, these are all variations on the corona theme.
• **Panatelas** (7 x 38) are usually longer than coronas, but they are dramatically thinner. They also have an open foot and closed head.
• **Lonsdales** (6 3/4 by 42) are thicker than panatelas, but longer than coronas.

The irregular shapes, or figurados, encompass every out-of-the ordinary-shaped cigar. The following list comprises the major types:

• **Pyramid:** It has a pointed, closed head and widens to an open foot.
• **Belicoso:** A small pyramid-shaped cigar with a rounded head rather than a point.
• **Torpedo:** A shape with a pointed head, a closed foot and a bulge in the middle.
• **Perfecto:** This looks like the cigar in cartoons with two closed rounded ends and a bulge in the middle.
• **Culebra:** Three panatelas braided together.
• **Diademas:** A giant cigar 8 inches or longer. Most often it has an open foot, but occasionally it will come with a perfecto or closed foot.

Remember, even with these "classic" irregular shapes, there are variations among manufacturers. Some cigars called belicosos look like pyramids, and some called torpedos look like pyramids because they do not have a perfecto tip. Confusing? Yes, it is.

Unfortunately, it really is self-defeating to try to talk about "classic" or "normal" ranges for any cigars on the market today. The basic shape designations can vary so greatly from company to company that they make little sense. Once you've become comfortable with the terminology, however, ask your tobacconist what the exact dimensions are of the cigar you like to smoke. Use that as your

The Macanudo Crown

Of all premium-cigar makers, only Macanudo
crowns the head of every one of its cigars.
Unlike a flat head, a crowned cigar head does
not bend or break under pressure. Perfectly
rounded and supported by the tobacco
beneath the cigar's wrapper leaf, a crowned
head makes a cigar easier to cut, smoother to
draw and more satisfying to smoke.

MACANUDO.
True Cigar Taste

base to branch out to bigger or smaller, longer or shorter cigars. And, don't assume because you like a Churchill from one company that you're going to get the same-size cigar with that name from another manufacturer.

There are some other designations that are worth knowing because they refer to the style of packing. An 8-9-8 designation, for instance, simply means that the cigars are stacked in three rows inside the box, eight on the bottom, nine in the middle and eight on top. They usually come in a distinctive round-sided box. Amatista refers to a glass jar of 50 cigars, originally packaged by H. Upmann, which was developed for smokers who wanted a "factory fresh" smoke. Finally, there are tubos, cigars that are packed in aluminum, glass or even wooden tubes; a tightly sealed tube will keep cigars fresh for a long period of time. Some cigars are also box-pressed, meaning they are put inside a box so tightly that they acquire a soft, squarish appearance.

IF ITS LEGENDARY IMAGE DOESN'T TEMPT YOU,
SURELY THE RICHNESS OF ITS FLAVOR
AND AROMA WILL

MONTECRISTO

Experience this legendary "cigar of cigars" for yourself.
Some temptations are just too great to ignore.

Taste

We all know that individuals are attracted to different taste sensations, and the taste of a cigar is no exception. We all have our personal preferences—but anyone can learn to distinguish a bad cigar from an excellent one.

While smoking a cigar is the central act in appreciating it, there's more to it than just putting it in your mouth and puffing away. Professional tobacco experts and experienced smokers practice some basic steps in connoisseurship that are worth every cigar lover's effort to master.

Forming an overall impression of a cigar means using all of your senses: sight, touch, smell, taste and even your hearing. First, sight and touch go hand in hand. The first thing that you

Danny DeVito

STEPHEN WAYDA

do when you remove a cigar from a box, or from your humidor, is inspect it. Even if this act is only subconscious, the appearance and feel of the cigar wrapper tell a story, and several lessons about taste can be learned from the outside of any cigar. Then, listen to it. Roll the cigar between fingers in order to determine the moisture content of the wrapper and the filler. It should be firm, but should give a little when squeezed, and there shouldn't be any rustling or crackling of the leaves.

A wrapper does not make or break a cigar. But it plays an important role because it provides texture and beauty, and is your first contact with the personality and character of a cigar. Even before you light up, seeing and feeling a wrapper with nice silky oil and without visual blemishes should give you certain expectations. Wrapper appearance will vary depending upon where the leaf was grown.

The best wrappers from Cuba are indeed like silk, with exceedingly close cell structure—they don't feel like vegetable matter because their surface is so smooth. These wrappers have an elasticity and strength often lacking in wrapper leaves from other countries.

By contrast, a Cameroon wrapper shows oil in its bumpy surface, called

Demi Moore

"tooth" in the tobacco industry. These bumps are a good sign that great taste and aroma will follow, even if the texture of the leaf isn't silky. Wrappers from Connecticut and Ecuador are somewhat close in surface texture, though not in color. Better Ecuadoran leaf has less tooth, is smooth to the touch, and has a mattelike appearance. The Connecticut wrapper shows more color depth, a bit more tooth and a nice shine.

Despite the differences in oils, seeing oil in any wrapper leaf indicates that the cigar has been well-humidified (oil secretes from tobacco at 70 to 72 percent humidity) and that the smoke should be relatively cool. A cool smoke is a tastier one, because it means the tobacco isn't carbonizing or overheating, which can limit the flavors.

If you see cracks or ripples in the surface of the wrapper leaf, you know that the cigar was exposed to cycles of over-humidification and excessive dryness. This, too, is important. If the cigar is forced through rapid cycles of expansion and contraction, the internal construction is destroyed. A cigar with internal damage will smoke unevenly, or "plug," drawing uneven-

STEPHEN WAYDA

Excalibur
by Hoyo de Monterrey

Finest of Their Kind In the Best of Taste

Since 1845 our master cigar-makers developed a technique to marry the full-bodied flavor of the English market wrapper with the supreme mildness of the Claro into a world-class, hand-made cigar like Excalibur.

Our craftsmen make sure that every precious long-filler leaf, binder and wrapper that goes into each Excalibur is hand-bunched in the traditional, time-honored way, then packed in a Spanish cedar Boite Nature Box to enhance the seasoning and taste to guarantee a classic smoke that is truly the finest of its kind.

Available at Fine Tobacconists Everywhere. There are eight sizes and shapes available in English Claro and Rich Maduro to satisfy the most discriminating smoker.

Imported by Danby-Palacio Division

VILLAZON & CO., INC.
25 Park Way, Upper Saddle River, NJ 07458

Sold under the brand name
Excalibur in the U.K. and Continental Europe
and other Foreign Markets.

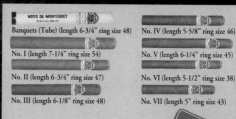

Banquets (Tube) (length 6-3/4" ring size 48)

No. I (length 7-1/4" ring size 54)

No. II (length 6-3/4" ring size 47)

No. III (length 6-1/8" ring size 48)

No. IV (length 5-5/8" ring size 46)

No. V (length 6-1/4" ring size 45)

No. VI (length 5-1/2" ring size 38)

No. VII (length 5" ring size 43)

Introduce a little civility back into your life with premium, conveniently sized Excalibur Miniatures.

INTRODUCING
15 YEAR
CASK STRENGTH GLENFIDDICH®

It has taken fifteen long years to create this masterpiece. Slowly and patiently in Dufftown, Scotland, selected casks of extraordinary whisky have been carefully married to yield a single malt scotch of remarkable character, rich bouquet and full flavor. Because there are fridays and then, there are Fridays.

The Friday Scotch

(continued)

ly. This may still occur due to faulty construction, but your chances are better with a perfect wrapper than with a broken one.

After lighting your cigar, look at the ash. According to most cigar experts, a white ash is better than a gray one. This is not merely an aesthetic issue; better soil produces whiter ash and more taste. Soil can be manipulated through fertilization, but if too much magnesium (a key ingredient in producing white ash) is added to the mix, the ash will flake, and nobody wants a messy cigar, even if the ash is white. Gray ash may hint at deficiencies in the soil, thus in the flavor.

A final visual cue is the burn rate. You can taste a cigar that is burning improperly because an uneven burn distorts the flavor of the blend. Simply put, a cigar is designed to burn different tobaccos evenly throughout the length of the smoke. A cigar may start off mild and grow stronger or change in some other way; these changes can be attributed to the location of the tobaccos. Thus, if a cigar burns unevenly, the delicate balance designed to produce a particular flavor or taste is disturbed, and the cigar will not taste right.

The sense of taste is located mainly on the tongue and to a lesser

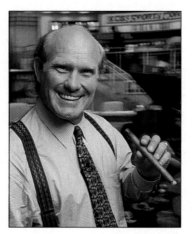

Terry Bradshaw

degree on the roof of the mouth. There exist only four basic tastes: sweet, sour, salty and bitter. Everything else is either a combination of these four or a combination of taste and aroma. Although food flavor descriptors are now being used, most tobacco men stick with words like acidic, salty, bitter, sweet, bite, sour, smooth, heavy, full-bodied, rich and balanced. Aroma too is important, and most cigar makers not only taste for flavors, but smell for aroma at the same time.

It takes many different types of tobacco to come up with a blend of tastes that works. And to reach a consistent taste, one that stays the same year after year, is the most difficult task for any cigar maker. No two leaves of tobacco are the same, and no two cigars can be the same year to year.

Cigar makers utilize different tobaccos to try to compensate for nature. They continually seek a blend that will achieve consistency and at the same time create some flavor complexity. A good blend uses tobaccos from different geographic zones, varieties, grades and harvests, so that the cigar will be complete and balanced.

Achieving this balance is difficult. There are an infinite number of variables that can alter the taste of any blend: soil, tobacco variety, climate, ground condition, curing, the harvester, fermentation, manufacturing process and the humidity of the cigar.

Two especially important factors in taste are aging and construction. Aging provides smoothness, richness and roundness—qualities you won't find in a cigar right from the roller's table.

Even with the finest blend in the world, a poorly constructed cigar will be less enjoyable than a perfectly made cigar of only modest blend. A loose draw (a cigar that burns fast, letting a lot of smoke pass through quickly because it is underfilled) will increase smoking temperature, destroying taste. A tight draw, on the other hand, reduces the sensitivity of the taste buds; drawing less smoke means having less to taste. Moreover, a tight draw may extinguish more frequently, and relighting makes a cigar harsh.

The variability of cigars may be one of the most essential things a consumer should remember. Cigars

Whoopi Goldberg

are handmade products, produced by skilled artisans in quantities of anywhere from 100 to 300 a day, depending on the size of the cigar and the manufacturing process. Like any handmade item, cigars are subject to human error. A bit too much tobacco here, a bit too little there, or a fatigued hand applying the wrong amount of pressure can completely alter the final product. All manufacturers inadvertantly let the occasional faulty cigar slip through their quality control system and reach the marketplace. What should a consumer do? Accept the reality, throw out the cigar and light up a new one. It's extremely unlikely that the next one will be flawed unless you are smoking a second-rate brand.

And, once you're smoking your favorite cigar, you won't even have to think about the complex set of processes that brought the cigar to your hand. It will most likely taste as great as the last one, and you'll already be looking forward to the next one.

JOHN HARDING

26

A FAMILY PORTRAIT

Astral®, Don Tomás® Special Edition, Don Tomás® International and Don Tomás®:
The premium cigar brands of United States Tobacco International.
The finest tobacco leaves, are grown and harvested, then lovingly rolled by hands trained
in the classic Cuban tradition. A size, shape and taste to please every cigar lover.

For distribution information, call toll free: 888-6-CIGAR-1

U.S. TOBACCO INTERNATIONAL, INC.

Cutting and Lighting

Cutting and lighting are more than just essential steps in cigar smoking; when done with ease and perfection the ritual is a sign of a true connoisseur. It is important for a cigar smoker to master the procedure because an improper cut can destroy a cigar. The smoke can become hot, the cigar may burn unevenly, or the wrapper leaf may unravel—allowing bits of unsightly tobacco to lodge in the smoker's teeth. When a cigar smoker is comfortable with his technique he can sit back and enjoy a smoke with

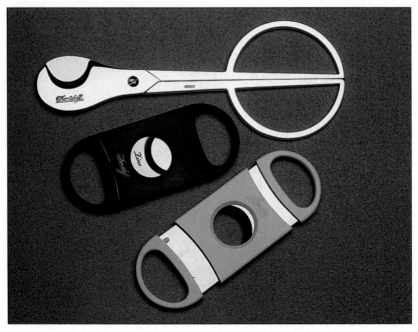

GENE COLEMAN

Cutters by Davidoff.

Most
critics agree
that our cigar
is better than
many Cuban
cigars.

And the
rest of them,
well, they're
just wrong.

The Signature Collection,
outranked 6 top Cuban
brands in a blind tasting.

1-888-477-2447
www.caribbeancigar.com

confidence.

Each smoker has a favorite way to snip off the end of a cigar. A ritual so personal is subject to inflexible opinions about right and wrong methods, and the choice of method is often traceable to the mentor who taught a given smoker to appreciate cigars. Regardless of method,

Neptune lighters from Prometheus.

the same wrapper leaf but has been shaped with a knife to be wrapped around the head end of the cigar, which is secured with the same kind of glue. The latter technique is obvious in some cigars because instead of being smoothed out underneath the flag, the leaf is twisted

though—whether wedge, guillotine, scissors, bull's-eye, piercer, knife or teeth—the quality of the cutting tool often relates directly to the quality of the cut. And there are a few basic rules that can lead to a perfect cut.

If mistakes are made in the cut, it may be because the smoker doesn't understand how cigars are made. All premium handmade cigars are closed off at one end (called the "head") in the manufacturing process. In some cases, this closure is made with a separate piece of the tobacco leaf called a "cap," usually cut from the same wrapper leaf that's on the cigar. It is secured with a special vegetable-base glue. Others are finished off with a "flag," a piece of leaf that is part of

off in a pigtail. In all cases, the cap or flag closes off the wrapper and binder leaves that hold the filler leaves together in the "bunch."

The goal of a guillotine or scissors cut is to clip off enough of the end to expose the filler leaves, but to leave enough of the cap or flag on to keep the wrapper on the cigar. That usually means a cut of about two millimeters, or about one-sixteenth of an inch. If you're not into metrics or rulers, another safe gauge is to look for the "shoulder" of the cigar. In a flat-end cigar, it may be quite noticeable; in a rounded end, it's a little harder to find but basically it's where the curve of the end straightens out. In a well-made cigar, the cap or flag usually

YOUR QUALITY OF LIFE DEPENDS UPON THE CHOICES YOU MAKE...

Don Lino

HAND MADE

extends over the shoulder. A cut made at the shoulder, or just a touch above, may be perfect.

Guillotine cutters must be kept sharp. Once they become dull, the blade begins to "push" the tobacco leaves, often tearing the side of the cigar away from the blade. To achieve a clean cut with a single-blade guillotine, the cigar should be positioned against the far side of the opening, the blade brought to rest against the cigar, and the end snipped with a sharp or quick thrust. Most single-blade guillotines also have a pocket for the blade; these must be regularly cleaned of tobacco pieces, or the blade may jam. Beware of inexpensive guillotine cutters with a single blade; they can damage cigars.

Double-bladed guillotines eliminate the problem of the cigar's far side being torn by an improper stroke of the blade. Be sure the cigar is flush against one blade before attempting to make a cut. The cutting motion should be crisp. These cutters should also be cleaned, but their design usually prevents jamming; an annual cleaning should be enough.

Scissors are more problematic. A good scissors must be properly balanced between the handles and the clipping edges. If not, it is very hard to hold the cigar steady against one of the cutting blades to get a clean cut. Also, if the hinge doesn't allow for a long movement of your fingers, it can be very hard to get a straight cut across the end of the cigar. But again, the same principle applies—you want

to cut off enough of the cigar to expose the filler leaves without removing all of the cap.

One of the most popular cutters today leaves a V-shaped wedge in the end of the cigar. A greater surface area of the filler bunch is exposed than in a straight cut across the end. But smokers who like to chew the end of their cigars should be wary of a wedge cut. If too much pressure is applied to the end of the cigar, the wedge can collapse. This causes an accumulation of moisture and tars, and can make the draw tighter. If you pull too hard on the cigar, it can make the cigar smoke hotter and harsher.

Two other types of cutters, a bull's-eye and a piercer, accomplish the same basic cut: putting a hole in the end of the cigar without damaging the cap's adhesion to the cigar. The bull's-eye uses a hollow-tip cutter that is turned in a quick circular motion. Experts advise against making the hole too deep; a too-deep cut can draw the air and smoke down toward the middle of the cigar, making it smoke hotter. The same caution should be used with the piercer, which often looks like an auger.

Many people swear by a simple knife or one-sided razor blade. Although the free blade requires a steady hand, the depth and angle of the cut, especially in a V-shaped wedge, can be gauged precisely according to the smoker's preference. The key to a successful knife cut is the sharpness of the blade. But unlike

some guillotine cutters, a knife blade can be sharpened on a whetstone.

No article on cutting would be complete without the simplest cutting device of all: your teeth. This way is certainly convenient—you always have your teeth with you. But experts, many of whom incidentally make a living selling fancy cutters in addition to cigars, argue that only the very skilled teeth cutter can ensure a good, clean cut every time. They argue you can't see the cigar, you don't know exactly where the cut is being made, and you run the risk the cap and wrapper. The element of bad manners: out the tobacco can be uns ut in a pinch, teeth always w

Let's dispel a few about lighting cigars. Ye e of a wooden match or a ce called a "spill" is elegant can be effective. But it's of e-consuming and unwieldy se it takes more than one mat properly light a cigar. There any good butane lighter is ar cient cigar smoker's companio e one caveat concerns fluid light While lighter manufacturers di this, it is a fact that oil-

taste to a ga, so you must be careful not to draw too heavily when using this type of lighter. Fluid lighters are dependable, though, and tend to have a lot of lights in them.

Now you're ready to light. Cool smoke is the goal of a perfect light. There is a simple rule to follow: Never let the cigar touch the flame. When you light up, hold the cigar at a 45-degree angle above the flame, just far enough away so that the tip of the flame dances up to the cigar but never quite touches it. Then, to assure a proper light, rotate the cigar in your hand so that the foot of the

JEFF HARRIS

34

cigar lights all the way around. When a lightly burning ring surrounds the tip of the cigar and begins to creep toward the center of the foot, blow out lightly through the cigar. Not everyone does this, but it makes sense; rather than breathing a first puff of lighter (or match-born sulfur) gases into the cigar, your first exhalation will rid the tobacco of these unwanted flavors.

Then you are ready to begin smoking. Do so by continuing to rotate the cigar as you take your first few puffs. This will regulate the burn, ensure that it is even and prevent "tunneling," which is when one side of the cigar burns faster than the other. This technique applies to all forms of lighting: matches, cedar strips or lighters.

Some people wonder if a cigar

wax vapors can ruin its taste. If you're using matches, long ones are preferable. If you use short ones, strike two at one time, let the sulfur burn off and then commence lighting—by using two, you get a broader flame and make it easier to get an even light.

Lighters are the most portable source of fire, and most can be lit with one hand while the other holds the cigar. A good lighter should have a certain heft; some are cut from solid blocks of brass and feel like it. But as important as the weight is the feel in your hand, like a good knife. It should be balanced and fit the size of your palm.

Opening the lighter should be effortless. The cap should swing open smoothly, and the hinge mechanism should be silent. (A hollow or clunky sound can indicate inferior materi-

minute can ensure a smooth, cool smoke, sometimes that isn't feasible. You may be on the telephone, or in a conversation with someone, and just forget to keep puffing. If your cigar goes out, by all means, relight it—just use the same caution in lighting it as you would with a fresh cigar. However, be aware that after a couple of relights, a cigar can begin to get harsh.

If you insist on spills or matches, there are a few rules to follow. You may use a candle to light a spill, but never use a candle to light a cigar;

ly if you're lighting a cigar. The flame should be adjustable, and should be fat, again something that is more important for a cigar smoker than a cigarette smoker. Some cigar lighters actually have two flames.

In the end, the goal is to have a trouble-free light. Since you'll be using it frequently, look for a lighter that feels comfortable and works in all situations including windy ones. If a lighter is not only functional but attractive, you'll be carrying it around like a pocket watch forever.

Storing and Carrying Cigars

The cigar revolution of the 1990's has spawned a surge in humidor sales. One of the hallmarks of a true cigar aficionados is ownership of a well-made humidor that will provide the special environment needed to care for precious cigars.

A humidor should maintain a cigar at its peak of "smokability." This isn't simple, because a humidor must re-create the tropical or semi-tropical environment in which most cigar tobacco is grown and where most fine, hand-rolled premium cigars are manufactured and aged. Makeshift tropical environments—like a steamy bathroom or a zippered plastic bag with a moist paper towel—don't work well.

A cigar is composed of multiple layers of tobacco. In an inconsistently humid environment like a shower stall, the outside of the cigar will dry

once the mist is cut off, but the inside of the cigar will still be damp. The inside "bunch" of tobacco will swell while the wrapper contracts and splits open, destroying your investment.

The most crucial characteristic of a fine humidor is that it provides a consistently tropical environment (about 68-70 degrees Fahrenheit and 70-72 percent humidity) over a long period of time. Remember, this doesn't only mean how often you need to add water to the humidification system; it also means that 20 years from now the box lid hasn't warped and the hinges still open easily and quietly.

Diamond Crown's Biltmore humidor

JAMES WORRELL

Davidoff accoutrements... for those who are obsessed with quality.

Davidoff-New York
535 Madison Avenue
800.548.4623

Davidoff-Beverly Hills
232 Via Rodeo
800.328.0039

For Your Nearest Davidoff Retailer Call 800.328.4365

Reputable humidor manufacturers include Diamond Crown, Davidoff, Danny Marshall, Dunhill, Elie Bleu, Michel Perrenoud and Savinelli. Excellent larger humidors, really standing floor cases and even credenza size boxes, are also being made today by manufacturers such as J. Pendergast, Kreitman-Thelan, Vinotemp and others.

The components of a good humidor can be judged easily. Starting from the inside of the box, look for details like perfectly squared and fitted seams. You shouldn't see any glue, and a gap in a joint spells trouble because it provides an exit for moisture, eventually resulting in warping. Cedar is the best wood for the inside of a humidor because of its ability to enhance the aging process. It allows the various tobaccos in a cigar the chance to "marry" so that the cigar is not composed of separate tobacco flavors, but of subtle nuances of taste.

The rim of the box should be constructed uniformly, with tight tolerances, so that the lid closes with the solid feel of a Mercedes Benz car door. An inner lip, especially a lower one, will protect cigars from dry outside air. This is all the more necessary in a box without a lock, because only the weight of the lid will keep it tightly shut. A humidor lid should never close like a safe, however, because if no air were allowed to circulate, musty smells would destroy your cigars. The entire box should be balanced, both when left closed and when opened. (The last thing you want is to have your box tumble off the desk because the lid is too heavy or bounces when lifted.)

Of course, a perfectly constructed box is worthless if it has no means of providing humidity. At one time old apple cores were thought to do this nicely, but modern humidification systems are more reliable. Most humidifiers rely on some variety of sponges, chemical compounds or plain bottles to provide moisture. However, remember that prime cigar aging demands constant humidity levels. Usually, humidor instruction manuals proclaim low maintenance. But once you've prepared the humidor for use—try wiping the interior with a damp cloth before loading it up with cigars—you should rely as much on the "feel" of the cigars inside as on the humidification sys-

JAMES WORRELL

38

**Daniel Marshall's
Ambiente humidor**

tem. If the cigars feel dry even though the humidity gauge reads 70 percent, you should check the device.

Other practical features, in order of importance, are: a tray, which provides the owner the option of storing cigars at more than one level so that they are exposed to varying degrees of humidity (always place parched cigars as far as possible from the humidification device so they will regain humid-

on larger units.

Keep in mind that in a home or office, a humidor shouldn't overwhelm its surroundings. Deciding where to put your new purchase before buying it might help you find a humidor that will both look good and function well. If you made the right choice, twenty years from now—when your son starts to covet your humidor—you will know for certain that your investment was worthwhile. You didn't buy a mere "box."

Another key question is what to do with cigars when you travel across the country, or across town for a big dinner. The best travel humidors and cigar cases are designed to keep cigars in perfect, smokable condition. Constructed of little more than metal, wood, leather and thread, they are just as simple and refined as what

for holding cutting instruments, which are occasionally added to humidors. A hygrometer, while fancy-looking, is seldom accurate even in the most expensive desk-top models.

The appearance of your humidor is entirely up to you. A deep, rich lacquer finish is beautiful and functional and should be judged as you would the finish of a dining-room table. Also, a felt bottom will serve as protection for both the box and the surface where it sits. Handles are often helpful additions, especially

flawless design.

Cases, whether telescoping, multi-fingered, open (without separate cigar dividers), tubular or some combination of the above, should always do at least two things exceptionally well: protect and hold your cigars. The equation is simple—you want whatever cigars you smoke most often to fit easily into your cigar case.

If you smoke a longer cigar, a telescoping case will be necessary. And if you smoke various ring gauges during the course of the same day, avoid fingered cases which are constructed to

J.G. Pendergast humidor

hold specific ring gauges and will not stretch to hold larger sizes.

If you smoke the same ring gauge consistently, a fingered case is a good bet because it will keep your cigars from rolling around or rubbing against the interior of the case, especially when you get down to the last cigar. Open cases have no safeguards to prevent your cigars from rattling around once you've removed one or two.

If you'll be stowing a two-, three- or four-fingered case in your glove compartment for your drive to and from the office or for weekend jaunts in the country, any good quality case will do. Thick leather, of almost any hide, is tough and will resist the minor jostling caused by potholes and traffic jams.

If upon your arrival at work you're going to remove the case from the car and stow it in your coat pocket, be sure that it will fit. Most four-fingered models are very wide, and unless your chest size and tailor are cooperative, you might look like you're packing a weapon.

Aside from a standard check for stitch quality and uniform construction—with no rough edges showing—picking out a leather case that will protect your cigars is an easy task. A good case should slide open with minimal effort (test this by putting some of your own cigars into the case), and should be lined, to protect your cigars from leathery aromas and prevent the wrapper leaf from catching on any rough inner hide. Choosing a cigar case is much like buying new shoes: quality (which includes durability), fit, ease of use and style are the most important factors, in that order.

If your travel entails bumping (literally) into strangers, take more

"Agnes, have you seen my Don Diegos?"

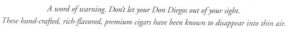

A word of warning. Don't let your Don Diegos out of your sight.
These hand-crafted, rich-flavored, premium cigars have been known to disappear into thin air.

care in selecting a case—
or consider a wooden or
silver tube. Tubes are
both bulky and heavy,
but they can certainly
take more abuse than
leather, and they will
keep a cigar fresh for up
to 72 hours. If you mind
the extra weight but still
need heavy-duty protec-
tion, opt for a telescoping
case with very thick
leather.

Once you've selected
a case or tube suitable
for your needs, use it
wisely. Slide fresh cigars
into your case in the
morning, and be sure to
remove any unsmoked cig-

Ducas humidors for Nat Sherman in Buffalo Green and Colorado Black.

ars at night, returning them to storage in your humidor. Most cases will
not keep cigars fresh for more than a
day. And whatever you do, never
store a partially smoked cigar in a
case—the aroma will linger, affect-
ing every cigar placed in the case
long after this careless mistake.

Unlike cases, travel humidors
are too big for local commuting. The
smallest models hold five Churchill-
size cigars (one more cigar than the
largest standard case), and are much
too big to fit in a jacket pocket. The
advantage to this bulk is that a travel humidor will keep cigars fresh
much longer than all pocket-sized
cases because it comes with a
humidification unit.

Even though a travel humidor is
designed for a multiday trip and a
case is not, your expectations for both
products should be similar. Again,
remember the size and shape of your
cigars, and be certain that the box
will accommodate them. Then
inspect the details. Look for features
like solid rear hinges, preferably of
the "piano" variety, which stretch the
length of the box. Also, be certain
that the humidification unit inside
the box will stay put while you sprint
to catch a plane or toss your luggage
into the back of a taxicab.

If all goes well, both you and your
cigars will arrive in fine condition,
ready to smoke away the troubles of
an all-too-fast modern age.

GENE COLEMAN

Buying Cigars

A favorite story among cigar merchants, as told by the late Zino Davidoff, concerns the destruction of the Dunhill shop in London during the German blitz of World War II. In the aftermath of the bombing the store manager's first priority—at 2 a.m.—was to inform Prime Minister Winston Churchill that his cigars were safe. We should all be so lucky as to receive such devoted attention!

In reality, with the large number of cigar customers today, it is very hard for a tobacconist to get to know his clientele personally. However, a good tobacconist is still the best resource a cigar smoker can have. So take the time to get to know yours. Make sure that he knows what you like to smoke. Maybe over time you'll get lucky; when he receives a shipment of hard-to-get cigars, he'll put aside a few for you.

Having a hometown tobacconist

RICK FRIEDMAN/BLACK STAR

León Jimenes
Premium Cigars

AGING

"Aging appears to be a simple process, as simple as storing. This may be true for many cigars. But for León Jimenes, it is an appreciation of time. Time that begins with the harvest and extends to a point of perfection... solely determined by knowledge. Only then, are León Jimenes cigars ready to be enjoyed."

Guillermo León

doesn't solve the question of what you do when you're on the road. Being in a strange city without cigars can be frustrating. What should you look for when judging whether a tobacconist has his act together?

If you ask a tobacconist for cigars and he shows you into a walk-in humidor where moist air caresses your face, and you almost need a sweater because the temperature is right around 70 degrees, you know you're in the right place. Tobacconists who take the time, trouble and expense to construct a properly humidified environment where cigars are kept in perfect smoking condition are definitely worth the detour. If you are at all in doubt about the storage conditions, ask to pick up a cigar. Feel it. If it is supple and its oils are clearly intact, then you can pretty much rest assured that the cigar you buy will be ready to smoke.

What are some of the trouble signs? First of all, if you are shown a glass counter display case that looks

like it's been there forever, be sure to check out the cigars. Some of the humidification units in this type of display case are not very efficient, or they require regular maintenance that they may not always get. The evidence will be in the cigars themselves. Again, there is no substitute for asking to feel a cigar. If you're not allowed to touch, be suspicious.

You may also want to ask about the freshness of the cigars. If the store looks as if it pays more attention to

JOHN RIZZO/BLACK STAR

46

DANNEMANN

El noble cigarillo

Os charutos pequenos Dannemann são famosos em muitos países do mundo. Suas ligas misturadas conforme antigas receitas bem guardadas, suas capas das melhores proveniências do mundo e o seu preparo cuidadoso garantem um prazer exclusivo.

Fabricados com licença da Cia. Brasileira de Charutos Dannemann e Dannemann AG

NEW AROMA

20 SMALL CIGARS, DANNEMANN

DANNEMANN

MOODS

El noble cigarillo

GET IN THE MOODS.

Moods is a premium cigarillo with an exciting aroma. It combines a unique filler blend with a rich, silky wrapper to deliver a short, fully satisfying smoke. Its aroma is its most outstanding feature. You'll be surprised by the way it enhances your surroundings. That's why Moods is becoming Europe's favorite cigarillo with smokers and non-smokers alike. Taste it, share the exciting aroma

DANNEMANN

gifts and magazines than to smok-
ables, you may not have any idea how
long the cigars in the display case
have been there. A store with heavy
traffic will turn over its inventory
more frequently. In high-volume outlets, even counter-style humidification
units may be completely satisfactory
because consumer demand forces the
owner to pay attention to his cigars.

Some additional factors are
important if you are trying to estab-
lish a long-term relationship with a
tobacconist. Is he willing to entertain
your requests for special orders, or
does he insist that you try one of his
"store brands"? The latter phenomenon may indicate that the tobacconist is most interested in selling
what he has in stock. On the other
hand, if you're smoking a particular
brand, and the tobacconist says he
has several brands that are similiar to
your favorite, try them out. You're
likely to get a cigar that you like, and
in the future you'll have an alterna-
tive if for some reason the store runs
out of your preferred smoke.

Today, it's important to find a
tobacconist who is following the cigar
market closely. Because of the boom
in cigar sales in the last few years,

new brands and sizes are coming on
the market monthly. A good tobacconist will know what's available and
what kind of tobacco is being used in
the cigar, and if he or she knows your
preferences, he may be able to recommend some new cigars that suit your
taste.

There's another new factor to
consider in any visit to a retailer.
Around the country, one of the most
common retailer complaints is how
customers treat cigars on the shelf.
Although we do recommend that you
ask to touch cigars, touching does
not require squeezing so hard the
wrapper breaks. A gentle pressure on
the cigar tells you all you need to
know about its condition. You should
also be considerate of the shopper
behind you. You may have seen
tobacco men breathe deeply from the
open foot of a cigar, but don't try it
yourself. First of all, the average consumer doesn't have a clue what he's
smelling for. And if you have the
urge to try the smell test in a retail
environment, think about the guy
coming in after you or the dozens
who've been there before you. It's not
necessary to determine the quality or
condition of the cigar.

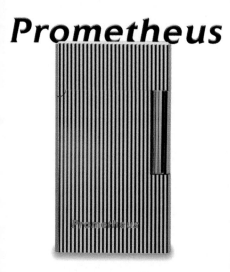

Prometheus

Prometheus
MADE IN FRANCE

Prometheus International, Inc.

5680 Bandini Blvd., Bell, CA 90201-6407, U.S.A.
Telephone (213) 261-7200 • Facsimile (213) 261-0801

Cigar smokers of the world -

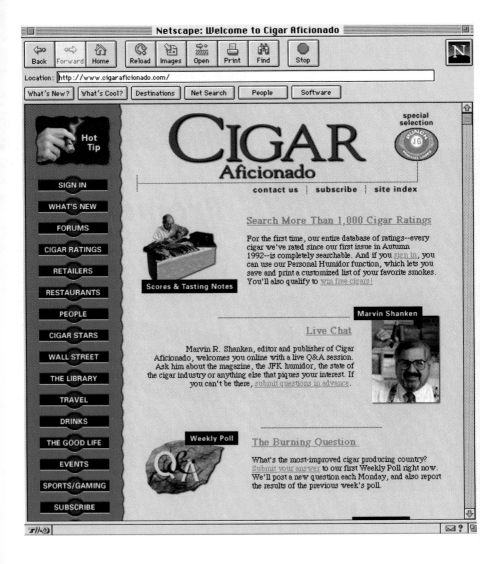

Back | Forward | Home | Reload | Images | Open | Print | Find | Stop

Location: http://www.cigaraficionado.com/

What's New? | What's Cool? | Destinations | Net Search | People | Software

CIGAR
Aficionado

special selection

contact us | subscribe | site index

Hot Tip

SIGN IN
WHAT'S NEW
FORUMS
CIGAR RATINGS
RETAILERS
RESTAURANTS
PEOPLE
CIGAR STARS
WALL STREET
THE LIBRARY
TRAVEL
DRINKS
THE GOOD LIFE
EVENTS
SPORTS/GAMING
SUBSCRIBE

Scores & Tasting Notes

Search More Than 1,000 Cigar Ratings

For the first time, our entire database of ratings--every cigar we've rated since our first issue in Autumn 1992--is completely searchable. And if you sign in, you can use our Personal Humidor function, which lets you save and print a customized list of your favorite smokes. You'll also qualify to win free cigars!

Marvin Shanken

Live Chat

Marvin R. Shanken, editor and publisher of Cigar Aficionado, welcomes you online with a live Q&A session. Ask him about the magazine, the JFK humidor, the state of the cigar industry or anything else that piques your interest. If you can't be there, submit questions in advance.

Weekly Poll

The Burning Question

What's the most-improved cigar producing country? Submit your answer to our first Weekly Poll right now. We'll post a new question each Monday, and also report the results of the previous week's poll.

you have a new virtual home!

Cigar Aficionado, your source for the most in-depth information on hand-made cigars and the artisans who make them is on the World Wide Web. Find a wealth of information online including:

- **Cigar Ratings**
- **Retail Tobacconists**
- **Cigar Friendly Restaurants**
- **Live Chats**
- **Bulletin Boards**
- **Lifestyle Information**
- **Publicly Traded Cigar Companies**
- **Betting Lines and Scores**
- **People of *Cigar Aficionado* - industry stars as well as other fascinating personalities**

It's all here plus much more!
Please visit us at:
http://www.cigaraficionado.com

Cognacs and Brandies

Somewhere in the medieval past, a distiller took grapes—the fruit of the vine—and transformed them into a fine distilled spirit. Today, that spirit is known as Cognac when it comes from a small, clearly defined area known by that name in France; Armagnac when it's from the region of that name near Cognac; or simply brandy when it comes from anywhere else.

Cognac is considered the pinnacle of grape brandies. On its label you may find a variety of designations indicating origin, aging and blend. If the town of Cognac is the center of a bull's-eye, then the six areas where grapes for use in Cognac can be grown extend in roughly concentric circles out from the center. At the center is Grande Champagne, a small area from which the best Cognacs are considered to come. Then there is Petit Champagne, which despite its name is larger than Grande Champagne. The other four

DAN WAGNER

ONYX
The Gem of Maduro

The most precious

maduro cigars.

Handcrafted

in the Dominican

Republic from

the finest tobaccos

to be the best

in their class.

areas in descending order of quality are Borderies, Fins Bois, Bons Bois and Boi Communs or Ordinaries.

Today, most Cognac comes from a single grape variety, Ugni Blanc, and after fermentation the grapes go through a double distillation. Then Cognac is aged in French oak barrels. There are three designations which indicate length of aging: V.S., which is aged less than four and a half years; V.S.O.P., is aged more than four and a half years; and X.O., or Napoleon, which indicates Cognacs aged more than six and a half years.

After aging, one of the real arts of Cognac comes into play—the blending. A master blender will often use grapes from a variety of regions or sources to arrive at a consistent final

Courtney Grant Winston

54

product. A designation of "Fine Champagne" means 50 percent of the grapes come from the Grande Champagne. If all the grapes are from either the Grande or Petite Champagne regions, the Cognac label may state this.

Some Cognac makers also produce extra special Cognacs with names like Martell Extra, Rémy Martin Louis XIII, Hennessey Paradis, Courvoisier Initiale Extra and Hine Triomphe. While all of these contain Cognacs that are aged considerably longer than six and a half years, even up to 70 years in some cases, they are legally bound only to have no Cognac less than six and a half years old. Names of other outstanding producers include Delamain, Frapin, Pierre Ferrand, A.E. Dor, A. de Fussigny, A. Hardy and Louis Royer.

Armagnac is similar to Cognac but only goes through a single distillation. It is considered a bit rougher than Cognac but purists believe it has a truer "grapey" flavor. It is also aged in oak barrels, and unlike Cognac, it can be bottled with a specific vintage date. Some brands to consider are Sempe, Larressingle, Darroze and Marquis de Caussade.

Spanish brandy is also a fine spirit. These brandies use a different grape variety, and are often richer and darker in appearance with a sweeter flavor on the palate. Top brands include Cardenal Mendoza, Lepanto, Duque de Alba and Carlos X.

American brandy has made huge strides in the last 10 years. Two producers, Carneros Alambic and Germain-Robin, are producing pot still products; as the brandies get more barrel aging, they are being blended into top quality products. Recently, Paul Masson also launched an aged brandy into the U.S. market.

The simple grape-based spirits that do not undergo significant barrel aging include grappa, a clear liquid, and various forms of marc, a spirit made from the leftover grape must after the harvest. Grappas are primarily Italian, although some American producers, such as Sebastiani, have been creating fine grappas. They have strong grape flavors, and are clean, striking spirits. In recent years, grappas made from single grape varieties, often with even more pronounced flavors, have arrived on the market.

Cognac, though, is the traditional choice in many countries for the perfect accompaniment to a great cigar. The intensity of the spirit is an especially good match for a robust hand-rolled cigar. Add a cup of coffee, and you have what the French call the "Three C's": Coffee, Cognac and Cigars.

...no comment

Port

It's almost a standard scene in any Victorian novel or play: the English gentlemen retire to the drawing room for a glass of Port and a cigar. A reflection of the cigar's glowing ember shimmers in the dark, nearly black, liquid in their glasses.

Port is a fortified wine. Port begins like any other wine—on a grapevine. But to be called Port, the vineyards, known as quintas, must be located in Portugal's Upper Douro Valley. The grapes are harvested and then crushed in shallow open concrete containers called lagars or in stainless steel vats. The wines are fermented to about 5 percent alcohol and then brandy is added to bring the solution to about 20 percent alcohol. The fortification process preserves the natural sweetness in the wine.

There are several different types of Port. Vintage Port is designated by the producer or shipper, and is a statement on the overall quality of the vintage. The decision is made in the spring following the second winter of the harvest. For instance, the 1985 vintage was declared in the spring of 1987. The producers taste the wine frequently. If a vintage is declared, the wines must be aged in wood casks for two years before bottling.

Vintage years are usually declared two or three times a decade, although not all the major houses agree on any single year. In the '60s, vintages were declared in 1960, 1963, 1966 and by a few houses in 1967; the '70s brought 1970, 1975 and 1977 and two houses in 1978; in the '80s, a banner decade, vintages were declared in 1980, 1982, 1983 and 1985. A dry spell of six years followed. Now, both 1991 and 1992 have been declared vintage years.

The top producers of vintage Port are Graham, Fonseca, Taylor and Quinta do Noval, although the latter is better known for its rare Nacional. Other producers include Cockburn, Croft, Dow, Ferreira, Sandeman and Warre. Great Ports can last a lifetime. Ports from the 1963 vintage, for instance, have not reached their peak, and 1955 and 1945 are still drinking marvelously.

If a vintage is not declared, then the fortified wine may be used in

Quinta do Seixo 1983, Offley Boa Vista 1983 and the 1987 and 1991 Taylor Quinta de Vargellas.

In addition, Port producers make tawny Ports that have received even more wood-aging. They are designated as 10-year-old, 20-year-old and 40-year-old, although this refers to the average age of the fortified wines used in the blend, not the absolute age of the blend. They tend to be lighter and show a nut-tier, more mature character. Finally,

Ports known as "late bottled vintage" or "vintage character" or saved for nonvintage or tawny Ports. "Late bottled vintage port" carries a vintage date, and receives more barrel-aging before bottling so that it is ready to drink sooner than the classic vintage Port. Most Ports may be blended from the wines of several different vineyards, but single vineyard Ports have also become common on the market. Some of the better ones are Ferreira's

there is the nonvintage Port category, which is much less expensive. It's hard to separate the various designations in this category; some producers call it "ruby Port," others "vintage character." In general, it should have about five years of barrel-aging to smooth it out. Nearly every Port producer makes a nonvintage port, and most cost less than $15 a bottle. Look for Churchill's Finest Reserve, Noval LB and Fonseca Bin 27.

RICK MARIANI

Scotch and Irish Whiskey

If there is a spirit that "marries" its flavors perfectly with cigars, Scotch is certainly the top candidate. This concoction of water and peat-smoked, malted barley is often redolent of smoky, charcoal-like flavors that go well with a fine cigar.

Most Scotch whisky is blended, often using dozens of fine malt spirits from distinct distilleries that are then blended with neutral grain spirits. The proportion of nonbarley grain spirits in a blended Scotch is a closely guarded secret, often passed down from one family generation or master blender to the next. Blends can vary in taste, and descriptors such as dry, sweet, smooth, smoky, peaty, salty, complex, balanced, clean and soft are used to describe the taste. The exact character of blended Scotch is determined by the barley malt, the ratio of malt to neutral spirits and the length and type of aging. Some blended Scotch brands include Chivas Regal; Crown Royal; Dewars; J&B; Cutty Sark; Johnnie Walker Red, Black and Blue; White Horse; Grants; Clan MacGregor; Passport and Teacher's.

A real phenomenon in the United States is the rise in popularity

JEFF HARRIS

THE EMBARGO DOESN'T MATTER ANYMORE.
CUBAN TASTE IS HERE.

The first 100% Cuban seed tobacco cigar with true Cuban taste made outside of Cuba. MiCubano is produced in Nicaragua, but the difference ends there. The filler, binder and wrapper leaf are all grown from Cuban seed. All the tobacco is grown and cured in the Cuban tradition. All MiCubanos are hand made in a factory owned and supervised by a Cuban expatriate. And the packaging is uniquely Cuban. But what distinguishes the taste of MiCubano is the quality of its blend and its wrapper - the only wrapper ever grown outside of Cuba that rivals its Cuban counterpart. Many have tried, but all have failed ... until MiCubano. MiCubano and true Cuban taste are here.

MiCubano
~650~
100% Cuban Seed Tobacco

of single malt Scotch whiskies. Several brands are part of any well-stocked bar today: Glenfiddich, Glenlivet, The Macallan, Highland Park, Glenmorangie, Aberlour, the Dalmore, Cardhu and Laphroaig. A host of others, rarer and harder to find, evoke images of ancient Scotland: Talisker, Lagavulin, Bunnahabhain, Bruichladdich, Oban and Edradour. Single malts differ from blended Scotches in that they are the product of a single distillery, so the inherent character of that distillery shines through. The distillery's home region is also a contributing factor; the big five are Islay, Speyside, Lowlands, Highlands and Campbeltown, and each is considered to have its own distinguishing features. Single malts also exhibit the differences between the two different types of barrels used in aging Scotch: old Sherry barrels or Bourbon barrels. Each imparts its own character, but it is generally agreed that Sherry casks impart a slight sweetness to a Scotch whisky while Bourbon is more neutral.

Irish whiskey also occupies a favorite niche in the world of grain-based spirits. In the United States, the two most widely available are Jameson's and Old Bushmills. Most Irish whiskey is triple-distilled, creating a more neutral-tasting spirit than most Scotch whisky. Also, Old Bushmills is primarily a grain spirit with only a small touch of malt. Recently, Old Bushmills created an all single malt product called Bushmills Malt.

Serious Scotch drinkers, especially single malt aficionados, prefer their beverage neat or at most, on the rocks. But Scotch and water or Scotch and soda are certainly accepted drinks. Given Scotch's popularity in the postwar years, bartenders also created a host of exotic Scotch-based cocktails: Rob Roy (Scotch and sweet vermouth) and Rusty Nail (Scotch and Drambuie) are just two.

But if you're intent on exploring the marriage of peat-smoked barley and a fine hand-rolled cigar, stick to the unadulterated versions.

JOYCE OUDKERK POOL

INSIDER INFORMATION

If you really love cigars, the publisher of *Cigar Aficionado* has created a monthly newsletter especially for you. With more ratings for cigars from such leading regions as the Dominican Republic, Honduras and Jamaica. More coverage on new releases. And prices and availability of cigars in tobacco shops and duty-free outlets around the world.

Plus, each issue of ***Marvin Shanken's Cigar Insider*** includes up-to-the-minute news on the world's finest cigar stores, the latest auction prices, investments, travel tips, duty-free prices, special cigar events, **industry reports** **that will keep you on top of the premium cigar market, and much more.** Every issue of *Cigar Insider* will also give you expanded coverage of Cuban cigars — production, brands, new sizes, availability worldwide, you name it!

Become a Charter Subscriber to *Cigar Insider* and receive this priceless information for just $60 a year. *(This exclusive newsletter is not available on any newsstand, only by subscription direct from the publisher.)* Your satisfaction is guaranteed. If you're not happy for any reason, we'll send you a full refund for all unmailed issues. Just call or write today.

SUBSCRIBE NOW!

CALL 1-800-644-4395

Rum

Like a great cigar, rum is a child of the tropics. But its origins are at least 3,000 years older. The fermented juice of sugar cane was produced first in Asia, made its way through North Africa to Spain and finally arrived in the New World. It was a barter commodity that helped drive the slave trade and much of commerce in the seventeenth and eighteenth centuries.

The majority of rum is of the clear or white variety. It is the fuel for a host of fun cocktails that starts with rum and cola, moves on through Daiquiris, Planter's Punch and Pina Coladas, and ends with mixtures of just about any fruit juice known to man. Rum is the ultimate mixable.

But in recent years, the world has discovered what Latins have known

A TRADITION RETURNS

La Regenta

The epicurean Canary Island cigar
selected for many royal European
humidors. Naturally cured,
meticulously aged, handcrafted
in The Old World tradition.

Marcos Miguel Tobacco Corporation
New Jersey: 1-800-473-0770
Dallas: 1-800-905-2441

for centuries: a dark, aged rum offers the same enjoyment and smooth character as an aged Cognac, single malt Scotch or Bourbon. After about five years of aging in charred oak barrels, the natural molasses colors turn amber and golden, and the flavors of maturity—vanilla, nuts, spices—come out on the palate.

Rum begins as molasses, using the by-product that remains after the crystallized sugar has been removed from sugar cane stalk. (There are other methods using cane juice and syrup, but they tend not to produce a product of equal quality.) This fact puts rum producers one step ahead of whiskey or vodka makers; in these grain-based products, starches from the grains must first be transformed into sugar.

The range of fermentation and distillation techniques that follows is remarkably diverse, making the word rum almost impossible to define. Some rum makers use a natural, slow fermentation of up to 12 days; others use a controlled fermentation with a secret yeast that produces results in a couple of days. Some use pot stills, much like Cognac stills, to refine their raw spirits; others use modern column stills that tend to produce cleaner, more neutral spirits.

Rum is then aged in used white-oak Bourbon barrels, with some charring of the insides to add color and flavor to the rum; the length of aging is determined by the maker's taste preferences. Almost all of the so-called aged or dark rums are blends of rums of different ages. United States law requires that any age statement on the label must refer to the youngest rum used in the blend, so a five-year-old rum cannot contain rums with less than five years of aging, but could include rums up to eight or ten years old.

Some of the aged rums available in America are Appleton Estate (Jamaica), Bacardi Añejo and Bacardi Gold Reserve (Puerto Rico), Bermúdez Aniversario (Dominican Republic), Ron Botran (Guatemala), Brugal (Dominican Republic), Flor de Caña (Nicaragua), Gosling's Black Seal (Bermuda), Mount Gay (Barbados), Myers's Rum (Jamaica), Pampero Aniversario (Venezuela) and Zacapa Centenario (Guatemala).

Connoisseurs can often identify rums based on their country of origin. Puerto Rican rums tend to be light. Barbados, Martinique, Nicaragua, Trinindad and the Virgin Islands produce medium-bodied rums. And the rums from Bermuda, Guatemala and Jamaica are usually the heaviest and darkest. The best rums are slow-fermented, distilled in pot stills and aged a long time.

Some professional cigar tasters in the Caribbean use rum to cleanse their palates between cigars. The reason is simple: the flavors and aromas of the tropics enhance the overall experience of smoking a cigar.

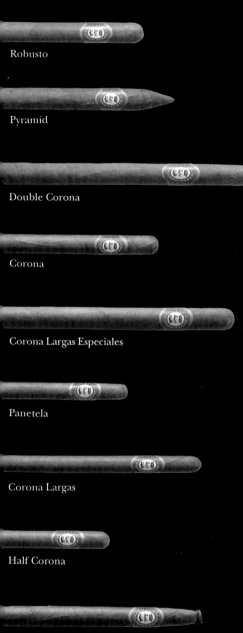

Robusto

Pyramid

Double Corona

Corona

Corona Largas Especiales

Panetela

Corona Largas

Half Corona

El Conde De Guell Sr.

A proud heritage makes them a discriminating choice today.

Not many cigars can boast of a heritage of excellence that can be traced to the 17th century. Tabacalera cigars from La Flor de la Isabela continue a lineage of products that are handcrafted in the tradition brought to the Philippines from Cuba by the Spanish conquistadores.

The heritage lives on, with each leaf properly aged, perfectly blended, and deftly rolled to create a most enjoyable cigar. La Flor de la Isabela preserves the tradition, so you may savor every cigar-smoking experience.

TABACALERA

LA FLOR DE LA ISABELA
Since 1881

Bourbon

Bourbon is America's own, a homegrown whiskey that was invented in frontier-era Kentucky. Legend has it that a "white lightning" maker, Elijah Craig, suffered a warehouse fire that charred some of his shipping barrels. He filled them with freshly distilled spirit anyway. When the shipment arrived in New Orleans, the liquid had an amber color and a noticeably softer flavor.

Bourbon is a strictly regulated spirit. To be called Bourbon, it must be made from at least 51 percent corn; most distillers use 65 to 75 percent with a percentage of wheat or other grains often included in the fermentation mash. Bourbon must age a minimum of two years in new white-oak barrels that have

been charred. No additives or colors are permitted. Though Bourbon can be made anywhere in the United States, only that made in Kentucky can have Bourbon on the label. Names like Jim Beam, Heaven Hill, Ancient Age, Early Times, Old Crow, Old Grand-Dad and Wild Turkey are engraved in Bourbon drinkers' minds.

Some other great American

KEN LEVINSON

whiskeys aren't called Bourbon, but are made in similar fashion, and often taste very much the same, too. Jack Daniel's and George Dickel are two Tennessee whiskeys. Jack Daniel's differs from Bourbon in that it is charcoal-filtered; its upscale brother, Gentleman Jack, receives two charcoal filterings. Both have a sweeter, smokier taste.

There's been a revolution in Bourbon-making during recent years: small-batch and single-barrel products are the fashion of the day. Most Bourbons are blends of several hundred different barrels that have been aged in huge warehouses and then mixed together to get a uniform taste. But "boutique" Bourbons may be a blend of only 20 barrels, or in several cases, are bottled from only one barrel. They usually carry a premium price, although some, like Maker's Mark, are around $20 in most markets. Other well-known brands are Basil Hayden, Booker's 107, Blanton's, Elijah Craig, Hancock's Reserve, Knob Creek, Rock Hill Farms and

Wild Turkey Rare Breed. You'll also find some "cask-strength" Bourbons in this group; they are bottled straight from the barrel without being cut with water, and the proofs may range up to 126.

Drinking Bourbon, whatever its origin, is a ritual that is as personal as shaving. Some people swear Bourbon should be consumed straight, others say cut with water, others insist that a couple of cubes of ice is all you need. The character of the Bourbon will change depending on the amount of water mixed in; some open up with floral and spice flavors, while others just taste watered down. Try your brand each way, and you'll find the right way for you. As for other drinks, Bourbon and ginger ale and the Whiskey Sour (shaken with sugar and lemon juice) are old favorites. And don't forge the Mint Julep, not really much more than Bourbon poured over cracked ice and mint leaves with a little sugar. Purists, however, reject anything but straight, pure Bourbon in their glass.

CHAPTER 11

Cigar Tasting Notes

Listed By Size *and* Score

I n this section you will find complete descriptions and tasting notes for the 1040 cigars rated by *Cigar Aficionado* since its founding in 1992. They are arranged in these categories:

1) double coronas, Churchills, corona gordas, lonsdales, coronas, robustos, petit coronas, panatelas, and odd-sized, straight-sided cigars
2) unusually shaped cigars such as torpedos and pyramids (grouped together in the figurado category here)
3) a separate listing for the dark-wrapped cigars known as maduros

Of course, the cigar's score, arrived at by a panel of senior editors of *Cigar Aficionado* in blind tastings, is also listed here.

All cigars are rated on a 100 point scale. The scoring system is as follows:
95–100: classic
90–94: outstanding
80–89: very good to excellent
70–79: average to good commercial quality
below 70: don't waste your money
N/A: Not Available

A cigar's final score reflects judgments made in four categories:

Appearance and Construction. The cigar is examined for quality of the wrapper and construction. The testers look for things like oiliness, firmness and overall consistency of wrapper color. Bulging veins, excessive spotting, marks and a rough finish are defects.

Smoking Characteristics. The way the cigar burns is evaluated; this includes the evenness of the burn and the color of the ash. The cigar's draw is also judged here.

Flavor. The tasters look for mild-, medium- and full-bodied characteristics. A description is then written about the taste of the cigar, which may include everything from cocoa beans and coffee to wet hay and grass. Spiciness is also a key factor. The "finish," or length of time that the flavors stay in the mouth, is noted as well.

Overall Impression. This is the taster's own opinion based on his summary of the cigar's characteristics.

The guide is formatted in three different ways. Following the tasting notes, you will find 1) a section with the cigars listed by country of origin and then by score within each size category; 2) an alphabetical listing by brand.

Cigar Tasting Notes

Listed By Size and Score

DOUBLE CORONA

Most of the following Double Corona tasting notes appeared in the Spring 1995 issue of Cigar Aficionado. Exceptions are indicated by a date in parentheses at the end of the tasting note.

HOYO DE MONTERREY **96**
DOUBLE CORONA
Cuba • *Size:* 7⅝" x 49 *Filler/Binder/Wrapper:* Cuba
An extraordinary full-bodied smoke. This cigar is filled with cocoa and coffee-bean flavors backed up by smooth woody and leathery notes. It has a perfect draw and a toastlike aroma.
U.S.: N/A • U.K.: £10.10

RAMON ALLONES **94**
GIGANTES
Cuba • *Size:* 7⅝" x 49 *Filler/Binder/Wrapper:* Cuba
This cigar has a smooth, creamy texture with strong pepper and spice notes and a sweet, intense, nutty character on the finish.
U.S.: N/A • U.K.: £9.90

FUENTE FUENTE OPUS **93**
X DOUBLE CORONA
Dominican Republic • *Size:* 7⅝" x 49 *Filler/Binder/Wrapper:* Dom. Rep.

A beautiful reddish-brown wrapper delivers flavors of spices, leather and coffee beans. It has a very earthy, perfumed aroma.
U.S.: $9.00 • U.K.: N/A

CUBA ALIADOS **92**
CHURCHILL
Honduras • *Size:* 7¼" x 54 *Filler/Wrapper:* Ecuador *Binder/*
A cigar with a beautiful dark-brown wrapper. It has strong flavors of spice and cocoa beans with solid, earthy tobacco characteristics. Some inconsistency was noted.
U.S.: $3.00 • U.K.: £4.10

DAVIDOFF DOUBLE **92**
"R"
Dominican Republic • *Size:* 7½" x 50 *Filler/Binder:* Dom. Rep. *Wrapper:* U.S.A./Conn. Shade
This very spicy cigar also has strong flavors of cedar wood and coffee, and a smooth, creamy finish that lingers on the palate.
U.S.: $16.50 • U.K.: £19.00

PARTAGAS LUSITANIA **92**
Cuba • *Size:* 7⅝" x 49 *Filler/Binder/Wrapper:* Cuba
A rich, full-bodied cigar that has cedar and leathery flavors with strong hints of

chestnuts and cinnamon.
U.S.: N/A • U.K.: £9.90

BELINDA PRIME **91**
MINISTER
Honduras • *Size:* 7½" x 50 *Filler:* Dom. Rep., Honduras *Binder:* Honduras *Wrapper:* Ecuador
An excellent draw supports this smooth-tasting cigar. It has flavors of spice and nuts, and a cedar taste that rounds out the solid tobacco core.
U.S.: $2.25 • U.K.: N/A

LA GLORIA CUBANA **91**
SOBERANOS
U.S.A. • *Size:* 8" x 52 *Filler:* Dom. Rep, Nicaragua *Binder:* Dom. Rep. *Wrapper:* Ecuador
This cigar has strong flavors of spice and leather and delivers a smooth, full-bodied smoke.
U.S.: $2.60 • U.K.: N/A

PUNCH DOUBLE **91**
CORONA
Cuba • *Size:* 7⅝" x 49 *Filler/Binder/Wrapper:* Cuba
This is a strong cigar, with excellent tobacco character and a long finish. It has flavors of spice and leather that give it an earthy, almost herbal, complexity.
U.S.: N/A • U.K.: £10.10

A bond as
old as history and
deep as Caribbean
tradition.

Bacardi rum and
a fine cigar.

Savor the richness.
Bacardi Select
& *La Gloria Cubana*.

Ron
BACARDI
SELECT

*A select blend
of the world's richest rums
slowly aged in oak barrels.
The rums are charcoal-filtered
before their marriage
in the oak, resulting in a
distinctly smooth dark rum.*

PUERTO RICAN RUM

MEDALS AWARDED TO BACARDI

SAVINELLI E.L.R. 91
CHURCHILL
Dominican Republic • *Size:* 7¼" x 48 *Filler/Binder:* Dom. Rep. *Wrapper:* U.S.A./ Conn. Shade
A very attractive cigar with a good draw and a wonderful core of spicy flavors backed up by mild coffee notes.
U.S.: $7.50 • U.K.: N/A

LA UNICA NO. 100 90
Dominican Republic • *Size:* 8½" x 52 *Filler/Binder:* Dom. Rep. *Wrapper:* U.S.A./Conn. Shade
A well-balanced cigar with an earthy character. It has sweet spice flavors such as nutmeg and a pleasant, nutty component.
U.S.: $2.55 • U.K.: N/A

MACANUDO VINTAGE 90
CABINET SELECTION NO. 1
Jamaica • *Size:* 7½" x 49 *Filler:* Dom. Rep., Jamaica *Binder:* Mexico *Wrapper:* U.S.A./Conn. Shade
A cigar with a medium-bodied smoke, woody, leathery characteristics and some mild, spicy flavors.
U.S.: $8.50 • U.K.: N/A

HOYO DE MONTERREY 89
EXCALIBUR NO. 1
Honduras • *Size:* 7¼" x 54 *Filler:* Nica., Hon., Dom. Rep. *Binder:* Ecuador *Wrapper:* U.S.A./Conn. Shade
A really gorgeous cigar, with a medium-brown colored wrapper and an oily sheen. It smokes like a dream with

delicious coffee, tobacco flavors and a long, rich finish. (12/01/92)
U.S.: $2.80 • U.K.: N/A

PRIMO DEL REY 89
SOBERANO
Dominican Republic • *Size:* 7½" x 50 *Filler:* Dom. Rep. *Binder:* U.S.A. *Wrapper:* Brazil
A solid, full-bodied smoke that has strong elements of coffee and sweet spices such as nutmeg that give it a refined character.
U.S.: $2.50 • U.K.: N/A

ROMEO Y JULIETA 89
VINTAGE NO. 5
Dominican Republic • *Size:* 7½" x 50 *Filler:* Dom. Rep. *Binder:* Mexico *Wrapper:* U.S.A./Conn. Shade
A medium-bodied cigar that has a light, nutty character with some flavors of mild, sweet spices such as nutmeg.
U.S.: $6.50 • U.K.: N/A

DON JUAN PRESIDENTE 88
Nicaragua • *Size:* 8½" x 50 *Filler/Binder:* Nicaragua, Dom. Rep. *Wrapper:* U.S.A./Conn. Shade
A mild, smooth cigar. It has sweet flavors of vanilla and cinnamon with some nuttiness.
U.S.: $2.65 • U.K.: N/A

JOYA DE NICARAGUA 88
VIAJANTE
Nicaragua • *Size:* 8½" x 52 *Filler/Binder/Wrapper:* Nicaragua

A solid cigar with rich, sweet spice flavors of cinnamon and chocolate and a creamy finish.
U.S.: $3.05 • U.K.: N/A

LA GLORIA CUBANA 88
CHURCHILL
U.S.A. • *Size:* 7" x 50 *Filler/Binder:* Dom. Rep., Brazil, Mexico *Wrapper:* Ecuador
Rich and decadent smoke. The wrapper is dark brown, with a great sheen. It is a full-bodied, powerful cigar with fascinating caramel, chocolate flavors and a mouth-filling texture. (12/01/92)
U.S.: $1.75 • U.K.: N/A

OSCAR SUPREME 88
Dominican Republic • *Size:* 8" x 48 *Filler/Binder:* Dom. Rep. *Wrapper:* U.S.A./Conn. Shade
This cigar has solid tobacco flavors and a steely, mineral characteristic that is backed up a distinct spiciness.
U.S.: $7.15 • U.K.: £7.50

PAUL GARMIRIAN 88
GOURMET DOUBLE CORONA
Dominican Republic • *Size:* 7⅝" x 50 *Filler/Binder:* Dom. Rep. *Wrapper:* U.S.A./Conn. Shade
A very pleasant, attractive, medium-bodied smoke with mild, sweet spice flavors and a creamy aftertaste.
U.S.: $9.50 • U.K.: £8.95

"Fidel Castro thought I had left Cuba with only the clothes on my back. But my secrets were locked in my heart."

After Fidel Castro came to power, Ramón Cifuentes could no longer make his Partagas® cigars in Cuba. Skilled hands and the Cuban leaf were far too scarce. In contrast, the Dominican Republic now has the Caribbean's finest cigar-makers and richest soil. And only Partagas cigars are still made under the watchful eyes of the same man who made them long ago in Cuba.

PARTAGAS

The cigar that knew Cuba when.

POR LARRAÑAGA **88**
FABULOSO
Dominican Republic • *Size:*
7" x 50 *Filler/Binder:* Dom.
Rep. *Wrapper:* U.S.A./
Conn. Shade
A mellow, medium-bodied
cigar that has some earthy
elements, almost flintlike,
but with a good solid depth
of spicy flavors.
U.S.: $4.50 • U.K.: N/A

SOSA SOBERANO **88**
Dominican Republic • *Size:*
7½" x 52 *Filler:* Dom. Rep.,
Brazil *Binder:* Honduras
Wrapper: Ecuador
A rich, chocolate-brown
wrapper. This cigar delivers a
very spicy and nutty smoke,
but our tasters noted some
young tobacco that dimin-
ished the cigar's complexity.
U.S.: $2.85 • U.K.: N/A

8-9-8 COLLECTION **87**
CHURCHILL
Jamaica • *Size:* 7½" x 49
Filler: Jamaica, Dom. Rep.
Binder: Mexico *Wrapper:*
U.S.A./Conn. Shade
This is a well-made, mild
cigar with a smooth wrapper
and a good draw. It has a rich
taste with some mild spice
and nut flavors.
U.S.: $6.75 • U.K.: N/A

CRUZ REAL **87**
CHURCHILL NO. 14
Mexico • *Size:* 7½" x 50
Filler/Binder/Wrapper: Mexico
A rustic cigar with an easy
draw. It is medium bodied
and has good, spicy aromas
and flavors.
U.S.: $3.88 • U.K.: £3.00

DUNHILL PERAVIAS **87**
Dominican Republic •
Size: 7" x 50 *Filler/Binder:*
Dom. Rep., Brazil *Wrapper:*
U.S.A./Conn. Shade
This is a very enjoyable cigar
with intriguing leafy, nutty aro-
mas and flavors and a velvety-
feel in the mouth. It burns
extremely well, with a nearly
perfect, even draw. (12/01/92)
U.S.: $4.75 • U.K.: £6.30

EL REY DEL MUNDO **87**
FLOR DEL MUNDO
Honduras • *Size:* 7½" x 54
Filler: Dom. Rep, Honduras
Binder/Wrapper: Honduras
Inconsistent. Several tasters
had cigars with too tight a
draw. It does have some
smooth, spicy flavors and a
woody, earthy aftertaste but
may need more aging.
U.S.: $3.50 • U.K.: N/A

LICENCIADOS **87**
PRESIDENTE
Dominican Republic • *Size:*
8" x 50 *Filler/Binder:* Dom.
Rep. *Wrapper:* U.S.A./
Conn. Shade
This is a good, medium-bod-
ied cigar with an earthy ele-
ment that combines smooth
nut and mild spice flavors.
U.S.: $2.40 • U.K.: N/A

NAT SHERMAN **87**
LANDMARK SELECTION
DAKOTA
Dominican Republic • *Size:*
7½" x 49 *Filler:* Dom. Rep.,
Mexico *Binder:* Mexico
Wrapper: Cameroon
A full-bodied cigar that has
strong pepper flavors and a
woody, earthy character.
U.S.: $4.90 • U.K.: N/A

ROYAL JAMAICA **87**
CHURCHILL
Dominican Republic • *Size:*
8" x 51 *Filler:* Jamaica,
Dom. Rep. Indonesia
Binder: Indonesia *Wrapper:*
Cameroon
An interesting medium-bod-
ied cigar with a smooth
creaminess and solid flavors
of chocolate and mild spice.
U.S.: $4.60 • U.K.: N/A

SANTA CLARA 1830 **87**
NO. 1
Mexico • *Size:* 7½" x 52
Filler/Binder/Wrapper: Mexico
A straightforward, medium-
bodied cigar with flavors of
mild spices and a bit of nutti-
ness.
U.S.: $2.50 • U.K.: £4.00

THOMAS HINDS **87**
HONDURAN SELECTION
PRESIDENTE
Honduras • *Size:* 8½" x 52
Filler/Binder: Honduras
Wrapper: Ecuador
A brownsih-green wrapper
offers a rather firm draw. It
has mild, smooth flavors of
creamy spice and a solid
tobacco core.
U.S.: N/A • U.K.: N/A

ASHTON AGED **86**
MADURO NO. 60
Dominican Republic • *Size:*
7½" x 52 *Filler/Binder:* Dom.
Rep. *Wrapper:* U.S.A./
Conn. Broadleaf
This maduro-style cigar has a
mild, smooth character with
a backbone of sweet spices
and pepper.
U.S.: $5.00 • U.K.: N/A

Want to come up for a drink sometime?

REMY MARTIN

100% fine champagne cognac from the heart of the most celebrated growing region in France.

To learn more about cognac and the world of Rémy Martin, call 1-800-678-REMY for our 10-minute video. Complimentary, while supplies last; offer expires 5-31-97.

Cigar Aficionado's "Big Smoke"

An Evening to Celebrate the Pleasures of Fine Cigars and the Good Life.
Sample Handmade Cigars from Around the World and the Best Spirits and
Wines. Explore Cigar Accessories, Watches and Jewelry. Enjoy Food from
Leading Local "Cigar Friendly" Restaurants.

1997

APRIL 15, FAIRMONT HOTEL, CHICAGO
Session 1 4:30-7 pm, Session 2 7:30-10 pm

MAY 7, MARRIOTT COPLEY, BOSTON
7-10 pm

MAY 22, MARRIOTT MARQUIS, NEW YORK CITY
Session 1 4:30-7 pm, Session 2 7:30-10 pm

OCTOBER 31, BALLY'S, LAS VEGAS
6:30-9:30 pm

NOVEMBER 1, BALLY'S, LAS VEGAS
6:30-9:30 pm

NOVEMBER 25, MARRIOTT MARQUIS, NEW YORK CITY
Session 1 4:30-7 pm, Session 2 7:30-10 pm

1998 dates and cities will be announced.

$150 PER TICKET.
Fax: 212 481-1523   Web Site: www.cigaraficionado.com
Include: Name, address, phone, fax, # tickets, city, time,
credit card #, expiration date, billing zip.

A portion of net proceeds will benefit CaP Cure,
the research organization seeking a cure for prostate cancer.

BAUZA FABULOSO **86**
Dominican Republic • *Size:*
7½" x 50 *Filler:* Dom. Rep.,
Nicaragua *Binder:* Mexico
Wrapper: Cameroon
A smooth-tasting cigar with
some exotic floral aromas and
flavors. It has some unusual
herbal, earthy tones on the
palate.
U.S.: $2.55 • U.K.: N/A

DON LINO HAVANA **86**
RESERVE CHURCHILL
Honduras • *Size:* 7½" x 50
Filler/Binder: Honduras
Wrapper: U.S.A./Conn.
Shade
This is a smooth-tasting cigar
with some perfumed aromas,
but a slightly dry, strawlike
finish.
U.S.: $5.35 • U.K.: N/A

NAT SHERMAN CITY **86**
DESK TRIBUNE
Dominican Republic • *Size:*
7½" x 50 *Filler/Binder:* Dom.
Rep. *Wrapper:* Mexico
This maduro cigar offers
plenty of sweet spice flavors
and some chocolate ele-
ments. It is medium bodied
with a rich finish.
U.S.: $4.35 • U.K.: N/A

PARTAGAS NO. 10 **86**
Dominican Republic •
Size: 7½" x 49 *Filler:* Dom.
Rep., Mexico *Binder:*
Mexico *Wrapper:* Cameroon
A mild cigar with spicy, dry
woody flavors. It also has
some solid tobacco notes.
U.S.: $4.00 • U.K.: N/A

PETRUS DC HAVANA **86**
Honduras • *Size:* 7¾"
x 50 *Filler/Binder/Wrapper:*
Honduras
Young tobacco may have
affected this cigar. It has
good flavors of spice, nuts
and coffee, but it was a little
rough.
U.S.: $4.25 • U.K.: N/A

ZINO VERITAS **86**
Honduras • *Size:* 7" x 50
Filler/Binder/Wrapper:
Honduras
A real smoothie; this cigar
has a lovely medium-brown
wrapper with an oily texture.
It is medium-bodied with fla-
vors of nutmeg and chocolate
and a delicious aftertaste.
(12/01/92)
U.S.: $6.40 • U.K.: N/A

ASHTON CHURCHILL **85**
Dominican Republic •
Size: 7½" x 50 *Filler/Binder:*
Dom. Rep. *Wrapper:*
U.S.A./Conn. Shade
This is delicate and light,
with lovely creamy and floral
flavors, and a refreshing
aftertaste. An attractive
afternoon cigar. (12/01/92)
U.S.: $3.25 • U.K.: N/A

CUESTA-REY **85**
DOMINICAN NO. 2
Dominican Republic • *Size:*
7¼" x 48 *Filler/Binder:* Dom.
Rep. *Wrapper:* U.S.A./
Conn. Shade
This cigar is finished a bit
roughly, and it has a dry taste
with a woody finish.
U.S.: $2.75 • U.K.: £4.25

DON LINO CHURCHILL **85**
Honduras • *Size:* 8" x 50
Filler/Binder: Dom. Rep.
Wrapper: U.S.A./Conn.
Shade
This is a very light-wrapped
cigar with a nice creamy nut-
tiness and some solid tobacco
flavors.
U.S.: $2.65 • U.K.: N/A

EL SUBLIMADO **85**
CHURCHILL
Dominican Republic • *Size:*
8" x 50 *Filler/Binder:* Dom.
Rep. *Wrapper:* U.S.A./
Conn. Shade
This cigar is medium bodied,
with some spicy flavors and
an unusual and pleasant per-
fumed, herbal taste.
U.S.: $12.00 • U.K.: N/A

JOSE BENITO **85**
PRESIDENTE
Dominican Republic • *Size:*
7¾" x 50 *Filler:* Dom. Rep.
Binder: Central America
Wrapper: Cameroon
This is a rich-tasting, medi-
um-bodied cigar that has
some creamy coffee flavors
and a core of spiciness.
U.S.: $3.60 • U.K.: N/A

LA FINCA BOLIVARES **85**
Nicaragua • *Size:* 7½" x 50
Filler/Binder/Wrapper:
Nicaragua
This cigar burned a little hot.
It has some pepper and nut-
meg flavors, but with a rustic
edge to them.
U.S.: $2.00 • U.K.: N/A

LA HOJA SELECTA **85**
COSIAC
U.S.A. • *Size:* 7" x 49 *Filler/ Binder:* Dom. Rep., Nicaragua *Wrapper:* U.S.A./ Conn. Shade
Another winner from El Credito Cigars, this is a wonderfully constructed cigar, with an attractive medium-brown wrapper. The La Hoja Selecta double corona is mild, with pretty, nutty flavors and a slightly bitter aftertaste. (12/01/92)
U.S.: $1.95 • U.K.: N/A

MACANUDO PRINCE **85**
PHILIP
Jamaica • *Size:* 7½" x 49 *Filler:* Dom. Rep., Jamaica *Binder:* Mexico *Wrapper:* U.S.A./Conn. Shade
This cigar seemed to have a little bite, but with some nice wood and nut flavors.
U.S.: $4.00 • U.K.: N/A

PLEIADES ALDEBARAN **85**
Dominican Republic • *Size:* 8½" x 50 *Filler/Binder:* Dom. Rep. *Wrapper:* U.S.A./ Conn. Shade
This is a mild cigar with light, creamy tobacco character and some mild, spicy flavors.
U.S.: $10.06 • U.K.: N/A

PUNCH DIADEMAS **85**
Honduras • *Size:* 7½" x 50 *Filler:* Hon., Nica., Dom. Rep. *Binder/Wrapper:* Ecuador
Another no-nonsense double corona. Very good-looking cigar with a smooth finish and a fine texture. The

Diademas smokes steady and easy, with light, grassy, earthy flavors and a slightly bitter finish. (12/01/92)
U.S.: $3.40 • U.K.: N/A

PUNCH CHATEAU L **85**
Honduras • *Size:* 7½" x 52 *Filler/Binder/Wrapper:* Honduras
A dark-brown wrapper. It has rich, spicy flavors with solid cocoa bean notes, but there is a woodsy-earthy tone that detracts in this cigar.
U.S.: $2.90 • U.K.: N/A

THE GRIFFIN'S **85**
PRESTIGE
Dominican Republic • *Size:* 8" x 48 *Filler/Binder:* Dom. Rep. *Wrapper:* U.S.A./ Conn. Shade
A cigar with some solid tobacco characteristics and spiciness—but with vegetal flavors that detract.
U.S.: $5.45 • U.K.: N/A

AVO NO. 3 **84**
Dominican Republic • *Size:* 7½" x 52 *Filler/Binder:* Dom. Rep. *Wrapper:* U.S.A./Conn. Shade
This is a cigar with a dry taste on the finish but some nutty, mild spice flavors.
U.S.: $6.25 • U.K.: N/A

CASA BLANCA **84**
PRESIDENTE
Dominican Republic • *Size:* 7½" x 50 *Filler:* Dom. Rep. *Binder:* Mexico *Wrapper:* U.S.A./Conn. Shade
A very mild cigar with a solid grassy, dry-paper character, but it has a light, creamy finish.
U.S.: $2.15 • U.K.: N/A

DON LINO COLORADO **84**
PRESIDENTE
Honduras • *Size:* 7½" x 50 *Filler/Binder:* Honduras, Nicaragua *Wrapper:* U.S.A./ Conn. Shade
A very mild, light cigar with some sweet, dry aromas and flavors.
U.S.: $8.00 • U.K.: N/A

JOYA DE NICARAGUA **83**
CHURCHILL
Nicaragua • *Size:* 6⅞" x 49 *Filler/Binder/Wrapper:* Nicaragua
This is not the most complex cigar, but it has plenty of flavor. Medium-brown wrapper with a slightly rough finish, it is a little underfilled making it soft when pressed between your fingers. Nonetheless, it shows captivating nutty, coffee character and lovely, velvety texture. (12/01/92)
U.S.: $2.20 • U.K.: £3.00

LA FONTANA **83**
MICHELANGELO
Honduras • *Size:* 7½" x 52 *Filler:* Honduras *Binder:* Mexico *Wrapper:* U.S.A./ Conn. Shade
This is a very loosely filled cigar with a hot draw. It has dry, strawlike flavors and a very dry, papery finish.
U.S.: $3.15 • U.K.: N/A

LEON JIMENES NO. 1 83
Dominican Republic •
Size: 7½" x 50 *Filler/Binder:*
Dom. Rep. *Wrapper:*
U.S.A./Conn. Shade
A very light, mellow smoke
with some creamy, mild spice
flavors but a flat, neutral finish.
U.S.: $5.50 • U.K.: N/A

ROMEO Y JULIETA 83
CHURCHILL
Dominican Republic • *Size:*
7" x 50 *Filler:* Brazil, Dom.
Rep. *Binder:* U.S.A./Conn.
Broadleaf *Wrapper:*
Cameroon
This cigar has tons of interesting earthy, rich flavors, but
it is a little overfilled and
hard. While smoking, it has
plenty of nutty, coffee, earthy
aromas and flavors with a
long aftertaste. (12/01/92)
U.S.: $2.30 • U.K.: N/A

ROYAL JAMAICA GIANT 83
CORONA
Dominican Republic • *Size:*
7½" x 49 *Filler:* Jamaica
Binder: Java *Wrapper:*
Cameroon
An individualistic smoke
with earthy aromas as you
puff away. It is lovely to look
at with a fine, medium-
brown wrapper and firm construction. The flavors are
delicious with lots of walnut
and coffee character.
(12/01/92)
U.S.: $3.10 • U.K.: £7.00

V CENTENNIAL 83
PRESIDENTE
Honduras • *Size:* 8" x 50
Filler: Dom. Rep., Honduras,
Nicaragua *Binder:* Mexico
Wrapper: U.S.A./Conn.
Shade
A mild cigar with a rough,
light-brown wrapper. It has a
grassy, dry-paper taste with a
hint of spice.
U.S.: $5.75 • U.K.: N/A

VUELTABAJO GIGANTE 83
Dominican Republic • *Size:*
8½" x 52 *Filler/Binder:* Dom.
Rep. *Wrapper:* U.S.A./
Conn. Shade
This mild cigar has very sim-
ple, light flavors that tend
toward dry wood and paper.
And it has some sour notes.
U.S.: $2.75 • U.K.: N/A

TE-AMO CHURCHILL 82
Mexico • *Size:* 7½" x 50
Filler/Binder/Wrapper: Mexico
An extremely mild cigar with
a very hot, loose draw that
has grassy and vegetal flavors.
U.S.: $3.05 • U.K.: N/A

TROYA EXECUTIVE 82
NO. 72
Dominican Republic • *Size:*
7¼" x 50 *Filler/Binder:* Dom.
Rep. *Wrapper:* U.S.A./
Conn. Shade
A mild cigar with a very yel-
low-brown wrapper. It is medi-
um bodied with some creamy
flavors. A simple smoke.
U.S.: $3.70 • U.K.: N/A

EL RICO HABANO 80
GRAN HABANERO
DELUXE
U.S.A. • *Size:* 7¼" x 50
Filler: Nicaragua, Ecuador,
Dom. Rep. *Binder:* Dom.
Rep. *Wrapper:* Ecuador
A medium-bodied cigar with
decent, earthy flavor, but it
lacks complexity.
U.S.: $2.35 • U.K.: N/A

BACCARAT CHURCHILL 79
Honduras • *Size:* 7" x 50
Filler: Honduras *Binder:*
Mexico *Wrapper:* U.S.A./
Conn. Shade
Rather unusual in style, the
Baccarat has light chocolate
and tobacco flavors although
its sweet wrapper may not be
to everyone's liking. It is
well-constructed and
extremely firm, but some
members of the smoking
panel were put off by the
sweetness of the
cigar. (12/01/92)
U.S.: $1.75 • U.K.: N/A

PEÑAMIL NO. 57 69
Canary Islands • *Size:*
7½" x 50 *Filler:* Special
Blend *Binder:* Dom. Rep.
Wrapper: U.S.A./Conn.
Shade
It is hard to find something
nice to say about this cigar.
The wrapper was so brittle
that it broke in most of our
smokers' hands. Worse, it
burnt as fast as a quickly burn-
ing fuse. Forget it. (12/01/92)
U.S.: $4.85 • U.K.: N/A

CHURCHILL

Most of the following Churchill tasting notes appeared in the Autumn 1995 issue of Cigar Aficionado. Exceptions are indicated by a date in parentheses at the end of the tasting note.

ROMEO Y JULIETA CHURCHILL **92**
Cuba • *Size:* 7" x 47 *Filler/Binder/Wrapper:* Cuba
This remains the benchmark Cuban Churchill. It is filled with a deep, rich spiciness, strong cocoa bean flavors and a lingering rich finish.
U.S.: N/A • U.K.: £9.70

PUNCH CHURCHILL **91**
Cuba • *Size:* 7" x 47 *Filler/Binder/Wrapper:* Cuba
A very smooth, full-bodied cigar with a rich earthiness, leather and sweet spices like nutmeg and a pleasing woody finish.
U.S.: N/A • U.K.: £9.70

BOLIVAR CORONA GIGANTES **90**
Cuba • *Size:* 7" x 47 *Filler/Binder/Wrapper:* Cuba
A cigar filled with spices, including cinammon and nutmeg, and a pleasant sweetness that finishes in a complex earthiness.
U.S.: N/A • U.K.: £9.70

DON JUAN CHURCHILL **90**
Nicaragua • *Size:* 7" x 49 *Filler/Wrapper:* Nicaragua *Binder:* Dom. Rep.
A very smooth-tasting cigar with flavors of toast and nuts and a strong spicy tobacco

finish with a nutmeg quality.
U.S.: $2.30 • U.K.: N/A

QUAI D'ORSAY IMPERIALES **90**
Cuba • *Size:* 7" x 47 *Filler/Binder/Wrapper:* Cuba
A rich-tasting cigar with toasted bread and cinnamon flavors and a lingering finish.
(09/01/93)
U.S.: N/A • France.: 55FF

ARTURO FUENTE DOUBLE CHATEAU **89**
Dominican Republic • *Size:* 6¼" x 50 *Filler/Binder:* Dom. Rep. *Wrapper:* U.S.A./Conn. Shade
A beautifully made cigar with an even brown color and good draw. It has medium- to full-bodied quality with pepper and spice flavors.
U.S.: $2.65 • U.K.: N/A

ARTURO FUENTE CHURCHILL **89**
Dominican Republic • *Size:* 7¼" x 48 *Filler/Binder:* Dom. Rep. *Wrapper:* Cameroon
A rich, medium-bodied cigar with a solid, sweet spiciness and a strong component of coffee beans that finishes just a touch dry.
U.S.: $2.50 • U.K.: N/A

COHIBA ESPLENDIDOS **89**
Cuba • *Size:* 7" x 47 *Filler/Binder/Wrapper:* Cuba
A full-bodied cigar with black cherrylike notes, and a woody spiciness on the palate. A firm, almost tough draw.
U.S.: N/A • U.K.: £17.60

CUBA ALIADOS VALENTINO NO. 1 **89**
Honduras • *Size:* 7" x 47 *Filler/Binder:* Honduras, Dom. Rep. *Wrapper:* Ecuador
This medium-bodied cigar has rich, flavorful character with a smooth, toasty texture and includes a spiciness and a cedar-box quality.
U.S.: $2.95 • U.K.: N/A

FLOR DE CAÑO DIADEMAS **89**
Cuba • *Size:* 7" x 47 *Filler/Binder/Wrapper:* Cuba
A full-bodied cigar with an earthy character, and a full range of leather and sweet spice flavors like nutmeg.
U.S.: N/A • U.K.: £9.70

MONTECRISTO CHURCHILL **89**
Dominican Republic • *Size:* 7" x 48 *Filler/Binder:* Dom. Rep. *Wrapper:* U.S.A./Conn. Shade
A very well-made, medium-bodied cigar with a creamy character and flavor notes of leather, light spices and a toasted butter finish.
U.S.: $6.95 • U.K.: N/A

MONTECRUZ NO. 200 NATURAL CLARO **89**
Dominican Republic • *Size:* 7¼" x 46 *Filler:* Dom. Rep, Brazil *Binder:* Dom. Rep. *Wrapper:* U.S.A./Conn. Shade
A very well-made cigar with a good draw and a floral aroma. It has a creaminess tinged with sweet spice, nuts and a hint of leather.
U.S.: $3.70 • U.K.: N/A

PARTAGAS NO. 10 **89**
Dominican Republic •
Size: 7½" x 49 *Filler:* Dom.
Rep., Mexico *Binder:*
Mexico *Wrapper:* Cameroon
A well-made cigar with a
solid medium-bodied smoke.
It has nutty flavors around a
very spicy core and a nice
coffee bean finish.
U.S.: $4.25 • U.K.: N/A

SAINT LUIS REY **89**
CHURCHILL
Cuba • *Size:* 7" x 47 *Filler/
Binder/Wrapper:* Cuba
This is a powerful cigar with
a rich cocoa bean character
and a touch of leather and
nuts, but with a short finish.
U.S.: N/A • U.K.: £9.00

8-9-8 COLLECTION **88**
CHURCHILL
Jamaica • *Size:* 7½" x 49
Filler: Jamaica, Dom. Rep.
Binder: Mexico *Wrapper:*
U.S.A./Conn. Shade
A well-made cigar with floral
notes on the palate, a nice
spiciness and an elegant
finish.
U.S.: $6.75 • U.K.: N/A

DIANA SILVIUS **88**
CHURCHILL
Dominican Republic • *Size:*
7" x 50 *Filler/Binder:* Dom.
Rep. *Wrapper:* U.S.A./
Conn. Shade
A medium-bodied cigar with a
spicy, peppery flavor and a long
spicy finish. Some inconsistency.
U.S.: $5.80 • U.K.: N/A

HOYO DE MONTERREY **88**
CHURCHILL
Cuba • *Size:* 7" x 47 *Filler/
Binder/Wrapper:* Cuba
This cigar has some exotic
spice flavors including nut-
meg and cinnamon, but it
has a dry finish.
U.S.: N/A • U.K.: £9.70

JUAN CLEMENTE **88**
CHURCHILL
Dominican Republic • *Size:*
6⅞" x 46 *Filler/Binder:* Dom.
Rep. *Wrapper:* U.S.A./
Conn. Shade
This is a rich-tasting but
medium-bodied cigar with
earthy flavors and a spicy
character.
U.S.: $4.90 • U.K.: £5.75

LA UNICA NO. 200 **88**
Dominican Republic • *Size:*
7" x 49 *Filler/Binder:* Dom.
Rep. *Wrapper:* U.S.A./
Conn. Shade
A nice medium-bodied cigar
with complex flavors includ-
ing nuts, sweet spices and
black pepper.
U.S.: $2.40 • U.K.: £4.00

LOS LIBERTADORES **88**
MAMBISES
Dominican Republic • *Size:*
6⅞" x 48 *Filler/Binder:* Dom.
Rep. *Wrapper:* U.S.A./
Conn. Shade
A mild- to medium-bodied
cigar with a light woody
spiciness, and some espresso
coffee bean on an otherwise
woody finish.
U.S.: $6.95 • U.K.: N/A

MONTECRUZ SUN- **88**
GROWN NO. 200
Dominican Republic • *Size:*
7¼" x 46 *Filler/Binder:* Dom.
Rep., Brazil *Wrapper:*
Indonesia
A well-made cigar with some
leathery notes, earthy com-
plexity and a smooth, creamy
finish.
U.S.: $3.70 • U.K.: N/A

NAT SHERMAN **88**
EXCHANGE SELECTION
OXFORD NO. 5
Dominican Republic • *Size:*
7" x 49 *Filler:* Dom. Rep.,
Mexico, Jamaica *Binder:*
Mexican *Wrapper:* U.S.A./
Conn. Shade
This is a good solid cigar with
some earthiness, spicy flavors
and a nice woody finish.
U.S.: $5.85 • U.K.: N/A

OLOR COLOSSOS **88**
Dominican Republic •
Size: 7½" x 48 *Filler/Binder:*
Dom. Rep. *Wrapper:*
U.S.A./Conn. Shade
A spicy cigar with a very nice
silky pepper quality that leads
into a fairly neutral finish.
U.S.: $2.60 • U.K.: N/A

SAVINELLI E.L.R. **88**
CHURCHILL
Dominican Republic • *Size:*
7¼" x 48 *Filler/Binder:* Dom.
Rep. *Wrapper:* U.S.A./
Conn. Shade
A medium-bodied cigar with
a smooth nutty character and
a creamy texture that leads
into a soft spicy finish.
U.S.: $7.50 • U.K.: N/A

SOSA CHURCHILL **88**
Dominican Republic • *Size:*
6¹⁵⁄₁₆ x 49 *Filler:* Dom. Rep.
Binder: Honduras *Wrapper:*
Ecuador
This is a spicy and peppery-
tasting cigar with hints of mild
cocoa flavors that end with a
nutty, slightly dry finish.
U.S.: $2.85 • U.K.: N/A

THOMAS HINDS **88**
HONDURAN SELECTION
CHURCHILL
Honduras • *Size:* 7" x 49
Filler/Binder: Honduras
Wrapper: Ecuador
This is a well-made cigar
with a rich spiciness. It has a
bit of young tobacco, but is a
solid-tasting cigar.
U.S.: $3.45 • Canada: $3.85

AVO NO. 5 **87**
Dominican Republic •
Size: 6¼" x 46 *Filler/Binder:*
Dom. Rep. *Wrapper:*
U.S.A./Conn. Shade
An elegant smoke with a
rich, spicy component that
includes flavors of nutmeg
and other sweet spices. A
slightly dry finish.
U.S.: $6.05 • U.K.: N/A

CARRINGTON NO. 5 **87**
Dominican Republic •
Size: 6⅛" x 46 *Filler/Binder:*
Dom. Rep. *Wrapper:*
U.S.A./Conn. Shade
A mild- to medium-bodied
cigar with a solid core of
spice, and a good toasty fla-
vor.
U.S.: $4.20 • U.K.: N/A

EL REY DEL MUNDO **87**
TAINOS
Cuba • *Size:* 7" x 47 *Filler/*
Binder/Wrapper: Cuba
Uneven construction hurts
this simple mild cigar with a
grassy taste and a light spicy
finish. (09/01/93)
U.S.: N/A • U.K.: £8.36

JULIA MARLOWE **87**
MONARCH
Dominican Republic • *Size:*
7" x 48 *Filler/Binder:* Dom.
Rep. *Wrapper:* Ecuador
A smooth-smoking cigar
with a good balance of spice
and tobacco flavors, although
there is a tendency to finish
with a bit of a bite.
(09/01/93)
U.S.: $2.30 • U.K.: N/A

NAT SHERMAN **87**
DAKOTA
Dominican Republic • *Size:*
7½" x 49 *Filler:* Jam., Mex.,
Dom. Rep. *Binder:* Mexico
Wrapper: Cameroon
This uncomplicated cigar
with a medium-brown wrap-
per delivers a taste of dark-
roasted coffee and a mild
spiciness. (09/01/93)
U.S.: $4.30 • U.K.: N/A

NAT SHERMAN **87**
GOTHAM SELECTION
NO. 500
Dominican Republic • *Size:*
7" x 50 *Filler/Binder:* Dom.
Rep. *Wrapper:* U.S.A./
Conn. Shade
A pleasant medium- to full-
bodied cigar with a spiciness
on the palate and an earthy
creaminess on the finish.
U.S.: $6.35 • U.K.: N/A

POR LARRAÑAGA **87**
FABULOSO
Dominican Republic • *Size:*
7" x 50 *Filler/Binder:* Dom.
Rep. *Wrapper:* U.S.A./
Conn. Shade
A smooth and creamy cigar
with a good balance and a
core of spice and coffee notes
that finishes with a slightly
woody and earthy taste.
U.S.: $4.50 • U.K.: N/A

PUNCH GRAND CRU **87**
MONARCH
Honduras • *Size:* 6¼" x 48
Filler: Nicaragua, Dom. Rep.
Binder: U.S.A./Conn.
Broadleaf *Wrapper:* Ecuador,
Honduras
An attractive cigar with a
light floral character, but sev-
eral tasters noted a hot,
slightly harsh finish.
(09/01/93)
U.S.: $5.00 • U.K.: N/A

SANTA ROSA **87**
CHURCHILL
Honduras • *Size:* 7" x 49
Filler/Binder: Nicaragua,
Honduras, Dom. Rep.
Wrapper: U.S.A./Conn.
Shade
A good, solid, medium-bod-
ied cigar with a spicy core of
flavors, a smooth texture and
a spicy finish.
U.S.: $2.90 • U.K.: N/A

V CENTENNIAL **87**
CHURCHILL
Honduras • *Size:* 7" x 48
Filler: Dom. Rep, Honduras,
Nicaragua *Binder:* Mexico
Wrapper: U.S.A./Conn.
Shade

A medium-bodied cigar that has a solid, spicy core and a smooth, creamy character with a cedarwood finish.
U.S.: $5.25 • U.K.: N/A

AVO XO MAESTOSO 86
Dominican Republic •
Size: 7" x 48 *Filler/Binder:*
Dom. Rep. *Wrapper:*
U.S.A./Conn. Shade
A medium-bodied cigar that has mild flavors of nuts and leather, backed up by a bit of spiciness.
U.S.: $8.80 • U.K.: N/A

CACIQUE NO. 7 86
Dominican Republic •
Size: 6⅞" x 46 *Filler/Binder:*
Dom. Rep. *Wrapper:*
U.S.A./Conn. Shade
A medium-bodied cigar with some pleasant, toasty notes, and an earthy quality of woods and mushrooms.
U.S.: $2.60 • U.K.: N/A

CUESTA-REY CABINET 86
8-9-8
Dominican Republic • *Size:*
7" x 49 *Filler/Binder:* Dom.
Rep. *Wrapper:* U.S.A./
Conn. Shade
This is a nice, medium-bodied smoke with some nutty flavors and a slightly dry, woody finish.
U.S.: $2.50 • U.K.: £5.50

DAVIDOFF 86
ANIVERSARIO NO. 2
Dominican Republic • *Size:*
7" x 48 *Filler/Binder:* Dom.
Rep. *Wrapper:* U.S.A./
Conn. Shade
This cigar offers up a range of cream and nut flavors and a

firm draw, but it has a bit of sourness on the finish.
U.S.: $14.10 • U.K.: £15.40

DON DIEGO 86
MONARCH
Dominican Republic •
Size: 7¼ x 47 *Filler/Binder:*
Dom. Rep. *Wrapper:*
U.S.A./Conn. Shade
This mellow straightforward cigar has a beautiful dark-brown wrapper, and rich flavors of mild coffee and nut.
(09/01/93)
U.S.: $3.40 • U.K.: N/A

DUNHILL CABRERAS 86
Dominican Republic •
Size: 7" x 48 *Filler/Binder:*
Dom. Rep., Brazil *Wrapper:*
U.S.A./Conn. Shade
This is a mild, creamy cigar with a mild coffee flavor and a smooth character overall. It has a mild finish.
U.S.: $6.30 • U.K.: N/A

EL REY DEL MUNDO 86
DOUBLE CORONA
Honduras • *Size:* 7" x 48
Filler/Binder: Honduras, Dom.
Rep. *Wrapper:* Ecuador
A medium-bodied cigar. It has a strong woody component with a balance of coffeelike flavors.
U.S.: $3.00 • U.K.: N/A

FONSECA 10-10 86
Dominican Republic • *Size:*
7" x 50 *Filler:* Dom. Rep.
Binder: Mexico *Wrapper:*
U.S.A./Conn. Shade
This is a medium-bodied cigar with smooth flavors that include cream and sweet nuts, but with a somewhat

tight draw.
U.S.: $4.25 • U.K.: N/A

JOSÉ MARTÍ MARTÍ 86
Dominican Republic •
Size: 7¼" x 50 *Filler/Binder:*
Dom. Rep. *Wrapper:*
U.S.A./Conn. Shade
This is a mild- to medium-bodied cigar. It has some light spiciness, an overall woody character and a dry finish.
U.S.: $3.00 • U.K.: N/A

LA RESERVA NO. 2 86
Honduras • *Size:* 6½"
x 48 *Filler:* Dom. Rep.,
Honduras *Binder:* Ecuador
Wrapper: U.S.A./Conn.
Shade
A straightforward smooth-smoking cigar with an attractive dark-brown wrapper. It has ample mild spice and pepper flavors. (09/01/93)
U.S.: $2.75 • U.K.: N/A

LEMPIRA CHURCHILL 86
Honduras • *Size:* 7" x 48
Filler/Binder: Honduras, Dom.
Rep. *Wrapper:* U.S.A./
Conn. Shade
A cigar with good balance and a smooth taste backed up by spice and pepper flavors.
U.S.: $3.25 • U.K.: N/A

LEON JIMENES NO. 2 86
Dominican Republic •
Size: 7" x 47 *Filler/Binder:*
Dom. Rep. *Wrapper:*
U.S.A./Conn. Shade
A cigar with a firm draw and a very pronounced nutty flavor that opens up to a solid tobacco flavor.
U.S.: $4.25 • U.K.: N/A

Montesino Gran Corona 86

Dominican Republic • *Size:* 6¼" x 48 *Filler/Binder:* Dom. Rep., Brazil *Wrapper:* U.S.A./Conn. Sun-Grown
This well-made light-bodied cigar comes on quickly with a mild creaminess, but overall is slightly grassy and has a tangy finish. (09/01/93)
U.S.: $1.85 • U.K.: N/A

Troya No. 63 86

Dominican Republic • *Size:* 6⅞" x 46 *Filler/Binder:* Dom. Rep. *Wrapper:* U.S.A./Conn. Shade
A very nicely balanced, medium-bodied cigar with a firm draw, earthy aroma and a mix of flavors including toast and sweet spices.
U.S.: $2.85 • U.K.: N/A

Zino Veritas 86

Honduras • *Size:* 7" x 50 *Filler/Binder/Wrapper:* Honduras
An attractive cigar with a floral aroma and flavor notes of spice and leather on the palate that extend into the finish.
U.S.: $7.10 • U.K.: N/A

Baccarat Churchill 85

Honduras • *Size:* 7" x 50 *Filler/Wrapper:* Honduras *Binder:* Mexico
Despite a touch of sweet gum on the wrapper, this cigar still has solid tobacco flavors, a bit of spice and a nice tanginess.
U.S.: $2.05 • U.K.: N/A

Bances Corona Inmensa 85

Honduras • *Size:* 6¼" x 48 *Filler/Binder:* Honduras, Dom. Rep. Nicaragua *Wrapper:* Ecuador
This is a spicy cigar with a solid core of earthy flavors that end with a slightly dry finish.
U.S.: $2.55 • U.K.: N/A

Caballeros Churchill 85

Dominican Republic • *Size:* 7" x 50 *Filler/Binder:* Dom. Rep. *Wrapper:* U.S.A./ Conn. Shade
A cigar with strong herbal notes and a smooth balance, with a creamy character and a fairly spicy finish.
U.S.: $3.50 • U.K.: N/A

Camacho Churchill 85

Honduras • *Size:* 7" x 48 *Filler/Binder/Wrapper:* Honduras
A cigar with a fine floral aroma, and flavors of toast and nuts, but with a fairly flat, dry finish.
U.S.: $2.75 • U.K.: N/A

El Rico Habano Double Corona 85

U.S.A. • *Size:* 7" x 47 *Filler:* Dom. Rep., Ecuador, Nicaragua *Binder/Wrapper:* Ecuador
The oily, dark brown wrapper gives a full-bodied smoke with an earthy aroma. It has some spice, but also has a youthful harshness.
U.S.: $2.35 • U.K.: N/A

Joya de Nicaragua Churchill 85

Nicaragua • *Size:* 6⅞" x 49 *Filler/Binder/Wrapper:* Nicaragua
Showed some inconsistency, but has a nice, spicy character with a nutty aroma and a slightly dry finish.
U.S.: $2.40 • U.K.: N/A

Los Libertadores Reserve Special Churchill 85

Dominican Republic • *Size:* 6⅞" x 49 *Filler/Binder:* Dom. Rep. *Wrapper:* U.S.A./ Conn. Shade
This cigar tastes of young tobacco, but has a nice creaminess and a touch of pepper on a dry finish.
U.S.: $7.20 • U.K.: N/A

Macanudo Vintage No. 1 85

Jamaica • *Size:* 7½" x 49 *Filler:* Jamaica, Dom. Rep. Mexico *Binder:* Mexico *Wrapper:* U.S.A./Conn. Shade
This is a well-made medium-bodied cigar with some flavors of nuts and a light spiciness.
U.S.: $8.75 • U.K.: N/A

Maya Churchill 85

Honduras • *Size:* 6⅞" x 49 *Filler/Binder:* Honduras, Dom. Rep. *Wrapper:* U.S.A./Conn. Shade
This mild cigar has a nice woody finish that comes out of good, solid, nutty flavors.
U.S.: $2.50 • U.K.: N/A

ONYX NO. 646 **85**
Dominican Republic • *Size:*
6⅝" x 46 *Filler:* Dom. Rep.,
Mexico *Binder:* Indonesia
Wrapper: Mexico
A maduro cigar with roasted
nut and coffee bean flavors that
finishes with sweet spice notes.
U.S.: $2.30 • U.K.: N/A

PUNCH CHATEAU L **85**
Honduras • *Size:* 7¼"
x 54 *Filler/Binder:* Honduras,
Nicaragua, Dom. Rep.
Wrapper: Ecuador
This cigar has a good draw
with a nice rich spicy taste,
and a slightly woody finish.
U.S.: $3.05 • U.K.: N/A

RAMON ALLONES **85**
REDONDOS
Dominican Republic • *Size:*
7½" x 49 *Filler:* Dom. Rep.,
Mexico *Binder:* Mexico
Wrapper: Cameroon
This is a well-balanced cigar
with a toasty character and a
nice solid spiciness on the
palate.
U.S.: $3.95 • U.K.: N/A

ROMEO Y JULIETA **85**
VINTAGE NO. 4
Dominican Republic • *Size:*
7" x 48 *Filler:* Dom. Rep.
Binder: Mexico *Wrapper:*
U.S.A./Conn. Shade
This is a nice, mild cigar that
has some mild spice and cof-
fee flavors, but with a slightly
dry finish.
U.S.: $6.00 • U.K.: N/A

ASHTON PRIME **84**
MINISTER
Dominican Republic • *Size:*
7" x 48 *Filler/Binder:* Dom.
Rep. *Wrapper:* U.S.A./
Conn. Shade
A nice-looking mild cigar
with a touch of spice and
dried fruit, but has a flinty
finish, and the bite of young
tobacco.
U.S.: $3.90 • U.K.: N/A

ASHTON CHURCHILL **84**
Dominican Republic • *Size:*
7½" x 52 *Filler/Binder:* Dom.
Rep. *Wrapper:* U.S.A./
Conn. Shade
This is a well-made mild
cigar that has some spicy fla-
vors but with some young
tobacco tastes.
U.S.: $4.50 • U.K.: N/A

BAUZA CASA GRANDE **84**
Dominican Republic •
Size: 6¼" x 48 *Filler:* Dom.
Rep., Nicaragua *Binder:*
Mexico *Wrapper:* Cameroon
A well-made cigar that has a
sweetish tobacco character
with some sweet spices, but
shows some young tobacco
notes.
U.S.: $2.75 • U.K.: N/A

CREDO MAGNIFICAT **84**
Dominican Republic •
Size: 6⅞" x 46 *Filler/Binder:*
Dom. Rep. *Wrapper:*
U.S.A./Conn. Shade
A well-made cigar that suf-
fers somewhat from young
tobacco. A bit raw but with
some solid flavors of nuts and
wood on the palate.
U.S.: $4.95 • U.K.: N/A

CUBA ALIADOS **84**
CHURCHILL EXTRA
Honduras • *Size:* 7¼" x 54
Filler: Dom. Rep *Binder/*
Wrapper: Ecuador
This cigar has a very firm
draw and a cedary character.
Overall, it lacks depth and
complexity.
U.S.: $3.25 • U.K.: £4.30

CUESTA-REY **84**
DOMINICAN NO. 2
Dominican Republic • *Size:*
7¼" x 48 *Filler/Binder:* Dom.
Rep. *Wrapper:* U.S.A./
Conn. Shade
A nice, light, spicy cigar with
some nuttiness. It shows a bit
of youth with a slightly green
wood finish.
U.S.: $2.95 • U.K.: £6.20

H. UPMANN **84**
MONARCH
Dominican Republic •
Size: 7" x 47 *Filler/Binder:*
Dom. Rep. *Wrapper:*
Indonesia
This cigar has a rough wrap-
per and a firm draw. It has a
slightly sour taste with a core
of spicy and nutty flavors.
U.S.: $4.00 • U.K.: N/A

HABANA GOLD BLACK **84**
LABEL CHURCHILL
Honduras • *Size:* 7½" x 46
Filler/Binder: Nicaragua,
Honduras *Wrapper:* Ecuador
This easy-drawing cigar has
some spice on the palate and
a flinty finish that ends a bit
dry.
U.S.: $5.00 • U.K.: N/A

JOSE BENITO CHURCHILL **84**

Dominican Republic • *Size:* 7" x 50 *Filler:* Dom. Rep. *Binder:* Central America *Wrapper:* Cameroon
A nice, medium-bodied cigar with a floral aroma and a sweet tobacco character with good balance.
U.S.: $2.85 • U.K.: N/A

LA AURORA BRISTOL ESPECIAL **84**

Dominican Republic • *Size:* 6⅛" x 48 *Filler/Binder:* Dom. Rep. *Wrapper:* Cameroon
A slightly tight, mild cigar with a pleasant earthy quality that has some nutty flavors. Some inconsistency noted.
U.S.: $2.10 • U.K.: N/A

LA FONTANA DA VINCI **84**

Honduras • *Size:* 6⅞" x 48 *Filler/Binder:* Honduras *Wrapper:* U.S.A./Conn. Shade This cigar's sweet wrapper isn't for everybody, but it is a well-made, light mild smoke with a slightly grassy and creamy flavor. (09/01/93)
U.S.: $2.25 • U.K.: N/A

SANTA DAMIANA CABINET SELECTION No. 800 **84**

Dominican Republic • *Size:* 7" x 50 *Filler/Binder:* Dom. Rep. *Wrapper:* U.S.A./Conn. Shade
A pleasant mild- to medium-bodied cigar with a creamy, smooth character and flavors of nuts, with a touch of spice and a dry finish.
U.S.: $8.00 • U.K.: N/A

TE-AMO PRESIDENTE **84**

Mexico • *Size:* 7" x 50 *Filler/Binder/Wrapper:* Mexico
A distinct, peppery cigar with a minerallike finish.
U.S.: $2.90 • U.K.: N/A

TEMPLE HALL No. 700 **84**

Jamaica • *Size:* 7½" x 49 *Filler:* Jamaica, Dom. Rep., Mexico *Binder:* Mexico *Wrapper:* Cameroon
This is a pleasant, mild- to medium-bodied cigar with a touch of spice and vanilla.
U.S.: $5.50 • U.K.: N/A

HOYO DE MONTERREY DOUBLE CORONA **83**

Honduras • *Size:* 6¼" x 48 *Filler/Binder:* Honduras, Nicaragua, Dom. Rep. *Wrapper:* Ecuador
An oily wrapper with some strong spicy elements and a creamy character with a slightly dry finish.
U.S.: $2.50 • U.K.: N/A

LAS CABRILLAS DESOTO **83**

Honduras • *Size:* 6⅞" x 50 *Filler/Binder:* Mexico, Nicaragua *Wrapper:* U.S.A./Conn. Shade
A smooth-tasting cigar with a good balance of creaminess and a soft, leathery taste.
U.S.: $1.85 • U.K.: N/A

MACANUDO PRINCE PHILIP **83**

Jamaica • *Size:* 7½" x 49 *Filler:* Jamaica, Dom. Rep., Mexico *Binder:* Mexico *Wrapper:* U.S.A./Conn. Shade
A mild cigar with an earthy quality and a creamy texture.
U.S.: $4.20 • U.K.: N/A

PRIMO DEL REY CLUB SELECCION REGALS **83**

Dominican Republic • *Size:* 7" x 50 *Filler/Binder:* Dom. Rep. *Wrapper:* U.S.A./Conn. Shade
Inconsistency noted. This cigar had some good spicy character but also had a dry, slightly papery finish.
U.S.: $2.10 • U.K.: N/A

ROYAL JAMAICA GIANT CORONA **83**

Dominican Republic • *Size:* 7½" x 49 *Filler:* Dom. Rep., Jamaica, Sumatra *Binder:* Cameroon *Wrapper:* Indonesia
This cigar showed some tightness in the draw and had a sweet nut flavor and a mild coffee bean finish.
U.S.: $3.70 • U.K.: N/A

SANTA DAMIANA SELECCION No. 100 **83**

Dominican Republic • *Size:* 6¼" x 48 *Filler/Binder:* Dom. Rep. *Wrapper:* U.S.A./Conn. Shade
A cigar with some cedary components. Overall it has a dry, woody character.
U.S.: $7.00 • U.K.: N/A

TRESADO SELECCION No. 200 **83**

Dominican Republic • *Size:* 7" x 48 *Filler:* Dom. Rep. *Binder:* Cameroon *Wrapper:* Indonesia
A mild, smooth cigar with a floral character and a woody finish.
U.S.: $1.85 • U.K.: N/A

VUELTABAJO CHURCHILL — 83

Dominican Republic • *Size:* 7" x 48 *Filler/Binder:* Dom. Rep. *Wrapper:* U.S.A./ Conn. Shade
A medium-bodied cigar with a smooth, nutty character and a pleasing, mildly earthy finish.
U.S.: $2.80 • U.K.: N/A

CUBITA 2000 — 82

Dominican Republic • *Size:* 7" x 50 *Filler/Binder:* Dom. Rep. *Wrapper:* U.S.A./Conn. Shade
While this cigar is well-made, it has a sharp peppery taste that turns into a sweetish flavor.
U.S.: $5.00 • U.K.: N/A

HOYO DE MONTERREY EXCALIBUR BANQUET — 82

Honduras • *Size:* 6¼" x 48 *Filler:* Nicaragua, Honduras, Dom. Rep. *Binder:* Honduras *Wrapper:* U.S.A./ Conn. Shade
Showed inconsistency. This cigar has a mild spiciness but was hampered by apparently young tobacco and a slightly hot finish.
U.S.: $5.55 • U.K.: £5.29

HOYO DE MONTERREY SULTAN — 82

Honduras • *Size:* 7¼" x 54 *Filler/Binder:* Honduras, Nicaragua, Dom. Rep. *Wrapper:* Ecuador
This medium- to full-bodied cigar has some spiciness, but is dominated by dry, balsawood flavors that have a faint vegetal quality.
U.S.: $3.05 • U.K.: N/A

PAUL GARMIRIAN CHURCHILL — 82

Dominican Republic • *Size:* 7" x 48 *Filler/Binder:* Dom. Rep. *Wrapper:* U.S.A./ Conn. Shade
This medium-bodied cigar has a very mild, spicy note, but ends up with a relatively flat finish.
U.S.: $8.00 • U.K.: £7.90

PETRUS CHURCHILL — 82

Honduras • *Size:* 7" x 50 *Filler/Binder:* Honduras *Wrapper:* Ecuador
A fairly rough-looking cigar with some nut and mild spice notes, and a dry, woody finish.
U.S.: $3.50 • U.K.: £7.50

PRIMO DEL REY SOBERANO — 82

Dominican Republic • *Size:* 7½" x 50 *Filler:* Dom. Rep. *Binder:* U.S.A. *Wrapper:* Indonesia
A mild cigar with some nutty flavors, but an inconsistent construction and an unattractive wrapper.
U.S.: $2.50 • U.K.: N/A

PUNCH GRAND CRU DIADEMAS — 82

Honduras • *Size:* 7¼" x 54 *Filler/Binder:* Honduras, Nicaragua, Dom. Rep *Wrapper:* Ecuador
This cigar has some peppery and spicy notes, but ends on the vegetal side with a dry finish.
U.S.: $4.05 • U.K.: N/A

PLEIADES SIRIUS — 81

Dominican Republic • *Size:* 6⅞" x 46 *Filler/Binder:* Dom. Rep. *Wrapper:* U.S.A./Conn. Shade
This cigar had draw problems. It also had very dry flavors including orange peel, and a touch of spice on the finish.
U.S.: $5.25 • U.K.: N/A

PRIMO DEL REY ARISTOCRAT — 81

Dominican Republic • *Size:* 6¼" x 48 *Filler/Binder:* Dom. Rep. *Wrapper:* U.S.A./ Conn. Shade
A veiny rough wrapper produces slightly dried out flavors that hint at cocoa beans, and has a sharp finish.
U.S.: $1.95 • U.K.: N/A

PUNCH DOUBLE CORONA — 81

Honduras • *Size:* 6¼" x 48 *Filler/Binder:* Honduras, Nicaragua, Dom. Rep. *Wrapper:* Ecuador
This cigar has some coffee and pepper flavors, but ends with a neutral, flat taste.
U.S.: $2.50 • U.K.: N/A

HOYO DE MONTERREY EXCALIBUR NO. 1 — 80

Honduras • *Size:* 7¼" x 54 *Filler/Binder:* Honduras, Nicaragua, Dom. Rep *Wrapper:* U.S.A./Conn. Shade
This cigar had an unusual flower-like aroma, and a very grassy flavor element and a dry finish.
U.S.: $3.40 • U.K.: £3.80

ORNELAS CHURCHILL   79
Mexico • Size: 7" x 49
Filler/Binder/Wrapper: Mexico
An unusually green wrapper.
It has some sweet tobacco
quality but shows evidence of
young tobacco, and an over-
all vegetal quality.
U.S.: $5.00   •   U.K.: N/A

SANTA CLARA NO. 2   78
Mexico • Size: 6½" x 48
Filler/Binder/Wrapper: Mexico
This cigar has an extremely
rough, sandpapery wrapper. It
also has a very dry character,
with a balsa-wood flavor and
a papery finish.
U.S.: $2.20   •   U.K.: £3.50

CORONA GORDA

Most of the following Corona
Gorda tasting notes appeared in
the Winter 1996/97 issue of
Cigar Aficionado. Exceptions
are indicated by a date in
parentheses at the end of the
tasting note.

HOYO DE MONTERREY   92
EPICURE NO. 1
Cuba • Size: 5⅝" x 46   Filler/
Binder/Wrapper: Cuba
A well-balanced cigar with a
powerful, full-bodied spici-
ness. There is a complex
earthiness on the palate with
hints of nutmeg. A long finish.
U.S.: N/A   •   U.K.: £8.87

PADRON 1964   92
ANNIVERSARY SERIES
EXCLUSIVO
Nicaragua • Size: 5½" x 50
Filler/Binder/Wrapper:
Nicaragua

This is an excellent cigar. It
is filled with smooth spice
flavors. There's a hint of ripe
berries and a strong earthy,
leathery finish. Well made
with a beautiful wrapper.
U.S.: $7.20   •   U.K.: N/A

FUENTE FUENTE OPUS   91
X FUENTE FUENTE
Dominican Republic • Size:
5⅝" x 46   Filler/Binder/
Wrapper: Dom. Rep.
A powerhouse of flavors,
including cocoa and coffee
beans and roasted nuts, as
well as some sweet spices
such as nutmeg. It has a dark,
oily wrapper.
U.S.: $8.75   •   U.K.: N/A

ROMEO Y JULIETA   91
EXHIBICION NO. 3
Cuba • Size: 5⅝" x 46
Filler/Binder/Wrapper: Cuba
A hint of youth, but this is a
full-bodied, flavorful cigar.
Strong hints of cinnamon
and coffee beans on a
smooth, easy draw. Will
improve with age.
U.S.: N/A   •   U.K.: £7.99

BELINDA CABINET   89
Honduras • Size: 5⅝"
x 45   Filler: Dom. Rep.,
Honduras   Binder: Honduras
Wrapper: Ecuador
An attractive, medium-bod-
ied cigar with a smooth spici-
ness and creamy, coffee fla-
vor. (06/01/94)
U.S.: $1.65   •   U.K.: N/A

COHIBA SIGLO IV   89
Cuba • Size: 5⅝" x 46
Filler/Binder/Wrapper: Cuba

This cigar has a solid coffee
bean character and is loaded
with a core of spiciness. It is
medium- to full-bodied with
a smooth, leathery finish.
U.S.: N/A   •   U.K.: £12.36

EL RICO HABANO   89
GRAN CORONA
Dominican Republic • Size:
5¼" x 46   Filler: Nicaragua,
Ecuador   Binder: Dom. Rep.
Wrapper: Ecuador
An excellent cigar. It has a
solid spiciness and a core of
earthy, woody flavors that
linger on the finish. Well
made with a nice, oily wrapper.
U.S.: $2.80   •   U.K.: N/A

FLOR DE GONZALEZ   89
EXTRA CORONA
U.S.A. • Size: 6" x 50   Filler/
Binder: Dom. Rep., Honduras
Wrapper: Ecuador
This is a very pretty wrapper.
It offers an elegant smoke of
herbal spices and a solid core
of earthy tobacco flavors.
There are also hints of nuts
on the medium- to full-bod-
ied smoke.
U.S.: $4.75   •   U.K.: N/A

HOYO DE MONTERREY   89
EXCALIBUR NO. 3
Honduras • Size: 6¼" x 50
Filler/Binder: Honduras
Wrapper: U.S.A./Conn.
Shade
A good, solid smoke with
toasty aromas and nice fla-
vors of coffee and roasted
nuts that finish on a cedary
note. (06/01/94)
U.S.: $2.80   •   U.K.: £4.00

LEMPIRA TORO 89
Honduras • *Size:* 6" x 50
Filler: Honduras, Nicaragua
Binder: Dom. Rep. *Wrapper:*
U.S.A./Conn. Shade
A rich, earthy cigar. It has
flavors of roasted nuts, coffee
beans and a hint of cocoa.
There is a little spice on a
medium finish.
U.S.: $3.60 • U.K.: N/A

AVO NO. 2 88
Dominican Republic •
Size: 6" x 50 *Filler/Binder:*
Dom. Rep. *Wrapper:*
U.S.A./Conn. Shade
A simple, well-made cigar
with nutmeg and cedary fla-
vors and a nice, medium-
length finish. (06/01/94)
U.S.: $5.50 • U.K.: N/A

DON LINO HAVANA 88
RESERVE TORO
Honduras • *Size:* 5½" x 46
Filler/Binder: Honduras
Wrapper: U.S.A./Conn. Shade
A very spicy , medium- to
full-bodied cigar. It has notes
of dried citrus on the palate
with rich flavors of coffee
beans and spice.
U.S.: $4.30 • U.K.: N/A

EL REY DEL MUNDO 88
CHOIX SUPREME
Honduras • *Size:* 6⅛" x 49
Filler: Dom. Rep., Honduras
Binder: Honduras *Wrapper:*
Ecuador
A predominantly nutty char-
acter on this medium- to full-
bodied cigar. It has flavors of
chestnuts on the palate, and
a pleasant spicy and coffee
bean finish.
U.S.: $3.50 • U.K.: N/A

FLOR DE FLOREZ 88
CABINET SELECTION
FLOREZ FLOREZ
Honduras • *Size:* 5¼" x 46
Filler/Binder/Wrapper:
Nicaragua
This is a smooth-tasting cigar
with a mild flavor. There are
hints of spice and a note of
cocoa beans. The finish holds
this cigar back.
U.S.: $6.50 • U.K.: N/A

MACANUDO HYDE 88
PARK CAFE
Jamaica • *Size:* 5½" x 49
Filler/Binder: Mexico, Dom.
Rep. *Wrapper:* U.S.A./
Conn. Shade
This is a well-rounded cigar
with a good balance of nutty
and straightforward tobacco
flavors.
U.S.: $4.45 • U.K.: N/A

OLOR PACO 88
Dominican Republic •
Size: 6" x 50 *Filler/Binder:*
Dom. Rep. *Wrapper:*
U.S.A./Conn. Shade
An unusual floral character
makes this an attractive
cigar. There are flavors of
coffee, ripe berries and mild,
sweet spices. There is a rich,
woody finish.
U.S.: $3.70 • U.K.: N/A

SOSA GOVERNOR 88
Dominican Republic •
Size: 6" x 50 *Filler:* Dom.
Rep. *Binder:* Honduras
Wrapper: Ecuador
A well-made cigar. It a mild-
to medium-bodied smoke
that has hints of spice and
some coffee beans, and a
woody finish.
U.S.: $3.55 • U.K.: N/A

V CENTENNIAL 88
NUMERO 2
Honduras • *Size:* 6" x 50
Filler: Dom. Rep., Honduras,
Nicaragua *Binder:* Mexico
Wrapper: U.S.A./Conn. Shade
A full-flavored cigar, with
sweet components of dried
fruit and a solid core of nutti-
ness. It should improve with
some aging.
U.S.: $4.95 • U.K.: N/A

ASHTON DOUBLE 87
MAGNUM
Dominican Republic • *Size:*
6" x 50 *Filler/Binder:* Dom.
Rep. *Wrapper:* U.S.A./
Conn. Shade
A well-made cigar that has a
nutty character over a solid
spicy core. There is a slight
herbal dryness on the finish.
U.S.: $6.75 • U.K.: N/A

BOLIVAR CORONA 87
EXTRA
Cuba • *Size:* 5⅝" x 46
Filler/Binder/Wrapper: Cuba
Another Cuban cigar with
some inconsistencies. It has a
solid earthy core of flavors
with some spice and wood on
the finish.
U.S.: N/A • U.K.: £7.58

CARA MIA TORO 87
Canary Islands • *Size:* 6"
x 50 *Filler/Binder:* Canary
Islands, Dom. Rep., Brazil
Wrapper: U.S.A./Conn. Shade
A cigar with an earthy character and a solid core of mild
spices, coffee beans and
leather flavors. A medium to
short finish.
U.S.: $6.50 • U.K.: N/A

CUBA ALIADOS NO. 4 **87**
Honduras • *Size:* 5½"
x 46 *Filler:* Dom. Rep.,
Brazil *Binder:* Ecuador
Wrapper: Ecuador/Sumatra
A smooth-tasting cigar with
some herbal and earthy fla-
vors and a mild, spicy under-
tone. (06/01/94)
U.S.: $2.00 • U.K.: N/A

CUESTA-REY **87**
CENTENNIAL
COLLECTION
DOMINICAN NO. 60
Dominican Republic • *Size:*
6" x 50 *Filler/Binder:* Dom.
Rep. *Wrapper:* U.S.A./
Conn. Shade
A solid cigar with a core of
straightforward tobacco fla-
vors. It has a nutty character
with some notes of sweet
herbs and mild spices.
U.S.: $3.60 • U.K.: £5.75

DA VINCI MONALISA **87**
Honduras • *Size:* 6" x 50
Filler: Honduras, Nicaragua,
Dom. Rep. *Binder:* Dom.
Rep. *Wrapper:* Ecuador
A medium-bodied cigar with
a complex herbal earthiness.
There are strong nutty flavors
on a creamy texture.
U.S.: $8.65 • U.K.: N/A

DON LEO ROBUSTO **87**
Dominican Republic •
Size: 5½" x 50 *Filler/Binder:*
Dom. Rep. *Wrapper:*
U.S.A./Conn. Shade
A medium-bodied smoke
with a pleasant tang. It has
hints of nuts and a dry fruit
character. There is a bit of
spice on the finish.
U.S.: $3.70 • U.K.: N/A

DON TOMAS SPECIAL **87**
EDITION NO. 500
Honduras • *Size:* 5½" x 46
Filler: Dom. Rep., Nicaragua
Binder/Wrapper: Honduras
A very well-balanced cigar. It
has leather and spices and
strong hints of nuts on the
palate. It has a smooth tex-
ture on the finish.
U.S.: $4.00 • U.K.: N/A

EL REY DEL MUNDO **87**
GRAN CORONAS
Cuba • *Size:* 5⅝" x 46
Filler/Binder/Wrapper: Cuba
An earthy, rich-tasting cigar
with cinnamon notes. It's a
little rustic, but a smooth
woody finish balances out
the cigar.
U.S.: N/A • France: 46FF

H. UPMANN **87**
CHURCHILL
Dominican Republic • *Size:*
5⅝" x 46 *Filler/Binder:* Dom.
Rep. *Wrapper:* Indonesia
A solid spicy smoke. It has
some saltiness on the palate
and an earthy core with some
wood flavors on the finish.
U.S.: $3.75 • U.K.: N/A

HABANICA SERIE 546 **87**
Nicaragua • *Size:* 5¼"
x 46 *Filler/Binder/Wrapper:*
Nicaragua
A beautiful, oily sheen on
this dark brown wrapper. It
has complex flavors of cocoa
and anise, with an earthy
spiciness. A short finish.
U.S.: $5.20 • U.K.: N/A

HOYO DE MONTERREY **87**
CORONA
Honduras • *Size:* 5⅝" x 46
Filler/Binder: Honduras,
Nicaragua, Dom. Rep.
Wrapper: Ecuador
A very spicy cigar with an
earthy character. There are
flavors of nuts and cedar on
the medium- to full-bodied
smoke. Finishes a bit dry.
U.S.: $2.50 • U.K.: N/A

HOYO DE MONTERREY **87**
GOVERNOR
Honduras • *Size:* 6⅛" x 50
Filler/Binder: Honduras,
Nicaragua, Dom. Rep.
Wrapper: Ecuador
A good cigar with a core of
herbal and earthy notes. It's
well made with some spice
and wood on the finish.
U.S.: $2.75 • U.K.: N/A

LA GLORIA CUBANA **87**
EXTRA
U.S.A. • *Size:* 6¼" x 46
Filler: Dom. Rep., Nica.
Binder: Nicaragua *Wrapper:*
Ecuador
A toasty, floral aroma with a
solid pepper-spice core of fla-
vors that give character to
this full-bodied cigar.
(06/01/94)
U.S.: $1.75 • U.K.: N/A

NAT SHERMAN **87**
GOTHAM SELECTION
NO. 711
Dominican Republic • *Size:*
6" x 50 *Filler/Binder:* Dom.
Rep. *Wrapper:* U.S.A./
Conn. Shade
A smooth-tasting, well-bal-
anced cigar. It has a creamy
character with coffee bean

and mild nut flavors, and with a mild, light spice finish.
U.S.: $6.90 • U.K.: N/A

ONYX NO. 650 **87**
Dominican Republic •
Size: 6" x 50 *Filler:* Dom.
Rep., Mexico *Binder:*
Indonesia *Wrapper:* Mexico
A medium-bodied cigar with a maduro-style wrapper. The Onyx has solid flavors of chocolate and an even burn. (06/01/94)
U.S.: $2.35 • U.K.: N/A

PARTAGAS ALMIRANTE **87**
Dominican Republic •
Size: 6¼" x 47 *Filler:* Jam., Dom. Rep., Mex. *Binder:*
Mexico *Wrapper:* Cameroon
A flavorful cigar with a medium-bodied spiciness. It has a slightly dry finish. (06/01/94)
U.S.: $3.40 • U.K.: N/A

PETERSON TORO **87**
Dominican Republic • *Size:*
6" x 50 *Filler:* Dom. Rep.
Binder: Ecuador *Wrapper:*
U.S.A./Conn. Shade
This is a smooth, medium- to full-bodied cigar. It has flavors of the earth, with leathery notes on the palate. Will benefit from aging.
U.S.: $7.00 • U.K.: N/A

PUNCH PUNCH **87**
Cuba • *Size:* 5⅝" x 46
Filler/Binder/Wrapper: Cuba
An earthy character overpowers some spiciness. A good draw on a medium-bodied smoke.
U.S.: N/A • U.K.: £7.87

ROMEO Y JULIETA **87**
VINTAGE NO. 2
Dominican Republic • *Size:*
6" x 46 *Filler:* Dom. Rep.
Binder: Mexico *Wrapper:*
U.S.A./Conn. Shade
This is a medium-bodied cigar that has solid tobacco flavors and hints of cedar and coffee. (06/01/94)
U.S.: $4.75 • U.K.: N/A

ROYAL JAMAICA **87**
DIRECTOR
Dominican Republic • *Size:*
6" x 45 *Filler:* Jamaica
Binder: Indonesia *Wrapper:*
Cameroon
This cigar has straightforward flavors of cedar and herbs, with a medium-length finish. (06/01/94)
U.S.: $3.10 • U.K.: N/A

SAVINELLI E.L.R. **87**
DOUBLE CORONA
Dominican Republic • *Size:*
6" x 50 *Filler/Binder:* Dom.
Rep. *Wrapper:* U.S.A./
Conn. Shade
A medium-bodied cigar with some solid leather and coffee bean notes. It has a mild finish.
U.S.: $7.25 • U.K.: N/A

8-9-8 ROBUSTO **86**
Jamaica • *Size:* 5½" x 49
Filler: Jamaica, Dom. Rep.
Binder: Mexico *Wrapper:*
U.S.A./Conn. Shade
A pleasant mild- to medium-bodied cigar. It has flavors of nuts with a cedary undertone. It's very well made and has a nice woody finish.
U.S.: $7.75 • U.K.: N/A

ARTURO FUENTE FLOR **86**
FINA 8-5-8
Dominican Republic • *Size:*
6" x 47 *Filler/Binder:* Dom.
Rep. *Wrapper:* Cameroon
A strong peppery flavor dominates this cigar. There is a dusty, earthy quality to the finish that is a little dry.
U.S.: $3.10 • U.K.: N/A

CUBITA NO. 700 **86**
Dominican Republic •
Size: 6" x 50 *Filler/Binder:*
Dom. Rep. *Wrapper:*
U.S.A./Conn. Shade
The cigar exhibits some youth. But there is a rich, earthy quality to the flavors with leather and woody tastes on a medium-length finish.
U.S.: $5.25 • U.K.: N/A

DON MELO CORONA **86**
EXTRA
Honduras • *Size:* 5½" x 46
Filler/Binder/Wrapper:
Honduras
A spicy smoke. It has a woody character and a medium body, but some vegetal notes on the finish.
U.S.: $2.95 • U.K.: N/A

DON TOMAS CORONA **86**
Honduras • *Size:* 5½" x
50 *Filler/Binder/Wrapper:*
Honduras
A nice, brown wrapper on a cigar that has pleasant cinnamon-spice and cedar flavors with a smooth aftertaste. (06/01/94)
U.S.: $1.90 • U.K.: N/A

LICENCIADOS TORO 86
Dominican Republic • *Size:* 6" x 50 *Filler/Binder:* Dom. Rep. *Wrapper:* U.S.A./Conn. Shade
A straightforward, medium-bodied cigar. It has a light nuttiness and an herbal character. A woody finish.
U.S.: $4.10 • U.K.: N/A

MACANUDO VINTAGE 86
CABINET SELECTION
1993
Jamaica • *Size:* 5½" x 49 *Filler/Binder:* Mexico, Dom. Rep. *Wrapper:* U.S.A./Conn. Shade
A well-made cigar. There is a fresh, clean quality to this medium-bodied cigar. It has flavors of nuts and cedar, and an overall sweet character.
U.S.: $9.75 • U.K.: N/A

MONTECRISTO 86
CORONA GRANDE
Dominican Republic • *Size:* 5¼" x 46 *Filler/Binder:* Dom. Rep. *Wrapper:* U.S.A./Conn. Shade
This is a medium-bodied cigar with a fresh, clean character. There are hints of spice and a dry woody finish.
U.S.: $6.75 • U.K.: N/A

NAT SHERMAN VIP 86
SELECTION CARNEGIE
Dominican Republic • *Size:* 6" x 48 *Filler/Binder:* Dom. Rep. *Wrapper:* U.S.A./Conn. Shade
An earthy cigar with solid spice and roasted coffee-bean flavors. It burns well and has a good draw. (06/01/94)
U.S.: $4.40 • U.K.: N/A

PAUL GARMIRIAN 86
CONNOISSEUR
Dominican Republic • *Size:* 6" x 50 *Filler/Binder:* Dom. Rep. *Wrapper:* U.S.A./Conn. Shade
A pleasant smooth-smoking cigar. There is a solid spiciness in this cigar, and it has a woody finish. Should improve with age.
U.S.: $8.70 • U.K.: £8.00

PUNCH SUPER 86
ROTHSCHILD
Honduras • *Size:* 5¼" x 50 *Filler:* Honduras *Binder/Wrapper:* Ecuador
A cigar with spiciness on the palate, but finishes with a slightly vegetal character. (06/01/94)
U.S.: $2.00 • U.K.: N/A

PUROS INDIOS 86
CORONA GORDA
Honduras • *Size:* 6" x 50 *Filler:* Brazil, Dom. Rep., Nicaragua *Binder/Wrapper:* Ecuador
A core of earthiness, with a spicy character. This cigar is great looking with an oily dark wrapper. It has a clean, sweet woody finish.
U.S.: $4.75 • U.K.: N/A

SANTA ROSA TORO 86
Honduras • *Size:* 6" x 50 *Filler/Binder:* Honduras *Wrapper:* Ecuador
This cigar shows its youth. The slight bite and young wood tastes should mellow with age. Medium- to full-bodied, and it is well made.
U.S.: $4.00 • U.K.: N/A

TE-AMO TORO 86
Mexico • *Size:* 6" x 50 *Filler/Binder/Wrapper:* Mexico
Although this cigar has some coarse qualities, it is filled with a peppery core of flavors that mellows as it smokes.
U.S.: $2.80 • U.K.: N/A

BERING HISPANOS 85
Honduras • *Size:* 6" x 50 *Filler/Binder:* Honduras, Mexico, Dom. Rep. Nicaragua *Wrapper:* U.S.A./Conn. Shade
This cigar has a creamy core that has a straightforward saltiness. There are hints of the earth and a woodiness on the finish.
U.S.: $1.85 • U.K.: N/A

C.A.O. CORONA 85
GORDA
Honduras • *Size:* 6" x 50 *Filler:* Nicaragua, Mexico *Binder:* Honduras *Wrapper:* U.S.A./Conn. Shade
Another young cigar. It is well made, but there is a strong, sharp vegetal character. There are hints of dried orange peel and pepper notes.
U.S.: $6.98 • U.K.: N/A

CASA BLANCA DELUXE 85
Dominican Republic • *Size:* 6" x 50 *Filler:* Dom. Rep. *Binder:* Mexico *Wrapper:* U.S.A./Conn. Shade
A mild, mellow smoke. There are some hints of sweet herbs, wood and leather on a mild finish.
U.S.: $2.50 • U.K.: £4.00

DAVIDOFF NO. 5000 **85**
Dominican Republic •
Size: 5⅝" x 46 *Filler/Binder:*
Dom. Rep. *Wrapper:*
U.S.A./Conn. Shade
A smooth-tasting cigar with
some wood and herbal notes
on the palate. It has a light
body on the finish.
U.S.: $9.55 • U.K.: £9.74

DON ASA CORONA **85**
Honduras • *Size:* 5½"
x 50 *Filler/Binder/Wrapper:*
Honduras
An attractive medium-brown
wrapper. It is a mellow smoke
with a nutty character, some
exotic eastern spices, but
with a hint of vegetal notes
on the finish.
U.S.: $1.95 • U.K.: N/A

DON LINO TORO **85**
Honduras • *Size:* 5½"
x 46 *Filler/Binder:* Honduras
Wrapper: U.S.A./Conn.
Shade
This is an easy-smoking, mild
cigar. It has some herbal and
nut flavors on the palate and
a slightly drying finish.
U.S.: $2.75 • U.K.: N/A

DUNHILL CONDADOS **85**
Dominican Republic •
Size: 6" x 48 *Filler/Binder:*
Dom. Rep., Brazil *Wrapper:*
U.S.A./Conn. Shade
This is a very nice, mellow
smoke. It has a strong herbal
character and it has a mild,
spicy finish.
U.S.: $6.00 • U.K.: £6.35

FLOR DE FLOREZ **85**
CORONA
Honduras • *Size:* 6" x 50
Filler/Binder: Honduras
Wrapper: U.S.A./Conn.
Shade
A medium-bodied smoke
with a creamy texture and a
light spicy flavor.
U.S.: $3.90 • U.K.: N/A

HABANICA SERIE 646 **85**
Nicaragua • *Size:* 6" x 46
Filler/Binder/Wrapper:
Nicaragua
A pretty dark brown colorado
wrapper. It has sweet spice
flavors, and as it warms up a
sweet woody character comes
out. A short finish holds it
back.
U.S.: $6.00 • U.K.: N/A

HAVANA CLASSICO **85**
ROBUSTO LARGO
U.S.A. • *Size:* 6" x 50 *Filler:*
Dom. Rep., Mexico,
Indonesia *Binder/Wrapper:*
Ecuador
A light cigar with mild
smoke. It's got some sweet
wood and herbal flavors. It
takes a while to get going.
U.S.: $5.85 • U.K.: N/A

MONTECRUZ SUN- **85**
GROWN NO. 201
Dominican Republic • *Size:*
6¼" x 46 *Filler/Binder:* Dom.
Rep., Brazil *Wrapper:*
Cameroon
This cigar is a bit rough, but
it delivers a spicy, medium-
bodied flavor and a slightly
hot finish. (06/01/94)
U.S.: $3.00 • U.K.: N/A

PAUL GARMIRIAN **85**
EPICURE
Dominican Republic • *Size:*
5½" x 50 *Filler/Binder:* Dom.
Rep. *Wrapper:* U.S.A./
Conn. Shade
This mild, light-bodied cigar
has a spicy character, but is
dominated by woody flavors
and a dry finish. (06/01/94)
U.S.: $6.80 • U.K.: £6.75

PUNCH CHATEAU M **85**
Honduras • *Size:* 5¼"
x 46 *Filler/Binder:* Honduras,
Nicaragua, Dom. Rep.
Wrapper: Ecuador
A nice-looking cigar with a
medium-brown wrapper.
There are hints of cocoa
bean and leather on a medi-
um-bodied smoke. Finishes a
bit dry.
U.S.: $2.75 • U.K.: N/A

ROMANTICOS **85**
LEONARDO
Dominican Republic • *Size:*
6" x 50 *Filler/Binder:* Dom.
Rep. *Wrapper:* U.S.A./
Conn. Shade
A mild cigar with a smooth,
creamy taste. There are hints
of herbs, but it has a very
short finish.
U.S.: $5.20 • U.K.: N/A

SAINT LUIS REY **85**
SERIE A
Honduras • *Size:* 6" x 50
Filler/Binder/Wrapper:
Honduras
This is a rich-tasting cigar.
Flavors of toast and coffee
beans with some hints of
leather on the rather short
finish.
U.S.: $3.90 • U.K.: N/A

TEMPLE HALL NO. 550 85
Jamaica • *Size:* 5½" x 49
Filler/Binder: Mexico, Dom.
Rep. *Wrapper:* U.S.A./
Conn. Shade
This is a mild, straightfor-
ward cigar. It has hints of
spice on a woody finish.
U.S.: $5.95 • U.K.: N/A

THOMAS HINDS 85
NICARAGUA
SELECTION SHORT
CHURCHILL
Nicaragua • *Size:* 6" x 50
Filler/Binder/Wrapper:
Nicaragua
A well-made cigar with a
solid medium-bodied smoke.
It has a creamy texture and
finishes a bit woody and flat.
U.S.: $5.70 • Canada: $8.65

BLAIR ROBUSTO 84
Honduras • *Size:* 6" x 50
Filler/Binder: Honduras
Wrapper: Ecuador
This cigar showed some
inconsistency. It had a salty
character. There are flavors
of sweet herbs on the palate.
U.S.: $4.70 • U.K.: N/A

DON DIEGO GRANDE 84
Dominican Republic •
Size: 6" x 50 *Filler/Binder:*
Dom. Rep. *Wrapper:*
U.S.A./Conn. Shade
A pleasant, mild cigar. It has
some hints of nutty flavors
and a clean, fresh finish.
U.S.: $4.50 • U.K.: N/A

DON TOMAS TORO 84
Honduras • *Size:* 5½"
x 46 *Filler/Binder/Wrapper:*
Honduras, Nicaragua*Filler:*

Honduras, Nicaragua
Binder/Wrapper: Honduras
A creamy cigar with nut and
herbal spiciness. It's a little
young with a dry finish.
U.S.: $2.60 • U.K.: £4.50

H. UPMANN CORSARIO 84
Dominican Republic •
Size: 5½" x 50 *Filler/Binder:*
Dom. Rep. *Wrapper:*
Cameroon
Inconsistent. Rough flavors
marred several tasters' cigars;
sweet, dried citrus notes were
evident in others. (06/01/94)
U.S.: $4.50 • U.K.: N/A

JOYA DE NICARAGUA 84
TORO
Nicaragua • *Size:* 6" x 50
Filler/Binder: Nicaragua
Wrapper: Ecuador
A mild- to medium-bodied
cigar. It has nutty and sweet
spice notes and feels a bit oily
on the palate. A mild, dry
woody finish.
U.S.: $3.55 • U.K.: N/A

MACABI CORONA 84
EXTRA
Dominican Republic • *Size:*
6" x 50 *Filler:* Dom. Rep.,
Nicaragua *Binder:* Mexico
Wrapper: U.S.A./Conn.
Shade
This cigar seems fairly dry on
the palate. There are some
sweet pepper flavors, and it
also finishes dry.
U.S.: $3.75 • U.K.: N/A

MACANUDO VINTAGE 84
CABINET SELECTION
1993 VIII
Jamaica • *Size:* 5½" x 49
Filler/Binder: Mexico, Dom.

Rep. *Wrapper:* U.S.A./
Conn. Shade
A pleasant, mild cigar with
plenty of nutty flavor. It has a
crisp and clean character and
it finishes with a light woody
quality.
U.S.: $11.25 • U.K.: N/A

MACANUDO CRYSTAL 84
CAFE
Jamaica • *Size:* 5½" x 50
Filler/Binder: Mexico, Dom.
Rep. *Wrapper:* U.S.A./
Conn. Shade
A well-made cigar. It is mild-
to medium-bodied with a
slightly woody finish. There
is some dryness on the palate
and there are some grassy
notes.
U.S.: $4.80 • U.K.: N/A

TRESADO SELECTION 84
NO. 300
Dominican Republic •
Size: 6" x 46 *Filler:* Dom.
Rep. *Binder:* Cameroon
Wrapper: Indonesia
This cigar has a salty charac-
ter. There are hints of cedar
and pepper.
U.S.: $2.35 • U.K.: N/A

VARGAS RESERVA 84
SENADORES
Canary Islands • *Size:* 5½" x
46 *Filler:* Canary Islands,
Dom. Rep. *Binder/Wrapper:*
Indonesia
Inconsistent performance. At
its best, some hints of sweet
spices and a woody finish.
U.S.: $7.00 • U.K.: N/A

AVO XO INTERMEZZO 83
Dominican Republic •
Size: 5½" x 50 *Filler/Binder:*

Dom. Rep. *Wrapper:*
U.S.A./Conn. Shade
There is mild spiciness in this
medium-bodied cigar, but
young tobacco produced a bit
of sourness on the finish.
(06/01/94)
U.S.: $8.25 • U.K.: N/A

CABAÑAS ROYALE 83
Dominican Republic •
Size: 5⅝" x 46 *Filler/Binder:*
Dom. Rep. *Wrapper:*
Mexico
A rough, dark wrapper pro-
duces a spicy smoke with
solid tobacco flavors, but a
slightly vegetal finish.
(06/01/94)
U.S.: $2.20 • U.K.: N/A

DON LINO ORO TORO 83
Honduras • *Size:* 5½" x 46
Filler/Binder/Wrapper:
Honduras
A sweet, herbal flavor on a
medium-bodied cigar, but
with a burnt citrus aroma and
finish. (06/01/94)
U.S.: $2.50 • U.K.: N/A

DON XAVIER CORONA 83
Canary Islands • *Size:*
5⅝" x 46 *Filler/Binder:*
Canary Islands, Dom. Rep.,
Brazil *Wrapper:* U.S.A./
Conn. Shade
A mild cigar. It has a light body
with a clean, woody finish.
U.S.: $7.80 • U.K.: N/A

EL REY DEL MUNDO 83
ROBUSTO LARGA
Honduras • *Size:* 6" x 50
Filler: Dom. Rep., Honduras
Binder/Wrapper: Honduras
Inconsistent. A medium-bod-
ied cigar with a dried herbal,

tobacco character. (06/01/94)
U.S.: $3.00 • U.K.: N/A

H. UPMANN MAGNUM 83
Cuba • *Size:* 5⅝" x 46
Filler/Binder/Wrapper: Cuba
Very inconsistent. Three
tasters had a loose fill with a
quick burn. Some pepper and
spiciness at its best. But not
up to par.
U.S.: N/A • U.K.: £8.69

JUAN CLEMENTE CLUB 83
SELECTION NO. 1
Dominican Republic • *Size:*
6" x 50 *Filler/Binder:* Dom.
Rep. *Wrapper:* U.S.A./
Conn. Shade
A pleasant mild cigar with a
light cedary aroma and some
hints of nuts and sweet herbs
on the palate. A light finish.
U.S.: $8.70 • U.K.: N/A

MAYA MAYA 83
Honduras • *Size:* 6" x 50
Filler/Binder: Honduras,
Nicaragua *Wrapper:* U.S.A./
Conn. Shade
There are strong elements of
dry spices and woodiness on
this slow-starting cigar. It has
a salty character and is rather
roughly constructed.
U.S.: $3.05 • U.K.: N/A

MORRO CASTLE 83
CORONA GORDA
Nicaragua • *Size:* 6" x 50
Filler/Binder: Nicaragua
Wrapper: Ecuador
This is a rather rough, rustic
cigar. There are some cedar
and herbal notes on a rough
finish.
U.S.: $4.65 • U.K.: N/A

OSCAR NO. 500 83
Dominican Republic •
Size: 5½" x 50 *Filler/Binder:*
Dom. Rep. *Wrapper:*
U.S.A./Conn. Shade
Showed some inconsistency.
But tasters noted a light- to
medium-bodied smoke with a
creamy texture and some
spiciness.
U.S.: $7.50 • U.K.: £6.80

PRIMO DEL REY 83
ALMIRANTE
Dominican Republic • *Size:*
6" x 50 *Filler/Binder:* Dom.
Rep. *Wrapper:* Indonesia
A cigar with a salty charac-
ter. There is an earthiness
here and some herbal notes.
U.S.: $2.50 • U.K.: N/A

PUNCH SUPERIOR 83
Honduras • *Size:* 5½"
x 48 *Filler/Binder/Wrapper:*
Honduras
A cigar with some harshness
on the palate and vegetal flavors. But an earthy aroma
and finish provide some character. (06/01/94)
U.S.: $2.90 • U.K.: N/A

SANTA DAMIANA 83
SELECTION NO. 300
Dominican Republic • *Size:*
5½" x 46 *Filler/Binder:* Dom.
Rep. *Wrapper:* U.S.A./
Conn. Shade
This cigar shows evidence of
young tobacco. It has some
sharp vegetal edges, but there
are flavors of coffee beans on
its medium-bodied smoke.
U.S.: $6.50 • U.K.: N/A

CANARIO D'ORO 82
INMENSO
Dominican Republic • *Size:*
5½" x 49 *Filler/Binder/*
Wrapper: Mexico, Dom.
Rep.*Filler:* Mexico, Dom.
Rep. *Binder/Wrapper:*
Mexico
A bit of youth shows through
on the wrapper. There's some
sweet herb flavors and the
cigar exhibits a light, nutty
character.
U.S.: $2.55 • U.K.: N/A

MICUBANO NO. 650 82
Nicaragua • *Size:* 6" x 50
Filler/Binder/Wrapper:
Nicaragua
A slightly vegetal character
masks some spicy notes on
the palate. A short finish.
U.S.: $3.50 • U.K.: N/A

NAT SHERMAN 82
EXCHANGE SELECTION
TRAFALGAR NO. 4
Dominican Republic • *Size:*
6" x 47 *Filler:* Dom. Rep.,
Mexico *Binder:* Mexico
Wrapper: U.S.A./Conn.
Shade
This cigar shows some youth.
It has a smooth round char-
acter with some herbal fla-
vors and a hint of pepper. A
papery finish.
U.S.: $6.10 • U.K.: N/A

PETRUS TABACAGE 89 82
CORONA SUBLIME
Honduras • *Size:* 5½" x 46
Filler/Binder: Honduras
Wrapper: Ecuador
A quite mild cigar with a
mild herbal character and a
very dry finish.
U.S.: $4.15 • U.K.: N/A

TE-AMO SATISFACTION 82
Mexico • *Size:* 6" x 46
Filler/Binder/Wrapper: Mexico
A cigar with some pepper fla-
vors. But it is dominated by a
dry, vegetal character.
U.S.: $2.50 • U.K.: N/A

THOMAS HINDS 82
HONDURAN SELECTION
SHORT CHURCHILL
Honduras • *Size:* 6" x 50
Filler/Binder: Honduras
Wrapper: Ecuador
A cigar with a cedary charac-
ter. There are hints of pepper
and a bit of sweetness on the
mild- to medium-bodied
smoke.
U.S.: $4.40 • Canada: $6.95

VUELTABAJO TORO 82
Dominican Republic •
Size: 6" x 50 *Filler/Binder:*
Dom. Rep. *Wrapper:*
U.S.A./Conn. Shade
This cigar has a very drying
effect on the palate. It is
mild, with small hints of nuts
and a floral note, with a dry
woody finish.
U.S.: $3.35 • U.K.: N/A

CACIQUE APACHE 81
Dominican Republic •
Size: 6" x 50 *Filler/Binder:*
Dom. Rep. *Wrapper:*
U.S.A./Conn. Shade
A very herbal cigar with
some grassy notes on the
palate. It is light and has
some nuttiness on the finish.
U.S.: $2.95 • U.K.: N/A

HOYO DE MONTERREY 81
EXCALIBUR NO. 4
Honduras • *Size:* 5⅞" x 46
Filler/Binder: Honduras,

Nicaragua, Dom. Rep.
Wrapper: U.S.A./Conn.
Shade
A very mild-tasting cigar. It
has a hint of vanilla and pepper, but a paper-thin character. There are hints of grassi-
ness and herbal flavors.
U.S.: $3.35 • U.K.: N/A

PRIMO DEL REY ROYAL 81
CORONA
Dominican Republic • *Size:*
6" x 46 *Filler/Binder:* Dom.
Rep. *Wrapper:* Indonesia
A cigar with a salty, vegetal
tone. It is quite rustic, and its
tobacco character brings it
around.
U.S.: $2.30 • U.K.: N/A

CALLE OCHO GORDITO 80
LARGO
U.S.A. • *Size:* 6" x 50 *Filler:*
Honduras, Nicaragua, Dom.
Rep. *Binder/Wrapper:*
Ecuador
A rustic cigar. It has a papery,
balsa wood quality and a
slightly dry finish.
U.S.: $6.25 • U.K.: N/A

CRUZ REAL NO. 19 80
Mexico • *Size:* 6" x 50
Filler/Binder/Wrapper: Mexico
This is a rustic cigar. Mild
flavors of spice and dried fruit
are present, but it has a very
dry, woody finish.
U.S.: $4.15 • U.K.: N/A

MATCH PLAY 80
TURNBERRY
Dominican Republic • *Size:*
6" x 50 *Filler/Binder:* Dom.
Rep. *Wrapper:* Ecuador
The cigar has some bite to it.
There are hints of pepper and

dry nuts, but some raw flavors of mint on the finish.
U.S.: $4.90 • U.K.: N/A

NAT SHERMAN MANHATTAN SELECTION SUTTON **80**
Dominican Republic • Size: 5½" x 49 Filler: Dom. Rep. Binder/Wrapper: Mexico
Rough construction. This cigar has a stemmy, vegetal character and a fast burn that finishes harshly. (06/01/94)
U.S.: $3.20 • U.K.: N/A

PARTAGAS NATURALES **80**
Dominican Republic • Size: 5½" x 50 Filler/Binder: Mexico, Dom. Rep. Wrapper: Cameroon
This is a fairly rustic smoke. It has an overall vegetal character, with some slight spice notes on the finish.
U.S.: $4.60 • U.K.: N/A

CARRINGTON NO. 7 **79**
Dominican Republic • Size: 6" x 50 Filler/Binder: Dom. Rep. Wrapper: U.S.A./Conn. Shade
A coarse cigar with a vegetal character. It is very mouth-drying, with a flat, dry woody finish.
U.S.: $4.86 • U.K.: N/A

LA FINCA JOYA **79**
Nicaragua • Size: 6" x 50 Filler/Binder/Wrapper: Nicaragua
While there are some hints of nutty flavors, this is a very rough, rustic cigar with some sharp tastes on the finish.
U.S.: $2.00 • U.K.: N/A

SANTA CLARA NO. 6 **79**
Mexico • Size: 6" x 50 Filler/Binder/Wrapper: Mexico, NicaraguaFiller: Mexico, Nicaragua Binder/Wrapper: Mexico
There are some earthy and spicy flavors in this cigar. But it showed inconsistent construction and ended up very dry and woody on the finish.
U.S.: $2.50 • U.K.: N/A

HENRY CLAY BREVAS A LA CONSERVA **78**
Dominican Republic • Size: 5⅝" x 46 Filler/Binder: Dom. Rep. Wrapper: U.S.A./Conn. Shade
A very rustic cigar. It is a bit hot on the palate, and there are funky, earthy flavors, with a flat, dry woody finish.
U.S.: $2.75 • U.K.: N/A

TORCEDOR TORO **78**
Nicaragua • Size: 6" x 50 Filler/Binder: Nicaragua Wrapper: Honduras
A poorly constructed cigar. It is rough and coarse, with a strong salty component and a dry, vegetal character.
U.S.: $2.80 • U.K.: N/A

TESORO DE COPAN CORONA **77**
Honduras • Size: 5¼" x 46 Filler/Binder: Honduras Wrapper: Ecuador
A cigar with a vegetal character. It seems young and green, and has a very drying element on the palate.
U.S.: $3.30 • U.K.: N/A

LONSDALE

Most of the following Lonsdale tasting notes appeared in the Autumn 1996 issue of Cigar Aficionado. Exceptions are indicated by a date in parentheses at the end of the tasting note.

COHIBA SIGLO III **95**
Cuba • Size: 6" x 42 Filler/Binder/Wrapper: Cuba
A great addition to a great line of cigars. It is gorgeous to look at with its rich brown, smooth wrapper and gives loads of pleasure with every puff. An opulent smoke with great finesse and class. (03/01/93)
U.S.: N/A • U.K.: £10.00

QUINTERO CHURCHILL **92**
Cuba • Size: 6½" x 42 Filler/Binder/Wrapper: Cuba
A powerful, full-bodied cigar with a deep nutty aroma and strong flavors of clove and nutmeg, with a cocoa-like finish. (03/01/94)
U.S.: N/A • Switzerland: 6 SF

CUBA ALIADOS LONSDALE **91**
Honduras • Size: 6½" x 42 Filler: Dom. Rep. Binder/Wrapper: Ecuador
A rich, powerful cigar packed with spice, cocoa and coffee flavors and an exotic floral finish. A great dark-brown wrapper. (03/01/94)
U.S.: $2.20 • U.K.: N/A

RAFAEL GONZALES **91**
LONSDALE
Cuba • *Size:* 6½" x 42 *Filler/
Binder/Wrapper:* Cuba
A dark-brown wrapper burns
evenly on this full-bodied
cigar, which has flavors of
coffee and cocoa and a solid
spicy core. (03/01/94)
U.S.: N/A • U.K.: £6.95

SANCHO PANZA **91**
MOLINAS
Cuba • *Size:* 6½" x 42 *Filler/
Binder/Wrapper:* Cuba
A well-balanced cigar with
smooth spiciness. There are
hints of dark coffee flavors
and dried citrus notes, with a
long spicy finish.
U.S.: N/A • Switzerland: 9SF

BOLIVAR GOLD MEDAL **90**
Cuba • *Size:* 6½" x 42
Filler/Binder/Wrapper: Cuba
A full-flavored cigar with a
toasty aroma and a nutty
spiciness that ends with a bit
of cedary aftertaste. (03/01/94)
U.S.: N/A • U.K.: £7.40

COHIBA SIGLO V **90**
Cuba • *Size:* 6⅝" x 43
Filler/Binder/Wrapper: Cuba
This cigar has a white peppery
taste and is loaded with coffee
and cream flavors. It is well
balanced with a medium to
full body and a cedary finish.
U.S.: N/A • U.K.: £15.15

H. UPMANN LONSDALE **90**
Cuba • *Size:* 6½" x 42
Filler/Binder/Wrapper: Cuba
A well-made, full-bodied
cigar that has an earthy
aroma and complex flavors of

spice and dried fruits.
(03/01/94)
U.S.: N/A • U.K.: £6.95

LA GLORIA CUBANA **90**
MEDAILLE D'OR NO. 2
Cuba • *Size:* 6⅔" x 43 *Filler/
Binder/Wrapper:* Cuba
A well-made cigar that burns
beautifully. It is well balanced and has a core of
leathery flavors with a perfumed character, and a long,
earthy finish.
U.S.: N/A • U.K.: 59FF

ROMEO Y JULIETA **90**
CORONA GRANDE
Cuba • *Size:* 6½" x 42 *Filler/
Binder/Wrapper:* Cuba
This is a full-bodied, rich
smoke. It has cedar and spice
flavors, including nutmeg,
and an overall pepper spice
character with a long, coffee
bean finish.
U.S.: N/A • Switzerland: 9SF

TROYA CETRO **90**
Dominican Republic •
Size: 6¼" x 44 *Filler/Binder:*
Dom. Rep. *Wrapper:*
U.S.A./Conn. Shade
This cigar has a medium
body with a solid spicy flavor
and a rich, almost leathery
mouth feel on the finish.
(03/01/94)
U.S.: $2.45 • U.K.: N/A

DAVIDOFF NO. 4000 **89**
Dominican Republic •
Size: 6" x 42 *Filler/Binder:*
Dom. Rep. *Wrapper:*
U.S.A./Conn.
A firm cigar with attractive
aromas and elegant coffee

and nut flavors. (03/01/94)
U.S.: $7.60 • U.K.: £9.10

DAVIDOFF GRAN CRU **89**
NO. 1
Dominican Republic • *Size:*
6" x 42 *Filler/Binder:* Dom.
Rep. *Wrapper:* U.S.A./
Conn. Shade
A beautiful brown wrapper
on a finely constructed cigar
that delivers a spicy pepper
flavor and a cedary finish.
(03/01/94)
U.S.: $7.90 • U.K.: £8.70

HOYO DE MONTERREY **89**
LE HOYO DES DIEUX
Cuba • *Size:* 6" x 42 *Filler/
Binder/Wrapper:* Cuba
A spicy, well-rolled cabinet
cigar with rich flavors and an
earthy aftertaste. (03/01/94)
U.S.: N/A • U.K.: £6.96

MACANUDO AMATISTA **89**
Jamaica • *Size:* 6¼" x 42
Filler: Mex., Jamaica, Dom.
Rep. *Binder:* Mexico
Wrapper: U.S.A./Conn.
Shade
A very well-balanced cigar
with medium-bodied flavors,
which include cocoa and
mild spices, and a long, mild
finish. (03/01/94)
U.S.: $4.05 • U.K.: N/A

V CENTENNIAL CETRO **89**
Honduras • *Size:* 6½"
x 44 *Filler/Binder:* Dom.
Rep., Mex., Nica., Hon.
Wrapper: U.S.A./Conn.
Shade
A medium-bodied cigar with
a core of earthy flavors that
have a hint of spiciness. It

finishes smoothly. (03/01/94)
U.S.: $3.75 • U.K.: N/A

ARTURO FUENTE 88
RESERVA NO. 1
Dominican Republic • *Size:*
6½" x 42 *Filler/Binder:* Dom.
Rep. *Wrapper:* Cameroon
A very well-balanced cigar
with sweetish, round tobacco
aromas that turn to aged
spice flavors on the palate.
(03/01/94)
U.S.: $5.75 • U.K.: N/A

ARTURO FUENTE 88
SPANISH LONSDALE
Dominican Republic • *Size:*
6½" x 42 *Filler/Binder:* Dom.
Rep. *Wrapper:* Cameroon
A cigar filled with earthy,
spicy flavors. It's well-made
and has a long, smooth fin-
ish. (03/01/94)
U.S.: $1.65 • U.K.: N/A

DON TOMAS SUPREMO 88
Honduras • *Size:* 6¼" x 42
Filler/Binder: Honduras
Wrapper: Honduras, Sumatra
A well-made cigar with a
good draw that has a rich
aroma and a nutty flavor.
(03/01/94)
U.S.: $1.60 • U.K.: N/A

FONSECA 8-9-8 88
Dominican Republic •
Size: 6" x 43 *Filler:* Dom.
Rep. *Binder:* Mexico
Wrapper: U.S.A./Conn.
Shade
A mild cigar that has a hint
of dry wood on the palate,
but also tastes of coffee and
spice. (03/01/94)
U.S.: $3.00 • U.K.: N/A

LA GLORIA CUBANA 88
MEDAILLE D'OR NO. 1
U.S.A. • *Size:* 6¾" x 43
Filler/Binder: Dom. Rep.,
Nicaragua *Wrapper:*
Ecuador
A rich, full-bodied smoke
with leathery, earthy notes
and a solid spicy and coffee
core of flavors. (03/01/94)
U.S.: $1.70 • U.K.: N/A

MONTECRISTO NO. 1 88
Cuba • *Size:* 6½" x 42
Filler/Binder/Wrapper: Cuba
A medium- to full-bodied
cigar with some mellow spiciness. It is smooth and well
balanced with a floral character and some hints of cedar.
U.S.: N/A • U.K.: £9.00

PARTAGAS NO. 1 88
Cuba • *Size:* 6⅝" x 43
Filler/Binder/Wrapper: Cuba
This cigar showed inconsis-
tency of young tobacco.
Some tasters noted solid
spices with a strong earthy
core of flavors. Needs aging.
U.S.: N/A • Switzerland: 10SF

PARTAGAS 8-9-8 88
Cuba • *Size:* 6⅝" x 43
Filler/Binder/Wrapper: Cuba
Another cigar with some
youthful characteristics. But
it also is rich and full-bodied
with a good, solid hazelnut
quality on the palate and a
woody finish. Will improve
with age.
U.S.: N/A • U.K.: £9.20

PARTAGAS NO. 1 88
Dominican Republic •
Size: 6¾" x 43 *Filler:* Dom.
Rep., Mexico *Binder:*
Mexico *Wrapper:* Cameroon
This is a well-balanced,
smooth smoke with a solid
spicy core and a touch of
earthiness on the palate.
There is a light, woody finish.
U.S.: $4.20 • U.K.: N/A

PARTAGAS 8-9-8 88
Dominican Republic •
Size: 6⅞" x 44 *Filler:* Dom.
Rep., Mexico *Binder:*
Mexico *Wrapper:* Cameroon
A well-made cigar with a
smooth taste. It has notes of
nuts and spices, with a strong
hint of herbs. It has a medi-
um body and a pleasant finish.
U.S.: $4.75 • U.K.: N/A

SAINT LUIS REY 88
LONSDALE
Cuba • *Size:* 6½" x 42 *Filler/
Binder/Wrapper:* Cuba
This is a solid, spicy cigar
with a sweet cocoa-bean
backbone. A touch rustic,
but very rich and tasty.
U.S.: N/A • Switzerland: 9SF

SAVINELLI E.L.R. 88
NO. 3 LONSDALE
Dominican Republic • *Size:*
6¼" x 43 *Filler/Binder:* Dom.
Rep. *Wrapper:* U.S.A./
Conn. Shade
A medium- to full-bodied
cigar. It has a solid, earthy
and leathery character with a
hint of sweet herbs and a
hazelnut finish.
U.S.: $6.00 • U.K.: N/A

BERING PLAZA **87**
Honduras • *Size:* 6"
x 43 *Filler:* Mex., Dom.
Rep., Hon. *Binder:*
Honduras *Wrapper:* Mexico
A solid-smoking cigar with
pepper flavors that come
through a good, easy draw.
(03/01/94)
U.S.: $ .95 • U.K.: N/A

BOLIVAR INMENSA **87**
Cuba • *Size:* 6⅝" x 43
Filler/Binder/Wrapper: Cuba
A well-made cigar with
good balance and a core of
red spices. But it finishes a
little dry.
U.S.: N/A • Switzerland: 9SF

DON LINO NO. 5 **87**
Honduras • *Size:* 6¼" x
44 *Filler/Binder:* Honduras
Wrapper: U.S.A./Conn. Shade
A medium-bodied cigar with
a solid spiciness and flavors
of light, creamy coffee. It
smokes easily and has a
cedarwood finish.
U.S.: $2.65 • U.K.: N/A

EL REY DEL MUNDO **87**
LONSDALE
Cuba • *Size:* 6⅜" x 42 *Filler/
Binder/Wrapper:* Cuba
A full-flavored cigar with some
sweet spice and cedar wood
flavors. It also has some under-
tones of earth and leather. But
it showed inconsistency.
U.S.: N/A • U.K.: £7.75

EL REY DEL MUNDO **87**
LONSDALE
Honduras • *Size:* 7" x 43
Filler/Binder: Honduras
Wrapper: Ecuador

A smooth and well-balanced
smoke. There are some hints
of mint and cedar, and then
some nuts and sweet wood on
the finish.
U.S.: $3.50 • U.K.: N/A

JOSE BENITO PALMA **87**
Dominican Republic •
Size: 6" x 43 *Filler:* Dom.
Rep. *Binder:* Honduras
Wrapper: Cameroon
A spicy aroma on this well-
made, medium-bodied cigar
leads to smooth, mild flavors
of nutmeg and pepper.
(03/01/94)
U.S.: $2.00 • U.K.: N/A

JOYA DE NICARAGUA **87**
NO. 1
Nicaragua • *Size:* 6⅝" x 44
Filler/Binder: Nicaragua
Wrapper: Ecuador
A sweet nut flavor dominates
this medium-bodied cigar. It
has solid notes of herbs that
build into spicy flavors, and it
has a spicy finish.
U.S.: $2.55 • U.K.: N/A

LA FINCA ROMEO **87**
Nicaragua • *Size:* 6½" x
42 *Filler/Binder/Wrapper:*
Nicaragua
A cigar with a creamy texture. It has plenty of nutty
flavors on the palate and a
sweet, cedary finish.
U.S.: $1.60 • U.K.: N/A

LICENCIADOS **87**
EXCELENTE
Dominican Republic • *Size:*
6¼" x 43 *Filler/Binder:* Dom.
Rep. *Wrapper:* U.S.A./
Conn. Shade

A well-made cigar with
spice and nuts on the mid-
palate with a woody, slightly
short finish.
U.S.: $3.00 • U.K.: N/A

MONTECRISTO NO. 1 **87**
Dominican Republic •
Size: 6½" x 44 *Filler/Binder:*
Dom. Rep. *Wrapper:*
U.S.A./Conn. Shade
A solid medium-bodied cigar.
It has a core of cocoa bean
flavors, with hints of sweet
spices and a pleasant, sweet
wood finish.
U.S.: $6.50 • U.K.: N/A

MONTESINO NO. 1 **87**
Dominican Republic •
Size: 6¼" x 43 *Filler/Binder:*
Dom. Rep. *Wrapper:*
U.S.A./Conn. Shade
A cigar with a spicy attack
on the palate, but with a
short finish. Well-made.
(03/01/94)
U.S.: $1.70 • U.K.: N/A

PADRON PALMA **87**
Honduras • *Size:* 6⁷⁄₁₆"
x 42 *Filler/Binder/Wrapper:*
Nicaragua
A cool, smooth smoke with
strong hints of roasted coffee
flavors. It also has some sweet
spices on the palate with a
perfumed, but rather short,
finish.
U.S.: $2.60 • U.K.: N/A

PARTAGAS HUMITUBE **87**
Dominican Republic •
Size: 6¼" x 43 *Filler:* Dom.
Rep. *Binder:* Mexico
Wrapper: Cameroon
This cigar comes across as
quite rustic with some good

spiciness. It has a smoothness on the palate, with a sweet woody character.
U.S.: $4.75 • U.K.: N/A

POR LARRAÑAGA **87**
CETROS
Dominican Republic • *Size: 6⅞" x 42 Filler/Binder:* Dom. Rep. *Wrapper:* U.S.A./ Conn. Shade
A nice, smooth-tasting cigar. It has some hints of toastiness on the palate and there is a good creamy texture.
U.S.: $4.50 • U.K.: N/A

RAMON ALLONES "B" **87**
Dominican Republic • *Size: 6½" x 42 Filler:* Dom. Rep., Mexico *Binder:* Mexico *Wrapper:* Cameroon
A smooth brown wrapper leads to a mild, medium-bodied spiciness with cedar and coffee flavors. (03/01/94)
U.S.: $3.00 • U.K.: N/A

SOSA NO. 1 **87**
Dominican Republic • *Size: 6½" x 43 Filler:* Dom. Rep., Brazil *Binder:* Honduras *Wrapper:* Ecuador
A medium-bodied cigar with toasted nut aromas, smooth, creamy, coffee flavors and a sweet, spicy finish. (03/01/94)
U.S.: $2.25 • U.K.: N/A

THOMAS HINDS **87**
NICARAGUAN
SELECTION LONSDALE
Nicaragua • *Size: 6⅔" x 43 Filler/Binder/Wrapper:* Nicaragua
A nice oily wrapper. This cigar has solid notes of coffee grounds and a good spiciness,

with a slight mineral finish.
U.S.: $4.30 • Canada: $4.95

8-9-8 COLLECTION **86**
LONSDALE
Jamaica • *Size: 6½" x 42 Filler:* Jamaica, Dom. Rep. *Binder:* Mexico *Wrapper:* U.S.A./Conn. Shade
A very well-made cigar. It has some solid notes of spice and nuts on the palate that finish a bit short and on the dry, woody side.
U.S.: $7.00 • U.K.: N/A

ASHTON 8-9-8 **86**
Dominican Republic • *Size: 6½" x 44 Filler/Binder:* Dom. Rep. *Wrapper:* U.S.A./Conn. Shade
A very pleasant, creamy cigar. It has strong flavors of nuts, with hints of leather and nutmeg.
U.S.: $4.40 • U.K.: £3.75

AVO NO. 1 **86**
Dominican Republic • *Size: 6⅔" x 42 Filler:* Dom.Rep. *Binder:* Dom. Rep. *Wrapper:* U.S.A./ Conn. Shade
This is a medium-bodied cigar that needs some aging. But it is smooth and woody with a slight floral aroma. There are nuts and dried citrus flavors on the palate.
U.S.: $5.85 • U.K.: N/A

BAUZA MEDAILLE **86**
D'ORO NO. 1
Dominican Republic • *Size: 6⅞" x 44 Filler:* Dom. Rep. , Nicaragua *Binder:* Mexico *Wrapper:* Ecuador

A very peppery cigar with a solid woody core of flavors. It has a smooth taste.
U.S.: $3.35 • U.K.: N/A

DON DIEGO LONSDALE **86**
Dominican Republic • *Size: 6⅝" x 42 Filler/Binder:* Dom. Rep. *Wrapper:* U.S.A./Conn. Shade
A good medium-bodied cigar. It has a touch of pepper at first, which rounds out to a creamy, toasty character with a hint of spiciness.
U.S.: $3.50 • U.K.: N/A

DON MELO CORONA **86**
GORDA
Honduras • *Size: 6¼" x 44 Filler/Binder/Wrapper:* Honduras
An oily, dark wrapper makes this an attractive cigar. It is a bit dry on the palate, with some hints of leathery and earthy flavors.
U.S.: $2.90 • U.K.: N/A

ENCANTO ELEGANTE **86**
Honduras • *Size: 7" x 44 Filler/Binder/Wrapper:* Honduras
Some inconsistency in construction for this cigar. But it is very spicy, with a nice earthy texture. There are hints of citrus fruit and a tanginess on the finish.
U.S.: $2.90 • U.K.: N/A

MACANUDO VINTAGE 86
CABINET NO. 2

Jamaica • *Size*: 6⁵⁄₁₆" x 43
Filler: Dom. Rep., Jamaica,
Mexico *Binder*: Mexico
Wrapper: U.S.A./Conn.
Shade
This is a good mild- to medium-bodied cigar with a strong element of nuttiness on the palate. It finishes a little dry, but has a woody character.
U.S.: $8.50 • U.K.: N/A

MONTE CANARIO 86
NUNCIO

Canary Islands • *Size*: 6³⁄₄" x 44 *Filler*: Canary Islands, Dom. Rep. *Binder*: Dom. Rep. *Wrapper*: U.S.A./ Conn. Shade
A well-made cigar with a good balance of flavors that include dried citrus and leather notes. It has a woody finish.
U.S.: $6.25 • U.K.: N/A

MONTE CANARIO 86
IMPERIALES

Canary Islands • *Size*: 6½" x 42 *Filler*: Canary Islands, Dom. Rep. *Binder*: Dom. Rep. *Wrapper*: U.S.A./ Conn. Shade
A medium-bodied cigar with a sweet herbal character. It has hints of leather and earthiness with a smooth finish.
U.S.: $6.00 • U.K.: N/A

PETRUS TABACAGE 89 86
NO. 2

Honduras • *Size*: 6¼" x 44
Filler: Nicaragua *Binder*: Honduras *Wrapper*: Ecuador
A very nice smooth-tasting cigar. It has some strong hints

of leather with a spicy, floral finish.
U.S.: $4.10 • U.K.: N/A

PRIMO DEL REY 86
SELECCION NO. 1

Dominican Republic • *Size*: 6 13/16 x 42 *Filler*: Dom. Rep., Brazil *Binder*: U.S.A. *Wrapper*: Indonesia
A pleasant medium-bodied smoke. It has some sweet pepper and earth notes on the palate, and a woody finish.
U.S.: $2.30 • U.K.: N/A

PUNCH NO. 1 86

Honduras • *Size*: 6½" x 43 *Filler*: Nica., Hon., Dom. Rep. *Binder*: Ecuador *Wrapper*: U.S.A./Conn. Shade
This easy-drawing cigar is well-balanced with an herbal spiciness, but it has a fairly short finish. (03/01/94)
U.S.: $2.00 • U.K.: N/A

RAMON ALLONES 86
CRYSTALS

Dominican Republic • *Size*: 6³⁄₄" x 42 *Filler*: Dom. Rep., Mexico *Binder*: Mexico *Wrapper*: Cameroon
This cigar is a bit rough, but it has a good woody character and flavor elements of nuts and mild spices with a slightly mineral finish.
U.S.: $4.35 • U.K.: N/A

ROMEO Y JULIETA 86
VINTAGE NO. 1

Dominican Republic • *Size*: 6" x 43 *Filler*: Dom. Rep. *Binder*: Mexico *Wrapper*: U.S.A./Conn. Shade

A solidly spicy cigar with a medium body that finishes with a dried-wood character. (03/01/94)
U.S.: $4.50 • U.K.: N/A

SAINT LUIS REY 86
LONSDALE

Honduras • *Size*: 6½" x 44
Filler/Binder/Wrapper: Honduras
A medium-bodied cigar that is a bit coarse, but it's packed with complex sweet herb and toast-like flavors. It ends a bit dry.
U.S.: $3.00 • U.K.: N/A

SANTA ROSA CETROS 86

Honduras • *Size*: 6" x 42
Filler/Binder/Wrapper: Honduras
Mild nut and spice flavors dominate this cigar that starts a bit slow, but builds to a smooth, pleasant smoke. (03/01/94)
U.S.: $2.00 • U.K.: N/A

TRESADO SELECCION 86
NO. 400

Dominican Republic • *Size*: 6⅝ x 44 *Filler*: Dom. Rep. *Binder*: Cameroon *Wrapper*: Indonesia
Some inconsistency. But a cigar with good balance and sweetish character. It has hints of coffee bean flavors and a sweet wood character.
U.S.: $1.85 • U.K.: N/A

TROYA NO. 54 86
ELEGANTE

Dominican Republic • *Size*: 7" x 43 *Filler/Binder*: Dom. Rep. *Wrapper*: U.S.A./ Conn. Shade

This is a well-balanced and smooth-tasting cigar. It has some flavors of toast and cream.
U.S.: $4.00 • U.K.: N/A

VERACRUZ RESERVE ESPECIAL **86**
Mexico • *Size:* 6½" x 42
Filler/Binder/Wrapper: Mexico
A light-tasting cigar that smokes easily with some spicy flavors. (03/01/94)
U.S.: $5.00 • U.K.: N/A

ARTURO FUENTE SELECCION PRIVADA NO. 1 **85**
Dominican Republic • *Size:* 6¾" x 44 *Filler/Binder:* Dom. Rep. *Wrapper:* Cameroon
This is a smooth, well-balanced cigar. It has a light peppery flavor with hints of sweet nuts.
U.S.: $2.75 • U.K.: N/A

BELINDA CORONA GRANDE **85**
Honduras • *Size:* 6¼" x 44
Filler/Binder: Honduras
Wrapper: Ecuador
This cigar has a short finish. But it has a creamy texture with smooth flavors of nuts and an earthy herbalness.
U.S.: $1.80 • U.K.: N/A

C.A.O. LONSDALE **85**
Honduras • *Size:* 7" x 44
Filler: Nicaragua, Mexico
Binder: Honduras *Wrapper:* U.S.A./Conn. Shade
A nice, well-balanced cigar. It has a strong cedarwood finish and some hints of leather and sweet spices on the palate.
U.S.: $4.95 • U.K.: N/A

CUESTA-REY CABINET NO. 95 **85**
Dominican Republic • *Size:* 6¼" x 42 *Filler:* Dom. Rep. *Binder:* Dom.Rep. *Wrapper:* Cameroon
A pleasant, spicy cigar. It has some hints of chocolate and earthiness on the palate, but ends with a rather dry, woody finish.
U.S.: $2.20 • U.K.: N/A

CUESTA-REY CABINET SELECTION NO. 1884 **85**
Dominican Republic • *Size:* 6¼" x 44 *Filler/Binder:* Dom. Rep. *Wrapper:* U.S.A./Conn. Shade
A mild- to medium-bodied cigar with a smooth taste of nuts and herbs. It has a mild spicy finish.
U.S.: $2.40 • U.K.: N/A

DON ASA CETROS NO. 2 **85**
Honduras • *Size:* 6½" x 44 *Filler/Binder/Wrapper:* Honduras
A very well-balanced and harmonious cigar with hints of sweet spices, woodiness and a slightly herbal flavor. A dry finish.
U.S.: $2.00 • U.K.: N/A

DON LINO HAVANA RESERVE NO. 1 **85**
Honduras • *Size:* 6½" x 44 *Filler/Binder:* Honduras *Wrapper:* U.S.A./Conn. Shade
A mild, smooth-tasting cigar. It has a creamy texture with some herb and wood flavors, and a bit of saltiness. A woody finish.
U.S.: $4.65 • U.K.: N/A

DON TOMAS HONDURAN SPECIAL EDITION NO. 200 **85**
Honduras • *Size:* 6½" x 44
Filler: Dom. Rep., Nicaragua
Binder/Wrapper: Honduras
This is a mellow smoke with a strong nutty component. Showed some inconsistency in performance. It has some solid coffeelike flavors.
U.S.: $4.60 • U.K.: N/A

DON VITO CAPO **85**
Dominican Republic • *Size:* 6¾" x 44 *Filler/Binder:* Dom. Rep. *Wrapper:* U.S.A./Conn. Shade
A well-made cigar with an oily wrapper. It has a creamy texture, with a solid pepper spice core, and a sweet cedar finish.
U.S.: $4.25 • U.K.: N/A

H. UPMANN DIRECTOR ROYALE **85**
Dominican Republic • *Size:* 6⅝" x 42 *Filler/Binder:* Dom. Rep. *Wrapper:* Indonesia
A cigar dominated by a salty character. It has some spice and a slightly dry finish.
U.S.: $4.25 • U.K.: N/A

HOYO DE MONTERREY NO. 1 **85**
Honduras • *Size:* 6½" x 43
Filler/Binder: Honduras, Nicaragua, Dom. Rep.
Wrapper: Ecuador
A very well-made cigar with a pleasant floral character. There is a bit of young tobacco evident on the palate, and it should improve with age.
U.S.: $2.75 • U.K.: N/A

MACABI NO. 1　**85**
U.S.A. • *Size:* 6¾" x 44
Filler: Dom. Rep., Nicaragua
Binder: Mexico　*Wrapper:*
U.S.A./Conn. Shade
A young cigar that starts out
slow, but it warms up to
pleasant flavors of sweet
herbs with an overall creamy
texture.
U.S.: $3.10　•　U.K.: N/A

MACANUDO BARON　**85**
DE ROTHSCHILD
Jamaica • *Size:* 6½" x 42
Filler: Dom. Rep., Jamaica,
Mexico　*Binder:* Mexico
Wrapper: U.S.A./Conn.
Shade
A very well-made cigar. It
has a creamy texture on a
mild body, with a slight tang.
It has a slightly dry finish.
U.S.: $4.00　•　U.K.: N/A

MONTECRUZ NO. 210　**85**
Dominican Republic •
Size: 6½" x 42　*Filler/Binder:*
Dom. Rep., Brazil　*Wrapper:*
U.S.A./Conn. Shade
A well-made cigar with rich
flavors of spice and coffee. It
has an elegant finish with
cedar-wood tones. (03/01/94)
U.S.: $2.65　•　U.K.: N/A

NAT SHERMAN　**85**
GOTHAM SELECTION
NO. 1400
Dominican Republic • *Size:*
6¼" x 44　*Filler/Binder:* Dom.
Rep.　*Wrapper:* U.S.A./
Conn. Shade
A spicy smoke with a white
peppery note. It has a slightly
earthy quality, with a woody
finish, and some hints of cof-
fee bean on the palate. It

burns well.
U.S.: $5.60　•　U.K.: N/A

PRIMO DEL REY　**85**
PRESIDENTE
Dominican Republic • *Size:*
6¹³⁄₁₆ x 44　*Filler:* Dom. Rep.,
Brazil　*Binder:* U.S.A.
Wrapper: Indonesia.
A well-made cigar that has a
tinge of mineral flavors. It
turns creamy and herbal with
an earthy aroma.
U.S.: $2.85　•　U.K.: N/A

PRIMO DEL REY　**85**
CHAVON
Dominican Republic • *Size:*
6½" x 41　*Filler:* Dom. Rep.,
Brazil　*Binder:* U.S.A.
Wrapper: Indonesia
This cigar starts out quite
salty, but it builds into a solid
core of spiciness with hints of
nutmeg. A woody finish.
U.S.: $1.85　•　U.K.: N/A

PUNCH LONSDALE　**85**
Honduras • *Size:* 6½" x 43
Filler/Binder: Honduras,
Nicaragua, Dom. Rep.
Wrapper: Ecuador
A pleasant, mild- to medium-
bodied cigar. It has a mild,
woody character with a
slightly dry wood finish.
U.S.: $2.75　•　U.K.: N/A

RAMON ALLONES　**85**
PRIVADA A
Dominican Republic • *Size:*
7" x 45　*Filler:* Dom. Rep.,
Mexico　*Binder:* Mexico
Wrapper: Cameroon
A pleasant, mild- to medium-
bodied smoke with a light
creaminess, a hint of nuts

and spices, and a fresh finish.
U.S.: $4.20　•　U.K.: N/A

SANTA CLARA NO. 3　**85**
Mexico • *Size:* 6⅝" x 43
Filler/Binder/Wrapper: Mexico
This cigar starts slowly, but it
builds to some nutty flavors
with a smooth-tasting orange
peel quality. It is a medium-
bodied smoke.
U.S.: $2.15　•　U.K.: N/A

SOSA FAMILY　**85**
SELECTION NO. 1
Dominican Republic • *Size:*
6¾" x 43　*Filler/Binder:* Dom.
Rep.　*Wrapper:* U.S.A./
Conn. Shade
A solid peppery cigar, but it
lacks depth. There are some
vegetal notes on a rather
short finish.
U.S.: $3.85　•　U.K.: N/A

TE-AMO MEDITATION　**85**
Mexico • *Size:* 6" x 42
Filler/Binder/Wrapper: Mexico
A solid cigar with straight
tobacco flavors, but a dry,
woody finish. (03/01/94)
U.S.: $2.10　•　U.K.: N/A

THOMAS HINDS　**85**
HONDURAN SELECTION
SUPREMOS
Honduras • *Size:* 6⅔" x 43
Filler/Binder: Honduras
Wrapper: Ecuador
This is an herbal cigar domi-
nated by a woody character.
It has some hints of spice on
the palate, and is a mild- to
medium-bodied smoke.
U.S.: $3.25 • Canada: $3.95

ZINO MOUTON CADET 85
No. 1
Honduras • *Size:* 6½" x 44
Filler/Binder/Wrapper:
Honduras
A medium-bodied cigar with
a hint of sweet spice on the
palate. It is dominated by an
herbal character with a dry
woody finish.
U.S.: $6.30 • U.K.: $5.50

ASTRAL LUJOS 84
Honduras • *Size:* 6½" x
44 *Filler:* Dom. Rep.,
Nicaragua *Binder/Wrapper:*
Honduras
A mild-tasting cigar with a
strong dry, herbal character.
Some inconsistency in per-
formance. It has a hint of
earthiness on a dry finish.
U.S.: $6.50 • U.K.: N/A

CARA MIA LONSDALE 84
Canary Islands • *Size:*
6½" x 42 *Filler/Binder:*
Canary Island, Brazil, Dom.
Rep. *Wrapper:* U.S.A./
Conn. Shade
A smooth-tasting cigar with
some mild hints of cream,
and a meaty note. It has an
overall floral character.
U.S.: $6.00 • U.K.: N/A

CASA BLANCA 84
LONSDALE
Dominican Republic • *Size:*
6½" x 42 *Filler:* Dom. Rep.,
Brazil *Binder:* Mexico
Wrapper: U.S.A./Conn. Shade
A very young cigar. It has
some cinnamon and dried
citrus elements on the
palate, and there are some
strong woody notes. Needs
to be aged.
U.S.: $2.25 • U.K.: N/A

CUESTA-REY CAPTIVA 84
Dominican Republic • *Size:*
6¾₆" x 42 *Filler/Binder:* Dom.
Rep. *Wrapper:* U.S.A./
Conn. Shade
A mild- to medium-bodied
cigar dominated by woody
flavors. It has a hint of nutti-
ness on the palate.
U.S.: $3.25 • U.K.: £5.75

DIANA SILVIUS 84
CORONA
Dominican Republic • *Size:*
6½" x 42 *Filler/Binder:* Dom.
Rep. *Wrapper:* U.S.A./
Conn. Shade
This is a well-made cigar. It
has some solid notes of cedar
and tobacco character with a
slightly tangy finish.
U.S.: $5.80 • U.K.: N/A

DON JUAN NUMERO 84
UNO
Nicaragua • *Size:* 6⅝" x 44
Filler: Nicaragua, Dom. Rep.
Binder: Mexico *Wrapper:*
U.S.A./Conn. Shade
A decent medium-bodied
cigar. It has some vegetal
notes and a salty character,
but there are some hints of
nuts on the palate.
U.S.: $2.55 • U.K.: N/A

DON LINO No. 1 84
Honduras • *Size:* 6½" x 44
Filler/Binder: Honduras
Wrapper: U.S.A./Conn. Shade
A well-made, medium-bod-
ied cigar dominated by sweet
herbal notes. While there are
some leathery tones on the
finish, it is dry.
U.S.: $3.15 • U.K.: N/A

DON TOMAS CORONA 84
GRANDE
Honduras • *Size:* 6½" x 44
Filler/Binder/Wrapper:
Honduras, Nicaragua *Filler:*
Honduras, Nicaragua
Binder/Wrapper: Honduras
This is a soft, spicy cigar with
a creamy character. It is
medium-bodied and has a
woody finish.
U.S.: $4.10 • U.K.: $5.49

DON XAVIER 84
LONSDALE
Canary Islands • *Size:* 6⅝" x
42 *Filler/Binder:* Canary
Islands, Dom. Rep., Brazil
Wrapper: U.S.A./Conn. Shade
A mild cigar with a good
creamy texture. It has mild
flavors of herbs.
U.S.: $7.75 • U.K.: N/A

F.D. GRAVE LONSDALE 84
Honduras • *Size:* 6¼" x
44 *Filler:* Dom. Rep.,
Honduras, U.S.A. *Binder/
Wrapper:* U.S.A.
A cigar with a good woody
character and a soft touch of
sweet herbs. A pleasant
aroma with hints of mint.
U.S.: $2.15 • U.K.: N/A

HOYO DE MONTERREY 84
AMBASSADOR
Honduras • *Size:* 6¼" x 44
Filler/Binder: Honduras,
Nicaragua, Dom. Rep.
Wrapper: Ecuador
This mild- to medium-bodied
cigar has some sweet, mild
spice flavors. It is a bit dry on
the finish.
U.S.: $2.60 • U.K.: N/A

JOSÉ MARTÍ PALMA   84
Dominican Republic •
Size: 7" x 42   *Filler:* Dom.
Rep.   *Binder:* Mexico
Wrapper: U.S.A./Conn.
Shade
A pleasant, nutty cigar with a
very creamy character. It is a
light-tasting, mild cigar with
an attractive wrapper.
U.S.: $3.00 • U.K.: N/A

JUAN CLEMENTE GRAN 84
CORONA
Dominican Republic • *Size:*
6" x 42   *Filler/Binder:* Dom.
Rep.   *Wrapper:* U.S.A./
Conn. Shade
This cigar has a woody aroma
and flavor and, as it gets
going, takes on a rustic,
earthy character. (03/01/94)
U.S.: $3.55 • U.K.: N/A

JUAN CLEMENTE CLUB 84
SELECTION NO. 3
Dominican Republic • *Size:*
7" x 44   *Filler/Binder:* Dom.
Rep.   *Wrapper:* U.S.A./
Conn. Shade
Good core of sweet herb and
nut flavors. It has a slightly
dry finish.
U.S.: $7.60 • U.K.: N/A

LA UNICA NO. 300   84
Dominican Republic •
Size: 6¾" x 44   *Filler/Binder:*
Dom. Rep.   *Wrapper:*
U.S.A./Conn. Shade
An oily wrapper. This mild-
to medium-bodied cigar has a
sweet spicy character with
some light coffee-like flavors.
U.S.: $2.50 • U.K.: N/A

MONTECRUZ   84
SUN-GROWN NO. 210
Dominican Republic • *Size:*
6½" x 42   *Filler/Binder:* Dom.
Rep., Brazil   *Wrapper:*
Indonesia
A pleasant mild- to medium-
bodied smoke. It has a light
brown wrapper and a strong
mineral character with a hint
of spice.
U.S.: $3.50 • U.K.: N/A

NAT SHERMAN   84
LANDMARK SELECTION
ALGONQUIN
Dominican Republic • *Size:*
6¾" x 43   *Filler:* Dom. Rep.
Binder: Mexico   *Wrapper:*
Cameroon
This is a pleasant, full-bodied
cigar that is a bit hot, but has
a core of spiciness. (03/01/94)
U.S.: $4.75 • U.K.: N/A

OLOR LONSDALE   84
Dominican Republic •
Size: 6½" x 42   *Filler/Binder:*
Dom. Rep.   *Wrapper:*
U.S.A./Conn. Shade
A cigar with a pleasant floral
note on the finish. It has
some nut and herb flavors.
U.S.: $3.60 • U.K.: N/A

PRIMO DEL REY   84
SELECCION NO. 2
Dominican Republic • *Size:*
6¼" x 42   *Filler:* Dom. Rep.,
Brazil   *Binder:* U.S.A.
Wrapper: Indonesia
This is a solid, medium-bod-
ied cigar with a good earthy
character and some sweet
wood and herbal flavors. A
nice, easy smoke.
U.S.: $2.00 • U.K.: N/A

PUNCH AMATISTA   84
Honduras • *Size:* 6¼" x
44   *Filler/Binder:* Honduras,
Nicaragua, Dom. Rep.
Wrapper: Ecuador
There are some flavors of
dried citrus fruit, with an
overall woody character. It
has a slightly herbal finish.
U.S.: $1.75 • U.K.: N/A

ROMEO Y JULIETA   84
PALMA
Dominican Republic • *Size:*
6" x 43   *Filler:* Dom. Rep.,
Brazil   *Binder:* U.S.A./Conn.
Broadleaf   *Wrapper:*
Cameroon
Mild pepper flavors show
through in this medium-bod-
ied cigar. (03/01/94)
U.S.: $1.95 • U.K.: N/A

ROYAL JAMAICA   84
CORONA GRANDE
Dominican Republic • *Size:*
6½" x 42   *Filler:* Jamaica
Binder: Cameroon   *Wrapper:*
Indonesia
This cigar has a very salty
character. There are hints of
black pepper and some cedar-
wood, but it finishes quite
dry.
U.S.: $3.50 • U.K.: N/A

TESOROS DE COPAN   84
CETROS
Honduras • *Size:* 6¼" x 44
Filler: Nicaragua   *Binder/*
Wrapper: Honduras
A decent yellow-brown
wrapper. This cigar still has
some grassy notes on the
palate, with touches of wood
and earth flavors. A dry
woody finish.
U.S.: $3.20 • U.K.: N/A

THE GRIFFIN'S NO. 300   84

Dominican Republic • *Size:* 6¼" x 44 *Filler/Binder:* Dom. Rep. *Wrapper:* U.S.A./Conn. Shade
This cigar has leathery flavors and a mild spiciness on the palate. It is well balanced and has a sweet, woody finish.
U.S.: $4.90 • U.K.: £6.00

ZINO TRADITION   84

Honduras • *Size:* 6¼" x 44 *Filler/Binder:* Honduras *Wrapper:* Ecuador
A well-balanced cigar that should improve with age. It has some herb and nut flavors on a creamy core. A dry finish.
U.S.: $6.00 • U.K.: N/A

AL-CAPONE CORONA GRANDE   83

Nicaragua • *Size:* 6¾" x 43 *Filler/Binder:* Nicaragua *Wrapper:* Brazil
This cigar has a smooth, cedary flavor with some notes of sweet coffee. It is medium-bodied and finishes with a slightly woody note.
U.S.: $3.50 • U.K.: N/A

BACCARAT LUCHADORES   83

Honduras • *Size:* 6" x 43 *Filler/Binder/Wrapper:* Honduras
A cigar that uses sweet gum to secure the wrapper. Not for everybody, but it's well-made, with solid tobacco flavors. (03/01/94)
U.S.: $1.30 • U.K.: N/A

BAUZA JAGUAR   83

Dominican Republic • *Size:* 6½" x 42 *Filler:* Dom. Rep., Nicaragua *Binder:* Mexico *Wrapper:* Ecuador
There is a hint of spiciness on the palate of this fairly straightforward cigar. It rounds out on the finish with a sweet woody note.
U.S.: $3.20 • U.K.: N/A

CANARIO D'ORO LONSDALE   83

Dominican Republic • *Size:* 6½" x 43 *Filler:* Dom. Rep., Mexico *Binder/Wrapper:* Mexico
A medium-bodied cigar with hints of spice and wood on the palate, and a woody finish.
U.S.: $2.25 • U.K.: N/A

CIFUENTES LONSDALE   83

Dominican Republic • *Size:* 6½" x 42 *Filler:* Dom. Rep, Mexico *Binder:* Cameroon *Wrapper:* U.S.A./Conn. Shade
A well-made cigar. It has solid flavors of herbs with a mild, woody finish.
U.S.: $10.60 • U.K.: N/A

CUBITA 8-9-8   83

Dominican Republic • *Size:* 6¾" x 43 *Filler/Binder:* Dom. Rep. *Wrapper:* U.S.A./Conn. Shade
A light, easy-smoking cigar with medium-bodied smoke. It has hints of anise and pepper, but with an overall paper-like, or dry woody character.
U.S.: $4.75 • U.K.: N/A

CUESTA-REY CENTENNIAL COLLECTION DOMINICAN NO. 4   83

Dominican Republic • *Size:* 6½" x 42 *Filler/Binder:* Dom. Rep. *Wrapper:* U.S.A./Conn. Shade
A cigar with a noted salty character. It has some strong vegetal notes and a mouth-drying finish.
U.S.: $2.40 • U.K.: £5.40

DON TOMAS CETROS   83

Honduras • *Size:* 6½" x 44 *Filler/Binder/Wrapper:* Honduras, Nicaragua *Filler:* Honduras, Nicaragua *Binder/Wrapper:* Honduras
A light and simple cigar. It has some vegetal character and a bit of tang on the palate. A dry finish.
U.S.: $3.00 • U.K.: N/A

DUNHILL DIAMANTES   83

Dominican Republic • *Size:* 6⅝" x 42 *Filler/Binder:* Dom. Rep., Brazil *Wrapper:* U.S.A./Conn. Shade
A nice-looking Connecticut shade wrapper. This cigar has some earthy qualities, but overall it has a slightly vegetal character with a dry woody finish.
U.S.: $4.65 • U.K.: N/A

GILBERTO OLIVA NUMERO 1   83

Honduras • *Size:* 6½" x 44 *Filler/Binder:* Dom. Rep., Nicaragua *Wrapper:* Ecuador
A young cigar. But it has some good spicy flavors and a smooth, creamy texture. Give it time.
U.S.: $3.40 • U.K.: N/A

H. UPMANN 83
LONSDALE
Dominican Republic • *Size:*
6⅝" x 42 *Filler/Binder:* Dom.
Rep. *Wrapper:* Indonesia
A slightly rustic cigar with
some spiciness on the palate.
It has a vegetal character and
a woody finish.
U.S.: $3.50 • U.K.: N/A

LEON JIMENES NO. 3 83
Dominican Republic •
Size: 6½" x 42 *Filler/Binder:*
Dom. Rep. *Wrapper:*
U.S.A./Conn. Shade
A very yellow wrapper on a
cigar that has a dry and herbal
character. There is a hint of
curry spice on its mild- to
medium-bodied smoke.
U.S.: $4.50 • U.K.: N/A

MONTESINO CESAR 83
NO. 2
Dominican Republic • *Size:*
6¼" x 44 *Filler/Binder:* Dom.
Rep. *Wrapper:* U.S.A./
Conn. Shade
This cigar burns well with a
firm draw. It has a strong woody
character with a woody finish.
There are hints of spiciness.
U.S.: $2.30 • U.K.: N/A

NAT SHERMAN 83
EXCHANGE SELECTION
BUTTERFIELD NO. 8
Dominican Republic • *Size:*
6½" x 42 *Filler:* Dom. Rep.
Binder: Mexico *Wrapper:*
U.S.A./Conn. Shade
A straightforward cigar with
hints of nuttiness and
creaminess and a touch of
spice, but with a very dry,
neutral finish.
U.S.: $5.60 • U.K.: N/A

PADRON 1964 83
ANNIVESARY SERIES
SUPERI
Honduras • *Size:* 6" x 42
Filler/Binder/Wrapper:
Nicaragua
This cigar has a strong herbal
character. There are some
hints of cocoa and leather on
the palate with a perfume-
like aroma. Mild.
U.S.: $6.30 • U.K.: N/A

PADRON AMBASSDOR 83
Honduras • *Size:* 6⅞" x
42 *Filler/Binder/Wrapper:*
Nicaragua
A mild- to medium-bodied
smoke with solid flavors of
nuts and herbs.
U.S.: $2.80 • U.K.: N/A

RAMON ALLONES 83
TRUMPS
Dominican Republic • *Size:*
6¼" x 43 *Filler:* Dom. Rep.,
Mexico *Binder:* Mexico
Wrapper: Cameroon
A rustic cigar. It has a
smooth taste with some sweet
notes, and a woody finish.
U.S.: $4.50 • U.K.: N/A

SANTA ROSA CORONA 83
Honduras • *Size:* 6½" x
44 *Filler/Binder/Wrapper:*
Honduras
A dry woodiness dominates
this medium-bodied cigar. It
has some strong vegetal flavors.
U.S.: $3.25 • U.K.: N/A

LA FLOR DOMINICANA 82
ALCALDE
Dominican Republic • *Size:*
6½" x 44 *Filler/Binder:* Dom.

Rep. *Wrapper:* U.S.A./
Conn. Shade
A nicely made cigar with a
slightly peppery taste. It has a
sharp finish.
U.S.: $5.50 • U.K.: N/A

PRIMO DEL REY 82
LONSDALE
Dominican Republic • *Size:*
6½" x 42 *Filler:* Dom. Rep.,
Brazil *Binder:* U.S.A.
Wrapper: Indonesia
A rustic-style cigar. It has a
strong salty component and
some dry vegetal flavors.
U.S.: $1.85 • U.K.: N/A

SANTA DAMIANA 82
NO. 700
Dominican Republic • *Size:*
6½" x 42 *Filler/Binder:* Dom.
Rep. *Wrapper:* U.S.A./
Conn. Shade
This cigar shows some youth.
But it has a creamy texture
with a backbone of pepper
flavors. A woody finish.
U.S.: $6.00 • U.K.: N/A

TE-AMO RELAXATION 82
Mexico • *Size:* 6⅞" x 44
Filler/Binder/Wrapper: Mexico
A rather rustic cigar with
straightforward, dry vegetal
flavors. It has a dry, balsa-
wood finish.
U.S.: $2.65 • U.K.: N/A

TEMPLE HALL 82
NO. 625
Jamaica • *Size:* 6¼" x 45
Filler: Dom. Rep., Mexico,
Jamaica *Binder:* Mexico
Wrapper: U.S.A./Conn. Shade
This has some sweet spice
notes on a very woody char-
acter. It is mild- to medium-

bodied and has a rather neutral finish.
U.S.: $5.45 • U.K.: N/A

BACCARAT NO. 1 81
Honduras • *Size:* 7" x 44
Filler/Wrapper: Honduras
Binder: Mexico
This cigar has sweet gum on the wrapper. While somewhat neutral, it has a mild nuttiness and creaminess that is pleasant.
U.S.: $2.15 • U.K.: N/A

**HOYO DE MONTERREY 81
CHURCHILL**
Honduras • *Size:* 6¼" x 45
Filler/Binder: Honduras, Nicaragua, Dom. Rep.
Wrapper: Ecuador
A cigar that shows its youth. It has some hot spiciness and a dry finish. It's well made and should improve with age.
U.S.: $2.60 • U.K.: N/A

OSCAR NO. 300 81
Dominican Republic •
Size: 6¼" x 44 *Filler/Binder:* Dom. Rep. *Wrapper:* U.S.A./Conn. Shade
A fairly roughly made cigar. It has strong hot spices on the palate and tends to be a bit harsh, with a vegetal, woody finish.
U.S.: $6.20 • U.K.: £7.75

PUNCH PUNCH 81
Honduras • *Size:* 6¼" x 45 *Filler/Binder:* Honduras, Nicaragua, Dom. Rep.
Wrapper: Ecuador
A relatively mild cigar with a sharp spiciness and vegetal flavors, and a balsa-wood finish.
U.S.: $2.60 • U.K.: N/A

TE-AMO CELEBRATION 81
Mexico • *Size:* 6¹¹⁄₁₆"
x 44 *Filler/Binder/Wrapper:* Mexico
A mild, herbal cigar. There's a bit of a perfume quality to it. The finish is dry.
U.S.: $3.00 • U.K.: N/A

**NAT SHERMAN 80
MANHATTAN
SELECTION GRAMERCY**
Dominican Republic • *Size:* 6¼" x 43 *Filler:* Dom. Rep.
Binder/Wrapper: Mexico
This cigar has a salty character. It has some herbal and wood flavors, and a woody, earthy finish.
U.S.: $3.60 • U.K.: N/A

**TE-AMO PARK AVENUE 80
NEW YORK**
Mexico • *Size:* 6⅝" x 42
Filler/Binder/Wrapper: Mexico
A young cigar with a strong vegetal character. There is some hot spiciness on the palate, but it burns quickly.
U.S.: $2.30 • U.K.: N/A

VUELTABAJO LONSDALE 80
Dominican Republic •
Size: 7" x 43 *Filler/Binder:* Dom. Rep. *Wrapper:* U.S.A./Conn. Shade
A rather flat neutral cigar. It has a vegetal and dry woody character. There is a hint of spice on the palate.
U.S.: $3.00 • U.K.: N/A

**LAS CABRILLAS PONCE 79
DE LEON**
Honduras • *Size:* 6⅝" x 44
Filler: Nicaragua, Mexico
Binder: Mexico *Wrapper:* U.S.A./Conn. Shade

This is a very rough, rustic cigar. It is mild, but with a dry papery character and an overall grassy flavor.
U.S.: $1.95 • U.K.: N/A

BANCES CAZADORES 78
Honduras • *Size:* 6¼"
x 43 *Filler:* Nicaragua
Binder: Mexico *Wrapper:* Ecuador
Hints of coffee and cocoa, but this cigar turns hot and has some slight vegetal flavors. (03/01/94)
U.S.: $ .85 • U.K.: N/A

**ORNELAS LTD. 78
COGNAC**
Mexico • *Size:* 6¼" x 42
Filler/Binder/Wrapper: Mexico
A strange-tasting cigar. It warms up to a pungent sweetness, but has a slightly harsh finish.
U.S.: $9.50 • U.K.: N/A

ORNELAS NO. 1 78
Mexico • *Size:* 6¼" x 44
Filler/Binder/Wrapper: Mexico
A very rustic cigar with a rough-looking wrapper. It has a very salty character and a hint of wood on the finish.
U.S.: $4.75 • U.K.: N/A

**PAUL GARMIRIAN 78
LONSDALE**
Dominican Republic • *Size:* 6½" x 42 *Filler/Binder:* Dom. Rep. *Wrapper:* U.S.A./Conn. Shade
This cigar is dominated by balsa wood and grassy elements. It has a very harsh attack and finishes very dry in the mouth.
U.S.: $6.80 • U.K.: £6.50

SOSA LONSDALE **78**
Dominican Republic •
Size: 6½" x 43 *Filler:* Dom.
Rep. *Binder:* Honduras
Wrapper: Ecuador
A dull greenish-brown wrapper. It has funky flavors of
wet hay and earthy dried
herbs, and finishes quite dry
on the palate.
U.S.: $2.90 • U.K.: N/A

CAMACHO NO. 1 **76**
Honduras • *Size:* 7" x 44
Filler/Binder: Honduras
Wrapper: Ecuador
This is a very rustic cigar
with a rough wrapper. It has
some hints of spice, but has
an earthy, funky character
with a barklike finish.
Inconsistent.
U.S.: $2.75 • U.K.: N/A

CRUZ REAL NO. 1 **76**
Mexico • *Size:* 6⅝" x 42
Filler/Binder/Wrapper: Mexico
A rough cigar. It is hot, and
while it has some pepper
notes on the palate, it also
has an earthy funkiness.
U.S.: $3.40 • U.K.: N/A

ORNELAS NO. 1 **69**
VANILLA
Mexico • *Size:* 6¾" x 44
Filler/Binder/Wrapper: Mexico
Beware. Not for connoisseurs. The vanilla flavoring is
perfumelike and sickly sweet,
and tastes more like pipe
tobacco. In a humidor, it
contaminates other cigars. If
you must, keep it separately.
U.S.: $6.00 • U.K.: N/A

CORONA

*Most of the following Corona
tasting notes appeared in the
Spring 1996 issue of* Cigar
Aficionado. *Exceptions are
indicated by a date in parentheses at the end of the tasting
note.*

BOLIVAR CORONA **91**
Cuba • *Size:* 5½" x 42
Filler/Binder/Wrapper: Cuba
A rich, earthy cigar with a
solid core of nuts and spices
and a very smooth balance.
A long spicy finish.
U.S.: N/A • U.K.: £6.80

EL REY DEL MUNDO **91**
CORONA DE LUXE
Cuba • *Size:* 5½" x 42 *Filler/
Binder/Wrapper:* Cuba
Although a little young, this
cigar exhibits great spice,
including cinnamon, and a
strong earthy finish that lasts.
Very well-made.
U.S.: N/A • U.K.: £6.65

H. UPMANN CORONA **91**
Cuba • *Size:* 5½" x 42
Filler/Binder/Wrapper: Cuba
Always a great smoke for a
corona. The H. Upmann is
bursting with complex coffee,
roasted nut and tobacco flavors. Buy a box and enjoy.
(03/01/93)
U.S.: N/A • U.K.: £5.85

LA FINCA CORONA **91**
Nicaragua • *Size:* 5½" x
42 *Filler/Binder/Wrapper:*
Nicaragua
A rich-tasting cigar with a
lot of depth. It has flavors of
spice, raisins and cedar. It is
well-balanced and has a
smooth finish.
U.S.: $1.40 • U.K.: N/A

MONTESINO **91**
DIPLOMATICO
Dominican Republic • *Size:*
5½" x 43 *Filler/Binder:* Dom.
Rep. *Wrapper:* U.S.A./
Conn. Shade
A very well-made cigar. It has
an earthy depth, with delicious sweet spice flavors of
cinnamon and strong nut elements, including walnuts. A
smooth, long-lasting finish.
U.S.: $1.90 • U.K.: N/A

HOYO DE MONTERREY **90**
LE HOYO DU ROI
Cuba • *Size:* 5½" x 42
Filler/Binder/Wrapper: Cuba
A full-bodied, rich cigar with
nutmeg and earthy flavors. It
is very well-balanced with a
long, cedery finish.
U.S.: N/A • U.K.: £7.35

PUROS INDIOS NO. 4 **90**
ESPECIAL
Honduras • *Size:* 5½" x 44
Filler: Brazil, Nicaragua,
Dom. Rep. *Binder/Wrapper:*
Ecuador
A rich, full-bodied cigar
filled with nutmeg and cinnamon spices, with a great
nutty character on the
palate. It has a long, earthy
finish with a hint of cocoa.
U.S.: $3.25 • U.K.: N/A

CASA BLANCA **89**
CORONA
Dominican Republic • *Size:*
5½" x 42 *Filler:* Dom. Rep.,
Brazil *Binder:* Mexico
Wrapper: U.S.A./Conn. Shade

A good-tasting cigar with notes of spice and cedar. It has excellent oils in the wrapper and a smooth, herb-like character on the finish.
U.S.: $1.85 • U.K.: N/A

JOSÉ MARTÍ 1868   **89**
CORONA
Honduras • Size: 5⅝" x 45
Filler: Dom. Rep., Honduras Binder: Honduras Wrapper: Ecuador
A complex, medium-bodied cigar. It has an earthy character, with notes of leather, herbs and roasted nuts, and a dark, woody finish.
U.S.: $1.50 • U.K.: N/A

PUNCH CORONA   **89**
Cuba • Size: 5½" x 42
Filler/Binder/Wrapper: Cuba
This is a spicy cigar with some leather notes. It finishes with a dry, woody flavor.
U.S.: N/A • U.K.: £6.45

RAMON ALLONES   **89**
CORONA
Cuba • Size: 5½" x 42 Filler/Binder/Wrapper: Cuba
A cigar with a firm draw. It has fancy chocolate and almond flavors, but shows its youth despite a solid tobacco core.
U.S.: N/A • U.K.: £6.65

ROMEO Y JULIETA   **89**
CORONA
Cuba • Size: 5½" x 42 Filler/Binder/Wrapper: Cuba
A slightly rough boxed cigar. It has good spice and a dose of nut flavors with a smooth, leathery finish.
U.S.: N/A • U.K.: £6.80

SAVINELLI   **89**
EXTRAORDINAIRE
Dominican Republic • Size: 5½" x 44 Filler/Binder: Dom. Rep. Wrapper: U.S.A./Conn. Shade
This medium-bodied cigar has a smooth, creamy nut element, and solid tobacco flavors in an earthy core. It has a long, spicy finish with wood notes.
U.S.: $5.75 • U.K.: N/A

CREDO ANTHANOR   **88**
Dominican Republic • Size: 5¼" x 42 Filler/Binder: Dom. Rep. Wrapper: U.S.A./Conn. Shade
A good medium-bodied cigar. It has flavors of dried orange peel with a nutty, spicy component and a well-balanced finish.
U.S.: $4.80 • U.K.: N/A

DAVIDOFF GRAN CRU   **88**
NO. 2
Dominican Republic • Size: 5⅝" x 43 Filler/Binder: Dom. Rep. Wrapper: U.S.A./Conn. Shade
A well-made, medium-bodied cigar with excellent spice flavors, including nutmeg. There's a solid, nutty core and a pleasant finish.
U.S.: $8.60 • U.K.: £7.96

HOYO DE MONTERREY   **88**
NO. 55
Honduras • Size: 5¼" x 43 Filler/Binder: Honduras, Nicaragua, Dom. Rep. Wrapper: Ecuador
There are hints of chocolate and nuts in this richly flavored, medium-bodied cigar.

There is a sweet woody note on the finish.
U.S.: $1.10 • U.K.: N/A

LA GLORIA CUBANA   **88**
GLORIAS
U.S.A. • Size: 5½" x 43
Filler: Dom. Rep., Nicaragua Binder: Nicaragua Wrapper: Ecuador
A solid, medium-bodied cigar with strong spice and cedar notes, and flavors of chocolate. It has a strong spicy finish.
U.S.: $2.50 • U.K.: N/A

LEMPIRA CORONA   **88**
Honduras • Size: 5½" x 42 Filler: Honduras, Nicaragua Binder: Dom. Rep. Wrapper: U.S.A./Conn. Shade
A rustic cigar with a pleasant cedary finish. It has flavors of nutmeg and cinnamon.
U.S.: $2.25 • U.K.: N/A

MONTECRISTO NO. 3   **88**
Cuba • Size: 5½" x 42
Filler/Binder/Wrapper: Cuba
A smooth but full-bodied cigar with a solid core of exotic spices, including cinnamon and nutmeg, and a pleasing cedary finish.
U.S.: N/A • U.K.: £7.80

OLOR MOMENTOS   **88**
Dominican Republic • Size: 5½" x 43 Filler/Binder: Dom. Rep. Wrapper: U.S.A./Conn. Shade
A sweet finish on a medium-bodied cigar. This cigar has a roasted chestnut flavor and creamy, herbal character with mild spices.
U.S.: $2.35 • U.K.: N/A

PADRON 1964   **88**
ANNIVERSARY SERIES
CORONA
Honduras • *Size:* 6" x 42
Filler/Binder/Wrapper:
Nicaragua
Although it is slightly tight, this cigar is packed with good spices and a hint of chocolate. It's well-balanced with a medium-bodied smoke.
U.S.: $5.05 • U.K.: N/A

PUNCH CAFE ROYAL   **88**
Honduras • *Size:* 5⅝" x
44 *Filler/Binder:* Honduras, Nicaragua, Dom.Rep.
Wrapper: Ecuador
This cigar has good nut flavors, including hints of chestnuts. It has a mild, spicy finish and is well-balanced overall.
U.S.: $2.65 • U.K.: N/A

ARTURO FUENTE   **87**
RESERVA NO. 3
Dominican Republic • *Size:* 5½" x 44 *Filler/Binder:* Dom. Rep. *Wrapper:* Cameroon
An attractive dark-brown wrapper. This cigar has an earthy quality with smooth flavors, but a dry wood finish.
U.S.: $6.75 • U.K.: N/A

AVO NO. 7   **87**
Dominican Republic •
Size: 6" x 44 *Filler/Binder:* Dom. Rep. *Wrapper:*
U.S.A./Conn. Shade
This cigar, a medium-bodied smoke, offers some herbal notes followed by strong chestnut flavors and an overall toast-like character.
U.S.: $5.20 • U.K.: N/A

BELINDA BREVA   **87**
CONSERVA
Honduras • *Size:* 5½" x 43
Filler: Dom. Rep., Honduras
Binder: Honduras *Wrapper:*
Ecuador
A cigar with medium-bodied character. It has solid flavors of nuts and a core of spiciness. There is a good toasty finish.
U.S.: $1.30 • U.K.: N/A

BERING CORONA   **87**
ROYALE
Honduras • *Size:* 6" x 41
Filler/Binder: Honduras, Mexico, Dom. Rep, Nicaragua *Wrapper:* Mexico
This is a medium-bodied cigar with a solid spicy core of flavors. It has a leathery aroma and a pleasing tobacco character.
U.S.: $1.35 • U.K.: N/A

C.A.O. CORONA   **87**
Honduras • *Size:* 6" x 42
Filler: Nicaragua, Mexico
Binder: Honduras *Wrapper:*
U.S.A./Conn. Shade
This cigar has a firm draw, but a pleasant toasty, creamy character. There's a bit of dry straw in the flavor, but it has a well-balanced finish.
U.S.: $4.25 • U.K.: N/A

CARRINGTON NO. 2   **87**
Dominican Republic •
Size: 6" x 42 *Filler/Binder:* Dom. Rep. *Wrapper:*
U.S.A./Conn. Shade
This smooth-tasting cigar has a light, spicy character, with some earthy tones.
U.S.: $3.65 • U.K.: N/A

CUESTA-REY   **87**
DOMINICAN NO. 5
Dominican Republic • *Size:* 5½" x 43 *Filler/Binder:* Dom. Rep. *Wrapper:* U.S.A./ Conn. Shade
A well-balanced cigar that shows a pleasing smooth, creamy texture with hints of spice and leather and solid tobacco flavors.
U.S.: $2.75 • U.K.: £4.25

DON DIEGO CORONA   **87**
MAJOR TUBE
Dominican Republic • *Size:* 5½" x 42 *Filler/Binder:* Dom. Rep. *Wrapper:* U.S.A./ Conn. Shade
A firm draw on a medium-bodied cigar. It has a creamy tobacco character and some hints of a toastlike flavor.
U.S.: $2.95 • U.K.: N/A

DON LINO PETIT   **87**
CETRO
Honduras • *Size:* 5½" x 42 *Filler/Binder:* Honduras *Wrapper:* U.S.A.
A pleasing, mild cigar with a flinty character and hints of toasted nuts.
U.S.: $2.30 • U.K.: N/A

DON TOMAS MATADOR   **87**
Honduras • *Size:* 5½" x 42 *Filler/Binder/Wrapper:* Honduras
An interesting cigar with a spicy quality that has an earthy hint, but it ends with a sweet wood finish.
U.S.: $2.40 • U.K.: N/A

HOYO DE MONTERREY 87
CAFE ROYAL
Honduras • *Size:* 5⅝" x 43
Filler/Binder: Honduras,
Nicaragua, Dom. Rep.
Wrapper: Ecuador
This is a well-made cigar
with an oily wrapper. It has a
smooth herbal core of flavors
with a good woody finish.
U.S.: $2.65 • U.K.: N/A

MACANUDO VINTAGE 87
NO. 3
Jamaica • *Size:* 5⁵⁄₁₆" x 43
Filler: Dom. Rep., Jam.
Binder: Mexico *Wrapper:*
U.S.A./Conn. Shade
Although some tightness was
noted in the draw, this cigar
has a good creamy texture with
a strong flavor of chestnuts and
a pleasant toasty finish.
U.S.: $8.00 • U.K.: N/A

MONTECRISTO NO. 3 87
Dominican Republic • *Size:*
5½" x 44 *Filler/Binder:* Dom.
Rep. *Wrapper:* U.S.A./
Conn. Shade
A well-made, medium-bod-
ied cigar with a solid, nutty
character. It has some
smooth herb and sweet spice
flavors, including nutmeg.
U.S.: $4.50 • U.K.: N/A

MONTECRUZ SUN- 87
GROWN NO. 220
Dominican Republic • *Size:*
5½" x 42 *Filler/Binder:* Dom.
Rep., Brazil *Wrapper:*
Cameroon
This cigar delivers a creami-
ness with a backbone of spicy
flavors. It has a medium-bod-
ied character.
U.S.: $3.40 • U.K.: N/A

NAT SHERMAN 87
LANDMARK SELECTION
HAMPSHIRE
Dominican Republic • *Size:*
5½" x 42 *Filler:* Jam., Mex.,
Dom. Rep. *Binder:* Mexico
Wrapper: Cameroon
This is a good-looking cigar
with solid tobacco flavors,
some notes of chestnuts and
chocolate with a mild, pep-
pery finish.
U.S.: $5.30 • U.K.: N/A

NAT SHERMAN 87
METROPOLITAN
SELECTION ANGLER
Dominican Republic • *Size:*
5½" x 43 *Filler/Binder:* Dom.
Rep. *Wrapper:* U.S.A./
Conn. Shade
An earthiness dominates this
cigar. The medium-bodied
smoke has rich flavors of
leather and toast and a pleas-
ant woody finish.
U.S.: $6.00 • U.K.: N/A

ROMEO Y JULIETA 87
VINTAGE NO. 1
Dominican Republic • *Size:*
6" x 43 *Filler:* Dom. Rep.
Binder: Mexico *Wrapper:*
U.S.A./Conn. Shade
A cigar with a smooth,
creamy texture. It has a touch
of sweet spices and nutmeg,
and a floral character.
U.S.: $5.75 • U.K.: N/A

SANTA CLARA NO. 5 87
Mexico • *Size:* 6" x 43
Filler/Binder/Wrapper: Mexico
A well-made cigar packed
with spices, it has a toasty
herbal character, with hints
of nuts and coffee. A smooth,
easy smoke.
U.S.: $2.00 • U.K.: £3.10

TROYA NO. 27 87
Dominican Republic •
Size: 5½" x 42 *Filler/Binder:*
Dom. Rep. *Wrapper:*
U.S.A./Conn. Shade
A good, solid medium-bodied
cigar. It has hints of nuts and
flowers. It is smooth and mellow.
U.S.: $3.25 • U.K.: N/A

ASHTON AGED 86
MADURO NO. 20
Dominican Republic • *Size:*
5½" x 44 *Filler/Binder:* Dom.
Rep. *Wrapper:* U.S.A
This cigar has sweet herbal notes
and a pleasant toasty flavor.
U.S.: $4.65 • U.K.: N/A

BANCES BREVAS 86
Honduras • *Size:* 5½"
x 43 *Filler/Binder:* Honduras,
Nicaragua, Dom. Rep.
Wrapper: Ecuador
A cigar with a flinty charac-
ter on the palate. There are
some spicy pepper flavors and
a nice cedary finish.
U.S.: $1.10 • U.K.: N/A

CRUZ REAL NO. 2 86
Mexico • *Size:* 6" x 42
Filler/Binder/Wrapper: Mexico
A tart smoke with some
slightly vegetal tones, but a
spicy backbone that includes
hints of black pepper.
U.S.: $3.15 • U.K.: N/A

FELIPE GREGORIO 86
SERENO
Honduras • *Size:* 5¼" x 42
Filler/Binder/Wrapper:
Honduras
This is a medium-bodied
cigar with an earthy charac-
ter. It has some nut and herb
flavors with a smooth, well-
balanced finish.
U.S.: $4.70 • U.K.: N/A

117

FONSECA 8-9-8 86
Dominican Republic •
Size: 6" x 43 *Filler/Binder:*
Dom. Rep. *Wrapper:*
U.S.A./Conn. Shade
This cigar has a nice nutty
flavor with hints of spice and
dried orange peel, and a
strong woody finish.
U.S.: $3.50 • U.K.: N/A

H. UPMANN CORONA 86
Dominican Republic •
Size: 5½" x 42 *Filler/Binder:*
Dom. Rep. *Wrapper:*
Indonesia
A medium-bodied cigar with
a tangy character and a mild
spice note on the palate. A
slighty earthy finish.
U.S.: $2.80 • U.K.: N/A

HABANA GOLD BLACK 86
LABEL CORONA
Honduras • *Size:* 6" x 44
Filler/Binder: Nicaragua
Wrapper: Indonesia
A mild cigar with a creamy
character. It has some leather
and toast notes with a
smooth herbal finish.
U.S.: $4.25 • U.K.: N/A

HOYO DE MONTERREY 86
SUPER HOYO
Honduras • *Size:* 5½" x 44
Filler: Nica., Hon., Dom.
Rep. *Binder:* Honduras
Wrapper: Ecuador
A young-tasting cigar. It has
a pungent earthy aroma, with
some vegetal flavors and a
slightly toasty taste.
U.S.: $1.60 • U.K.: N/A

JOSE BENITO PALMA 86
Dominican Republic •
Size: 6" x 43 *Filler:* Dom.

Rep. *Binder:* Honduras
Wrapper: Cameroon
Even-keeled corona with
medium-bodied, fresh,
creamy, tobacco aromas and
flavors and a light aftertaste.
A good everyday corona.
(03/01/93)
U.S.: $1.90 • U.K.: N/A

JUAN CLEMENTE CLUB 86
SELECTION NO. 4
Dominican Republic • *Size:*
5¾" x 42 *Filler/Binder:* Dom.
Rep. *Wrapper:* U.S.A./
Conn. Shade
A good-looking, medium-
bodied cigar. It has good
spice and herb flavors and
shows a solid construction.
U.S.: $7.05 • U.K.: N/A

LICENCIADOS NO. 4 86
Dominican Republic • *Size:*
5½" x 42 *Filler/Binder:* Dom.
Rep. *Wrapper:* U.S.A./
Conn. Shade
A mild- to medium-bodied
cigar. It has some rich creamy
flavors and a solid core of nut-
tiness, with a woody finish.
U.S.: $2.10 • U.K.: N/A

MACABI MEDIA 86
CORONA
U.S.A. • *Size:* 5½" x 43
Filler: Dom. Rep., Nicaragua
Binder: Mexico *Wrapper:*
U.S.A./Conn. Shade
A well-balanced cigar with a
good floral character. It has
nut and spice flavors and a
light, woody finish.
U.S.: $2.65 • U.K.: N/A

MACANUDO DUKE OF 86
DEVON
Jamaica • *Size:* 5½" x 42
Filler: Dom. Rep., Jamaica
Binder: Mexico *Wrapper:*
U.S.A./Conn. Shade
A straightforward, mild- to
medium-bodied cigar with
solid notes of nuts and light
coffee flavors, and a good
cedary finish.
U.S.: $3.85 • U.K.: N/A

PADRON LONDRES 86
Nicaragua • *Size:* 5½"
x 42 *Filler/Binder:* Nicaragua
Wrapper: Ecuador
A rich-tasting cigar with
some dark, sweet flavors like
chocolate. But a very firm
draw was noted.
U.S.: $1.85 • U.K.: N/A

PARTAGAS CORONA 86
Cuba • *Size:* 5½" x 42
Filler/Binder/Wrapper: Cuba
Another cigar that exhibits
signs of youthfulness. But it
has a spicy core of flavors and
an interesting herbal and
woody finish.
U.S.: N/A • U.K.: £6.80

PARTAGAS SABROSOS 86
Dominican Republic •
Size: 5⅞" x 43 *Filler/Binder:*
Mexico, Dom. Rep.
Wrapper: Cameroon
A rustic cigar that had a
loose draw, some strong
grassy flavors and a wood
component.
U.S.: $4.15 • U.K.: N/A

PARTAGAS NO. 2 86
Dominican Republic •
Size: 5⅞" x 44 *Filler:* Dom.

Rep., Mexico *Binder:* Mexico *Wrapper:* Cameroon This cigar has a rough-looking wrapper. But it has some nut and spice flavors on the palate, and a dry woody finish.
U.S.: $3.95 • U.K.: N/A

PAUL GARMIRIAN 86
CORONA
Dominican Republic • *Size:* 5½" x 42 *Filler/Binder:* Dom. Rep. *Wrapper:* U.S.A./ Conn. Shade
A good-tasting, medium-bodied cigar with baked bread flavors of cinnamon and nutmeg. There is a sweet tobacco character with a slightly leathery finish.
U.S.: $6.00 • U.K.: £5.60

RAMON ALLONES 86
PRIVADA D
Dominican Republic • *Size:* 5" x 42 *Filler/Binder:* Mexico, Dom. Rep. *Wrapper:* Cameroon
This is more of a petite corona in size, but if you're into spicy, peppery food, try this one. With a dark-brown wrapper and a slow draw, it's medium-bodied with a strong, spicy, savory style. (03/01/93)
U.S.: $2.35 • U.K.: N/A

SANTA ROSA NO. 4 86
Honduras • *Size:* 5½" x 42 *Filler/Binder:* Honduras *Wrapper:* Ecuador
A good medium-bodied smoke. It has a flinty character, but a core of nuttiness, and a smooth herbal texture.
U.S.: $2.40 • U.K.: N/A

THOMAS HINDS 86
HONDURAN SELECTION
CORONA
Honduras • *Size:* 5½" x 42 *Filler/Binder:* Honduras *Wrapper:* Ecuador
Although it has a mild finish, this cigar has some leather and floral notes, with a hint of chocolate.
U.S.: $2.05 • Canada: $2.40

VUELTABAJO CORONA 86
Dominican Republic • *Size:* 5¼" x 42 *Filler/Binder:* Dom. Rep. *Wrapper:* U.S.A./Conn. Shade
A good draw leads into a medium-bodied smoke with solid tobacco flavors. It has a peppery finish with a cedary character.
U.S.: $2.70 • U.K.: N/A

ZINO MOUTON-CADET 86
NO. 1
Honduras • *Size:* 6½" x 44 *Filler/Binder:* Honduras *Wrapper:* U.S.A./Conn. Shade
Another no-nonsense, very good corona. Well made with a fine light brown wrapper, it shows lovely spicy, slightly herbal aromas and flavors and a light aftertaste. (03/01/93)
U.S.: $5.50 • U.K.: N/A

BAUZA GRECOS 85
Dominican Republic • *Size:* 5½" x 42 *Filler:* Dom. Rep., Nicaragua *Binder:* Mexico *Wrapper:* Cameroon
A spicy cigar with a light backbone of nut flavors and mild chocolate. It is still young.
U.S.: $2.50 • U.K.: N/A

BERING IMPERIAL 85
Honduras • *Size:* 5¼" x 42 *Filler/Binder:* Honduras, Mexico, Dom. Rep., Nicaragua *Wrapper:* Mexico
A bit rough. But it shows a nice herbal complexity with an earthy backbone and a nice toasty finish.
U.S.: $1.35 • U.K.: N/A

CAMACHO 85
NACIONALES
Dominican Republic • *Size:* 5½" x 44 *Filler/Binder/ Wrapper:* Honduras
Tasters noted a sweet tobacco taste with a floral character. There's a bit of spice with a mild, earthy finish.
U.S.: $2.25 • U.K.: N/A

DON DIEGO CORONA 85
Dominican Republic • *Size:* 5⅝" x 42 *Filler/Binder:* Dom. Rep. *Wrapper:* U.S.A./Conn. Shade
A smooth-tasting, mild cigar that has some floral notes and a slight nutty flavor, but an overall papery character.
U.S.: $2.85 • U.K.: N/A

DON MELO PETIT 85
CORONA
Honduras • *Size:* 5½" x 42 *Filler/Binder/Wrapper:* Honduras, Nicaragua *Filler:* Honduras, Nicaragua *Binder/Wrapper:* Honduras
This cigar has a medium-bodied character. There are flavors of nuts and a hint of leather and coffee. A short finish.
U.S.: $2.35 • U.K.: N/A

DUNHILL VALVERDES 85
Dominican Republic •
Size: 5½" x 42 *Filler/Binder:*
Dom. Rep., Brazil *Wrapper:*
U.S.A./Conn. Shade
A creamy-tasting cigar. It is
medium-bodied with solid
spice and herbal flavors and a
light, woody finish.
U.S.: $3.90 • U.K.: £5.70

DUNHILL TABARAS 85
Dominican Republic •
Size: 5½" x 42 *Filler/Binder:*
Dom. Rep., Brazil *Wrapper:*
U.S.A./Conn. Shade
This is a mellow cigar with a
smooth, mild texture filled
with creamy notes and some
light, nutty flavors.
U.S.: $5.90 • U.K.: £6.30

EL RICO HABANO 85
CORONA
U.S.A. • *Size:* 5½" x 42
Filler: Dom. Rep., Nicaragua
Binder: Nicaragua *Wrapper:*
Ecuador
Loads of flavor in this mid-
dle-of-the-road cigar. Oily,
with a rich-brown wrapper, it
shows enticing aromas and
flavors of coffee and cinna-
mon and a rich long finish.
(03/01/93)
U.S.: $1.30 • U.K.: N/A

H. UPMANN CORONA 85
MAJOR TUBE
Dominican Republic • *Size:*
5⅛" x 42 *Filler/Binder:* Dom.
Rep. *Wrapper:* Indonesia
A solid, medium-bodied
smoke. Strong earthy notes
dominate hints of nuts and
sweet spices.
U.S.: $3.10 • U.K.: N/A

HOYO DE MONTERREY 85
CORONA
Cuba • *Size:* 5½" x 42 *Filler/
Binder/Wrapper:* Cuba
A pleasant cigar that shows
signs of youth. It has spicy
flavors, but overall a woody,
herbal character with some
bite.
U.S.: N/A • U.K.: £6.80

HOYO DE MONTERREY 85
EXCALIBUR NO. 5
Honduras • *Size:* 6¼" x 43
Filler: Nica., Hon., Dom.
Rep. *Binder:* Honduras
Wrapper: Ecuador
This is always a very good
cigar. Medium brown col-
ored, it's firmly made with a
sure and even draw. Plenty of
chocolate, spice aromas and
flavors. (03/01/93)
U.S.: $2.30 • U.K.: N/A

LA AURORA NO. 4 85
Dominican Republic •
Size: 5¼" x 42 *Filler/Binder:*
Dom. Rep. *Wrapper:*
Cameroon
A mild cigar with a pleasing
woody spiciness and a hint of
nuts.
U.S.: $1.85 • U.K.: N/A

LEON JIMENES NO. 4 85
Dominican Republic •
Size: 5⅜" x 42 *Filler/Binder:*
Dom. Rep. *Wrapper:*
U.S.A./Conn. Shade
A cigar with a medium-bod-
ied smoke. It has a light
spiciness with a cedary
aroma.
U.S.: $3.55 • U.K.: N/A

LOS LIBERTADORES 85
INSURRECTOS
Dominican Republic • *Size:*
5½" x 42 *Filler/Binder:* Dom.
Rep. *Wrapper:* U.S.A./
Conn. Shade
A mild cigar with solid tobac-
co flavors and character. A
bit of spice on the finish.
U.S.: $3.98 • U.K.: N/A

MACANUDO HAMPTON 85
COURT
Jamaica • *Size:* 5¼" x 42
Filler: Dom. Rep., Jamaica
Binder: Mexico *Wrapper:*
U.S.A./Conn. Shade
A mild cigar with flavors of
nuts and a pleasant creamy
texture. Smooth and mellow.
U.S.: $4.00 • U.K.: N/A

MAYA PETIT CORONA 85
Honduras • *Size:* 5½"
x 42 *Filler/Binder:* Honduras,
Nicaragua *Wrapper:* U.S.A./
Conn. Shade
A medium-bodied cigar that
offers hints of earthiness and
herbs. It has toasty notes in
the aroma and on the palate.
U.S.: $2.00 • U.K.: N/A

MONTECRUZ SUN- 85
GROWN TUBOS
Dominican Republic • *Size:*
6" x 42 *Filler/Binder:* Dom.
Rep., Brazil *Wrapper:*
Indonesia
Although tasters noted a
pleasant, nutty complexity,
this cigar finished with a
metallic taste. But it has a
good earthy spiciness and a
touch of sweet tobacco flavor.
U.S.: $3.75 • U.K.: N/A

TRESADO SELECCION NO. 500   85
Dominican Republic • *Size:* 5½" x 42 *Filler:* Dom. Rep. *Binder:* Cameroon *Wrapper:* Indonesia
A woody character dominates this cigar. It has some hints of pepper and a fairly neutral finish.
U.S.: $1.60 • U.K.: N/A

ASHTON CORONA   84
Dominican Republic • *Size:* 5½" x 44 *Filler/Binder:* Dom. Rep. *Wrapper:* U.S.A./Conn. Shade
A nice, mild cigar with some light spicy flavors and a pleasant herbal character.
U.S.: $4.10 • U.K.: N/A

CANARIA D'ORO CORONA   84
Dominican Republic • *Size:* 5½" x 43 *Filler:* Dom. Rep., Mexico *Binder/Wrapper:* Mexico
A mild cigar with a decent draw. It is rustic-looking but provides some light nuttiness and dry, woody finish.
U.S.: $2.10 • U.K.: N/A

EL REY DEL MUNDO HABANA CLUB   84
Honduras • *Size:* 5½" x 42 *Filler:* Dom. Rep., Honduras *Binder:* Honduras *Wrapper:* Ecuador
A smooth-tasting cigar with a hint of nuts and a floral character. It ends with a dry finish.
U.S.: $3.50 • U.K.: N/A

EL SUBLIMADO CORONA   84
Dominican Republic • *Size:* 6" x 44 *Filler/Binder:* Dom. Rep. *Wrapper:* U.S.A./Conn. Shade
A very yellow wrapper. This mild- to medium-bodied cigar has straw-like herbal notes with a creamy coffee flavor and a light woody finish.
U.S.: $3.00 • U.K.: £10.00

HENRY CLAY BREVAS   84
Dominican Republic • *Size:* 5½" x 42 *Filler/Binder:* Dom. Rep. *Wrapper:* U.S.A./Conn. Shade
There is some spice in this cigar, with some coffee flavors. It has a slightly earthy quality on the dry finish.
U.S.: $2.25 • U.K.: N/A

JOSÉ MARTÍ CORONA   84
Dominican Republic • *Size:* 5½" x 42 *Filler:* Dom. Rep. *Binder:* Mexico *Wrapper:* U.S.A./Conn. Shade
A smooth, mellow cigar with a creamy texture and mild herbal character.
U.S.: $2.25 • U.K.: N/A

KNOCKANDO NO. 3   84
Dominican Republic • *Size:* 5¾" x 41 *Filler/Binder:* Dom. Rep. *Wrapper:* U.S.A./Conn. Shade
Aptly named after the single malt Scotch, this cigar has an appealing nutty character. It's well made with a surefire draw and gives plenty of pleasure until the last puff. (03/01/93)
U.S.: $6.75 • U.K.: N/A

LA UNICA NO. 500   84
Dominican Republic • *Size:* 5½" x 42 *Filler/Binder:* Dom. Rep. *Wrapper:* U.S.A./Conn. Shade
A greenish-brown cigar with a slightly rough construction. It has a weedy character with some mild wood on the finish.
U.S.: $2.35 • U.K.: N/A

LAS CABRILLAS MAGELLAN   84
Honduras • *Size:* 6" x 42 *Filler:* Nicaragua, Mexico *Binder:* Mexico *Wrapper:* U.S.A./Conn. Shade
A medium-bodied cigar with a balsa-wood tone and a dry, papery finish. There's a touch of white-pepper flavor.
U.S.: $1.65 • U.K.: N/A

LICENCIADOS SUPREME MADURO NO. 200   84
Dominican Republic • *Size:* 5" x 42 *Filler/Binder:* Dom. Rep. *Wrapper:* U.S.A./Conn. Shade
A good maduro cigar. It has flavors of coffee and cola, with a solid spicy finish and an overall mild character.
U.S.: $2.75 • U.K.: N/A

MICUBANO NO. 542   84
Nicaragua • *Size:* 5" x 42 *Filler/Binder/Wrapper:* Nicaragua
All tasters noted a tight draw on this otherwise medium-bodied cigar. It has some smooth, creamy flavors with a hint of earthiness.
U.S.: $3.10 • U.K.: N/A

POR LARRAÑAGA NACIONALES — 84

Dominican Republic • *Size:* 5½" x 42 *Filler/Binder:* Dom. Rep. *Wrapper:* U.S.A./ Conn. Shade
This is a well-balanced, medium-bodied cigar. It has some good hints of nuts with a creamy texture.
U.S.: $3.60 • U.K.: N/A

PRIMO DEL REY NO. 4 — 84

Dominican Republic • *Size:* 5½" x 42 *Filler/Binder:* Dom. Rep. *Wrapper:* Indonesia
This cigar has a light, salty character with some mild, light tobacco flavors and an earthy finish.
U.S.: $1.65 • U.K.: N/A

PUNCH NO. 75 — 84

Honduras • *Size:* 5½" x 43 *Filler:* Nica., Hon., Dom. Rep. *Binder/Wrapper:* Ecuador
Although there is a hint of a vegetal quality in this cigar, it has a solid peppery core. Needs time to age.
U.S.: $1.60 • U.K.: N/A

SOSA BREVAS — 84

Dominican Republic • *Size:* 5½" x 43 *Filler:* Dom. Rep. *Binder:* Honduras *Wrapper:* Ecuador
A cigar with some vegetal notes on the palate, but it finishes with a light spiciness and earthiness.
U.S.: $2.50 • U.K.: N/A

THOMAS HINDS NICARAGUAN SELECTION CORONA — 84

Nicaragua • *Size:* 5½" x 42 *Filler/Binder/Wrapper:* Nicaragua
A cigar dominated by some woody flavors with a creamy texture. There is a smoothness here with a light, spicy finish.
U.S.: $3.70 • U.K.: C$3.95

8-9-8 COLLECTION CORONA — 83

Dominican Republic • *Size:* 5½" x 42 *Filler:* Jamaica, Dom. Rep. *Binder:* Mexico *Wrapper:* U.S.A./Conn. Shade
A medium-bodied smoke with a smooth texture and some spice, but an overall dry, papery character.
U.S.: $5.50 • U.K.: N/A

CABALLEROS CORONA — 83

Dominican Republic • *Size:* 5¼" x 43 *Filler/Binder:* Dom. Rep. *Wrapper:* U.S.A./Conn. Shade
A cigar with a creamy texture and mild character. It has an easy-smoking buttery flavor with a slightly cedary finish.
U.S.: $2.80 • U.K.: N/A

JOYA DE NICARAGUA NO. 6 — 83

Nicaragua • *Size:* 6" x 42 *Filler/Binder/Wrapper:* Nicaragua
This cigar is rustic, with slightly sour herbal flavors, although it has a touch of spice on the finish.
U.S.: $2.20 • U.K.: N/A

LA HOJA SELECTA CETROS DE ORO — 83

U.S.A. • *Size:* 5¼" x 43 *Filler/Binder:* Dom. Rep., Mexico, Brazil *Wrapper:* U.S.A./Conn. Shade
Straightforward corona with pleasing herbal, tobacco character. Very handsome and well-constructed but perhaps a little one-dimensional in flavor. (03/01/93)
U.S.: $1.65 • U.K.: N/A

NAT SHERMAN CITY DESK GAZETTE — 83

Dominican Republic • *Size:* 6" x 42 *Filler/Binder/Wrapper:* Dom. Rep.
A maduro cigar. It has an earthy character with flavors of nuts and herbs and a solid tobacco core.
U.S.: $4.00 • U.K.: N/A

ONYX NO. 642 — 83

Dominican Republic • *Size:* 6" x 42 *Filler:* Dom. Rep., Mexico *Binder:* Indonesia *Wrapper:* Mexico
A slightly rough maduro with a smooth, round flavor and a touch of sweet spice on the palate.
U.S.: $2.50 • U.K.: N/A

PUNCH ROYAL CORONATION — 83

Honduras • *Size:* 5¼" x 44 *Filler/Binder:* Honduras, Nicaragua, Dom. Rep. *Wrapper:* Ecuador
This medium-bodied cigar has some vegetal notes with a leathery flavor, and some spice on a long finish. Shows its youth.
U.S.: $2.35 • U.K.: N/A

ROMEO Y JULIETA **83**
CORONA
Dominican Republic • *Size:*
5½" x 44 *Filler:* Dom. Rep.,
U.S.A. *Binder:* U.S.A./
Conn. Broadleaf *Wrapper:*
Cameroon
A good everyday smoke you
won't get bored with. The
wrapper is a little rough and
uneven in color, but there's
plenty of spicy, nutmeg and
tobacco aromas and flavors.
(03/01/93)
U.S.: $1.80 • U.K.: N/A

V CENTENNIAL **83**
CORONA
Honduras • *Size:* 5½" x 42
Filler: Honduras, Dom.Rep.,
Nicaragua *Binder:* Mexico
Wrapper: U.S.A./Conn. Shade
Some inconsistency noted.
This cigar shows some nutty
flavors and a bit of spice, but
a flat finish.
U.S.: $3.00 • U.K.: N/A

ZINO DIAMONDS **83**
Honduras • *Size:* 5½"
x 40 *Filler/Binder:* Honduras
Wrapper: U.S.A./Conn.
Shade
A small cigar. It has a light,
mild character with some
nutty flavors and a smooth
woody finish.
U.S.: $4.20 • U.K.: N/A

PETERSON CORONA **82**
Dominican Republic •
Size: 5¼" x 43 *Filler:* Dom.
Rep. *Binder:* Ecuador
Wrapper: U.S.A./Conn. Shade
A rather rustic, rough cigar.
It has a straw-like character
and a dry spice finish.
U.S.: $6.00 • U.K.: N/A

BACCARAT PETIT **81**
CORONA
Honduras • *Size:* 5½" x 42
Filler/Wrapper: Honduras
Binder: Mexico
This cigar has a light, sweet
gum on the wrapper. It has
pleasing notes of tobacco, but
a strawlike flavor on the
palate.
U.S.: $1.60 • U.K.: N/A

PLEIADES ORION **81**
Dominican Republic •
Size: 5¼" x 42 *Filler/Binder:*
Dom. Rep. *Wrapper:*
U.S.A./Conn. Shade
This cigar has a dry, papery
character with some hints of
grass on an otherwise creamy
texture.
U.S.: $5.48 • U.K.: N/A

DON JUAN CETRO **80**
Nicaragua • *Size:* 6" x 43
Filler: Nicaragua *Binder:*
Dom. Rep. *Wrapper:*
U.S.A./Conn. Shade
A mild cigar. It has some
decent tobacco components,
but overall is a little rough,
and a vegetal character domi-
nates.
U.S.: $2.00 • U.K.: N/A

TE-AMO MEDITATION **80**
Mexico • *Size:* 6" x 42
Filler/Binder/Wrapper: Mexico
A cigar with a tight draw and
salty character with flavors of
straw and paper. A hint of
pepper spice on the finish.
U.S.: $2.30 • U.K.: N/A

LA REGENTA NO. 3 **78**
Canary Islands • *Size:*
5⅝" x 42 *Filler/Binder:* Dom.
Rep., Brazil *Wrapper:*
U.S.A./Conn. Shade
Slightly difficult to draw and
even harder to get any serious flavor. Extremely mild in
character with a light coffee
and cream character and a
short aftertaste. (03/01/93)
U.S.: $2.30 • U.K.: N/A

ROBUSTO

*Most of the following Robusto
tasting notes appeared in the
Winter 1994/95 issue of Cigar
Aficionado. Exceptions are
indicated by a date in parentheses at the end of the tasting
note.*

BOLIVAR ROYAL **95**
CORONAS
Cuba • *Size:* 5" x 50 *Filler/
Binder/Wrapper:* Cuba
A powerful, spicy smoke with
rich, earthy flavors of leather,
sweet spices like cinnamon
and nutmeg and a dash of
chocolate. It delivers a
smooth, nutty, long-lasting
finish.
U.S.: N/A • U.K.: £6.08

HOYO DE MONTERREY **94**
EPICURE NO. 2
Cuba • *Size:* 5" x 50 *Filler/
Binder/Wrapper:* Cuba
A rich, full-bodied smoke
filled with solid spice, sweet
coffee-bean and cocoa-bean
flavors and a long, spicy finish.
U.S.: N/A • U.K.: £6.64

FLOR DE CAÑO SHORT 93 CHURCHILL
Cuba • *Size:* 5" x 50 *Filler/ Binder/Wrapper:* Cuba
A rich, full-flavored smoke with lots of spice and cinnamon and mild cocoa-bean flavors.
U.S.: N/A • U.K.: £5.61

COHIBA ROBUSTO 92
Cuba • *Size:* 5" x 50 *Filler/ Binder/Wrapper:* Cuba
This cigar's wrapper has a nice sheen. It is a rich smoke that smooths out quickly to full-bodied, earthy flavors of nutmeg and cocoa with a long, spicy finish.
U.S.: N/A • U.K.: £10.12

ARTURO FUENTE OPUS 90 X ROBUSTO
Dominican Republic • *Size:* 5¼" x 50 *Filler/Binder/ Wrapper:* Dom. Rep.
A strong, full-bodied smoke with rich flavors of sweet spices and a leathery, cedar-box character.
U.S.: $8.00 • U.K.: N/A

RAMON ALLONES 90 SPECIALLY SELECTED
Cuba • *Size:* 5" x 50 *Filler/ Binder/Wrapper:* Cuba
A rich, full-bodied cigar with spice and coffee flavors and a nice nut-and-cedar finish.
U.S.: N/A • U.K.: £5.96

ARTURO FUENTE DON 89 CARLOS ROBUSTO
Dominican Republic • *Size:* 5" x 50 *Filler/Binder:* Dom. Rep. *Wrapper:* Cameroon
A nice, oily wrapper. This is a full-bodied cigar with rich,

spicy flavors and a long, spicy finish.
U.S.: $7.00 • U.K.: N/A

FONSECA 5-50 89
Dominican Republic • *Size:* 5" x 50 *Filler:* Dom. Rep. *Binder:* Mexico *Wrapper:* U.S.A./Conn. Shade
A well-balanced, medium-bodied cigar with mild spices and a soft, mellow character that includes hints of cocoa and caramel.
U.S.: $3.50 • U.K.: N/A

ROMEO Y JULIETA 89 EXHIBICION NO. 4
Cuba • *Size:* 5" x 48 *Filler/ Binder/Wrapper:* Cuba
This cigar has a strong, earthy component with leather and pepper flavors and a long, spicy finish.
U.S.: N/A • U.K.: £5.92

V CENTENNIAL 89 ROBUSTO
Honduras • *Size:* 5" x 50 *Filler:* Dom. Rep., Honduras, Nicaragua *Binder:* Mexico *Wrapper:* U.S.A./Conn. Shade
This cigar has mild coffee-bean flavors and a smooth spiciness on a solid tobacco core.
U.S.: $3.75 • U.K.: N/A

ASHTON MAGNUM 88
Dominican Republic • *Size:* 5" x 50 *Filler/Binder:* Dom. Rep. *Wrapper:* U.S.A./Conn. Shade
A pleasant, medium-bodied cigar with solid flavors of mild spices and an earthy quality on the finish. Scored 82 in Vol. 1, No. 1.
U.S.: $3.35 • U.K.: N/A

CANARIA D'ORO 88 ROTHSCHILD
Dominican Republic • *Size:* 4½" x 50 *Filler/Binder/ Wrapper:* Mexico, Dom. Rep.*Filler:* Mexico, Dom. Rep. *Binder/Wrapper:* Mexico
A mild, fragrant cigar that has a mild, creamy character with solid hints of spice on the palate.
U.S.: $1.50 • U.K.: N/A

DUNHILL ALTAMIRA 88
Dominican Republic • *Size:* 5" x 48 *Filler/Binder:* Dom. Rep. *Wrapper:* U.S.A./ Conn. Shade
A pretty, medium-brown wrapper leads into a well-balanced tobacco character with mild spice and nut flavors.
U.S.: $5.00 • U.K.: £5.65

ENCANTO ROTHSCHILD 88
Honduras • *Size:* 4½" x 50 *Filler/Binder/Wrapper:* Honduras
This cigar comes with an attractive brown wrapper. It has rich, spicy flavors with notes of coffee beans and a long aftertaste.
U.S.: $2.00 • U.K.: N/A

LICENCIADOS WAVELL 88
Dominican Republic • *Size:* 5" x 50 *Filler/Binder:* Dom. Rep. *Wrapper:* U.S.A./Conn. Shade
A well-balanced, well-made cigar with light, creamy flavors and a dried, sweet-fruit and cedar character.
U.S.: $2.20 • U.K.: N/A

PARTAGAS SERIES D NO. 4 — 88

Cuba • *Size:* 5" x 50 *Filler/Binder/Wrapper:* Cuba
A solid, rich cigar with mellow spiciness and coffee flavors and a good balance on the finish. Can be slow to start.
U.S.: N/A • U.K.: £6.52

POR LARRAÑAGA ROBUSTO — 88

Dominican Republic • *Size:* 5" x 50 *Filler/Binder:* Dom. Rep. *Wrapper:* U.S.A./Conn. Shade
This is a well-made cigar with a firm draw. It has nice chestnut and sweet spice elements on the palate and a smooth, mild finish.
U.S.: $3.60 • U.K.: N/A

ZINO MOUTON-CADET NO. 6 — 88

Honduras • *Size:* 5" x 50 *Filler/Binder:* Honduras *Wrapper:* Ecuador
There is a creamy smoothness to this mellow cigar, which has a long, mild spice finish and an elegant character.
U.S.: $6.00 • Switzerland: 6SF

AVO XO INTERMEZZO — 87

Dominican Republic • *Size:* 5½" x 50 *Filler/Binder:* Dom. Rep. *Wrapper:* U.S.A./Conn. Shade
A pretty wrapper with a nice sheen. This cigar has woody flavors and a pleasant, spicy finish.
U.S.: $6.75 • U.K.: N/A

DAVIDOFF SPECIAL "R" — 87

Dominican Republic • *Size:* 4⅞" x 50 *Filler/Binder:* Dom. Rep. *Wrapper:* U.S.A./Conn. Shade
A cigar with some solid spice notes, but it has a bit of sourness on the finish and a dry wood character.
U.S.: $8.25 • U.K.: £11.12

DON TOMAS SPECIAL EDITION NO. 300 — 87

Honduras • *Size:* 5" x 50 *Filler/Binder/Wrapper:* Honduras
A woody, earthy complexity highlights this medium-bodied cigar with a pretty brown wrapper.
U.S.: $3.45 • U.K.: N/A

MACANUDO HYDE PARK — 87

Jamaica • *Size:* 5½" x 49 *Filler:* Dom. Rep., Jamaica *Binder:* Mexico *Wrapper:* U.S.A./Conn. Shade
This is a mild, light, creamy smoke with a hint of nuttiness and a delicate cedar aroma.
U.S.: $3.20 • U.K.: N/A

PLEIADES PLUTON — 87

Dominican Republic • *Size:* 5" x 50 *Filler/Binder:* Dom. Rep. *Wrapper:* U.S.A./Conn. Shade
This cigar is a creamy smoke with solid spice notes. It burns very well and has a satisfying mild tobacco aftertaste.
U.S.: $5.35 • U.K.: N/A

ROYAL JAMAICA ROBUSTO — 87

Dominican Republic • *Size:* 4½" x 49 *Filler:* Jamaica *Binder:* Java *Wrapper:* Cameroon
A nice brown wrapper. This is a medium-bodied cigar with well-balanced flavors of mild spices.
U.S.: $2.20 • U.K.: N/A

VUELTABAJO ROBUSTO — 87

Dominican Republic • *Size:* 4¼" x 52 *Filler/Binder:* Dom. Rep. *Wrapper:* U.S.A./Conn. Shade
This is a solid, mild cigar with some hints of nuts and light, spicy flavors with a light, creamy aftertaste.
U.S.: $2.10 • U.K.: N/A

H. UPMANN PEQUEÑOS 100 — 86

Dominican Republic • *Size:* 4½" x 50 *Filler/Binder:* Dom. Rep., Brazil *Wrapper:* Cameroon
This is a good, all-around robusto. With a dark brown wrapper, it is very well-made and gives a good draw. Attractive rich espresso flavors and a medium finish. (09/01/92)
U.S.: $1.50 • U.K.: N/A

H. UPMANN CABINET SELECTION NO. 100 — 86

Dominican Republic • *Size:* 4¼" x 50 *Filler/Binder:* Dom. Rep. *Wrapper:* Cameroon
A dark-wrapped cigar with strong, dark spice flavors as well as hints of chocolate. There is a bit of tartness on the palate and finish.
U.S.: $4.20 • U.K.: N/A

HOYO DE MONTERREY 86
ROTHSCHILD
Honduras • Size: 4½" x 50
Filler/Binder: Honduras
Wrapper: U.S.A./Conn.
Shade
This full-bodied cigar has
some solid spice and pepper
flavors with a woody finish.
U.S.: $1.55 • U.K.: N/A

NAT SHERMAN VIP 86
SELECTION ASTOR
Dominican Republic • Size:
4½" x 50 Filler/Binder: Dom.
Rep. Wrapper: U.S.A./
Conn. Shade
A light cigar with a smooth
draw and a mild, spicy flavor
that turns to a dried-wood
character on the finish.
U.S.: $4.40 • U.K.: N/A

NAT SHERMAN HOST 86
SELECTION HOBART
Honduras • Size: 5" x 50
Filler: Honduras Binder:
Mexico Wrapper: U.S.A./
Conn. Shade
A cigar with light, grassy fla-
vors and a smooth, mild fin-
ish that contains some medi-
um spiciness.
U.S.: $3.40 • U.K.: N/A

PARTAGAS ROBUSTO 86
Dominican Republic •
Size: 4½" x 49 Filler/Binder:
Mexico, Dom. Rep.
Wrapper: Cameroon
A medium-bodied cigar with
a strong earthy component
and some mild, spicy flavors
on a dry finish.
U.S.: $2.95 • U.K.: N/A

ROMEO Y JULIETA 86
VINTAGE NO. 3
Dominican Republic • Size:
4½" x 50 Filler: Dom. Rep.
Binder: Mexico Wrapper:
U.S.A./Conn. Shade
This cigar has a strong herbal
component, yet soft spice fla-
vors round out the texture
through a long finish.
U.S.: $5.00 • U.K.: N/A

SANTA DAMIANA 86
SELECCION NO. 500
Dominican Republic • Size: 5"
x 50 Filler/Binder: Dom. Rep.
Wrapper: U.S.A./Conn. Shade
A medium-bodied cigar with a
strong cedary note on the palate
and a smooth, mellow finish.
U.S.: $5.50 • U.K.: N/A

THOMAS HINDS 86
HONDURAN SELECTION
ROBUSTO
Honduras • Size: 5" x 50
Filler/Binder: Honduras
Wrapper: Ecuador
This cigar has some solid
earthy flavors and a light,
vegetal quality.
U.S.: $1.95 • Canada: $2.25

ARTURO FUENTE 85
CHATEAU FUENTE
ROTHSCHILD
Dominican Republic • Size:
5" x 50 Filler/Binder: Dom.
Rep. Wrapper: U.S.A./
Conn. Shade
Some inconsistency in this
cigar. Good spice flavors with
several woody notes. Former-
ly called Chateau Rothschild.
U.S.: $1.90 • U.K.: N/A

ASHTON AGED 85
MADURO NO. 10
Dominican Republic • Size:
5" x 50 Filler/Binder: Dom.
Rep. Wrapper: U.S.A./
Conn. Broadleaf
A solid cigar with a dark
wrapper. It has some good,
spicy flavors and a nice
tobacco finish.
U.S.: $3.75 • U.K.: N/A

CABALLEROS 85
ROTHSCHILD
Dominican Republic • Size:
5" x 50 Filler/Binder: Dom.
Rep. Wrapper: U.S.A./
Conn. Shade
A cigar with some solid
tobacco flavors. It also has a
light, spicy character with
medium-bodied smoke.
U.S.: $3.00 • U.K.: N/A

DON LINO COLORADO 85
ROBUSTO
Honduras • Size: 5½" x 50
Filler: Nicaragua, Honduras
Binder: U.S.A./Connecticut
Broadleaf Wrapper: U.S.A./
Conn. Shade
A firm, well-made cigar with
solid, nutty flavors and a
woody character yet a hot,
almost metallic finish.
U.S.: $5.20 • U.K.: N/A

DON TOMAS 85
ROTHSCHILD
Honduras • *Size:* 4½" x 50
Filler/Binder/Wrapper: Honduras
A cigar with some rough
spots and a tendency toward
a loose fill. But it has a solid
spicy core with good tobacco
flavors.
U.S.: $1.65 • U.K.: N/A

EL SUBLIMADO 85
REGARDETE
Dominican Republic • *Size:*
4½" x 50 *Filler/Binder:* Dom.
Rep. *Wrapper:* U.S.A./
Conn. Shade
Some inconsistencies in this
cigar. Overall, it has a mild
character with some spicy fla-
vors and a decent, smooth
finish.
U.S.: $8.00 • France: 68FF

H. UPMANN CABINET 85
SELECTION ROBUSTO
Dominican Republic • *Size:*
4¼" x 50 *Filler/Binder:* Dom.
Rep. *Wrapper:* Cameroon
A cigar with some earthy,
herbaceous flavors overlaid
with light spices.
U.S.: $4.20 • U.K.: N/A

JUAN CLEMENTE 85
ROTHSCHILD
Dominican Republic • *Size:*
4⅞" x 50 *Filler/Binder:* Dom.
Rep. *Wrapper:* U.S.A./
Conn. Shade
This cigar has strong, spicy
flavors yet is marred by a
heavy, dry-wood undertone
and a short finish.
U.S.: $4.70 • U.K.: N/A

LA GLORIA CUBANA 85
WAVELL
U.S.A. • *Size:* 5" x 50
Filler: Dom. Rep., Nicaragua
Binder: Nicaragua *Wrapper:*
Ecuador
A cigar with a clean finish,
mild spiciness and some exot-
ic floral flavors on the palate.
U.S.: $2.15 • U.K.: N/A

LEON JIMENES 85
ROBUSTO
Dominican Republic • *Size:*
5½" x 50 *Filler/Binder:* Dom.
Rep. *Wrapper:* U.S.A./
Conn. Shade
This cigar shows some incon-
sistency in its construction,
although it has a pleasant
cedary flavor tinged with
spice.
U.S.: $4.35 • U.K.: N/A

MACANUDO VINTAGE 85
NO. 5
Jamaica • *Size:* 5½" x 49
Filler: Dom. Rep., Jamaica
Binder: Mexico *Wrapper:*
U.S.A./Conn. Shade
A light, easy-smoking cigar
that tends toward some grassy
and straw flavors.
U.S.: $7.00 • U.K.: N/A

MONTECRISTO 85
ROBUSTO
Dominican Republic • *Size:*
4¼" x 50 *Filler/Binder:* Dom.
Rep., Brazil *Wrapper:*
Cameroon
This cigar has some earthy,
herbal notes that blend at
first into a slight harshness;
however, it ends with nut
and mild spice flavors.
U.S.: $6.00 • U.K.: N/A

PARTAGAS NATURAL 85
Dominican Republic •
Size: 5½" x 49 *Filler/Binder:*
Mexico, Dom. Rep.
Wrapper: Cameroon
A well-made, medium-bod-
ied cigar that has some mild
spice components and a
clean tobacco finish.
U.S.: $3.20 • U.K.: N/A

BACCARAT HAVANA 84
SELECTION ROBUSTO
Honduras • *Size:* 5" x 50
Filler/Wrapper: Honduras
Binder: Mexico
A cigar with sweet gum on
the wrapper. It is mild with
some light spicy notes.
U.S.: $1.70 • U.K.: N/A

CUBA ALIADOS 84
ROTHSCHILD
Honduras • *Size:* 5" x 50
Filler: Dom. Rep. *Binder/
Wrapper:* Ecuador
This is a pretty but simple
cigar. It has slightly vegetal
and earthy flavors and a
smooth, medium-bodied tex-
ture.
U.S.: $2.20 • U.K.: £2.20

DIANA SILVIUS 84
ROBUSTO
Dominican Republic • *Size:*
4⅞" x 52 *Filler/Binder:* Dom.
Rep. *Wrapper:* U.S.A./
Conn. Shade
This cigar had some nice
pepper flavors yet it burned a
little hot. Several tasters
noted a harsh aftertaste.
U.S.: $5.30 • U.K.: N/A

DON LINO ROBUSTO **84**
Honduras • *Size:* 5½"
x 50 *Filler/Binder:* Sumatra
Wrapper: U.S.A./Conn.
Shade
There is a tart, almost sour
quality to this cigar. It has
some dry, grassy flavors that
turn to soft, creamy notes on
the finish.
U.S.: $2.10 • U.K.: N/A

DUNHILL ROMANAS **84**
Dominican Republic •
Size: 4½" x 50 *Filler/Binder:*
Dom. Rep. *Wrapper:*
U.S.A./Conn. Shade
A cigar with flavors of spice
and a toasted, almost burnt,
aroma.
U.S.: $4.45 • U.K.: £5.10

JOSE BENITO **84**
ROTHSCHILD
Dominican Republic • *Size:*
4¾" x 50 *Filler:* Dom. Rep.
Binder: Honduras *Wrapper:*
Cameroon
This cigar starts slowly, but
offers pleasant spice flavors
on a smooth texture.
U.S.: $2.15 • U.K.: N/A

JUAN CLEMENTE CLUB **84**
SELECTION NO. 2
Dominican Republic • *Size:*
4½" x 46 *Filler/Binder:* Dom.
Rep. *Wrapper:* U.S.A./
Conn. Shade
Inconsistent. Some tasters
noted strong spicy and cedar
flavors. Others found it harsh
and sour.
U.S.: $5.75 • U.K.: N/A

LA UNICA NO. 400 **84**
Dominican Republic •
Size: 4½" x 50 *Filler/Binder:*
Dom. Rep. *Wrapper:*
U.S.A./Conn. Shade
This is a rough cigar that has
a solid, spicy flavor and a
mild nuttiness.
U.S.: $1.65 • U.K.: N/A

NAT SHERMAN **84**
MANHATTAN
SELECTION SUTTON
Dominican Republic • *Size:*
5½" x 49 *Filler:* Dom. Rep.
Binder/Wrapper: Mexico
An unattractive wrapper. It
has a toasty aroma, but lacks
some spice and yields a flat,
almost bitter finish.
U.S.: $3.80 • U.K.: N/A

PAUL GARMIRIAN **84**
SERIES NO. 2
Dominican Republic • *Size:*
4¾" x 48 *Filler/Binder:* Dom.
Rep. *Wrapper:* U.S.A./
Conn. Shade
This cigar's wrapper has a
gummy vegetal character
that masks some complex
spice flavors. It has a sharp,
biting finish.
U.S.: $6.40 • U.K.: £6.35

ROMEO Y JULIETA **84**
ROTHSCHILD
Dominican Republic • *Size:*
5" x 50 *Filler:* Dom. Rep.,
Brazil *Binder:* U.S.A./
Connecticut Broadleaf
Wrapper: Cameroon
This is a very mild cigar with
a dry, papery flavor, although
it offers a hint of spice.
U.S.: $2.10 • U.K.: N/A

SOSA WAVELL **84**
Dominican Republic •
Size: 4¾" x 50 *Filler:* Dom.
Rep., Brazil *Binder:*
Honduras *Wrapper:* Ecuador
A pleasant cigar with a slight-
ly vegetal quality, yet it also
has a tangy and spicy finish.
U.S.: $2.25 • U.K.: N/A

TEMPLE HALL **84**
NO. 550
Jamaica • *Size:* 5½" x 50
Filler: Dom. Rep., Jamaica
Binder: Mexico *Wrapper:*
U.S.A./Conn. Shade
This is a light, creamy cigar
with a simple, grassy element
and some green or immature
flavors.
U.S.: $5.20 • U.K.: N/A

AVO NO. 9 **83**
Dominican Republic •
Size: 4¾" x 48 *Filler/Binder:*
Dom. Rep. *Wrapper:*
U.S.A./Conn. Shade
A cigar with earthy aromas,
but with slightly sour, acidic
flavors.
U.S.: $4.75 • U.K.: N/A

BAUZA ROBUSTO **83**
Dominican Republic •
Size: 5½" x 50 *Filler:* Dom.
Rep., Nicaragua *Binder:*
Mexico *Wrapper:* Cameroon
This cigar has a sour bite on
the palate, although some
tasters noted a spicy after-
taste.
U.S.: $2.25 • U.K.: N/A

DON LINO HAVANA **83**
RESERVE ROBUSTO
Honduras • *Size:* 5½" x 50
Filler: Connecticut broadleaf

Binder: Sumatra *Wrapper:*
U.S.A./Conn. Shade
Grassy flavors tend to domi-
nate this mild cigar with a
firm draw.
U.S.: $3.95 • U.K.: N/A

EL REY DEL MUNDO 83
ROBUSTO
Honduras • *Size:* 5" x 54
Filler/Binder/Wrapper:
Honduras
A quite unattractive wrapper.
Inconsistencies in the draw
were noted, but otherwise it
has some woody, spicy flavors.
U.S.: $2.50 • U.K.: N/A

LAS CABRILLAS 83
CORTEZ
Honduras • *Size:* 4¾" x 50
Filler: Dom. Rep., Mexico
Binder: Mexico *Wrapper:*
U.S.A./Conn. Shade
This mild cigar has some
construction flaws, but it dis-
plays some light floral and
dried-fruit flavors.
U.S.: $1.20 • U.K.: N/A

MONTECRUZ SUN- 83
GROWN ROBUSTO
Dominican Republic • *Size:*
4½" x 49 *Filler/Binder:* Dom.
Rep., Brazil *Wrapper:*
Cameroon
A medium-bodied cigar with
earthy, vegetal flavors. It
offers some hints of spice on
the finish.
U.S.: $2.20 • U.K.: N/A

PRIMO DEL REY 83
NO. 100
Dominican Republic • *Size:*
4½" x 50 *Filler/Binder:* Dom.
Rep. *Wrapper:* Brazil

A nice, well-balanced cigar
with some creamy flavors of
mild coffee and a hint of spice.
U.S.: $1.70 • U.K.: N/A

PUNCH ROTHSCHILD 83
Honduras • *Size:* 4½"
x 50 *Filler/Binder:* Honduras,
Nicaragua, Dom. Rep.
Wrapper: U.S.A./Conn.
Shade
A loose fill in this cigar cre-
ates a hot, spicy draw that
mellows a bit to some nut
and wood flavors.
U.S.: $1.55 • U.K.: N/A

PUNCH GRAND CRU 83
ROBUSTO
Honduras • *Size:* 5¼" x 50
Filler/Binder/Wrapper:
Honduras
This is a straightforward cigar
that lacks a bit of depth. But
it shows some flavors of spice
and a good balance.
U.S.: $3.25 • U.K.: N/A

CRUZ REAL NO. 25 82
Mexico • *Size:* 5½" x 52
Filler/Binder: Mexico
Wrapper: Sumatra
A rather rough wrapper leads
into a dry wood, almost cedary
flavor that lacks complexity.
U.S.: $2.60 • U.K.: £3.50

EL REY DEL MUNDO 82
ROBUSTO DE MANUEL
Honduras • *Size:* 5" x 54
Filler/Binder/Wrapper:
Honduras
A solid cigar that lacks some
complexity. It has dry, straw-
like flavors with some woody
notes, but a short finish.
U.S.: $2.50 • U.K.: N/A

TE-AMO TORITO 82
Mexico • *Size:* 4¾" x 50
Filler/Binder/Wrapper: Mexico
Irregular construction hurts
this cigar. It has a medium-
bodied character with spice
and strong cedar compo-
nents.
U.S.: $1.90 • U.K.: N/A

TROYA NO. 18 82
Dominican Republic •
Size: 4¾" x 50 *Filler/Binder:*
Dom. Rep. *Wrapper:*
U.S.A./Conn. Shade
This cigar has a loose draw
that creates a grassy, papery
smoke with a bite.
U.S.: $2.80 • U.K.: N/A

DON RAMOS 81
ROTHSCHILD
Honduras • *Size:* 4½" x 50
Filler: Hon., Dom. Rep., Ecu.
Binder: U.S.A. *Wrapper:*
Ecuador
Attractive and pleasant, the
Don Ramos has light grassy
aromas and delicate coffee,
dusty flavors. It draws well
although a little quick.
Overall, a pleasing smoke.
(09/01/92)
U.S.: N/A • U.K.: £2.71

JOYA DE NICARAGUA 81
CONSUL
Nicaragua • *Size:* 4½" x 52
Filler/Binder/Wrapper:
Nicaragua
A rough, rustic smoke with
some creamy notes, but with
dry, strawlike flavors and a
sharp bite on the finish.
U.S.: $1.75 • U.K.: N/A

BELINDA MEDAGLIA D'ORO **80**
Honduras • Size: 4½" x 50
Filler: Dom. Rep., Honduras
Binder: Honduras Wrapper: Ecuador
This cigar shows rough construction and an earthy flavor component with a hot, almost metallic finish.
U.S.: $1.80 • U.K.: N/A

LA INVICTA MAGNUM NO. 2 **79**
Honduras • Size: 4½" x 50
Filler: Dom. Rep., Nica., Hon. Binder: Ecuador
Wrapper: U.S.A./Conn. Shade
A quick easy smoke is the best way to describe this cigar. Very fast draw with nutty aromas, it is medium-bodied with rather neutral flavors. Nothing not to like about it but not much to get excited about. (09/01/92)
U.S.: N/A • U.K.: £2.81

PETRUS ROTHSCHILD **74**
Honduras • Size: 4¾" x 50 Filler/Binder/Wrapper: Honduras
A consistently underfilled cigar. It burns hot with harsh, chemical flavors and has a dry, balsa-wood, papery character.
U.S.: $2.40 • U.K.: N/A

LA HOJA SELECTA PALAIS ROYAL **72**
U.S.A. • Size: 4¼" x 50
Filler/Binder: Dom. Rep., Bra., Mex. Wrapper: U.S.A./Conn. Shade
Inconsistency hurts this cigar. The wrapper is uneven and the entire cigar is loosely rolled. It smokes too fast and gives very grassy, strawlike flavors. Not a complete write off, but it could be better. (09/01/92)
U.S.: $1.70 • U.K.: N/A

PETIT CORONA

Most of the following Petit Corona tasting notes appeared in the Summer 1995 issue of Cigar Aficionado. Exceptions are indicated by a date in parentheses at the end of the tasting note.

COHIBA SIGLO I **93**
Cuba • Size: 4" x 40
Filler/Binder/Wrapper: Cuba
A lot of flavor in a small cigar. Beautifully crafted with a rich chocolate wrapper, it is soft-textured and sumptuous to smoke, with dark chocolate and spice aromas and flavors. (03/01/93)
U.S.: N/A • U.K.: £6.00

EL RICO HABANO PETIT-HABANO **89**
U.S.A. • Size: 5" x 40
Filler: Nicaragua, Dom. Rep. Binder/Wrapper: Ecuador
This cigar has excellent flavors of tobacco, coffee and spicy pepper. The cigar also has a sweet wood/cedary finish.
U.S.: $1.45 • U.K.: N/A

MONTECRISTO NO. 4 **89**
Cuba • Size: 5" x 42 Filler/Binder/Wrapper: Cuba
A perfumed aroma makes this an attractive cigar. It has smooth, round flavors of herbed spices. It is full bodied and spicy.
U.S.: N/A • U.K.: £5.75

MONTESINO DIPLOMATICO **89**
Dominican Republic • Size: 5½" x 43 Filler/Binder: Dom. Rep. Wrapper: U.S.A./Conn. Shade
A well-made cigar with a good draw and a toasty aroma. There are earthy, medium-bodied flavors mixed with herbal and spice notes.
U.S.: $1.60 • U.K.: N/A

PARTAGAS PETIT CORONA **89**
Cuba • Size: 5" x 42 Filler/Binder/Wrapper: Cuba
A beautiful, oily wrapper leads into a smoke with excellent leather and sweet spice flavors. It has a light, smooth finish.
U.S.: N/A • U.K.: £5.50

ROMEO Y JULIETA PETIT CORONA **89**
Cuba • Size: 5" x 42 Filler/Binder/Wrapper: Cuba
An elegant cigar with rich, spicy flavors. It is well-made and is rich looking and has a long, full-bodied finish.
U.S.: N/A • U.K.: £5.50

8-9-8 COLLECTION CORONA **88**
Jamaica • Size: 5½" x 42
Filler: Jamaica, Dom. Rep. Binder: Mexico Wrapper: U.S.A./Conn. Shade
This cigar has very nice creamy flavors with touches of sweet spice like nutmeg and pepper. Well made.
U.S.: $4.75 • U.K.: N/A

DAVIDOFF GRAN CRU No. 4 — 88

Dominican Republic • *Size:* 5" x 40 *Filler/Binder:* Dom. Rep. *Wrapper:* U.S.A./ Conn. Shade
A cigar with a medium-bodied smoke. It has a smooth creamy texture and good spicy flavors.
U.S.: $5.95 • U.K.: £7.00

DAVIDOFF GRAN CRU No. 3 — 88

Dominican Republic • *Size:* 5" x 42 *Filler/Binder:* Dom. Rep. *Wrapper:* U.S.A./ Conn. Shade
This cigar showed some lack of maturity, with young tobacco characteristics. But it has some nice spice and sweet woody flavors.
U.S.: $6.85 • U.K.: N/A

HOYO DE MONTERREY EXCALIBUR No. 7 — 88

Honduras • *Size:* 5" x 43 *Filler/Binder:* Honduras, Nicaragua, Dom. Rep. *Wrapper:* U.S.A./Conn. Shade
A pleasant cigar with an earthy complexity. At its core, there are smooth, creamy pepper flavors. It ends on a rich leathery note.
U.S.: $2.25 • U.K.: £2.13

MACANUDO LORD CLARIDGE — 88

Jamaica • *Size:* 5½" x 38 *Filler:* Dom. Rep., Jamaica, Mexico *Binder:* Mexico *Wrapper:* U.S.A./Conn. Shade
A nicely balanced cigar with a firm draw that has a smooth

creamy texture, and a buttered toast component on the palate. The finish tastes like rich leather.
U.S.: $2.95 • U.K.: N/A

MACANUDO VINTAGE No. 3 — 88

Jamaica • *Size:* 5½" x 42 *Filler:* Dom. Rep. , Jamaica, Mexico *Binder:* Mexico *Wrapper:* U.S.A./Conn. Shade
This rich cigar has a slightly rough construction, but it is filled with earthy, robust flavors with hints of coffee beans. It has a long, nutty finish.
U.S.: $7.00 • U.K.: N/A

AVO No. 8 — 87

Dominican Republic • *Size:* 5½" x 40 *Filler/Binder:* Dom. Rep. *Wrapper:* U.S.A./Conn. Shade
This cigar has pleasant floral aromas. There are sweet nutmeg flavors, and a hint of coffee beans and creaminess on the palate.
U.S.: $5.40 • U.K.: N/A

BACCARAT PETIT CORONA — 87

Honduras • *Size:* 5½" x 42 *Filler/Wrapper:* Honduras *Binder:* Mexico
Although it showed some inconsistency, this cigar had a well-balanced, smooth taste, and contained solid notes of spice and coffee.
U.S.: $1.40 • U.K.: N/A

BOLIVAR PETIT CORONA — 87

Cuba • *Size:* 5" x 42 *Filler/ Binder/Wrapper:* Cuba

A well-made, medium-bodied cigar with a good draw. It has some strong elements of coffee and a hint of spice. But it has a flat finish.
U.S.: N/A • U.K.: £5.50

EL REY DEL MUNDO HABANA CLUB — 87

Honduras • *Size:* 5½" x 42 *Filler:* Dom. Rep., Honduras *Binder/Wrapper:* Honduras
Clean tobacco flavors dominate this well-made cigar with a dark brown wrapper. There is a solid, well-balanced core of cedar and sweet spice notes.
U.S.: $3.00 • U.K.: N/A

HOYO DE MONTERREY SUPER HOYO — 87

Honduras • *Size:* 5½" x 44 *Filler/Binder:* Honduras, Nicaragua, Dom. Rep. *Wrapper:* Ecuador
Although it is a bit rustic-looking, this is a pleasant cigar with some spice and coffee flavors.
U.S.: $1.35 • U.K.: N/A

MACANUDO HAMPTON COURT — 87

Jamaica • *Size:* 5¾" x 43 *Filler:* Dom. Rep., Jamaica, Mexico *Binder:* Mexico *Wrapper:* U.S.A./Conn. Shade
A very well-made mild cigar. It has a good draw and an even burn, and solid flavors of tobacco and sweet wood. A coffee bean character comes out on the finish.
U.S.: $3.50 • U.K.: N/A

PLEIADES ANTARES 87
Dominican Republic •
Size: 5½" x 40 *Filler/Binder:*
Dom. Rep. *Wrapper:*
U.S.A./Conn. Shade
A mellow cigar that has an
interesting aroma of roasting
meat. There are fruity flavors
reminiscent of mango and a
smooth nutty finish.
U.S.: $4.15 • U.K.: N/A

PRIMO DEL REY NO. 4 87
Dominican Republic •
Size: 5½" x 42 *Filler:* Dom.
Rep. *Binder:* U.S.A.
Wrapper: Brazil
A full-bodied cigar with a
rich, oily smoke. There are
strong sweet spice flavors like
nutmeg, and a smooth, leath-
ery tone to the finish.
U.S.: $1.40 • U.K.: N/A

THOMAS HINDS 87
HONDURAN SELECTION
CORONA
Honduras • *Size:* 5½" x 42
Filler/Binder: Honduras
Wrapper: Ecuador
A cigar with a generally easy
draw, and a range of flavors
that include dry wood and
paper. There is a good level
of spiciness on the finish.
U.S.: $2.05 • U.K.: N/A

ZINO MOUTON-CADET 87
NO. 5
Honduras • *Size:* 5" x 42
Filler/Binder: Honduras
Wrapper: Ecuador
A mild cigar with a slightly
easy draw. The cigar has pro-
nounced notes of cedar and
some solid spicy notes.
U.S.: $4.70 • U.K.: N/A

ARTURO FUENTE 86
PETIT CORONA
Dominican Republic • *Size:*
5" x 38 *Filler/Binder:* Dom.
Rep. *Wrapper:* Cameroon
A well-made cigar with a firm
draw. It has an oily texture to
the smoke, and interesting
sweetish tobacco flavors along
with a solid cedary finish.
U.S.: $1.65 • U.K.: N/A

CUBA ALIADOS 86
REMEDIOS
Honduras • *Size:* 5½" x 42
Filler: Dom. Rep., Brazil
Binder/Wrapper: Ecuador
A cigar that needs more
aging. It has some solid
earthy tones with flavors of
spice and coffee, and a nice
light woody character.
U.S.: $2.00 • U.K.: N/A

CUESTA-REY 86
DOMINICAN NO. 5
Dominican Republic • *Size:*
5½" x 42 *Filler/Binder:* Dom.
Rep. *Wrapper:* U.S.A./
Conn. Shade
A well-made cigar that
lacked a bit of balance. It has
some nice nutty and toasty
flavors, and it ends with a
mild spiciness.
U.S.: $2.30 • U.K.: £3.45

DON DIEGO PETIT 86
CORONA
Dominican Republic • *Size:*
5⅛" x 42 *Filler/Binder:* Dom.
Rep. *Wrapper:* U.S.A./
Conn. Shade
A nice, mild smoke.
Although it lacks complexity,
the cigar has a creamy tex-
ture with some fruit-like fla-
vors that provide balance.
U.S.: $2.15 • U.K.: N/A

DON TOMAS BLUNT 86
Honduras • *Size:* 5"
x 42 *Filler/Binder/Wrapper:*
Honduras
A pleasant, well-made cigar
with a mild creaminesss, and
a solid underlying core of
spiciness.
U.S.: $1.45 • U.K.: N/A

H. UPMANN TUBOS 86
Dominican Republic •
Size: 5½" x 42 *Filler/Binder:*
Dom. Rep. *Wrapper:*
Cameroon
Although this cigar has a
creamy texture, the flavors
tend toward dry wood and
light spice. It has an easy
draw.
U.S.: $2.70 • U.K.: N/A

H. UPMANN PETIT 86
CORONA
Dominican Republic •
Size: 5⅛" x 42 *Filler/Binder:*
Dom. Rep. *Wrapper:*
Indonesia
A well-made cigar although
it appears a bit rough. It has a
cream and nut character, and
it is smooth and well bal-
anced.
U.S.: $2.25 • U.K.: N/A

HOYO DE MONTERREY 86
LE HOYO DU PRINCE
Cuba • *Size:* 5" x 40 *Filler/
Binder/Wrapper:* Cuba
A decent cigar with some
nice toasty aromas. The fla-
vors tend toward cedar wood
and sweet spices.
U.S.: N/A • U.K.: £5.55

NAT SHERMAN **86**
LANDMARK SELECTION
HAMPSHIRE
Dominican Republic • *Size:*
5½" x 42 *Filler:* Dom. Rep.,
Jamaica, Mexico *Binder:*
Mexico *Wrapper:* Cameroon
A pretty, dark-brown wrapper
produces nice earthy flavors
that hint at spice and mush-
rooms. A dry balsa wood
character is offset by some
earthy qualities on the finish.
U.S.: $4.80 • U.K.: N/A

OLOR MOMENTOS **86**
Dominican Republic •
Size: 5½" x 43 *Filler/Binder:*
Dom. Rep. *Wrapper:*
U.S.A./Conn. Shade
A cigar with an attractive
oily wrapper. It is a bit dry on
the palate with some woody
flavors, but there are hints of
herbs in the aroma and on
the finish.
U.S.: $1.70 • U.K.: N/A

PAUL GARMIRIAN **86**
PETIT CORONA
Dominican Republic • *Size:*
5" x 43 *Filler/Binder:* Dom.
Rep. *Wrapper:* U.S.A./
Conn. Shade
A medium-bodied smoke
that has creamy and mild
spice qualities, and a mild
woody finish.
U.S.: $5.30 • U.K.: £5.20

POR LARRAÑAGA **86**
PETIT CETROS EN
CEDRO
Dominican Republic • *Size:*
5" x 38 *Filler/Binder:* Dom.
Rep. *Wrapper:* U.S.A./
Conn. Shade

A well-balanced, medium-
bodied cigar that has herb
and pepper flavors and a
toasty, almost leathery aroma.
U.S.: $3.00 • U.K.: N/A

PUNCH ROYAL **86**
SELECTION NO. 12
Cuba • *Size:* 5" x 42 *Filler/*
Binder/Wrapper: Cuba
A cigar with a very sweet fla-
vor profile that includes but-
terscotch and burnt caramel.
It has a very woody compo-
nent on the finish.
U.S.: N/A • U.K.: £5.20

ZINO DIAMONDS **86**
Honduras • *Size:* 5½"
x 40 *Filler/Binder:* Honduras
Wrapper: Ecuador
A light-wrappered cigar with
a good spicy core of flavors,
and some hints of herbs.
U.S.: $4.55 • U.K.: N/A

DAVIDOFF NO. 2000 **85**
Dominican Republic •
Size: 5" x 42 *Filler/Binder:*
Dom. Rep. *Wrapper:*
U.S.A./Conn. Shade
A medium-bodied cigar with
a nice, mild nuttiness. It fin-
ishes with a nice dose of spice
that is balanced by an overall
creamy texture.
U.S.: $6.25 • U.K.: £8.00

DON LINO PETIT **85**
CETRO
Honduras • *Size:* 5½" x 42
Filler/Binder: Honduras
Wrapper: U.S.A./Conn.
Shade
A mild cigar with a nutty
character. It has a good draw
and a creamy texture.
U.S.: $1.95 • U.K.: N/A

HOYO DE MONTERREY **85**
EXCALIBUR NO. 6
Honduras • *Size:* 5½" x 38
Filler/Binder: Honduras,
Nicaragua, Dom. Rep.
Wrapper: U.S.A./Conn.
Shade
Some inconsistency in this
cigar. A loose, hot draw was
noted by several tasters. But
there are some earthy tobacco
flavors, and the cigar settles
down after a brief harshness.
U.S.: $2.40 • U.K.: £2.17

PADRON LONDRES **85**
Nicaragua • *Size:* 5½"
x 42 *Filler/Binder/Wrapper:*
Nicaragua
A pretty box-pressed cigar. A
mild smoke, it tastes of cocoa
beans and has some light
woody notes.
U.S.: $1.60 • U.K.: N/A

PUNCH ELITE **85**
Honduras • *Size:* 5¼"
x 44 *Filler/Binder:* Honduras,
Nicaragua, Dom. Rep.
Wrapper: Ecuador
This cigar is a medium-bod-
ied smoke. There are nutmeg
and burnt spice flavors, and
an overall woody character.
U.S.: $.90 • U.K.: N/A

RAMON ALLONES **85**
SIZE D
Dominican Republic • *Size:*
5" x 42 *Filler:* Dom. Rep.,
Mexico *Binder:* Mexico
Wrapper: Cameroon
A cigar with an attractive
dark-brown wrapper. But it is
dominated by woody and
very light, dry spice flavors.
U.S.: $3.00 • U.K.: N/A

SANCHO PANZA NON PLUS 85
Cuba • *Size:* 5" x 42 *Filler/Binder/Wrapper:* Cuba
Although this cigar shows some nice flavors of coffee and cream, it lacks complexity and depth in its medium-bodied smoke.
U.S.: N/A • U.K.: N/A

BAUZA GRECOS 84
Dominican Republic • *Size:* 5½" x 42 *Filler:* Dom. Rep., Nicaragua *Binder:* Mexico *Wrapper:* Cameroon
A mild cigar with a short, dry finish. It has some flowery aromas and flavors, with a touch of spice.
U.S.: $1.80 • U.K.: N/A

BAUZA PETIT CORONA 84
Dominican Republic • *Size:* 5" x 38 *Filler:* Dom. Rep., Nicaragua *Binder:* Mexico *Wrapper:* Cameroon
A pleasant smoke that has a sweet tobacco characteristic and some dry spice flavors.
U.S.: $1.60 • U.K.: N/A

BERING IMPERIAL 84
Honduras • *Size:* 5¼" x 42 *Filler/Wrapper:* Mexico, Dom. Rep., Honduras *Binder:* Honduras
This is a mild cigar. It has some light earthy flavors backed up by a hint of spice that ends with a somewhat dry finish.
U.S.: $1.15 • U.K.: N/A

JOSE BENITO PETITE 84
Dominican Republic • *Size:* 5½" x 38 *Filler:* Dom. Rep. *Binder:* Central

America *Wrapper:* Cameroon
A medium-bodied cigar with a decent construction and draw, and a creamy-textured smoke with wood and nut flavors.
U.S.: $2.10 • U.K.: N/A

LA FINCA CORONA 84
Nicaragua • *Size:* 5½" x 42 *Filler/Binder/Wrapper:* Nicaragua
A medium-bodied cigar. It has hints of spice, leather and nuts, and a decent core of tobacco flavors.
U.S.: $1.40 • U.K.: N/A

LOS LIBERTADORES INSURRECTOS 84
Dominican Republic • *Size:* 5½" x 42 *Filler/Binder:* Dom. Rep. *Wrapper:* U.S.A./Conn. Shade
A nice-looking, yellowish-brown Connecticut wrapper. The cigar has a good draw, but it also has dry, straw-like flavors and a mild, vegetal finish.
U.S.: $3.98 • U.K.: N/A

MACANUDO PETIT CORONA 84
Jamaica • *Size:* 5" x 38 *Filler:* Dom. Rep., Jamaica, Mexico *Binder:* Mexico *Wrapper:* U.S.A./Conn. Shade
This is a mild, elegant cigar with a toasty aroma. Flavors of dry spice and wood dominate.
U.S.: $2.40 • U.K.: N/A

MONTECRUZ SUN-GROWN NO. 230 84
Dominican Republic • *Size:* 5" x 42 *Filler/Binder:* Dom. Rep., Brazil *Wrapper:* Cameroon
A nice cigar with medium body. Although it has some light spice and citrus flavors, it finishes a bit flat and dry.
U.S.: $2.45 • U.K.: N/A

PARTAGAS NO. 4 84
Dominican Republic • *Size:* 5" x 38 *Filler/Binder:* Mexico, Dom. Rep., Jamaica *Wrapper:* Cameroon
This is a mild cigar with a good draw. There is dryness in the smoke, but there are some flavors of white pepper and flint, and an overall herbal character.
U.S.: $2.40 • U.K.: N/A

QUINTERO MEDIAS CORONAS 84
Cuba • *Size:* 5" x 40 *Filler/Binder/Wrapper:* Cuba
This cigar showed some rough construction, but it has nice flavors of sweet spice and dry cedar wood.
U.S.: N/A • U.K.: N/A

TRESADO SELECCION NO. 500 84
Dominican Republic • *Size:* 5½" x 42 *Filler:* Dom. Rep. *Binder:* Cameroon *Wrapper:* Indonesia
This cigar has a mild- to medium-bodied character. There are some spicy flavors, and it has a smooth round finish.
U.S.: $1.30 • U.K.: N/A

TROYA CLASICO 84
Dominican Republic •
Size: 5½" x 42 *Filler/Binder:*
Dom. Rep. *Wrapper:*
U.S.A./Conn. Shade
A cigar with a flinty character,
and a toasty aroma with some
nutty flavors. A dry finish.
U.S.: $6.00 • U.K.: N/A

DON LINO NO. 4 83
Honduras • *Size:* 5" x 42
Filler/Binder: Honduras
Wrapper: U.S.A./Conn. Shade
A well-made cigar with a
firm draw. Mild sweet spice
flavors support a medium-
bodied smoke.
U.S.: $1.75 • U.K.: N/A

H. UPMANN CORONA 83
MAJOR
Dominican Republic •
Size: 5⅟₁₆" x 42 *Filler/Binder:*
Dom. Rep. *Wrapper:*
Cameroon
A rustic cigar with papery,
vegetal flavors. There is a
touch of spice, but it is domi-
nated by a woodiness and a
green character.
U.S.: $2.70 • U.K.: N/A

HOYO DE MONTERREY 83
NO. 55
Honduras • *Size:* 5¼" x 43
Filler/Binder: Honduras,
Nicaragua, Dom. Rep.
Wrapper: Ecuador
A bit rustic, middle of the
road smoke that has some
spicy flavors, and a bit of dry-
ness on the palate.
U.S.: $0.90 • U.K.: N/A

JOYA DE NICARAGUA 83
PETITE
Nicaragua • *Size:* 5½" x 38
Filler/Binder/Wrapper:
Nicaragua
This cigar had some young
tobacco. As a result, there
were some ammonia-like aro-
mas and tastes. It had an over-
all dry paper characteristic.
U.S.: $1.65 • U.K.: N/A

MONTECRUZ SUN- 83
GROWN CEDAR AGED
Dominican Republic • *Size:*
5" x 42 *Filler/Binder:* Dom.
Rep., Brazil *Wrapper:*
Cameroon
A medium-bodied cigar with
hints of coffee bean flavors,
but a rough, earthy character.
U.S.: $2.80 • U.K.: N/A

ROYAL JAMAICA PETIT 83
CORONA
Dominican Republic • *Size:*
5" x 40 *Filler:* Jamaica,
Dom. Rep., Sumatra *Binder:*
Java *Wrapper:* Cameroon
A mild cigar with a tight
draw. It has some soft,
creamy flavors with nutty
components.
U.S.: $2.40 • U.K.: N/A

TE-AMO NO. 4 83
Mexico • *Size:* 5" x 42
Filler/Binder/Wrapper: Mexico
This cigar showed some construction flaws. It had a hot
draw, and some vegetal flavors that mar otherwise
pleasant spicy qualities.
U.S.: $1.80 • U.K.: N/A

VUELTABAJO CORONA 83
Dominican Republic •
Size: 5¾" x 42 *Filler/Binder:*
Dom. Rep. *Wrapper:*
U.S.A./Conn. Shade
This is a nice cigar with some
solid tobacco characteristics,
but it has some unusual fla-
vors of strong hot spices with
a meaty aroma.
U.S.: $2.15 • U.K.: N/A

EL REY DEL MUNDO 82
TINOS
Honduras • *Size:* 5½" x 38
Filler: Dom. Rep., Honduras
Binder/Wrapper: Honduras
This cigar had a loose fill and
a hot draw. It is spicy, but the
hot smoke leaves a flat, dry
taste in the mouth.
U.S.: $1.75 • U.K.: N/A

LICENCIADOS SUPREME 82
MADURO NO. 200
Dominican Republic • *Size:*
5½" x 42 *Filler/Binder:* Dom.
Rep. *Wrapper:* U.S.A./
Conn. Broadleaf
A maduro-style cigar with an
earthy aroma. It is well-bal-
anced with a fruity, almost
melon-like, flavor backed up
by cedar.
U.S.: $2.20 • U.K.: N/A

LICENCIADOS NO. 4 82
Dominican Republic •
Size: 5½" x 42 *Filler/Binder:*
Dom. Rep. *Wrapper:*
U.S.A./Conn. Shade
This cigar's roasted nut
aroma is attractive. But it
also had a stale spice flavor,
and a very papery finish.
U.S.: $1.65 • U.K.: N/A

NAT SHERMAN VIP **82**
SELECTION BARNUM
GLASS TUBE
Dominican Republic • *Size:*
5½" x 42 *Filler/Binder:* Dom.
Rep. *Wrapper:* U.S.A./
Conn. Shade
A light-bodied cigar with
some slightly sour, acidic
tones, and a vegetal charac-
ter that is balanced on the
finish with a touch of spice.
U.S.: $5.70 • U.K.: N/A

BANCES UNIQUE **81**
Honduras • *Size:* 5½"
x 38 *Filler/Binder:* Honduras,
Nicaragua, Dom. Rep.
Wrapper: Ecuador
A rustic cigar with a tight draw.
Nuts and sweet spices domi-
nate its flavors, but it suffered
from uneven construction.
U.S.: $0.75 • U.K.: N/A

CASA BLANCA **81**
CORONA
Dominican Republic • *Size:*
5½" x 42 *Filler:* Dom. Rep.
Binder: Mexico *Wrapper:*
U.S.A./Conn. Shade
This mild cigar has some
interesting nutty aromas and
spicy flavors, but with an
overall dry wood character
and finish.
U.S.: $1.90 • U.K.: £2.50

FONSECA COSACOS **81**
Cuba • *Size:* 5⅓" x 42
Filler/Binder/Wrapper: Cuba
A very rough, unattractive
wrapper. The cigar is loosely
filled, and has a grassy, sour
flavor.
U.S.: N/A • U.K.: N/A

H. UPMANN PETIT **81**
CORONA
Cuba • *Size:* 5" x 42 *Filler/
Binder/Wrapper:* Cuba
A cigar with a very tight
draw. Although it has some
nice citrus-style flavors, it
ended up lacking complexity.
U.S.: N/A • U.K.: £5.50

CARRINGTON NO. 4 **80**
Dominican Republic •
Size: 5½" x 40 *Filler/Binder:*
Dom. Rep. *Wrapper:*
U.S.A./Conn. Shade
A rough wrapper on this mild
cigar gives a dried out char-
acter to the flavors. It tastes
of paper, and some spice on a
hot finish.
U.S.: $3.40 • U.K.: £3.00

NAT SHERMAN HOST **80**
SELECTION HAMILTON
Honduras • *Size:* 5½" x 42
Filler: Honduras *Binder:*
Mexico *Wrapper:* U.S.A./
Conn. Shade
A cigar with a very mild tobac-
co character. There are flavors
of orange peel and some spice
but with a dry finish.
U.S.: $2.85 • U.K.: N/A

CORTESIA NO. 1 **79**
Honduras • *Size:* 5½"
x 40 *Filler/Binder:* Honduras,
Nicaragua, Dom. Rep.
Wrapper: Ecuador
A loose fill creates a hot
draw, and fills the mouth
with a dry woody, balsa-like
flavor. It also has a metallic
finish.
U.S.: $1.30 • U.K.: N/A

HOYO DE MONTERREY **70**
SABROSAS
Honduras • *Size:* 5" x 40
Filler: Honduras, Nicaragua,
Dom. Rep. *Binder/Wrapper:*
Ecuador
This cigar has very little
tobacco taste, and it is domi-
nated by dry paper and burnt
leaf flavors. The finish has a
sharp bite.
U.S.: $0.70 • U.K.: N/A

PANATELA

*All of the following Panatela
tasting notes appeared in the
Fall 1994 issue of Cigar
Aficionado.*

CHATEAU DE LA **91**
FUENTE PETIT
LANCERO
Dominican Republic • *Size:*
6" x 38 *Filler/Binder/
Wrapper:* Dom. Rep.
A beautiful, reddish-brown
wrapper and an easy, elegant
draw. Complex flavors of
robust spices with undertones
of cedar and leather produce
a rich, full character.
U.S.: $9.50 • U.K.: N/A

MONTECRISTO **91**
ESPECIAL NO. 2
Cuba • *Size:* 6" x 38 *Filler/
Binder/Wrapper:* Cuba
A smooth, mellow smoke
with medium body and fla-
vors of nutmeg. A dried-cit-
rus/spicy character builds as
the cigar burns down.
U.S.: N/A • U.K.: £7.35

COHIBA CORONA ESPECIAL 89
Cuba • *Size:* 6" x 38 *Filler/Binder/Wrapper:* Cuba
A firm, well-made cigar produces well-rounded flavors of spices and nuts and has a solid tobacco character with an earthy, chocolaty finish.
U.S.: N/A • U.K.: £11.35

PUNCH NINFAS 88
Cuba • *Size:* 7" x 38 *Filler/Binder/Wrapper:* Cuba
A cigar with toasty aromas and smooth, full-bodied flavors with touches of cedar and spice.
U.S.: N/A • U.K.: £4.85

V CENTENNIAL NUMERO 1 88
Honduras • *Size:* 7½" x 38 *Filler:* Dom. Rep., Honduras, Nicaragua *Binder:* Nicaragua *Wrapper:* U.S.A./Conn. Shade
A beautiful, oily, brown wrapper delivers a rich spiciness and a medium body with a bit of a tang.
U.S.: $4.50 • U.K.: N/A

AVO XO PRELUDIO 87
Dominican Republic • *Size:* 6" x 40 *Filler/Binder:* Dom. Rep. *Wrapper:* U.S.A./Conn. Shade
A smooth, brown wrapper. It has some cedar-wood flavors and a spicy backbone.
U.S.: $7.00 • U.K.: N/A

BELINDA BELINDAS 87
Honduras • *Size:* 6½" x 36 *Filler:* Dom. Rep., Honduras *Binder:* Honduras *Wrapper:* Ecuador

A dark-brown-wrapped cigar with a rich spiciness that is held back only by a mild, short finish.
U.S.: $1.40 • U.K.: N/A

CUESTA-REY CABINET NO. 2 87
Dominican Republic • *Size:* 7" x 36 *Filler/Binder:* Dom. Rep. *Wrapper:* Cameroon
A dark-brown wrapper produces a nice, mild spiciness with a slightly sweet, cocoa finish.
U.S.: $2.00 • U.K.: N/A

DAVIDOFF NO. 2 87
Dominican Republic • *Size:* 6" x 38 *Filler/Binder:* Dom. Rep. *Wrapper:* U.S.A./Conn. Shade
A rich, brown-red wrapper with a slightly tight draw. Creamy, nutty flavors are backed up by a mild spiciness.
U.S.: $8.25 • U.K.: £9.25

JUAN CLEMENTE PANATELA 87
Dominican Republic • *Size:* 6½" x 34 *Filler/Binder:* Dom. Rep. *Wrapper:* U.S.A./Conn. Shade
A well-made cigar with a full, rich tobacco flavor, a good, spicy character and a sweet, cocoa-bean component.
U.S.: $2.95 • U.K.: £2.75

LA GLORIA CUBANA PANATELA DELUXE 87
U.S.A. • *Size:* 7" x 37 *Filler:* Dom. Rep., Nicaragua *Binder/Wrapper:* Ecuador
This cigar has strong, delicious, spicy notes, but it finishes a bit short and flat.
U.S.: $1.75 • U.K.: N/A

PAUL GARMIRIAN PANATELA 87
Dominican Republic • *Size:* 7½" x 38 *Filler/Binder:* Dom. Rep. *Wrapper:* U.S.A./Conn. Shade
A full-flavored smoke with some spice and toasted-nut notes. It is elegant and well-balanced, but has a tight draw.
U.S.: $6.80 • U.K.: £6.75

TEMPLE HALL NO. 685 87
Jamaica • *Size:* 6⅛" x 34 *Filler:* Dom. Rep., Mexico *Binder:* Mexico *Wrapper:* U.S.A./Conn. Shade
A light-wrappered cigar with a solid draw leads to a smooth, creamy flavor and some spice notes.
U.S.: $4.25 • U.K.: N/A

ASHTON PANATELA 86
Dominican Republic • *Size:* 6" x 36 *Filler/Binder:* Dom. Rep. *Wrapper:* U.S.A./Conn. Shade
A well-made cigar with a good draw. This cigar has a spicy, pepper character and solid tobacco flavors.
U.S.: $2.80 • U.K.: N/A

CUESTA-REY DOMINICAN NO. 3 86
Dominican Republic • *Size:* 7" x 36 *Filler/Binder:* Dom. Rep. *Wrapper:* U.S.A./Conn. Shade
A well-made cigar with a light-brown wrapper. It has mild, spicy flavors and a smooth, flinty aftertaste.
U.S.: $2.25 • U.K.: N/A

DON TOMAS SPECIAL 86
EDITION NO. 400
Honduras • *Size:* 7" x 36
Filler/Binder/Wrapper: Honduras
A smooth-drawing cigar with
a mellow tobacco character
that is backed up by a mild
spiciness.
U.S.: $2.00 • U.K.: N/A

HOYO DE MONTERREY 86
LE HOYO DU DAUPHIN
Cuba • *Size:* 6" x 38 *Filler/
Binder/Wrapper:* Cuba
A spicy, peppery cigar with
an easy elegance and a firm
draw. A beautiful, brown
wrapper.
U.S.: N/A • U.K.: £6.75

LA FINCA FLORA 86
Nicaragua • *Size:* 7"
x 36 *Filler/Binder/Wrapper:*
Nicaragua
A medium-bodied cigar with
some spicy flavors and a well-
balanced presence in the
mouth.
U.S.: $1.30 • U.K.: N/A

MAYA PALMA FINA 86
Honduras • *Size:* 6⅞"
x 36 *Filler/Binder:* Honduras,
Dom. Rep. *Wrapper:*
U.S.A./Conn. Shade
This cigar has a good, solid
draw and mild flavors of
spices and nuts.
U.S.: $1.50 • U.K.: N/A

MONTECRISTO 86
ESPECIAL
Cuba • *Size:* 7½" x 38 *Filler/
Binder/Wrapper:* Cuba
This is a smooth-tasting cigar
with solid notes of pepper
spice and a pleasant cedar-
wood finish.
U.S.: N/A • U.K.: £9.15

ARTURO FUENTE 85
PANATELA FINA
Dominican Republic • *Size:*
7" x 38 *Filler/Binder:* Dom.
Rep. *Wrapper:* Cameroon
A cigar with fine aromas and
a spicy flavor that has notes
of nuts and sweet wood.
U.S.: $1.75 • U.K.: N/A

CARRINGTON NO. 3 85
Dominican Republic •
Size: 7" x 36 *Filler/Binder:*
Dom. Rep. *Wrapper:*
U.S.A./Conn. Shade
An elegant smoke with a
smooth mellowness. A good,
firm draw produces some
mild spice and toast flavors.
U.S.: $3.30 • U.K.: N/A

DON LINO HAVANA 85
RESERVE PANATELA
Honduras • *Size:* 7" x 36
Filler/Binder: Sumatra
Wrapper: U.S.A./Conn.
Shade
The draw is a bit tight. There
is some nutty spiciness, but
the flavors tend toward a
vegetal, dry-paper finish.
U.S.: $3.65 • U.K.: N/A

DON TOMAS PANATELA 85
LARGAS
Honduras • *Size:* 7" x 38
Filler/Binder/Wrapper:
Honduras
This cigar has a tight draw,
but it has nut and spice fla-
vors and solid tobacco core.
U.S.: $1.80 • U.K.: N/A

MACANUDO 85
PORTOFINO
Jamaica • *Size:* 7" x 34
Filler: Dom. Rep., Mex., Jam.

Binder: Mexico *Wrapper:*
U.S.A. Shade
A delicate, light-brown wrapper leads to spicy and peppery flavors and a mild,
cedary aftertaste.
U.S.: $3.20 • U.K.: N/A

ROMEO Y JULIETA 85
SHAKESPEARE
Cuba • *Size:* 6½" x 28
Filler/Binder/Wrapper: Cuba
This cigar has some solid,
spicy notes, but draws a bit
hot from a slightly loose fill.
U.S.: N/A • U.K.: £4.20

ZINO MOUTON-CADET 85
NO. 2
Honduras • *Size:* 6" x 35
Filler/Binder: Honduras
Wrapper: Ecuador
A creamy, light cigar with
some straightforward flavors
although some tasters noted a
vegetal, grassy note.
U.S.: $4.95 • U.K.: N/A

CASA BLANCA 84
PANATELA
Dominican Republic • *Size:*
6" x 36 *Filler:* Dom. Rep.
Binder: Mexico *Wrapper:*
U.S.A./Conn. Shade
A tight draw produces some
hot, vegetal flavors although
some spice comes through on
the finish.
U.S.: $1.25 • U.K.: £2.50

DUNHILL PANATELA 84
Canary Islands • *Size:*
6" x 30 *Filler/Binder:* Canary
Is. *Wrapper:* Cameroon
A mild cigar with smooth,
earthy flavors and a light,
creamy finish.
U.S.: $2.90 • U.K.: N/A

MONTECRUZ 84
TUBULARES SUN
GROWN
Dominican Republic • *Size:*
6⅛" x 36 *Filler/Binder:* Dom.
Rep., Brazil *Wrapper:*
Cameroon
A rustic, rough-looking cigar
with some spice and coffee
flavors, but a flat, dry, balsa-
wood finish.
U.S.: $2.75 • U.K.: N/A

ROMEO Y JULIETA 84
BELVEDERE
Cuba • *Size:* 5½" x 39 *Filler/*
Binder/Wrapper: Cuba
A pleasant cigar with some
woody flavors and spicy
notes. A tight draw.
U.S.: N/A • U.K.: £4.50

THE GRIFFIN'S NO. 84
400
Dominican Republic • *Size:*
6" x 38 *Filler/Binder:* Dom.
Rep. *Wrapper:* U.S.A./
Conn. Shade
A medium-brown wrapper.
Slightly vegetal, but with
some spicy backbone and a
tangy presence in the mouth.
A bit of heat on the finish.
U.S.: $3.95 • Switzerland: 6.60SF

COHIBA LANCERO 83
Cuba • *Size:* 7½" x 38
Filler/Binder/Wrapper: Cuba
This cigar was too tight.
Great tobacco flavors, but
the draw is simply too hard to
smoke.
U.S.: N/A • U.K.: £14.10

DAVIDOFF NO. 1 83
Dominican Republic •
Size: 7½" x 38 *Filler/Binder:*
Dom. Rep. *Wrapper:*
U.S.A./Conn. Shade
This mild, light wrapper
delivers some mild herbal fla-
vors; but there is an unpleas-
ant, short, balsa-wood finish.
U.S.: $9.30 • U.K.: £11.25

DUNHILL FANTINO 83
Dominican Republic •
Size: 7" x 28 *Filler/Binder:*
Dom. Rep. *Wrapper:*
U.S.A./Conn. Shade
This smooth cigar has a
medium-length finish with
some mild, peppery notes.
U.S.: $3.30 • U.K.: £3.60

EL REY DEL MUNDO 83
ELEGANTE
Cuba • *Size:* 6¼" x 28 *Filler/*
Binder/Wrapper: Cuba
A nice, oily, brown wrapper
that shows a solid, spicy-nut
core of flavors, but otherwise
it is a bit bland and one-
dimensional.
U.S.: N/A • U.K.: £4.05

HOYO DE MONTERREY 83
EXCALIBUR NO. 7
Honduras • *Size:* 5" x 43
Filler/Binder: Honduras
Wrapper: U.S.A./Conn.
Shade
A dark, rough wrapper. This
cigar has some burnt spice
flavors and a dryness on the
palate.
U.S.: $2.10 • U.K.: N/A

MACANUDO VINTAGE 83
NO. 7
Jamaica • *Size:* 7½" x 38
Filler: Dom. Rep., Mex., Jam.
Binder: Mexico *Wrapper:*
U.S.A./Conn. Shade
This cigar has a tight draw
and a dry, balsa-wood flavor
that ends up tasting neutral.
U.S.: $7.00 • U.K.: N/A

NAT SHERMAN 83
EXCHANGE SELECTION
MURRAY HILL NO. 7
Dominican Republic • *Size:*
6" x 38 *Filler:* Dom. Rep.,
Mex., Jam. *Binder:* Mexico
Wrapper: U.S.A./Conn.
Shade
This light-yellow-brown cigar
has mild, creamy flavors, but
it is tightly rolled and has a
tough draw.
U.S.: $4.90 • U.K.: N/A

ROYAL JAMAICA TUBE 83
NO. 2
Dominican Republic • *Size:*
6½" x 34 *Filler:* Jamaica
Binder: Java *Wrapper:*
Cameroon
A well-made cigar with a
brown wrapper. A good, spicy
component overlays a simple
tobacco core.
U.S.: $3.00 • U.K.: N/A

BAUZA FLORETE 82
Dominican Republic •
Size: 6⅞" x 35 *Filler:*
Nicaragua, Dom. Rep.
Binder: Mexico *Wrapper:*
Cameroon
An overall tight draw with
some solid spice flavors.
U.S.: $1.55 • U.K.: N/A

DON DIEGO ROYAL PALMA — 82

Dominican Republic • Size: 6⅛" x 36 Filler/Binder: Dom. Rep. Wrapper: U.S.A./ Conn. Shade
A mild, easy smoke that burns a bit hot, but with some smooth, nut and dry, coffee-bean flavors.
U.S.: $2.50 • U.K.: N/A

LICENCIADOS PANATELA LINDAS — 82

Dominican Republic • Size: 7" x 38 Filler: Dom. Rep. Binder: Honduras Wrapper: U.S.A./Conn. Shade
A very tight draw limits this cigar. But the mild, slightly dry finish has hints of herbs and nuts.
U.S.: $1.50 • U.K.: N/A

NAT SHERMAN LANDMARK SELECTION METROPOLE — 82

Dominican Republic • Size: 6" x 34 Filler: Dom. Rep., Hon., Jam., Brazil Binder: Mexico Wrapper: Cameroon
A mellow smoke with some perfumed aromas and mild flavors.
U.S.: $3.90 • U.K.: N/A

PARTAGAS TUBOS — 82

Dominican Republic • Size: 7" x 38 Filler: Dom. Rep., Mex., Jam. Binder: Mexico Wrapper: Cameroon
An unattractive wrapper with a good draw and a medium-bodied tobacco character. A short but spicy finish.
U.S.: $3.30 • U.K.: N/A

PLEIADES ANTARES — 82

Dominican Republic • Size: 5½" x 40 Filler/Binder: Dom. Rep. Wrapper: U.S.A./Conn. Shade
A tight draw on this mild cigar. There are some spicy notes, but it has a flat, menthollike finish.
U.S.: $3.95 • France: 26FF

POR LARRAÑAGA DELICADOS — 82

Dominican Republic • Size: 6½" x 36 Filler/Binder: Dom. Rep. Wrapper: U.S.A./Conn. Shade
An inconsistent cigar. It has some smooth tobacco flavors and light, dry finish.
U.S.: $2.55 • U.K.: N/A

AVO NO. 4 — 81

Dominican Republic • Size: 7" x 38 Filler/Binder: Dom. Rep. Wrapper: U.S.A./Conn. Shade
This cigar appears well-made, but a tough draw leads into a dry, one-dimensional flavor. Some pepper notes, but with a bite.
U.S.: $4.80 • U.K.: N/A

BANCES UNIQUE — 81

Honduras • Size: 5½" x 38 Filler: Nicaragua Binder: Mexico Wrapper: Ecuador
This cigar has a firm, solid draw with a decent spiciness. An unattractive wrapper.
U.S.: $.70 • U.K.: N/A

DUNHILL DOMINICAN SAMANAS — 81

Dominican Republic • Size: 6" x 38 Filler/Binder: Dom.

Rep. Wrapper: U.S.A./Conn. Shade
A yellow-brown wrapper on a light, mild cigar. It has some creamy spice, yet also grassy flavors and aromas.
U.S.: $3.30 • U.K.: £4.45

JOYA DE NICARAGUA NO. 5 — 81

Nicaragua • Size: 5½" x 38 Filler/Binder/Wrapper: Nicaragua
This cigar has a sourness and an overall vegetal character, although some light spice comes through on the finish.
U.S.: $1.50 • U.K.: N/A

TE-AMO TORERO — 81

Mexico • Size: 6⁵⁄₁₆" x 35 Filler/Binder/Wrapper: Mexico
A nice-looking cigar, but with a very tight draw. Some dryness on the palate creates a mild smoothness yet it lacks flavor.
U.S.: $1.80 • U.K.: N/A

EL REY DEL MUNDO TINOS — 80

Honduras • Size: 5½" x 38 Filler: Dom. Rep., Honduras Binder/Wrapper: Honduras
A mild cigar with some vegetal and dry-metallic flavors. Not very well-made. Several tasters noted hard draws.
U.S.: $1.75 • U.K.: N/A

EL RICO HABANO NO. 1 — 80

U.S.A. • Size: 7½" x 38 Filler: Dom. Rep. Binder: Nicaragua Wrapper: Ecuador
A tight draw with a spicy character and a dry, coffee-bean flavor.
U.S.: $2.50 • U.K.: N/A

HOYO DE MONTERREY **80**
DELIGHTS
Honduras • *Size:* 6¼" x 37
Filler/Binder: Honduras
Wrapper: U.S.A./Conn.
Shade
This cigar smokes solidly
with some straightforward,
spice flavors, but with a hot
aftertaste and finish.
U.S.: $.85 • U.K.: N/A

LA AURORA PALMAS **80**
EXTRA
Dominican Republic • *Size:*
6¼" x 35 *Filler:* U.S.A./
Connecticut Broadleaf
Binder: Sumatra *Wrapper:*
U.S.A./Conn. Broadleaf
This rustic cigar has a burnt
taste with some vegetal notes
and very little spice.
U.S.: $1.65 • U.K.: N/A

DON LINO PANATELAS **79**
Honduras • *Size:* 7"
x 36 *Filler/Binder:* Sumatra
Wrapper: U.S.A./Conn.
Shade
A pretty wrapper doesn't
deliver. The cigar has a tough
draw with bitter flavors and a
short, flat finish.
U.S.: $1.75 • U.K.: N/A

DON TOMAS **78**
INTERNATIONAL
SELECTION NO. 4
Honduras • *Size:* 7" x 36
Filler/Binder/Wrapper:
Honduras
A very tight draw with hot,
harsh spices and a camphor
element on the palate.
U.S.: $2.25 • U.K.: N/A

SOSA SANTE FE **78**
Dominican Republic •
Size: 6" x 35 *Filler:* Dom.
Rep., Brazil *Binder:*
Honduras *Wrapper:* Ecuador
Some inconsistency. A mild
cigar with a smooth, medium
body, but a sharp vegetal finish.
U.S.: $1.80 • U.K.: N/A

DON JUAN LINDAS **77**
Nicaragua • *Size:* 5½"
x 38 *Filler/Binder/Wrapper:*
Nicaragua, Mexico*Filler:*
Nicaragua, Mexico *Binder/
Wrapper:* Nicaragua
An underfilled cigar that
burns hot with a bitter, sour
presence in the mouth and
some dry, grassy flavors.
U.S.: $1.10 • U.K.: N/A

H. UPMANN **76**
NATURALES
Dominican Republic • *Size:*
6⅛" x 36 *Filler/Binder:* Dom.
Rep. *Wrapper:* Cameroon
This cigar has a tart charac-
ter; a loose fill produces hot,
dry flavors of paper and balsa.
U.S.: $2.50 • U.K.: N/A

ODD-SIZED

*The following tasting notes
appeared in the March/April
1997 issue of* Cigar Aficionado.

HOYO DE MONTERREY **93**
PARTICULARES
Cuba • *Size:* 9¼" x 47 *Filler/
Binder/Wrapper:* Cuba
A full-bodied smoke. This
cigar has an aroma of roasted
coffee, a smooth easy draw and
rich flavors of coffee beans and
an earthy, spicy core.
U.S.: N/A • U.K.: N/A

MONTECRISTO "A" **91**
Cuba • *Size:* 9¼" x 47
Filler/Binder/Wrapper: Cuba
A great-looking cigar, with
an oily sheen on the wrapper. An excellent draw leads
to a sweet spice, nutmeg flavor with an earthy under-
tone. Starts out with a mild
finish that intensifies. Great
balance.
U.S.: N/A • U.K.: £24.00

PADRON MAGNUM **91**
Nicaragua • *Size:* 9" x 50
Filler/Binder/Wrapper:
Nicaragua
A smooth, well-balanced,
medium-bodied smoke. It has
strong, solid flavors of nuts
and coffee beans. It is a very
well-made cigar.
U.S.: $5.45 • U.K.: N/A

ROMEO Y JULIETA **91**
FABULOSO
Cuba • *Size:* 9¼" x 47 *Filler/
Binder/Wrapper:* Cuba
This is an attractive cigar
with an oily wrapper. It starts
out tight, then loosens, opening up to a complex blend of
sweet spice and cedar wood
flavors on a long finish.
U.S.: N/A • U.K.: £5.60

ARTURO FUENTE DON **90**
CARLOS NO. 3
Dominican Republic • *Size:*
5½" x 44 *Filler/Binder:* Dom.
Rep. *Wrapper:* Cameroon
This cigar has a full-bodied
character. There are hints of
sweet spices, a solid core of
cedar wood and a sweet nutmeg component. A spicy
finish.
U.S.: $6.25 • U.K.: N/A

DIAMOND CROWN   **90**
ROBUSTO NO. 4
Dominican Republic • *Size:*
5½" x 54 *Filler/Binder:* Dom.
Rep. *Wrapper:* U.S.A./
Conn. Shade
A medium-bodied cigar with
an excellent balance of fla-
vors. There is a good tobacco
core, with a perfumed, floral
character and a nutty finish.
U.S.: $9.50 • U.K.: N/A

EL REY DEL MUNDO   **89**
ORIGINALE
Honduras • *Size:* 5⅞" x 45
Filler/Binder: Honduras
Wrapper: Ecuador
A rich tasting cigar with fla-
vors of toasted nuts and
baked cocoa beans. It has a
strong earthy spiciness on the
finish.
U.S.: $4.50 • U.K.: N/A

EVELIO ROBUSTO   **89**
Honduras • *Size:* 4¼"
x 54 *Filler:* Dom. Rep.,
Nicaragua *Binder:*
Nicaragua *Wrapper:*
Ecuador
A medium-bodied cigar with
a lot of spicy flavors. It has a
long finish with hints of
leather and the earth.
U.S.: $4.80 • U.K.: N/A

FONSECA 2-2   **89**
Dominican Republic •
Size: 4¼" x 40 *Filler/Binder:*
Dom. Rep. *Wrapper:*
U.S.A./Conn. Shade
This is a powerful little cigar.
It has good flavors of herbs
and nuts on a long, woody
finish.
U.S.: $2.65 • U.K.: N/A

ASHTON CABINET   **88**
SELECTION NO. 7
Dominican Republic • *Size:*
6¼" x 54 *Filler/Binder:* Dom.
Rep. *Wrapper:* U.S.A./
Conn. Shade
A well-made cigar with solid
flavors of pepper and nuts, and
a nice creamy character. There
are some floral notes, with a bit
of tangy youthfulness.
U.S.: $8.00 • U.K.: N/A

LA GLORIA CUBANA   **88**
GLORIAS EXTRA
Dominican Republic • *Size:*
6¼" x 46 *Filler/Binder:* Dom.
Rep., Nicaragua *Wrapper:*
Ecuador
A spicy, medium-bodied
cigar. It has good coffee bean
flavors on a solid herbal core
and a nice, spicy finish.
U.S.: $3.25 • U.K.: N/A

PUNCH CORONA   **88**
Honduras • *Size:* 6¼"
x 45 *Filler/Binder:* Honduras,
Nicaragua, Dom. Rep.
Wrapper: Ecuador
This is medium-to-full bodied
cigar with a strong sweet spice
character. There are notes of
sweet herbs, leather and dry
cedar with a touch of nuttiness.
U.S.: $2.80 • U.K.: N/A

PUNCH GRAND CRU   **88**
BRITANNIA
Honduras • *Size:* 6¼" x 50
Filler/Binder: Honduras,
Nicaragua, Dom. Rep.
Wrapper: U.S.A./Conn. Shade
This medium-bodied cigar is
filled with solid tobacco fla-
vors, backed with a cedary
tone, and a straightforward
herbalness.
U.S.: $4.55 • U.K.: N/A

ROMEO Y JULIETA   **88**
PRESIDENTE
Dominican Republic • *Size:*
7" x 43 *Filler:* Dom. Rep.,
Brazil *Binder:* U.S.A.
Wrapper: Indonesia
An earthy aroma leads into a
well-balanced, medium bod-
ied cigar. It has flavors of
spices, and a leathery, woody
finish.
U.S.: $3.85 • U.K.: N/A

DIAMOND CROWN   **87**
ROBUSTO NO. 5
Dominican Republic • *Size:*
4½" x 54 *Filler/Binder:* Dom.
Rep. *Wrapper:* U.S.A./
Conn. Shade
A well-made cigar with some
characteristics of youth. But
there is a solid core of cedar
flavors with hints of nuts and
a floral undertone.
U.S.: $8.50 • U.K.: N/A

ORNELAS 250   **87**
Mexico • *Size:* 9½" x 64
Filler/Binder/Wrapper: Mexico
Almost too big to enjoy, but
this cigar has a solid core of
sweet spice and nutty flavors
with a creamy aftertaste.
U.S.: $31.00 • U.K.: N/A

PARTAGAS CULEBRAS   **87**
Cuba • *Size:* 5¼" x 39
Filler/Binder/Wrapper: Cuba
An unusual cigar in the marketplace, the three-cigar
braid. It has a sweet woody
character, and decent construction. It's just odd-
looking.
U.S.: N/A • U.K.: £11.23

PARTAGAS LIMITED **87**
RESERVE REGALE
Dominican Republic • *Size:*
6¼" x 47 *Filler/Binder:*
Mexico, Dom. Rep.
Wrapper: Cameroon
This is a pleasant, medium-
bodied cigar with some hints of
spice and wood on the finish.
U.S.: $14.50 • U.K.: N/A

PARTAGAS LIMITED **87**
RESERVE ROYALE
Dominican Republic • *Size:*
6¼" x 43 *Filler/Binder:*
Mexico, Dom. Rep.
Wrapper: Cameroon
A flavorful, medium bodied
cigar with strong elements of
pepper and other spices. It
finishes with a good spiciness
and a hint of dry wood.
U.S.: $14.00 • U.K.: N/A

PAUL GARMIRIAN **87**
BOMBONE
Dominican Republic • *Size:*
3½" x 43 *Filler/Binder:* Dom.
Rep. *Wrapper:* U.S.A./
Conn. Shade
A well-balanced, small
smoke that has elements of
cream and cedar on the
palate, and a solid tobacco
aftertaste.
U.S.: $5.00 • U.K.: £5.00

ROYAL JAMAICA **87**
DOUBLE CORONA
Dominican Republic • *Size:*
7" x 45 *Filler:* Jamaica
Binder: Cameroon *Wrapper:*
Indonesia
This is a medium-to-full bod-
ied cigar. It has a very sweet
tobacco character with a core
of sweet spice flavors.
U.S.: $4.40 • U.K.: N/A

TE-AMO NEW YORK **87**
LAGUARDIA
Mexico • *Size:* 5" x 54 *Filler/
Binder/Wrapper:* Mexico
A well-made cigar with a
core of spiciness and an oth-
erwise herbal character. It
has some smoked woodiness
on the finish.
U.S.: $2.80 • U.K.: N/A

8-9-8 COLLECTION **86**
MONARCH
Jamaica • *Size:* 6¼" x 45
Filler: Jamaica, Dom. Rep.
Binder: Mexico *Wrapper:*
U.S.A./Conn. Shade
An elegant cigar. It is a mild,
mellow smoke with a creamy,
light spicy character and a
solid woody finish.
U.S.: $8.50 • U.K.: N/A

ARTURO FUENTE **86**
CHATEAU FUENTE
ROYAL SALUTE
Dominican Republic • *Size:*
7⅝" x 54 *Filler/Binder:* Dom.
Rep. *Wrapper:* U.S.A./
Conn. Shade
A well-balanced, medium-
bodied cigar with a creamy,
herbal character and a hint
of woodiness on the finish.
U.S.: $4.45 • U.K.: N/A

BERING BARONS **86**
Honduras • *Size:* 7¼"
x 42 *Filler:* Dom. Rep.,
Mexico, Nicaragua,
Honduras *Binder:* Honduras
Wrapper: Mexico
A cigar with an earthy charac-
ter. There are flavors of sweet
spice and a woody finish.
U.S.: $2.25 • U.K.: N/A

C.A.O. GOLD **86**
CORONA GORDA
Nicaragua • *Size:* 6½" x 50
Filler/Binder: Nicaragua
Wrapper: Ecuador
A cigar with suppleness and a
smooth draw. It has an herbal
character with a few hints of
spice, and a slightly earthy,
rough finish
U.S.: $7.10 • U.K.: N/A

CASA BLANCA **86**
JEROBOAM
Dominican Republic • *Size:*
10" x 66 *Filler:* Dom. Rep.,
Brazil *Binder:* Mexico
Wrapper: U.S.A./Conn. Shade
A huge cigar. But there is a
plenty of flavor packed into it.
This cigar has a creamy char-
acter with some hints of herbs.
U.S.: $3.25 • U.K.: N/A

DIAMOND CROWN **86**
ROBUSTO NO. 1
Dominican Republic • *Size:*
8½" x 54 *Filler/Binder:* Dom.
Rep. *Wrapper:* U.S.A./
Conn. Shade
This is a very well-balanced,
medium-bodied cigar. It has
nutty flavors, with a slight
floral character and a light
peppery finish.
U.S.: $16.50 • U.K.: N/A

GILBERTO OLIVA **86**
VIAJANTE
Nicaragua • *Size:* 6" x 52
Filler/Binder: Dom. Rep.,
Nicaragua *Wrapper:*
Ecuador
A solid, medium-bodied
smoke. It has a creamy char-
acter with some herbal fla-
vors and a peppery note on
the finish.
U.S.: $4.60 • U.K.: N/A

HAVANA CLASSICO 86
MALECON
U.S.A. • *Size:* 9" x 60 *Filler:*
Dom. Rep., Mexico,
Indonesia *Binder/Wrapper:*
Ecuador
A giant. This cigar has a
grassy core with a slight
earthiness, and some nutty
flavors.
U.S.: $17.00 • U.K.: N/A

HOYO DE MONTERREY 86
CHURCHILL
Honduras • *Size:* 6¼" x 45
Filler/Binder: Honduras,
Nicaragua, Dom. Rep.
Wrapper: Ecuador
A cigar with some floral notes
in the aroma. It has some cof-
fee bean and cedar flavors on
the finish, and an overall
mild, herbal character.
U.S.: $2.60 • U.K.: N/A

HOYO DE MONTERREY 86
DEMITASSE
Honduras • *Size:* 4" x 39
Filler/Binder: Honduras,
Nicaragua, Dom. Rep.
Wrapper: Ecuador
This is a small cigar. For its
size, it has some good earthy
flavors, with wood and spice
notes on the finish.
U.S.: $.90 • U.K.: N/A

MONTECRISTO DOUBLE 86
CORONA
Dominican Republic • *Size:*
6¼" x 50 *Filler/Binder:* Dom.
Rep. *Wrapper:* U.S.A./
Conn. Shade
This is a solid, mild-to-medi-
um body cigar. It has a woody
character with some hints of
nuts, and a slightly vegetal
finish.
U.S.: $8.00 • U.K.: N/A

SANCHO PANZA 86
SANCHOS
Cuba • *Size:* 9¼" x 47 *Filler/
Binder/Wrapper:* Cuba
A cigar with very light, mild
characteristics. It has a
cedary note on the palate
with some papery flavors.
U.S.: N/A • U.K.: £5.60

BELINDA CABINET 85
Honduras • *Size:* 5⅝"
x 45 *Filler/Binder:* Honduras
Wrapper: Ecuador
A medium-bodied cigar with
some woody and earthy flavors. Although it shows some
youth, it should improve
with age.
U.S.: $1.65 • U.K.: N/A

BERING CORONADOS 85
Honduras • *Size:* 5⁷⁄₁₆"
x 45 *Filler/Wrapper:* Mexico,
Dom. Rep., Nicaragua,
Honduras *Binder:* Honduras
A mild- to-medium-bodied
cigar. It has a perfumed quali-
ty with light, earthy aromas
and a light spiciness.
U.S.: $1.50 • U.K.: N/A

CANARIO D'ORO 85
SUPREMOS
Dominican Republic • *Size:*
7" x 45 *Filler/Binder/
Wrapper:* Mexico, Dom.
Rep.*Filler:* Mexico, Dom.
Rep. *Binder/Wrapper:*
Mexico
This is a solid, spicy cigar
with an earthy character. It
finishes a little dry. A well-
made smoke.
U.S.: $2.75 • U.K.: N/A

EVELIO ROBUSTO 85
LARGA
Honduras • *Size:* 6" x 54
Filler: Dom. Rep., Nicaragua
Binder: Nicaragua *Wrapper:*
Ecuador
This cigar has evidence of
young tobacco. There are
strong flavors of herbs with
some hints of sweet spice.
Should improve with age.
U.S.: $5.60 • U.K.: N/A

JOSÉ MARTÍ REMEDIO 85
Dominican Republic •
Size: 5½" x 45 *Filler:* Nic.,
Hon., Dom. Rep. *Binder:*
Honduras *Wrapper:* Ecuador
This cigar shows medium-
bodied complexity with a
earthy aroma, but it has a
short finish with a bit of
dryness.
U.S.: $2.25 • U.K.: N/A

NESTOR 747 CABINET 85
SERIES NO. 2
Honduras • *Size:* 4¼" x 54
Filler: Honduras *Binder:*
Nicaragua *Wrapper:*
Ecuador
Although this cigar has a dry
finish, there are some nut
and spice flavors on the
palate. It is a bit young.
U.S.: $4.50 • U.K.: N/A

PARTAGAS ALMIRANTE 85
Dominican Republic •
Size: 6¼" x 47 *Filler/Binder:*
Mexico, Dom. Rep.
Wrapper: Cameroon
This peppery cigar has some
coffee bean flavors, and an
earthy characteristic. It fin-
ishes a little harsh.
U.S.: $4.65 • U.K.: N/A

EL REY DEL MUNDO RECTANGULARE   84

Honduras • *Size:* 5⅝" x 45
Filler/Binder: Honduras
Wrapper: Ecuador
A medium bodied cigar with
hints of dried orange peel,
and a mintiness on top of a
solid tobacco character. It is
young.
U.S.: $2.75 • U.K.: N/A

MONTECRUZ SUN-GROWN INDIVIDUALES   84

Dominican Republic • *Size:*
8" x 46 *Filler/Binder:* Dom.
Rep., Brazil *Wrapper:*
Indonesia
Good balance with a woody,
earthy character and some
sweet, white pepper flavors.
It finishes a little flat.
U.S.: $11.00 • U.K.: N/A

TE-AMO NEW YORK WALL STREET   84

Mexico • *Size:* 6" x 52 *Filler/Binder/Wrapper:* Mexico
A medium-bodied cigar with
a decent balance. It has an
herbal character with some
hints of woodiness.
U.S.: $3.20 • U.K.: N/A

BERING CORONA GRANDE   83

Honduras • *Size:* 6¼" x 46
Filler/Wrapper: Mexico,
Nicaragua, Dom. Rep.,
Honduras *Binder:* Honduras
A medium-bodied cigar that
has some woody flavors and
an overall vegetal character.
U.S.: $1.85 • U.K.: N/A

PETRUS TABACAGE 89 NO. 4   83

Honduras • *Size:* 5⅝" x 38
Filler: Nicaragua *Binder:*
Honduras *Wrapper:* Ecuador
A slightly salty cigar with
some hints of spice on the
palate and a dry finish.
U.S.: $3.00 • U.K.: N/A

CRUZ REAL NO. 28   82

Mexico • *Size:* 8½"
x 54 *Filler/Binder/Wrapper:*
Mexico
A rustic, rough cigar with a
loose fill. It has a vegetal
pungency, and some hints of
wood and spice.
U.S.: $6.25 • U.K.: N/A

EL REY DEL MUNDO CORONA   82

Honduras • *Size:* 5⅝" x 45
Filler/Binder: Honduras
Wrapper: Ecuador
This cigar shows some youth.
it has decent flavors but
overall is a little rough.
U.S.: $2.75 • U.K.: N/A

JOYA DE NICARAGUA NO. 1   82

Nicaragua • *Size:* 6⅝" x 44
Filler/Binder: Nicaragua
Wrapper: Ecuador
A cigar with flat, woody fla-
vors that leave the palate a
bit dry. It is mild and light-
bodied.
U.S.: $3.05 • U.K.: N/A

LAS CABRILLAS BALBOA   82

Honduras • *Size:* 7½" x 54
Filler/Binder: Mexico, Dom.
Rep. *Wrapper:* U.S.A./
Conn. Shade
This is a rustic cigar made
with young tobacco. It has
some spiciness and an overall
herbal character.
U.S.: $2.60 • U.K.: N/A

PRIMO DEL REY CHURCHILL   82

Dominican Republic • *Size:*
6¼" x 48 *Filler/Binder:* Dom.
Rep., U.S.A., Brazil
Wrapper: Indonesia
A cigar with a mild- to-medium-
bodied character. It has herbal
flavors, and it is well-made.
U.S.: $2.60 • U.K.: N/A

ROYAL JAMAICA NO. 1 TUBE   82

Dominican Republic • *Size:*
6" x 45 *Filler:* Jamaica
Binder: Cameroon *Wrapper:*
Indonesia
A cigar with a slightly tight
draw. It is a little rough on
the palate, but it has some
solid tobacco flavors and a
slight earthiness.
U.S.: $4.80 • U.K.: N/A

TE-AMO CEO   82

Mexico • *Size:* 8½" x 52
Filler/Binder/Wrapper: Mexico
A cigar with earthy qualities
and very herb-like flavors. It's
a little rough around the
edges, but with some underlying strength.
U.S.: $4.00 • U.K.: N/A

CALLE OCHO EMBAJADOR — 81

U.S.A. • *Size:* 9" x 60 *Filler:* Honduras, Dom. Rep., Mexico, Nicaragua *Binder/Wrapper:* Ecuador
A simple, very large cigar with straightforward flavors. It has an overall herbal character and a rather flat finish.
U.S.: $17.00 • U.K.: N/A

EL REY DEL MUNDO ROBUSTO ZAVALLA — 81

Honduras • *Size:* 5" x 54 *Filler/Binder:* Honduras *Wrapper:* Ecuador
A cigar with a tight draw. It has some decent medium-bodied herbal flavors, but a flat finish.
U.S.: $3.00 • U.K.: N/A

JOSÉ MARTÍ MACEO — 81

Dominican Republic • *Size:* 6⅞" x 45 *Filler:* Dom. Rep., Brazil *Binder:* Mexico, Sumatra *Wrapper:* U.S.A./Conn. Shade
A rustic cigar. There is an overall creaminess on the palate, but it has a slightly grassy undertone.
U.S.: $3.25 • U.K.: N/A

PLEIADES SATURNE — 81

Dominican Republic • *Size:* 8" x 46 *Filler/Binder:* Dom. Rep. *Wrapper:* U.S.A./Conn. Shade
A cigar with a strong dry herbal character. It is light-bodied and has a dry wood finish.
U.S.: $10.35 • U.K.: N/A

THE GRIFFIN'S NO. 200 — 81

Dominican Republic • *Size:* 7" x 44 *Filler/Binder:* Dom. Rep. *Wrapper:* U.S.A./Conn. Shade
A somewhat harsh cigar with very dry, papery flavors. It has some spice on the finish.
U.S.: $6.20 • U.K.: N/A

BACCARAT NO. 1 — 80

Honduras • *Size:* 7" x 44 *Filler/Binder/Wrapper:* Honduras
This cigar has sweet gum on the wrapper. There are some hints of spice on the palate, but there was some inconsistency in construction, including a loose draw.
U.S.: $2.90 • U.K.: N/A

NAT SHERMAN MORGAN — 80

Dominican Republic • *Size:* 7" x 42 *Filler/Binder:* Dom. Rep. *Wrapper:* U.S.A./Conn. Shade
A simple cigar with a light vegetal character. There is a hint of nuttiness on an otherwise dry finish.
U.S.: $4.80 • U.K.: N/A

ROYAL JAMAICA GOLIATH — 80

Dominican Republic • *Size:* 9" x 64 *Filler:* Jamaica *Binder:* Cameroon *Wrapper:* Indonesia
Lives up to its name. It's got an undertone of damp earthiness, and showed some inconsistency with its tight draw.
U.S.: $9.10 • U.K.: N/A

BERING CASINOS — 79

Honduras • *Size:* 7⅛" x 42 *Filler:* Dom. Rep. Mexico, Nicaragua, Honduras *Binder:* Honduras *Wrapper:* U.S.A./Conn. Shade
This cigar is dominated by dry grassy flavors and a hint of sweet tobacco on the finish. The construction is a little rough.
U.S.: $2.75 • U.K.: N/A

PLEIADES NEPTUNE — 79

Dominican Republic • *Size:* 7½" x 42 *Filler/Binder:* Dom. Rep. *Wrapper:* U.S.A./Conn. Shade
A flat finish and a dry papery character dominate this cigar. It is light-bodied, and there is a hint of a spice on the palate.
U.S.: $9.35 • U.K.: N/A

PUNCH AFTER DINNER — 74

Honduras • *Size:* 7¼" x 45 *Filler/Binder:* Honduras, Nicaragua, Dom. Rep. *Wrapper:* Ecuador
A very rustic cigar. It also had a poor draw. There are some hints of coffee bean and spice on the palate, but it was hard to get past the poor construction.
U.S.: $2.25 • U.K.: N/A

FIGURADO

Most of the following Figurado tasting notes appeared in the Winter 1995/96 issue of Cigar Aficionado. Exceptions are indicated by a date in parentheses at the end of the tasting note.

ROMEO Y JULIETA FABULOSO — 96
Cuba • *Size:* 9" x 47   *Filler/Binder/Wrapper:* Cuba
Superbly crafted, and it burns perfectly. It's rich and teeming with tobacco character, yet the Fabuloso remains elegant and refined. (06/01/93)
U.S.: N/A • U.K.: £15.00

MONTECRISTO "A" — 95
Cuba • *Size:* 9½" x 47
Filler/Binder/Wrapper: Cuba
Wonderfully crafted with a deep-colored, smooth wrapper. It burns perfectly and delivers rich yet mellow coffee and cedar flavors. (06/01/93)
U.S.: N/A • U.K.: £18.00

MONTECRISTO NO. 2 — 94
Cuba • *Size:* 6⅛" x 52
Filler/Binder/Wrapper: Cuba
The benchmark torpedo. It is loaded with rich, complex flavors such as cinnamon, strong full-bodied notes of chocolate and leather, and a long spicy finish.
U.S.: N/A • U.K.: £9.80

DIPLOMATICOS NO. 2 — 92
Cuba • *Size:* 6⅛" x 52
Filler/Binder/Wrapper: Cuba
A well-balanced cigar with a strong earthy characteristic and a complex core of spicy flavors that ends in a long finish.
U.S.: N/A • France: 62FF

FUENTE FUENTE OPUS X NO. 2 — 92
Dominican Republic • *Size:* 6¼" x 52   *Filler/Binder/Wrapper:* Dom. Rep.
A beautiful, oily wrapper. This cigar has an excellent draw and is loaded with spice and nut flavors, with solid notes of cedar. A long earthy finish.
U.S.: $12.00 • U.K.: N/A

PUNCH DIADEMAS EXTRA — 92
Cuba • *Size:* 9" x 47   *Filler/Binder/Wrapper:* Cuba
The Diademas Extra has a beautiful, oily wrapper and is superbly made. It smokes wonderfully and shows loads of spicy, peppery and nutty character yet remains very refined. (06/01/93)
U.S.: N/A • U.K.: N/A

PUROS INDIOS PIRAMIDES NO. 1 — 92
Honduras • *Size:* 7½" x 60
Filler: Brazil, Dom. Rep., Nicaragua *Binder/Wrapper:* Ecuador
A full-flavored cigar loaded with sweet earthy flavors including cocoa and leather, with a coffee bean character on the palate.
U.S.: $6.50 • U.K.: N/A

MONTECRISTO ESPECIAL NO. 1 — 91
Cuba • *Size:* 7½" x 38   *Filler/Binder/Wrapper:* Cuba
A benchmark for this size. It's silky and smooth with cedar, chocolate and spice highlights and a long, flavorful aftertaste. (06/01/93)
U.S.: N/A • U.K.: £9.00

BOLIVAR BELICOSO FINO — 90
Cuba • *Size:* 5½" x 52   *Filler/Binder/Wrapper:* Cuba
A beautiful, small torpedo. This full-bodied smoke has a strong spiciness and a sweet earthy quality with a pleasant tangy finish.
U.S.: N/A • U.K.: £8.25

PUROS INDIOS PIRAMIDES NO. 2 — 90
Honduras • *Size:* 6½" x 46
Filler: Brazil, Dom. Rep., Nicaragua *Binder/Wrapper:* Ecuador
This is a rich-tasting pyramid with lots of spice and nuts on the palate and a long earthy finish. Well made with a smooth draw.
U.S.: $5.50 • U.K.: N/A

ROMEO Y JULIETA BELICOSO — 90
Cuba • *Size:* 5½" x 52   *Filler/Binder/Wrapper:* Cuba
A handsome pyramid with a gray hue. It draws well and is full-bodied with a rich, peppery, spicy character and a long finish. (06/01/93)
U.S.: N/A • U.K.: £7.00

SANTIAGO CABANA TORPEDO — 90
U.S.A. • *Size:* 6¼" x 54
Filler: Dom. Rep., Honduras, Nicaragua *Binder/Wrapper:* Ecuador
A very nice medium-bodied cigar. Nutty flavors, including chestnuts, dominate and there is a pleasant sweet spice character with hints of nutmeg. Medium-length finish.
U.S.: $9.95 • U.K.: N/A

ARTURO FUENTE   **89**
HEMINGWAY
SIGNATURE
Dominican Republic • *Size:*
6" x 46   *Filler/Binder:* Dom.
Rep.   *Wrapper:* Cameroon
A beautiful dark wrapper. A
smooth, rich cigar with an
earthy combination of spice,
pepper and leather flavors
and a cedary finish.
U.S.: $3.85 • U.K.: N/A

ARTURO FUENTE   **89**
HEMINGWAY SHORT
STORY
Dominican Republic • *Size:*
4¼" x 49   *Filler/Binder:* Dom.
Rep.   *Wrapper:* Cameroon
This cigar's unique size makes
blind tasting impossible. It is
packed with flavors of pep-
per, spice and espresso coffee.
U.S.: $2.85 • U.K.: N/A

ASHTON CABINET   **89**
SELECTION NO. 10
Dominican Republic • *Size:*
7½" x 52   *Filler/Binder:* Dom.
Rep.   *Wrapper:* U.S.A./
Conn. Shade
A mild- to medium-bodied
cigar. It has a delicious combination of creaminess and a
cocoa bean flavor with sweetish tobacco flavors. A slightly
dry woody finish.
U.S.: $11.00 • U.K.: N/A

AVO XO FANTASIA   **89**
PYRAMID
Dominican Republic • *Size:*
5½" x 50   *Filler/Binder:* Dom.
Rep.   *Wrapper:* U.S.A./
Conn. Shade
A rich, spicy cigar. It has
earthy flavors of leather and
chocolate but with a smooth

balance. A bit youthful, and
should improve with age.
U.S.: $7.50 • U.K.: N/A

CUBA ALIADOS   **89**
PIRAMIDES NO. 2
Honduras • *Size:* 6½" x 46
Filler/Binder: Honduras, Dom.
Rep.   *Wrapper:* Ecuador
This full-bodied smoke has a
rustic edge. There are well-
balanced flavors of pepper
and spice.
U.S.: $5.00 • U.K.: N/A

H. UPMANN NO. 2   **89**
Cuba • *Size:* 6⅛" x 52
Filler/Binder/Wrapper: Cuba
A full-bodied smoke with fla-
vors of cocoa bean and nut-
meg, and a strong nutty core.
A smooth, peppery finish. It
is a little young.
U.S.: N/A • U.K.: £8.40

ASHTON CABINET   **88**
SELECTION NO. 3
Dominican Republic • *Size:*
6" x 46   *Filler/Binder:* Dom.
Rep.   *Wrapper:* U.S.A./
Conn. Shade
A medium-bodied cigar with
a creamy texture and a solid
core of nutty flavors that lead
into a light spiciness.
U.S.: $7.00 • U.K.: N/A

EL REY DEL MUNDO   **88**
GRANDES DE ESPAÑA
Cuba • *Size:* 7½" x 38   *Filler/
Binder/Wrapper:* Cuba
Extremely well crafted and
easy to draw. Medium-bodied
with rich, nutty, coffee aro-
mas and flavors and a linger-
ing aftertaste. (06/01/93)
U.S.: N/A • U.K.: N/A

EL RICO HABANO   **88**
NO. 1
U.S.A. • *Size:* 7½" x 38
Filler: Dom. Rep., Nicaragua
Binder: Nicaragua   *Wrapper:*
Ecuador
A thin cigar packed with fla-
vor. It burns extremely well
and fills your mouth with
rich, spicy flavors and a soft,
smooth texture. (06/01/93)
U.S.: $1.75 • U.K.: N/A

MACABI BELICOSO   **88**
FINO
U.S.A. • *Size:* 6¼" x 52
Filler: Dom. Rep., Nicaragua
Binder: Mexico   *Wrapper:*
U.S.A./Conn. Shade
A smooth-tasting cigar with
nice flavors of nuts and cin-
namon and a creamy texture.
U.S.: $5.00 • U.K.: N/A

OSCAR NO. 700   **88**
Dominican Republic • *Size:*
7" x 54   *Filler/Binder:* Dom.
Rep.   *Wrapper:* U.S.A.
This cigar has a pleasant
herbal aroma, and offers up
flavors of nuts and spice on
the palate. It finishes with
hints of dry spices.
U.S.: $9.70 • U.K.: N/A

PAUL GARMIRIAN   **88**
BELICOSO
Dominican Republic • *Size:*
6¼" x 52   *Filler/Binder:* Dom.
Rep.   *Wrapper:* U.S.A./
Conn. Shade
A medium-bodied cigar with
rich, spicy flavors. It has a
solid, earthy tobacco backbone
but lacks a bit of intensity.
U.S.: $8.20 • U.K.: £8.10

PAUL GARMIRIAN   88
CELEBRATION
Dominican Republic • *Size:* 9" x 50 *Filler/Binder:* Dom. Rep. *Wrapper:* U.S.A./ Conn. Shade
A flavor-packed smoke that burns extremely well. It has peppery aromas and flavors and a rich finish. (06/01/93)
U.S.: $12.80 • U.K.: £12.50

SOSA FAMILY   88
SELECTION NO. 2
Dominican Republic • *Size:* 6¼" x 54 *Filler/Binder:* Dom. Rep. *Wrapper:* U.S.A./ Conn. Shade
A cigar with strong nut and toast flavors. It has a medium-bodied smoke. A well-made, attractive cigar.
U.S.: $6.00 • U.K.: N/A

TEMPLE HALL   88
BELICOSO
Jamaica • *Size:* 6" x 50 *Filler:* Jamaica, Dom. Rep., Mexico *Binder:* Mexico *Wrapper:* U.S.A./Conn. Shade
A well-balanced, medium-bodied cigar with a light spiciness that smooths out through a creamy and nutty core. A woody finish.
U.S.: $5.75 • U.K.: N/A

ASHTON VINTAGE   87
CABINET NO. 1
Dominican Republic • *Size:* 9" x 52 *Filler/Binder:* Dom. Rep. *Wrapper:* U.S.A./ Conn. Shade
Another big cigar, yet it shows reserve. It's mild and fresh with light coffee, slightly herbal aromas and flavors. (06/01/93)
U.S.: $10.50 • U.K.: N/A

ASHTON VINTAGE   87
CABINET SELECTION NO. 2
Dominican Republic • *Size:* 7" x 47 *Filler/Binder:* Dom. Rep. *Wrapper:* U.S.A./ Conn. Shade
A medium-bodied cigar with a smooth, creamy texture that rounds out to straightforward, nutty flavors with a touch of spice.
U.S.: $9.00 • U.K.: N/A

AVO BELICOSO   87
Dominican Republic • *Size:* 6" x 50 *Filler/Binder:* Dom. Rep. *Wrapper:* U.S.A./ Conn. Shade
This is a mellow cigar with medium-bodied smoke. It has a floral aroma with solid flavors of toasted nuts and a creamy, sweetish character.
U.S.: $7.00 • U.K.: N/A

CARRINGTON NO. 8   87
Dominican Republic • *Size:* 6⅞" x 60 *Filler/Binder:* Dom. Rep. *Wrapper:* U.S.A./ Conn. Shade
A pleasant, mild smoke with a creamy texture and a walnut-like flavor with an earthy finish.
U.S.: $6.00 • U.K.: N/A

COHIBA LANCERO   87
Cuba • *Size:* 7½" x 38 *Filler/Binder/Wrapper:* Cuba
Our tasters found the Lancero too tightly rolled and difficult to draw, but it can be rich and harmonious with a coffee, nutty character. (06/01/93)
U.S.: N/A • U.K.: £13.50

CUBA ALIADOS   87
PIRAMIDES
Honduras • *Size:* 7½" x 60 *Filler/Binder:* Honduras, Dom. Rep. *Wrapper:* Ecuador
There are hints of cocoa bean in this big pyramid. It has solid flavors of toast and roasted nuts.
U.S.: $7.00 • U.K.: N/A

DAVIDOFF SPECIAL   87
"T"
Dominican Republic • *Size:* 6" x 52 *Filler/Binder:* Dom. Rep. *Wrapper:* U.S.A./Conn. Shade
This is a pleasant medium-bodied cigar that has a soft spicy character and a creamy texture, but with a flat finish.
U.S.: $10.30 • U.K.: £11.25

EL REY DEL MUNDO   87
FLOR DE LLANEZA
Honduras • *Size:* 6½" x 54 *Filler/Binder:* Honduras, Dom. Rep *Wrapper:* Ecuador
This is a full-flavored cigar showing good balance and notes of leather with an earthy quality. It has a slightly dry, flat finish.
U.S.: $4.50 • U.K.: N/A

FONSECA   87
TRIANGULARE
Dominican Republic • *Size:* 5½" x 56 *Filler:* Dom. Rep. *Binder:* Mexico *Wrapper:* U.S.A./Conn. Shade
A cigar with a mellow quality and a medium body. It has a dry spiciness and a pleasant, creamy texture with a long finish.
U.S.: $6.25 • U.K.: N/A

**LA GLORIA CUBANA 87
MEDAILLE D'OR NO. 1**
Cuba • *Size:* 7⅛" x 36 *Filler/
Binder/Wrapper:* Cuba
Hard to draw, but it burns
evenly and delivers light coffee
and clove aromas and flavors.
(06/01/93)
U.S.: N/A • U.K.: N/A

**LA GLORIA CUBANA 87
PIRAMIDES**
U.S.A. • *Size:* 7¼" x 56
Filler: Dom. Rep., Nicaragua
Binder/Wrapper: Ecuador
This is a medium-bodied
style for this brand. It has
solid spicy flavors and a
woody finish.
U.S.: $6.00 • U.K.: N/A

**LOS LIBERTADORES 87
FIGURADO**
Dominican Republic • *Size:*
6½" x 52 *Filler/Binder:* Dom.
Rep. *Wrapper:* U.S.A./
Conn. Shade
A well-balanced, medium-
bodied cigar. It has flavors of
sweet nuts and toast with a
light finish.
U.S.: $7.50 • U.K.: N/A

**MACANUDO DUKE OF 87
WINDSOR**
Jamaica • *Size:* 6" x 50
Filler: Jamaica, Dom. Rep.,
Mexico *Binder:* Mexico
Wrapper: U.S.A./Conn.
Shade
This is a mellow cigar with a
mild to medium body. It has
some delicate spice notes on
otherwise woody flavors, and
it has a bit of a tangy finish.
U.S.: $4.75 • U.K.: N/A

MONTECRISTO NO. 2 87
Dominican Republic •
Size: 6" x 50 *Filler/Binder:*
Dom. Rep. *Wrapper:* U.S.A.
A mild- to medium-bodied
cigar with a nice earthy qual-
ity and flavors of spice and
nuts with a light, well-bal-
anced finish.
U.S.: $8.95 • U.K.: N/A

**NAT SHERMAN METRO. 87
SELECTION
METROPOLITAN**
Dominican Republic • *Size:*
7" x 52 *Filler/Binder:* Dom.
Rep. *Wrapper:* U.S.A./
Conn. Shade
A mellow cigar with plenty
of nuttiness on the palate. It
has a slightly balsa-like fin-
ish, but a spiciness compen-
sates for the dryness.
U.S.: $8.25 • U.K.: N/A

**ROMEO Y JULIETA 87
CELESTIAL FINO**
Cuba • *Size:* 5¼" x 46 *Filler/
Binder/Wrapper:* Cuba
It looks a little coarse with a
rough wrapper, but this pyramid
smokes well, with an enticing
rosemary, spicy character and a
smooth texture. (06/01/93)
U.S.: N/A • U.K.: £7.00

**TROYA TORPEDO 87
NO. 81**
Dominican Republic • *Size:*
7" x 54 *Filler/Binder:* Dom.
Rep. *Wrapper:* U.S.A./
Conn. Shade
A well-made medium-bodied
cigar with strong nut and
solid tobacco flavors. It also
has a spicy character with a
ripe finish.
U.S.: $5.00 • U.K.: N/A

**V CENTENNIAL 87
TORPEDO**
Honduras • *Size:* 7" x 54
Filler: Dom. Rep., Nicaragua,
Honduras *Binder:* Mexico
Wrapper: U.S.A./Conn.
Shade
A well-balanced cigar. It has
some spice and coffee flavors.
A solid, medium-bodied
smoke.
U.S.: $6.00 • U.K.: N/A

**ARTURO FUENTE 86
HEMINGWAY CLASSIC**
Dominican Republic • *Size:*
7" x 48 *Filler/Binder:* Dom.
Rep. *Wrapper:* Cameroon
This cigar has a medium
body with a dry spice character. It has a slightly dry finish
with a solid core of tobacco
flavors.
U.S.: $4.75 • U.K.: N/A

**ARTURO FUENTE 86
HEMINGWAY
MASTERPIECE**
Dominican Republic • *Size:*
9¼" x 52 *Filler/Binder:* Dom.
Rep. *Wrapper:* Cameroon
Powerful and rich smoke.
Good draw and full-bodied
with rich coffee taste and
spicy flavors. (06/01/93)
U.S.: $7.00 • U.K.: N/A

AVO PYRAMIDE 86
Dominican Republic •
Size: 7" x 54 *Filler/Binder:*
Dom. Rep. *Wrapper:*
U.S.A./Conn. Shade
This cigar has a sweet spice
quality with hints of leather
and wood. There is a tangi-
ness on the finish.
U.S.: $7.00 • U.K.: N/A

AVO PETIT BELICOSO 86
Dominican Republic • *Size:* 4¾" x 50 *Filler/Binder:* Dom. Rep. *Wrapper:* U.S.A./Conn. Shade
A medium-bodied cigar with some inconsistency; nuts and nutmeg flavors with notes of cocoa beans. A slightly woody finish.
U.S.: $5.60 • U.K.: N/A

C.A.O. 86
TRIANGULARES
Honduras • *Size:* 7" x 54 *Filler:* Nicaragua, Mexico *Binder:* Honduras *Wrapper:* U.S.A./Conn. Shade
A nice, mild cigar. It has a nutty quality with a good toast-like flavor.
U.S.: $6.75 • U.K.: N/A

EL SUBLIMADO 86
TORPEDO
Dominican Republic • *Size:* 7" x 54 *Filler/Binder:* Dom. Rep. *Wrapper:* U.S.A.
This well-made cigar has some floral aromas and a core of nutty flavors.
U.S.: $14.00 • U.K.: N/A

FELIPE GREGORIO 86
BELICOSO
Honduras • *Size:* 6⅛" x 54 *Filler/Binder/Wrapper:* Honduras
A medium-bodied cigar with medium-length finish. There are earthy flavors with a mild spiciness.
U.S.: $7.10 • U.K.: £10.00

LA GLORIA CUBANA 86
TORPEDO NO. 1
U.S.A. • *Size:* 6½" x 54 *Filler:* Dom. Rep., Nicaragua *Binder:* Nicaragua *Wrapper:* Ecuador
This cigar has strong toasty flavors with an earthy leatheryness. But a bit of sourness was noted by several tasters.
U.S.: $5.00 • U.K.: N/A

LOS LIBERTADORES 86
FIGURADO RESERVA
ESPECIAL
Dominican Republic • *Size:* 6½" x 52 *Filler/Binder:* Dom. Rep. *Wrapper:* U.S.A./ Conn. Shade
This is a mild- to medium-bodied cigar that has a creamy nut quality with a light spicy finish.
U.S.: $7.50 • U.K.: N/A

MACANUDO DUKE OF 86
WELLINGTON
Jamaica • *Size:* 8½" x 38 *Filler:* Jam., Mex., Dom. Rep. *Binder:* Mexico *Wrapper:* U.S.A./Conn. Shade
A little difficult to draw, but it has a very good, light coffee taste and a spicy character with a fresh finish. (06/01/93)
U.S.: $4.15 • U.K.: N/A

PAUL GARMIRIAN 86
BELICOSO FINO
Dominican Republic • *Size:* 5½" x 52 *Filler/Binder:* Dom. Rep. *Wrapper:* U.S.A./ Conn. Shade
A cigar with rich spice flavors notes, but with a slightly dry cedary finish.
U.S.: $7.80 • U.K.: £7.75

PETRUS ANTONIUS 86
Honduras • *Size:* 5" x 54 *Filler/Binder:* Honduras, Nicaragua *Wrapper:* Ecuador
A mild- to medium-bodied cigar that has a creamy, salty-nut flavor on the palate and a well-balanced finish.
U.S.: $4.00 • U.K.: £7.00

POR LARRAÑAGA 86
PYRAMID
Dominican Republic • *Size:* 6" x 50 *Filler/Binder:* Dom. Rep. *Wrapper:* U.S.A.
This is a mild- to medium-bodied cigar with a light creaminess and a slightly dry woody finish.
U.S.: $5.95 • U.K.: N/A

SANCHO PANZA 86
BELICOSO
Cuba • *Size:* 5½" x 52 *Filler/ Binder/Wrapper:* Cuba
A well-made cigar that has an herbal aroma and leather and spice flavors, but it finishes a little dry.
U.S.: N/A • U.K.: £8.25

THOMAS HINDS 86
HONDURAN SELECTION
TORPEDO
Honduras • *Size:* 6" x 52 *Filler/Binder:* Honduras *Wrapper:* Ecuador
A very pleasant, medium-bodied cigar with a core of earthy tobacco flavors and a light finish.
U.S.: $3.90 • Canada: $4.45

ASTRAL PERFECCION 85
Honduras • *Size:* 7" x 48
Filler/Binder/Wrapper:
Honduras, Nicaragua*Filler:*
Honduras, Nicaragua
Binder/Wrapper: Honduras
A mild-tasting cigar with
some dry wood/paper notes
that round out into a mild
spiciness and a woody finish.
U.S.: $6.40 • U.K.: N/A

CASA BLANCA 85
JEROBOAM
Dominican Republic • *Size:*
10" x 66 *Filler:* Dom. Rep.,
Brazil *Binder:* Mexico
Wrapper: U.S.A./Conn.
Shade
So large it's a little overwhelm-
ing to smoke. Yet it burns
extremely well and the smoke
is smooth and cool. The
Jeroboam is rich in character.
(06/01/93)
U.S.: $5.00 • U.K.: N/A

DON LINO HAVANA 85
RESERVE TORPEDO
CLASSICO
Honduras • *Size:* 7" x 48
Filler/Binder: Honduras
Wrapper: U.S.A./Conn.
Shade
A mild cigar with a nutty and
creamy texture. It is well-
made with a good draw.
U.S.: $5.25 • U.K.: N/A

EL REY DEL MUNDO 85
FLOR DE LAVONDA
Honduras • *Size:* 6½" x 52
Filler/Binder: Honduras, Dom.
Rep. *Wrapper:* Ecuador
This is a pleasant, mild
smoke. It has light herblike
flavors.
U.S.: $3.25 • U.K.: N/A

HABANA GOLD BLACK 85
LABEL TORPEDO
Honduras • *Size:* 6" x 52
Filler/Binder: Nicaragua,
Honduras *Wrapper:*
Indonesia
A medium-bodied cigar with
nut and spice flavors that end
on a slightly vegetal finish.
U.S.: $5.00 • U.K.: N/A

PUNCH GRAND CRU 85
PRINCE CONSORT
Honduras • *Size:* 8½" x 52
Filler: Nica., Hon., Dom.
Rep. *Binder:* U.S.A./
Connecticut Broadleaf
Wrapper: Ecuador, Honduras
A little inconsistent among
our tasters, but it shows
medium-bodied, earthy, cit-
rusy character and a smooth,
soft texture. (06/01/93)
U.S.: $4.40 • U.K.: N/A

ROMEO Y JULIETA 85
ROMEO
Dominican Republic • *Size:*
6" x 46 *Filler:* Dom. Rep.,
Brazil *Binder:* U.S.A.
Wrapper: Cameroon
Some hints of exotic spices
and coffee bean flavors. It is a
little rustic and rough.
U.S.: $3.25 • U.K.: N/A

ROYAL JAMAICA PARK 85
LANE
Dominican Republic • *Size:*
6" x 47 *Filler:* Jamaica,
Dom. Rep., Indonesia
Binder: Cameroon *Wrapper:*
Indonesia
A good medium-bodied cigar.
It has a pleasant spicy flavor
with a tangy finish.
U.S.: $3.70 • U.K.: N/A

TE-AMO FIGURADO 85
Mexico • *Size:* 6⅝"
x 50 *Filler/Binder/Wrapper:*
Mexico
This cigar has a deep earthiness and a strong pepper
influence in the flavor, but
with a bit of steeliness on the
palate and a dry wood finish.
U.S.: $2.95 • U.K.: N/A

THE GRIFFIN'S DON 85
BERNARDO
Dominican Republic • *Size:*
9" x 46 *Filler/Binder:* Dom.
Rep. *Wrapper:* U.S.A./
Conn. Shade
A large cigar that burns well
and exhibits elegant, spicy
flavors. (06/01/93)
U.S.: $6.60 • U.K.: N/A

HOYO DE MONTERREY 84
CULEBRA
Honduras • *Size:* 6¼" x 35
Filler: Nica., Hon., Dom.
Rep. *Binder:* U.S.A./
Connecticut Broadleaf
Wrapper: Ecuador, Sumatra
Fun and quick to smoke with
an even burn and light, fresh
aromas and flavors. (06/01/93)
U.S.: $3.40 • U.K.: N/A

LAS CABRILLAS 84
MAXIMILIAN
Honduras • *Size:* 7" x 55
Filler: Nicaragua, Mexico
Binder: Mexico *Wrapper:*
U.S.A./Conn. Shade
A cigar with cedary and
slightly baked flavors, includ-
ing roasted cocoa. A firm
draw and a somewhat vegetal
finish.
U.S.: $2.60 • U.K.: N/A

PARTAGAS PRESIDENTE 84
Cuba • *Size:* 6⅛" x 47
Filler/Binder/Wrapper: Cuba
This cigar shows extreme
youth and some inconsisten-
cy in the draw. But it has a
rich, spicy core of flavors.
U.S.: N/A • France: 61FF

**TE-AMO GRAN 84
PYRAMIDE**
Mexico • *Size:* 7¼" x 54
Filler/Binder/Wrapper: Mexico
A rough-looking cigar.
Although it has a slightly veg-
etal, grassy tone, it also deliv-
ers some spicy pepper flavors.
U.S.: $3.10 • U.K.: N/A

**THE GRIFFIN'S 84
NO. 100**
Dominican Republic • *Size:*
7" x 38 *Filler/Binder:* Dom.
Rep. *Wrapper:* U.S.A./
Conn. Shade
Slightly rough and coarse
looking, and it doesn't burn
evenly. But it has pleasant,
creamy, spicy flavors and a
delicate texture. (06/01/93)
U.S.: $4.40 • U.K.: N/A

**VUELTABAJO 84
PYRAMIDE**
Dominican Republic •
Size: 7" x 50 *Filler/Binder:*
Dom. Rep. *Wrapper:*
U.S.A./Conn. Shade
A straightforward cigar. It
has a mild, creamy character
with a touch of pepper. A
slightly metallic aftertaste.
U.S.: $4.25 • U.K.: N/A

ASTRAL FAVORITO 83
Honduras • *Size:* 7"
x 48 *Filler/Binder/Wrapper:*
Honduras, Nicaragua*Filler:*

Honduras, Nicaragua
Binder/Wrapper: Honduras
This cigar has a firm draw, a
sweet woody quality and a
nice nutty flavor, but a slight
bitterness on the finish.
U.S.: $6.40 • U.K.: N/A

AVO NO. 4 83
Dominican Republic •
Size: 7" x 38 *Filler/Binder:*
Dom. Rep. *Wrapper:*
U.S.A./Conn. Shade
Rather rough and unfinished
looking, but it has decent
earthy aromas and flavors.
Some tasters noted an off-
putting grassy character.
(06/01/93)
U.S.: $4.75 • U.K.: N/A

**DON LINO COLORADO 83
TORPEDO**
Honduras • *Size:* 7" x 48
Filler/Binder: Honduras,
Nicaragua *Wrapper:* U.S.A.
An attractive reddish-brown
wrapper. It has some spicy
flavors, but an overall grassy,
herbal quality and a woody
finish.
U.S.: $6.25 • U.K.: N/A

**NAT SHERMAN VIP 83
SELECTION ZIGFIELD
FANCY TAIL**
Dominican Republic • *Size:*
6¼" x 38 *Filler/Binder:* Dom.
Rep. *Wrapper:* U.S.A./
Conn. Shade
An inconsistent draw. It has
some pleasant toast and spice
notes on the palate, but a dry,
woody finish.
U.S.: $5.00 • U.K.: N/A

TE-AMO PIRAMIDE 83
Mexico • *Size:* 6¼" x 50
Filler/Binder/Wrapper: Mexico
A cigar with plenty of pepper
taste. It also has a flinty fla-
vor, and some inconsistency
was noted in the draw.
U.S.: $2.30 • U.K.: N/A

**DAVIDOFF 82
ANIVERSARIO NO.1**
Dominican Republic • *Size:*
7½" x 38 *Filler/Binder:* Dom.
Rep. *Wrapper:* U.S.A./
Conn. Shade
Light-colored and a fairly
rough wrapper. The No. 1 is
very mild with grassy, pep-
pery flavors and a hot finish.
(06/01/93)
U.S.: $16.50 • U.K.: N/A

DAVIDOFF NO. 1 82
Dominican Republic •
Size: 7½" x 38 *Filler/Binder:*
Dom. Rep. *Wrapper:*
U.S.A./Conn. Shade
Very good draw for this sleek
cigar, and it's exceedingly
mild and smooth with a light,
creamy character—almost
verging on bland. (06/01/93)
U.S.: $9.00 • U.K.: N/A

DUNHILL CENTENAS 82
Dominican Republic •
Size: 6" x 50 *Filler/Binder:*
Dom. Rep., Brazil *Wrapper:*
U.S.A./Conn. Shade
This cigar is smooth-tasting
with some vegetal flavors and
a touch of spice on the finish.
U.S.: $8.00 • U.K.: £8.35

ORIENT EXPRESS **82**
EXPRESSO
Honduras • *Size:* 6" x 48
Filler: Nicaragua, Mexico
Binder: Dom. Rep. *Wrapper:*
Ecuador
A somewhat rustic and rough
cigar with a tartness on the
palate. A straightforward
smoke.
U.S.: $10.50 • U.K.: N/A

PADRON 1964 ANN. **82**
SERIES PIRAMIDE
Honduras • *Size:* 6⅞" x 52
Filler/Binder/Wrapper:
Nicaragua
A spicy cigar with plenty of
pepper notes, but it finishes a
little short and harsh.
U.S.: $8.00 • U.K.: N/A

SOSA PIRAMIDES **80**
Dominican Republic •
Size: 7" x 64 *Filler:* Dom.
Rep. *Binder:* Honduras
Wrapper: Ecuador
This is a mild, light cigar
with a loose draw that turns
hot. It finishes with a fairly
dry, burnt wood flavor.
U.S.: $5.00 • U.K.: N/A

MADURO

*Most of the following Maduro
tasting notes appeared in the
Summer 1996 issue of* Cigar
Aficionado. *Exceptions are
indicated by a date in parentheses at the end of the tasting
note.*

EL REY DEL MUNDO **91**
ROBUSTO SUPREMA
Honduras • *Size:* 7" x 54
Filler: Dom. Rep., Honduras
Binder/Wrapper: Honduras

This cigar has an oily, dark-
brown wrapper and a pleasant combination of pungent/
sweet flavors including
chocolate, roasted nuts and
spice. A long finish enhances
this pleasant cigar. (12/01/93)
U.S.: $3.50 • U.K.: N/A

DON LINO CHURCHILL **90**
Honduras • *Size:* 7"
x 50 *Filler/Binder:* Honduras
Wrapper: U.S.A./Conn.
Broadleaf
This cigar has a dark, smooth
wrapper and woody flavors
that turn spicy on the finish.
(12/01/93)
U.S.: $2.55 • U.K.: N/A

LA GLORIA CUBANA **90**
WAVELL
U.S.A. • *Size:* 5" x 50 *Filler:*
Dom. Rep., Nica., Ecu.
Binder: Ecuador *Wrapper:*
U.S.A./Conn. Shade
A very dark, oily wrapper.
This cigar has a rich, creamy
taste that is filled with sweet,
spicy flavors. (12/01/93)
U.S.: $1.65 • U.K.: N/A

BANCES PRESIDENT **89**
Honduras • *Size:* 8½"
x 52 *Filler:* Nicaragua,
Honduras *Binder:* Mexico
Wrapper: Ecuador
A cool, big cigar with medi-
um-bodied smoke and flavors
of chocolate, coffee and
sweet spices. (12/01/93)
U.S.: $2.60 • U.K.: N/A

LA GLORIA CUBANA **89**
CHURCHILL
U.S.A. • *Size:* 7" x 50 *Filler:*
Dom. Rep., Nicaragua

Binder: Ecuador *Wrapper:*
U.S.A./Conn. Broadleaf
A cigar with an oily, black-
brown wrapper that delivers
rich spicy flavors and
smooth, round tobacco tastes
on a short finish. (12/01/93)
U.S.: $1.90 • U.K.: N/A

TRESADO SELECTION **89**
No. 200
Dominican Republic •
Size: 7" x 48 *Filler/Binder:*
Dom. Rep. *Wrapper:*
Indonesia
A very well-made cigar with
a good draw. It has flavors of
cloves and other sweet spices
and a solid tobacco taste on
the finish. (12/01/93)
U.S.: $1.70 • U.K.: N/A

ARTURO FUENTE **88**
CHATEAU FUENTE
Dominican Republic • *Size:*
4½" x 50 *Filler/Binder:* Dom.
Rep. *Wrapper:* U.S.A./
Conn. Sun-Grown
This rich-tasting cigar has a
smoky, coffee character with
a medium body. (12/01/93)
U.S.: $1.75 • U.K.: N/A

CUBA ALIADOS **88**
CHURCHILL DELUXE
Honduras • *Size:* 7¼" x 54
Filler: Dom. Rep. *Binder/
Wrapper:* Ecuador
This cigar has great mouth-feel
with a solid, pepper-and-spice
flavor core and a smooth, mild
finish. (12/01/93)
U.S.: $3.00 • U.K.: N/A

CUESTA-REY CABINET **88**
No. 1884
Dominican Republic • *Size:*
6¼" x 44 *Filler/Binder:* Dom.

Rep. *Wrapper:* U.S.A./
Conn. Broadleaf
This rustic-looking cigar has
strong chocolate flavors and
a smooth earthiness on the
finish. (12/01/93)
U.S.: $1.75 • U.K.: N/A

JOYA DE NICARAGUA 88
MADURO DELUXE
ROBUSTO
Nicaragua • *Size:* 4¾" x 52
Filler/Binder: Nicaragua
Wrapper: Costa Rica
This is a rich-tasting maduro.
It has strong cocoa bean fla-
vors and a long sweet finish.
It is well made with a good
oily wrapper and a good draw.
U.S.: $3.25 • U.K.: N/A

ONYX NO. 650 88
Dominican Republic •
Size: 6" x 50 *Filler:* Dom.
Rep., Mexico *Binder:*
Indonesia *Wrapper:* Mexico
A very well-made maduro. It
starts out slowly, but builds
into a solid core of sweet spicy
flavors. It has strong woody
elements on the finish.
U.S.: $3.05 • U.K.: N/A

PADRON 3000 88
MADURO
Nicaragua • *Size:* 5½" x 52
Filler/Binder/Wrapper:
Nicaragua
A cigar with a strong spicy
character and a range of cof-
fee-style flavors. It is rich-
tasting with an earthy finish.
U.S.: $2.90 • U.K.: N/A

SOSA ROTHSCHILD 88
MADURO
Dominican Republic • *Size:*
4¾" x 49 *Filler:* Dom. Rep.,

Brazil *Binder:* Honduras
Wrapper: U.S.A./Conn.
Broadleaf
This cigar has a sharp, sweet-
ish beginning on the palate
and then shifts to flavors of
pepper and spice. (12/01/93)
U.S.: $1.90 • U.K.: N/A

SOSA CHURCHILL 88
MADURO
Dominican Republic • *Size:*
6¹⁵⁄₁₆" x 49 *Filler:* Dom. Rep.
Binder: Honduras *Wrapper:*
U.S.A./Conn. Broadleaf
This is a light-colored
maduro with an oily wrapper.
It has a combination of
woodiness and sweet herbs,
with a good, earthy finish.
U.S.: $3.30 • U.K.: N/A

ASHTON AGED 87
MADURO NO. 30
Dominican Republic • *Size:*
6¾" x 44 *Filler/Binder:* Dom.
Rep. *Wrapper:* U.S.A./
Conn. Broadleaf
A lush, dark-brown wrapper
helps deliver a dark chocolate aroma with a light, spicy
flavor on the palate and a hint
of sweetness. An enjoyable,
pleasant finish. (12/01/93)
U.S.: $3.75 • U.K.: N/A

BANCES CORONA 87
INMENSA
Honduras • *Size:* 6¾" x 48
Filler: Nicaragua, Honduras
Binder: Mexico *Wrapper:*
Ecuador
A well-made maduro with a
smooth, oily wrapper. It has
rich coffee flavors and a light,
almost-sweet taste on the
palate. (12/01/93)
U.S.: $2.10 • U.K.: N/A

CASA BLANCA 87
DELUXE
Dominican Republic •
Size: 6" x 50 *Filler:* Dom.
Rep. *Binder:* Mexico
Wrapper: U.S.A./Conn.
Shade
A very dark, well-made
maduro. It has flavors of
dried citrus and cocoa and a
long, peppery finish.
U.S.: $2.15 • U.K.: £3.50

CRUZ REAL NO. 14 87
Mexico • *Size:* 7½"
x 50 *Filler/Binder/Wrapper:*
Mexico
This cigar has a sweet, earthy
character. There are flavors
of sweet wood and pepper
with a long finish.
U.S.: $3.60 • U.K.: N/A

CUBA ALIADOS 87
CORONA DELUXE
Honduras • *Size:* 6½" x 45
Filler: Dom. Rep. *Binder/
Wrapper:* Ecuador
A smooth brown-black wrap-
per with good construction. A
nice draw leads to mild spice
flavors and smooth finish.
(12/01/93)
U.S.: $2.40 • U.K.: N/A

CUESTA-REY 87
DOMINICAN NO. 2
Dominican Republic • *Size:*
7½" x 48 *Filler/Binder:* Dom.
Rep. *Wrapper:* U.S.A./
Conn. Broadleaf
There are well-balanced fla-
vors of leather, nuts and hints
of cocoa and coffee beans. It
has an overall sweet tobacco
character and a mild finish.
U.S.: $3.25 • U.K.: N/A

DON DIEGO PRIVADA 87
NO. 1
Dominican Republic • Size:
6⅛" x 43 Filler/Binder: Dom.
Rep., Brazil Wrapper:
U.S.A./Conn. Broadleaf
A medium-bodied smoke with
good maduro characteristics
and a mild chocolate taste on
a smooth finish. (12/01/93)
U.S.: $3.25 • U.K.: N/A

HENRY CLAY BREVAS 87
DE LA CONSERVA
Dominican Republic • Size:
5⅝" x 46 Filler/Binder: Dom.
Rep., Brazil Wrapper:
U.S.A./Conn. Broadleaf
This is a solid maduro with a
shiny wrapper. It has hints of
cocoa bean and a slight burnt
toast character with some
sweet spice on the finish.
U.S.: $2.50 • U.K.: N/A

HOYO DE MONTERREY 87
EXCALIBUR NO. 3
Honduras • Size: 6⅛" x 48
Filler/Binder: Honduras,
Nicaragua, Dom. Rep. Wrapper: U.S.A./Conn. Broadleaf
A well-made maduro with a
good, smooth taste. It has a
mild cocoa bean character
with herbal notes, and a long
spicy finish.
U.S.: $3.60 • U.K.: £3.07

LA FINCA ROBUSTO 87
Nicaragua • Size: 4½"
x 50 Filler/Binder/Wrapper:
Nicaragua
This cigar has an herbal
character. The medium-bodied smoke has flavors of pepper and sweet chocolate, and
a long spicy finish.
U.S.: $1.60 • U.K.: N/A

LICENCIADOS WAVELL 87
MADURO
Honduras • Size: 5" x 50
Filler/Binder: Dom. Rep.
Wrapper: U.S.A./Conn.
Broadleaf
A well-made maduro. It has a
sweet character with a cola
flavor and some dark spices.
A medium-length finish.
U.S.: $2.90 • U.K.: N/A

PADRON EXECUTIVE 87
MADURO
Nicaragua • Size: 7½" x 50
Filler/Binder/Wrapper:
Nicaragua
A big, well-made maduro. It
has excellent balance, good
mild spice flavors and a
woody, leathery finish.
U.S.: $3.75 • U.K.: N/A

PETRUS DOUBLE 87
CORONA
Honduras • Size: 7¾" x 50
Filler/Binder/Wrapper:
Honduras
A well-balanced cigar with a
smooth, cream taste and flavors
of citrus and nuts with a solid
tobacco finish. (12/01/93)
U.S.: $3.85 • U.K.: N/A

PRIMO DEL REY 87
SOBERANO MADURO
Dominican Republic • Size:
7½" x 50 Filler/Binder: Dom.
Rep. Wrapper: U.S.A./
Conn. Broadleaf
A cigar with a good coffee-style aroma. It has a solid
tang on the palate, and flavors of dried orange peel, a
hint of butterscotch and a
short, woody finish.
U.S.: $2.90 • U.K.: N/A

PUNCH PITA MADURO 87
Honduras • Size: 6⅛"
x 50 Filler/Binder: Honduras,
Nicaragua, Dom. Rep.
Wrapper: U.S.A./Conn.
Broadleaf
A smooth-tasting cigar with
solid sweet spice notes and
some deep coffee bean flavors. There are hints of nuts
and wood on the palate. It
has a dry finish.
U.S.: $2.60 • U.K.: N/A

ROMEO Y JULIETA 87
ROTHSCHILD
Dominican Republic • Size:
5" x 50 Filler/Binder: Dom.
Rep. Wrapper: U.S.A./
Conn. Broadleaf
A rich, black-brown cigar
with hints of coffee and spice
on the palate. A sightly
woody finish comes through
the medium-bodied smoke.
(12/01/93)
U.S.: $2.10 • U.K.: N/A

ROYAL JAMAICA 87
CORONA
Dominican Republic • Size:
5½" x 40 Filler: Jamaica
Binder: Indonesia Wrapper:
Mexico
A smooth-tasting cigar with
a rich, black wrapper. It has
rich coffee and roasted nut
flavors, but a mild finish.
(12/01/93)
U.S.: $2.30 • U.K.: N/A

SOSA WAVELL MADURO 87
Dominican Republic •
Size: 4¾" x 50 Filler: Dom.
Rep. Binder: Honduras
Wrapper: U.S.A./Conn.
Broadleaf

A cigar filled with spicy flavors and a complex earthy quality. It smokes well and has a smooth medium-bodied finish.
U.S.: $2.95 • U.K.: N/A

TROYA NO. 18 ROTHSCHILD MADURO 87
Dominican Republic • Size: 4½" x 50 Filler/Binder: Dom. Rep. Wrapper: Ecuador
A light maduro with flavors of coffee beans and a smooth, long finish. It is a medium-bodied smoke.
U.S.: $4.00 • U.K.: N/A

ARTURO FUENTE CORONA IMPERIAL 86
Dominican Republic • Size: 6½" x 46 Filler/Binder: Dom. Rep. Wrapper: U.S.A./Conn. Sun-Grown
A black-wrapped cigar with mild spiciness and nutty, coffee flavors. It finishes a bit hot. (12/01/93)
U.S.: $1.80 • U.K.: N/A

ASHTON AGED MADURO NO. 50 86
Dominican Republic • Size: 7" x 48 Filler/Binder: Dom. Rep. Wrapper: U.S.A./Conn. Broadleaf
A well-balanced cigar. It has some toast and wood flavors with a hint of cocoa bean, and a short, herbal finish.
U.S.: $5.40 • U.K.: N/A

CANARIA D'ORO ROTHSCHILD MADURO 86
Dominican Republic • Size: 4½" x 49 Filler/Wrapper: Mexico, Dominican Republic Binder: U.S.A.

A strong spicy core carries this cigar. The construction is a bit rough and it has dry, woody finish.
U.S.: $2.00 • U.K.: N/A

EL REY DEL MUNDO DELUXE 86
Honduras • Size: 6⅞" x 48 Filler: Dom. Rep., Honduras Binder: Honduras Wrapper: U.S.A./Conn. Broadleaf
A brownish-black-wrappered cigar that delivers spicy and burnt chocolate flavors on the palate. A well-balanced cigar. (12/01/93)
U.S.: $3.50 • U.K.: N/A

EL REY DEL MUNDO FLOR DEL MUNDO MADURO 86
Honduras • Size: 7¼" x 52 Filler/Binder: Honduras, Dom. Rep. Wrapper: Ecuador
A cigar with a shiny maduro wrapper. It has a core of spicy flavors and hints of cocoa bean, toast and leather on the medium-bodied smoke. A short finish.
U.S.: $4.00 • U.K.: N/A

ENCANTO TORO MADURO 86
Honduras • Size: 6" x 50 Filler/Binder/Wrapper: Honduras
A cigar with well-balanced flavors. It has some sweet spice and nut qualities, and a long finish with some spice.
U.S.: $2.75 • U.K.: N/A

F.D. GRAVE CHURCHILL 86
Honduras • Size: 7¼" x 50 Filler: Dom. Rep., Honduras, U.S.A. Binder: U.S.A.

Wrapper: U.S.A./Conn. Broadleaf
A smooth-tasting cigar. It has a creaminess and flavors of pepper, licorice and herbs. A good medium-bodied smoke.
U.S.: $2.50 • U.K.: N/A

FONSECA 5-50 86
Dominican Republic • Size: 5" x 50 Filler: Dom. Rep. Binder: Mexico Wrapper: U.S.A./Conn. Broadleaf
A smooth, almost-black wrapper gives this cigar a range of medium-bodied, spicy flavors that finish with a chocolaty, nutty taste. (12/01/93)
U.S.: $3.00 • U.K.: N/A

HAVANA CLASSICO ROBUSTO 86
U.S.A. • Size: 5" x 50 Filler: Dom. Rep., Mexico, Nicaragua Binder/Wrapper: Ecuador
A medium-bodied cigar with a light woodiness and hints of mild herbs. It has a slightly earthy finish.
U.S.: $5.70 • U.K.: N/A

HOYO DE MONTERREY GOVERNOR MADURO 86
Honduras • Size: 6⅛" x 50 Filler/Binder: Honduras, Nicaragua, Dom. Rep. Wrapper: U.S.A./Conn. Broadleaf
A smooth-tasting cigar with flavors of dried citrus and a spicy cedar-box character. It has a light woody finish.
U.S.: $2.60 • U.K.: N/A

LA UNICA NO. 200   **86**
Dominican Republic •
Size: 7" x 49 *Filler/Binder:*
Dom. Rep. *Wrapper:*
U.S.A./Conn. Broadleaf
A cigar with a sweet flavor
profile. There are hints of
coffee and pepper. It has a
dry, woody finish.
U.S.: $2.70 • U.K.: N/A

MONTESINO   **86**
DIPLOMATICO
Dominican Republic • *Size:*
5½" x 42 *Filler/Binder:* Dom.
Rep. *Wrapper:* U.S.A./
Conn. Sun-Grown
A cigar with sweet flavors
that range from exotic floral
notes to licorice. An interest-
ing smoke. (12/01/93)
U.S.: $1.35 • U.K.: N/A

MONTESINO GRAN   **86**
CORONA
Dominican Republic • *Size:*
6¾" x 48 *Filler/Binder:* Dom.
Rep. *Wrapper:* U.S.A./
Conn. Sun-Grown
This well-made corona draws
well and has burnt sugar and
spicy flavors on the palate
and a short but tangy finish.
(12/01/93)
U.S.: $1.85 • U.K.: N/A

NAT SHERMAN CITY   **86**
DESK TRIBUNE
Dominican Republic • *Size:*
7½" x 50 *Filler/Binder:* Dom.
Rep. *Wrapper:* Mexico
A well-balanced cigar with a
spicy sweetness. There are
hints of earthiness on the
palate and the finish.
U.S.: $4.35 • U.K.: N/A

ORNELAS ROBUSTO   **86**
MADURO
Mexico • *Size:* 4¼" x 49
Filler/Binder/Wrapper: Mexico
A mild- to medium-bodied
cigar with a light spicy char-
acter. There are hints of nut
and cedar-box flavors and it
has a woody finish.
U.S.: $5.50 • U.K.: N/A

PADRON PADRON   **86**
2000 MADURO
Nicaragua • *Size:* 5" x 50
Filler/Binder/Wrapper:
Nicaragua
A rich-tasting maduro with
plenty of spice and hints of
coffee. It has an earthy finish.
U.S.: $2.35 • U.K.: N/A

PADRON CHURCHILL   **86**
MADURO
Nicaragua • *Size:* 6⅞" x 46
Filler/Binder/Wrapper:
Nicaragua
A mild- to medium-bodied
cigar with a combination of
vegetal and herbal elements
that turn into a sweet spici-
ness on the palate and finish.
U.S.: $2.95 • U.K.: N/A

PRIMO DEL REY NO.   **86**
100 MADURO
Dominican Republic • *Size:*
4½" x 50 *Filler/Binder:* Dom.
Rep. *Wrapper:* U.S.A./
Conn. Broadleaf
A rather light-colored
maduro. It has some leathery,
earthy qualities and tart,
spicy flavors with a dry finish.
U.S.: $2.10 • U.K.: N/A

PUNCH CHATEAU M   **86**
Honduras • *Size:* 6¾" x 46
Filler: Nica., Hon., Dom.

Rep. *Binder/Wrapper:*
Ecuador
This rich-looking maduro
delivers spicy flavors with a
sweetish, burnt chocolate finish. A nice, well-rounded
cigar. (12/01/93)
U.S.: $1.80 • U.K.: N/A

PUNCH DOUBLE   **86**
CORONA
Honduras • *Size:* 6¾" x 48
Filler: Nica., Hon., Dom.
Rep. *Binder:* U.S.A./Conn
Broadleaf *Wrapper:* U.S.A./
Conn. Shade
A well-made cigar with a
smooth draw. It has clean
tobacco flavors and hints of
sweet chocolate and spice on
a mild finish. (12/01/93)
U.S.: $2.20 • U.K.: N/A

PUNCH ROTHSCHILD   **86**
MADURO
Honduras • *Size:* 4½" x 50
Filler/Binder: Honduras,
Nicaragua, Dom. Rep.
Wrapper: U.S.A./Conn.
Broadleaf
A cigar with an earthy charac-
ter. There are hints of wood
and coffee beans on the palate.
It has mild pepper flavors.
U.S.: $2.00 • U.K.: N/A

PUROS INDIOS   **86**
CHURCHILL MADURO
Honduras • *Size:* 7¼" x 52
Filler: Nicaragua, Dom. Rep.,
Brazil, Jamaica *Binder/*
Wrapper: Ecuador
This cigar has flavors of nuts
and coffee, with a leathery
aroma. The finish is rather
short, but has a touch of spice.
U.S.: $7.40 • U.K.: N/A

PUROS INDIOS CORONA **86**
GORDA MADURO
Honduras • *Size:* 6" x 52
Filler: Nicaragua, Dom. Rep.,
Brazil, Jamaica *Binder/*
Wrapper: Ecuador
A medium-bodied maduro
cigar with a solid core of pep-
per spice. There are also
fruity and creamy elements
with a good, woody finish.
U.S.: $4.25 • U.K.: N/A

ROYAL JAMAICA **86**
CHURCHILL MADURO
Dominican Republic • *Size:*
8" x 51 *Filler:* Jamaica
Binder: Cameroon *Wrapper:*
Mexico
A good, medium-bodied
cigar. It has a strong, sweet
spiciness, with elements of
coffee and cocoa bean fla-
vors. A spicy finish.
U.S.: $5.40 • U.K.: N/A

TE-AMO MAXIMO **86**
CHURCHILL MADURO
Mexico • *Size:* 7" x 54 *Filler/*
Binder/Wrapper: Mexico
A cigar that starts out slowly
but has some solid notes of
spice, including dry pepper fla-
vors, and a hint of roasted nuts.
U.S.: $3.35 • U.K.: N/A

TEMPLE HALL ESTATES **86**
NO. 450
Dominican Republic • *Size:*
4½" x 49 *Filler:* Mex., Jam.,
Dom. Rep. *Binder:* U.S.A./
Connecticut Shade
Wrapper: Mexico
A dark-black wrapper with a
slightly tough draw. Rich fla-
vors of coffee and nuts.
(12/01/93)
U.S.: $4.50 • U.K.: N/A

ARTURO FUENTE **85**
CHURCHILL
Dominican Republic • *Size:*
7" x 48 *Filler/Binder:* Dom.
Rep. *Wrapper:* U.S.A./
Conn. Sun Grown
This medium-bodied cigar
has a slight sweetness on the
palate and strong flavors of
sweet nuts and spice.
(12/01/93)
U.S.: $2.15 • U.K.: N/A

ASHTON AGED **85**
MADURO NO. 40
Dominican Republic • *Size:*
6" x 50 *Filler/Binder:* Dom.
Rep. *Wrapper:* U.S.A./
Conn. Broadleaf
A cigar with a sweet tobacco
character. There are hints of
cinnamon and a smooth nut-
tiness. The finish is light.
U.S.: $5.00 • U.K.: N/A

C.A.O. CHURCHILL **85**
MADURO
Honduras • *Size:* 8" x 50
Filler: Nicaragua, Mexico
Binder: Honduras *Wrapper:*
U.S.A./Conn. Broadleaf
A fairly mild cigar. It has
some notes of raw nuts and a
woody, mild finish.
U.S.: $7.00 • U.K.: N/A

DON TOMAS **85**
PRESIDENTES
Honduras • *Size:* 7½" x 50
Filler/Binder: Honduras
Wrapper: U.S.A./Conn.
Broadleaf
A good, smooth smoke with
peppery spices and a light
finish. (12/01/93)
U.S.: $2.35 • U.K.: N/A

ENCANTO ROTHCHILD **85**
MADURO
Honduras • *Size:* 4½" x 50
Filler/Binder/Wrapper:
Honduras
A cigar with a perfume-like
character. There are some
sweet, nutty flavors and a
touch of pepper on the finish.
U.S.: $3.00 • U.K.: N/A

FONSECA 10-10 **85**
Dominican Republic •
Size: 6¼" x 49 *Filler:* Dom.
Rep. *Binder:* Mexico
Wrapper: U.S.A./Conn.
Broadleaf
This cigar has an oily, black
wrapper and a light body
with slightly sweet flavors. A
smooth smoke. (12/01/93)
U.S.: $3.50 • U.K.: N/A

HABANA GOLD WHITE **85**
LABEL CHURCHILL
Honduras • *Size:* 7" x 52
Filler/Binder/Wrapper:
Nicaragua
A cigar with a pleasant sweet
herbal character and a cedary
flavor. It has a smooth finish.
U.S.: $5.50 • U.K.: N/A

HOYO DE MONTERREY **85**
EXCALIBUR NO. 2
Honduras • *Size:* 7" x 46
Filler: Hon., Nica., Dom.
Rep. *Binder:* Ecuador
Wrapper: U.S.A./Conn.
Broadleaf
A good, dark wrapper. The
cigar has spicy, roasted coffee
flavors, but some dry wood and
vegetal notes on the finish.
(12/01/93)
U.S.: $2.75 • U.K.: N/A

**HOYO DE MONTERREY 85
EXCALIBUR NO. 1
MADURO**
Honduras • *Size:* 7¼" x 54
Filler/Binder: Honduras,
Nicaragua, Dom. Rep. *Wrapper:* U.S.A./Conn. Broadleaf
A well-made maduro. This
cigar has a hint of nutmeg
and sweet spices, with an
overall toasty character. It
has a mild nutty finish.
U.S.: $3.90 • U.K.: N/A

**HOYO DE MONTERREY 85
SULTAN MADURO**
Honduras • *Size:* 7¼" x 54
Filler/Binder: Honduras,
Nicaragua, Dom. Rep.
Wrapper: U.S.A./Conn.
Broadleaf
A cigar with a well-balanced
flavor of bittersweet chocolate around a nutty core. It
has a light, spicy finish.
U.S.: $3.50 • U.K.: N/A

**HOYO DE MONTERREY 85
ROTHSCHILD MADURO**
Honduras • *Size:* 4½" x 50
Filler/Binder: Honduras,
Nicaragua, Dom. Rep. *Wrapper:* U.S.A./Conn. Broadleaf
This cigar has a sweet spice,
almost ginger-like, flavor.
There are strong notes of
nuts on the finish.
U.S.: $2.00 • U.K.: N/A

**MACANUDO PRINCE 85
PHILIP**
Dominican Republic • *Size:*
7½" x 49 *Filler:* Mex., Jam.,
Dom. Rep. *Binder:* U.S.A./
Connecticut Shade
Wrapper: Mexico
Rough construction hurts
this cigar, but it has peppery

flavors and a slightly spicy
finish. (12/01/93)
U.S.: $3.45 • U.K.: N/A

**NAT SHERMAN CITY 85
DESK DISPATCH**
Dominican Republic • *Size:*
6½" x 46 *Filler/Binder:* Dom.
Rep. *Wrapper:* Mexico
This is a solid maduro cigar
with dark coffee bean and
mild spice flavors. It has a
woody finish.
U.S.: $3.65 • U.K.: N/A

**NAT SHERMAN CITY 85
DESK TELEGRAPH**
Dominican Republic • *Size:*
6" x 50 *Filler/Binder:* Dom.
Rep. *Wrapper:* Mexico
A mild nuttiness dominates
this cigar. It has some light
spice and pepper notes on the
palate and a mild, woody finish.
U.S.: $3.95 • U.K.: N/A

ONYX NO. 642 85
Dominican Republic •
Size: 6" x 42 *Filler:* Dom.
Rep., Mexico *Binder:*
Indonesia *Wrapper:* Mexico
A tight draw limits this
cigar, but it has mild, earthy
flavors with a sweetish taste.
(12/01/93)
U.S.: $1.85 • U.K.: N/A

ONYX NO. 750 85
Dominican Republic •
Size: 7½" x 50 *Filler:* Dom.
Rep., Mexico *Binder:*
Indonesia *Wrapper:* Mexico
A well-constructed cigar,
although a tight draw was
noted. There are complex
flavors of chocolate with an
herbal character and a mild
coffee finish.
U.S.: $3.45 • U.K.: N/A

**ORNELAS CAFETERO 85
GRANDE**
Mexico • *Size:* 6½" x 46
Filler/Binder/Wrapper: Mexico
A mild cigar with well-balanced flavors of nuts and
toast. It has touch of flintiness on the finish.
U.S.: $5.30 • U.K.: N/A

PARTAGAS MADURO 85
Dominican Republic •
Size: 6¼" x 48 *Filler:* Dominican Republic, Mexico *Binder:*
U.S.A. *Wrapper:* Mexico
A mild- to medium-bodied
smoke. It has attractive spiciness and an herbal, woody
finish.
U.S.: $4.15 • U.K.: N/A

PRIMO DEL REY NO. 4 85
Dominican Republic •
Size: 5½" x 42 *Filler:* Dom.
Rep. *Binder:* U.S.A./
Connecticut *Wrapper:*
U.S.A./Conn. Broadleaf
A mild-flavored cigar with
touches of spice and an earthy
finish that make it a straightforward smoke. (12/01/93)
U.S.: $1.25 • U.K.: N/A

**PRIMO DEL REY 85
ALMIRANTE MADURO**
Dominican Republic • *Size:*
6" x 50 *Filler/Binder:* Dom.
Rep. *Wrapper:* U.S.A./
Conn. Broadleaf
A solid maduro with wood
and spice flavors. It has a
slightly papery finish.
U.S.: $2.20 • U.K.: N/A

**PUNCH CHATEAU L 85
MADURO**
Honduras • *Size:* 7¼" x 54
Filler/Binder: Honduras,

160

Nicaragua, Dom. Rep. *Wrapper:* U.S.A./Conn. Broadleaf A cigar with an herbal character. There are hints of buttered toast with a slightly burnt flavor.
U.S.: $3.50 • U.K.: N/A

ROYAL JAMAICA 85 CORONA GRANDE
Dominican Republic • *Size:* 6½" x 42 *Filler:* Jamaica *Binder:* Indonesia *Wrapper:* Mexico
An easy-smoking cigar filled with a solid, rich taste and some sweet flavors. It has a smooth finish. (12/01/93)
U.S.: $2.65 • U.K.: N/A

SANTA CLARA 1830 85 NO. 6
Mexico • *Size:* 6" x 51 *Filler/ Binder/Wrapper:* Mexico
A pleasant, but basic, maduro with a spicy, chocolate flavor and one of the tasting's longest aftertastes. (12/01/93)
U.S.: $1.55 • U.K.: N/A

TE-AMO TORITO 85 MADURO
Mexico • *Size:* 4¼" x 50 *Filler/Binder/Wrapper:* Mexico
A cigar with lots of earthy elements and a sweet spiciness. There is a strong woody character on the finish.
U.S.: $2.05 • U.K.: N/A

V CENTENNIAL 85 ROBUSTO MADURO
Honduras • *Size:* 5" x 50 *Filler:* Dom. Rep., Nicaragua, Honduras *Binder/Wrapper:* Mexico

A medium-bodied cigar with a slightly sweet character. It has mild spice, citrus and wood flavors with a slight saltiness on the finish.
U.S.: $3.75 • U.K.: N/A

ASHTON AGED 84 MADURO NO. 60
Dominican Republic • *Size:* 7½" x 52 *Filler/Binder:* Dom. Rep. *Wrapper:* U.S.A./ Conn. Broadleaf
A big cigar with a medium body and loads of spice on the palate, but it finishes dry and sharp. (12/01/93)
U.S.: $4.50 • U.K.: N/A

BELINDA EXCELLENTE 84
Honduras • *Size:* 6" x 50 *Filler:* Dom. Rep., Honduras *Binder:* Honduras *Wrapper:* Ecuador
A cigar with a strong woody character. There are some light, spicy flavors and a leather note on the finish.
U.S.: $2.00 • U.K.: N/A

C.A.O. ROBUSTO 84 MADURO
Honduras • *Size:* 4½" x 50 *Filler:* Nicaragua, Mexico *Binder:* Honduras *Wrapper:* U.S.A./Conn. Broadleaf
There are some hints of pepper in this cigar. It has a dry woodiness on the palate and some vegetal flavors. It has a woody finish.
U.S.: $4.80 • U.K.: N/A

CABAÑAS CORONA 84
Dominican Republic • *Size:* 5½" x 42 *Filler/Binder:* Dom. Rep. *Wrapper:* Mexico

A tight draw limits this otherwise well-balanced cigar. It has spice and nut flavors and a medium finish. (12/01/93)
U.S.: $1.80 • U.K.: N/A

CABAÑAS EXQUISITO 84 MADURO
Dominican Republic • *Size:* 6½" x 48 *Filler/Binder:* Dom. Rep. *Wrapper:* Mexico
This brownish-black-wrappered cigar has slightly sweet, milk-chocolate flavors and a long finish. (12/01/93)
U.S.: $2.25 • U.K.: N/A

CRUZ REAL NO. 19 84
Mexico • *Size:* 6" x 50 *Filler/Binder/Wrapper:* Mexico
A mild-tasting maduro with an earthy, herbal character. It has some perfume- like flavors and a woody finish.
U.S.: $3.60 • U.K.: N/A

CUESTA-REY CABINET 84 NO. 95
Dominican Republic • *Size:* 6¼" x 42 *Filler/Binder:* Dom. Rep. *Wrapper:* U.S.A./ Conn. Broadleaf
A firmly packed cigar that delivers nut and roasted-coffee flavors and has a slightly sweet finish. (12/01/93)
U.S.: $1.55 • U.K.: N/A

DON LINO 84 ROTHSCHILD MADURO
Honduras • *Size:* 4½" x 50 *Filler/Binder/Wrapper:* Honduras
A cigar with light touches of nuts, herbs and a slight hint of pepper on the finish.
U.S.: $2.40 • U.K.: N/A

DON TOMAS TORO **84**
MADURO
Honduras • *Size:* 5½" x 46
Filler/Binder/Wrapper:
Honduras, Nicaragua *Filler:*
Honduras, Nicaragua
Binder/Wrapper: Honduras
A rough-looking wrapper. It
has a touch of spiciness, and
a woody component with a
semisweet finish that has a
hint of coffee beans in it.
U.S.: $2.75 • U.K.: N/A

FLAMENCO BREVAS A **84**
LA CONSERVA
Dominican Republic • *Size:*
5⁵⁄₁₆" x 42 *Filler/Binder:* Dom.
Rep. *Wrapper:* U.S.A./
Conn. Broadleaf
A medium-bodied cigar that
seems too tightly packed, but
has rich flavors of spice and
pepper. (12/01/93)
U.S.: $1.90 • U.K.: N/A

HABANA GOLD WHITE **84**
LABEL ROBUSTO
Honduras • *Size:* 5" x 50
Filler/Binder/Wrapper:
Nicaragua
A cigar with an overall
woody character. There are
some notes of dried citrus fla-
vors, and sweet herbal notes
with a sweet finish.
U.S.: $4.60 • U.K.: N/A

HENRY CLAY BREVA **84**
FINA MADURO
Dominican Republic • *Size:*
6½" x 48 *Filler/Binder:* Dom.
Rep., Brazil *Wrapper:*
U.S.A./Conn. Broadleaf
A cigar with some hints of
coffee beans, but an overall
herbal character. It has an
earthy finish.
U.S.: $2.35 • U.K.: N/A

JOYA DE NICARAGUA **84**
MADURO DELUXE
PRESIDENTE
Nicaragua • *Size:* 7½" x 50
Filler/Binder: Nicaragua
Wrapper: Costa Rica
This cigar seems quite young.
It has some herbal flavors
and is tangy with a hint of
cocoa beans on the finish.
U.S.: $4.00 • U.K.: N/A

LA UNICA NO. 400 **84**
Dominican Republic •
Size: 4½" x 50 *Filler/Binder:*
Dom. Rep. *Wrapper:*
U.S.A./Conn. Broadleaf
A slightly rough finish. This
cigar has some woodiness on
the palate with a solid citrus
note. It is well-balanced.
U.S.: $2.35 • U.K.: N/A

LAS CABRILLAS **84**
CORTEZ MADURO
Honduras • *Size:* 4¾" x 50
Filler: Nicaragua, Mexico
Binder/Wrapper: Mexico
A mild cigar with some
charred flavors. But it also
has some dry spice and
cedary components on the
palate with a woody finish.
U.S.: $1.45 • U.K.: N/A

LICENCIADOS SUPREME **84**
MADURO NO. 400
Dominican Republic • *Size:*
6" x 50 *Filler/Binder:* Dom.
Rep. *Wrapper:* U.S.A./
Conn. Shade
A mild cigar with flavors of
roasted nuts and a complex
espresso and coffee bean
character. It has an excellent
draw, and burns evenly and
smoothly.
U.S.: $3.10 • U.K.: N/A

ORNELAS CHURCHILL **84**
MADURO
Mexico • *Size:* 7" x 49 *Filler/
Binder/Wrapper:* Mexico
A cigar with a medium-
length finish. It has flavors of
toast and leather with a hint
of cedar wood.
U.S.: $6.30 • U.K.: N/A

PETRUS NO. 2 **84**
Honduras • *Size:* 6¼"
x 44 *Filler/Binder/Wrapper:*
Honduras
A rich-tasting cigar filled
with spice and an attractive,
light, fruity aftertaste.
However, showed inconsis-
tency. (12/01/93)
U.S.: $2.65 • U.K.: N/A

PETRUS TABACAGE 89 **84**
CHURCHILL
Honduras • *Size:* 7" x 50
Filler: Nicaragua *Binder:*
Honduras *Wrapper:* Ecuador
A cigar with flavors of nuts
and a hint of dry citrus. It has
a very dry finish.
U.S.: $4.85 • U.K.: N/A

TE-AMO CHURCHILL **84**
MADURO
Mexico • *Size:* 7½" x 50
Filler/Binder/Wrapper: Mexico
A mild cigar with a mellow,
slightly spicy character. It has
a solid pepper note and a
woody finish.
U.S.: $3.25 • U.K.: N/A

TE-AMO TORO **84**
MADURO
Mexico • *Size:* 6" x 50 *Filler/
Binder/Wrapper:* Mexico
A quite mild cigar with some
hints of cocoa bean and some
vegetal flavors with a dry,
woody finish.
U.S.: $2.65 • U.K.: N/A

TE-AMO SATISFACTION 84
MADURO
Mexico • *Size:* 6" x 46 *Filler/Binder/Wrapper:* Mexico
A cigar with a light, easy taste. It has some spice on the palate and a solid woody finish.
U.S.: $2.35 • U.K.: N/A

THOMAS HINDS 84
NICARAGUAN SELECTION ROBUSTO MADURO
Nicaragua • *Size:* 5" x 50 *Filler/Binder/Wrapper:* Nicaragua
This medium-bodied maduro has very peppery flavors and a ripe, dried-citrus core, but with a dry finish.
U.S.: $4.45 • Canada: $4.95

THOMAS HINDS 84
NICARAGUAN SELECTION CORONA GORDA MADURO
Nicaragua • *Size:* 6" x 50 *Filler/Binder/Wrapper:* Nicaragua
A cigar with a mild spiciness. It has some pepper flavors and a woody finish.
U.S.: $4.75 • Canada: $5.45

TROYA NO. 63 84
CHURCHILL MADURO
Dominican Republic • *Size:* 6⅞" x 46 *Filler/Binder:* Dom. Rep. *Wrapper:* Ecuador
This is a well-balanced cigar with nutty and leathery flavors. It has a woody finish with a hint of earthiness.
U.S.: $5.00 • U.K.: N/A

V CENTENNIAL 84
CHURCHILL MADURO
Honduras • *Size:* 6⅞" x 48 *Filler:* Dom. Rep., Nicaragua, Honduras *Binder/Wrapper:* Mexico
A cigar with a light, sweet perfume-like character and herbal tones. It has some spicy flavors and a soft, dry woody finish.
U.S.: $5.25 • U.K.: N/A

V CENTENNIAL 84
NUMERO 2 MADURO
Honduras • *Size:* 6" x 50 *Filler:* Dom. Rep., Nicaragua, Honduras *Binder/Wrapper:* Mexico
An earthy cigar with hints of dark chocolate and anise. It has a short but sweet finish.
U.S.: $4.50 • U.K.: N/A

ASHTON AGED 83
MADURO NO. 10
Dominican Republic • *Size:* 5" x 50 *Filler/Binder:* Dom. Rep. *Wrapper:* U.S.A./Conn. Broadleaf
This cigar has a spicy core of flavors and a quite dry, woody finish.
U.S.: $4.90 • U.K.: N/A

CASA BLANCA 83
PRESIDENTE
Dominican Republic • *Size:* 7½" x 50 *Filler:* Dom. Rep. *Binder:* Mexico *Wrapper:* U.S.A./Conn. Broadleaf
A well-made maduro. It has a strong woody element on the palate with a hint of herbs and nuts.
U.S.: $2.30 • U.K.: N/A

LICENCIADOS TOROS 83
Dominican Republic • *Size:* 6" x 50 *Filler:* Dom. Rep. *Binder:* Honduras *Wrapper:* U.S.A./Conn. Broadleaf
A rough black wrapper delivers very spicy flavors. Overall it is a good cigar with a light finish. (12/01/93)
U.S.: $1.70 • U.K.: N/A

MACANUDO DUKE 83
OF DEVON
Jamaica • *Size:* 5½" x 42 *Filler:* Mex., Jam., Dom. Rep. *Binder:* U.S.A./Connecticut Shade *Wrapper:* Mexico
A big, well-made cigar that offers mild pepper and toasted nut flavors. (12/01/93)
U.S.: $2.85 • U.K.: N/A

SANTA CLARA 1830 83
NO. 1
Mexico • *Size:* 7" x 51 *Filler/Binder/Wrapper:* Mexico
A rustic, medium-brown wrapper that offers rich, spicy smoke with a cedary, cinnamon note. A slightly hot finish. (12/01/93)
U.S.: $1.85 • U.K.: N/A

TE-AMO PRESIDENTE 83
MADURO
Mexico • *Size:* 7" x 50 *Filler/Binder/Wrapper:* Mexico
A smooth-tasting cigar with a solid woody component, and a mild nuttiness and light spiciness on the finish.
U.S.: $3.10 • U.K.: N/A

THOMAS HINDS NICARAGUAN SELECTION CHURCHILL MADURO — 83

Nicaragua • *Size:* 7" x 49
Filler/Binder/Wrapper:
Nicaragua
An unusual cigar. It has a fresh, herbal aroma that leads into a sweet spice and dried orange peel character. It is mild, with some slightly vegetal flavors.
U.S.: $4.80 • Canada: $5.95

TRESADO SELECTION NO. 500 — 83

Dominican Republic •
Size: 5½" x 42 *Filler/Binder:*
Dom. Rep. *Wrapper:*
Indonesia
This brownish maduro-style cigar has a light, delicate character with a hint of spice on the palate. (12/01/93)
U.S.: $1.20 • U.K.: N/A

TROYA NO. 45 CETRO — 83

Dominican Republic •
Size: 6" x 44 *Filler/Binder:*
Dom. Rep. *Wrapper:*
U.S.A./Conn. Broadleaf
Inconsistent construction hurts this cigar, but some tasters noted floral flavors and a peppery finish.
(12/01/93)
U.S.: $1.45 • U.K.: N/A

CRUZ REAL NO. 24 — 82

Mexico • *Size:* 4½"
x 50 *Filler/Binder/Wrapper:*
Mexico
A cigar with a slightly rough wrapper. It has hints of toast and leather on the palate and a tangy finish.
U.S.: $3.15 • U.K.: N/A

ENCANTO CHURCHILL MADURO — 82

Honduras • *Size:* 6⅞" x 49
Filler/Binder/Wrapper:
Honduras
A mild cigar with an herbal flavor profile. There is a light spiciness on the palate.
U.S.: $3.00 • U.K.: N/A

LAS CABRILLAS BALBOA MADURO — 82

Honduras • *Size:* 7½" x 54
Filler: Nicaragua, Mexico
Binder/Wrapper: Mexico
This cigar has a rough construction. It has some burnt caramel flavors and a soft peppery finish.
U.S.: $2.25 • U.K.: N/A

PETRUS TABACAGE 89 ROTHSCHILD — 81

Honduras • *Size:* 4¼" x 50
Filler: Nicaragua *Binder:*
Honduras *Wrapper:* Ecuador
A cigar with a tangy quality that may denote youth. It has some herbal, woody characteristics and a touch of sweetness on the palate.
U.S.: $3.55 • U.K.: N/A

SANTA ROSA SANCHO PANZA MADURO — 81

Honduras • *Size:* 4½" x 50
Filler/Binder: Honduras *Wrapper:* U.S.A./Conn. Broadleaf
A cigar with unusually ripe fruit flavors. There is an earthy and woody quality to the finish.
U.S.: $3.00 • U.K.: N/A

TE-AMO ROBUSTO MADURO — 81

Mexico • *Size:* 5½" x 54
Filler/Binder/Wrapper: Mexico
This cigar exhibits some spicy characteristics, but with a rather stale, grassy finish.
U.S.: $2.60 • U.K.: N/A

LICENCIADOS NO. 4 — 80

Dominican Republic •
Size: 5¼" x 43 *Filler:* Dom.
Rep. *Binder:* Honduras *Wrapper:* U.S.A./Conn. Broadleaf
Inconsistent construction; delivers chocolate and tobacco flavors even though it has a short, hot aftertaste. (12/01/93)
U.S.: $1.30 • U.K.: N/A

LICENCIADOS PRESIDENTE — 80

Dominican Republic • *Size:*
8" x 50 *Filler:* Dom. Rep.
Binder: Honduras *Wrapper:*
U.S.A./Conn. Broadleaf
A tough cigar that either burns quickly and hot or is too tight to draw. The short finish has a bite. (12/01/93)
U.S.: $1.95 • U.K.: N/A

ORNELAS CAFETERO CHICO MADURO — 79

Mexico • *Size:* 5½" x 46
Filler/Binder/Wrapper: Mexico
This cigar has a tight draw. Some tasters noted stale and burnt-leaf flavors. Overall, it had a dry, balsa-wood character.
U.S.: $4.90 • U.K.: N/A

PETRUS TABACAGE 89 CORONA SUBLIME — 78

Honduras • *Size:* 5½" x 46
Filler: Nicaragua *Binder:*
Honduras *Wrapper:* Ecuador
This cigar was very young with a gummy quality to the wrapper. But it had some solid spice notes, with an overall tangy character.
U.S.: $3.75 • U.K.: N/A

CHAPTER 12

Cigars

Listed by Size *and* Country

RATING	BRAND	SIZE

DOUBLE CORONA

CUBA

96 Hoyo de Monterrey Double Corona 7⅝" x 49

94 Ramon Allones Gigantes 7⅝" x 49

92 Partagas Lusitania 7⅝" x 49

91 Punch Double Corona 7⅝" x 49

DOMINICAN REPUBLIC

93 Fuente Fuente Opus X Double Corona 7⅝" x 49

92 Davidoff Double "R" 7½" x 50

91 Savinelli E.L.R. Churchill 7¼" x 48

90 La Unica No. 100 8½" x 52

89 Primo del Rey Soberano 7½" x 50

89 Romeo y Julieta Vintage No. 5 7½" x 50

88 Oscar Supreme 8" x 48

88 Paul Garmirian Gourmet Double Corona 7⅝" x 50

88 Por Larrañaga Fabuloso 7" x 50

88 Sosa Soberano 7½" x 52

87 Dunhill Peravias 7" x 50

87 Licenciados Presidente 8" x 50

87 Nat Sherman Landmark Selection Dakota 7½" x 49

87 Royal Jamaica Churchill 8" x 51

86 Ashton Aged Maduro No. 60 7½" x 52

86 Bauza Fabuloso 7½" x 50

86 Nat Sherman City Desk Tribune 7½" x 50

86 Partagas No. 10 7½" x 49

85 Ashton Churchill 7½" x 50

85 Cuesta-Rey Dominican No. 2 7¼" x 48

85 El Sublimado Churchill 8" x 50

85 Jose Benito Presidente 7¼" x 50

85 Pleiades Aldebaran 8½" x 50

85 The Griffin's Prestige 8" x 48

84 Avo No. 3 7½" x 52

84 Casa Blanca Presidente 7½" x 50

83 Leon Jimenes No. 1 7½" x 50

83 Romeo y Julieta Churchill 7" x 50

83 Royal Jamaica Giant Corona 7½" x 49

83 Vueltabajo Gigante 8½" x 52

82 Troya Executive No. 72 7¼" x 50

HONDURAS

92 Cuba Aliados Churchill 7¼" x 54

91 Belinda Prime Minister 7½" x 50

89 Hoyo de Monterrey Excalibur No. 1 7¼" x 54

87 El Rey del Mundo Flor del Mundo 7½" x 54

87   Thomas Hinds Honduran Selection Presidente 8½" x 52

86   Don Lino Havana Reserve Churchill 7½" x 50

86   Petrus DC Havana 7¼" x 50

86   Zino Veritas 7" x 50

85   Don Lino Churchill 8" x 50

85   Punch Diademas 7½" x 50

85   Punch Chateau L 7½" x 52

84   Don Lino Colorado Presidente 7½" x 50

83   La Fontana Michelangelo 7½" x 52

83   V Centennial Presidente 8" x 50

79   Baccarat Churchill 7" x 50

JAMAICA

90   Macanudo Vintage Cabinet Selection No. 1 7½" x 49

87   8-9-8 Collection Churchill 7½" x 49

85   Macanudo Prince Philip 7½" x 49

CANARY ISLANDS

69   Peñamil No. 57 7½" x 50

MEXICO

87   Cruz Real Churchill No. 14 7½" x 50

87   Santa Clara 1830 No. 1 7½" x 52

82   Te-Amo Churchill 7½" x 50

NICARAGUA

88   Don Juan Presidente 8½" x 50

88   Joya de Nicaragua Viajante 8½" x 52

85   La Finca Bolivares 7½" x 50

83   Joya de Nicaragua Churchill 6⅞" x 49

U.S.A.

91   La Gloria Cubana Soberanos 8" x 52

88   La Gloria Cubana Churchill 7" x 50

85   La Hoja Selecta Cosiac 7" x 49

80   El Rico Habano Gran Habanero Deluxe 7¼" x 50

CHURCHILL

CUBA

92   Romeo y Julieta Churchill 7" x 47

91   Punch Churchill 7" x 47

90   Bolivar Corona Gigantes 7" x 47

90   Quai d'Orsay Imperiales 7" x 47

89   Cohiba Esplendidos 7" x 47

89   Flor de Caño Diademas 7" x 47

89   Saint Luis Rey Churchill 7" x 47

88   Hoyo de Monterrey Churchill 7" x 47

87   El Rey del Mundo Tainos 7" x 47

DOMINICAN REPUBLIC

89   Arturo Fuente Double Chateau 6¼" x 50

89   Arturo Fuente Churchill 7¼" x 48

89   Montecristo Churchill 7" x 48

89   Montecruz No. 200 Natural Claro 7¼" x 46

89   Partagas No. 10 7½" x 49

88   Diana Silvius Churchill 7" x 50

88   Juan Clemente Churchill 6¼" x 46

88   La Unica No. 200 7" x 49

88   Los Libertadores Mambises 6⅞" x 48

88   Montecruz Sun-Grown No. 200 7¼" x 46

88   Nat Sherman Exchange Selection Oxford No. 5 7" x 49

88   Olor Colossos 7½" x 48

88 Savinelli E.L.R. Churchill 7¼" x 48

88 Sosa Churchill 6¹⁵⁄₁₆ x 49

87 Avo No. 5 6¾" x 46

87 Carrington No. 5 6⅞" x 46

87 Julia Marlowe Monarch 7" x 48

87 Nat Sherman Dakota 7½" x 49

87 Nat Sherman Gotham Selection No. 500 7" x 50

87 Por Larrañaga Fabuloso 7" x 50

86 Avo XO Maestoso 7" x 48

86 Cacique No. 7 6⅞" x 46

86 Cuesta-Rey Cabinet 8-9-8 7" x 49

86 Davidoff Aniversario No. 2 7" x 48

86 Don Diego Monarch 7¼ x 47

86 Dunhill Cabreras 7" x 48

86 Fonseca 10-10 7" x 50

86 José Martí Martí 7¼" x 50

86 Leon Jimenes No. 2 7" x 47

86 Montesino Gran Corona 6¾" x 48

86 Troya No. 63 6⅞" x 46

85 Caballeros Churchill 7" x 50

85 Los Libertadores Reserve Special Churchill 6⅞" x 49

85 Onyx No. 646 6⅝" x 46

85 Ramon Allones Redondos 7½" x 49

85 Romeo y Julieta Vintage No. 4 7" x 48

84 Ashton Prime Minister 7" x 48

84 Ashton Churchill 7½" x 52

84 Bauza Casa Grande 6¾ x 48

84 Credo Magnificat 6⅞" x 46

84 Cuesta-Rey Dominican No. 2 7¼" x 48

84 H. Upmann Monarch 7" x 47

84 Jose Benito Churchill 7" x 50

84 La Aurora Bristol Especial 6⅜" x 48

84 Santa Damiana Cabinet Selection No. 800 7" x 50

83 Primo del Rey Club Seleccion Regals 7" x 50

83 Royal Jamaica Giant Corona 7½" x 49

83 Santa Damiana Seleccion No. 100 6¾" x 48

83 Tresado Seleccion No. 200 7" x 48

83 Vueltabajo Churchill 7" x 48

82 Cubita 2000 7" x 50

82 Paul Garmirian Churchill 7" x 48

82 Primo del Rey Soberano 7½" x 50

81 Pleiades Sirius 6⅞" x 46

81 Primo del Rey Aristocrat 6¾" x 48

HONDURAS

89 Cuba Aliados Valentino No. 1 7" x 47

88 Thomas Hinds Honduran Selection Churchill 7" x 49

87 Punch Gran Cru Monarch 6¾" x 48

87 Santa Rosa Churchill 7" x 49

87 V Centennial Churchill 7" x 48

86 El Rey del Mundo Double Corona 7" x 48

86 La Reserva No. 2 6½" x 48

86 Lempira Churchill 7" x 48

86 Zino Veritas 7" x 50

85 Baccarat Churchill 7" x 50

85 Bances Corona Inmensa 6¾" x 48

85 Camacho Churchill 7" x 48

85 Maya Churchill 6⅞" x 49

85 Punch Chateau L 7¼" x 54

84 Cuba Aliados Churchill Extra 7¼" x 54

84 Habana Gold Black Label Churchill 7½" x 46

84   La Fontana Da Vinci   6⅞" x 48

83   Hoyo de Monterrey Double Corona
      6¼" x 48

83   Las Cabrillas Desoto   6⅞" x 50

82   Hoyo de Monterrey Excalibur
      Banquet   6¼" x 48

82   Hoyo de Monterrey Sultan   7¼" x 54

82   Petrus Churchill   7" x 50

82   Punch Grand Cru Diademas   7¼" x 54

81   Punch Double Corona   6¼" x 48

80   Hoyo de Monterrey Excalibur No. 1
      7¼" x 54

JAMAICA

88   8-9-8 Collection Churchill   7½" x 49

85   Macanudo Vintage No. 1   7½" x 49

84   Temple Hall No. 700   7½" x 49

83   Macanudo Prince Philip   7½" x 49

MEXICO

84   Te-Amo Presidente   7" x 50

79   Ornelas Churchill   7" x 49

78   Santa Clara No. 2   6½" x 48

NICARAGUA

90   Don Juan Churchill   7" x 49

85   Joya de Nicaragua Churchill   6⅞" x 49

U.S.A.

85   El Rico Habano Double Corona
      7" x 47

CORONA GORDA

CUBA

92   Hoyo de Monterrey Epicure No. 1
      5⅜" x 46

91   Romeo y Julieta Exhibicion No. 3
      5⅜" x 46

89   Cohiba Siglo IV   5⅝" x 46

87   Bolivar Corona Extra   5⅜" x 46

87   El Rey del Mundo Gran Coronas
      5⅜" x 46

87   Punch Punch   5⅜" x 46

83   H. Upmann Magnum   5⅜" x 46

DOMINICAN REPUBLIC

91   Fuente Fuente Opus X Fuente
      Fuente   5⅝" x 46

89   El Rico Habano Gran Corona
      5¼" x 46

88   Avo No. 2   6" x 50

88   Olor Paco   6" x 50

88   Sosa Governor   6" x 50

87   Ashton Double Magnum   6" x 50

87   Cuesta-Rey Centennial Collection
      Dominican No. 60   6" x 50

87   Don Leo Robusto   5½" x 50

87   H. Upmann Churchill   5⅝" x 46

87   Nat Sherman Gotham Selection
      No. 711   6" x 50

87   Onyx No. 650   6" x 50

87   Partagas Almirante   6¼" x 47

87   Peterson Toro   6" x 50

87   Romeo y Julieta Vintage No. 2
      6" x 46

87   Royal Jamaica Director   6" x 45

87   Savinelli E.L.R. Double Corona
      6" x 50

86   Arturo Fuente Flor Fina 8-5-8
      6" x 47

86   Cubita No. 700   6" x 50

86   Licenciados Toro   6" x 50

86 **Montecristo Corona Grande** 5¾" x 46

86 **Nat Sherman VIP Selection Carnegie** 6" x 48

86 **Paul Garmirian Connoisseur** 6" x 50

85 **Casa Blanca Deluxe** 6" x 50

85 **Davidoff No. 5000** 5⅝" x 46

85 **Dunhill Condados** 6" x 48

85 **Montecruz Sun-Grown No. 201** 6¼" x 46

85 **Paul Garmirian Epicure** 5½" x 50

85 **Romanticos Leonardo** 6" x 50

84 **Don Diego Grande** 6" x 50

84 **H. Upmann Corsario** 5½" x 50

84 **Macabi Corona Extra** 6" x 50

84 **Tresado Selection No. 300** 6" x 46

83 **Avo XO Intermezzo** 5½" x 50

83 **Cabañas Royale** 5⅝" x 46

83 **Juan Clemente Club Selection No. 1** 6" x 50

83 **Oscar No. 500** 5½" x 50

83 **Primo del Rey Almirante** 6" x 50

83 **Santa Damiana Selection No. 300** 5½" x 46

82 **Canaria d'Oro Inmenso** 5½" x 49

82 **Nat Sherman Exchange Selection Trafalgar No. 4** 6" x 47

82 **Vueltabajo Toro** 6" x 50

81 **Cacique Apache** 6" x 50

81 **Primo del Rey Royal Corona** 6" x 46

80 **Match Play Turnberry** 6" x 50

80 **Nat Sherman Manhattan Selection Sutton** 5½" x 49

80 **Partagas Naturales** 5½" x 50

79 **Carrington No. 7** 6" x 50

78 **Henry Clay Brevas a la Conserva** 5⅝" x 46

HONDURAS

89 **Belinda Cabinet** 5⅝" x 45

89 **Hoyo de Monterrey Excalibur No. 3** 6¼" x 50

89 **Lempira Toro** 6" x 50

88 **Don Lino Havana Reserve Toro** 5½" x 46

88 **El Rey del Mundo Choix Supreme** 6⅛" x 49

88 **Flor de Florez Cabinet Selection Florez Florez** 5¾" x 46

88 **V Centennial Numero 2** 6" x 50

87 **Cuba Aliados No. 4** 5½" x 46

87 **Da Vinci Monalisa** 6" x 50

87 **Don Tomas Special Edition No. 500** 5½" x 46

87 **Hoyo de Monterrey Governor** 6⅛" x 50

87 **Hoyo de Monterrey Corona** 5⅝" x 46

86 **Don Melo Corona Extra** 5½" x 46

86 **Don Tomas Corona** 5½" x 50

86 **Punch Super Rothschild** 5¼" x 50

86 **Puros Indios Corona Gorda** 6" x 50

86 **Santa Rosa Toro** 6" x 50

85 **Bering Hispanos** 6" x 50

85 **C.A.O. Corona Gorda** 6" x 50

85 **Don Asa Corona** 5½" x 50

85 **Don Lino Toro** 5½" x 46

85 **Flor de Florez Corona** 6" x 50

85 **Punch Chateau M** 5¾" x 46

85 **Saint Luis Rey Serie A** 6" x 50

84 **Blair Robusto** 6" x 50

84 **Don Tomas Toro** 5½" x 46

83 **Don Lino Oro Toro** 5½" x 46

83 **El Rey del Mundo Robusto Larga** 6" x 50

83 **Maya Maya** 6" x 50

83 Punch Superior 5½" x 48

82 Petrus Tabacage 89 Corona Sublime 5½" x 46

82 Thomas Hinds Honduran Selection Short Churchill 6" x 50

81 Hoyo de Monterrey Excalibur No. 4 5⅜" x 46

77 Tesoros de Copan Corona 5¼" x 46

JAMAICA

88 Macanudo Hyde Park Cafe 5½" x 49

86 8-9-8 Collection Robusto 5½" x 49

86 Macanudo Vintage Cabinet Selection 1993 5½" x 49

85 Temple Hall No. 550 5½" x 49

84 Macanudo Vintage Cabinet Selection 1993 VIII 5½" x 49

84 Macanudo Crystal Cafe 5½" x 50

CANARY ISLANDS

87 Cara Mia Toro 6" x 50

84 Vargas Reserva Senadores 5½" x 46

83 Don Xavier Corona 5⅜" x 46

MEXICO

86 Te-Amo Toro 6" x 50

82 Te-Amo Satisfaction 6" x 46

80 Cruz Real No. 19 6" x 50

79 Santa Clara No. 6 6" x 50

NICARAGUA

92 Padron 1964 Anniversary Series Exclusivo 5½" x 50

87 Habanica Serie 546 5¼" x 46

85 Habanica Serie 646 6" x 46

85 Thomas Hinds Nicaraguan Selection Short Churchill 6" x 50

84 Joya de Nicaragua Toro 6" x 50

83 Morro Castle Corona Gorda 6" x 50

82 MiCubano No. 650 6" x 50

79 La Finca Joya 6" x 50

78 Torcedor Toro 6" x 50

U.S.A.

89 Flor de Gonzalez Extra Corona 6" x 50

87 La Gloria Cubana Extra 6¼" x 46

85 Havana Classico Robusto Largo 6" x 50

80 Calle Ocho Gordito Largo 6" x 50

LONSDALE

CUBA

95 Cohiba Siglo III 6" x 42

92 Quintero Churchill 6½" x 42

91 Rafael Gonzales Lonsdale 6½" x 42

91 Sancho Panza Molinas 6½" x 42

90 Bolivar Gold Medal 6½" x 42

90 Cohiba Siglo V 6¾" x 43

90 H. Upmann Lonsdale 6½" x 42

90 La Gloria Cubana Medaille d'Or No. 2 6 2/3" x 43

90 Romeo y Julieta Corona Grande 6½" x 42

89 Hoyo de Monterrey Le Hoyo des Dieux 6" x 42

88 Montecristo No. 1 6½" x 42

88 Partagas No. 1 6¾" x 43

88 Partagas 8-9-8 6¾" x 43

88 Saint Luis Rey Lonsdale 6½" x 42

87 Bolivar Inmensa 6¾" x 43

87 El Rey del Mundo Lonsdale 6¾" x 42

DOMINICAN REPUBLIC

90 Troya Cetro 6¼" x 44

89 Davidoff No. 4000 6" x 42

89 Davidoff Gran Cru No. 1 6" x 42

88 Arturo Fuente Reserva No. 1
6½" x 42

88 Arturo Fuente Spanish Lonsdale
6½" x 42

88 Fonseca 8-9-8 6" x 43

88 Partagas No. 1 6¼" x 43

88 Partagas 8-9-8 6⅛" x 44

88 Savinelli E.L.R. No. 3 Lonsdale
6¼" x 43

87 Jose Benito Palma 6" x 43

87 Licenciados Excelente 6¼" x 43

87 Montecristo No. 1 6½" x 44

87 Montesino No. 1 6¼" x 43

87 Partagas Humitube 6¼" x 43

87 Por Larrañaga Cetros 6⅛" x 42

87 Ramon Allones "B" 6½" x 42

87 Sosa No. 1 6½" x 43

86 Ashton 8-9-8 6½" x 44

86 Avo No. 1 6¾" x 42

86 Bauza Medaille D'Oro No. 1
6⅞" x 44

86 Don Diego Lonsdale 6⅝" x 42

86 Primo del Rey Seleccion No. 1
6¹³⁄₁₆ x 42

86 Ramon Allones Crystals 6¼" x 42

86 Romeo y Julieta Vintage No. 1
6" x 43

86 Tresado Seleccion No. 400 6⅝ x 44

86 Troya No. 54 Elegante 7" x 43

85 Arturo Fuente Seleccion Privada
No. 1 6¼" x 44

85 Cuesta-Rey Cabinet No. 95
6¼" x 42

85 Cuesta-Rey Cabinet Selection No.
1884 6¼" x 44

85 Don Vito Capo 6¼" x 44

85 H. Upmann Director Royale
6⅝" x 42

85 Montecruz No. 210 6½" x 42

85 Nat Sherman Gotham Selection
No. 1400 6¼" x 44

85 Primo del Rey Presidente 6¹¹⁄₁₆ x 44

85 Primo del Rey Chavon 6½" x 41

85 Ramon Allones Privada A 7" x 45

85 Sosa Family Selection No. 1
6¼" x 43

84 Casa Blanca Lonsdale 6½" x 42

84 Cuesta-Rey Captiva 6⁵⁄₁₆" x 42

84 Diana Silvius Corona 6½" x 42

84 José Martí Palma 7" x 42

84 Juan Clemente Gran Corona 6" x 42

84 Juan Clemente Club Selection No. 3
7" x 44

84 La Unica No. 300 6¼" x 44

84 Montecruz Sun-Grown No. 210
6½" x 42

84 Nat Sherman Landmark Selection
Algonquin 6¼" x 43

84 Olor Lonsdale 6½" x 42

84 Primo del Rey Seleccion No. 2
6¼" x 42

84 Romeo y Julieta Palma 6" x 43

84 Royal Jamaica Corona Grande
6½" x 42

84 The Griffin's No. 300 6¼" x 44

83 Bauza Jaguar 6½" x 42

83 Canaria d'Oro Lonsdale 6½" x 43

83 Cifuentes Lonsdale 6½" x 42

83 Cubita 8-9-8 6¼" x 43

83 Cuesta-Rey Centennial Collection
Dominican No. 4 6½" x 42

83   Dunhill Diamantes 6⅝" x 42

83   H. Upmann Lonsdale 6⅝" x 42

83   Leon Jimenes No. 3 6½" x 42

83   Montesino Cesar No. 2 6¼" x 44

83   Nat Sherman Exchange Selection Butterfield No. 8 6½" x 42

83   Ramon Allones Trumps 6¼" x 43

82   La Flor Dominicana Alcalde 6½" x 44

82   Primo del Rey Lonsdale 6½" x 42

82   Santa Damiana No. 700 6½" x 42

81   Oscar No. 300 6¼" x 44

80   Nat Sherman Manhattan Selection Gramercy 6¼" x 43

80   Vueltabajo Lonsdale 7" x 43

78   Paul Garmirian Lonsdale 6½" x 42

78   Sosa Lonsdale 6½" x 43

HONDURAS

91   Cuba Aliados Lonsdale 6½" x 42

89   V Centennial Cetro 6½" x 44

88   Don Tomas Supremo 6¼" x 42

87   Bering Plaza 6" x 43

87   Don Lino No. 5 6¼" x 44

87   El Rey del Mundo Lonsdale 7" x 43

87   Padron Palma 6⁷⁄₁₆" x 42

86   Don Melo Corona Gorda 6¼" x 44

86   Encanto Elegante 7" x 44

86   Petrus Tabacage 89 No. 2 6¼" x 44

86   Punch No. 1 6½" x 43

86   Saint Luis Rey Lonsdale 6½" x 44

86   Santa Rosa Cetros 6" x 42

85   Belinda Corona Grande 6¼" x 44

85   C.A.O. Lonsdale 7" x 44

85   Don Asa Cetros No. 2 6½" x 44

85   Don Lino Havana Reserve No. 1 6½" x 44

85   Don Tomas Honduran Special Edition No. 200 6½" x 44

85   Hoyo de Monterrey No. 1 6½" x 43

85   Punch Lonsdale 6½" x 43

85   Thomas Hinds Honduran Selection Supremos 6⅝" x 43

85   Zino Mouton-Cadet No. 1 6½" x 44

84   Astral Lujos 6½" x 44

84   Don Lino No. 1 6½" x 44

84   Don Tomas Corona Grande 6½" x 44

84   F.D. Grave Lonsdale 6¼" x 44

84   Hoyo de Monterrey Ambassador 6¼" x 44

84   Punch Amatista 6¼" x 44

84   Tesoros de Copan Cetros 6¼" x 44

84   Zino Tradition 6¼" x 44

83   Baccarat Luchadores 6" x 43

83   Don Tomas Cetros 6½" x 44

83   Gilberto Oliva Numero 1 6½" x 44

83   Padron 1964 Anniversary Series Superi 6" x 42

83   Padron Ambassdor 6⅞" x 42

83   Santa Rosa Corona 6½" x 44

81   Baccarat No. 1 7" x 44

81   Hoyo de Monterrey Churchill 6¼" x 45

81   Punch Punch 6¼" x 45

79   Las Cabrillas Ponce de Leon 6⅝" x 44

78   Bances Cazadores 6¼" x 43

76   Camacho No. 1 7" x 44

JAMAICA

89   Macanudo Amatista 6¼" x 42

86   8-9-8 Collection Lonsdale 6½" x 42

86   Macanudo Vintage Cabinet No. 2 6⁹⁄₁₆" x 43

85   Macanudo Baron de Rothschild
6½" x 42

82   Temple Hall No. 625 6¼" x 45

CANARY ISLANDS

86   Monte Canario Nuncio 6¼" x 44

86   Monte Canario Imperiales 6½" x 42

84   Cara Mia Lonsdale 6½" x 42

84   Don Xavier Lonsdale 6⅜" x 42

MEXICO

86   Veracruz Reserve Especial 6½" x 42

85   Santa Clara No. 3 6⅜" x 43

85   Te-Amo Meditation 6" x 42

82   Te-Amo Relaxation 6⅜" x 44

81   Te-Amo Celebration 6¹¹⁄₁₆" x 44

80   Te-Amo Park Avenue New York
6⅜" x 42

78   Ornelas Ltd. Cognac 6¼" x 42

78   Ornelas No. 1 6¼" x 44

76   Cruz Real No. 1 6⅜" x 42

69   Ornelas No. 1 Vanilla 6¼" x 44

NICARAGUA

87   Joya de Nicaragua No. 1 6⅜" x 44

87   La Finca Romeo 6½" x 42

87   Thomas Hinds Nicaraguan Selection
Lonsdale 6 2/3" x 43

84   Don Juan Numero Uno 6⅜" x 44

83   Al-Capone Corona Grande 6¼" x 43

U.S.A.

88   La Gloria Cubana Medaille D'Or
No. 1 6¼" x 43

85   Macabi No. 1 6¼" x 44

CORONA

CUBA

91   Bolivar Corona 5½" x 42

91   El Rey del Mundo Corona De Luxe
5½" x 42

91   H. Upmann Corona 5½" x 42

90   Hoyo de Monterrey Le Hoyo du Roi
5½" x 42

89   Punch Corona 5½" x 42

89   Ramon Allones Corona 5½" x 42

89   Romeo y Julieta Corona 5½" x 42

88   Montecristo No. 3 5½" x 42

86   Partagas Corona 5½" x 42

85   Hoyo de Monterrey Corona
5½" x 42

DOMINICAN REPUBLIC

91   Montesino Diplomatico 5½" x 43

89   Casa Blanca Corona 5½" x 42

89   Savinelli Extraordinaire 5½" x 44

88   Credo Anthanor 5¼" x 42

88   Davidoff Gran Cru No. 2 5⅜" x 43

88   Olor Momentos 5½" x 43

87   Arturo Fuente Reserva No. 3
5½" x 44

87   Avo No. 7 6" x 44

87   Carrington No. 2 6" x 42

87   Cuesta-Rey Dominican No. 5
5½" x 43

87   Don Diego Corona Major Tube
5½" x 42

87   Montecristo No. 3 5½" x 44

87   Montecruz Sun-Grown No. 220
5½" x 42

87 Nat Sherman Landmark Selection Hampshire 5½" x 42

87 Nat Sherman Metropolitan Selection Angler 5½" x 43

87 Romeo y Julieta Vintage No. 1 6" x 43

87 Troya No. 27 5½" x 42

86 Ashton Aged Maduro No. 20 5½" x 44

86 Fonseca 8-9-8 6" x 43

86 H. Upmann Corona 5½" x 42

86 Jose Benito Palma 6" x 43

86 Juan Clemente Club Selection No. 4 5¼" x 42

86 Licenciados No. 4 5½" x 42

86 Partagas Sabrosos 5⅞" x 43

86 Partagas No. 2 5⅞" x 44

86 Paul Garmirian Corona 5½" x 42

86 Ramon Allones Privada D 5" x 42

86 Vueltabajo Corona 5¼" x 42

85 Bauza Grecos 5½" x 42

85 Camacho Nacionales 5½" x 44

85 Don Diego Corona 5⅞" x 42

85 Dunhill Valverdes 5½" x 42

85 Dunhill Tabaras 5½" x 42

85 H. Upmann Corona Major Tube 5⅞" x 42

85 La Aurora No. 4 5¼" x 42

85 Leon Jimenes No. 4 5⁵⁄₁₆" x 42

85 Los Libertadores Insurrectos 5½" x 42

85 Montecruz Sun-Grown Tubos 6" x 42

85 Tresado Seleccion No. 500 5½" x 42

84 Ashton Corona 5½" x 44

84 Canaria d'Oro Corona 5½" x 43

84 El Sublimado Corona 6" x 44

84 Henry Clay Brevas 5½" x 42

84 José Martí Corona 5½" x 42

84 Knockando No. 3 5¾" x 41

84 La Unica No. 500 5½" x 42

84 Licenciados Supreme Maduro No. 200 5" x 42

84 Por Larrañaga Nacionales 5½" x 42

84 Primo del Rey No. 4 5½" x 42

84 Sosa Brevas 5½" x 43

83 Caballeros Corona 5¼" x 43

83 Nat Sherman City Desk Gazette 6" x 42

83 Onyx No. 642 6" x 42

83 Romeo y Julieta Corona 5½" x 44

82 Peterson Corona 5¼" x 43

81 Pleiades Orion 5¼" x 42

HONDURAS

90 Puros Indios No. 4 Especial 5½" x 44

89 José Martí 1868 Corona 5⅜" x 45

88 Hoyo de Monterrey No. 55 5¼" x 43

88 Lempira Corona 5½" x 42

88 Padron 1964 Anniversary Series Corona 6" x 42

88 Punch Cafe Royal 5⅜" x 44

87 Belinda Breva Conserva 5½" x 43

87 Bering Corona Royale 6" x 41

87 C.A.O. Corona 6" x 42

87 Don Lino Petit Cetro 5½" x 42

87 Don Tomas Matador 5½" x 42

87 Hoyo de Monterrey Cafe Royal 5⅜" x 43

86 Bances Brevas 5½" x 43

86 Felipe Gregorio Sereno 5¼" x 42

86 Habana Gold Black Label Corona 6" x 44

86 Hoyo de Monterrey Super Hoyo 5½" x 44

86 Santa Rosa No. 4 5½" x 42

86 Thomas Hinds Honduran Selection Corona 5½" x 42

86 Zino Mouton-Cadet No. 1 6½" x 44

85 Bering Imperial 5¼" x 42

85 Don Melo Petit Corona 5½" x 42

85 Hoyo de Monterrey Excalibur No. 5 6¼" x 43

85 Maya Petit Corona 5½" x 42

84 El Rey del Mundo Habana Club 5½" x 42

84 Las Cabrillas Magellan 6" x 42

84 Punch No. 75 5½" x 43

83 Punch Royal Coronation 5¼" x 44

83 V Centennial Corona 5½" x 42

83 Zino Diamonds 5½" x 40

81 Baccarat Petit Corona 5½" x 42

JAMAICA

87 Macanudo Vintage No. 3 5⅞" x 43

86 Macanudo Duke of Devon 5½" x 42

85 Macanudo Hampton Court 5¼" x 42

83 8-9-8 Collection Corona 5½" x 42

CANARY ISLANDS

78 La Regenta No. 3 5⅞" x 42

MEXICO

87 Santa Clara No. 5 6" x 43

86 Cruz Real No. 2 6" x 42

80 Te-Amo Meditation 6" x 42

NICARAGUA

91 La Finca Corona 5½" x 42

86 Padron Londres 5½" x 42

84 MiCubano No. 542 5" x 42

84 Thomas Hinds Nicaraguan Selection Corona 5½" x 42

83 Joya de Nicaragua No. 6 6" x 42

80 Don Juan Cetro 6" x 43

U.S.A.

88 La Gloria Cubana Glorias 5½" x 43

86 Macabi Media Corona 5½" x 43

85 El Rico Habano Corona 5½" x 42

83 La Hoja Selecta Cetros de Oro 5¼" x 43

ROBUSTO

CUBA

95 Bolivar Royal Coronas 5" x 50

94 Hoyo de Monterrey Epicure No. 2 5" x 50

93 Flor de Caño Short Churchill 5" x 50

92 Cohiba Robusto 5" x 50

90 Ramon Allones Specially Selected 5" x 50

89 Romeo y Julieta Exhibicion No. 4 5" x 48

88 Partagas Series D No. 4 5" x 50

DOMINICAN REPUBLIC

90 Arturo Fuente Opus x Robusto 5¼" x 50

89 Arturo Fuente Don Carlos Robusto 5" x 50

89 Fonseca 5-50 5" x 50

88 Ashton Magnum 5" x 50

88 Canaria d'Oro Rothschild 4½" x 50

88 Dunhill Altamira 5" x 48

88 Licenciados Wavell 5" x 50

88 Por Larrañaga Robusto 5" x 50

87 Avo XO Intermezzo 5½" x 50

87 Davidoff Special "R" 4⅞" x 50

87 Pleiades Pluton 5" x 50

87 Royal Jamaica Robusto 4½" x 49

87 Vueltabajo Robusto 4¼" x 52

86 H. Upmann Pequeños 100 4½" x 50

86 H. Upmann Cabinet Selection No. 100 4¼" x 50

86 Nat Sherman VIP Selection Astor 4½" x 50

86 Partagas Robusto 4½" x 49

86 Romeo y Julieta Vintage No. 3 4½" x 50

86 Santa Damiana Seleccion No. 500 5" x 50

85 Arturo Fuente Chateau Fuente Rothschild 5" x 50

85 Ashton Aged Maduro No. 10 5" x 50

85 Caballeros Rothschild 5" x 50

85 El Sublimado Regardete 4½" x 50

85 H. Upmann Cabinet Selection Robusto 4¼" x 50

85 Juan Clemente Rothschild 4⅞" x 50

85 Leon Jimenes Robusto 5½" x 50

85 Montecristo Robusto 4¼" x 50

85 Partagas Natural 5½" x 49

84 Diana Silvius Robusto 4⅞" x 52

84 Dunhill Romanas 4½" x 50

84 Jose Benito Rothschild 4¼" x 50

84 Juan Clemente Club Selection No. 2 4½" x 46

84 La Unica No. 400 4½" x 50

84 Nat Sherman Manhattan Selection Sutton 5½" x 49

84 Paul Garmirian Series No. 2 4¼" x 48

84 Romeo y Julieta Rothschild 5" x 50

84 Sosa Wavell 4¼" x 50

83 Avo No. 9 4¼" x 48

83 Bauza Robusto 5½" x 50

83 Montecruz Sun-Grown Robusto 4½" x 49

83 Primo del Rey No. 100 4½" x 50

82 Troya No. 18 4¼" x 50

HONDURAS

89 V Centennial Robusto 5" x 50

88 Encanto Rothschild 4½" x 50

88 Zino Mouton-Cadet No. 6 5" x 50

87 Don Tomas Special Edition No. 300 5" x 50

86 Hoyo de Monterrey Rothschild 4½" x 50

86 Nat Sherman Host Selection Hobart 5" x 50

86 Thomas Hinds Honduran Selection Robusto 5" x 50

85 Don Lino Colorado Robusto 5½" x 50

85 Don Tomas Rothschild 4½" x 50

84 Baccarat Havana Selection Robusto 5" x 50

84 Cuba Aliados Rothschild 5" x 50

84 Don Lino Robusto 5½" x 50

83 Don Lino Havana Reserve Robusto 5½" x 50

83 El Rey del Mundo Robusto 5" x 54

83 Las Cabrillas Cortez 4¼" x 50

83 Punch Rothschild 4½" x 50

83 Punch Grand Cru Robusto 5¼" x 50

82 El Rey del Mundo Robusto de Manuel 5" x 54

81 Don Ramos Rothschild 4½" x 50

80 Belinda Medaglia d'Oro 4½" x 50

79   La Invicta Magnum No. 2 4½" x 50

74   Petrus Rothschild 4¼" x 50

JAMAICA

87   Macanudo Hyde Park 5½" x 49

85   Macanudo Vintage No. 5 5½" x 49

84   Temple Hall No. 550 5½" x 50

MEXICO

82   Cruz Real No. 25 5½" x 52

82   Te-Amo Torito 4¼" x 50

NICARAGUA

81   Joya de Nicaragua Consul 4½" x 52

U.S.A.

85   La Gloria Cubana Wavell 5" x 50

72   La Hoja Selecta Palais Royal
      4¼" x 50

PETIT CORONA

CUBA

93   Cohiba Siglo I 4" x 40

89   Montecristo No. 4 5" x 42

89   Partagas Petit Corona 5" x 42

89   Romeo y Julieta Petit Corona
      5" x 42

87   Bolivar Petit Corona 5" x 42

86   Hoyo de Monterrey Le Hoyo du
      Prince 5" x 40

86   Punch Royal Selection No. 12
      5" x 42

85   Sancho Panza Non Plus 5" x 42

84   Quintero Medias Coronas 5" x 40

81   Fonseca Cosacos 5⅓" x 42

81   H. Upmann Petit Corona 5" x 42

DOMINICAN REPUBLIC

89   Montesino Diplomatico 5½ " x 43

88   Davidoff Gran Cru No. 4 5" x 40

88   Davidoff Gran Cru No. 3 5" x 42

87   Avo No. 8 5½" x 40

87   Pleiades Antares 5½" x 40

87   Primo del Rey No. 4 5½" x 42

86   Arturo Fuente Petit Corona 5" x 38

86   Cuesta-Rey Dominican No. 5
      5½" x 42

86   Don Diego Petit Corona 5⅛" x 42

86   H. Upmann Tubos 5⅛6" x 42

86   H. Upmann Petit Corona 5¹⁄₁₆" x 42

86   Nat Sherman Landmark Selection
      Hampshire 5½" x 42

86   Olor Momentos 5½" x 43

86   Paul Garmirian Petit Corona 5" x 43

86   Por Larrañaga Petit Cetros en Cedro
      5" x 38

85   Davidoff No. 2000 5" x 42

85   Ramon Allones Size D 5" x 42

84   Bauza Grecos 5½" x 42

84   Bauza Petit Corona 5" x 38

84   Jose Benito Petite 5½" x 38

84   Los Libertadores Insurrectos 5½" x 42

84   Montecruz Sun-Grown No. 230
      5" x 42

84   Partagas No. 4 5" x 38

84   Tresado Seleccion No. 500 5½" x 42

84   Troya Clasico 5½" x 42

83   H. Upmann Corona Major 5¹⁄₁₆" x 42

83   Montecruz Sun-Grown Cedar Aged
      5" x 42

83   Royal Jamaica Petit Corona 5" x 40

83   Vueltabajo Corona 5¾" x 42

82 Licenciados Supreme Maduro No. 200 5½" x 42

82 Licenciados No. 4 5½" x 42

82 Nat Sherman VIP Selection Barnum Glass Tube 5½" x 42

81 Casa Blanca Corona 5½" x 42

80 Carrington No. 4 5½" x 40

HONDURAS

88 Hoyo de Monterrey Excalibur No. 7 5" x 43

87 Baccarat Petit Corona 5½" x 42

87 El Rey del Mundo Habana Club 5½" x 42

87 Hoyo de Monterrey Super Hoyo 5½" x 44

87 Thomas Hinds Honduran Selection Corona 5½" x 42

87 Zino Mouton-Cadet No. 5 5" x 42

86 Cuba Aliados Remedios 5½" x 42

86 Don Tomas Blunt 5" x 42

86 Zino Diamonds 5½" x 40

85 Don Lino Petit Cetro 5½" x 42

85 Hoyo de Monterrey Excalibur No. 6 5½" x 38

85 Punch Elite 5¼" x 44

84 Bering Imperial 5¼" x 42

83 Don Lino No. 4 5" x 42

83 Hoyo de Monterrey No. 55 5¼" x 43

82 El Rey del Mundo Tinos 5½" x 38

81 Bances Unique 5½" x 38

80 Nat Sherman Host Selection Hamilton 5½" x 42

79 Cortesia No. 1 5½" x 40

70 Hoyo de Monterrey Sabrosas 5" x 40

JAMAICA

88 8-9-8 Collection Corona 5½" x 42

88 Macanudo Lord Claridge 5½" x 38

88 Macanudo Vintage No. 3 5½" x 42

87 Macanudo Hampton Court 5¼" x 43

84 Macanudo Petit Corona 5" x 38

MEXICO

83 Te-Amo No. 4 5" x 42

NICARAGUA

85 Padron Londres 5½" x 42

84 La Finca Corona 5½" x 42

83 Joya de Nicaragua Petite 5½" x 38

U.S.A.

89 El Rico Habano Petit-Habano 5" x 40

PANATELA

CUBA

91 Montecristo Especial No. 2 6" x 38

89 Cohiba Corona Especial 6" x 38

88 Punch Ninfas 7" x 38

86 Hoyo de Monterrey Le Hoyo du Dauphin 6" x 38

86 Montecristo Especial 7½" x 38

85 Romeo y Julieta Shakespeare 6½" x 28

84 Romeo y Julieta Belvedere 5½" x 39

83 Cohiba Lancero 7½" x 38

83 El Rey del Mundo Elegante 6¼" x 28

DOMINICAN REPUBLIC

91 Chateau de la Fuente Petit Lancero 6" x 38

87 Avo XO Preludio 6" x 40

87 Cuesta-Rey Cabinet No. 2 7" x 36

87 Davidoff No. 2 6" x 38

87 Juan Clemente Panatela 6½" x 34

87 Paul Garmirian Panatela 7½" x 38

86 Ashton Panatela 6" x 36

86 Cuesta-Rey Dominican No. 3 7" x 36

85 Arturo Fuente Panatela Fina 7" x 38

85 Carrington No. 3 7" x 36

84 Casa Blanca Panatela 6" x 36

84 Montecruz Tubulares Sun-Grown 6⅛" x 36

84 The Griffin's No. 400 6" x 38

83 Davidoff No. 1 7½" x 38

83 Dunhill Fantino 7" x 28

83 Nat Sherman Exchange Selection Murray Hill No. 7 6" x 38

83 Royal Jamaica Tube No. 2 6½" x 34

82 Bauza Florete 6⅞" x 35

82 Don Diego Royal Palma 6⅛" x 36

82 Licenciados Panatela Lindas 7" x 38

82 Nat Sherman Landmark Selection Metropole 6" x 34

82 Partagas Tubos 7" x 38

82 Pleiades Antares 5½" x 40

82 Por Larrañaga Delicados 6½" x 36

81 Avo No. 4 7" x 38

81 Dunhill Dominican Samanas 6" x 38

80 La Aurora Palmas Extra 6¾" x 35

78 Sosa Sante Fe 6" x 35

76 H. Upmann Naturales 6⅛" x 36

HONDURAS

88 V Centennial Numero 1 7½" x 38

87 Belinda Belindas 6½" x 36

86 Don Tomas Special Edition No. 400 7" x 36

86 Maya Palma Fina 6⅞" x 36

85 Don Lino Havana Reserve Panatela 7" x 36

85 Don Tomas Panatela Largas 7" x 38

85 Zino Mouton-Cadet No. 2 6" x 35

83 Hoyo de Monterrey Excalibur No. 7 5" x 43

81 Bances Unique 5½" x 38

80 El Rey del Mundo Tinos 5½" x 38

80 Hoyo de Monterrey Delights 6¼" x 37

79 Don Lino Panatelas 7" x 36

78 Don Tomas International Selection No. 4 7" x 36

JAMAICA

87 Temple Hall No. 685 6⅞" x 34

85 Macanudo Portofino 7" x 34

83 Macanudo Vintage No. 7 7½" x 38

CANARY ISLANDS

84 Dunhill Panatela 6" x 30

MEXICO

81 Te-Amo Torero 6 9/16" x 35

NICARAGUA

86 La Finca Flora 7" x 36

81 Joya de Nicaragua No. 5 5½" x 38

77 Don Juan Lindas 5½" x 38

U.S.A.

87 La Gloria Cubana Panatela Deluxe 7" x 37

80 El Rico Habano No. 1 7½" x 38

ODD-SIZED

CUBA

93   Hoyo de Monterrey Particulares 9¼" x 47

91   Montecristo "A" 9¼" x 47

91   Romeo y Julieta Fabuloso 9¼" x 47

87   Partagas Culebras 5¼" x 39

86   Sancho Panza Sanchos 9¼" x 47

DOMINICAN REPUBLIC

90   Arturo Fuente Don Carlos No. 3 5½" x 44

90   Diamond Crown Robusto No. 4 5½" x 54

89   Fonseca 2-2 4¼" x 40

88   Ashton Cabinet Selection No. 7 6¼" x 54

88   La Gloria Cubana Glorias Extra 6¼" x 46

88   Romeo y Julieta Presidente 7" x 43

87   Diamond Crown Robusto No. 5 4½" x 54

87   Partagas Limited Reserve Regale 6¼" x 47

87   Partagas Limited Reserve Royale 6¼" x 43

87   Paul Garmirian Bombone 3½" x 43

87   Royal Jamaica Double Corona 7" x 45

86   Arturo Fuente Chateau Fuente Royal Salute 7⅞" x 54

86   Casa Blanca Jeroboam 10" x 66

86   Diamond Crown Robusto No. 1 8½" x 54

86   Montecristo Double Corona 6¼" x 50

85   Canaria d'Oro Supremos 7" x 45

85   José Martí Remedio 5½" x 45

85   Partagas Almirante 6¼" x 47

84   Montecruz Sun-Grown Individuales 8" x 46

82   Primo del Rey Churchill 6¼" x 48

82   Royal Jamaica No. 1 Tube 6" x 45

81   José Martí Maceo 6⅞" x 45

81   Pleiades Saturne 8" x 46

81   The Griffin's No. 200 7" x 44

80   Nat Sherman Morgan 7" x 42

80   Royal Jamaica Goliath 9" x 64

79   Pleiades Neptune 7½" x 42

HONDURAS

89   El Rey del Mundo Originale 5⅝" x 45

89   Evelio Robusto 4¼" x 54

88   Punch Corona 6¼" x 45

88   Punch Grand Cru Britannia 6¼" x 50

86   Bering Barons 7¼" x 42

86   Hoyo de Monterrey Churchill 6¼" x 45

86   Hoyo de Monterrey Demitasse 4" x 39

85   Belinda Cabinet 5⅝" x 45

85   Bering Coronados 5⅛₆" x 45

85   Evelio Robusto Larga 6" x 54

85   Nestor 747 Cabinet Series No. 2 4¼" x 54

84   El Rey del Mundo Rectangulare 5⅝" x 45

83   Bering Corona Grande 6¼" x 46

83   Petrus Tabacage 89 No. 4 5⅝" x 38

82   El Rey del Mundo Corona 5⅝" x 45

82   Las Cabrillas Balboa 7½" x 54

81	El Rey del Mundo Robusto Zavalla 5" x 54		91	Montecristo Especial No. 1 7½" x 38
80	Baccarat No. 1 7" x 44		90	Bolivar Belicoso Fino 5½" x 52
79	Bering Casinos 7⅛" x 42		90	Romeo y Julieta Belicoso 5½" x 52
74	Punch After Dinner 7¼" x 45		89	H. Upmann No. 2 6⅛" x 52
			88	El Rey del Mundo Grandes De España 7½" x 38

J A M A I C A

86 8-9-8 Collection Monarch 6¼" x 45

M E X I C O

87 Ornelas 250 9½" x 64

87 Te-Amo New York LaGuardia 5" x 54

84 Te-Amo New York Wall Street 6" x 52

82 Cruz Real No. 28 8½" x 54

82 Te-Amo CEO 8½" x 52

N I C A R A G U A

91 Padron Magnum 9" x 50

86 C.A.O. Gold Corona Gorda 6½" x 50

86 Gilberto Oliva Viajante 6" x 52

82 Joya de Nicaragua No. 1 6⅝" x 44

U . S . A .

86 Havana Classico Malecon 9" x 60

81 Calle Ocho Embajador 9" x 60

FIGURADO

C U B A

96 Romeo y Julieta Fabuloso 9" x 47

95 Montecristo "A" 9½" x 47

94 Montecristo No. 2 6⅛" x 52

92 Diplomaticos No. 2 6⅛" x 52

92 Punch Diademas Extra 9" x 47

87 Cohiba Lancero 7½" x 38

87 La Gloria Cubana Medaille d'Or No. 1 7⅛" x 36

87 Romeo y Julieta Celestial Fino 5¾" x 46

86 Sancho Panza Belicoso 5½" x 52

84 Partagas Presidente 6⅛" x 47

D O M I N I C A N R E P U B L I C

92 Fuente Fuente Opus x No. 2 6¼" x 52

89 Arturo Fuente Hemingway Signature 6" x 46

89 Arturo Fuente Hemingway Short Story 4¼" x 49

89 Ashton Cabinet Selection No. 10 7½" x 52

89 Avo XO Fantasia Pyramid 5½" x 50

88 Ashton Cabinet Selection No. 3 6" x 46

88 Oscar No. 700 7" x 54

88 Paul Garmirian Belicoso 6¼" x 52

88 Paul Garmirian Celebration 9" x 50

88 Sosa Family Selection No. 2 6¼" x 54

87 Ashton Vintage Cabinet No. 1 9" x 52

87 Ashton Vintage Cabinet Selection No. 2 7" x 47

87 Avo Belicoso 6" x 50

87 Carrington No. 8 6⅞" x 60

87 Davidoff Special "T" 6" x 52

87 Fonseca Triangulare 5½" x 56

87 Los Libertadores Figurado 6½" x 52

87 Montecristo No. 2 6" x 50

87 Nat Sherman Metropolitan Selection Metropolitan 7" x 52

87 Troya Torpedo No. 81 7" x 54

86 Arturo Fuente Hemingway Classic 7" x 48

86 Arturo Fuente Hemingway Masterpiece 9¼" x 52

86 Avo Pyramide 7" x 54

86 Avo Petit Belicoso 4¼" x 50

86 El Sublimado Torpedo 7" x 54

86 Los Libertadores Figurado Reserva Especial 6½" x 52

86 Paul Garmirian Belicoso Fino 5½" x 52

86 Por Larrañaga Pyramid 6" x 50

85 Casa Blanca Jeroboam 10" x 66

85 Romeo y Julieta Romeo 6" x 46

85 Royal Jamaica Park Lane 6" x 47

85 The Griffin's Don Bernardo 9" x 46

84 The Griffin's No. 100 7" x 38

84 Vueltabajo Pyramide 7" x 50

83 Avo No. 4 7" x 38

83 Nat Sherman VIP Selection Zigfield Fancy Tail 6¼" x 38

82 Davidoff Aniversario No. 1 7½" x 38

82 Davidoff No. 1 7½" x 38

82 Dunhill Centenas 6" x 50

80 Sosa Piramides 7" x 64

HONDURAS

92 Puros Indios Piramides No. 1 7½" x 60

90 Puros Indios Piramides No. 2 6½" x 46

89 Cuba Aliados Piramides No. 2 6½" x 46

87 Cuba Aliados Piramides 7½" x 60

87 El Rey del Mundo Flor de Llaneza 6½" x 54

87 V Centennial Torpedo 7" x 54

86 C.A.O. Triangulares 7" x 54

86 Felipe Gregorio Belicoso 6⅛" x 54

86 Petrus Antonius 5" x 54

86 Thomas Hinds Honduran Selection Torpedo 6" x 52

85 Astral Perfeccion 7" x 48

85 Don Lino Havana Reserve Torpedo Classico 7" x 48

85 El Rey del Mundo Flor de Lavonda 6½" x 52

85 Habana Gold Black Label Torpedo 6" x 52

85 Punch Grand Cru Prince Consort 8½" x 52

84 Hoyo de Monterrey Culebra 6¼" x 35

84 Las Cabrillas Maximilian 7" x 55

83 Astral Favorito 7" x 48

83 Don Lino Colorado Torpedo 7" x 48

82 Orient Express Expresso 6" x 48

82 Padron 1964 Anniversary Series Piramide 6⅛" x 52

JAMAICA

88 Temple Hall Belicoso 6" x 50

87 Macanudo Duke of Windsor 6" x 50

86 Macanudo Duke of Wellington 8½" x 38

MEXICO

85 Te-Amo Figurado 6⅝" x 50

84 Te-Amo Gran Pyramide 7¼" x 54

83 Te-Amo Piramide 6¼" x 50

U . S . A .

90 Santiago Cabana Torpedo 6¼" x 54

88 El Rico Habano No. 1 7½" x 38

88 Macabi Belicoso Fino 6¼" x 52

87 La Gloria Cubana Piramides 7¼" x 56

86 La Gloria Cubana Torpedo No. 1
6½" x 54

MADURO

D O M I N I C A N
R E P U B L I C

89 Tresado Selection No. 200 7" x 48

88 Arturo Fuente Chateau Fuente
4½" x 50

88 Cuesta-Rey Cabinet No. 1884
6¼" x 44

88 Onyx No. 650 6" x 50

88 Sosa Rothschild Maduro 4¼" x 49

88 Sosa Churchill Maduro 6¹⁵⁄₁₆ x 49

87 Ashton Aged Maduro No. 30
6¼" x 44

87 Casa Blanca Deluxe 6" x 50

87 Cuesta-Rey Dominican No. 2
7½" x 48

87 Don Diego Privada No. 1 6⅝" x 43

87 Henry Clay Brevas de la Conserva
5⅝" x 46

87 Licenciados Wavell Maduro 5" x 50

87 Primo del Rey Soberano Maduro
7½" x 50

87 Romeo y Julieta Rothschild 5" x 50

87 Royal Jamaica Corona 5½" x 40

87 Sosa Wavell Maduro 4¾" x 50

87 Troya No. 18 Rothschild Maduro
4½" x 50

86 Arturo Fuente Corona Imperial
6½" x 46

86 Ashton Aged Maduro No. 50 7" x 48

86 Canaria d'Oro Rothschild Maduro
4½" x 49

86 Fonseca 5-50 5" x 50

86 La Unica No. 200 7" x 49

86 Montesino Diplomatico 5½" x 42

86 Montesino Gran Corona 6¾" x 48

86 Nat Sherman City Desk Tribune
7½" x 50

86 Primo del Rey No. 100 Maduro
4½" x 50

86 Royal Jamaica Churchill Maduro
8" x 51

85 Arturo Fuente Churchill 7" x 48

85 Ashton Aged Maduro No. 40 6" x 50

85 Fonseca 10-10 6¼" x 49

85 Nat Sherman City Desk Dispatch
6½" x 46

85 Nat Sherman City Desk Telegraph
6" x 50

85 Onyx No. 642 6" x 42

85 Onyx No. 750 7½" x 50

85 Partagas Maduro 6¼" x 48

85 Primo del Rey No. 4 5½" x 42

85 Primo del Rey Almirante Maduro
6" x 50

85 Royal Jamaica Corona Grande
6½" x 42

84 Ashton Aged Maduro No. 60
7½" x 52

84 Cabañas Corona 5½" x 42

84 Cabañas Exquisito Maduro 6½" x 48

84 Cuesta-Rey Cabinet No. 95 6¼" x 42

84 Flamenco Brevas A La Conserva
5⁵⁄₁₆" x 42

84 Henry Clay Brevas Fina Maduro
6½" x 48

84 La Unica No. 400 4½" x 50

84 Licenciados Supreme Maduro
No. 400 6" x 50

84 Troya No. 63 Churchill Maduro
6⅛" x 46

83 Ashton Aged Maduro No. 10
5" x 50

83 Casa Blanca Presidente 7½" x 50

83 Licenciados Toros 6" x 50

83 Tresado No. 500 5½" x 42

83 Troya No. 45 Cetro 6" x 44

80 Licenciados No. 4 5¼" x 43

80 Licenciados Presidente 8" x 50

HONDURAS

91 El Rey del Mundo Robusto Suprema
7" x 54

90 Don Lino Churchill 7" x 50

89 Bances President 8½" x 52

88 Cuba Aliados Churchill Deluxe
7¼" x 54

87 Bances Corona Inmensa 6¼" x 48

87 Cuba Aliados Corona Deluxe 6½" x 45

87 Hoyo de Monterrey Excalibur No. 3
6⅛" x 48

87 Petrus Double Corona 7¼" x 50

87 Punch Pita Maduro 6⅛" x 50

86 El Rey del Mundo Deluxe 6⅞" x 48

86 El Rey del Mundo Flor del Mundo
Maduro 7¼" x 52

86 Encanto Toro Maduro 6" x 50

86 F.D. Grave Churchill 7¾" x 50

86 Hoyo de Monterrey Governor
Maduro 6⅛" x 50

86 Punch Chateau M 6¾" x 46

86 Punch Double Corona 6¾" x 48

86 Punch Rothschild Maduro 4½" x 50

86 Puros Indios Churchill Maduro
7¼" x 52

86 Puros Indios Corona Gorda Maduro
6" x 52

85 C.A.O. Churchill Maduro 8" x 50

85 Don Tomas Presidentes 7½" x 50

85 Encanto Rothchild Maduro 4½" x 50

85 Habana Gold White Label Churchill
7" x 52

85 Hoyo de Monterrey Excalibur No. 2
7" x 46

85 Hoyo de Monterrey Excalibur No. 1
Maduro 7¼" x 54

85 Hoyo de Monterrey Sultan Maduro
7¼" x 54

85 Hoyo de Monterrey Rothschild
Maduro 4½" x 50

85 Punch Chateau L Maduro 7¼" x 54

85 V Centennial Robusto Maduro
5" x 50

84 Belinda Excellente 6" x 50

84 C.A.O. Robusto Maduro 4½" x 50

84 Don Lino Rothschild Maduro 4½" x 50

84 Don Tomas Toro Maduro 5½" x 46

84 Habana Gold White Label Robusto
5" x 50

84 Las Cabrillas Cortez Maduro 4¾" x 50

84 Petrus No. 2 6¼" x 44

84 Petrus Tabacage 89 Churchill 7" x 50

84 V Centennial Churchill Maduro
6⅛" x 48

84 V Centennial Numero 2 Maduro
6" x 50

82 Encanto Churchill Maduro 6⅛" x 49

82 Las Cabrillas Balboa Maduro 7½" x 54

81 Petrus Tabacage 89 Rothschild
4¼" x 50

81 Santa Rosa Sancho Panza Maduro
4½" x 50

78 Petrus Tabacage 89 Corona Sublime
5½" x 46

JAMAICA

86 Temple Hall Estates No. 450
4½" x 49

85 Macanudo Prince Philip 7½" x 49

83 Macanudo Duke of Devon 5½" x 42

MEXICO

87 Cruz Real No. 14 7½" x 50

86 Ornelas Robusto Maduro 4¾" x 49

86 Te-Amo Maximo Churchill Maduro
7" x 54

85 Ornelas Cafetero Grande 6½" x 46

85 Santa Clara 1830 No. 6 6" x 51

85 Te-Amo Torito Maduro 4¾" x 50

84 Cruz Real No. 19 6" x 50

84 Ornelas Churchill Maduro 7" x 49

84 Te-Amo Churchill Maduro 7½" x 50

84 Te-Amo Toro Maduro 6" x 50

84 Te-Amo Satisfaction Maduro 6" x 46

83 Santa Clara 1830 No. 1 7" x 51

83 Te-Amo Presidente Maduro 7" x 50

82 Cruz Real No. 24 4½" x 50

81 Te-Amo Robusto Maduro 5½" x 54

79 Ornelas Cafetero Chico Maduro
5½" x 46

NICARAGUA

88 Joya de Nicaragua Maduro Deluxe
Robusto 4¾" x 52

88 Padron 3000 Maduro 5½" x 52

87 La Finca Robusto 4½" x 50

87 Padron Executive Maduro 7½" x 50

86 Padron 2000 Maduro 5" x 50

86 Padron Churchill Maduro 6⅞" x 46

84 Joya de Nicaragua Maduro Deluxe
Presidente 7½" x 50

84 Thomas Hinds Nicaraguan Selection
Robusto Maduro 5" x 50

84 Thomas Hinds Nicaraguan Selection
Corona Gorda Maduro 6" x 50

83 Thomas Hinds Nicaraguan Selection
Churchill Maduro 7" x 49

U.S.A.

90 La Gloria Cubana Wavell 5" x 50

89 La Gloria Cubana Churchill 7" x 50

86 Havana Classico Robusto 5" x 50

VINTAGE

CUBA

98 Montecristo No. 1 Seleccion
Suprema 6½" x 42

97 Cabanas No. 751 Alfred Dunhill
6½" x 42

97 Romeo y Julieta Seleccion Suprema
Cedro 6½" x 42

95 H. Upmann No. 22 Seleccion
Suprema 4½" x 55

95 H. Upmann No. 4 Alfred Dunhill
6½" x 46

93 La Corona Churchill 6½" x 46

93 Partagas No. 6 Seleccion Superba
4½" x 40

92 Belinda Belindas 5½" x 42

92 Flor de Farach Palmeras 5" x 38

92 Montecristo No. 4 Seleccion
Suprema 5" x 42

89 Ramon Allones Ideales 6½" x 40

89 Romeo y Julieta Sun-Grown Brevas
5½" x 44

87 Ramon Allones No. 66 (perfecto)
6" x n/a

86 Henry Clay Coronas 5½" x 42

CHAPTER 13

Cigars

Listed by Brand

Brand	Category	Size	Rating

8-9-8 COLLECTION

JAMAICA

Churchill *Churchill* 7½" x 49 • **88**

Churchill *Double Corona* 7½" x 49 • **87**

Corona *Corona* 5½" x 42 • **83**

Corona *Petit Corona* 5½" x 42 • **88**

Lonsdale *Lonsdale* 6½" x 42 • **86**

Monarch *Odd* 6¾" x 45 • **86**

Robusto *Corona Gorda* 5½" x 49 • **86**

AL-CAPONE

NICARAGUA

Corona Grande *Lonsdale* 6¼" x 43 • **83**

ARTURO FUENTE

DOMINICAN REPUBLIC

Chateau Fuente *Maduro* 4½" x 50 • **88**

Chateau Fuente Rothschild *Robusto*
5" x 50 • **85**

Chateau Fuente Royal Salute *Odd*
7⅝" x 54 • **86**

Churchill *Churchill* 7¼" x 48 • **89**

Churchill *Maduro* 7" x 48 • **85**

Corona Imperial *Maduro* 6½" x 46 • **86**

Don Carlos No. 3 *Odd* 5½" x 44 • **90**

Don Carlos Robusto *Robusto* 5" x 50 • **89**

Double Chateau *Churchill* 6¼" x 50 • **89**

Flor Fina 8-5-8 *Corona Gorda* 6" x 47 • **86**

Hemingway Classic *Figurado* 7" x 48 • **86**

Hemingway Masterpiece *Figurado*
9¼" x 52 • **86**

Hemingway Short Story *Figurado*
4¼" x 49 • **89**

Hemingway Signature *Figurado*
6" x 46 • **89**

Opus X Robusto *Robusto* 5¼" x 50 • **90**

Panatela Fina *Panatela* 7" x 38 • **85**

Petit Corona *Petit Corona* 5" x 38 • **86**

Reserva No. 1 *Lonsdale* 6½" x 42 • **88**

Reserva No. 3 *Corona* 5½" x 44 • **87**

Seleccion Privada No. 1 *Lonsdale*
6¼" x 44 • **85**

Spanish Lonsdale *Lonsdale* 6½" x 42 • **88**

ASHTON

DOMINICAN REPUBLIC

8-9-8 *Lonsdale* 6½" x 44 • **86**

Aged Maduro No. 10 *Robusto* 5" x 50 • **85**

Aged Maduro No. 10 *Maduro* 5" x 50 • **83**

Aged Maduro No. 20 *Corona*
5½" x 44 • **86**

Aged Maduro No. 30 *Maduro*
6¼" x 44 • **87**

Aged Maduro No. 40 *Maduro* 6" x 50 • **85**

Aged Maduro No. 50 *Maduro* 7" x 48 • **86**

Aged Maduro No. 60 *Maduro*
7½" x 52 • **84**

Aged Maduro No. 60 *Double Corona*
7½" x 52 • **86**

Cabinet Selection No. 3 *Figurado*
6" x 46 • **88**

Cabinet Selection No. 7 *Odd* 6¼" x 54 • **88**

Cabinet Selection No. 10 *Figurado*
7½" x 52 • **89**

Churchill *Churchill* 7½" x 52 • **84**

Churchill *Double Corona* 7½" x 50 • **85**

Corona *Corona* 5½" x 44 • **84**

Double Magnum *Corona Gorda*
6" x 50 • **87**

Magnum *Robusto* 5" x 50 • **88**

Panatela *Panatela* 6" x 36 • **86**

Prime Minister *Churchill* 7" x 48 • **84**

Vintage Cabinet No. 1 *Figurado*
9" x 52 • **87**

Vintage Cabinet Selection No. 2 *Figurado*
7" x 47 • **87**

ASTRAL

HONDURAS

Favorito *Figurado* 7" x 48 • **83**

Lujos *Lonsdale* 6½" x 44 • **84**

Perfeccion *Figurado* 7" x 48 • **85**

AVO

DOMINICAN REPUBLIC

Belicoso *Figurado* 6" x 50 • **87**

No. 1 *Lonsdale* 6⅔" x 42 • **86**

No. 2 *Corona Gorda* 6" x 50 • **88**

No. 3 *Double Corona* 7½" x 52 • **84**

No. 4 *Figurado* 7" x 38 • **83**

No. 4 *Panatela* 7" x 38 • **81**

No. 5 *Churchill* 6¼" x 46 • **87**

No. 7 *Corona* 6" x 44 • **87**

No. 8 *Petit Corona* 5½" x 40 • **87**

No. 9 *Robusto* 4¼" x 48 • **83**

Petit Belicoso *Figurado* 4¼" x 50 • **86**

Pyramide *Figurado* 7" x 54 • **86**

AVO XO

DOMINICAN REPUBLIC

Fantasia Pyramid *Figurado* 5½" x 50 • **89**

Intermezzo *Corona Gorda* 5½" x 50 • **83**

Intermezzo *Robusto* 5½" x 50 • **87**

Maestoso *Churchill* 7" x 48 • **86**

Preludio *Panatela* 6" x 40 • **87**

BACCARAT

HONDURAS

Churchill *Churchill* 7" x 50 • **85**

Churchill *Double Corona* 7" x 50 • **79**

Havana Selection Robusto *Robusto*
5" x 50 • **84**

Luchadores *Lonsdale* 6" x 43 • **83**

No. 1 *Lonsdale* 7" x 44 • **81**

No. 1 *Odd* 7" x 44 • **80**

Petit Corona *Corona* 5½" x 42 • **81**

Petit Corona *Petit Corona* 5½" x 42 • **87**

BANCES

HONDURAS

Brevas *Corona* 5½" x 43 • **86**

Cazadores *Lonsdale* 6¼" x 43 • **78**

Corona Inmensa *Churchill* 6¼" x 48 • **85**

Corona Inmensa *Maduro* 6¼" x 48 • **87**

President *Maduro* 8½" x 52 • **89**

Unique *Panatela* 5½" x 38 • **81**

Unique *Petit Corona* 5½" x 38 • **81**

BAUZA

DOMINICAN REPUBLIC

Casa Grande *Churchill* 6¾" x 48 • **84**

Fabuloso *Double Corona* 7½" x 50 • **86**

Florete *Panatela* 6⅛" x 35 • **82**

Grecos *Corona* 5½" x 42 • **85**

Grecos *Petit Corona* 5½" x 42 • **84**

Jaguar *Lonsdale* 6½" x 42 • **83**

Medaille D'Oro No. 1 *Lonsdale* 6⅞" x 44 • **86**

Petit Corona *Petit Corona* 5" x 38 • **84**

Robusto *Robusto* 5½" x 50 • **83**

BELINDA

CUBA

Belindas *Vintage* 5½" x 42 • **92**

BELINDA

HONDURAS

Belindas *Panatela* 6½" x 36 • **87**

Breva Conserva *Corona* 5½" x 43 • **87**

Cabinet *Corona Gorda* 5⅝" x 45 • **89**

Cabinet *Odd* 5⅝" x 45 • **85**

Corona Grande *Lonsdale* 6¼" x 44 • **85**

Excellente *Maduro* 6" x 50 • **84**

Medaglia d'Oro *Robusto* 4½" x 50 • **80**

Prime Minister *Double Corona* 7½" x 50 • **91**

BERING

HONDURAS

Barons *Odd* 7¼" x 42 • **86**

Casinos *Odd* 7⅛" x 42 • **79**

Corona Grande *Odd* 6¼" x 46 • **83**

Corona Royale *Corona* 6" x 41 • **87**

Coronados *Odd* 5⅜₆" x 45 • **85**

Hispanos *Corona Gorda* 6" x 50 • **85**

Imperial *Corona* 5¼" x 42 • **85**

Imperial *Petit Corona* 5¼" x 42 • **84**

Plaza *Lonsdale* 6" x 43 • **87**

BLAIR

HONDURAS

Robusto *Corona Gorda* 6" x 50 • **84**

BOLIVAR

CUBA

Belicoso Fino *Figurado* 5½" x 52 • **90**

Corona *Corona* 5½" x 42 • **91**

Corona Extra *Corona Gorda* 5⅝" x 46 • **87**

Corona Gigantes *Churchill* 7" x 47 • **90**

Gold Medal *Lonsdale* 6½" x 42 • **90**

Inmensa *Lonsdale* 6⅜" x 43 • **87**

Petit Corona *Petit Corona* 5" x 42 • **87**

Royal Coronas *Robusto* 5" x 50 • **95**

CABALLEROS

DOMINICAN REPUBLIC

Churchill *Churchill* 7" x 50 • **85**

Corona *Corona* 5¼" x 43 • **83**

Rothschild *Robusto* 5" x 50 • **85**

CABAÑAS

CUBA

No. 751 Alfred Dunhill *Vintage*
6½" x 42 • **98**

CABAÑAS

DOMINICAN REPUBLIC

Corona *Maduro* 5½" x 42 • **84**
Exquisito Maduro *Maduro* 6½" x 48 • **84**
Royale *Corona Gorda* 5⅜" x 46 • **83**

CACIQUE

DOMINICAN REPUBLIC

Apache *Corona Gorda* 6" x 50 • **81**
No. 7 *Churchill* 6⅛" x 46 • **86**

CALLE OCHO

U.S.A.

Embajador *Odd* 9" x 60 • **81**
Gordito Largo *Corona Gorda* 6" x 50 • **80**

CAMACHO

DOMINICAN REPUBLIC

Nacionales *Corona* 5½" x 44 • **85**

CAMACHO

HONDURAS

Churchill *Churchill* 7" x 48 • **85**
No. 1 *Lonsdale* 7" x 44 • **76**

CANARIA D'ORO

DOMINICAN REPUBLIC

Corona *Corona* 5½" x 43 • **84**
Inmenso *Corona Gorda* 5½" x 49 • **82**
Lonsdale *Lonsdale* 6½" x 43 • **83**
Rothschild *Robusto* 4½" x 50 • **88**
Rothschild Maduro *Maduro* 4½" x 49 • **86**
Supremos *Odd* 7" x 45 • **85**

C.A.O.

HONDURAS

Churchill Maduro *Maduro* 8" x 50 • **85**
Corona *Corona* 6" x 42 • **87**
Corona Gorda *Corona Gorda* 6" x 50 • **85**
Lonsdale *Lonsdale* 7" x 44 • **85**
Robusto Maduro *Maduro* 4½" x 50 • **84**
Triangulares *Figurado* 7" x 54 • **86**

C.A.O.

NICARAGUA

Gold Corona Gorda *Odd* 6½" x 50 • **86**

CARA MIA

CANARY ISLANDS

Lonsdale *Lonsdale* 6½" x 42 • **84**
Toro *Corona Gorda* 6" x 50 • **87**

CARRINGTON

DOMINICAN REPUBLIC

No. 2 *Corona* 6" x 42 • **87**
No. 3 *Panatela* 7" x 36 • **85**
No. 4 *Petit Corona* 5½" x 40 • **80**
No. 5 *Churchill* 6⅛" x 46 • **87**
No. 7 *Corona Gorda* 6" x 50 • **79**
No. 8 *Figurado* 6⅛" x 60 • **87**

CASA BLANCA

DOMINICAN REPUBLIC

Corona *Corona* 5½" x 42 • **89**
Corona *Petit Corona* 5½" x 42 • **81**
Deluxe *Corona Gorda* 6" x 50 • **85**
Deluxe *Maduro* 6" x 50 • **87**
Jeroboam *Figurado* 10" x 66 • **85**
Jeroboam *Odd* 10" x 66 • **86**
Lonsdale *Lonsdale* 6½" x 42 • **84**
Panatela *Panatela* 6" x 36 • **84**
Presidente *Double Corona* 7½" x 50 • **84**
Presidente *Maduro* 7½" x 50 • **83**

CHATEAU DE LA FUENTE

DOMINICAN REPUBLIC
Petit Lancero *Panatela* 6" x 38 • **91**

CIFUENTES

DOMINICAN REPUBLIC
Lonsdale *Lonsdale* 6½" x 42 • **83**

COHIBA

CUBA

Corona Especial *Panatela* 6" x 38 • **89**
Esplendidos *Churchill* 7" x 47 • **89**
Lancero *Figurado* 7½" x 38 • **87**
Lancero *Panatela* 7½" x 38 • **83**
Robusto *Robusto* 5" x 50 • **92**
Siglo I *Petit Corona* 4" x 40 • **93**
Siglo III *Lonsdale* 6" x 42 • **95**
Siglo IV *Corona Gorda* 5⅝" x 46 • **89**
Siglo V *Lonsdale* 6⅛" x 43 • **90**

CORTESIA

HONDURAS
No. 1 *Petit Corona* 5½" x 40 • **79**

CREDO

DOMINICAN REPUBLIC
Anthanor *Corona* 5¼" x 42 • **88**
Magnificat *Churchill* 6⅛" x 46 • **84**

CRUZ REAL

MEXICO

Churchill No. 14 *Double Corona*
    7½" x 50 • **87**
No. 1 *Lonsdale* 6⅛" x 42 • **76**
No. 2 *Corona* 6" x 42 • **86**
No. 14 *Maduro* 7½" x 50 • **87**
No. 19 *Maduro* 6" x 50 • **84**
No. 19 *Corona Gorda* 6" x 50 • **80**
No. 24 *Maduro* 4½" x 50 • **82**
No. 25 *Robusto* 5½" x 52 • **82**
No. 28 *Odd* 8½" x 54 • **82**

CUBA ALIADOS

HONDURAS

Churchill *Double Corona* 7¼" x 54 • **92**
Churchill Deluxe *Maduro* 7¼" x 54 • **88**
Churchill Extra *Churchill* 7¼" x 54 • **84**
Corona Deluxe *Maduro* 6½" x 45 • **87**
Lonsdale *Lonsdale* 6½" x 42 • **91**
No. 4 *Corona Gorda* 5½" x 46 • **87**
Piramides *Figurado* 7½" x 60 • **87**
Piramides No. 2 *Figurado* 6½" x 46 • **89**
Remedios *Petit Corona* 5½" x 42 • **86**
Rothschild *Robusto* 5" x 50 • **84**
Valentino No. 1 *Churchill* 7" x 47 • **89**

CUBITA

DOMINICAN REPUBLIC

2000 *Churchill* 7" x 50 • **82**
8-9-8 *Lonsdale* 6¾" x 43 • **83**
No. 700 *Corona Gorda* 6" x 50 • **86**

CUESTA-REY

DOMINICAN REPUBLIC

Cabinet 8-9-8 *Churchill* 7" x 49 • **86**
Cabinet No. 2 *Panatela* 7" x 36 • **87**
Cabinet No. 95 *Lonsdale* 6¼" x 42 • **85**
Cabinet No. 95 *Maduro* 6¼" x 42 • **84**
Cabinet Selection No. 1884 *Lonsdale*
   6¾" x 44 • **85**
Cabinet No. 1884 *Maduro* 6¼" x 44 • **88**
Captiva *Lonsdale* 6¹⁄₁₆" x 42 • **84**
Centennial Collection Dominican No. 4
   Lonsdale 6½" x 42 • **83**

Centennial Collection Dominican No. 60
   Corona Gorda 6" x 50 • **87**
Dominican No. 2 *Churchill* 7¼" x 48 • **84**
Dominican No. 2 *Double Corona*
   7¼" x 48 • **85**
Dominican No. 2 *Maduro* 7½" x 48 • **87**
Dominican No. 3 *Panatela* 7" x 36 • **86**
Dominican No. 5 *Corona* 5½" x 43 • **87**
Dominican No. 5 *Petit Corona*
   5½" x 42 • **86**

DAVIDOFF

DOMINICAN REPUBLIC

Aniversario No.1 *Figurado* 7½" x 38 • **82**
Aniversario No. 2 *Churchill* 7" x 48 • **86**
Double "R" *Double Corona* 7½" x 50 • **92**
Gran Cru No. 1 *Lonsdale* 6" x 42 • **89**
Gran Cru No. 2 *Corona* 5⅝" x 43 • **88**
Gran Cru No. 3 *Petit Corona* 5" x 42 • **88**
Gran Cru No. 4 *Petit Corona* 5" x 40 • **88**
No. 1 *Panatela* 7½" x 38 • **83**
No. 1 *Figurado* 7½" x 38 • **82**
No. 2 *Panatela* 6" x 38 • **87**
No. 2000 *Petit Corona* 5" x 42 • **85**
No. 4000 *Lonsdale* 6" x 42 • **89**
No. 5000 *Corona Gorda* 5⅝" x 46 • **85**
Special "R" *Robusto* 4⅞" x 50 • **87**
Special "T" *Figurado* 6" x 52 • **87**

DA VINCI

HONDURAS

Monalisa *Corona Gorda* 6" x 50 • **87**

DIAMOND CROWN

DOMINICAN REPUBLIC

Robusto No. 1 *Odd* 8½" x 54 • **86**
Robusto No. 4 *Odd* 5½" x 54 • **90**
Robusto No. 5 *Odd* 4½" x 54 • **87**

DIANA SILVIUS

DOMINICAN REPUBLIC

Churchill *Churchill* 7" x 50 • **88**
Corona *Lonsdale* 6½" x 42 • **84**
Robusto *Robusto* 4⅞" x 52 • **84**

DIPLOMATICOS

CUBA

No. 2 *Figurado* 6⅛" x 52 • **92**

DON ASA

HONDURAS

Cetros No. 2 *Lonsdale* 6½" x 44 • **85**
Corona *Corona Gorda* 5½" x 50 • **85**

DON DIEGO

DOMINICAN REPUBLIC

Corona *Corona* 5⅝" x 42 • **85**
Corona Major Tube *Corona* 5½" x 42 • **87**
Grande *Corona Gorda* 6" x 50 • **84**
Lonsdale *Lonsdale* 6⅝" x 42 • **86**
Monarch *Churchill* 7¼ x 47 • **86**
Petit Corona *Petit Corona* 5⅛" x 42 • **86**
Privada No. 1 *Maduro* 6⅝" x 43 • **87**
Royal Palma *Panatela* 6⅛" x 36 • **82**

DON JUAN

NICARAGUA

Cetro *Corona* 6" x 43 • **80**
Churchill *Churchill* 7" x 49 • **90**
Lindas *Panatela* 5½" x 38 • **77**
Numero Uno *Lonsdale* 6⅝" x 44 • **84**
Presidente *Double Corona* 8½" x 50 • **88**

DON LEO

DOMINICAN REPUBLIC

Robusto *Corona Gorda* 5½" x 50 • **87**

DON LINO

HONDURAS

Churchill *Double Corona* 8" x 50 • **85**
Churchill *Maduro* 7" x 50 • **90**
Colorado Presidente *Double Corona* 7½" x 50 • **84**
Colorado Robusto *Robusto* 5½" x 50 • **85**
Colorado Torpedo *Figurado* 7" x 48 • **83**
Havana Reserve Churchill *Double Corona* 7½" x 50 • **86**
Havana Reserve No. 1 *Lonsdale* 6½" x 44 • **85**
Havana Reserve Panatela *Panatela* 7" x 36 • **85**
Havana Reserve Robusto *Robusto* 5½" x 50 • **83**
Havana Reserve Toro *Corona Gorda* 5½" x 46 • **88**
Havana Reserve Torpedo Classico *Figurado* 7" x 48 • **85**
No. 1 *Lonsdale* 6½" x 44 • **84**
No. 4 *Petit Corona* 5" x 42 • **83**

No. 5 *Lonsdale* 6¼" x 44 • **87**
Oro Toro *Corona Gorda* 5½" x 46 • **83**
Panatelas *Panatela* 7" x 36 • **79**
Petit Cetro *Corona* 5½" x 42 • **87**
Petit Cetro *Petit Corona* 5½" x 42 • **85**
Robusto *Robusto* 5½" x 50 • **84**
Rothschild **Maduro** *Maduro* 4½" x 50 • **84**
Toro *Corona Gorda* 5½" x 46 • **85**

DON MELO
HONDURAS

Corona Extra *Corona Gorda* 5½" x 46 • **86**
Corona Gorda *Lonsdale* 6¼" x 44 • **86**
Petit Corona *Corona* 5½" x 42 • **85**

DON RAMOS
HONDURAS

Rothschild *Robusto* 4½" x 50 • **81**

DON TOMAS
HONDURAS

Blunt *Petit Corona* 5" x 42 • **86**
Cetros *Lonsdale* 6½" x 44 • **83**
Corona *Corona Gorda* 5½" x 50 • **86**
Corona Grande *Lonsdale* 6½" x 44 • **84**
Honduran Special Edition No. 200
 Lonsdale 6½" x 44 • **85**
International Selection No. 4 *Panatela*
 7" x 36 • **78**
Matador *Corona* 5½" x 42 • **87**
Panatela Largas *Panatela* 7" x 38 • **85**
Presidentes *Maduro* 7½" x 50 • **85**
Rothschild *Robusto* 4½" x 50 • **85**

Special Edition No. 300 *Robusto*
 5" x 50 • **87**
Special Edition No. 400 *Panatela*
 7" x 36 • **86**
Special Edition No. 500 *Corona Gorda*
 5½" x 46 • **87**
Supremo *Lonsdale* 6¼" x 42 • **88**
Toro *Corona Gorda* 5½" x 46 • **84**
Toro **Maduro** *Maduro* 5½" x 46 • **84**

DON VITO
DOMINICAN REPUBLIC

Capo *Lonsdale* 6¼" x 44 • **85**

DON XAVIER
CANARY ISLANDS

Corona *Corona Gorda* 5⅝" x 46 • **83**
Lonsdale *Lonsdale* 6⅝" x 42 • **84**

DUNHILL
CANARY ISLANDS

Panatela *Panatela* 6" x 30 • **84**

DUNHILL
DOMINICAN REPUBLIC

Altamira *Robusto* 5" x 48 • **88**
Cabreras *Churchill* 7" x 48 • **86**
Centenas *Figurado* 6" x 50 • **82**
Condados *Corona Gorda* 6" x 48 • **85**
Diamantes *Lonsdale* 6⅝" x 42 • **83**
Dominican Samanas *Panatela* 6" x 38 • **81**
Fantino *Panatela* 7" x 28 • **83**
Peravias *Double Corona* 7" x 50 • **87**

Romanas *Robusto* 4½" x 50 • **84**

Tabaras *Corona* 5½" x 42 • **85**

Valverdes *Corona* 5½" x 42 • **85**

EL REY DEL MUNDO

CUBA

Corona De Luxe *Corona* 5½" x 42 • **91**

Elegante *Panatela* 6¼" x 28 • **83**

Gran Coronas *Corona Gorda* 5⅝" x 46 • **87**

Grandes De España *Figurado* 7½" x 38 • **88**

Lonsdale *Lonsdale* 6⅛" x 42 • **87**

Tainos *Churchill* 7" x 47 • **87**

EL REY DEL MUNDO

HONDURAS

Choix Supreme *Corona Gorda*
6⅛" x 49 • **88**

Corona *Odd* 5⅝" x 45 • **82**

Deluxe *Maduro* 6⅛" x 48 • **86**

Double Corona *Churchill* 7" x 48 • **86**

Flor de Lavonda *Figurado* 6½" x 52 • **85**

Flor de Llaneza *Figurado* 6½" x 54 • **87**

Flor del Mundo *Double Corona*
7½" x 54 • **87**

Flor del Mundo Maduro *Maduro*
7¼" x 52 • **86**

Habana Club *Corona* 5½" x 42 • **84**

Habana Club *Petit Corona* 5½" x 42 • **87**

Lonsdale *Lonsdale* 7" x 43 • **87**

Originale *Odd* 5⅝" x 45 • **89**

Rectangulare *Odd* 5⅝" x 45 • **84**

Robusto *Robusto* 5" x 54 • **83**

Robusto Larga *Corona Gorda* 6" x 50 • **83**

Robusto Suprema *Maduro* 7" x 54 • **91**

Robusto Zavalla *Odd* 5" x 54 • **81**

Robusto de Manuel *Robusto* 5" x 54 • **82**

Tinos *Panatela* 5½" x 38 • **80**

Tinos *Petit Corona* 5½" x 38 • **82**

EL RICO HABANO

DOMINICAN REPUBLIC

Gran Corona *Corona Gorda* 5¼" x 46 • **89**

EL RICO HABANO

U.S.A.

Corona *Corona* 5½" x 42 • **85**

Double Corona *Churchill* 7" x 47 • **85**

Gran Habanero Deluxe *Double Corona*
7¼" x 50 • **80**

No. 1 *Figurado* 7½" x 38 • **88**

No. 1 *Panatela* 7½" x 38 • **80**

Petit-Habano *Petit Corona* 5" x 40 • **89**

EL SUBLIMADO

DOMINICAN REPUBLIC

Churchill *Double Corona* 8" x 50 • **85**

Corona *Corona* 6" x 44 • **84**

Regardete *Robusto* 4½" x 50 • **85**

Torpedo *Figurado* 7" x 54 • **86**

ENCANTO

HONDURAS

Churchill Maduro *Maduro* 6¼" x 49 • **82**

Elegante *Lonsdale* 7" x 44 • **86**

Rothschild *Robusto* 4½" x 50 • **88**

Rothschild Maduro *Maduro* 4½" x 50 • **85**

Toro Maduro *Maduro* 6" x 50 • **86**

EVELIO

HONDURAS

Robusto *Odd* 4¼" x 54 • **89**

Robusto Larga *Odd* 6" x 54 • **85**

F.D. GRAVE

HONDURAS

Churchill *Maduro* 7¼" x 50 • **86**

Lonsdale *Lonsdale* 6¼" x 44 • **84**

FELIPE GREGORIO

HONDURAS

Belicoso *Figurado* 6⅛" x 54 • **86**

Sereno *Corona* 5¼" x 42 • **86**

FLAMENCO

DOMINICAN REPUBLIC

Brevas a La Conserva *Maduro*
5⅞" x 42 • **84**

FLOR DE CAÑO

CUBA

Diademas *Churchill* 7" x 47 • **89**

Short Churchill *Robusto* 5" x 50 • **93**

FLOR DE FARACH

CUBA

Palmeras *Vintage* 5" x 38 • **92**

FLOR DE FLOREZ

HONDURAS

Cabinet Selection Florez Florez *Corona
Gorda* 5¼" x 46 • **88**

Corona *Corona Gorda* 6" x 50 • **85**

FLOR DE GONZALEZ

U.S.A.

Extra Corona *Corona Gorda* 6" x 50 • **89**

FONSECA

CUBA

Cosacos *Petit Corona* 5¼" x 42 • **81**

FONSECA

DOMINICAN REPUBLIC

2-2 *Odd* 4¼" x 40 • **89**

5-50 *Maduro* 5" x 50 • **86**

5-50 *Robusto* 5" x 50 • **89**

8-9-8 *Corona* 6" x 43 • **86**

8-9-8 *Lonsdale* 6" x 43 • **88**

10-10 *Churchill* 7" x 50 • **86**

10-10 *Maduro* 6¼" x 49 • **85**

Triangulare *Figurado* 5½" x 56 • **87**

FUENTE FUENTE OPUS X

DOMINICAN REPUBLIC

Double Corona *Double Corona*
7⅝" x 49 • **93**

Fuente Fuente *Corona Gorda* 5⅝" x 46 • **91**

No. 2 *Figurado* 6¼" x 52 • **92**

GILBERTO OLIVA

HONDURAS

Numero 1 *Lonsdale* 6½" x 44 • **83**

GILBERTO OLIVA

NICARAGUA

Viajante *Odd* 6" x 52 • **86**

H. UPMANN

CUBA

Corona *Corona* 5½" x 42 • **91**

Lonsdale *Lonsdale* 6½" x 42 • **90**

Magnum *Corona Gorda* 5⅝" x 46 • **83**

No. 2 *Figurado* 6⅛" x 52 • **89**

No. 4 Alfred Dunhill *Vintage* 6½" x 46 • **95**

No. 22 Alfred Dunhill Seleccion Suprema *Vintage* 4½" x 55 • **94**

Petit Corona *Petit Corona* 5" x 42 • **81**

H. UPMANN

DOMINICAN REPUBLIC

Cabinet Selection No. 100 *Robusto* 4¼" x 50 • **86**

Cabinet Selection Robusto *Robusto* 4¼" x 50 • **85**

Churchill *Corona Gorda* 5⅝" x 46 • **87**

Corona *Corona* 5½" x 42 • **86**

Corona Major *Petit Corona* 5⅛₆" x 42 • **83**

Corona Major Tube *Corona* 5⅛" x 42 • **85**

Corsario *Corona Gorda* 5½" x 50 • **84**

Director Royale *Lonsdale* 6⅝" x 42 • **85**

Lonsdale *Lonsdale* 6⅝" x 42 • **83**

Monarch *Churchill* 7" x 47 • **84**

Naturales *Panatela* 6⅛" x 36 • **76**

Pequenos 100 *Robusto* 4½" x 50 • **86**

Petit Corona *Petit Corona* 5⅛₆" x 42 • **86**

Tubos *Petit Corona* 5⅛₆" x 42 • **86**

HABANA GOLD

HONDURAS

Black Label Churchill *Churchill* 7½" x 46 • **84**

Black Label Corona *Corona* 6" x 44 • **86**

Black Label Torpedo *Figurado* 6" x 52 • **85**

White Label Churchill *Maduro* 7" x 52 • **85**

White Label Robusto *Maduro* 5" x 50 • **84**

HABANICA

NICARAGUA

Serie 546 *Corona Gorda* 5¼" x 46 • **87**

Serie 646 *Corona Gorda* 6" x 46 • **85**

HAVANA CLASSICO

U.S.A.

Malecon *Odd* 9" x 60 • **86**

Robusto *Maduro* 5" x 50 • **86**

Robusto Largo *Corona Gorda* 6" x 50 • **85**

HENRY CLAY

CUBA

Coronas *Vintage* 5½" x 42 • **86**

HENRY CLAY

DOMINICAN REPUBLIC

Brevas *Corona* 5½" x 42 • **84**

Brevas a la Conserva *Corona Gorda*
5⅝" x 46 • **78**

Brevas de la Conserva *Maduro*
5⅝" x 46 • **87**

Brevas Fina Maduro *Maduro* 6½" x 48 • **84**

HOYO DE MONTERREY

CUBA

Churchill *Churchill* 7" x 47 • **88**

Corona *Corona* 5½" x 42 • **85**

Double Corona *Double Corona*
7⅝" x 49 • **96**

Epicure No. 1 *Corona Gorda* 5⅝" x 46 • **92**

Epicure No. 2 *Robusto* 5" x 50 • **94**

Le Hoyo des Dieux *Lonsdale* 6" x 42 • **89**

Le Hoyo du Dauphin *Panatela* 6" x 38 • **86**

Le Hoyo du Prince *Petit Corona*
5" x 40 • **86**

Le Hoyo du Roi *Corona* 5½" x 42 • **90**

Particulares *Odd* 9¼" x 47 • **93**

HOYO DE MONTERREY

HONDURAS

Ambassador *Lonsdale* 6¼" x 44 • **84**

Cafe Royal *Corona* 5⅝" x 43 • **87**

Churchill *Lonsdale* 6¼" x 45 • **81**

Churchill *Odd* 6¼" x 45 • **86**

Corona *Corona Gorda* 5⅝" x 46 • **87**

Culebra *Figurado* 6¼" x 35 • **84**

Delights *Panatela* 6¼" x 37 • **80**

Demitasse *Odd* 4" x 39 • **86**

Double Corona *Churchill* 6¼" x 48 • **83**

Excalibur Banquet *Churchill* 6¼" x 48 • **82**

Excalibur No. 1 *Churchill* 7¼" x 54 • **80**

Excalibur No. 1 *Double Corona*
7¼" x 54 • **89**

Excalibur No. 1 Maduro *Maduro*
7¼" x 54 • **85**

Excalibur No. 2 *Maduro* 7" x 46 • **85**

Excalibur No. 3 *Corona Gorda*
6¼" x 50 • **89**

Excalibur No. 3 *Maduro* 6⅛" x 48 • **87**

Excalibur No. 4 *Corona Gorda*
5⅝" x 46 • **81**

Excalibur No. 5 *Corona* 6¼" x 43 • **85**

Excalibur No. 6 *Petit Corona* 5½" x 38 • **85**

Excalibur No. 7 *Panatela* 5" x 43 • **83**

Excalibur No. 7 *Petit Corona* 5" x 43 • **88**

Governor *Corona Gorda* 6⅛" x 50 • **87**

Governor Maduro *Maduro* 6⅛" x 50 • **86**

No. 1 *Lonsdale* 6½" x 43 • **85**

No. 55 *Corona* 5¼" x 43 • **88**

No. 55 *Petit Corona* 5¼" x 43 • **83**

Rothschild *Robusto* 4½" x 50 • **86**

Rothschild Maduro *Maduro* 4½" x 50 • **85**

Sabrosas *Petit Corona* 5" x 40 • **70**

Sultan *Churchill* 7¼" x 54 • **82**

Sultan Maduro *Maduro* 7¼" x 54 • **85**

Super Hoyo *Corona* 5½" x 44 • **86**

Super Hoyo *Petit Corona* 5½" x 44 • **87**

JOSE BENITO

DOMINICAN REPUBLIC

Churchill *Churchill* 7" x 50 • **84**

Palma *Corona* 6" x 43 • **86**

Palma *Lonsdale* 6" x 43 • **87**

Petite *Petit Corona* 5½" x 38 • **84**

Presidente *Double Corona* 7¼" x 50 • **85**

Rothschild *Robusto* 4¼" x 50 • **84**

JOSÉ MARTÍ

DOMINICAN REPUBLIC

Corona *Corona* 5½" x 42 • **84**

Maceo *Odd* 6⅞" x 45 • **81**

Martí *Churchill* 7¼" x 50 • **86**

Palma *Lonsdale* 7" x 42 • **84**

Remedio *Odd* 5½" x 45 • **85**

JOSÉ MARTÍ 1868

HONDURAS

Corona *Corona* 5¾" x 45 • **89**

JOYA DE NICARAGUA

NICARAGUA

Churchill *Churchill* 6⅞" x 49 • **85**

Churchill *Double Corona* 6⅞" x 49 • **83**

Consul *Robusto* 4½" x 52 • **81**

Maduro Deluxe Presidente *Maduro*
7½" x 50 • **84**

Maduro Deluxe Robusto *Maduro*
4¼" x 52 • **88**

No. 1 *Lonsdale* 6⅜" x 44 • **87**

No. 1 *Odd* 6⅜" x 44 • **82**

No. 5 *Panatela* 5½" x 38 • **81**

No. 6 *Corona* 6" x 42 • **83**

Petite *Petit Corona* 5½" x 38 • **83**

Toro *Corona Gorda* 6" x 50 • **84**

Viajante *Double Corona* 8½" x 52 • **88**

JUAN CLEMENTE

DOMINICAN REPUBLIC

Churchill *Churchill* 6¾" x 46 • **88**

Club Selection No. 1 *Corona Gorda*
6" x 50 • **83**

Club Selection No. 2 *Robusto* 4½" x 46 • **84**

Club Selection No. 3 *Lonsdale* 7" x 44 • **84**

Club Selection No. 4 *Corona* 5¼" x 42 • **86**

Gran Corona *Lonsdale* 6" x 42 • **84**

Panatela *Panatela* 6½" x 34 • **87**

Rothschild *Robusto* 4⅞" x 50 • **85**

JULIA MARLOWE

DOMINICAN REPUBLIC

Monarch *Churchill* 7" x 48 • **87**

KNOCKANDO

DOMINICAN REPUBLIC

No. 3 *Corona* 5¼" x 41 • **84**

LA AURORA

DOMINICAN REPUBLIC

Bristol Especial *Churchill* 6¾" x 48 • **84**

No. 4 *Corona* 5¼" x 42 • **85**

Palmas Extra *Panatela* 6¼" x 35 • **80**

LA CORONA

CUBA

Churchill *Vintage* 6½" x 46 • **93**

LA FINCA

NICARAGUA

Bolivares *Double Corona* 7½" x 50 • **85**
Corona *Corona* 5½" x 42 • **91**
Corona *Petit Corona* 5½" x 42 • **84**
Flora *Panatela* 7" x 36 • **86**
Joya *Corona Gorda* 6" x 50 • **79**
Robusto *Maduro* 4½" x 50 • **87**
Romeo *Lonsdale* 6½" x 42 • **87**

LA FLOR DOMINICANA

DOMINICAN REPUBLIC

Alcalde *Lonsdale* 6½" x 44 • **82**

LA FONTANA

HONDURAS

Da Vinci *Churchill* 6⅞" x 48 • **84**
Michelangelo *Double Corona* 7½" x 52 • **83**

LA GLORIA CUBANA

CUBA

Medaille d'Or No. 1 *Figurado* 7⅛" x 36 • **87**
Medaille d'Or No. 2 *Lonsdale* 6⅔" x 43 • **90**

LA GLORIA CUBANA

DOMINICAN REPUBLIC

Glorias Extra *Odd* 6¼" x 46 • **88**

LA GLORIA CUBANA

U.S.A.

Churchill *Double Corona* 7" x 50 • **88**

Churchill *Maduro* 7" x 50 • **89**
Extra *Corona Gorda* 6¼" x 46 • **87**
Glorias *Corona* 5½" x 43 • **88**
Medaille D'Or No. 1 *Lonsdale*
    6¼" x 43 • **88**
Panatela Deluxe *Panatela* 7" x 37 • **87**
Piramides *Figurado* 7¼" x 56 • **87**
Soberanos *Double Corona* 8" x 52 • **91**
Torpedo No. 1 *Figurado* 6½" x 54 • **86**
Wavell *Maduro* 5" x 50 • **90**
Wavell *Robusto* 5" x 50 • **85**

LA HOJA SELECTA

U.S.A.

Cetros de Oro *Corona* 5¼" x 43 • **83**
Cosiac *Double Corona* 7" x 49 • **85**
Palais Royal *Robusto* 4¼" x 50 • **72**

LA INVICTA

HONDURAS

Magnum No. 2 *Robusto* 4½" x 50 • **79**

LA REGENTA

CANARY ISLANDS

No. 3 *Corona* 5⅝" x 42 • **78**

LA RESERVA

HONDURAS

No. 2 *Churchill* 6½" x 48 • **86**

LA UNICA

DOMINICAN REPUBLIC

No. 100 *Double Corona* 8½" x 52 • **90**
No. 200 *Churchill* 7" x 49 • **88**
No. 200 *Maduro* 7" x 49 • **86**
No. 300 *Lonsdale* 6¼" x 44 • **84**
No. 400 *Robusto* 4½" x 50 • **84**
No. 400 *Maduro* 4½ x 50 • **84**
No. 500 *Corona* 5½" x 42 • **84**

LAS CABRILLAS

HONDURAS

Balboa *Odd* 7½" x 54 • **82**
Balboa Maduro *Maduro* 7½" x 54 • **82**
Cortez *Robusto* 4¼" x 50 • **83**
Cortez Maduro *Maduro* 4¼" x 50 • **84**
Desoto *Churchill* 6⅞" x 50 • **83**
Magellan *Corona* 6" x 42 • **84**
Maximilian *Figurado* 7" x 55 • **84**
Ponce de Leon *Lonsdale* 6⅞" x 44 • **79**

LEMPIRA

HONDURAS

Churchill *Churchill* 7" x 48 • **86**
Corona *Corona* 5½" x 42 • **88**
Toro *Corona Gorda* 6" x 50 • **89**

LEON JIMENES

DOMINICAN REPUBLIC

No. 1 *Double Corona* 7½" x 50 • **83**
No. 2 *Churchill* 7" x 47 • **86**
No. 3 *Lonsdale* 6½" x 42 • **83**

No. 4 *Corona* 5⅜6" x 42 • **85**
Robusto *Robusto* 5½" x 50 • **85**

LICENCIADOS

DOMINICAN REPUBLIC

Excelente *Lonsdale* 6¼" x 43 • **87**
No. 4 *Corona* 5½" x 42 • **86**
No. 4 *Maduro* 5¼" x 43 • **80**
No. 4 *Petit Corona* 5½" x 42 • **82**
Panatela Lindas *Panatela* 7" x 38 • **82**
Presidente *Double Corona* 8" x 50 • **87**
Presidente *Maduro* 8" x 50 • **80**
Supreme Maduro No. 200 *Corona*
5" x 42 • **84**
Supreme Maduro No. 200 *Petit Corona*
5½" x 42 • **82**
Supreme Maduro No. 400 *Maduro*
6" x 50 • **84**
Toro *Corona Gorda* 6" x 50 • **86**
Toro *Maduro* 6" x 50 • **83**
Wavell *Robusto* 5" x 50 • **88**
Wavell Maduro *Maduro* 5" x 50 • **87**

LOS LIBERTADORES

DOMINICAN REPUBLIC

Figurado *Figurado* 6½" x 52 • **87**
Figurado Reserva Especial *Figurado*
6½" x 52 • **86**
Insurrectos *Corona* 5½" x 42 • **85**
Insurrectos *Petit Corona* 5½" x 42 • **84**
Mambises *Churchill* 6⅞" x 48 • **88**
Reserve Special Churchill *Churchill*
6⅞" x 49 • **85**

MACABI

DOMINICAN REPUBLIC
Corona Extra *Corona Gorda* 6" x 50 • **84**

MACABI

U.S.A.

Belicoso Fino *Figurado* 6¼" x 52 • **88**
Media Corona *Corona* 5½" x 43 • **86**
No. 1 *Lonsdale* 6¼" x 44 • **85**

MACANUDO

JAMAICA

Amatista *Lonsdale* 6¼" x 42 • **89**

Baron de Rothschild *Lonsdale*
6½" x 42 • **85**

Crystal Cafe *Corona Gorda* 5½" x 50 • **84**

Duke of Devon *Corona* 5½" x 42 • **86**

Duke of Devon *Maduro* 5½" x 42 • **83**

Duke of Wellington *Figurado* 8½" x 38 • **86**

Duke of Windsor *Figurado* 6" x 50 • **87**

Hampton Court *Corona* 5¼" x 42 • **85**

Hampton Court *Petit Corona* 5¼" x 43 • **87**

Hyde Park *Robusto* 5½" x 49 • **87**

Hyde Park Cafe *Corona Gorda*
5½" x 49 • **88**

Lord Claridge *Petit Corona* 5½" x 38 • **88**

Petit Corona *Petit Corona* 5" x 38 • **84**

Portofino *Panatela* 7" x 34 • **85**

Prince Philip *Churchill* 7½" x 49 • **83**

Prince Philip *Double Corona* 7½" x 49 • **85**

Prince Philip *Maduro* 7½" x 49 • **85**

Vintage Cabinet Selection No. 1 *Double
Corona* 7½" x 49 • **90**

Vintage Cabinet No. 2 *Lonsdale*
6⁹⁄₁₆" x 43 • **86**

Vintage Cabinet Selection 1993 *Corona
Gorda* 5½" x 49 • **86**

Vintage Cabinet Selection 1993 VIII
Corona Gorda 5½" x 49 • **84**

Vintage No. 1 *Churchill* 7½" x 49 • **85**

Vintage No. 3 *Corona* 5⁹⁄₁₆" x 43 • **87**

Vintage No. 3 *Petit Corona* 5½" x 42 • **88**

Vintage No. 5 *Robusto* 5½" x 49 • **85**

Vintage No. 7 *Panatela* 7½" x 38 • **83**

MATCH PLAY

DOMINICAN REPUBLIC
Turnberry *Corona Gorda* 6" x 50 • **80**

MAYA

HONDURAS

Churchill *Churchill* 6¼" x 49 • **85**

Maya *Corona Gorda* 6" x 50 • **83**

Palma Fina *Panatela* 6¼" x 36 • **86**

Petit Corona *Corona* 5½" x 42 • **85**

MICUBANO

NICARAGUA

No. 542 *Corona* 5" x 42 • **84**

No. 650 *Corona Gorda* 6" x 50 • **82**

MONTE CANARIO

CANARY ISLANDS
Imperiales *Lonsdale* 6½" x 42 • **86**
Nuncio *Lonsdale* 6¼" x 44 • **86**

MONTECRISTO

CUBA

"**A**" *Figurado* 9½" x 47 • **95**
"**A**" *Odd* 9¼" x 47 • **91**
Especial *Panatela* 7½" x 38 • **86**
Especial No. 1 *Figurado* 7½" x 38 • **91**
Especial No. 2 *Panatela* 6" x 38 • **91**
No. 1 *Lonsdale* 6½" x 42 • **88**
No. 1 Seleccion Suprema *Vintage*
6½" x 42 • **98**
No. 2 *Figurado* 6⅛" x 52 • **94**
No. 3 *Corona* 5½" x 42 • **88**
No. 4 *Petit Corona* 5" x 42 • **89**
No. 4 Seleccion Suprema *Vintage*
5" x 42 • **92**

MONTECRISTO

DOMINICAN REPUBLIC

Churchill *Churchill* 7" x 48 • **89**
Corona Grande *Corona Gorda*
5¼" x 46 • **86**
Double Corona *Odd* 6¼" x 50 • **86**
No. 1 *Lonsdale* 6½" x 44 • **87**
No. 2 *Figurado* 6" x 50 • **87**
No. 3 *Corona* 5½" x 44 • **87**
Robusto *Robusto* 4¼" x 50 • **85**

MONTECRUZ

DOMINICAN REPUBLIC

No. 200 Natural Claro *Churchill*
7¼" x 46 • **89**
No. 210 *Lonsdale* 6½" x 42 • **85**
Sun-Grown Cedar Aged *Petit Corona*
5" x 42 • **83**
Sun-Grown Individuales *Odd* 8" x 46 • **84**

Sun-Grown No. 200 *Churchill*
7¼" x 46 • **88**
Sun-Grown Tubos *Corona* 6" x 42 • **85**
Sun-Grown No. 201 *Corona Gorda*
6¼" x 46 • **85**
Sun-Grown No. 210 *Lonsdale*
6½" x 42 • **84**
Sun-Grown No. 220 *Corona* 5½" x 42 • **87**
Sun-Grown No. 230 *Petit Corona*
5" x 42 • **84**
Sun-Grown Robusto *Robusto* 4½" x 49 • **83**
Tubulares Sun Grown *Panatela*
6⅛" x 36 • **84**

MONTESINO

DOMINICAN REPUBLIC

Cesar No. 2 *Lonsdale* 6¼" x 44 • **83**
Diplomatico *Corona* 5½" x 43 • **91**
Diplomatico *Maduro* 5½" x 42 • **86**
Diplomatico *Petit Corona* 5½ " x 43 • **89**
Gran Corona *Churchill* 6¼" x 48 • **86**
Gran Corona *Maduro* 6¼" x 48 • **86**
No. 1 *Lonsdale* 6¼" x 43 • **87**

MORRO CASTLE

NICARAGUA

Corona Gorda *Corona Gorda* 6" x 50 • **83**

NAT SHERMAN

DOMINICAN REPUBLIC

City Desk Dispatch *Maduro* 6½" x 46 • **85**
City Desk Gazette *Corona* 6" x 42 • **83**
City Desk Telegraph *Maduro* 6" x 50 • **85**
City Desk Tribune *Double Corona*
7½" x 50 • **86**

City Desk Tribune *Maduro* 7½" x 50 • **86**

Dakota *Churchill* 7½" x 49 • **87**

Exchange Selection Butterfield No. 8
Lonsdale 6½" x 42 • **83**

Exchange Selection Murray Hill No. 7
Panatela 6" x 38 • **83**

Exchange Selection Oxford No. 5
Churchill 7" x 49 • **88**

Exchange Selection Trafalgar No. 4
Corona Gorda 6" x 47 • **82**

Gotham Selection No. 500 *Churchill*
7" x 50 • **87**

Gotham Selection No. 711 *Corona Gorda*
6" x 50 • **87**

Gotham Selection No. 1400 *Lonsdale*
6¼" x 44 • **85**

Landmark Selection Algonquin *Lonsdale*
6¼" x 43 • **84**

Landmark Selection Dakota *Double Corona*
7½" x 49 • **87**

Landmark Selection Hampshire *Corona*
5½" x 42 • **87**

Landmark Selection Hampshire *Petit
Corona* 5½" x 42 • **86**

Landmark Selection Metropole *Panatela*
6" x 34 • **82**

Manhattan Selection Gramercy *Lonsdale*
6¼" x 43 • **80**

Manhattan Selection Sutton *Corona Gorda*
5½" x 49 • **80**

Manhattan Selection Sutton *Robusto*
5½" x 49 • **84**

Metropolitan Selection Angler *Corona*
5½" x 43 • **87**

Metropolitan Selection Metropolitan
Figurado 7" x 52 • **87**

Morgan *Odd* 7" x 42 • **80**

VIP Selection Astor *Robusto* 4½" x 50 • **86**

VIP Selection Barnum Glass Tube *Petit
Corona* 5½" x 42 • **82**

VIP Selection Carnegie *Corona Gorda*
6" x 48 • **86**

VIP Selection Zigfield Fancy Tail *Figurado*
6¼" x 38 • **83**

NAT SHERMAN

HONDURAS

Host Selection Hamilton *Petit Corona*
5½" x 42 • **80**

Host Selection Hobart *Robusto*
5" x 50 • **86**

NESTOR 747

HONDURAS

Cabinet Series No. 2 *Odd* 4¼" x 54 • **85**

OLOR

DOMINICAN REPUBLIC

Colossos *Churchill* 7½" x 48 • **88**

Lonsdale *Lonsdale* 6½" x 42 • **84**

Momentos *Corona* 5½" x 43 • **88**

Momentos *Petit Corona* 5½" x 43 • **86**

Paco *Corona Gorda* 6" x 50 • **88**

ONYX

DOMINICAN REPUBLIC

No. 642 *Corona* 6" x 42 • **83**

No. 642 *Maduro* 6" x 42 • **85**

No. 646 *Churchill* 6¾" x 46 • **85**

No. 650 *Corona Gorda* 6" x 50 • **87**

No. 650 *Maduro* 6" x 50 • **88**

No. 750 *Maduro* 7½" x 50 • **85**

ORIENT EXPRESS

HONDURAS

Expresso *Figurado* 6" x 48 • **82**

ORNELAS

MEXICO

250 *Odd* 9½" x 64 • **87**

Cafetero Chico Maduro *Maduro*
5½" x 46 • **79**

Cafetero Grande *Maduro* 6½" x 46 • **85**

Churchill *Churchill* 7" x 49 • **79**

Churchill Maduro *Maduro* 7" x 49 • **84**

Ltd. Cognac *Lonsdale* 6¼" x 42 • **78**

No. 1 *Lonsdale* 6¼" x 44 • **78**

No. 1 Vanilla *Lonsdale* 6¼" x 44 • **69**

Robusto Maduro *Maduro* 4¼" x 49 • **86**

OSCAR

DOMINICAN REPUBLIC

No. 300 *Lonsdale* 6¼" x 44 • **81**

No. 500 *Corona Gorda* 5½" x 50 • **83**

No. 700 *Figurado* 7" x 54 • **88**

Supreme *Double Corona* 8" x 48 • **88**

PADRON

HONDURAS

1964 Anniversary Series Corona *Corona*
6" x 42 • **88**

1964 Anniversary Series Piramide
Figurado 6⅞" x 52 • **82**

1964 Annivesary Series Superi *Lonsdale*
6" x 42 • **83**

Ambassdor *Lonsdale* 6⅞" x 42 • **83**

Palma *Lonsdale* 6⁵⁄₁₆" x 42 • **87**

PADRON

NICARAGUA

1964 Anniversary Series Exclusivo
Corona Gorda 5½" x 50 • **92**

2000 Maduro *Maduro* 5" x 50 • **86**

3000 Maduro *Maduro* 5½" x 52 • **88**

Churchill Maduro *Maduro* 6⅞" x 46 • **86**

Executive Maduro *Maduro* 7½" x 50 • **87**

Londres *Corona* 5½" x 42 • **86**

Londres *Petit Corona* 5½" x 42 • **85**

Magnum *Odd* 9" x 50 • **91**

PARTAGAS

CUBA

8-9-8 *Lonsdale* 6⅜" x 43 • **88**

Corona *Corona* 5½" x 42 • **86**

Culebras *Odd* 5¼" x 39 • **87**

Lusitania *Double Corona* 7⅞" x 49 • **92**

No. 1 *Lonsdale* 6⅜" x 43 • **88**

No. 6 Seleccion Superba *Vintage*
4½" x 40 • **93**

Petit Corona *Petit Corona* 5" x 42 • **89**

Presidente *Figurado* 6⅜" x 47 • **84**

Series D No. 4 *Robusto* 5" x 50 • **88**

PARTAGAS

DOMINICAN REPUBLIC

8-9-8 *Lonsdale* 6¼" x 44 • **88**

Almirante *Corona Gorda* 6¼" x 47 • **87**

Almirante *Odd* 6¼" x 47 • **85**

Humitube *Lonsdale* 6¼" x 43 • **87**

Limited Reserve Regale *Odd* 6¼" x 47 • **87**

Limited Reserve Royale *Odd* 6¼" x 43 • **87**

Maduro *Maduro* 6¼" x 48 • **85**

Natural *Corona Gorda* 5½" x 50 • 80
Natural *Robusto* 5½" x 49 • 85
No. 1 *Lonsdale* 6¼" x 43 • 88
No. 2 *Corona* 5⅛" x 44 • 86
No. 4 *Petit Corona* 5" x 38 • 84
No. 10 *Churchill* 7½" x 49 • 89
No. 10 *Double Corona* 7½" x 49 • 86
Robusto *Robusto* 4½" x 49 • 86
Sabrosos *Corona* 5⅞" x 43 • 86
Tubos *Panatela* 7" x 38 • 82

PAUL GARMIRIAN

DOMINICAN REPUBLIC

Belicoso *Figurado* 6¼" x 52 • 88
Belicoso Fino *Figurado* 5½" x 52 • 86
Bombone *Odd* 3½" x 43 • 87
Celebration *Figurado* 9" x 50 • 88
Churchill *Churchill* 7" x 48 • 82
Connoisseur *Corona Gorda* 6" x 50 • 86
Corona *Corona* 5½" x 42 • 86
Epicure *Corona Gorda* 5½" x 50 • 85
Gourmet Double Corona *Double Corona* 7⅞" x 50 • 88
Lonsdale *Lonsdale* 6½" x 42 • 78
Panatela *Panatela* 7½" x 38 • 87
Petit Corona *Petit Corona* 5" x 43 • 86
Series No. 2 *Robusto* 4¼" x 48 • 84

PEÑAMIL

CANARY ISLANDS

No. 57 *Double Corona* 7½" x 50 • 69

PETERSON

DOMINICAN REPUBLIC

Corona *Corona* 5¼" x 43 • 82
Toro *Corona Gorda* 6" x 50 • 87

PETRUS

HONDURAS

Antonius *Figurado* 5" x 54 • 86
Churchill *Churchill* 7" x 50 • 82
DC Havana *Double Corona* 7¼" x 50 • 86
Double Corona *Maduro* 7¼" x 50 • 87
No. 2 *Maduro* 6¼" x 44 • 84
Rothschild *Robusto* 4¼" x 50 • 74
Tabacage 89 Churchill *Maduro* 7" x 50 • 84
Tabacage 89 Corona Sublime *Corona Gorda* 5½" x 46 • 82
Tabacage 89 Corona Sublime *Maduro* 5½" x 46 • 78
Tabacage 89 No. 2 *Lonsdale* 6¼" x 44 • 86
Tabacage 89 No. 4 *Odd* 5⅜" x 38 • 83
Tabacage 89 Rothschild *Maduro* 4¼" x 50 • 81

PLEIADES

DOMINICAN REPUBLIC

Aldebaran *Double Corona* 8½" x 50 • 85
Antares *Panatela* 5½" x 40 • 82
Antares *Petit Corona* 5½" x 40 • 87
Neptune *Odd* 7½" x 42 • 79
Orion *Corona* 5¼" x 42 • 81
Pluton *Robusto* 5" x 50 • 87
Saturne *Odd* 8" x 46 • 81
Sirius *Churchill* 6⅞" x 46 • 81

POR LARRAÑAGA

DOMINICAN REPUBLIC

Cetros *Lonsdale* 6⅞" x 42 • **87**

Delicados *Panatela* 6½" x 36 • **82**

Fabuloso *Churchill* 7" x 50 • **87**

Fabuloso *Double Corona* 7" x 50 • **88**

Nacionales *Corona* 5½" x 42 • **84**

Petit Cetros en Cedro *Petit Corona* 5" x 38 • **86**

Pyramid *Figurado* 6" x 50 • **86**

Robusto *Robusto* 5" x 50 • **88**

PRIMO DEL REY

DOMINICAN REPUBLIC

Almirante *Corona Gorda* 6" x 50 • **83**

Almirante Maduro *Maduro* 6" x 50 • **85**

Aristocrat *Churchill* 6¾" x 48 • **81**

Chavon *Lonsdale* 6½" x 41 • **85**

Churchill *Odd* 6¼" x 48 • **82**

Club Seleccion Regals *Churchill* 7" x 50 • **83**

Lonsdale *Lonsdale* 6½" x 42 • **82**

No. 4 *Corona* 5½" x 42 • **84**

No. 4 *Maduro* 5½" x 42 • **85**

No. 4 *Petit Corona* 5½" x 42 • **87**

No. 100 *Robusto* 4½" x 50 • **83**

No. 100 Maduro *Maduro* 4½" x 50 • **86**

Presidente *Lonsdale* 6$\frac{13}{16}$" x 44 • **85**

Royal Corona *Corona Gorda* 6" x 46 • **81**

Seleccion No. 1 *Lonsdale* 6$\frac{13}{16}$" x 42 • **86**

Seleccion No. 2 *Lonsdale* 6¼" x 42 • **84**

Soberano *Churchill* 7½" x 50 • **82**

Soberano *Double Corona* 7½" x 50 • **89**

Soberano Maduro *Maduro* 7½" x 50 • **87**

PUNCH

CUBA

Churchill *Churchill* 7" x 47 • **91**

Corona *Corona* 5½" x 42 • **89**

Diademas Extra *Figurado* 9" x 47 • **92**

Double Corona *Double Corona* 7⅝" x 49 • **91**

Ninfas *Panatela* 7" x 38 • **88**

Punch *Corona Gorda* 5⅝" x 46 • **87**

Royal Selection No. 12 *Petit Corona* 5" x 42 • **86**

PUNCH

HONDURAS

After Dinner *Odd* 7¼" x 45 • **74**

Amatista *Lonsdale* 6¼" x 44 • **84**

Cafe Royal *Corona* 5⅝" x 44 • **88**

Chateau L *Churchill* 7¼" x 54 • **85**

Chateau L *Double Corona* 7½" x 52 • **85**

Chateau L Maduro *Maduro* 7¼" x 54 • **85**

Chateau M *Maduro* 6¾" x 46 • **86**

Chateau M *Corona Gorda* 5¾" x 46 • **85**

Corona *Odd* 6¼" x 45 • **88**

Diademas *Double Corona* 7½" x 50 • **85**

Double Corona *Maduro* 6¾" x 48 • **86**

Double Corona *Churchill* 6¾" x 48 • **81**

Elite *Petit Corona* 5¼" x 44 • **85**

Britannia *Odd* 6¼" x 50 • **88**

Grand Cru Diademas *Churchill* 7¼" x 54 • **82**

Grand Cru Monarch *Churchill* 6¾" x 48 • **87**

Grand Cru Prince Consort *Figurado* 8½" x 52 • **85**

Grand Cru Robusto *Robusto* 5¼" x 50 • **83**

Lonsdale *Lonsdale* 6½" x 43 • 85

No. 1 *Lonsdale* 6½" x 43 • 86

No. 75 *Corona* 5½" x 43 • 84

Pita Maduro *Maduro* 6⅛" x 50 • 87

Punch *Lonsdale* 6¼" x 45 • 81

Rothschild *Robusto* 4½" x 50 • 83

Rothschild Maduro *Maduro* 4½" x 50 • 86

Royal Coronation *Corona* 5¼" x 44 • 83

Super Rothschild *Corona Gorda*
5¼" x 50 • 86

Superior *Corona Gorda* 5½" x 48 • 83

PUROS INDIOS

HONDURAS

Churchill Maduro *Maduro* 7¼" x 52 • 86

Corona Gorda *Corona Gorda* 6" x 50 • 86

Corona Gorda Maduro *Maduro*
6" x 52 • 86

No. 4 Especial *Corona* 5½" x 44 • 90

Piramides No. 1 *Figurado* 7½" x 60 • 92

Piramides No. 2 *Figurado* 6½" x 46 • 90

QUAI D'ORSAY

CUBA

Imperiales *Churchill* 7" x 47 • 90

QUINTERO

CUBA

Churchill *Lonsdale* 6½" x 42 • 92

Medias Coronas *Petit Corona* 5" x 40 • 84

RAFAEL GONZALES

CUBA

Lonsdale *Lonsdale* 6½" x 42 • 91

RAMON ALLONES

CUBA

Corona *Corona* 5½" x 42 • 89

Gigantes *Double Corona* 7⅛" x 49 • 94

Ideales *Vintage* 6½" x 40 • 89

No. 66 (perfecto) *Vintage* 6" x n/a • 87

Specially Selected *Robusto* 5" x 50 • 90

RAMON ALLONES

DOMINICAN REPUBLIC

"B" *Lonsdale* 6½" x 42 • 87

Crystals *Lonsdale* 6¼" x 42 • 86

Privada A *Lonsdale* 7" x 45 • 85

Privada D *Corona* 5" x 42 • 86

Redondos *Churchill* 7½" x 49 • 85

Size D *Petit Corona* 5" x 42 • 85

Trumps *Lonsdale* 6¼" x 43 • 83

ROMANTICOS

DOMINICAN REPUBLIC

Leonardo *Corona Gorda* 6" x 50 • 85

ROMEO Y JULIETA

CUBA

Alfred Dunhill Selection Sun-Grown
Breva *Vintage* 5½" x 44 • 89

Belicoso *Figurado* 5½" x 52 • 90

Belvedere *Panatela* 5½" x 39 • 84

Celestial Fino *Figurado* 5¼" x 46 • **87**

Churchill *Churchill* 7" x 47 • **92**

Corona *Corona* 5½" x 42 • **89**

Corona Grande *Lonsdale* 6½" x 42 • **90**

Exhibicion No. 3 *Corona Gorda*
  5⅜" x 46 • **91**

Exhibicion No. 4 *Robusto* 5" x 48 • **89**

Fabuloso *Figurado* 9" x 47 • **96**

Fabuloso *Odd* 9¼" x 47 • **91**

No. 758 Alfred Dunhill Ltd. Seleccion
  Vintage 6½" x 42 • **97**

Petit Corona *Petit Corona* 5" x 42 • **89**

Shakespeare *Panatela* 6½" x 28 • **85**

ROMEO Y JULIETA

DOMINICAN REPUBLIC

Churchill *Double Corona* 7" x 50 • **83**

Corona *Corona* 5½" x 44 • **83**

Palma *Lonsdale* 6" x 43 • **84**

Presidente *Odd* 7" x 43 • **88**

Romeo *Figurado* 6" x 46 • **85**

Rothschild *Maduro* 5" x 50 • **87**

Rothschild *Robusto* 5" x 50 • **84**

Vintage No. 1 *Corona* 6" x 43 • **87**

Vintage No. 1 *Lonsdale* 6" x 43 • **86**

Vintage No. 2 *Corona Gorda* 6" x 46 • **87**

Vintage No. 3 *Robusto* 4½" x 50 • **86**

Vintage No. 4 *Churchill* 7" x 48 • **85**

Vintage No. 5 *Double Corona* 7½" x 50 • **89**

ROYAL JAMAICA

DOMINICAN REPUBLIC

Churchill *Double Corona* 8" x 51 • **87**

Churchill Maduro *Maduro* 8" x 51 • **86**

Corona *Maduro* 5½" x 40 • **87**

Corona Grande *Lonsdale* 6½" x 42 • **84**

Corona Grande *Maduro* 6½" x 42 • **85**

Director *Corona Gorda* 6" x 45 • **87**

Double Corona *Odd* 7" x 45 • **87**

Giant Corona *Churchill* 7½" x 49 • **83**

Giant Corona *Double Corona* 7½" x 49 • **83**

Goliath *Odd* 9" x 64 • **80**

No. 1 Tube *Odd* 6" x 45 • **82**

Park Lane *Figurado* 6" x 47 • **85**

Petit Corona *Petit Corona* 5" x 40 • **83**

Robusto *Robusto* 4½" x 49 • **87**

Tube No. 2 *Panatela* 6½" x 34 • **83**

SAINT LUIS REY

CUBA

Churchill *Churchill* 7" x 47 • **89**

Lonsdale *Lonsdale* 6½" x 42 • **88**

SAINT LUIS REY

HONDURAS

Lonsdale *Lonsdale* 6½" x 44 • **86**

Serie A *Corona Gorda* 6" x 50 • **85**

SANCHO PANZA

CUBA

Belicoso *Figurado* 5½" x 52 • **86**

Molinas *Lonsdale* 6½" x 42 • **91**

Non Plus *Petit Corona* 5" x 42 • **85**

Sanchos *Odd* 9¼" x 47 • **86**

SANTA CLARA

MEXICO

No. 2 *Churchill* 6½" x 48 • **78**
No. 3 *Lonsdale* 6⅛" x 43 • **85**
No. 5 *Corona* 6" x 43 • **87**
No. 6 *Corona Gorda* 6" x 50 • **79**

SANTA CLARA 1830

MEXICO

No. 1 *Double Corona* 7½" x 52 • **87**
No. 1 *Maduro* 7" x 51 • **83**
No. 6 *Maduro* 6" x 51 • **85**

SANTA DAMIANA

DOMINICAN REPUBLIC

Cabinet Selection No. 800 *Churchill*
7" x 50 • **84**
No. 700 *Lonsdale* 6½" x 42 • **82**
Seleccion No. 100 *Churchill* 6¼" x 48 • **83**
Selection No. 300 *Corona Gorda*
5½" x 46 • **83**
Seleccion No. 500 *Robusto* 5" x 50 • **86**

SANTA ROSA

HONDURAS

Cetros *Lonsdale* 6" x 42 • **86**
Churchill *Churchill* 7" x 49 • **87**
Corona *Lonsdale* 6½" x 44 • **83**
No. 4 *Corona* 5½" x 42 • **86**
Sancho Panza Maduro *Maduro*
4½" x 50 • **81**
Toro *Corona Gorda* 6" x 50 • **86**

SANTIAGO CABANA

U.S.A.

Torpedo *Figurado* 6¼" x 54 • **90**

SAVINELLI

DOMINICAN REPUBLIC

E.L.R. Churchill *Churchill* 7¼" x 48 • **88**
E.L.R. Churchill *Double Corona*
7¼" x 48 • **91**
E.L.R. Double Corona *Corona Gorda*
6" x 50 • **87**
E.L.R. No. 3 Lonsdale *Lonsdale*
6¼" x 43 • **88**
Extraordinaire *Corona* 5½" x 44 • **89**

SOSA

DOMINICAN REPUBLIC

Brevas *Corona* 5½" x 43 • **84**
Churchill *Churchill* 6¹⁵⁄₁₆ x 49 • **88**
Churchill Maduro *Maduro* 6¹⁵⁄₁₆ x 49 • **88**
Family Selection No. 1 *Lonsdale*
6¼" x 43 • **85**
Family Selection No. 2 *Figurado*
6¼" x 54 • **88**
Governor *Corona Gorda* 6" x 50 • **88**
Lonsdale *Lonsdale* 6½" x 43 • **78**
No. 1 *Lonsdale* 6½" x 43 • **87**
Piramides *Figurado* 7" x 64 • **80**
Rothschild Maduro *Maduro* 4¼" x 49 • **88**
Sante Fe *Panatela* 6" x 35 • **78**
Soberano *Double Corona* 7½" x 52 • **88**
Wavell *Robusto* 4¼" x 50 • **84**
Wavell Maduro *Maduro* 4¼" x 50 • **87**

TE-AMO

MEXICO

Celebration *Lonsdale* 6¹¹⁄₁₆" x 44 • 81

CEO *Odd* 8½" x 52 • 82

Churchill *Double Corona* 7½" x 50 • 82

Churchill Maduro *Maduro* 7½" x 50 • 84

Figurado *Figurado* 6⅝" x 50 • 85

Gran Pyramide *Figurado* 7¼" x 54 • 84

Maximo Churchill Maduro *Maduro* 7" x 54 • 86

Meditation *Corona* 6" x 42 • 80

Meditation *Lonsdale* 6" x 42 • 85

New York LaGuardia *Odd* 5" x 54 • 87

New York Wall Street *Odd* 6" x 52 • 84

No. 4 *Petit Corona* 5" x 42 • 83

Park Avenue New York *Lonsdale* 6⅝" x 42 • 80

Piramide *Figurado* 6¼" x 50 • 83

Presidente *Churchill* 7" x 50 • 84

Presidente Maduro *Maduro* 7 " x 50 • 83

Relaxation *Lonsdale* 6⅝" x 44 • 82

Robusto Maduro *Maduro* 5½" x 54 • 81

Satisfaction *Corona Gorda* 6" x 46 • 82

Satisfaction Maduro *Maduro* 6" x 46 • 84

Torero *Panatela* 6⁹⁄₁₆" x 35 • 81

Torito *Robusto* 4¼" x 50 • 82

Torito Maduro *Maduro* 4¼ " x 50 • 85

Toro *Corona Gorda* 6" x 50 • 86

Toro Maduro *Maduro* 6" x 50 • 84

TEMPLE HALL

JAMAICA

Belicoso *Figurado* 6" x 50 • 88

Estates No. 450 *Maduro* 4½" x 49 • 86

No. 550 *Corona Gorda* 5½" x 49 • 85

No. 550 *Robusto* 5½" x 50 • 84

No. 625 *Lonsdale* 6¼" x 45 • 82

No. 685 *Panatela* 6⅛" x 34 • 87

No. 700 *Churchill* 7½" x 49 • 84

TESOROS DE COPAN

HONDURAS

Cetros *Lonsdale* 6¼" x 44 • 84

Corona *Corona Gorda* 5¼" x 46 • 77

THE GRIFFIN'S

DOMINICAN REPUBLIC

Don Bernardo *Figurado* 9" x 46 • 85

No. 100 *Figurado* 7" x 38 • 84

No. 200 *Odd* 7" x 44 • 81

No. 300 *Lonsdale* 6¼" x 44 • 84

No. 400 *Panatela* 6" x 38 • 84

Prestige *Double Corona* 8" x 48 • 85

THOMAS HINDS

HONDURAS

Honduran Selection Churchill *Churchill* 7" x 49 • 88

Honduran Selection Corona *Corona* 5½" x 42 • 86

Honduran Selection Corona *Petit Corona* 5½" x 42 • 87

Honduran Selection Presidente *Double Corona* 8½" x 52 • 87

Honduran Selection Robusto *Robusto* 5" x 50 • 86

Honduran Selection Short Churchill *Corona Gorda* 6" x 50 • 82

Honduran Selection Supremos *Lonsdale*
6¾" x 43 • **85**

Honduran Selection Torpedo *Figurado*
6" x 52 • **86**

THOMAS HINDS

NICARAGUA

Nicaraguan Selection Churchill Maduro
Maduro 7" x 49 • **83**

Nicaraguan Selection Corona *Corona*
5½" x 42 • **84**

Nicaraguan Selection Corona Gorda
Maduro *Maduro* 6" x 50 • **84**

Nicaraguan Selection Lonsdale *Lonsdale*
6¾" x 43 • **87**

Nicaraguan Selection Robusto Maduro
Maduro 5" x 50 • **84**

Nicaraguan Selection Short Churchill
Corona Gorda 6" x 50 • **85**

TORCEDOR

NICARAGUA

Toro *Corona Gorda* 6" x 50 • **78**

TRESADO

DOMINICAN REPUBLIC

Seleccion No. 200 *Churchill* 7" x 48 • **83**

Seleccion No. 200 *Maduro* 7" x 48 • **89**

Seleccion No. 300 *Corona Gorda*
6" x 46 • **84**

Seleccion No. 400 *Lonsdale* 6⅜ x 44 • **86**

Seleccion No. 500 *Corona* 5½" x 42 • **85**

Seleccion No. 500 *Maduro* 5½" x 42 • **83**

Seleccion No. 500 *Petit Corona*
5½" x 42 • **84**

TROYA

DOMINICAN REPUBLIC

Cetro *Lonsdale* 6¼" x 44 • **90**

Clasico *Petit Corona* 5½" x 42 • **84**

Executive No. 72 *Double Corona*
7¼" x 50 • **82**

No. 18 *Robusto* 4¼" x 50 • **82**

No. 18 Rothschild Maduro *Maduro*
4½" x 50 • **87**

No. 27 *Corona* 5½" x 42 • **87**

No. 45 Cetro *Maduro* 6" x 44 • **83**

No. 54 Elegante *Lonsdale* 7" x 43 • **86**

No. 63 Churchill 6⅞" x 46 • **86**

No. 63 Churchill Maduro *Maduro*
6⅞" x 46 • **84**

Torpedo No. 81 *Figurado* 7" x 54 • **87**

V CENTENNIAL

HONDURAS

Cetro *Lonsdale* 6½" x 44 • **89**

Churchill *Churchill* 7" x 48 • **87**

Churchill Maduro *Maduro* 6⅞" x 48 • **84**

Corona *Corona* 5½" x 42 • **83**

Numero 1 *Panatela* 7½" x 38 • **88**

Numero 2 *Corona Gorda* 6" x 50 • **88**

Numero 2 Maduro *Maduro* 6" x 50 • **84**

Presidente *Double Corona* 8" x 50 • **83**

Robusto *Robusto* 5" x 50 • **89**

Robusto Maduro *Maduro* 5" x 50 • **85**

Torpedo *Figurado* 7" x 54 • **87**

VARGAS

CANARY ISLANDS

Reserva Senadores *Corona Gorda*
5½" x 46 • **84**

VERACRUZ

MEXICO

Reserve Especial *Lonsdale* 6½" x 42 • **86**

VUELTABAJO

DOMINICAN REPUBLIC

Churchill *Churchill* 7" x 48 • **83**

Corona *Corona* 5¼" x 42 • **86**

Corona *Petit Corona* 5¼" x 42 • **83**

Gigante *Double Corona* 8½" x 52 • **83**

Lonsdale *Lonsdale* 7" x 43 • **80**

Pyramide *Figurado* 7" x 50 • **84**

Robusto *Robusto* 4¼" x 52 • **87**

Toro *Corona Gorda* 6" x 50 • **82**

ZINO

HONDURAS

Diamonds *Corona* 5½" x 40 • **83**

Diamonds *Petit Corona* 5½" x 40 • **86**

Mouton-Cadet No. 1 *Corona* 6½" x 44 • **86**

Mouton-Cadet No. 1 *Lonsdale*
6½" x 44 • **85**

Mouton-Cadet No. 2 *Panatela* 6" x 35 • **85**

Mouton-Cadet No. 5 *Petit Corona*
5" x 42 • **87**

Mouton-Cadet No. 6 *Robusto* 5" x 50 • **88**

Tradition *Lonsdale* 6¼" x 44 • **84**

Veritas *Churchill* 7" x 50 • **86**

Veritas *Double Corona* 7" x 50 • **86**

CHAPTER 14

Cigar Retailers

The cigar stores that follow are divided into two sections: United States and International. The stores in the United States are listed by state, and then alphabetically by city. International stores are listed by country, and then alphabetically by city.

UNITED STATES

Alabama

Cigar Limited
1027-A Opelika Rd.
Auburn 36830
(334) 821-3886

Little Anthony's Cigars
101 N. College St.
Auburn 36830
(334) 826-7054

BIRMINGHAM

The Briary
Brookwood Village N., 741-B
Birmingham 35209
(205) 871-2839

J Blackburn & Co.
2000 Galleria Pkwy., #226
Birmingham 35244
(205) 985-0409

Overton & Vine
3150 Overton Rd., Ste. 5
Birmingham 35223
(205) 967-1409

Puff & Browse
1901 6th Ave. N.
#175, Ste. 190
Birmingham 35203
(205) 251-9251

Tobacco Express #1
1813 Ctr. Point Pkwy.
Birmingham 35215
(205) 856-1155

Zachary Scott Cigars Co. Inc.
2402 Canterbury Rd.
Birmingham 35223
(205) 879-0059

Tobacco Express
1405 2nd Ave. SW
Cullman 35055
(205) 775-1212

Tobacco Road
219-A 2nd Ave. SE
Decatur 35601
(205) 355-8065

Dakota Coffee Works
3074-4 Ross Clark Circle
Dothan 36301
(334) 677-1718

Dakota Coffee Works
121 Southgate Rd.
Dothan 36301
(334) 702-8785

Tinder Box #360
10-C S. Church St.
Fairhope 36532
(334) 990-6779

Tobacco Shack
Eastern Shore Plaza, Hwy. 98
Fairhope 36532
(334) 928-9974

The Tobacco Express
3290 Florence Blvd.
Florence 35630
(205) 764-7641

Antonelli's
525 Broad St.
Gadsden 35901
(205) 543-7473

Great Spirits
3022 S. Memorial Pkwy., Ste. 100
Huntsville 35801
(205) 881-4496

Humidor Pipe Shop Inc.
2502 Memorial Pkwy. SW
Huntsville 35801
(205) 539-6431

The Tobacco Barn
2101 Airport Rd. N.
Jasper 35504
(205) 221-4564

Tobacco Junction
8890 Hwy. 72 W.
Madison 35758
(205) 890-0557

Tinder Box #215
3484 Bel Air Mall
Mobile 36606
(334) 473-1221

MONTGOMERY

Tobacco Leaf
6150 Atlanta Hwy.
Montgomery 36117
(334) 277-3880

Tobacco Road #3
2073 Coliseum Blvd.
Montgomery 36110
(334) 273-9905

Tobacco Road #4
7958 Vaughan Rd.
Montgomery 36116
(334) 273-9906

Tobacco Road
25405 Perdido Beach
Blvd., Ste. 14
Orange Beach 36561
(334) 981-6105

Alaska

ANCHORAGE

Brown Jug
4140 Old Seward
Hwy.
Anchorage 99503
(907) 563-3286

Pete's Tobacco Shop
3930 Mountain View
Anchorage 99508
(907) 274-7473

Sourdough News &
Tobacco
735 W. 4th Ave.
Anchorage 99501
(907) 274-6397

Tobacco Cash
601 E. Northern
Lights Blvd., Ste. L
Anchorage 99503
(907) 279-9411

Carrs Foodland Oak
And Keg
526 Gaffney Rd.
Fairbanks 99701
(907) 456-2089

Percy's
214 Front St.
Juneau 99801
(907) 463-3100

Arizona

The Kind
Connection
1174 Hwy. 95
Bullhead City 86442
(520) 754-1114

HB Cigars Courtesy
Of Homebrewers
Outpost
823 N. Humphreys
Flagstaff 86001
(520) 774-2488

GLENDALE

Cigarettes Cheaper!
Olive Sq., 5128 W.
Olive Ave.
Glendale 85302
(602) 937-3294

Cigarettes Cheaper!
Arrowhead Plaza,
20165 N. 67th
Ave., 122-B
Glendale 85308
(602) 572-6748

Cigarettes Cheaper!
Fry's Plaza, 6032 N.
67th Ave.
Glendale 85301
(602) 847-0263

Cigarettes Cheaper!
5116 W. Northern Ave.
Glendale 85301
(602) 842-9541

Cigarettes Cheaper!
Glendale Galleria,
5800 W. Peoria
Ave., D-100
Glendale 85302
(602) 412-8890

Stag Tobacconist
7700 W. Arrowhead
Towne Ctr., #2025
Glendale 85308
(602) 979-7500

Welcome Smokers
#34
15224 N. 59th Ave.,
Ste. 4
Glendale 85306
(602) 547-3635

The Beverage
House #6
2250 Hwy. 6070,
Ste. N.
Globe 85501
(520) 425-2912

Cigarettes Cheaper!
Goodyear Village,
378 N. Litchfield
Rd., #104
Goodyear 85338
(602) 932-9011

MESA

Cigarettes Cheaper!
Main St. Market-
place 1955 W.
Main St. #102
Mesa 85201
(602) 835-6094

Cigarettes Cheaper!
Megafoods Plaza,
1245 E. Southern
Ave.
Mesa 85204

(602) 507-1838

Cigarettes Cheaper!
Continental Plaza,
855 W. University
Dr. #10
Mesa 85201
(602) 834-0863

Cigarettes Cheaper!
Fitch Plaza, 323 E.
Brown Rd., #204
Mesa 85201
(602) 833-1391

Cigarettes Cheaper!
Barkley Sq., 1437 E.
Main St., #114
Mesa 85203
(602) 964-5837

DJ's Smoke Shop
2034 W. Southern
Ave.
Mesa 85202
(602) 461-9174

DJ's Smoke Shop
1206 E. Broadway Rd.
Mesa 85204
(602) 649-8893

Stag Tobacconist
6555 E. Southern
Ave., Ste. 2402
Mesa 85206
(602) 830-4134

Tinder Box #370
1312 W. Southern
Ave., Ste. 1
Mesa 85202
(602) 644-9300

PEORIA

Cigarettes Cheaper!
Fry's Food & Drug
Plaza (75th Ave.
& Cactus Rd.)
Peoria 85381
(602) 878-7537

Welcome Smokers
9210 W. Peoria
Ste. 7
Peoria 85345
(602) 878-3834

**Welcome Smokers
#33**
7530 W. Peoria
Ste. H
Peoria 85345
(602) 479-7550

PHOENIX

Christopher's
2398 E. Camelback,
Ste. 290
Phoenix 85016
(602) 957-3214

**Churchill's Fine
Cigars**
5021 N. 44th St.
Phoenix 85018
(602) 840-9080

**Cigarette Discount
Center**
4127 N. 7th Ave.
Phoenix 85013
(602) 212-1481

Cigarettes Cheaper!
2619 S. 21st St.
Phoenix 85034
(602) 273-6229

Cigarettes Cheaper!
Horizon Village #6,
1940 W. Indian Rd.
Phoenix 85015
(602) 631-4562

Cigarettes Cheaper!
Sunset Plaza,
3426 Bell Rd.
Phoenix 85023
(602) 789-6938

Cigarettes Cheaper!
Central Thomas
Ctr., 2811 N.
Central Ave.
Phoenix 85004
(602) 265-9221

Cigarettes Cheaper!
Mountain View
Marketplace Ctr.,
3131 E. Thunder-
bird Rd., 15-B
Phoenix 85032
(602) 992-7705

Cigarettes Cheaper!
Plaza 75, 4013 N.
75th Ave.
Phoenix 85033
(602) 846-2820

Cigarettes Cheaper!
3458 Van Buren Ctr.
Phoenix 85008
(602) 278-3880

Cigarettes Cheaper!
Mountain Park Plaza,
510 E. Baseline
Rd., #D-13
Phoenix 85040
(602) 304-1267

Knight Gallery
Paradise Valley Mall,
4550 E. Cactus
Rd., #40
Phoenix 85032
(602) 996-6610

**Smokin' Cigar
Company**
455 N. 3rd St.
Phoenix 85004
(602) 252-3422

**Sportsman's Fine
Wine & Spirit**
3205 E. Camelback Rd.
Phoenix 85018
(602) 955-7730

Stag Tobacconist
9627-A Metro
Parkway W.
Phoenix 85051
(602) 943-7517

Stag Tobacconist
3121 N. 3rd Ave.
Phoenix 85013
(602) 265-2748

**Tobacco & Pipes
Plus Inc.**
3245 E. Thomas Rd.
Phoenix 85018
(602) 955-5077

Welcome Smokers
717 W. Union Hills
Phoenix 85027
(602) 548-3370

**Welcome Smokers
#31**
12038 N. 35th Ave.,
Ste. 3
Phoenix 85029
(602) 938-9288

**Welcome Smokers
#32**
11801 N. 19th Ave.,
Ste. 5
Phoenix 85029
(602) 331-6051

**Welcome Smokers
#35**
717 W. Union Hills
Phoenix 85021
(602) 548-3370

**Welcome Smokers
#36**
9210 W. Peoria Ave.,
Ste. 7
Phoenix 85345
(602) 878-3834

Ye Old Pipe Shoppe
2017 E. Camelback Rd.
Phoenix 85016
(602) 955-9542

SCOTTSDALE

A Z Wine Company
2515 N. Scottsdale
Rd., #4
Scottsdale 85257
(602) 423-9305

Cigarettes Cheaper!
Fountain Plaza Ctr.,
7790 E. McDowell
Rd., #101
Scottsdale 85257
(602) 423-3438

Cigarettes Cheaper!
Camelback-Miller
Plaza, 4390 N.
Miller Rd., #D
Scottsdale 85251
(602) 949-1801

DJ's Smoke Shop
1412 N. Scottsdale Rd.
Scottsdale 85257
(602) 946-4509

Ford & Haig
Tobacconist
7076 5th Ave.
Scottsdale 85251
(602) 946-0608

Hiland Trading
Company
6917 E. Thomas Rd.
Scottsdale 85251
(602) 945-7050

Lonsdales Cigars
23535 N. Scottsdale Rd.
Scottsdale 85255
(602) 585-8330

Stag Tobacconist
7014 E. Camelback,
#2105
Scottsdale 85251
(602) 994-4282

The Village Smoke
Shop
8989 E. Via Linda,
Ste. 111
Scottsdale 85258
(602) 314-9898

Moore Coffee &
Cigars
180 Palo Verde
Circle
Sedona 86351
(520) 282-4502

Cigarettes Cheaper!
Kings Inn Ctr.,
10659 NW Grand
Ave., Ste. 8
Sun City 85351
(602) 974-8575

TEMPE

Cigarettes Cheaper!
Broadway
Marketplace,
2109 S. Rural Rd.
Tempe 85282
(602) 736-2434

Rural Road Liquors
7420 S. Rural Rd.
Tempe 85283
(602) 345-9110

Tempe Tobacco
7 W. Baseline
Tempe 85283
(602) 777-7710

TUCSON

Anthony's Cigar
Emporium
7866 N. Oracle Rd.
Tucson 85704
(520) 531-9155

Cigarettes Cheaper!
Fry's Randolph Plaza,
4188 E. 22nd St.
Tuscon 85711
(520) 748-0583

Crescent Tobacco
Shop And
Newsstand #1
216 E. Congress St.
Tuscon 85701
(520) 622-1559

Crescent Tobacco
Shop And
Newsstand #2
7037 E. Tanque-
Berde Rd.
Tuscon 85715
(520) 296-3102

The Moon Smoke
Shop
120 W. Grant Rd.
Tucson 85705
(602) 622-7261

Smoker's Emporium
4514 E. Broadway
Blvd.
Tucson 85711
(520) 321-0202

Smoker's Haven
Park Mall, 5870 E.
Broadway
Tucson 85711
(520) 747-8989

The Tinder Box
#248
3601 E. Broadway #47
Tucson 85716
(520) 326-7198

YUMA

Sentinel Tobacco
224 Main #114
Yuma 85364
(520) 539-0003

Territorial Tobacco
Company
1528 W. 14th St.
Yuma 85364
(520) 539-9441

Arkansas

Tobacco Mart
309 Watson St.
Benton 72015
(501) 315-1888

The Tobacco Store
110 Rainbow Dr.,
Hwy. 367
Cabot 72023
(501) 941-3179

Garmeister Cigars
136 Spring
Eureka Springs
72632
(501) 253-2988

FAYETTEVILLE

The Southern
Gentleman
21 W. Mountain
Fayetteville 72701
(501) 521-1422

Stogies Fine Cigars,
Tobacco And
Much More
One Center Sq.
Fayetteville 72701
(501) 621-6610

The Tobacco Shop
121 W. Township, #21
Fayetteville 72703
(501) 444-8311

FORT SMITH

Discount Tobacco
2000 Rogers Ave.
Fort Smith 72901
(501) 494-7740

Hot Off The Press
5220 Townson
Fort Smith 72901
(501) 646-3200

Puff & Stuff
9101 Hwy. 71 S.
Fort Smith 72908
(501) 646-0307

Taylor Pipe &
Tobacco
5304 Rogers Ave.
Fort Smith 72903
(800) 36-SMOKE

Tobacco Box Ltd.
Indian Mall
Jonesboro 72401
(501) 972-6420

Tobacco Super Store
2235 Caraway Rd.,
Ste. B
Jonesboro 72401
(501) 633-0099

Gatsby's Fine Cigars
200 N. Bowman
Little Rock 72211
(501) 664-2212

The Pipe & Tobacco
2908 S. University
Little Rock 72204
(501) 562-7473

Smoke Shoppe
7420 N. Hills Blvd.
North Little Rock
72116
(501) 835-6067

Tobacco Super
Store #27
2625 W. Kings Hwy.
Paragould 72450
(501) 239-8589

Stogies Fine Cigars,
Tobacco And
Much More
224 2nd St., Ste. J
Rogers 72756
(501) 621-6610

Davis Smoke Shop
East Gate Plaza, #2
Davis Building
Russellville 72801
(501) 968-6760

California

Agoura Liquor &
Deli
5003 Kanan Rd.
Agoura Hills 91301
(818) 991-3946

ALAMEDA

Cigarettes Cheaper!
2220-C S. Shore Ctr.
Alameda 94501
(510) 337-1879

Cigarettes Cheaper!
Marina Village Ctr.,
913 Marina
Village Pkwy.
Alameda 94501
(510) 749-9280

Mel's Land Mark
1240 High St. &
Encina Ave.
Alameda 94501
(510) 865-2646

Beverages & More
836 San Pablo Ave.
Albany 94706
(510) 525-9582

Cigarettes Cheaper!
Vinyard
Marketplace,
11338 Kenyon
Way, #7-C
Alta Loma 91737
(909) 941-1619

Smoke Shop
8722 Baseline Rd.
Alta Loma 91701
(909) 483-1917

Cigarettes Cheaper!
622 S. Brookhurst St.
Anaheim 92804
(714) 491-4981

Cigarettes Cheaper!
Food 4 Less Ctr.,
1608 Lemon St.
Anaheim 92801
(714) 447-3320

Vons Company
618 Michillinda
Ave.
Ancadia 91007
(310) 821-7208

Cigarettes Cheaper!
Angels Towne
Shopping Ctr., 274
S. Main St.
Angels Camp 95222
(209) 736-6735

Cigarettes Cheaper!
Terrace Shopping
Ctr., 2767 Lone
Tree Way
Antioch 94509
(510) 777-9795

Cigarettes Cheaper!
Kiowa Sq. Ctr.,
20783 Bear Valley
Rd.
Apple Valley 92308
(619) 240-0030

Deer Park Wine &
Spirits
783 Rio Del Mar
Blvd., #27
Aptos 95003
(408) 688-1228

Cigar Palace
139 E. Foothill Blvd.
Arcadia 91006
(818) 359-8582

Cigarettes Cheaper!
Arcadia Hub Ctr.,
733-D W. Naomi
Ave.
Arcadia 91007
(818) 821-4473

Cigarettes Cheaper!
Arroyo Town &
Country Sq., 1446
Grand Ave.
Arroyo Grande
93420
(805) 473-0992

Cigarettes Cheaper!
Food 4 Less Ctr.,
8310-B El Camino
Real
Atascadero 93422
(805) 466-4494

Cigarettes Cheaper!
Lucky Ctr., 1880
Bellevue Rd.
Atwater 95301
(209) 358-4744

AUBURN

Cigarettes Cheaper!
Auburn Town Ctr.,
350 Elm Ave.
Auburn 95603
(916) 885-9754

Cigarettes Cheaper!
Rock Creek Plaza,
2635 Bell Rd.
Auburn 95603
(916) 889-8752

**Old Town Cigar
Shop**
1111 Sacramento
St., Ste. E
Auburn 95603
(916) 887-9533

BAKERSFIELD

A Cellar Above
4705 Wilson
Bakersfield 93309
(805) 834-7757

Cigarettes Cheaper!
Ming Plaza, 3829
Ming Ave.
Bakersfield 93309
(805) 837-0603

Cigarettes Cheaper!
1656 Oak St.
Bakersfield 93301
(805) 325-9368

Cigarettes Cheaper!
Chester Loop
Shopping Ctr., 2431
N. Chester Ave.
Bakersfield 93308
(805) 399-7137

Cigarettes Cheaper!
2781 Calloway Dr.,
#500
Bakersfield 93312
(805) 587-0602

Cigarettes Cheaper!
Niles Center, 6221-A
Niles St.
Bakersfield 93305
(805) 363-5448

Cigarettes Cheaper!
Bakersfield Plaza
Ctr., 4106
California Ave.
Bakersfield 93309
(805) 633-1347

Gerry's Fine Cigars
2324 Brundage Lane
Bakersfield 93304
(805) 633-1440

**Hiland's Gift &
Tobacco**
East Hill Mall, 3000
Mall View Rd.,
#1051
Bakersfield 93306
(805) 872-7890

**John T's Pipe &
Tobacco**
84 Valley Plaza
Bakersfield 93304
(805) 832-7002

**Royal Cigar Of
Balboa**
609 E. Balboa
Balboa 92661
(714) 675-6429

Cigarettes Cheaper!
Park Plaza & Maine
4138 N. Main Ave.
Baldwin Park 91706
(818) 814-9952

Cigarettes Cheaper!
14525-H Baldwin
Park Town &
Country Dr.
Baldwin Park 91706
(818) 338-7546

Cigarettes Cheaper!
4457 Park Rd.
Benicia 94510
(707) 745-6691

Dave's Smoke Shop
2444 Durant Ave.
Berkeley 94704
(510) 883-0325

Juicy News II
3167 College Ave.
Berkeley 94705
(510) 601-8602

BEVERLY
HILLS

Al's Newsstand
216 S. Beverly Dr.
Beverly Hills 90212
(310) 278-6397

**Alfred Dunhill
Limited**
201 N. Rodeo Dr.
Beverly Hills 90210
(310) 274-5351

**Beverly Hills Hotel
Signature Shop**
9641 Sunset Blvd.
Beverly Hills 90210
(310) 276-2251

Davidoff Of Geneva
232 N. Rodeo Dr.
Beverly Hills 90210
(310) 278-8884

**Grand Havana
Room**
301 N. Canon Dr.
Beverly Hills 90210
(310) 274-8100

Nazareth's
350 N. Canon Dr.
Beverly Hills 90210
(310) 271-5863

**Thomas Hinds
Tobacconist**
9632 Santa Monica
Blvd.
Beverly Hills 90210
(310) 275-9702

Vendome #24
9153 W. Olympic
Blvd.
Beverly Hills 90212
(310) 276-9463

The Wine Merchant
9701 Santa Monica
Blvd.
Beverly Hills 90210
(310) 278-7322

John Pipe Shop
563 Pineknot Ave.
Big Bear Lake 92315
(909) 866-1755

**Jensen's Finest
Foods**
27264 Hwy. 189
Blue Jay 92317
(909) 337-8484

BREA

Brea Industries
300 S. Brea Blvd.
Brea 92621
(714) 990-5551

Cigarettes Cheaper!
The Gateway, 407 W.
Imperial Hwy., #1
Brea 92621
(714) 672-9976

Maxwell's Tobacco Shop
2500 E. Imperial
Hwy. Ste. 199
Brea 92821
(714) 256-2344

Cigar-A-Rama
11729 Barrington Ct.
Brentwood 90049
(310) 440-0402

Canyon Smoke Shop Inc.
7941 Beach Blvd. #F
Buena Park 90620
(714) 739-0894

Cigarettes Cheaper!
Lincoln Park Ctr.,
8976 Knott Ave.
Buena Park 90620
(714) 828-7258

Havana Studios
245 E. Olive Ave.,
Ste. 100
Burbank 91502
(818) 557-7600

Burlingame Tobacconist
1404 Burlingame Ave.
Burlingame 94010
(415) 343-3300

Smokes
48400 Seminole Dr.
#C-1
Cabazon 92230
(909) 849-4343

Cigar Lovers Two
2173 Ventura Blvd.
Camarillo 93010
(805) 388-8344

Cigarettes Cheaper!
Central Plaza
Shopping Ctr.,
740 Arneill Rd.
Camarillo 93010
(805) 383-0335

Bob & Jon's Bottle Shop
2292 Main St.
Cambria 93428
(805) 927-4909

Cambria Cargo Company
4044 Burton Dr.
Cambria 93428
(805) 927-2400

Cigarettes Cheaper!
Goldorado Ctr., 3490
Palmer Dr. #3K
Cameron Park
95682
(916) 672-9468

Ugly Al's Fine Cigars Inc.
7239 Corbin Ave.
Canoga Park 91306
(818) 709-1525

Cardiff Seaside Market
2087 San Elijo Ave.
Cardiff By Sea 92007
(619) 753-5445

Hiland's Gift & Tobacco
Plaza Camino Real,
2525 El Camino
Real, #206
Carlsbad 92008
(619) 434-2788

Village Cigar & Fine Gift
2959 State St.
Carlsbad 92008
(619) 730-0717

Carmel Pipe Shop
Lincoln South
of Ocean
Carmel By The Sea
93921
(408) 624-9737

Cigarettes Cheaper!
4949 Marconi,
Ste. G
Carmichael 95608
(916) 481-9501

Briar Rose
20700 S. Avalon
Blvd., #537
Carson 90746
(310) 538-1018

Cigarettes Cheaper!
Avalon Ctr., 20220-A
S. Avalon Blvd.
Carson 90746
(310) 719-9532

M & R Liquor
1024 Casitas Pass Rd.
Cartinteria 93013
(805) 684-3110

Cigarettes Cheaper!
Date Palm Shopping
Ctr., 35790 Date
Palm Dr.
Cathedral City
92234
(619) 324-5018

The Pipe Rack
2020 Ave. Of The
Stars, Level 2
Century City 90067
(310) 552-9842

M K's Cigar Box
19116 Pioneer Blvd.
Cerritos 90703
(310) 865-5111

Cigarettes Cheaper!
10216½ Mason Ave.
Chatsworth 91311
(818) 886-3379

CHICO

**Bidwell Cigar
Number 3**
243 W. 2nd St.
Chico 95928
(916) 842-8600

Cigarettes Cheaper!
Towne & Country
Ctr., 118 W. East
Ave., Ste. B
Chico 95926
(916) 896-0716

Cigarettes Cheaper!
University Sq., 1000-
B Sacramento Ave.
Chico 95926
(916) 342-3627

Cigarettes Cheaper!
Park Plaza Ctr.,
766 Mangrove Ave.
Chico 95926
(916) 345-4966

Rabbogliatti's
802 W. 5th St.
Chico 95928
(916) 342-9591

Cigarettes Cheaper!
County Fair
Shopping Ctr.,
12079 Central Ave.
Chino 91710
(909) 590-1325

Village Liquor
4117 Riverside Dr.
Chino 91710
(909) 627-3438

**Chino Hills Smoke
Shop**
2563-C Chino Hill
Pkwy.
Chino Hill 91709
(909) 597-1455

Cigarettes Cheaper!
Country Wood Ctr.,
1718 Robertson
Blvd.
Chowchilla 93610
(209) 665-5156

CHULA VISTA

Cigarettes Cheaper!
College Plaza, 945-F
Otay Lakes Rd.
Chula Vista 91913
(619) 216-1222

**La Villa Del
Tobacco**
1049 Cordova Dr.
Chula Vista 91910
(619) 482-7658

**Royalty Cigar
Company**
345 3rd Ave.
Chula Vista 91910
(619) 425-8905

Tinder Box
Chula Vista Ctr., 555
Broadway, #1010
Chula Vista 91910
(619) 262-4822

Tinder Box #147
6144 Sunrise Mall
Citrus Heights
95610
(800) 725-3231

**Claremont Tobacco
House**
272 W. 2nd St.
Claremont 91711
(714) 625-6321

O'Sullivan's Cigars
26 Mirango Ct.
Clayton 94517
(510) 672-9616

Cigarettes Cheaper!
1820 Shaw Ave.,
#104
Clovis 93611
(209) 298-7758

Cigarettes Cheaper!
Coalinga Shopping
Ctr., 139 West
Polk St.
Coalinga 93210
(209) 934-1196

Cigarettes Cheaper!
Olive Tree Plaza,
632 Edith Ave.
Corning 96021
(916) 824-6384

CORONA

**Arnett's Smoke
Shop**
1185 Magnolia Ave., #F
Corona 91719
(909) 340-2739

Cigarettes Cheaper!
Corona Market
Place, Bldg. B,
1501 Rimpau
Ave., #110
Corona 91719
(909) 272-1593

Cigarettes Cheaper!
Plaza On 6th St.,
1112 W. 6th St.,
#102
Corona 91720
(909) 272-2982

COSTA MESA

**Alfred Dunhill
Limited**
South Coast Plaza,
3333 Bristol St.
Costa Mesa 92626
(714) 641-0521

Cheer's Tobacco
1525 Mesa Verde Dr.
Costa Mesa 92626
(714) 662-2880

Long's Drug Store
175 E. 17th St.
Costa Mesa 92627
(714) 631-8860

Meerschaum King
88 Fair Dr.
Costa Mesa 92627
(714) 636-1897

Price Buster
Cigarettes
1175 Baker St.
Costa Mesa 92628
(714) 979-6841

Royal Cigar Society
1909 Harbor Blvd.
Costa Mesa 92627
(714) 646-0550

7 Day Liquors
891 Baker St., B-1
Costa Mesa 92626
(714) 540-2519

Smoke Shack
250 Ogle St.
Costa Mesa 92627
(800) 969-3005

Tinder Box #107
Crystal Ct. South
Coast Plaza, 3333
Bear St.
Costa Mesa 92626
(714) 540-8262

Cigarettes Cheaper!
10555 De Anza Blvd.
Cupertino 95014
(408) 252-9655

Cigarettes Cheaper!
Cypress West Ctr.,
4163 Ball Rd.
Cypress 90630
(714) 761-2766

Tobacco Club
5491 Ball Rd., #C
Cypress 90630
(714) 527-1363

Cigarettes Cheaper!
Westlake Shopping
Ctr., 19 Westlake
Mall
Daly City 94015
(415) 757-9957

Tinder Box #125
107-A Serramante Ctr.
Daly City 94015
(415) 756-1771

The Ritz Carlton
Gift Shop
One Ritz Carlton
Dana Point 92629
(714) 240-2000

Smoke-n-Ale Cigars
And Home
Brewers Supplies
24701 La Plaza, #103
Dana Point 92629
(714) 487-0880

Danville Cigar And
Fine Gifts
411 Hartz Ave.
Danville 94526
(510) 831-8899

Del Mar Hills
Liquors
2654 Del Mar
Heights Rd.
Del Mar 92014
(619) 481-8148

Primo Cigar
2670 Via De La
Valle, Ste. A-170
Del Mar 92014
(619) 259-0855

Cigarettes Cheaper!
Desert Hot Springs
Town Ctr.,
14208 Palm Dr.
Desert Hot Springs
92240
(619) 251-8853

Cigarettes Cheaper!
Towne Ctr. Village,
1127 S. Grand
Ave.
Diamond Bar 91765
(909) 860-7676

Royal Tobacco
7946 E. Florence
Ave.
Downey 90241
(310) 928-1113

Cigarette Store
6942 Village Pkwy.
Dublin 94568
(510) 829-9615

EL CAJON

Cigarettes Cheaper!
Plaza De Las Palmas,
1175 Avocado
Ave., #103
El Cajon 92020
(619) 588-4665

Smokers Depot
145 Jamacha Rd.
El Cajon 92021
(619) 440-3400

Tinder Box
329 Parkway Plaza
El Cajon 92020
(619) 440-1121

El Centro Liquor
401 State St.
El Centro 92243
(619) 353-4460

Mursuli Cigars
10733 Lower Azusa
Rd.
El Monte 91731
(818) 444-3443

Cigarettes Cheaper!
8557 Elk Grove Blvd.
Elk Grove 95624
(916) 686-2173

Cigarettes Cheaper!
Camden Shopping
Ctr., 9170 Elk
Grove-Florin Rd.
Elk Grove 95624
(916) 685-8720

ENCINITAS

Beverages & More
212 N. El Camino
Real
Encinitas 92024
(619) 943-6631

Cigarettes Cheaper!
Santa Fe Plaza, 425½
Santa Fe Dr.
Encinitas 92024
(619) 436-9128

Cigarettes Cheaper!
215-H S. El Camino
Real De La Plaza
Encinitas Ctr.
Encinitas 92024
(619) 633-4469

Puff & Stuff
335 First St.
Encinitas 92024
(619) 753-3839

ENCINO

Cigar Den
17933 Ventura Blvd.
Encino 91316
(818) 343-5768

Cigarettes Cheaper!
16060 Ventura
Blvd., #110
Encino 91436
(818) 789-6651

Cigarettes Cheaper!
Encino Oaks
Shopping Ctr.,
17330 Ventura
Blvd.
Encino 91316
(818) 981-7059

ESCONDIDO

Cigarettes Cheaper!
Ferrara Plaza, 2403
E. Valley Pkwy.
Escondido 92027
(619) 781-4279

**Holiday Wine
Cellars**
302 W. Mission
Escondido 92025
(619) 745-1200

**Tinder Box North
County Fair**
200 E. Via Rancho
Pkwy., Ste. 157
Escondido 92025
(619) 745-9230

**The Enchanted
Victorian Tobacco
& Gift Shop**
317 E St.
Eureka 95501
(707) 441-1888

John's Cigars
2211 Myrtle Ave.
Eureka 95501
(707) 444-8869

**John T's Unique
Gifts**
1419-B Solano Mall
Fairfield 94533
(707) 426-5566

D R Cigars
657 E. Bidwell St.
Folsom 95630
(916) 983-4278

Cigarettes Cheaper!
Fontana Sq.
Shopping Ctr.,
17151 Foothill
Blvd.
Fontana 92335
(909) 427-9098

Cigarettes Cheaper!
Palm Ct. at Empire
Ctr., 17122
Slover Ave.
Fontana 92331
(909) 428-7097

FOUNTAIN
VALLEY

Cigarettes Cheaper!
Westhaven Plaza,
Ste. J, 16027
Brookhurst St.
Fountain Valley
92728
(714) 531-2474

Cigarettes Cheaper!
Callens Corner,
18605 Brookhurst St.
Fountain Valley
92708
(714) 964-5492

Cigarettes Cheaper!
Magnolia Plaza,
9113 Garfield Ave.
Fountain Valley
92708
(714) 962-4289

H & H Tobacco
18225 S. Brookhurst, #6
Fountain Valley
92708
(714) 962-2927

**R & R Tobacco
Company**
10810 Warner Ave.
Fountain Valley
92708
(714) 964-8777

Cigarettes Cheaper!
Crossroads Shopping
Ctr., 39471
Fremont Blvd.
Fremont 94538
(510) 651-0441

Rock Stop
39494 Fremont
Fremont 94538
(510) 745-8118

FRESNO

Cigars Limited
4287 W. Swift Ave.
Fresno 93722
(209) 221-0161

Cigarettes Cheaper!
Hoover Market Pl.,
5730 N. 1st St.,
#113
Fresno 93710
(209) 448-0871

Cigarettes Cheaper!
C & O Shopping Ctr.,
4849 E. Olive Ave.
Fresno 93727
(209) 252-6705

Cigarettes Cheaper!
The Canyons Ctr.,
4910 E. Kings
Canyon Rd., #111
Fresno 93727
(209) 251-2033

Cigarettes Cheaper!
Sunset Sq., 7089 N.
Marks Ave., #104
Fresno 93711
(209) 438-0665

Cigars Limited
5132 Palm Ave.
Fresno 93704
(209) 221-0161

**Hardwick's Briar
Shoppe**
3402 N. Blackstone
Ave., #124
Fresno 93726
(209) 228-1389

Havanna's
2051 W. Bullard
Fresno 93711
(209) 439-4642

**John T's Pipe &
Tobacco**
581 E. Shaw Ave.
Fresno 93710
(209) 229-4253

Perfect Blend &
Fine Cigars
1294 N. Wisdom
Fresno 93728
(209) 486-0400

Wine Barrel
1105 E. Champlain Dr.
Fresno 93720
(209) 434-1057

FULLERTON

Cigarettes Cheaper!
Lucky Sq. Ctr., 307
N. Euclid St.
Fullerton 92632
(714) 773-0178

Cigarettes Cheaper!
Fullerton Ctr., 166
N. Raymond Ave.
Fullerton 92631
(714) 447-1333

Dome Liquors
3115 Yorba Linda
Blvd.
Fullerton 92631
(714) 524-0800

Red Cloud Fine
Cigar
118 W. Wilshire Ave.
Fullerton 92832
(714) 680-6200

GARDEN
GROVE

Cigarettes Cheaper!
Town & Country
Shopping Ctr.,
12841 Harbor Blvd.
Garden Grove
92640
(714) 530-4967

Cigarettes Cheaper!
Garden Promenade,
9877 Chapman
Ave., #D
Garden Grove
92641
(714) 636-1337

J & H Tobacco
11912 Valley View
Garden Grove
92645
(714) 895-6209

Cigarettes Cheaper!
Gardena Valley Ctr.,
244 W. Redondo
Beach Blvd.
Gardena 90247
(310) 329-8954

Cigarettes Cheaper!
340 E. 10th St.,
Space C
Gilroy 95020
(408) 847-2060

GLENDALE

Ceegar Gallery &
Lounge
109 S. Broadway
Glendale 91205
(818) 559-2170

Cigar Box
1325-A Glendale
Galleria
Glendale 91210
(818) 244-3344

Cigar Plus
309½ W. Broadway
Glendale 91204
(818) 547-3771

Garard Fine Cigars
154 S. Brand Blvd.
Glendale 91204
(818) 247-9701

Plaza Liquors
333 N. Verdugo Rd.
Glendale 91206
(818) 549-0556

Red Carpet Wines
& Spirits
400 E. Glen Oaks
Blvd.
Glendale 91207
(818) 247-5544

Smoke A Cigar Club
318 N. Brand Blvd.
Glendale 91203
(818) CIGAR 97

Glendora Cigars
614 W. Alosta Ave.
Glendora 91740
(818) 852-2255

Marty's Cigar &
Divan
109 W. Foothill Blvd.
Glendora 91741
(818) 852-9337

GRANADA HILLS

Cigarettes Cheaper!
16287 San Fernando
Mission Blvd.
Granada Hills 91344
(818) 368-8635

Cigarettes Cheaper!
16925 Devonshire St.
Granada Hills 91344
(818) 363-1855

Party Time Liquor
11902 Balboa Blvd.
Granada Hills 91344
(818) 360-1777

Cigarettes Cheaper!
Gold Country Ctr.,
12031 Sutton Way
Grass Valley 95945
(916) 272-5569

Station House
1381 E. Main St.
Grass Valley 95945
(916) 273-7979

Cigarettes Cheaper!
Heritage Oak
Shopping Ctr.,
1562 State Hwy.
99
Gridley 95948
(916) 846-3067

Cigarettes Cheaper!
Centennial Plaza
Shopping Ctr.,
1868 W. Lacey
Blvd.
Hanford 93230
(209) 584-6793

Cigarettes Cheaper!
Hawaiian Gardens
Town Ctr., 12140-C
Carson St.
Hawaiian Gardens
90716
(310) 421-7853

Cigarettes Cheaper!
El Segundo Plaza,
5063 El Segundo
Blvd.
Hawthorne 90250
(310) 675-9673

HAYWARD

Cigarettes Cheaper!
20930 Mission Blvd.
Hayward 94541
(510) 481-8037

Cigarettes Cheaper!
24703 Amador St., #8
Hayward 94544
(510) 732-5579

Cigarettes Cheaper!
Mission Plaza Ctr.,
26905 Mission
Blvd., #B
Hayward 94544
(510) 889-1447

HEALDSBURG

Cigarettes Cheaper!
Vineyard Plaza
Shopping Ctr.,
1087 Vine St.
Healdsburg 95448
(707) 431-2446

Indian Wells Cigar
113 Plaza St.
Healdsburg 95448
(707) 431-2800

**Root & Eastwood
Wine & Spirits**
1123 Vine St.
Healdsburg 95448
(707) 433-8311

**Sotoyome Tobacco
Company**
119 Plaza St.
Healdsburg 95448
(707) 433-3338

HEMET

Cigarettes Cheaper!
Stanford Ctr.,
41863-A E.
Florida Ave.
Hemet 92544
(909) 929-2504

Cigarettes Cheaper!
Sears Plaza,
565 San Jacinto St.
Hemet 92543
(909) 929-8708

Cigarettes Cheaper!
Village West, 3137
W. Florida Ave.
Hemet 92545
(909) 929-9931

**Holy Smoke
Tobacco**
3637 W. Florida
Ave.
Hemet 92545
(909) 925-1945

Cigarettes Cheaper!
Creekside Ctr., 1511
N. Sycamore Rd.
Hercules 94547
(510) 799-8765

Cigarettes Cheaper!
Hollywood Plaza,
4627 W. Santa
Monica Blvd.
Hollywood 90029
(213) 667-2574

HUNTINGTON BEACH

**The Cigar Room In
XI**
16400 Pacific Coast
Hwy., Ste. 120
Huntington Beach
92649
(310) 592-5290

Cigarettes Cheaper!
Edinger Plaza, 7596
Edinger Ave.
Huntington Beach
92647
(714) 842-8414

**Hiland's Gift &
Tobacco**
15931 Goldenwest St.
Huntington Beach
92647
(714) 897-1172

**Huntington Beach
Smoke Shop**
7194 Edinoer Ave.
Huntington Beach
92647
(714) 841-9929

K & B Cigars
15562 Graham St.
Huntington Beach
92649
(714) 899-9007

Liquor Warehouse
9092 Adams
Huntington Beach
92646
(714) 965-6000

Tobacco Road
Village Lane, 54200
N. Circle Dr.
Idyllwild 92549
(909) 659-3930

Tinder Box #186
333 Puente Hills
Mall
Industry 91748
(818) 965-7215

IRVINE

The Cigar Cellar
313 San Marino
Irvine 92614
(714) 852-8253

Diedrich Coffee
2144 Michaelson
Irvine 92612
(714) 260-1600

**Hiland's Gift &
Tobacco**
2272 Michelson,
#110
Irvine 92612
(714) 475-9986

Irvine Smoke Shop
165251 Carmen
Ave.
Irvine 92714
(714) 263-8939

Long's Drug Store
4880 Irvine Blvd.
Irvine 92620
(714) 505-1680

**Stafford Fine Wine
& Specialty**
17801 Main St.,
Ste. F
Irvine 92714
(714) 474-4416

Cigarettes Cheaper!
11960 W. Hwy. 88
Jackson 95642
(209) 223-9564

Cigarettes Cheaper!
Jackson Creek Plaza,
525-4 Hwy. 49
Jackson 95642
(916) 223-9570

Cigarettes Cheaper!
King City Shopping
Ctr., 510-Q Canal
St.
King City 93930
(408) 385-9297

**Cumulus Fine Cigar
& Lounge**
716 Foothill Blvd.
La Canada 91011
(818) 952-3137

The Cigar Box
2131 Vuelta Ct.
La Costa 92009
(619) 350-4500

Wine St.
6986 El Camino Real
La Costa 92009
(619) 431-8455

LA JOLLA

Cigar Cellar
1261 Prospect St.,
Ste. 2
La Jolla 92037
(619) 459-3255

Havana Club
2149 Avenida De La
Playa
La Jolla 92037
(619) 459-7787

Maxx Fine Cigars
909 Prospect, Ste.
150-B
La Jolla 92037
(619) 551-7047

**Spirits Of St.
Germain**
3251 Holiday Ct.,
Ste. 101
La Jolla 92037
(619) 455-1414

Beverages & More
8410 Ctr. Dr.
La Mesa 91942
(619) 461-6230

Tobac Royale
8291 La Mesa Blvd.
La Mesa 91941
(619) 464-6787

**Boley's Tobacco
Shop**
12234 La Mirada
Blvd.
La Mirada 90638
(310) 943-6546

Cigarettes Cheaper!
La Verne Town Ctr.,
2320 Foothill
Blvd.
La Verne 91750
(909) 596-6399

**Jackson Wine &
Spirits**
3524 Mount Diablo
Blvd.
Lafayette 94549
(510) 376-6000

**Mr. Bones Fine
Cigars**
325 Glenneyre
Laguna Beach 92651
(714) 454-8665

**Laguna Hill Smoke
Shop**
25614 Alicia Pkwy
Laguna Hills 92653
(714) 699-2651

**Southwest Gift &
Tobacco**
24155 Laguna Hills
Mall, #1750
Laguna Hills 92653
(714) 829-8474

**Price Buster
Cigarettes And
Quality Cigar**
22359 El Toro Rd.
Lake Forest 92630
(714) 699-0042

**Tobacco Barn Pipe
Shop**
23532 El Toro Rd., #13
Lake Forest 92630
(714) 830-7110

Cigarettes Cheaper!
Lakewood Sq.,
4019 Hardwick
Lakewood 90712
(310) 408-1188

**John's Cigar &
Spirit**
5932 E. Delamo
Blvd.
Lakewood 90713
(310) 421-6815

Chief Tobacco
5535 Woodruff Ave.
Lakewood City
90713
(310) 920-6065

LANCASTER

Cigarettes Cheaper!
Quartz Hill Towne
Ctr., 4073 W.
Ave. L
Lancaster 93536
(805) 948-9064

Cigarettes Cheaper!
Valley Central Ctr.,
44503 Valley
Central Way C-1
Lancaster 93536
(805) 948-9264

**London Pipe & Gift
Shop**
1120 W. Ave. K
Lancaster 93534
(805) 948-5352

Primo Cigars
Topanga Plaza Mall,
6600 Topanga
Canyon Blvd.
Lanoga Park 91303
(818) 992-1308

**Discount Cigarette
Outlets**
16129 Hawthorne
Blvd.
Lawndale 90260
(310) 542-5884

Cigarettes Cheaper!
Lemoore Plaza, 155
'A' Hanford-
Armona Rd.
Lemoore 93245
(209) 924-0154

LIVERMORE

Cigarettes Cheaper!
Pepper Tree Plaza, 863
E. Stanley Blvd.
Livermore 94550
(510) 449-3327

Cigarettes Cheaper!
Nob Hill Shopping
Ctr., 3024 Pacific
Ave.
Livermore 95242
(510) 606-7298

Jack Kavanagh
Liquor/Beverage
4068 E. Ave.
Livermore 94550
(510) 443-2434

Jack Kavanagh
Liquor/Beverage
1024 E. Stanley Blvd.
Livermore 94550
(510) 443-9463

Jack Kavanagh
Liquor/Beverage
4518 Las Positas Rd.
Livermore 94550
(510) 443-443

Cigarettes Cheaper!
Livingston Main St.
Plaza, 1471 "B"
St., #K
Livingston 95334
(209) 394-4267

LODI

Cigarettes Cheaper!
Cherokee Retail
Ctr., 550-G S.
Cherokee Lane
Lodi 95240
(209) 333-2568

Cigarettes Cheaper!
Vineyard Ctr., 784
W. Kettleman
Lane
Lodi 95240
(209) 365-6112

Fred's Puff N Stuff
228 W. Pine St.
Lodi 95240
(209) 334-1088

Cigarettes Cheaper!
Lompoc Mission
Plaza #1412 N.W.
H St., Ste. A
Lompoc 93436
(805) 737-9698

LONG BEACH

Churchill's
5844 Naples Plaza
Long Beach 90803
(310) 433-3994

Cigarettes Cheaper!
Los Coyotes Ctr.,
3368 Los Coyotes
Diagonal
Long Beach 90808
(310) 429-7272

Cigarettes Cheaper!
Food 4 Less Ctr.,
2183 South St.
#102-A
Long Beach 90805
(310) 423-2204

Havana Cigar Club
3939 E. Broadway
Long Beach 90803
(310) 433-8053

Hiland's Gift &
Tobacco
Von's Pavillion Ctr.,
5937 Spring St.
Long Beach 90808
(310) 425-3258

Joe R's Churchills
Of Long Beach
107 W. Broadway
Long Beach 90802
(310) 491-7300

Marina Tobacco
6244 E. Pacific
Coast Hwy.
Long Beach 90803
(310) 597-0095

Morry's Of Naples
5764 E. 2nd St.
Long Beach 90803
(310) 433-0405

Naples Pipe Shop
5662 E. 2nd St.
Long Beach 90803
(310) 439-8515

Golden Cigar
35-89 Taylor, Ste. 3
Loomis 95650
(916) 652-2010

Draeger's Market
342 1st St.
Los Altos 94022
(415) 948-9196

Edward's Pipe &
Tobacco
4546 El Camino
Real
Los Altos 94022
(415) 941-1228

LOS ANGELES

Ben's Smoke Shop
6423 Hollywood
Blvd.
Los Angeles 90028
(213) 467-5000

Beverage
Warehouse
4935 McConnell
Ave., Unit #21
Los Angeles 90066
(310) 306-2822

Brentwood Cigar
Club
11606 Chayote St.
Los Angeles 90049
(310) 440-3908

Century City
Tobacco
10250 Santa Monica
Blvd., #27
Los Angeles 90067
(310) 277-0760

Cigar Joint
7174 Melrose Ave.
Los Angeles 90046
(213) 930-2341

Cigar Joint
10921 Weyburn
Ave.
Los Angeles 90024
(310) 208-1121

Country Home
Tobacco
2240 S. Atlantic
Blvd.
Los Angeles 91754
(213) 721-1192

Cuvee Fine Wine &
Food
145 S. Robinson
Blvd.
Los Angeles 90048
(310) 271-43333

Kenny's Cellar
11151 W. Olympic
Blvd.
Los Angeles 90064
(310) 478-9463

La Plata Cigars Mfg.
1026 S. Grand Ave.
Los Angeles 90015
(213) 747-8561

Larchmont Village
Wine/Spirit
223 N. Larchmont
Blvd.
Los Angeles 90004
(213) 856-8699

Mel & Rose Liquor
& Deli
8344 Melrose Ave.
Los Angeles 90069
(213) 655-5557

Smoke N Stuff
750 W. 7th St.
Los Angeles 90017
(213) 627-0334

The Smoking
Section
7801 Melrose Ave.,
Unit #4
Los Angeles 90046
(213) 653-0328

The Tobacco
Merchant
7115 Melrose Ave.
Los Angeles 90046
(213) 931-3225

Wally's Liquor
2107 Westwood
Blvd.
Los Angeles 90025
(310) 475-0606

Cigarettes Cheaper!
Canal Farm
Shopping Ctr.,
341-H Pacheco
Blvd.
Los Banos 93635
(209) 827-1632

Joey's Menswear
52 N. Santa Cruz
Ave.
Los Gatos 95030
(408) 395-4497

The Studio
1 N. Santa Cruz Ave.
Los Gatos 95030
(408) 395-7078

Cigarettes Cheaper!
Madra Marketplace
Shopping Ct.,
2295-B,
W. Cleveland
Madera 93637
(209) 662-0442

MANHATTAN
BEACH

Beach Cities Cigar
1713 Artesia Blvd.
Manhattan Beach
90266
(310) 937-7977

Bristol Farms
1570 Rosecrans Ave.
Manhattan Beach
90266
(310) 643-5229

Manhattan Liquors
1157-A Artesia
Blvd.
Manhattan Beach
90266
(310) 374-3454

Royal Cigar Society
1145 N. Sepulveda
Blvd.
Manhattan Beach
90266
(310) 796-5577

Cigarettes Cheaper!
Raley's Union Sq.
Shopping, 1252
Lathrop Rd.
Manteca 95336
(209) 823-0169

Cigarettes Cheaper!
Seacrest Plaza Ste. B,
266 Reservation
Rd.
Marina 93933
(408) 384-3432

Tobacco Trader
4722$\frac{1}{4}$ Admiralty
Way
Marina Del Ray
90292
(310) 823-5831

The Cigar Post
5202 Cole Rd.
Mariposa 95338
(209) 742-6409

Cigar Box
311 D St.
Marysville 95901
(916) 742-4354

Beltramo's
1540 El Camino Real
Menlo Park 94025
(415) 325-2806

Draeger's Market
1010 University Dr.
Menlo Park 94026
(415) 688-0682

Old Knickerbockers
555 Santa Cruz Ave.
Menlo Park 94025
(415) 327-8769

Cigarettes Cheaper!
Raley's Yosemite N.,
3528 G St.
Merced 95340
(209) 384-3965

Sherlock Holmes
Tobacconist
1712 Canal St.
Merced 95340
(209) 723-9071

Telford's Pipe Shop
121 Strawberry
Village
Mill Valley 94941
(415) 388-0440

Vintage Wine &
Spirits
67 Throckmorton
Ave.
Mill Valley 94941
(415) 388-1626

Cigarettes Cheaper!
26861 Trabuco Rd.
D-1, Alicia/
Trabuco Ctr.
Mission Viejo 92961
(714) 830-2989

Hiland's Gift & Tobacco
27000 Crown Valley Pkwy., #814
Mission Viejo 92692
(714) 347-8665

MODESTO

Cigarettes Cheaper!
Lakes Shopping Ctr., 2601 N. Oakdale Rd.
Modesto 95355
(209) 523-7733

Cigarettes Cheaper!
1221 E. Orangeburg Ave., #6
Modesto 95350
(209) 577-4147

Cigarettes Cheaper!
901 N. Carpenter Rd.
Modesto 95351
(209) 579-1503

Cigarettes Cheaper!
2225 Plaza Pkwy., C-6
Modesto 95359
(209) 544-6824

Cigarettes Cheaper!
3848 McHenry Ave. #175
Modesto 95356
(209) 571-1284

Cigarettes Cheaper!
2100 Standiford Ave., Ste. E-4, Standiford Sq.
Modesto 95355
(209) 571-2823

Liquor Locker
2020 Standiford Ave., Ste. J-5
Modesto 95350
(209) 522-9112

Cigarettes Cheaper!
Foothill Park Plaza, 176 W. Foothill Blvd.
Monrovia 91016
(818) 303-8650

G & P Cigars
1433 N. Montabello Blvd.
Montabello 90640
(213) 887-0066

Paragon
9480 Central Ave.
Montclair 91763
(909) 621-9979

Cigarettes Cheaper!
541 Tyler St.
Monterey 93942
(408) 646-9248

Hellam's Tobacco Shop
423 Alvarado St.
Monterey 93940
(408) 373-2816

Cigarettes Cheaper!
Moorpark Town Ctr., 231 W. Los Angeles Ave.
Moorpark 93021
(805) 529-8390

Cigarettes Cheaper!
Cypress Plaza Shopping Ctr., 640 Quintana Way
Morro Bay 93442
(805) 772-1769

Beverages & More
Mountain View, 423 San Antonio Rd.
Mountain View 94040
(415) 949-1826

Cigarettes Cheaper!
Sierra Vista Plaza, 25100 Hancock Ave., #113
Murrieta 92562
(909) 698-9271

NAPA

Baker St. Tobacconist
3053 Jefferson St.
Napa 94558
(707) 252-2766

Brix Restaurant & Market
7377 St. Helena Hwy.
Napa 94558
(707) 944-2749

Cigarettes Cheaper!
River Park Shopping Ctr., 1441 Imola Ave. W.
Napa 94559
(707) 253-9565

Cigarettes Cheaper!
5841 Jarvis Ave.
Newark 94560
(510) 793-2910

John T's
1043 New Park Mall
Newark 94560
(510) 796-7033

Stagecoach Liquors Inc.
1536 Newbury Rd.
Newbury Park 91320
(805) 498-4343

NEWPORT BEACH

Accents On Newport Beach
Four Seasons Hotel, 690 Newport Ctr. Dr., Newport Beach 92660
(714) 640-2394

Cheer's Tobacco
177 Riverside Ave., #G, Newport Beach 92663
(714) 650-6510

Lido Cigar Room
3441 Via Lido, Ste. D
Newport Beach 92663
(714) 723-0595

Newport Tobacco
Fashion Island, 533 Newport Centre Dr., Newport Beach 92660
(714) 644-5153

Portofino Cigars
1000 W. Coast Hwy., Ste. D, Newport Beach 92663
(714) 650-0166

228

Romeo Et Juliette
1000 Bristol N.,
Ste. 7
Newport Beach
92660
(310) 430-2331

Smokin Cigars
Fashion Island
Newport Beach
92625
(714) 721-6833

NORTH HILLS

Cigarettes Cheaper!
Lucky Ctr., 15439
Parthenia St.
North Hills 91343
(818) 894-4998

Cigarettes Cheaper!
16154 Nordhoff St.,
#103
North Hills 91343
(818) 762-1546

Cigarettes Cheaper!
Norwood Ctr., 9048-
A Woodley Ave.
North Hills 91343
(818) 892-8781

Cigarettes Cheaper!
North Hollywood
Ctr., 5160
Vineland, #110
North Hollywood
91601
(818) 762-1546

Cigarettes Cheaper!
College Block
Shopping Ctr.,
9420 Reseda Blvd.
Northridge 91324
(818) 772-2051

Cigarettes Cheaper!
Paddison Sq., 12407
S. Norwalk Blvd.
Norwalk 90650
(310) 863-3913

Cigarettes Cheaper!
The Sq., 2055-A
Novato Blvd.
Novato 94947
(415) 893-9037

**The Humidor Fine
Cigars**
21 Hampshire Way
Novato 94945
(415) 892-3358

Cigarettes Cheaper!
Foothill Oaks
Shopping Ctr., 156
S. Maag Ave.
Oakdale 95361
(209) 848-8310

Mingo's Mercantile
40571 Hwy. 41
Oakhurst 93644
(209) 683-4878

OAKLAND

Beverages & More
525 Embarcadero
Oakland 94607
(510) 208-5126

**Grand Lake Smoke
Shop**
3206 Grand Ave.
Oakland 94610
(510) 268-4070

**The Piedmont
Tobbaconist**
17 Glen Ave.
Oakland 94611
(510) 652-PIPE

OCEANSIDE

Cigarettes Cheaper!
Oceanside Town &
Country, 1759-J
Oceanside Blvd.
Oceanside 92054
(619) 433-9343

Cigarettes Cheaper!
Plaza Rancho Del
Oro, 4170
Oceanside Blvd.,
#177-C
Oceanside 92056
(619) 732-0451

Cigarettes Cheaper!
Mission Douglas
Plaza, 3915
Mission Ave., #6
Oceanside 92056
(619) 967-9156

The Humidor
70 N. Ramone Ave.
Old Pasadena 91103
(818) 584-6383

ONTARIO

Cigarettes Cheaper!
Ontario Village Ctr.,
602-A W. Holt
Blvd.
Ontario 91762
(909) 988-9823

**David's Gift &
Tobacco**
1 Mills Circle,
Ste. 100
Ontario 91764
(909) 481-2200

**Ontario Smoke
Shop**
2538 S. Grove Ave.
#2-A
Ontario 91761
(909) 923-5090

ORANGE

Adray's
1809 W. Chapman
Ave.
Orange 92868
(714) 978-8500

**Aroma Italiano
Coffee House**
1948 N. Tustin
Orange 92865
(714) 282-2382

Cigarettes Cheaper!
Rusty Leaf Plaza,
2560 E. Chapman
Ave.
Orange 92669
(714) 289-8430

Cigarettes Cheaper!
Nohl Plaza, 1514 E.
Lincoln Ave.
Orange 92665
(714) 921-4558

Classic Cigar
7903 E. Santa Cruz
Ave.
Orange 92869
(714) 633-7549

Tinder Box #145
2183 Mall Of
Orange
Orange 92865
(714) 998-0792

Wine Exchange
2368 N. Orange
Mall
Orange 92865
(714) 974-1454

Cigarettes Cheaper!
Cable Park
Shopping Ctr.,
8811 Greenback
Lane
Orangeville 95662
(916) 987-9748

Cigarettes Cheaper!
Currier Sq. Ctr.,
2359-B Myers St.
Oroville 95965
(916) 534-3134

OXNARD

Cigar Lovers
2540 Vineyard Ave.
Oxnard 93030
(805) 485-6974

Cigarettes Cheaper!
Fremont Sq., 800 N.
Ventura Rd.,
Unit B
Oxnard 93030
(805) 278-9706

Cigarettes Cheaper!
1811-B Ventura Blvd.
Oxnard 93030
(805) 278-2011

Long's Drug Store
4445 Mission Blvd.
Pacific Beach 92109
(619) 273-0440

Previously Owned
4667 Cass St.
Pacific Beach 92109
(619) 272-5106

Cigarettes Cheaper!
Fairmont Ctr.,
797 Hickey Blvd.
Pacifica 94044
(415) 355-9509

PALM DESERT

Cigarettes Cheaper!
Palm Desert Country
Club Ctr., 42-335
Washington St., #D
Palm Desert 92260
(619) 345-9549

Cigarettes Cheaper!
Plaza De Monterey,
73-111 Country
Club Dr. #B-1
Palm Desert 92260
(619) 568-6216

The Humidor
73405 El Paseo,
Ste. 31A
Palm Desert 92260
(619) 568-1892

**Palm Desert
Tobacco**
73580 El Paseo #D
Palm Desert 92260
(619) 340-1954

**Palm Desert
Tobacco**
Palm Desert Town
Ctr., 72-840 Hwy.
111 G-235
Palm Desert 92260
(619) 340-3364

Cigarettes Cheaper!
1775 E. Palm
Canyon Dr.,
Rm. A-C
Palm Springs 93364
(619) 223-9570

Tinder Box #114
245 S. Palm Canyon
Dr., Ste. A-2
Palm Springs 92262
(619) 325-4041

PALMDALE

Cigarettes Cheaper!
Palmdale Ctr., 248
E. Palmdale Blvd.
Palmdale 92665
(805) 274-2985

Cigarettes Cheaper!
The Village Plaza
Ctr., 2321 South
Ave. E., E-2
Palmdale 93550
(805) 274-9328

**Hiland's Gifts &
Tobacco**
Antelope Valley
Mall, 1233 W.
Ave. P, #305
Palmdale 93551
(805) 538-9620

**Dominion Premium
Cigars**
2465 E. Bayshore
Rd., Ste. 301
Palo Alto 94303
(415) 354-0244

Mac's Smoke Shop
534 Emerson St.
Palo Alto 94301
(415) 323-3724

Cigarettes Cheaper!
Old Town Plaza,
6008-B Clarke Rd.
Paradise 95969
(916) 876-3275

PASADENA

Captain Tobacco
2371 E. Colorado
Blvd.
Pasadena 91107
(818) 795-4714

Cigar By Chivas
37 N. Arroyo Pkwy.
Pasadena 91103
(818) 395-7505

The Cigar Company
380 S. Lake Ave.
Pasadena 91101
(818) 792-2112

Cigarettes Cheaper!
Orangewood Plaza,
137 W. California
Blvd.
Pasadena 91105
(818) 795-8743

Mr. S Liquor Mart #5
2044 Colorado
Pasadena 91107
(818) 795-5700

Tinder Box #304
165 Plaza Pasadena
Pasadena 91101
(818) 449-6479

Cigarettes Cheaper!
Woodland Plaza, 181
Niblick Rd.
Paso Robles 93446
(805) 238-6988

Cregors
611 Spring St.
Paso Robles 93446
(805) 239-1917

Cigarettes Cheaper!
Perris Towne Ctr., 75
W. Nuevo Rd.,
Ste. 1
Perris 92571
(909) 943-9421

PETALUMA

A Man's World
39 Petaluma Blvd. N.
Petaluma 94952
(707) 778-9100

Cigarettes Cheaper!
Petaluma Gateway,
911 Lakeville Hwy.
Petaluma 94954
(707) 766-8131

Cigarettes Cheaper!
Plaza North
Shopping Ctr., 249
N. McDowell Blvd
Petaluma 94954
(707) 776-4847

Cigarettes Cheaper!
231-G N.H.
McDowell Blvd.
Petaluma 94954
(707) 776-0699

Cigarettes Cheaper!
Pacific Coast Plaza,
891 Oak Park
Blvd.
Pismo Beach 93449
(805) 473-1130

Cigarettes Cheaper!
Save Mart Ctr.,
2951-B Harbor St.
Pittsburg 94565
(510) 432-4466

PLACERVILLE

Cigarettes Cheaper!
Carriage Trade
Shopping Ctr.,
1438 Broadway
Placerville 95667
(916) 621-0386

**Hang Town
Humidor & Cigar
Co.**
135 Placerville Dr.
Placerville 95667
(916) 626-3475

The Wine Smith
346 Main St.
Placerville 95667
(916) 622-0516

Tobacco Loft
1920 Contra Costa
Blvd.
Pleasant Hill 94523
(510) 686-3440

Hoptech
3015 Hopyard Rd.,
Ste. E
Pleasanton 94588
(510) 426-1450

Tobacco Loft
4001-4 Santa Rita
Rd., Rose Pavilion
Pleasanton 94588
(510) 463-0100

Cigarettes Cheaper!
Pony Express Ctr.,
6454 Pony Express
Trail, #13
Pollock Pines 95726
(916) 647-8064

Express West
266 N. Euclid Ave.
Pomona 91762
(909) 988-1366

Cigarettes Cheaper!
Mandalay Village
Marketplace, 565
Channel Island
Blvd., 4A-8
Port Hueneme 93041
(805) 382-7616

Cigarettes Cheaper!
Porterville
Marketplace, 1283
W. Henderson
Porterville 93257
(209) 781-1461

John's Liquor
290 Alpine Rd.,
Ladera Shopping
Ctr.
Portola Valley 94028
(415) 854-6816

Cigarettes Cheaper!
Ranco Las Palmas
Ctr., 42-456 Bob
Hope Dr.
Rancho Mirage
92270
(619) 773-5099

Jensens Market
69-900 Frank
Sinatra Dr.
Rancho Mirage 92270
(619) 770-3355

Big Town Liquors
28733 S. Western
Ave.
Rancho Palos 90275
(310) 833-4401

Celebrity Cigars
29133 S. Western
Ave.
Rancho Palos Verdes
90275
(310) 832-4000

REDDING

Cigarettes Cheaper!
Westwood Village,
6478-F Westside
Rd.
Redding 96001
(916) 246-3722

Cigarettes Cheaper!
North Point Plaza,
125 Lake Blvd.
Redding 96003
(916) 246-3722

Tobacco & Brew
2143 Hilltop Dr.
Redding 96002
(916) 223-2049

REDLAND

**Arnett's Smoke
Shop**
446 N. Orange St.
Redland 92374
(909) 792-6161

The Cigar Box
617 Cypress Circle
Redland 92373
(909) 798-2828

Cigarettes Cheaper!
The Pavillion at
Redlands, 2094-H
W. Redlands Blvd.
Redland 92373
(909) 798-1556

**Bombay Cigar
Society**
209 Ave. I
Redondo Beach
90277
(310) 798-6568

**Broadway
Tobacconist**
2013 Broadway
Redwood City 94063
(415) 261-9657

Cigarettes Cheaper!
Five Points Plaza,
535 S. Riverside
Ave.
Rialto 92376
(909) 873-1373

Smoke Shop Rialto
2026-B N. Riverside
Ave.
Rialto 92377
(909) 820-6388

Cigarettes Cheaper!
Richmond Ctr.,
1170 McDonald
Ave., B-1
Richmond 94801
(510) 237-2862

Cigarettes Cheaper!
Ridgecrest Towne
Centre, 880-B, N.
China Lake Blvd.
Ridgecrest 93555
(619) 371-3227

RIVERSIDE

The Cigar Box
6519 Magnolia Ave.
Riverside 92506
(909) 786-0616

Cigarettes Cheaper!
Arlington Heights,
6160 Arlington
Ave., #C-8
Riverside 92504
(909) 352-1019

Cigarettes Cheaper!
Mission Grove Plaza,
301 E. Alessandro
Blvd., #3-F
Riverside 92508
(909) 789-2537

Cigarettes Cheaper!
Nexus Town Ctr.,
3410-E La Sierra
Ave.
Riverside 92506
(909) 352-1713

Cigarettes Cheaper!
Magnolia Town Ctr.,
6167 Magnolia
Ave.
Riverside 92506
(909) 779-0654

Cigarettes Cheaper!
Woodcrest Plaza,
17090 Van Buren
Blvd.
Riverside 92504
(909) 789-2830

Tinder Box
1283 Galleria At
Tyler
Riverside 92503
(909) 689-4401

**House Of Cigar &
Liquor**
400 S. Pacific Coast
Hwy.
Rodondo Beach
90277
(310) 540-7075

Palani's
44A Peninsula Ctr.
Rolling Hills 90274
(310) 541-6469

**Duffy's Liquor &
Cigar**
329 Vernon St.
Roosevelt 95678
(916) 783-3258

SACRAMENTO

Berkley Fine Wines
515 Pavilions Lane
Sacramento 95825
(916) 929-4422

Beverages & More
3106 Arden Way
Sacramento 95825
(916) 481-8651

**Briar Patch Smoke
Shop**
Arden Fair, 1689
Arden Way, Ste.
2006
Sacramento 95815
(916) 929-8965

**Chuck's Quality
Cigars & Etc.**
1328 Fulton Ave.
Sacramento 95825
(916) 488-0811

Cigarettes Cheaper!
Norwood Ctr., 4201
Norwood Ave.
Sacramento 95953
(916) 924-0816

Cigarettes Cheaper!
4215 Norwood Dr.,
Ste. 11
Sacramento 95853
(916) 924-0816

Cigarettes Cheaper!
8399 Folsom Blvd., #4
Sacramento 95826
(916) 386-3512

Cigarettes Cheaper!
3643 Bradshaw Rd.,
Ste. F
Sacramento 95827
(916) 366-0253

**Garcia Y Vega
Smoke Shop**
725 K St.
Sacramento 95814
(916) 447-0804

**Rodney's Cigars &
Liquor**
1000 J St.
Sacramento 95814
(916) 442-5998

**Tower Pipe &
Cigars**
2518 Land Park Dr.
Sacramento 95818
(916) 443-8466

ST. HELENA

**Baker St.
Tobacconist**
1150 Main St.
St. Helena 94574
(707) 963-8673

**St. Helena Grocery
Company**
607 St. Helena
Hwy. S.
St. Helena 94574
(707) 963-2662

**St. Helena Wine
Center**
1321 Main St.
St. Helena 94574
(707) 963-1313

**St. Helena Wine
Merchant**
699 St. Helena Hwy.
St. Helena 94574
(707) 963-7888

SALINAS

Cigarettes Cheaper!
Santa Rita Plaza,
1980 N. Main St.
Salinas 93906
(408) 449-3648

Cigarettes Cheaper!
Main St. Plaza, 1168
S. Main St.
Salinas 93901
(408) 758-5882

Grapes & Grains
385 Salinas
Salinas 93901
(408) 424-3482

**Ludwig's Smoke
Shop**
431 San Anselmo
Ave.
San Anselmo 94960
(415) 456-1820

**SAN
BERNARDINO**

Cigarettes Cheaper!
Super K Ctr., 136 W.
40th St.
San Bernardino
92719
(909) 881-5545

**Hiland's Gift &
Tobacco**
212 Inland Ctr.
San Bernardino
92408
(909) 885-8282

**Poor Richard's Pipe
Shop**
364 W. Highland
Ave., San
Bernardino 92405
(909) 883-7031

Ed's Smoke Shop
1221 San Carlos
Ave.
San Carlos 94070
(415) 591-6266

Elegant Tobacco
1272 El Camino
San Carlos 94070
(415) 591-0500

Bob's Fine Wines
470 Camme De
Estrella
San Clemente 92672
(714) 496-3313

SAN DIEGO

Bad Habits
3850 5th Ave.
San Diego 92103
(619) 298-6340

Beverages & More
11475 Carmel
Mountain Rd.
San Diego 92129
(619) 673-3892

The Black
5017 Newport Ave.
San Diego 92107
(619) 222-5498

**Captain Hunt
Tobacconist**
851-D W. Harbor Dr.
San Diego 92101
(619) 232-2938

**Cigar Cellar/Club
Robusto**
1640 Camino Del
Rio N., #1376
San Diego 92108
(619) 291-7391

Cigarettes Cheaper!
Balboa Mesa Ctr.,
5665-A Balboa
Ave., San Diego
(619) 278-5573

Cigarettes Cheaper!
University Sq. Ctr.,
5971 University
Ave., #310
San Diego 92115
(619) 229-0359

Cigarettes Cheaper!
Serra Mesa Ctr.,
3298-C Grayling
Dr., San Diego
92123
(619) 505-0332

Cigarettes Cheaper!
Southland Plaza, 655
   Saturn Blvd., #15-A
San Diego 92154
(619) 423-7065

Cigarettes Cheaper!
Plaza Rancho
   Penasquitas, 9929
   Carmel Mountain
   Rd., San Diego
   92129
(619) 780-0727

Cuban Cigar
   Factory
360 8th Ave.
San Diego 92101
(619) 238-2496

Fumar Cigar
1165-A Garnet
San Diego 92109
(619) 270-9227

Hemingway's
777 Front St.,
   Ste. 112
San Diego 92101
(619) 702-6446

Jug Liquor
4979 Cass St.
San Diego 92109
(619) 483-1374

Kensington Grill
4055 Adams Ave.
San Diego 92116
(619) 281-4014

Liberty Tobacco
7341 Clairemont
   Mesa Blvd.
San Diego 92111
(619) 292-1772

Racine & Laramie
2737 San Diego
   Ave., San Diego
   92110
(619) 291-7833

Smoker's Land
13295 Black
   Mountain Rd.
San Diego 92129
(619) 484-7373

Tinder Box
4465 La Jolla Village
   Dr., Ste. #H-38
San Diego 92122
(619) 262-4822

Tinder Box #115
Fashion Valley Mall
San Diego 92108
(619) 291-7337

The Village Spirit
   Shop
11936 Bernardo
   Plaza Dr.
San Diego 92128
(619) 487-4949

Vintage Wines Ltd
6904 Miramar Rd.,
   Ste. #101
San Diego 92121
(619) 549-2112

The Wine Bank
363 5th Ave.,
   Ste. 100
San Diego 91942
(619) 234-7487

Sharon Cigar &
   Tobacco
1371 W. Arrow Hwy.
San Dimas 91773
(909) 305-2199

SAN FRANCISCO

Alfred Dunhill
   Limited
250 Post St.
San Francisco 94108
(415) 781-3368

Ashbury Tobacco
1524 Haight St.
San Francisco 94117
(415) 552-5556

Beverages & More
201 Bayshore Blvd.
San Francisco 94124
(415) 648-1233

California Tobacco
   Center
1501 Polk St.
San Francisco 94109
(415) 885-5479

Cigarettes Cheaper!
17 Kearny St.
San Francisco 94108
(415) 986-6428

Cigarettes Cheaper!
123 Powell St.
San Francisco 94102
(415) 732-7746

D & M Liquors
2200 Fillmore
San Francisco 94115
(415) 346-1325

Grant's Pipe Shop
562 Market St.
San Francisco 94104
(415) 981-1000

Greystone Wine &
Liquor
4100 24th St.
San Francisco 94114
(415) 824-9646

Hennessy's Wines
& Spirits
3600 16th St.
San Francisco 94114
(415) 864-6677

The Humidor
2201 Union St.
San Francisco 94123
(415) 563-5181

Jim Mate Pipe Shop
575 Geary St.
San Francisco 94102
(415) 775-6634

The Jug Shop Inc.
1567 Pacific Ave.
San Francisco 94109
(415) 885-2922

Juicy News
2453 Fillmore St.
San Francisco 94115
(415) 441-3051

Michael's Liquors
2198 Union St.
San Francisco 94123
(415) 921-5700

Mr. Liquor
250 Taraval St.
San Francisco 94116
(415) 731-6222

N A Tobacco
1343 Polk St.
San Francisco 94109
(415) 776-5650

Plump Jack Wines
3201 Fillmore St.
San Francisco 94123
(415) 346-9870

Sherlock's Haven
Embarcadero
Center West, 275
Battery St.
San Francisco 94111
(415) 362-1405

Vendetta
12 Tillman Place
San Francisco 94108
(415) 397-7755

The Wine Club
953 Harrison St.
San Francisco 94107
(415) 512-9088

SAN JOSE

Beverages & More
14800 Camden Ave.
San Jose 95124
(408) 369-0990

Cigarettes Cheaper!
Almaden Oaks
Plaza, 6113
Meridian Ave.
San Jose 95120
(408) 927-6939

Cigarettes Cheaper!
7110 Santa Teresa
Blvd.
San Jose 95139
(408) 629-1287

Cigarettes Cheaper!
Berryessa Hills Shop-
ping Ctr., 1190 N.
Capitol Ave.
San Jose 95132
(408) 926-9618

Cigarettes Cheaper!
Park Almaden
Shopping Ctr., 950
Branham Lane
San Jose 95136
(408) 448-2866

Cigarettes Cheaper!
Winchester
Pavillion, 700 S.
Winchester Blvd. E.
San Jose 95128
(408) 260-1212

Cigarettes Cheaper!
Park Almaden Ctr.,
950 Branham Lane
San Jose 91536
(408) 448-8266

Metro Convenience
Center
73 Metro Dr.
San Jose 95110
(408) 437-0393

Mission Pipe Shop
812 Town Country
Village Dr.
San Jose 95128
(408) 241-8868

Smokers Paradise
3617 Union Ave.
San Jose 95124
(408) 377-1335

**Willow Glen Cigars
& Tobacco**
1068 Lincoln Ave.
San Jose 95125
(408) 283-9323

....

Prestige Cigar
32281 Camino
Capistrano, C-103
San Juan 92675
(714) 496-1199

Cigarettes Cheaper!
Plaza Del Rio Ctr.,
32301-D Camino
Capistrano
San Juan 92690
(714) 489-8121

**Jack Kavanagh
Liquor/Beverage**
1306 Bockman Rd.
San Lorenzo 94580
(510) 278-4336

Cigarettes Cheaper!
793 Foothill Blvd.
Ste. E
San Luis Obispo
93405
(805) 594-1850

**Sanctuary Tobacco
Shop**
1111 Chorro St.
San Luis Obispo
93401
(805) 543-1958

Cigarettes Cheaper!
San Marcos Lucky
Center, 1921 W.
San Marcos Blvd.,
#15
San Marcos 92069
(619) 599-6974

Cigarettes Cheaper!
Vallecitos Village
Center, 1250 E.
Mission Rd.
San Marcos 92069
(619) 738-3717

**Third Ave. News &
Tobacco**
36 E. 3rd
San Mateo 94401
(415) 579-5719

Tinder Box #142
139 Hillsdale Mall
San Mateo 94403
(415) 341-4945

Cigarettes Cheaper!
298-A El Portal Ctr.
San Pablo 94806
(510) 236-8568

Cigarettes Cheaper!
402 San Pablo
Towne Ctr.
San Pablo 94806
(510) 235-1866

Beverages & More
750 Francisco Blvd. W.
San Rafael 94901
(415) 456-8367

**Jack Kavanagh
Liquor/Beverage**
21001 San Ramon
Valley Blvd.
San Ramon 94583
(510) 828-6891

SANTA ANA

Cigarettes Cheaper!
McCalla Centre, 208
N. Harbor Blvd.,
#A6
Santa Ana 92703
(714) 265-0774

Cigarettes Cheaper!
Park Ctr., 1710 E.
17th St., #C
Santa Ana 92711
(714) 972-3977

Teri Cigar Company
310 E. 1st St.
Santa Ana 92701
(714) 541-9142

The Wine Club
2110 E. Macfadden,
Ste. E.
Santa Ana 92705
(714) 835-6485

SANTA
BARBARA

The Cigar Company
1005 Santa Barbara St.
Santa Barbara 93101
(805) 962-4427

Cigarettes Cheaper!
Magnolia Ctr., 5146
Hollister Ave.
Santa Barbara 93111
(805) 692-2136

**Santa Barbara Cigar
& Tobacco**
10 W. Figueroa St.
Santa Barbara 93101
(805) 963-1979

The Tinder Box
1307 State St.
Santa Barbara 93101
(805) 963-8464

The Wine Bistro
1280 Coast Village
Rd., Santa Barbara
93108
(805) 969-1356

SANTA
CLARA

Beverages & More
4175 Stevens Creek
Blvd., Santa Clara
95051
(408) 248-2776

**The Mission City
Cigar Company**
623 Azevedo Ct.
Santa Clara 95051
(408) 247-2022

The Wine Club
1200 Coleman Ave.
Santa Clara 95050
(408) 567-0900

SANTA CRUZ

Avenue Cigars
713 Pacific Ave.
Santa Cruz 95060
(408) 427-9747

Cigarettes Cheaper!
922 Soquel Ave.
Santa Cruz 95062
(408) 458-2744

Pipe Line
818 Pacific Ave.
Santa Cruz 95060
(408) 425-7473

SANTA
MARIA

Cigarettes Cheaper!
Acorn Plaza, 4869 S.
Bradley Rd., B-3
Santa Maria 93455
(805) 934-8158

Cigarettes Cheaper!
Broadway Pavilion,
2530-D S.
Broadway
Santa Maria 93455
(805) 922-8942

Cigarettes Cheaper!
North Broadway
Plaza, 1860 N.
Broadway
Santa Maria 93454
(805) 928-6962

SANTA
MONICA

Cigar Cellar
223-B Broadway
Santa Monica 90401
(310) 289-0292

**Hiland &
Collectible**
265 Santa Monica
Place, Ste. #265
Santa Monica 90401
(310) 394-1580

**Jerry's Liquor &
Wine**
2923 Wilshire Blvd.
Santa Monica 90403
(310) 828-5923

Royal Cigar Society
2814 Main St.
Santa Monica 90405
(310) 581-8555

Tinder Box Wilshire
2729 Wilshire Blvd.
Santa Monica 90403
(310) 828-2313

SANTA ROSA

Beverages & More
2090 Santa Rosa Ave.
Santa Rosa 95404
(707) 573-1544

Cigarettes Cheaper!
711 Stony Point Rd.,
8-B
Santa Rosa 94544
(707) 573-4748

Cigarettes Cheaper!
Raley's Fulton
Marketplace, 1425
Fulton Rd., #225
Santa Rosa 95403
(707) 575-1338

The Squire
346 Coddington
Mall
Santa Rosa 95401
(707) 573-8544

Tinder Box
2048 Santa Rosa
Plaza
Santa Rosa 95401
(707) 579-4442

Cigarettes Cheaper!
Santee Town Ctr.,
50-C Town Ctr. Dr.
Santee 92071
(619) 448-4889

**Gene Hiller Men's
Wear**
729 Bridgeway
Sausalito 94965
(415) 332-3636

Cigarettes Cheaper!
Scotts Village
Shopping Ctr.,
235-C Mt.
Herman Rd.
Scotts Valley 95066
(408) 461-9361

Romeo Et Juliette
1198 Pacific Coast
Hwy., Ste. E
Seal Beach 90740
(310) 430-2331

Cigarettes Cheaper!
Laguna Plaza
Shopping Ctr.,
1130 N. Fremont,
Ste. 203
Seaside 93955
(408) 899-1861

Cigarettes Cheaper!
5197 E. Los Angeles
Ave., C-3
Simi Valley 93063
(805) 520-4922

JM Enterprises
2235 1st St., Ste. #119
Simi Valley 93065
(805) 582-2454

El Rancho Market
2886 Mission Dr.
Solvang 93463
(805) 688-4300

Cigarettes Cheaper!
150 W. Stockton Rd.
Sonora 95370
(209) 533-0671

Cigarettes Cheaper!
Sonora Crossroads
Shopping, 1245
Sanguinetti Rd.
Sonora 95370
(209) 533-2305

Bay Briar Shoppe
2910 Daubenbiss
Ave.
Soquel 95073
(408) 462-1965

King's Liquor
2227 Lake Tahoe
Blvd.
South Lake Tahoe
96150
(716) 541-4614

STANTON

Cigarettes Cheaper!
Stanton Lucky Ctr.,
7034 Katella Ave.
Stanton 91436
(714) 373-9394

**Prissy's Smoke
Shop**
12136 Beach Blvd.
Stanton 90680
(714) 938-4990

STOCKTON

Cigarettes Cheaper!
1540 E. March Lane,
Ste. B-8
Stockton 95210
(209) 476-8097

Cigarettes Cheaper!
Eastland Plaza Ctr.,
678 Wilson Way
Stockton 95205
(209) 937-0914

Cigarettes Cheaper!
Colonial Plaza, 3255
W. Hammer Ln. #1
Stockton
(209) 472-0354

Cigarettes Cheaper!
Venetian Sq., 4555
N. Pershing Ave.,
#31
Stockton 95207
(209) 474-8037

Tobacco Leaf
209 Lincoln Ctr.
Stockton 95207
(209) 474-8216

STUDIO CITY

The Big Easy
12604 Ventura Blvd.
Studio City 91604
(818) 762-3279

Jumping Java
11919 Ventura Blvd.
Studio City 91604
(818) 980-4249

Vendome #28
11976 Ventura Blvd.
Studio City 91604
(818) 766-5272

American Rag
9175 San Fernando
Rd.
Sun Valley 91352
(818) 768-2020

**Murphy Ave.
Smoke Shop**
114 S. Murphy St.
Sunnyvale 94086
(408) 735-9127

Board Room
16822 Pacific Coast
Hwy.
Sunset Beach 90742
(310) 592-3770

Cigarettes Cheaper!
Taft Hills Plaza,1068
W. Kern
Taft 93268
(805) 763-0171

Cigarettes Cheaper!
18324 Oxnard St., #1
Tarzana 91356
(818) 342-2166

Party House
18839 Ventura Blvd.
Tarzana 91356
(818) 342-0355

Cigarettes Cheaper!
Red Apple Plaza,
785-K Tucker Rd.
Tehachapi 93561
(805) 823-0452

TEMECULA

The Cigar Source
42200 Moraga Rd.,
Ste. 41-H
Temecula 92591
(909) 676-6708

Cigarettes Cheaper!
Palm Plaza, 26489-B
Ynez Rd.
Temecula 92591
(909) 676-8207

**Old Towne Smoke
Shoppe**
28690 Front St.,
Ste. 320
Temecula 92590
(909) 699-1918

**Rosemead
Cigarettes &
Cigars**
5779 Rosemead
Blvd.
Temple City 91780
(818) 309-9021

Cigar House
1378-A Noah Moore
Park Rd.
Thousand Oaks
91360
(805) 374-0082

**Village Smoke
Shoppe**
3006 Thousand
Oaks Blvd.
Thousand Oaks
91360
(805) 495-9736

Liberson's Gourmet
10143 Riverside Dr.
Toluca Lake 91602
(818) 985-4310

V-Cut Smoke Shop
10600 Riverside Dr.
Toluca Lake 91602
(818) 766-9593

TORRANCE

The Cigar Room
22543 Hawthorne
Blvd.
Torrance 90505
(310) 375-4420

Cigarettes Cheaper!
Pacific Plaza Ctr.,
5015 Pacific Coast
Hwy.
Torrance 90505
(310) 373-7670

Tinder Box #136
71 Del Amo Fashion
Sq.
Torrance 90503
(310) 542-7975

Cigarettes Cheaper!
Madera Marketplace
Shopping, 3161 N.
Tracy Blvd.
Tracy 95376
(209) 836-5806

TRUCKEE

Cigarettes Cheaper!
Truckee Crossroads,
11377 Dearfield
Truckee 96161
(916) 582-8891

Cigart Gallery
10020 Donner Pass
Rd.
Truckee 96160
(916) 582-1580

Tourist Liquor
10092 Donner Pass
Rd.
Truckee 96161
(916) 582-3521

Cigarettes Cheaper!
Heritage Place
Shopping Ctr., 238
E. Cross St.
Tulare 93274
(209) 684-9084

Cigarettes Cheaper!
Turlock Town Ctr.,
529 N. Golden
State Blvd.
Turlock 95380
(209) 667-1409

Cigarettes Cheaper!
1805 Countryside Dr.
Turlock 95382
(209) 664-1736

Kelly's Mens Store
330 El Camino Real
Tustin 92780
(714) 731-1385

Cigarettes Cheaper!
31834 Alvarado
Blvd.
Union City 94587
(510) 487-1432

**Cigar Exchange
International**
134 N. 2nd Ave.,
Ste. G
Upland 91786
(909) 946-6782

Cigarettes Cheaper!
Mountain Sq. Ctr.,
286 S. Mountain
Ave.
Upland 91786
(909) 931-0851

**Havanah House
Cigar & Lounge**
7020 Greenleaf Ave.
Uptown Whittier
90602
(310) 698-2245

Cigarettes Cheaper!
Golden Hills
Shopping Ctr., 973
Alamo Dr.
Vacaville 95687
(707) 449-9094

Lil' Havana
1011 Mason St., Ste.
1Vacaville 95688
(707) 447-8678

Cheefa's Fine Cigars
23360 W. Valencia
Blvd. #E
Valencia 91355
(805) 253-1125

VENTURA

The Cigar Company
3845 Telegraph Rd.
Ventura 93003
(805) 494-1886

The Cigar Company
3498 Telegraph Rd.
Ventura 93003
(805) 642-7108

Cigarettes Cheaper!
Mission Plaza
Shopping Ctr., 51-
H W. Main St.
Ventura 93001
(805) 653-5134

Cigarettes Cheaper!
Victoria Plaza, 6108
Telegraph Rd.
Ventura 93003
(805) 658-6832

John T's
363 South Mills Rd.,
Ste. 1610
Ventura 93003
(209) 627-9252

**Mandell's Liquor &
Wine**
3915 Telegraph Rd.
Ventura 93003
(805) 642-1148

Salzers
5777 Valentine Rd.
Ventura 93003
(805) 639-2160

VICTORVILLE

Cigarettes Cheaper!
Liberty Village, 13790
Bear Valley Rd., E-2
Victorville 92392
(619) 241-5629

Cigarettes Cheaper!
Victor Valley Town
Ctr., 12209
Hesperia Rd., #20
Victorville 92392
(619) 243-7664

**Hiland's Gift &
Tobacco**
Mall Of Victor
Valley, 14400 Bear
Valley Rd., #11
Victorville 92392
(619) 241-5821

VISALIA

Cigarettes Cheaper!
Visalia Village, 2615
S. Mooney
Visalia 93277
(209) 741-9826

Cigarettes Cheaper!
North Pointe Ctr.,
1442 N. Bed Maddox
Visalia 93292
(209) 636-1208

John T's
2183 Mooney Blvd.
Visalia 93277
(209) 627-9252

VISTA

Cigarettes Cheaper!
Melrose Village
Plaza, 1621-H S.
Melrose Dr.
Vista 92083
(619) 727-4119

Cigarettes Cheaper!
Lucky Vista Ctr., 929
E. Vista Way
Vista 92084
(619) 726-4726

Cigarettes Cheaper!
Vons/Savon Ctr.,
948 S. Santa Fe Ave.
Vista 92084
(619) 724-8160

Cigars 'R' Us
1275 S. Santa Fe
Ave., Ste. 102
Vista 92083
(619) 630-9600

Pipes & Tobacco
512 E. Vista Way
Vista 92084
(619) 758-9881

Cigarettes Cheaper!
Walnut Hills Village,
20633-2 Amar Rd.
Walnut 91789
(909) 444-9196

S & H Tobacco
101 W. Central
Ave., Ste. D
Walnut 91789
(714) 671-0224

WALNUT
CREEK

Beverages & More
2900 N. Main St.
Walnut Creek 94596
(510) 472-0130

Cigarettes Cheaper!
1546 Palos Verdes
Mall
Walnut Creek 94596
(510) 935-9038

Cigarettes Cheaper!
Newell Ctr., 1485
   Newell Ave.
Walnut Creek 94596
(510) 944-0675

John T's
1200 W. Covina
   Pkwy., #597
West Covina 91790
(818) 338-8124

Cigarettes Cheaper!
Platt Village, 6436
   Platt Ave.
West Hill 91307
(818) 716-7097

Up In Smoke
8278 Santa Monica
   Blvd.
West Hollywood
   90046
(213) 654-8173

**Lakeside Marine
   Liquor Store**
32123 Lindero
   Canyon Rd.
West Lake Village
   91361
(818) 889-8389

WEST LOS
ANGELES

The Big Easy
1922 Westwood Blvd.
West Los Angeles
   90025
(310) 234-3279

Cigarettes Cheaper!
11221 National
   Blvd.
West Los Angeles
   90064
(310) 479-8779

**Politically
   Inc.orrect**
Cigar Shop &
   Lounge, 10850 W.
   Pico Blvd, #505
West Los Angeles
   90064
(310) 446-9979

The Wine House
2311 Cotner Ave.
West Los Angeles
   90064
(310) 479-3731

Cigarettes Cheaper!
North Ranch
   Gateway, 30819
   Thousand Oaks
   Blvd.
Westlake Village
   91362
(818) 991-2378

WHITTIER

Cigarettes Cheaper!
Santa Fe Springs
   Ctr., 13423
   Telegraph Rd.
Whittier 90605
(310) 946-9474

**Intermezzo's Of
   Uptown**
6740 Green Leaf
   Ave.
Whittier 90601
(310) 945-1349

**Uncle Frank's
   Cigars**
12909 Philadelphia
   St.
Whittier 90601
(310) 907-1935

**Whittier Cigarette
   & Cigar**
11803 Whittier
   Blvd.
Whittier City 90601
(310) 695-7870

WOODLAND
HILLS

The Cigar Company
21744 Ventura Blvd.
Woodland Hills
   91364
(818) 346-1505

**Discount Cigarette
   Outlets**
21849 Ventura Blvd.
Woodland Hills
   91364
(818) 883-2307

Green Jug Liquor
6307 Platt Ave.
Woodland Hills
   91367
(818) 88- 9463

Primo Cigars
20504 Ventura
   Blvd., #313
Woodland Hills
   91364
(818) 710-8035

Serra Cigar Company
4863 Topanga
   Canyon Blvd.
Woodland Hills
   91367
(818) 883-1217

**Roberts Of
   Woodside**
3015 Woodside Rd.
Woodside 94062
(415) 851-2640

Smoke Shop
20513 Yorba Linda
   Blvd.
Yorba Linda 92886
(714) 695-0532

Cigarettes Cheaper!
441-G Bridge St.
Yuba City 95991
(916) 673-3937

Colorado

**Aspen's Pen
   Perfecto**
645 E. Durant St.
Aspen 81611
(800) 250-5089

The Baggage Claim
307 S. Galena St.
Aspen 81611
(800) 845-6291

Avon Liquor
100 W. Beaver
   Creek Blvd.
Avon 81620
(970) 949-4384

BOULDER

The Cigarette Store
1750 15th St.
Boulder 80302
(303) 449-7089

Eads News
1715 28th St.
Boulder 80301
(303) 442-5900

**Harvest Wine &
   Spirits**
3075 Arapahoe Ave.
Boulder 80303
(303) 447-9832

Petty John's Liquor & Wine
613 S. Broadway
Boulder 80303
(303) 499-2337

COLORADO SPRINGS

Cheer's Liquor Mart
1105 N. Circle Dr.
Colorado Springs
80909
(719) 574-2244

Coaltrain Wine & Liquor
330 W. Uintah
Colorado Springs
80905
(719) 475-9700

Hathaway's Mag & Smoke
216 N. Tejon
Colorado Springs
80903
(719) 632-1441

Old West Cigar Company
303 E. Pike Peak Ave.
Colorado Springs
80903
(719) 635-2443

Rampart Liquors
7635 N. Union Blvd.
Colorado Springs
80920
(719) 599-0715

Sherlock's Pipes & Tobacco
3650 Austin Bluffs
Pkwy., Ste. #182
Colorado Springs
80918
(719) 598-4444

Southwest Wine & Spirits
1785 S. 8th St.
Colorado Springs
80906
(719) 389-0906

Stag Of Colorado Ltd.
750 Citadel Dr. E.,
Ste., 2214
Colorado Springs
80909
(719) 596-5363

Welcome Smokers #18
4437 N. Academy
Blvd,. Ste. B
Colorado Springs
80918
(719) 532-1747

Welcome Smokers #22
1904 E. Kiowaya
Colorado Springs 80903
(719) 471-0820

Welcome Smokers #7
815 S. Sierra Madre St.
Colorado Springs 80903
(719) 471-0854

Penelope's Restaurant
Bar & Market, 120 Elk Ave.
Crested Butte 81224
(970) 349-5178

DENVER

Argonaut Wine & Liquor
718 E. Colfax
Denver 80203
(303) 831-7788

Bonnie Brae
785 S. University Blvd.
Denver 80209
(303) 733-7263

Cigar & Tobacco World
5227 Leetsdale Dr.
Denver 80222
(303) 321-7308

Cigarette Store
2120 S. Broadway, Ste. #16
Denver 80210
(303) 715-1506

Eno Teca Lodo
1730 Wynkoop St.
Denver 80202
(303) 293-2887

Havana's Fine Cigars
2727 E. 2nd Ave.
Denver 80206
(303) 355-2003

Jerri's Tobacco Shops
1616 Glenarm
Denver 80202
(888) 825-3522

Key Liquors
2860 S. Colorado
Denver 80222
(303) 757-2277

Prince Philips
Tamarac Sq., 7777 E. Hampden
Denver 80231
(303) 695-1959

Smokers Inn
1685 S. Colorado Blvd., Unit K
Denver 80222
(303) 758-5030

The Tobacco Leaf
7111 W. Alameda, Unit N
Denver 80226
(303) 274-8721

The Vineyard
261 Fillmore
Denver 80206
(303) 355-8324

Durango Smoke Shop
113 W. College Dr.
Durango 81301
(970) 247-9115

Edward Pipe & Tobacco Shop
3439 S. Broadway
Englewood 80110
(303) 781-7662

Heritage Wine & Liquor
7475 E. Arapahoe Rd.
Englewood 80112
(303) 770-8212

Edwards Tobacco & Darts
3307 S. College, Unit 102-B
Fort Collins 80525
(970) 226-5311

Fish's Liquor Mart
1007 E. Harmony Rd.
Fort Collins 80525
(970) 223-3348

Welcome Smokers #21
275 Main St.
Frisco 80443
(970) 668-4901

Rem's Place
241 Grand Ave.
Grand Junction 81501
(970) 242-3136

West Lake Wine & Spirits
2024 35th Ave.
Greeley 80634
(303) 330-8466

Highlands Ranch Wine & Spirits
9455 S. University Blvd.
Highlands 80126
(303) 470-7000

The Cigarette Store #662
179 W. South Boulder Rd.
Lafayette 80026
(303) 665-7870

Cask & Barrel Limited
2205 Dover St.
Lakewood 80215
(303) 238-2774

Cigarette Express
6630 W. Colfax
Lakewood 80214
(303) 235-2755

LITTLETON

Alexander Liquors
11757 W. Kencaryl
Littleton 80127
(303) 979-7837

County Line Liquors
181 W. County Line Rd.
Littleton 80126
(303) 730-8211

Garbox
8100 W. Crestline Ave., Ste. A-15, Department 102
Littleton 80123
(303) 904-4893

The Nickle Cigar
6679 W. Ken Caryl Ave.
Littleton 80123
(303) 904-8760

Tony's Wine &
Specialty Beer
4991 E. Dry Creek
Rd.
Littleton 80122
(303) 770-4297

Tobacco Haven
10572-B Melody Dr.
North Glenns 80234
(303) 450-0953

PUEBLO

Cigars Ltd
307 S. Union Ave.
Pueblo 81003
(719) 542-4300

Welcome Smokers #1
401 N. Greenwood,
Ste. H
Pueblo 81003
(719) 543-6846

Welcome Smokers #15
951 U.S. Hwy. 50 W.
Pueblo 81008
(719) 545-3646

Welcome Smokers #17
249 Hwy. 50
Salida 81201
(719) 539-5475

Welcome Smokers #13
362 Main St.
Security 80911
(719) 390-5996

Welcome Smokers #19
401 N. Commercial
St.
Trinidad 81082
(719) 846-7512

The Baggage
Cheque
244 Wall St.
Vail 81657
(970) 476-1747

Apple Jack Liquors
3320 Youngfield St.
Wheat Ridge 80033
(303) 233-3331

Welcome Smokers #12
110 W. Midland
Woodland Park
80863
(719) 687-9890

Connecticut

The Hunter's Shop
539 Main St.
Branford 06405
(203) 488-8550

BYOB
847 Federal Rd.
Brookfield 06804
(203) 775-9020

CP Royal Tobacco
235 Federal Rd.
Brookfield 06804
(203) 775-6325

The Aperitif
50 Albany Tpke.,
Building 4 Unit C
Canton 06019
(203) 693-9373

Marisa's Cafe
168 Main St.
Cheshire 06410
(203) 699-9722

Timberline Office
Supply
265 Highland Ave.
Cheshire 06410
(203) 272-2088

Winslow Cigar
Company
470 W. Main St.
Cheshire 06410
(203) 271-3401

Post Wines & Spirit
230 Post Rd.
Cos Cob 06807
(203) 661-0292

Cigar Box
279 Main St.
Danbury 06810
(203) 748-5718

The Connecticut
Valley
Tobacconist
337 Hazard Ave.
Enfield 06082
(860) 763-4655

Olive Oyls
77 Main St.
Essex 06426
(203) 767-4909

Arcade Cigars
1636 Post Rd.
Fairfield 06430
(203) 259-1994

Golden Leaf Cigar
Shop
2248 Black Rock Tpke.
Fairfield 06430
(203) 735-3174

Cigar Cellar
771-A Farmington
Ave.
Farmington 06032
(860) 677-1901

GREENWICH

Greenwich Cigar
Store
91 Railroad Ave.
Greenwich 06830
(203) 622-9831

Tobacconist Of
Greenwich
8 Havemeyer Place
Greenwich 06830
(203) 869-5401

US Tobacco
1 Sound Shore Dr.
Greenwich 06830
(203) 622-3626

Guilford News &
Tobacco
1016 Boston Post
Rd.
Guilford 06437
(203) 453-1349

Budget Rite Liquors
1427 Dixwell Ave.
Hamden 06514
(203) 288-6397

The Calabash
Shoppe
2450 Whitney Ave.
Hamden 06518
(203) 248-6185

De La Concha Of
Hartford
1 Civic Ctr. Plaza
Hartford 06103
(203) 527-4291

The Tobacco Shop
55 Asylum St.
Hartford 06103
(860) 524-8577

Makayla's Cigar Store
679 Boston Post Rd.
Madison 06443
(203) 245-0469

Tobacco Road Ltd.
Connecticut Post Mall, 1201
Milford 06460
(203) 877-1957

Brewers
487 Rte. 111
Monroe 06468
(203) 459-2909

Knights & Names
Old Mystic Village
Mystic 06355
(860) 444-5211

Stogie's
80 Church St.
Naugatuck 06770
(203) 729-3031

Owl Shop
268 College St.
New Haven 06510
(203) 624-3250

Archway News
64 Bank St.
New Milford 06776
(203) 355-1557

J & J Tobacco
3273 Berlin Tpke.
Newington 06111
(860) 666-0439

Main St. Smoke Shop
155 Main St.
Oakville 06779
(860) 945-0020

Tobacco Plaza
1393 Boston Post Rd.
Old Saybrook 06475
(860) 388-4811

Wine & Liquor Outlet
528 Boston Post Rd.
Orange 06477
(203) 795-8302

Sam's Smoke Junction
71 Oxford Rd.
Oxford 06478
(203) 888-4995

Chief Catoonah Tobacconists
19 Bailey Ave.
Ridgefield 06877
(203) 438-4494

Century Service Center
940 Cromwell Ave.
Rocky Hill 06067
(860) 721-1145

Torpedoes Smoke Shop
922 Hopmeadow St.
Simsbury 06070
(860) 658-7502

Have A Cigar!
980 Sullivan Ave.
South Windsor 06074
(860) 644-5800

The Smoke Shop
Heritage Inn Arcade
Heritage Village
Southbury 06488
(203) 264-5075

Bull's Head News & Variety
51 High Ridge Rd.
Stamford 06905
(203) 359-0740

Smokin Sounds
1026 High Ridge Rd.
Stamford 06905
(203) 329-2808

Denby's Tobacco & Collectibles
908 White Plains Rd.
Trumbull 06611
(203) 261-8114

Executive Cigars
114 Tellar Rd.
Trumbull 06611
(203) 452-9154

Have A Cigar!
435 Hartford Tpke.
Vernon 06066
(860) 875-6556

Brass City Tobacconists
102 Grand St.
Waterbury 06702
(203) 754-7000

Best Cigar Company
769 Farmington Ave.
West Hartford 06119
(860) 570-1228

The Cigar Shop
52 La Salle Rd.
West Hartford 06107
(860) 236-5041

Cigar Port
7 Riverside Ave.
Westport 06880
(203) 454 (PUFF)

Westport Cigar Company
44 Railroad Place
Westport 06880
(203) 227-8996

JJ's News
255 Main St.
Windsor Locks 06096
(860) 627-9200

The Flaming Harmonica
70 Hawkins Rd.
Woodstock Valley 06282
(860) 974-2677

Delaware

Books & Tobacco
214 Lantana Dr.
Hockessin 19707
(302) 239-4224

Tobacco Outlet
Town Sq. Shopping Ctr., Rte. 113
Millsboro 19966
(302) 934-8045

Three Sons Smoke Shop
Farmers Market, 110 N. Dupont Hwy.
New Castle 19720
(302) 322-2116

NEWARK

CB Perkins #80
Christiana Mall, 328
Newark 19702
(302) 266-7200

Cigarette City Inc.
511 College Sq.
Newark 19711
(302) 369-8203

Cigarette City Inc.
238 Peoples Plaza
Newark 19702
(302) 836-4889

Greybeards Ltd.
805 Arbern Place
Newark 19711
(302) 234-0396

**Rehoboth Cigarette
Outlet & New**
2 The Marketplace
Rehoboth 19971
(302) 226-3151

**Greybeards Of
London**
201 Rehoboth Ave.
Rehoboth Beach
19971
(302) 227-4972

Steve's Emporium
508 Greenhill Ave.
Willmington 19805
(302) 654-8794

WILMINGTON

**Books & Tobacco
Inc.**
4555 Kirkwood Hwy.
Wilmington 19808
(302) 994-3156

**Brandywine
Cigarette And
Tobacco Outlet**
3101 Concord Pike
Wilmington 19803
(302) 478-3362

**Frank's Union
Liquors**
1902 W. 13th St.
Wilmington 19806
(302) 429-1978

**Kirkwood News &
Tobacco**
5998 Kirkwood Hwy.
Wilmington 19808
(302) 995-2881

**Kreston Liquor
Mart Inc.**
904 Concord Ave.
Wilmington 19802
(302) 652-3792

Peco's Liquors
522 Philadelphia
Pike
Wilmington 19809
(302) 762-5230

Tobacco Village
4011-B Concord Pike
Wilmington 19803
(302) 478-5075

District Of Columbia

**Calvert Woodley
Wines**
4339 Connecticut
Ave. NW
Washington, D.C.
20008
(202) 966-4400

Central Liquors
726 9th St. NW
Washington, D.C.
20001
(202) 737-2800

**Eagle Wine &
Liquor**
3345 M St. NW
Washington, D.C.
20007
(202) 333-5500

**Georgetown
Tobacco**
3144 M St. NW
Washington, D.C.
20007
(202) 338-5100

**Grand Havana
Room**
1220 19th St. NW
Washington, D.C.
20036
(202) 293-6848

J R Tobacco
1667 K St. NW
Washington, D.C.
20006
(202) 296-3872

Les Halles
1201 Pennsylvania
Ave. NW
Washington, D.C.
20004
(202) 347-6848

Paul's Liquors
5205 Wisconsin
Ave.
Washington, D.C.
20016
(202) 537-1900

Pearson Liquors
2436 Wisconsin
Ave. NW
Washington, D.C.
20007
(202) 333-6666

Schneider Liquors
300 Massachusetts
Ave.
Washington, D.C.
20002
(202) 543-9300

W Curtis Draper
640 14th NW
Washington, D.C.
20005
(202) 638-2555

**Wide World Of
Wines & Cigars**
2201 Wisconsin
Ave. NW
Washington, D.C.
20007
(202) 333-7500

Florida

**Amelia Liquors
South**
4924 First Coast Hwy.
Amelia Island 32034
(904) 261-7701

**The Ritz Carlton
Gift Shop**
4750 Amelia Island
Pkwy.
Amelia Island 32034
(904) 277-1100

The Wharf
973 Atlantic Blvd.
Atlantic Beach
32233
(904) 246-8616

Mike's Cigars
1030 Kane Concourse
Bay Harbor 33154
(305) 866-2277

BOCA RATON

**Bennington
Tobacconist**
Royal Palm Plaza
#80, 501 SE
Mizner Blvd.
Boca Raton 33432
(407) 391-1372

**Carmody Fine Wine
& Liquor**
6060 SW 18th St.
Boca Raton 33433
(407) 394-3766

**Crown Liquors &
Wine Merchants**
4131 N. Federal Hwy.
Boca Raton 33432
(407) 392-6366

**Crown Liquors &
Wine Merchants**
7154 Beracasa Way
Boca Raton 33433
(407) 391-6009

**Crown Liquors &
Wine Merchants**
757 S. Federal Hwy.
Boca Raton 33433
(407) 394-3828

**Garden Shop
Liquors**
7050 W. Palmetto
Park Rd.
Boca Raton 33433
(407) 368-7032

Hamptons Tobacco
Mizner Park
Boca Raton 33432
(407) 391-0012

**Palm Beach Cigar
Company**
9268 Lake Serena
Dr.
Boca Raton 33496
(561) 395-7175

**Palm Beach Cigar
Company Inc.**
4651 N. Dixie Hwy.
Boca Raton 33431
(561) 395-7175

PS Cigars
19575 8-A S. State
Rd. 7
Boca Raton 33498
(561) 482-9070

**Sabatino's Gourmet
Market**
8177 W. Glades Rd.
Boca Raton 33433
(407) 852-9289

Smoker's Gallery
302 Town Ctr.
Boca Raton 33431
(561) 416-1330

**Tinder Box
International**
5250 Town Ctr.
Circle, Ste. 113
Boca Raton 33432
(561) 338-8606

Bonita Smoke Shop
3300 Bonita Beach
Rd., Unit 104
Bonita Springs
34134
(941) 495-9296

Tobacco Road
26831 S. Tamiami
Trail, Unit 44

Bonita Springs
33923
(941) 947-8121

BOYNTON
BEACH

**Crown Liquors &
Wine Merchants**
564 SE 15th Ave.
Boynton Beach
33435
(407) 734-9463

Dan's News
640 E. Ocean Ave.
Boynton Beach
33435
(407) 737-0345

Smokers Gallery
801 N. Congress Ave.
Boynton Beach
33426
(407) 736-5533

Beers Unlimited
4428 Cortez Rd. W.
Bradenton 34210
(941) 761-0502

Smoke & Snuff
205 Desoto Sq. Mall
Bradenton 34205
(941) 747-9700

Smoke & Snuff
666 Brandon Town
Ctr.
Brandon 33511
(813) 654-2566

Cape Smoke Shop
3512 Del Prado
Blvd.
Cape Coral 33904
(941) 549-8809

Gourmet Captiva
14820 Captiva Dr.
Captiva Island
33924
(941) 472-4200

CLEARWATER

**Havana Cigar
Company**
28471 U.S. Hwy. 19 N.
Clearwater 34621
(813) 725-8815

Smoke & Snuff
104 Clearwater Mall
Clearwater 34624
(813) 796-1668

Smoker's Paradise
1251 S. Missouri Ave.
Clearwater 34616
(813) 446-2231

**Mr. D's Pipe &
Tobacco**
Countryside Mall,
Ste. 2033, 27001
U.S. 19 N.
Cleawater 34621
(813) 796-1220

**Wooden Indian
Cigar Store**
142 Minuteman
Cosway
Cocoa Beach 32931
(407) 868-1718

**Grumpy's Cigar
Pub**
9 Stone St.
Cocoa Village 32922
(407) 631-5430

Havana Ray's
3399 Virginia St. #670
Coconut Grove 33133
(305) 446-4003

CORAL
GABLES

**Bill's Pipe &
Tobacco Shop**
2309 Ponce de Leon
Blvd.
Coral Gables 33134
(305) 444-1764

Cigar Depot
1536 South Dixie Hwy.
Coral Gables 33146
(305) 665-0102

The Cigar Gallery
2920 Ponce de Leon
Blvd.
Coral Gables 33134
(305) 445-0100

**Crown Liquors &
Wine Merchants**
6731-51 Red Rd.
Coral Gables 33143
(305) 669-0225

Gables' Cigar Co.
2222 Ponce de Leon
Blvd., Ste. 302
Coral Gables 33134
(888) CIGAR-42

Sips and Cigars Inc.
9838 W. Sample Rd.
Coral Springs 33065
(954) 340-8860

The Smoke Shack
9469 W. Atlantic Blvd.
Coral Springs 33071
(954) 341-0821

Karen's Cigars
8360 Griffin Rd.
Davie 33328
(954) 252-0020

Tinder Box #199
2455 W. International Speedway
Daytona Beach 32114
(904) 253-0708

Tobacco Exotica
749 W. International
Speedway
Daytona Beach
32114
(904) 255-3782

Tobacco Exotica
3404 S. Atlantic
Daytona Beach
Shore 32118
(904) 761-2400

**Crown Liquors &
  Wine Merchants**
306 S. Federal Hwy.
Deerfield Beach
  33441
(954) 427-5274

El Grande Cigarro
632 E. Atlantic Ave.
Delray 33483
(561) 243-1663

City News II
14530 S. Military
  Trail
Delray Beach 33445
(407) 496-3166

Tobacco Trader
1652 Providence
  Blvd.
Deltona 32725
(904) 789-3994

DESTIN

**Classic Cigar &
  Wine Company**
9375 Hwy. 98 W.,
  Ste. 35
Destin 32541
(770) 886-1670

Flamingo Cafe
414 Hwy. 98 E.
Destin 32541
(904) 837-0961

Harbor Cigars
1021 Hwy. 98 E.,
  Ste. E.
Destin 32541
(904) 650-3111

Seaside Cigar
285 Hwy. 98 E.,
  Ste. D
Destin 32541
(904) 650-1600

FORT
LAUDERDALE

A Galaxy Of Maps
5975 N. Federal
  Hwy., Store 116
Fort Lauderdale
  33308
(954) 267-9000

Chester's Tobacco
7770 NW 44th St.
Fort Lauderdale
  33351
(954) 741-4888

Churchill's Inc.
8258 State Rd. 84
Fort Lauderdale
  33324
(954) 475-9431

City News Stand
4400 Bougain Villa Dr.
Fort Lauderdale
  33308
(954) 776-0940

**Crown Liquors &
  Wine Merchants**
2850 N. Federal Hwy.
Fort Lauderdale
  33306
(954) 566-5322

**Crown Liquors &
  Wine Merchants**
3518 N. Ocean
  Blvd.
Fort Lauderdale
  33308
(954) 566-2337

Mushroom Plus
903 Sunrise Lane
Fort Lauderdale
  33304
(954) 630-0615

67 Liquors
5479 N. Federal Hwy.
Fort Lauderdale
  33308
(954) 771-9000

67 Liquors
1311 SE 17th St.
Fort Lauderdale
  33316
(954) 767-9099

Smoke & Beanery
1225 E. Las Olas
  Blvd.
Fort Lauderdale
  33301
(954) 764-8566

Smokers Gallery
2356 E. Sunrise
  Blvd.
Fort Lauderdale
  33304
(954) 561-0002

Zgar Time
1880 NW 97th Ave.
Fort Lauderdale
  33322
(888) 699-4277

FORT MEYERS

**The Downtown
  Tobacco Shoppe**
2235 1st St., Ste. 104
Fort Meyers 33901
(941) 337-4662

Sir Richards
Christmans Village,
  320 McGregor
  Blvd.
Fort Meyers 33901
(941) 332-7722

Smoke & Snuff
139 Edison Mall
Fort Meyers 33901
(941) 939-2626

**Beach Tobacco
  Candy & Nut**
19041 San Carlos
  Blvd., Unit #7
Fort Meyers Beach
  33931
(813) 463-5177

**Discount Cigarettes
  Etc.**
17105 San Carlos
  Blvd., #B1
Fort Meyers Beach
  33931
(941) 482-1947

The Brass Pipe
2573 S. U.S. 1
Fort Pierce 34982
(407) 461-7451

**Roy's Wine &
  Liquor**
720 U.S. Hwy. 1
Fort Pierce 34950
(407) 461-3097

Herbs & Things
446 Racetrack Rd.
  NW, Ste. F
Fort Walton Beach
  32547
(904) 862-3220

GAINESVILLE

Knuckleheads
607 SW 27th St.
Gainesville 32607
(352) 373-0186

248

Modern Age Gift & Tobacco
1035 NW 76th Blvd.
Gainesville 32606
(352) 332-5100

Modern Age Gift & Tobacco
214 NW 13th St.
Gainesville 32601
(352) 371-4733

Smoke & Snuff
The Oaks Mall,
C-4, 6451 W.
Newberry Rd.
Gainesville 32605
(352) 331-3696

The Essence Of Smoke
1946 Hollywood Blvd.
Hollywood 33020
(800) 369-5940

Vlass's Curiosity Shop
974 Pine Tree Dr.
Indian Harbor Beach 32937
(407) 777-9460

JACKSONVILLE

Broudy's Liquors #3
7900 Hillman Plaza
Jacksonville 32244
(904) 777-2646

Broudy's Liquors #4
353 Marshlanding Pkwy.
Jacksonville 32205
(904) 273-6119

Casa Del Tobacco
4131 Southside Blvd., Ste.104
Jacksonville 32216
(904) 998-9993

Chefs Market II
4520-2 San Juan Ave.
Jacksonville 32210
(904) 387-1700

Edward's Of San Marco
2016 San Marco Blvd.
Jacksonville 32207
(904) 396-7990

Edwards Pipe & Tobacco
5566-23 Ft Caroline Rd.
Jacksonville 32277
(904) 745-6368

Gourmet's Delight
12401 Beit Blvd,
Ste. 7
Jacksonville 32246
(904) 641-1833

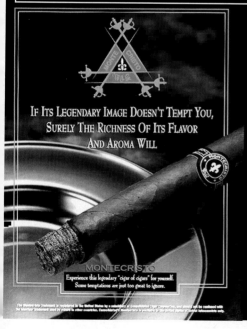

Nicotine
1021-B Park St.
Jacksonville 32204
(904) 354-0009

Player's Smoke Shop
4315-1 Brentwood Ave.
Jacksonville 32206
(904) 358-3388

Smoke & Snuff
2540 The Ave. S. Mall
Jacksonville 32256
(904) 363-2161

Tobacco Cove
3849 Bay Meadows Rd.
Jacksonville 32217
(904) 731-2890

The Tobacco Shop
17 N. Ocean St.
Jacksonville 32202
(904) 355-9319

Tobacco Village
4940 Blanding Blvd.
Jacksonville 32210
(904) 771-3200

Stogies Of Key Biscayne
260 Crandon Blvd., Ste. 12
Key Biscayne 33149
(305) 365-5885

Caribbean Cigar Factory
103400 Overseas Hwy.
Key Largo 33037
(305) 453-4014

KEY WEST

Caribbean Cigar Factory
112 Fitzpatrick
Key West 33040
(305) 292-9595

Conch Republic Cigar Factory
512 Green St.
Key West 33040
(800) 317-2167

Conch Spirits II
5390 U.S. #1
Key West 33040
(305) 292-9870

Key West Havana Cigar
1117 Duval St.
Key West 33040
(800) 217-4884

Kings Treasure Tobacco Of Key West
106 Duval St.
Key West 33040
(305) 294-4477

La Tobacoria
326 Duval St.
Key West 33040
(305) 294-3200

The Tobacco Shop
208 Duval St.
Key West 33040
(305) 293-0106

Cigar Bazaar
3865 Lake Emma Rd.
Lake Mary 32746
(407) 444-0403

Edwards Pipe & Tobacco
2118 S. Florida Ave.
Lakeland 33803
(941) 687-4168

Crown Liquors & Wine Merchants
5000 N. University Dr.
Lauderhill 33351
(305) 741-7070

Scents & Cigars
3122 N. Federal Hwy.
Lighthouse Point 33064
(954) 784-1177

67 Liquors
5360 N. Federal Hwy.
Lighthouse Point 33064
(954) 427-6967

The Tobacco Merchant
1877 W. State Rd.
Longwood 32750
(407) 767-0050

Tobacco Depot #2
23038 State Rd. 54
Lutz 33549
(813) 948-3844

The Ritz Carlton Gift Shop
100 S. Ocean Blvd.
Manalapan 33462
(407) 533-6000

Dangerous John Hubert's
Quay Village, #10, 12650 Overseas Hwy.
Marathon Key 33050
(305) 743-9299

Margate Newstand And Cigars
5430 W. Atlantic
Margate 33063
(954) 968-7563

Side Effects
2458 N. State Rd. 7
Margate 33063
(954) 979-6763

Tobacerie
1700 W. New Haven Ave.
Melbourne 32904
(407) 768-0170

MIAMI

Bob's Pipe Shop
Cutler Ridge Mall, 20505 S. Dixie Hwy.
Miami 33189
(305) 235-7434

Caribbean Cigar Factory
6265 SW 8th St.
Miami 33140
(305) 267-3911

Cigar Box
19501 Biscayne Blvd.
Miami 33180
(305) 936-8808

Cigar World Inc.
7286 SW 40th
Miami 33155
(305) 261-8002

Cigars & Things
4008 SW 57th Ave.
Miami 33155
(305) 666-1350

Coffee Works Plus
8349 NW 12th St.
Miami 33126
(305) 477-8151

Crossings Liquors
12993 SW 112th St.
Miami 33186
(305) 387-3675

El Credito Cigars
1106 SW 8th St.
Miami 33130
(305) 858-4162

Escudo Habanero LC
2101 SW 8th St.
Miami 33125
(305) 541-0050

Foremost Sunset
  Corners
8701 Sunset Dr.
Miami 33173
(305) 271-8492

Gulf Liquors And
  Wine Merchant
1836 SW 3rd Ave.
Miami 33129
(305) 854-4646

H & J Limited
7921 SW 40th St.,
Ste. 40
Miami 33155
(305) 261-9363

Harriel's Tobacco
  Shoppe
11401 S. Dixie Hwy.
Miami 33156
(305) 252-9010

Iggy's
7795 W. Flagler St.
Miami 33144
(305) 267-9511

King's Treasure
  Tobacco
401 Biscayne Blvd.,
Ste. 144
Miami 33132
(305) 374-5593

La Tradicion
  Cubana
226 E. Flagler St.
Miami 33131
(305) 374-2339

Macabi Cigars
3473 SW 8th St.
Miami 33135
(305) 446-2606

Macabi Cigars
13989 S. Dixie Hwy.
Miami 33176
(305) 259-7009

Nicks Cigar
 Company
7167 W.T. Flagler St.
Miami 33144
(305) 266-9907

Praido Roarigues
1850 NW 82nd Ave.
Miami 33126

Smoke Shop #2
1601 Biscayne Blvd.
Miami 33132
(305) 358-1886

Smoker's Gallery
888 SW 136th St., #435
Miami 33176
(305) 378-2300

Stogies Inc.
10101 SW 72nd St.
Miami 33173
(305) 279-4990

Tio Pepe Liquors
9800 SW 8th St.
Miami 33174
(305) 227-9663

Tobacco News
22 E. 3rd Ave.
Miami 33132
(305) 358-6865

Tobacco Taki
10341 SW 44th St.
Miami 33165
(305) 559-1591

MIAMI BEACH

Cigar Connection
Lincoln Rd. Mall,
 #534
Miami Beach 33139
(305) 594-2288

The Cuba Club
432 41st St.
Miami Beach 33140
(305) 604-9798

Cy's At Sobe
1504 Alton Rd.
Miami Beach 33139
(305) 532-5301

Q Cigars
17028 Collins Ave.
Miami Beach 33160
(305) 949-8080

Smokers Notch
425 Washington
 Ave.
Miami Beach 33139
(888) 53 SMOKE

Sobe Liquor
1609 Alton Rd.
Miami Beach 33139
(305) 674-1212

South Beach News
 & Tobacco
710 Washington
 Ave., #9
Miami Beach 33139
(305) 673-3002

Zelick's Tobacco
 Corp
326 Lincoln Rd.
Miami Beach 33139
(305) 538-1544

Zelicko Tobacco
Havana Republic,
 326 Lincoln Rd.
Miami Beach 33139
(305) 538-1544

Rich's Wine Cellar
6702 Main St.
Miami Lakes 33014
(954) 819-7454

The Cigar Bar
108 E. 3rd Ave.
Mount Dora 32757
(352) 735-CGAR

NAPLES

Bill Henry's
 Tobacco Road
200 Goodlette Rd.
 S., #8
Naples 33940
(941) 262-2098

Heaven
2950 Tamiami Trail N.
Naples 33940
(941) 649-6373

Rick's Discount
 Cigarettes &
 Cigars
8793 Tamiami Trail E.
Naples 34113
(941) 774-2888

Smoke & Snuff
Coastland Ctr.,
 G3A, 1988
 Tamiami Trail N.
Naples 34102
(941) 649-5599

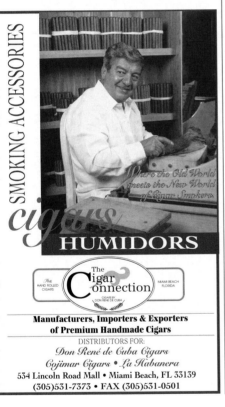

Eight 'til Late
241 3rd St.
Neptune Beach
32266
(904) 241-1127

The Tobacco Hut
Elfers Sq., 4036 S.
Madison St.
New Port Richey
34652
(813) 842-2139

La Havana Cabana Inc.
324-B Flagler Ave.
New Smyrna Beach
32169
(904) 426-5400

NORTH MIAMI

Crown Liquors & Wine Merchants
12555 Biscayne
Blvd.
North Miami 33181
(305) 892-9463

Encantada Cigars
1646 NE 123rd St.
North Miami 33181
(305) 891-4888

Laurenzo's
16385 W. Dixie
Hwy.
North Miami 33160
(305) 945-6381

Cigar Locator
17813 Biscayne
Blvd.
North Miami Beach
33160
(305) 931-1900

Smokers World
20097 Biscayne
Blvd.
North Miami Beach
33180
(305) 931-1117

Smoke Shop
4625 Tamiami Trail
N.
North Naples 34103
(941) 435-1862

LJ Fine Cigars & Tobacco
11585 N. U.S.
Hwy. 1
North Palm Beach
33408
(800) 486-1919

67 Liquors
1585 E. Oakland
Park Blvd.
Oakland Park 33304
(954) 565-0407

Smoke & Snuff
Paddock Mall,
Rm. 520
Ocala 34474
(352) 237-2883

Thoroughbred Tobacco Company
44 SE 1st Ave.,
Ste. #2
Ocala 34471
(352) 380-0629

Ortiz Inc. Cigar Elegante
6010 Hammock
Wood Dr.
Odessa 33556
(800) 962-2495

Mikes Tobacco & Gifts
226 S. Volusia Ave.
Orange City 32763
(904) 775-3707

Cigar Box
1910 Wells Rd.
Orange Park 32073
(904) 278-5065

ORLANDO

Art's Premium Cigars & Exquisite Accessories
1235 N. Orange
Ave., Ste. 201
Orlando 32804
(407) 895-9772

Cigar SA
10253 Neversink Ct.
Orlando 32817
(407) 384-9374

Heart's Liquor & Home Brew
5824 N. Orange
Blossom Trail
Orlando 32810
(407) 298-4103

Ol' Times
124 W. Pine St., Ste.
106, Orlando 32801
(407) 425-7879

The Pacino's Liquor & Restaurant
12523 State Rd.
Orlando 32836
(407) 827-1101

Perry Louis Fine Wine & Cigars
7635 Ashley Park
Ct., 504
Orlando 32835
(407) 522-4466

Pipe & Pouch Smoke Shop
53 N. Orange Ave.
Orlando 32801
(407) 841-7980

Smoke & Snuff
244 The Florida
Mall
Orlando 32809
(407) 826-5053

The Breakers News & Gourmet
1 S. County Rd.
Palm Beach 33480
(561) 655-6611

Hamptons Tobacco
247 Worth Ave.
Palm Beach 33480
(407) 835-0060

Smokers Gallery
3101 PGA Blvd.
Palm Beach Gardens
33410
(407) 694-9440

Harr's Surf-n-Turf
3235 Tampa Rd.
Palm Harbor 34684
(813) 787-6758

Wholly Smokes/ Unique Gifts #2
33959 U.S. Hwy.
19 N.
Palm Harbor 34684
(813) 771-0705

Jim's Pipe & Tobacco Shop
2400 Lisenby Ave.
Panama City 32405
(904) 785-1022

PEMBROKE PINES

Aficionado's Premium Cigars
112 S. Flamingo Rd.
Pembroke Pines
33027
(954) 431-9800

Cigar Box
11401 Pines Blvd.
Pembroke Pines
33026
(954) 433-7744

Cigar Box
10500 NW 7th St.
Pembroke Pines
33026
(954) 430-8974

Florida Tobacco Book & Novelty
7948 Pines Blvd.
Pembroke Pines
33024
(954) 963-4358

PENSACOLA

The Cigar Brewery
232 E. Main St.
Pensacola 32501
(904) 432-3995

Tinder Box
Cordova Mall, 5100
N. 9th Ave.
Pensacola 32504
(904) 477-4131

Tobacco Annies
8084 N. Davis Hwy.
Pensacola 32514
(904) 857-0798

Tobacco Depot #5
1816 Jim Redman
A-5
Plant City 33566
(813) 717-9048

PLANTATION

Cigar Hut & Tobacco Imports
Mercedes Executive
Plaza, 1848-A N.
University Dr.
Plantation 33322
(954) 370-0057

Crown Liquors & Wine Merchants
7620 Peters Rd.
Plantation 33324
(305) 475-9750

Sal's Smoke Shops
8130 W. Broward
Blvd.
Plantation 33324
(954) 452-7655

Cigars By Juan
2900 W. Sample Rd.,
#3225
Pompano Beach
33073
(954) 984-8939

White Ash
3201 E. Atlantic
Blvd.
Pompano Beach
33062
(954) 786-0290

Eight 'til Late
832-16 A1A N.
Ponte Vedra 32082
(904) 285-5356

Smoke & Snuff
865 Port Charlotte
Train Ctr., 1441
Tamiami Trail
Port Charlotte
33948
(941) 627-5640

PORT RICHEY

Only The Best
10154 U.S. Hwy.
19 N.
Port Richey 34668
(813) 861-7000

Smoke & Snuff
611 Gulfview Sq.
Mall, 9409 U.S. 19
Port Richey 34668
(813) 849-4746

Wholly Smokes/ Unique Gifts
11840 U.S. Hwy. 19
Port Richey 34668
(813) 863-0374

Tampa Bay Tobacco
318 Main St.
Safety Harbor 34695
(813) 726-6031

ST. AUGUSTINE

Broudy's Liquors #1
205 N. Ponce De
Leon Blvd.
St. Augustine 32095
(904) 829-6909

Broudy's Liquors #2
Anastasia Sq.
St. Augustine 32084
(904) 471-1751

St. Jorge Tobacco Shoppe
62 Spanish St., Unit B
St. Augustine 32084
(904) 825-2681

ST. PETERSBURG

Beers Unlimited
1490 S. Pasadena Ave.
St. Petersburg 33707
(813) 345-9905

Central Cigars
273 Central Ave.
St. Petersburg 33701
(813) 898-2442

Smoke & Snuff
886 Tyrone Sq. Mall
St. Petersburg 33710
(813) 381-9527

SARASOTA

Bennington Tobacco
5 Filmore Dr.
Sarasota 34236
(941) 388-1562

Holy Smoke
3100 N. Washington
Blvd.
Sarasota 34234
(941) 351-4606

Sarasota Wine Club
4607 S. Tamiami
Trail
Sarasota 34321
(941) 922-8216

Smoke & Snuff
68 Sarasota Sq. Mall,
820 Tamiami Trail
Sarasota 34238
(941) 921-6147

The Smoke Shop
106 Paradise Plaza
Sarasota 34239
(941) 955-6433

Smokin' Joe's
1467 Main St.
Sarasota 34236
(941) 365-3556

**Seminole Smoke
Shop**
7884 Seminole Mall
Seminole 33772
(813) 391-2783

Macabi Cigars
5861 Sunset Dr.
South Miami 33143
(305) 662-4417

**Los Passion De La
Vie**
613 Lincoln Rd.
South Miami Beach
33139
(305) 672-1174

Tobacco Depot #1
138 Mariner
Springhill 34609
(352) 688-1500

STUART

**Coffman's
Dowtown
Tobacco**
Post Office Arcade,
23-C W. Osceola St.
Stuart 34994
(561) 286-4781

**Coffman's Tobacco
Shop**
4320 SE Federal
Hwy.
Stuart 34997
(561) 287-5060

**Factory Direct
Handmade Cigars**
2201 SE Indian St.,
G-14
Stuart 34997
(407) 340-0488

Smokers Gallery
12801 W. Sunrise
Blvd., #563
Sunrise 33323
(954) 846-2631

TALLAHASSEE

**Leni's Coffee & Tea
Company**
1400 Village Sq.
Blvd., Ste. 29
Tallahassee 32312
(904) 668-3385

Smoke & Snuff
2055 Governors Sq.
Mall
Tallahassee 32301
(904) 877-8489

Smoke Shop Etc.
2810-2 Sharer Rd
Tallahassee 32312
(904) 385-9669

TAMPA

**Cammarata Cigar
Company**
4830 W. Kennedy,
Ste. 180
Tampa 33609
(813) 287-2654

**Charlie's Wine
Cellar**
533 S. Howard Ave.,
Ste. 2
Tampa 33606
(813) 254-1395

**Edwards Pipe &
Tobacco**
3235 Henderson
Blvd.
Tampa 33609
(813) 872-0723

Executive Cigars
15026 S. Fork Dr.
Tampa 33624
(813) 269-4375

**Gonzalez Havano
Cigar Company**
3304 W. Columbus
Dr., Ste. C
Tampa 33607
(813) 348-0343

**Hometown News &
Cigars**
1441 E. Fletcher
Ave., Ste. 121
Tampa 33612
(813) 977-6740

**Nick's Cigar
Company Of
Tampa**
2205 N. 20th St.
Tampa 33605
(813) 248-5628

Regional News
101 E. Kennedy
Blvd.
Tampa 33602
(813) 223-4043

**Rodriguez &
Menendez Cigar
Factory**
4321 N. Armenia Ave.
Tampa 33607
(813) 879-9740

Simons Market
3225 S. Macdill Ave.
Tampa 33629
(813) 839-2521

Smoke & Snuff
2015 Tampa Bay Ctr.
Tampa 33607
(813) 879-7071

Smoke & Snuff
West Shore Plaza,
#339
Tampa 33609
(813) 282-8776

**Tampa Rico Cigar
Company**
Third Floor Mini
Mall, Tampa
International
Tampa 33607
(813) 874-8997

Thompson & Co
5401 Hanger Ct.
Tampa 33634
(813) 884-6344

Tobacco Depot #4
13149 N., Dale
Mabry
Tampa 33618
(813) 968-1241

**Vincent & Tampa
Cigar Company**
2503 21st St.,
Tampa 33605
(813) 248-1511

B-21 Liquors
43380 U.S. Hwy. 19
Tarpon Springs
34689
(813) 937-5049

Don Gregory Cigar
1121 Penninsula Rd.
Tarpon Springs
34689
(917) 937-7562

The Tobacconist
119-B Bullard Pkwy.
Temple Terrace
33617
(813) 989-3133

Smoke Inn
Village Sq. Shopping
Ctr., 241 U.S.
Hwy. 1
Tequesta 33469
(561) 745-0600

The Pipe Den
1426 20th St.
Vero Beach 32960
(407) 569-1154

Jamestown Tobacco
319 Clematis St.,
Ste. 103
West Palm Beach
33401
(407) 659-7273

WINTER
PARK

Cigarz On The Ave.
333 Park Ave. S.
Winter Park 32789
(407) 647-2427

**East India Trading
Company**
East India Market,
610 W. Morse Blvd.
Winter Park 32789
(407) 647-7520

**Lee's Liquor Three
Inc.**
761 N. Orange Ave.
Winter Park 32789
(407) 645-3395

Tobacco Depot #3
36608 State Rd. 54
W.
Zephyrhills 33541
(813) 788-3806

Georgia

Vintage Bottle Shop
1720 Mars Hill Rd.
Acworth 30101
(770) 428-9686

ALPHARETTA

Cigar Merchant
9850 Nesbit Ferry,
Ste. 17
Alpharetta 30202
(770) 552-1942

Clubhouse Cigars
6000 Medlock
Bridge Pkwy.,
Ste. B-100
Alpharetta 30302
(770) 495-9330

**Old Crab Apple
Bottle Shop**
12280 Houze Rd.
Alpharetta 30201
(770) 475-3930

Tinder Box #368
North Point Mall,
1204 N. Point
Circle
Alpharetta 30202
(770) 569-0059

**Fire Points Bottle
Shop**
1655 S. Lumpkin St.
Athens 30606
(706) 543-6989

**Modern Age
Tobacco & Gift
Shop**
1087 Baxter St.
Athens 30606
(706) 549-6360

ATLANTA

**The Atlanta
Tobacco Company**
84 Upper Alabama
St.
Atlanta 30303
(404) 586-9636

**Buckhead Fine
Wine**
3906 Roswell Rd.,
Ste. C & D
Atlanta 30342
(404) 231-8566

**Buckhead Fine
Wine II**
1155 Mount Vernon
Rd., Ste. 470-480
Atlanta 30338
(770) 604-9500

Cigar Box
3393 Peachtree Rd. NE
Atlanta 30326
(404) 266-9901

Cigar Villa #2
4920 Roswell Rd.,
Ste. 31
Atlanta 30342
(404) 845-0801

**Corks Beverage
Depot**
2997 Cumberland
Circle
Atlanta 30339
(770) 437-0037

**Edward's Pipe &
Tobacco**
3137 Piedmont Rd.
Atlanta 30305
(404) 292-1721

Happy Herman's
2299 Cheshire
Bridge Rd.
Atlanta 30324
(404) 321-3012

Happy Herman's
204 Johnson Ferry
Rd.
Atlanta 30328
(404) 256-3354

Harris Teeter #170
Sage Hill Shopping
Ctr., 1799
Briarcliff Rd. NE
Atlanta 30306
(404) 607-1189

Jax Beer & Wine
5901 Roswell Rd.
Atlanta 30328
(404) 252-1443

Kroger Store
1700 Monroe Dr.
Atlanta 30324
(404) 872-0782

Metro News
3528 Browns Mill
Rd. SE
Atlanta 30354
(404) 684-0005

Murphy's
997 Virginia Ave.
Atlanta 30306
(404) 872-0904

**The Ritz Carlton
Gift Shop**
181 Peachtree St. NE
Atlanta 30303
(404) 659-0400

**The Ritz Carlton
Gift Shop**
3434 Peachtree Rd. NE
Atlanta 30326
(404) 237-2700

**Rosewell Hightower
Beverages**
8529 Rosewell Rd
Atlanta 30350
(770) 993-0810

Royal Cigar Co.
1776 Peachtree St. NE
Atlanta 30309
(404) 876-9422

**Sherrin's Tinder
Box At Lenox**
3393 Peachtree Rd
Atlanta 30326
(404) 231-9853

Urban Market Inc.
752 A & B North
Highland Ave.
Atlanta 30306
(404) 347-9746

AUGUSTA

**Marcella's Fine
Cigars & Tobacco**
2921 Washington
Rd.
Augusta 30909
(706) 737-0477

Tobacco & Gifts
592 Bobby Jones
Expy. Anderson
Plaza, Ste. 18
Augusta 30907
(706) 860-8386

Tobacco Land
3450 Wrightsboro
Rd., 1010 Augusta
Mall
Augusta 30909
(706) 738-8381

**Edwards Pipe &
Tobacco**
444 N. Indian Creek
Dr.
Clarkston 30021
(404) 292-1721

**Sweet Briar Smoke
Shop**
5592 H Whitesville Rd.
Columbus 31904
(706) 322-6467

Scottish Tobacco
425 Sigmund Rd.,
Ste. 117
Conyers 30207
(770) 922-5066

**Classic Cigar &
Wine Company**
1605 Woodridge Ct.
Cumming 30131
(904) 650-3355

**Beverage World
Package**
6731 Peachtree Ind.
Blvd.
Doraville 30360
(770) 441-0001

**Sheila's Gift &
Antique**
801 N. Madison Ave.
Douglas 31533
(912) 383-8803

Mistic Dreams
6229 Sairburn
Douglasville 30134
(770) 489-9490

**The Tinder Box
#331**
2100 Pleasant Hill
Rd., Ste. 105,
Gwimett Place
Duluth 30136
(770) 813-1248

**The Cigar
Merchant**
2472 Jett Ferry Rd.,
Ste. 410
Dunwoody 30338
(770) 671-1777

Tobacco Outlet #6
101 Kenwood Rd.,
Hwy. 85, Ste. 22
Fayetteville 30214
(770) 719-8977

Tobacco Outlet #1
1513 W. McIntosh Rd.
Griffin 30223
(770) 229-1666

Duke Of Dixie
341 Benson St.
Hartwell 30643
(706) 376-9283

Wise Buys #7
2702 Hwy. 16-W
Jackson 30233
(770) 228-5477

**Modern Age
Tobacco & Gifts**
7000 Tara Blvd.
Ste. D
Jonesboro 30236
(770) 472-1587

Tobacco Outlet #3
855 Spur 138
Jonesboro 30236
(770) 478-2691

Tinder Box #366
400 Barrett Pkwy.,
Town Ctr., Ste. 190
Kennesaw 30144
(770) 428-9075

Old South Tobacco
3706 Mercer
University Dr.
Macon 31204
(912) 477-5426

MARIETTA

**Bullocks Wine &
Spirits**
3612 Sandy Plains
Rd.
Marietta 30066
(770) 565-0017

Cigar Emporium
4719 Lower Roswell
Rd.
Marietta 30068
(770) 579-8280

Cigar Villa
700 Sandy Plains
Rd., Ste. A-15
Marietta 30066
(770) 919-0444

Continental Cigar
Company
172 Roswell St.
Marietta 30060
(770) 509-1178

Cubana Cigar
Company
3000 Canton Hills
Dr.
Marietta 30062
(770) 973-3090

Merchants Package
Store
1272 Johnson Ferry Rd.
Marietta 30068
(770) 321-9194

Minks Beer & Wine
2555 Delk Rd.
Marietta 30067
(770) 952-2337

Sherlocks
2156 Roswell Rd
Marietta 30062
(770) 971-6333

Sherlocks
135 Barrett Parkway
Marietta 30066
(770) 426-6744

This That & The
Other
2040 Cobb Pkwy. S.,
Ste. 44
Marietta 30060
(770) 984-8801

Harvard Wine &
Beverage
110 Old Evans Rd.
Martinez 30907
(706) 855-0060

The Ultimate Cigar
1381 Morrow
Industrial Blvd
Morrow 30260
(770) 968-9622

The Humidor Inc.
6669 Peachtree Indst
Blvd., Ste. H
Norcross 30092
(770) 448-5424

Tobacco Outlet #5
1210 Rockbridge
Rd., Space P
Norcross 30093
(770) 923-0086

Tobacco Outlet #4
3219 New Macland
Rd., Unit #2
Powder Springs
30073
(770) 943-8555

Georgia Cigar,
Tobacco & Coffee
Company
773 Hwy. 138, Ste. 4
Riverdale 30296
(770) 996-8182

Victor Sinclair
Cigars
201 Redfern Village
St. Simons Island
31522
(912) 634-1192

SAVANNAH

Habersham
Beverage
4618 Habersham St.
Savannah 31405
(912) 354-6477

O'Sullavan's
115 E. Broughton St.
Savannah 31401
(912) 232-4222

Ye Olde Tobacco
Shop
131 W. River St.
Savannah 31401
(912) 236-9384

Ye Olde Tobacco
Shop
280 Eisenhower Dr.
Savannah 31406
(800) 596-1425

Cigar Villa
3599 Atlanta Rd.
Smyrna 30080
(770) 433-1243

Tobacco Outlet #2
3791 S. Cobb Dr.,
Ste. J
Smyrna 30080
(770) 434-5160

Cigar Emporium
1525 E. Park Place
Stone Mountain
30087
(770) 879-7090

Up In Smoke Fine
Cigars
3983 Lavista Rd.,
Ste. 187
Tucker 30084
(770) 414-0033

Dixie Beverage
Outlet
8507 Hwy. 92
Woodstock 30189
(770) 924-0988

Hawaii

Kipuka Smoke Shop
308 Kam Ave. #102
Hilo 96720
(808) 961-5082

HONOLULU

Alfred Dunhill
Limited
2365 Kahakaua Ave.
Honolulu 96815
(808) 971-2020

Don Pablo Cigar
Company
1430 Kona St.,
Ste. 102
Honolulu 96814
(808) 944-1600

Little Big Man
Tobacco
1065 Kawaiahao St.,
Ste. 606
Honolulu 96814
(808) 256-6779

Premium Cigar
Company
1137 12th Ave.
Honolulu 96816
(808) 737-6662

R. Field Wine
Company
Ward Centre, 1200
Ala Moana Blvd.
Honolulu 96814
(808) 596-9463

Tobacco's Of Hawaii
512-101 Atkinson Dr.
Honolulu 96814
(808) 942-7833

Connoisseur Food & Wine
444 Hana Hwy.,
Unit A-1
Kahului 96732
(808) 871-9463

Stantons Of Maui
Maui Mall
Kahului 96732
(808) 877-3711

Hawaii Tobacco Company At Friends Expresso
151 Hekili St.
Kailua 96734
(808) 263-2233

Kona Wine Market
75-5626 Kuakini Hwy.
Kailua-Kona
(808) 329-9400

Hawaiian Hemp Company
Kawaihae Harbor Shopping Ctr.,
#11-C
Kawaihae 96743
(808) 882-7978

Sir Wilfreds/Lahaina
Hahaina Cannery Mall, 1221 Honoapiilani Hwy.
Lahaina Maui 96761
(808) 667-1941

Idaho

BOISE

Aged To Perfection
969 E. Park Ctr. Blvd.
Boise 83706
(208) 387-2739

Havana House Ltd.
220 W.T. Jefferson St.
Boise 83702
(208) 343-2907

Sturman's Smoke Shop
218 N. 10 St.
Boise 83702
(208) 338-3225

Tobacco Connection
725 Vista Ave.
Boise 83705
(208) 342-6330

Castaway Fly Fishing Shop
3620 N. Fruitland Lane
Coeur D' Alene 83814
(208) 765-3133

World Foods
6190 Sunshine St., Ste. 1
Coeur D' Alene 83814
(208) 765-8095

KETCHUM

Art & Soul
119 Lewis St.
Ketchum 83340
(208) 726-9123

Atkinsons' Market
Giacobbi Sq.
Ketchum 83340
(208) 726-5668

Iconoclast Pipe & Books
100 1st Ave. N.
Ketchum 83340
(208) 726-1564

H & J Tobacco
301 Main St.
Lewiston 83501
(208) 798-0871

Oasis Smoke Shop
1135 Blue Lakes Blvd. N.
Twin Falls 83301
(208) 734-1578

Illinois

Famous Liquors
85 E. Fullerton Ave.
Addison 60101
(630) 279-7070

Payless Tobacco
709B West Lake St.
Addison 60101
(708) 628-8177

Arp. Retail Inc.
12322 S. Cicero Ave.
Alsip 60658
(708) 597-6535

Rick's News & Tobacco
2528 College Ave.
Alton 62002
(618) 462-7425

ARLINGTON HEIGHTS

Arlington Pipe & Cigar Shop
3 W. Davis St.
Arlington Heights 60005
(847) 255-2263

Cigarettes Cheaper!
Southpoint Commons Ctr.,
708 E. Rand Rd.
Arlington Heights 60604
(847) 342-9460

Cigarettes Cheaper!
Arlington Towne Sq., 43 W. Golf Rd.
Arlington Heights 60604
(847) 718-0279

AURORA

Cigarettes Cheaper!
Aurora Commons Ctr., 1276-A N. Lake
Aurora 60506
(630) 897-7522

Cigarettes Cheaper!
West Aurora Plaza, 1989 W. Galena Blvd.
Aurora 60506
(630) 896-5617

Cigarettes Cheaper!
Farnsworth Plaza Ctr./1040 N. Farnsworth Ave.
Aurora 60505
(630) 375-1526

260

John's Smoke Shop
18 S. River
Aurora 60506
(708) 897-3920

Tinder Box
1462 Fox Valley Ctr.
Aurora 60504
(630) 898-9450

Payless Tobacco
227 N. Northwest
Hwy.
Barrington 60010
(847) 842-1080

**Robusto's Tobacco
Co.**
3620 North Belt W.
Belleville 62226
(618) 277-9414

P J Discount
202 W. Irving Park
Rd.
Bensonville 60106
(708) 350-2000

BLOOMINGTON

Cigarette Express
Market Sq., 1510 W.
Market St.
Bloomington 61701
(309) 828-7025

Famous Liquors
1404 E. Empire
Bloomington 61701
(309) 663-8303

Smoker's Choice Inc.
1212 Towanda Ave.
Bloomington 61701
(309) 828-1581

Cigarettes Cheaper!
10073 S. 76th Ave.
Bridgeview 60455
(708) 233-1531

Cigarettes Cheaper!
Bridgeview Cub Ctr.,
10272 S. Harlem
Bridgeview 60455
(708) 423-5492

Cigarettes Cheaper!
116 Broadview
Village Sq.
Broadview 60153
(708) 343-4086

BUFFALO GROVE

Cigar Exchange
470 Half Day Rd.
Buffalo Grove 60089
(847) 808-4444

Cigarettes Cheaper!
Woodland Commons,
480 Half Day Rd.
Buffalo Grove 60089
(847) 821-1601

Payless Tobacco
1169 Old McHenry
Rd.
Buffalo Grove 60089
(847) 821-8552

**Smokey Joe's
Cigarette Stop**
400 South Illinois Ave.
Carbondale 62901
(618) 529-1583

**Yester Year
Tobacconist**
200 W. Monroe
Carbondale 62901
(618) 457-8495

CAROL STREAM

Cigarettes Cheaper!
Heritage Plaza, 722
Army Trail Rd.
Carol Stream 60188
(630) 830-7251

Cigarettes Cheaper!
Northland Mall, 477
S. Schmale Ave.
Carol Stream 60188
(630) 871-1240

Payless Tobacco
1485 Fair Oak Rd.
Carol Stream 60188
(630) 830-2005

**Egor's Tobacco &
Gift Shop**
2 Wisconsin Ave.
Carpentersville
60110
(847) 428-7707

**Tool Masters Of
Cary**
360 NW Hwy.
Cary 60013
(847) 639-8994

Jon's Pipe Shop
509 E. Green St.
Champaign 61820
(217) 344-3459

Calliope Ct.
706 Jackson Ave.
Charleston 61920
(217) 348-1905

CHICAGO

**Alfred Dunhill
Limited**
Water Tower Place,
835 N. Michigan
Ave.
Chicago 60611
(312) 467-4455

Around The World
1044 W. Belmont
Chicago 60657
(773) 327-7975

Blue Havana
854 W. Belmont
Ave.
Chicago 60657
(312) 348-5000

Blue Havana
2709 N. Clark St.
Chicago 60614
(773) 542-8262

Cardinal Liquors
4905 N. Lincoln Ave.
Chicago 60625
(312) 561-0270

Casey's Liquors
1444 W. Chicago Ave.
Chicago 60622
(312) 243-2850

Cigarettes Cheaper!
The Hall Plaza, 4646
W. Diversey
Chicago 60639
(773) 545-4746

Cigarettes Cheaper!
Broadway Festival,
5318 N. Broadway
Chicago 60640
(773) 506-8426

Cigarettes Cheaper!
35 N. Wells #7
Chicago 60606
(315) 553-1998

Cigarettes Cheaper!
The Yards Plaza,
4632 S. Damen
Chicago 60609
(773) 843-0507

Cigarettes Cheaper!
6 E. Madison Ave.
Chicago 60602
(312) 553-1448

Cigarettes Cheaper!
Wisner Milwaukee
Plaza, 2851 N.
Milwaukee Ave.
Chicago 60618
(312) 862-9258

Decarlo Liquors
515 N. Western
Chicago 60612
(312) 226-4600

Double Corona
2058 W. Chicago
Ave.
Chicago 60622
(312) 342-7820

**Eastgate Wine &
Spirits**
446 W. Diversy
Pkwy.
Chicago 60614
(312) 327-1210

English Pipe Shop
15 S. La Salle St.
Chicago 60603
(312) 263-3922

**Four Friends Cigar
Shop**
3516 S. Halsted Ave.
Chicago 60609
(773) 927-5963

**Four Seasons/Gift
Shop**
120 E. Delaware
Place
Chicago 60611
(312) 280-8800

**Good Fellas Cigar
Shop**
5539 W. Montrose
Ave.
Chicago 60641
(312) 286-9747

**Habana House Of
Fine Cigars**
5510 W. Devon
Chicago 60646
(773) 763-2130

**Iwan Ries &
Company**
19 S. Wabash Ave.
Chicago 60603
(312) 372-1306

**Jack Schwartz
Importer**
175 W. Jackson
Chicago 60604
(312) 782-7898

**Old Chicago Smoke
Shop**
10 S. La Salle St.
Chicago 60603
(312) 236-9771

**Park West Liquor
& Smoke**
2581 N. Lincoln
Chicago 60614
(312) 935-8197

Rubovits Cigars
320 S. La Salle St.
Chicago 60604
(312) 939-3780

**Sam's Wine &
Spirits**
1720 N. Marcey St.
Chicago 60614
(312) 664-4394

333 Tobacco Shop
333 N. Michigan Ave.
Chicago 60601
(312) 782-4317

Up Down Tobacco
1550 N. Wells St.
Chicago 60610
(312) 337-8505

Valuemost Liquors
3263 N. Pulaski Rd.
Chicago 60641
(312) 725-4151

Worldwide Tobacco
1587 N. Milwaukee
Chicago 60622
(773) TOBACCO

Southtown Rx
1533 Chicago Rd.
Chicago Heights
60411
(708) 755-3500

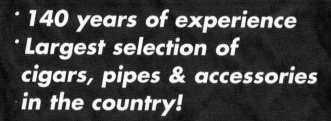

Cigarettes Cheaper!
The Commons Of
 Chicago Ridge
Chicago Ridge
 60415
(708) 499-3631

Cigarettes Cheaper!
West Town Ctr.,
 1300-F Ashland
 Ave.
Chicago/West Town
 60622
(773) 486-7830

Chiko Club Liquors
5202 W. 25th St.
Cicero 60650
(708) 656-5111

Prestige Wine &
 Liquors
1423 W. 55th St.
Country Side 60525
(708) 354-6969

Main St. Deli &
 Liquor
5425 S. Lagrange
Countryside 60525
(708) 354-0355

Cigarettes Cheaper!
Hillcrest Ctr., 1701
 N. Larkin #C-2
Crest Hill 60433
(815) 729-3822

Cardinal Wine &
 Spirits
305 Virginia St.
Crystal Lake 60014
(815) 459-4050

Tool Masters
5111 E. Terra Cotta
 Ave.
Crystal Lake 60014
(815) 459-8299

Moore's Tobacco Shop
8 Fountain Pl.
Danville 61832
(217) 431-3271

Famous Liquors
1321 N. Oakland
Decatur 62526
(217) 428-0632

Cigarettes Cheaper!
Deerfield Commons,
 718 Waukegan Rd.
 #12
Deerfield 60015
(847) 948-8659

Tribeca Cigar
 Company
5229 Main St.
Downers Grove
 60515
(630) 241-1200

ELGIN

Pied Piper Tobacco
 Shop
557 N. McLean Blvd.
Elgin 60123
(847) 695-8670

Prairie Rock
 Brewery
127 S. Grove
Elgin 60120
(847) 622-8888

The Smokin' Fox
269 S. State St.
Elgin 60123
(847) 608-9903

Cigarette People
2900 N. Harlem
 Ave.
Elmwood Park
 60635
(708) 453-2433

Evanston Pipe &
 Tobacco
923 Davis St.
Evanston 60201
(847) 328-0208

Smokey Bear
8701 S. Kedzie Ave.
Evergreen Park
 60805
(708) 499-0222

The Tinder Box
255 St. Clair Sq.
Fairview Heights
 62208
(618) 632-6160

Famous Liquors
7339 Madison St.
Forest Park 60130
(708) 366-2500

Cigarettes Cheaper!
Frankfort Crossing
 Ctr., 350 N.
 Lagrange Rd. B-1
Frankfort 60423
(815) 464-0678

Male Order Express
227 S. 3rd St.
Geneva 60134
(630) 208-6253

For Your Leisure
482 Forest Ave.
Glen Ellyn 60137
(630) 942-8830

Wash-n-Go Amoco
2 S. 780 Rte. 53
Glen Ellyn 60137
(630) 790-1881

Cigarettes Cheaper!
Plaza Westlake Ctr.,
2190
Bloomingdale Rd.
Glendale Heights
60139
(630) 980-1512

Stogies
1226 E. Lake St.
Hanover Park 60103
(630) 837-6828

Armanetti's
18244 S. Kedzie Ave.
Hazelcrest 60429
(708) 798-7700

HIGHLAND
PARK

Cigarettes Cheaper!
First Place Ctr., 1942
1st St.
Highland Park
60035
(847) 266-8671

Markus
International Inc.
484 Hillside Dr.
Highland Park
60035
(847) 43 FLAME

Old Chicago Smoke
Shop
221 Skokie Valley Rd.
Highland Park
60714
(847) 831-3311

Cigarettes Cheaper!
Hoffman Village
Ctr., 2545 W. Golf
Rd.
Hoffman Estate
60194
(847) 781-0620

Great Ash
5 North 105 Rte. 53,
Unit 16
Itasca 60143
(630) 773-2520

JOLIET

Lambert Amoco
Food Shop
928 W. Jefferson St.
Joliet 60436
(815) 725-4181

Lambert Amoco
Food Shop
1529 N. Broadway
Joliet 60435
(815) 726-8867

Tinder Box
Joliet Mall,
1034 Louis
Joliet 60431
(815) 439-1190

Cigarettes Cheaper!
Cossitt Landmark
Ctr., 8 N. La Grange
La Grange 60525
(708) 354-9116

Piper Of La Grange
13 S. La Grange Rd.
La Grange 60525
(708) 352-1882

The Marling
Tobacco Shop
1383 N. Western Ave.
Lake Forest 60045
(847) 234-2232

Cigarettes Cheaper!
Randall Plaza, 161
N. Randall Rd.
Lake In The Hills
60102
(847) 458-8401

Wine & Cigar Shop
884 S. Rand Rd.
Lake Zurich 60047
(847) 438-1922

Suburban News
And Concession
3300 W. Devon Ave.
Lincolnwood 60659
(847) 679-5577

LOMBARD

Cigarettes Cheaper!
Oxford Corners,
1267 S. Main St.
Lombard 60148
(630) 627-4650

Famous Liquors
105 E. Roosevelt Rd.
Lombard 60148
(630) 629-3330

Tinder Box
205 Yorktown Ctr.
Lombard 60148
(708) 495-2555

Cigarettes Cheaper!
Matteson Plaza,
4103 W. Lincoln
Hwy.
Matteson 60433
(708) 503-9058

Tobacco Plus Inc.
4718 W. Lincoln
Hwy.
Matteson 60443
(708) 748-5227

Tool Land
2350 W. Rte. 120
McHenry 60050
(815) 344-8299

Tobacco And Gift
City
3281 W. 115th St.
Merrionette Park
60655
(708) 489-5700

Baker St.
S. Park Mall, 4500
16th St.
Moline 61265
(309) 762-9267

Cut 'n' Puff
Pipe/Tobacco
Shop
1417 5th Ave.
Moline 61265
(309) 762-1819

Cigarettes Cheaper!
Settlers Landing
Mall, 1866
Douglas Rd.
Montgomery 60538
(630) 801-7710

Visit Chicago's longest and most lavishly stocked humidor!

Open Late and on Sunday

Up Down Tobacco — A Spectacular Cigar Smoker's Paradise!
1550 North Wells, Chicago • (312) 337-8025
Sunday – Friday 11a.m. to 11p.m., Saturday 10a.m. to 12p.m.
PROFESSIONAL TOBACCONISTS SINCE 1963

Cigarettes Cheaper!
1105 N. Mt.
Prospect Plaza
Mount Prospect
60056
(847) 398-5450

Gold Eagle Liquors
1721 Golf Rd.
Mount Prospect
60056
(847) 437-3500

Dicarlo Armanetti Liquors
425 Townline Rd.
Mundelein 60060
(847) 566-4600

Cigarettes Cheaper!
Ogden Mall, 1271 E.
Ogden Ave. #131
Naperville 60563
(630) 961-4715

Gentleman's Delight
24 W. 500 Maple
Ave., Ste. 104
Naperville 60540
(708) 961-2496

NILES

Cigarettes Cheaper!
Dempster Plaza,
8802 W. Dempster
St.
Niles 60714
(847) 299-0031

Cigarettes Cheaper!
Golf Rd. Ctr., 8353
W. Golf Rd.
Niles 60714
(847) 583-1205

Goldfinger Super Sales
7227 N. Harlem
Ave.
Niles 60174
(708) 647-7460

Cigarettes Cheaper!
Norridge Commons,
7048 Forest
Preserve Dr.
Norridge 60634
(708) 457-1820

Tobacco Express
5050 N. Cumberland
Ave.
Norridge 60656
(708) 452-8159

Cigarettes Cheaper!
N. Riverside Park
Plaza, 7335 25th
St.
North Riverside
60546
(708) 442-0244

NORTHBROOK

Cigar Heaven Inc.
2750 Dundee Rd.
Northbrook 60062
(847) 564-9600

Cigarettes Cheaper!
845 Sanders Rd.
Northbrook 60062
(847) 714-9228

Cigarettes Cheaper!
Northbrook Ctr.,
1131-A Church
St.
Northbrook 60062
(847) 509-8167

Cigarettes Cheaper!
Oak Lawn Ctr., 8830
S. Cicero Ave.
Oak Lawn 60453
(708) 423-3514

Cigarettes Cheaper!
Harlem North Ctr.,
7101 W. North Ave.
Oak Park 60302
(708) 386-0974

Cigarettes Cheaper!
Olympia Corners,
2424 Lincoln Hwy.
Olympia Fields
60461
(708) 503-9331

Cigarettes Cheaper!
Lakeview Plaza,
15874 La Grange Rd.
Orland Park 60462
(708) 873-1180

Smoker's Haven
15806 S. Harlem
Ave.
Orland Park 60462
(708) 633-8331

PALATINE

Burning Ambitions
19 N. Bothwell
Palatine 60067
(847) 358-0200

Cigarettes Cheaper!
1244 E. Dundee Rd.
Palatine 60067
(847) 359-3398

Dobby's World Wide Liquor/Wine
15 S. Brockway
Palatine 60067
(847) 359-0400

Puff 'n' Stuff
20434 N. Rand Rd.
Palatine 60074
(847) 550-0055

Sir Timothy
845-847 N.
Quentine Rd.
Palatine 60067
(847) 776-0976

Cigarettes Cheaper!
6541 W. 127th St.
Palos Heights 60463
(708) 388-0179

Cigarettes Cheaper!
9656 W. 131st St.
Palos Park 60464
(708) 361-5488

Around The World Cigar & Gifts
31½ S. Prospect Ave.
Park Ridge 60068
(847) 292-1219

Duffy's Eatery
4410 N. Rockwood
Rd.
Peoria 61614
(309) 685-9188

Lambert Amoco Food Shop
4802 Caton Farm Rd.
Plainfield 60544
(815) 436-7246

International House Of Wine
11302 W. Rte. 12
Richmond 60071
(815) 678-4573

ROCKFORD

Royal Liquor
3714 E. State St.
Rockford 61108
(815) 399-3418

Rudy's Cigars
Edgebrook Center,
1641 N. Alpine Rd.
Rockford 61107
(815) 223-2351

Tinder Box
Cherry Vale Mall
Rockford 61112
(815) 332-4656

Cigarettes Cheaper!
Rolling Meadows
Ctr., 3206 Kirchoff
Rd.
Rolling Meadows
60008
(847) 342-1598

**Lambert Amoco
Food Shop**
347 Independence
Blvd.
Romeoville 60446
(815) 886-4944

ROSELLE

Heroe's Unlimited
259 E. Irving Park Rd.
Roselle 60172
(630) 980-1080

**Payless Tobacco &
Liquor**
356 E. Irving Park Rd.
Roselle 60172
(708) 980-8299

Simply Cigars
350 E. Irving Park Rd.
Roselle 60172
(630) 529-9524

Tool Shed
417 Railroad Ave.
Round Lake 60073
(847) 546-6222

Tool Shed, Jr.
519 W. Rollins Rd.
Round Lake Beach
60073
(847) 740-8665

SCHAUMBURG

**The Cigar
Connoisseur**
839 E. Algonquin Rd.
Schaumburg 60173
(847) 925-1500

Cigarettes Cheaper!
2478 W.
Schaumburg Rd.
Schaumburg 60194
(847) 839-8314

**Country Sports
Cards And Fine
Cigars**
2261 W.
Schaumburg Rd.
Schaumburg 60194
(847) 534-9576

**Habana Cigar
House**
1404 E. Golf Rd.
Schaumburg 60173
(847) 517-4444

SKOKIE

**Cigar King
Downtown
Skokie**
8016 Lincoln
Skokie 60077
(800) CIGAR 51

**Gift & Tobacco
Emporium**
Village Crossing
Shopping Center,
7140 N. Carpenter
Skokie 60077
(847) 674-4283

**Gold Standard
Liquors**
5100 W. Dempster
Skokie 60077
(847) 674-4200

Tinder Box
125-E Old Orchard
Center
Skokie 60077
(847) 677-6717

SPRINGFIELD

**Cigars For
Aficionado's**
717 N. Grand Ave. E.
Springfield 62702
(217) 523-4357

Discount Tobacco
1715 Wabash Ave.
Springfield 62704
(217) 793-7272

**Epicures Choice
Smoke Shop**
Myers Bldg., 1 W.
Old State Capital
Plaza
Springfield 62701
(217) 523-9350

Famous Liquors
724 S. Grand Ave. E.
Springfield 62703
(217) 528-4377

Famous Liquors
1540 W. Wabash
Springfield 62704
(217) 793-2808

South Side Cigars
30 E. 34th St.
Steger 60475
(708) 754-6312

34th Street Cigars
83 E. 34th St.
Steger 60475
(708) 756-7494

Cigarette Express
21 Northpoint Plaza
Streator 61364
(815) 672-6161

Best Tobacco
310 E. State St.
Sycamore 60178
(815) 899-9164

Cigarettes Cheaper!
Tinley Park
Commons, 17161
S. Harlen Ave.
Tinley Park 60477
(708) 429-2925

Tobacco City
7943 W. 171st St.
Tinley Park 60477
(708) 532-1850

Tinder Box 191
120 Hawthorne
Center
Vernon Hills 60061
(847) 362-6655

Al's Smoke Shop Inc.
1 E. Park Blvd.
Villa Park 60181
(708) 279-2215

Cigarettes Cheaper!
Timberlake Center,
2239 N. Lewis
Ave.
Waukegan 60087
(847) 360-1529

Schrank's Smoke 'n Gun
2010 Washington
St.
Waukegan 60085
(847) 662-4034

Tinder Box
1116 Spring Hill
Mall
West Dundee 60118
(847) 428-6444

Willowbrook Liquors
6920 S. Rte. 83
Willowbrook 60514
(630) 654-0988

Cigary International
139 Skokie Blvd.
Wilmette 60091
(888) 244-2795

Harbor Bacco 'n' Beans
1707-7th St., Ste. 3
Winthrop Harbor
60096
(847) 731-7001

Tobacco World Inc.
11302 S. Harlem
Ave.
Worth 60482
(708) 448-0002

Cigarettes Cheaper!
Zion Plaza, 1315
21st St.
Zion 60099
(847) 746-3314

Indiana

Angola Tobacco Shop
2998 N. Wayne St.
Angola 46703
(219) 665-9142

Low Bob's
1405 N. Wayne
Angola 46703
(219) 665-1778

Low Bob's
1007-B W. 7th
Auburn 46706
(219) 927-8804

Low Bob's #67
343-8 1st St.
Beech Grove 46107
(317) 781-1841

Big Red Liquors
1110 N. College
Ave.
Bloomington 47404
(812) 332-9495

The Briar & The Burley
College Mall, 2968
E. 3rd St.
Bloomington 47401
(812) 332-3300

Cigarettes Cheaper!
Meridian Village
Plaza, 13664 N.
Meridian St.
Carmel 46032
(317) 582-1548

Kahns Fine Wine Market Place
313 E. Carmel Dr.
Carmel 46032
(317) 251-9463

Black Tie Smokes
203 Broadway
Chesterton 46304
(219) 921-5330

Theodore James Tobacconist
1076 Joliet St.
Dyer 46311
(219) 864-8800

Harry's Humidor
25416 County Rd. 6
Elkhart 46514
(219) 266-8223

Briar 'n' Bean
Eastland Mall, Ste.
121, 800 N.
Greenriver Rd.
Evansville 47715
(812) 479-8736

FORT WAYNE

Low Bob's
Gateway Plaza, 1575-
D Goshen Rd.
Fort Wayne 46808
(219) 471-3662

Quality Liquors
3107-09 E. State
Blvd.
Fort Wayne 46805
(219) 484-3201

Riegel's Pipe & Tobacco
624 S. Calhoun St.
Fort Wayne 46802
(219) 424-1429

Riegel's Pipe & Tobacco
Georgetown Square,
6556 E. State Blvd.
Fort Wayne 46815
(219) 493-2806

The Butt Hut
495 N. State
Rte. 127
Freemont 46737
(219) 833-1374

Granger Tobacco
12634 State Rd. 23
Granger 46530
(219) 271-7070

Tobacco City
234 W. Ridge Rd.
Griffith 46319
(219) 838-5500

Cigarettes Cheaper!
Columbia Plaza,
6421 Columbia
Ave.
Hammond 46320
(219) 931-2351

Cigarettes Cheaper!
Highland Plaza,
8337 Indianapolis
Blvd.
Highland 46322
(219) 838-9049

INDIANAPOLIS

Cigarettes Cheaper!
Shermon Commons,
3709 E.
Washington St.,
Ste. B
Indianapolis 46201
(317) 352-1713

DJ Discount Tobacco
5638 W. Washington St.
Indianapolis 46241
(317) 487-1392

Hardwickes Pipe & Tobacco
Monument Circle,
24 N. Meridian St.
Indianapolis 46204
(317) 635-7884

Hardwickes Pipe & Tobacco
743 Broad Ripple Ave.
Indianapolis 46220
(317) 257-5915

Kahns Fine Wines
5369 N. Keystone Ave.
Indianapolis 46220
(317) 251-9463

Pipe Puffer #2
1740 E. 86th St.
Indianapolis 46240
(317) 846-7473

Pipe Puffer Smoke Shop
2306-E S. County Line Rd.
Indianapolis 46227
(317) 881-2957

Tinder Box
Washington Square Mall, 10202 E. Washington St.
Indianapolis 46229
(317) 899-2811

Tinder Box
6020 E. 82nd
Indianapolis 46250
(813) 845-0806

Tobacco Barn
5302 W. 10th & Lindhurst
Indianapolis 46222
(317) 481-9700

Tobacco Outlet
8613 N. Michigan Rd.
Indianapolis 46268
(317) 334-9700

The Tobacco Shop
Lafayette Shoppes,
4660 W. 38th St.
Indianapolis 46254
(317) 299-6010

Village Smoke Shop
8910 S. Meridian St.
Indianapolis 46227
(317) 888-8122

Wine Gallery
4026 E. 82nd St. Ste. A-8
Indianapolis 46250
(317) 576-0108

Ybor's/Gibsons Indiana
49 W. Maryland St. Ste. H-3
Indianapolis 46204
(317) 951-1621

Leaf And Briar
9877 W. Country Rd.
Knightstown 46148
(317) 685-2623

Bogie's Stogies
107 N. 6th St.
Lafayette 47902
(317) 742-6771

MERRILLVILLE

Cigarettes Cheaper!
Merrillville Plaza,
1609 E. 80th St.
Merrillville 46010
(219) 793-9673

Cigarettes Cheaper!
Crossroads Plaza,
6120 Broadway
Merrillville 46410
(219) 985-0967

Tinder Box
2217 Southlake Mall
Merrillville 46410
(219) 769-4770

Cigarette Discount Outlet
4211 Franklin St.
Michigan City 46360
(219) 931-1507

The Golden Leaf
232 W. 4th St.
Michigan City 46360
(219) 872-9692

Tinder Box #273
110 University Park Mall
Mishawaka 46545
(219) 277-3440

MUNCIE

Brewster's
1750 W. University Ave.
Muncie 47303
(317) 935-9090

Low Bob's Discount Tobacco #2
1716 E. Memorial Dr.
Muncie 47302
(317) 281-1662

Sal's Tobacco Pipe & Coffee
3319 N. Everbrook Lane
Muncie 47304
(317) 286-7257

Village Tobacco Shoppe
414 N. Martin
Muncie 47303
(317) 284-9999

MUNSTER

Munster Smoke Shop
822 Ridge Rd.
Munster 46351
(219) 836-1993

Munster Tobacco Town
17 Ridge Rd.
Munster 46321
(219) 836-0158

Talumet Tobacco
8148 Talumet Ave.
Munster 46321
(219) 836-1900

Men's Toy Shop Inc.
Old Colonial Bldg.,
131 N. Van Buren
Nashville 47448
(812) 988-6590

Kaiser's Tobacco Store
415 E. Oak St.
New Albany 47150
(812) 945-2651

The Liquor Store
758 Westfield Rd.
Noblesville 46060
(317) 770-9199

Smoke House
60 S. Broadway
Peru 46970
(317) 473-9917

Low Bob's East
4521 National Rd. E.
Richmond 47374
(317) 935-1305

Cigarettes Cheaper!
The Crossroads
Center, 1505 U.S.
Rte. 41, Ste. A-16
Scheeville 46375
(219) 865-9564

SOUTH BEND

Bullseye Discount
Liquor
1818 S. Bend Ave.
South Bend 46637
(219) 273-0200

Club Lasalle
115 W. Colfax Ave.
South Bend 46601
(219) 288-1155

Tinder Box #171
1290 Scottsdale
Mall, Ste. 2045
South Bend 46614
(219) 291-7342

Tobacco Outlet
50532 U.S. 33 N.
South Bend 46637
(219) 277-7958

Wabash Cigar Store
Inc.
815 Wabash Ave.
Terre Haute 47807
(812) 232-1249

VALPARAISO

Cigarette Discount
Outlet
2814 Talumet Ave.
Valparaiso 46383
(219) 477-2726

Godfather Liquors
107 E. Morthland
(U.S. 30)
Valparaiso 46383
(219) 462-9512

Triangle Liquors
3210 N. Talumet
Valparaiso 46383
(219) 477-4849

Fort Knox Liquors
603 N. 15½ St.
Vincennes 47591
(812) 882-8014

Second Heaven
Smoke Lounge
445 Sagamore Pkwy. W.
West Lafayette
47906
(317) 497-3530

Iowa

Hyvee Food Store
3800 W. Lincoln
Way
Ames 50014
(515) 292-0205

C & C Smoker's
Outlet
121 N. Ankeny Blvd.
Ankeny 50021
(515) 964-9755

Regal Liquors
2880 Devils Glen
Rd.
Bettendorf 52722
(319) 332-0957

Jefferson St. Cigar
Shop
408 N. Main St.
Burlington 52601
(319) 754-6698

Hill St. News
2217 College St.
Cedar Falls 50613
(319) 277-7749

J.T. Connolly's
Tobacco Bowl
Westdale Mall,
2600 Edgewood Rd.
Cedar Rapids 52404
(319) 396-3533

Baker St.
Northpark Mall, 320
W. Kimberly Rd.
Davenport 52806
(319) 391-4055

David's Briar
Shoppe
944 Merle Hay Mall
Des Moines 50310
(515) 278-8701

Tobacco Outlet
3814 Douglas Ave.
Des Moines 50310
(515) 279-7813

Pipe Inn
Kennedy Mall
Dubuque 52002
(319) 556-5175

Stogies Smoke Shop
100 North Ct.
Fairfield 52556
(515) 472-9878

John's Grocery
401 E. Market St.
Iowa City 52245
(319) 337-2183

Regal Liquors
2818 North Ct.
Ottumwa 52501
(515) 683-4142

National Cigar
617 Sycamore St.
Waterloo 50703
(319) 234-5958

Pars And Cigars
1401 22nd St.
West Des Moines
50265
(515) 327-1255

Tinder Box #277
1551 Valley West
Mall
West Des Moines
50266
(515) 225-6011

Kansas

Hawkins Tobacco
& Gifts
1010 S. Kansas
Liberal 67901
(316) 624-3452

OVERLAND
PARK

Cigar & Tabac
Limited
6930 W. 105th St.
Overland Park
66212
(913) 642-9500

The Cigar Box
5275 W. 95th St.
Overland Park
66207
(913) 642-3443

Klein's Party Shop
7524 W. 119th St.
Overland Park
66213
(913) 451-2122

Mel's Party Shop
7709 W. 63rd St.
Overland Park
66202
(913) 262-4184

Metcalf Discount
Liquors
9296 Metcalf
Overland Park
66212
(913) 648-6999

The Pittsburgh
Smoker's Outlet
Store
201 S. Broadway
Pittsburgh 66762
(313) 232-5770

Overland Cigar &
Tobacco
730 S. Kansas Ave.
Topeka 66604
(913) 233-0808

Cheers & Beers
Connection
3300 N. Rock Rd.
Wichita 67226
(316) 636-2433

Welcome Smokers
5409 E. Harry
Wichita 67218
(316) 686-0847

Kentucky

The Party Source
95 Riviera Dr.
Bellevue 41073
(606) 291-4007

Bowling Green Pipe
& Tobacco
Shoppe
434 E. Main St.
Bowling Green
42101
(502) 843-9439

Tobacco For Less
1680 Cambell Lane
Ste. 112
Bowling Green
42104
(502) 843-9052

Tobacco For Less
306 W. Cumberland
Gap Pkwy.
Corbin 40701
(606) 526-9688

The Brew Works
1115 Main St.
Covington 41011
(606) 581-2739

Tinder Box #257
1020 Florence Mall
Florence 41042
(606) 525-6067

Tobacco For Less
625 South L. Roger
Wells Blvd.
Glasgow 42141
(502) 651-1679

Tobacco Mart
2872 U.S. Hwy. 41 N.
Henderson 42420
(502) 827-9406

LEXINGTON

Fayette Cigar Store
137 E. Main St.
Lexington 40507
(606) 252-6267

Lansdowne Wine &
Liquor
3329 Tates Creek Rd.
Lexington 40502
(606) 266-8475

Liquor Barn
921 Beaumont
Centre Pkwy.
Lexington 40513
(606) 223-1400

Liquor Barn
3040 Richmond Rd.
Lexington 40509
(606) 252-8800

Schwab's Pipes 'n
Stuff
Lexington Mall,
Richmond Rd.
Lexington 40502
(606) 266-1011

Strauss Tobacconist
Hyatt Gift Shop,
410 W. Vine
Lexington 40507
(606) 252-5142

LOUISVILLE

Kremer's Smoke
Shoppe
333 S. Preston St.
Louisville 40202
(502) 584-3332

Liquor Outlet
1800 South
Hurstbourne Pkwy.
Louisville 40220
(502) 491-0753

Old Town Wine &
Spirit
1529 Bardstown Rd.
Louisville 40205
(502) 451-8591

Oxmoor Smoke
Shoppe
7900 Shellyville Rd.
Louisville 40204
(502) 426-4706

Up In Smoke Ltd.
Cigar Shop
1431 Bardstown Rd.
Louisville 40204
(502) 451-1118

Cigar Emporium
Westland Park Plaza,
2702 Fredricka St.
Owensboro 42301
(502) 691-0802

The Tobacco Barn
5023 Hinkleville Rd.
Paducah 42001
(502) 442-7633

Louisiana

BATON ROUGE

The Burning Leaf
11848 Coursey Blvd.
Baton Rouge 70816
(504) 292-9004

Churchill's
7949 Jefferson Hwy.
Baton Rouge 70809
(504) 927-4211

Havana House Of Cigar
676 Jefferson Hwy.
Baton Rouge 70806
(504) 930-0309

Phillip's Bayou Humidor
1152 S. Acadian Thruway
Baton Rouge 70806
(504) 343-1152

Tobacco Rack
120 Bossier Crossroad
Bossier City 71111
(318) 752-2981

Jewel Caters & Gourmet
201 N. New Hampshire St.
Covington 70433
(504) 892-5746

Louisianna Star
409 N. Columbia St.
Covington 70433
(504) 893-8873

Tobacco Plus
115 E. 1st
Crowley 70526
(318) 783-8696

The Cigar Merchant
1001 Coolidge Blvd.
Lafayette 70503
(318) 233-9611

Shop-A-Lot
2707 Hazel St.
Lake Charles 70601
(318) 433-2846

Havanas Of Louisiana
4450 Hwy. 22
Mandeville 70471
(504) 674-9282

METAIRIE

Cafe Havana
3216 W. Esplanade, Ste. 240
Metairie 70002
(800) 489-6738

Cohiba Cigar Emporium
102-F Metairie Hts.
Metairie 70001
(504) 837-0380

Juliet's Cigar Parlor
3516 Veterans Blvd.
Metairie 70002
(504) 887-1234

Martin's Wine Cellar #2
714 Elmire Ave.
Metairie 70005
(504) 896-7300

The Tinder Box #261
Lakeside Shopping Center, 3301 Veterans Blvd.
Metairie 70002
(504) 834-5801

NEW ORLEANS

Cigar Emporium Of New Orleans
5243 Canal Blvd.
New Orleans 70124
(504) 483-6009

Dos Jefes Uptown Cigar Shop
5700 Magazine St.
New Orleans 70115
(504) 899-3030

The Epitome
729 St. Louis
New Orleans 70130
(504) 523-2844

The Humidor Room
137 Robert E. Lee Blvd.
New Orleans 70124
(504) 28 CGARS

Martin's Wine Cellar
38-27 Barronne St.
New Orleans 70115
(504) 899-7411

New Orleans Cigar Co.
201 St. Charles Ave., Ste. 125
New Orleans 70170
(504) 524-9631

The Tinder Box #197
5700 Read Blvd.
New Orleans 70127
(504) 242-2846

M.A.'s Smoke House
1736 E. 70th St.
Shreveport 71105
(318) 797-3138

Tobacco Rack
750 Southfield Rd.
Shreveport 71106
(318) 861-7765

Epitome Coffee/Cigar Bar
North Shore Square, 150 N. Shore Blvd.
Slidell 70460
(504) 781-9888

The Humidor
451 Red Oak St.
Slidell 70460
(504) 645-9060

The Tobacco Pouch
700-A St. Mary St.
Thibodaux 70301
(504) 447-3170

Mill Store
1880 Flanacher Rd.
Zachary 70791
(504) 654-6430

Maine

Stillwater Convenience
340 Stillwater Ave.
Bangor 04401
(207) 990-3354

Welch's Beverage & Tobacco
546 Hammond St.
Bangor 04401
(207) 945-0112

PORTLAND

Classic Cigars
53 Pleasant Ave., Ste. 2
Portland 04103
(207) 774-8119

Joe's Smoke Shop
665 Congress St.
Portland 04101
(207) 885-0141

R.S.V.P.
887 Forest Ave.
Portland 04103
(207) 773-8803

Beverage Mart
77 North Ave.
Skowhegan 04976
(207) 474-2312

The News Shop
321 Main Mall Rd.
South Portland 04106
(207) 780-9635

Maryland

ANNAPOLIS

A. Fader & Son
Annapolis Plaza
Annapolis 21401
(410) 841-5155

Annapolis Cigar Company
121 Main St.
Annapolis 21401
(410) 295-7400

Leader Drugs
2444 Solomon's
Island Rd. Ste. 208
Annapolis 21401
(410) 841-6773

The Smoke Shop
56 Maryland Ave.
Annapolis 21401
(410) 263-2066

Port Tack Limited
1264 Bay Dale Dr.
Arnold 21012
(301) 974-0800

BALTIMORE

A. Fader & Son
107 E. Baltimore
Baltimore 21202
(410) 685-5511

A. Fader & Son
Eastpoint Mall
Baltimore 21224
(410) 282-6622

Max's Trading Company
733 S. Broadway
Baltimore 21231
(410) 675-6297

Wells Liquors
6310 York Rd.
Baltimore 21212
(410) 435-2700

Whitemarsh Plaza Liquors
7968 Honego Blvd.
Baltimore 21236
(410) 931-4055

Decker Wine & Spirits
401 Baltimore Pike
Bel Air 21014
(410) 879-4400

South Station Gourmet
16 Bel Air S. Pkwy.
Unit 1, Ste. C
Bel Air 21015
(410) 569-2337

JB Sims Fine Tobaccos
4914 St. Elmo Ave.
Bethesda 20814
(301) 656-7123

The Brew Pot
13031 11th St.
Bowie 20715
(301) 805-6799

A. Fader & Son
40 West Shopping
Center
728 N. Rolling Rd.
Catonville 21228
(410) 744-9090

EASTON

Harrison's Wine & Spirits
207 N. Harrison
Easton 21601
(410) 822-5757

Town & Country Liquors
28248 St. Micheal's
Rd.
Easton 21601
(410) 822-1433

Wye River Cigar Company
The Gallery, 29 S.
Harrison St.
Easton 21601
(410) 822-5000

Oasis Liquors
2013 Pulaki Hwy.
Edgewood 21040
(410) 679-2600

Carrolltowne Liquors Inc.
6410 Ridge Rd.
Eldersburg 21784
(410) 795-6900

Jason Liquors
9339 Baltimore Rd.
Ellicott City 21402
(410) 465-2424

Stogies
3995 College Ave.
Ellicott City 21403
(410) 465-8358

Venice Wines & Liquors
431 Dual Hwy.
Flagerstown 21740
(301) 733-2819

Ronnie's Beverage Warehouse
1514 Rock Spring
Rd.
Forest Hill 21050
(410) 838-4566

Davidus Cigar Ltd.
1015 W. Patrick St.
Fredrick 21702
(301) 662-6606

JB Sims Fine Tobaccos II
12119 Darnestown
Rd.
Gaithersburg 20878
(301) 963-0109

Tobacco Shack
12615-D Wisteria Dr.
Germantown 20874
(301) 972-2905

Valley Tobacco Company
Hunt Valley Mall,
118 Shawn Rd.
Hunt Valley 21030
(410) 771-3493

Capital Plaza Smoke Shop
6200 Anapolis Rd.
Landover Hills
20784
(301) 341-2614

Signature Cigars
8610 Cherry Lane
Laurel 20707
(301) 470-4300

Rolling Rd. Tobacco
   Warehouse
1421 York Rd.
Lutherville 21093
(410) 339-7072

OCEAN CITY

94th Street
   Beer/Wine & Deli
9301 Coastal Hwy.
Ocean City 21842
(410) 524-7037

Sandbaggers
8101 Coastal Hwy.
Ocean City 21842
(410) 524-4410

Smoke Rings
4513 Coastal Hwy.
Ocean City 21842
(410) 289-3250

Smoke Rings
5 2nd St.
Ocean City 21842
(410) 289-1204

A. Fader & Son
Valley Village
   Shopping Center
Owings Mills 21117
(410) 363-7799

Shelly's Woodroast
1699 Rockville Pike
Rockville 20852
(301) 984-3300

Chesapeake Trading
   Company
102 Talbot St.
Saint Michaels 21663
(410) 745-9797

Flamingo Flats
406 Talbot St.
Saint Michaels 21663
(410) 745-2053

A. Fader & Son
25 W. Allegheny
Towson 21204
(410) 825-1467

The Other Side
15 W. Chesapeake Ave.
Towson 21204
(410) 337-9202

Massachusetts

Blanchard's Inc.
103 Harvard Ave.
Allston 02134
(617) 782-5588

Marty's Wine,
   Gourmet Food &
   Tobacco
193 Harvard Ave.
Allston 02134
(617) 782-3250

Andover Spa
9 Elm St.
Andover 01810
(508) 475-4750

The Cigar Emporium
   At Auburndale
   Wine & Spirits
2102 Common-
   wealth Ave.
Auburndale 02166
(617) 244-2772

Mall News
480 Boston Rd.
Billerica 01821
(508) 663-5946

BOSTON

Alfred Dunhill
   Limited
69 Newbury St.
Boston 02116
(617) 424-8600

Bauer Liquors
337 Newbury St.
Boston 02115
(718) 262-0083

Brookline Liquor
   Mart
1354 Common-
   wealth Ave.
Boston 02134
(617) 731-6644

Charles Street
   Liquors
143 Charles St.
Boston 02114
(617) 523-5051

Cigar Landing II
Faneuil Hall Market
   Place, Quincy
   Market Bldg.
Boston 02109
(617) 723- 0147

Cigar Masters
176 Newbury St.
Boston 02116
(617) 266-4400

David P Ehrlich
27 Court Sq.
Boston 02108
(617) 227-1720

Gloucester Street
Cigar Co.
34 Gloucester St.
Boston 02115
(617) 424-1000

The Humidor
800 Boylston St.
Boston 02199
(617) 262-5510

Humo
12 Stoneholm St.,
Ste. 502
Boston 02115
(617) 424-8490

L J Peretti
Company
2½ Park Square
Boston 02116
(617) 482-0218

State Street Smoke
Shop Inc.
107-A State St.
Boston 02109
(617) 227-7576

Brewster Package
Store
2655 Main St.
Brewster 02631
(508) 896-3412

Martignetti's
1650 Soldiers Field
Rd.
Brighton 02135
(617) 782-3700

Psych-O-Delic
1285 Belmont St.,
Rte. 123
Brockton 02401
(508) 559-0925

Brookline News &
Gift
313 Harvard St.
Brookline 02146
(617) 566-9634

The Cigar
Emporium At
Busa Liquors
182 Cambridge St.
Burlington 01803
(617) 272-1050

Cape Way Package
Store
3187 Cranberry
Hwy.
Buzzards Bay 02532
(508) 759-4291

Harvard Provisions
Company
94 Mt. Auburn St.
Cambridge 02138
(617) 547-6684

Leavitt & Pierce
1316 Massachusetts
Ave.
Cambridge 02138
(617) 547-0576

C B Perkins
Village Mall, 95
Washington St.
Canton 02021
(617) 575-1411

Cape Cod Package
Store
1495 Falmouth Rd.
Centerville 02632
(508) 775-2065

The Epicure
538 Main St.
Chatham 02633
(508) 945-0047

Harrington Wine &
Liquor
10 Summer St.
Chelmsford 01824
(508) 256-2711

K B Tobacco
168 Everett Ave.
Chelsea 02150
(617) 889-0012

Gary's Liquors
655 VFW Pkwy.
Chestnut Hill 02167
(617) 323-1122

Scrappy's Liquor
Locker
577 East St.
Chicopee 01020
(413) 594-9553

The Cigar Emporium
At Curtis Liquors
790 Rte. 3-A
Cohasset 02025
(617) 383-9800

EAST BOSTON

Heights News/
Cigar Pit
1006 Bennington St.
East Boston 02128
(617) 569-4450

House Of Cigars
262 Meridian St.
East Boston 02128
(617) 568-9737

Two Guys Smoke Shop
262 Meridian St.
East Boston 02128
(888) 224-4272

Torpedoes Landing
Colonial Inn Shops,
38 Water St.
Edgartown 02539
(508) 627-7964

Trader Fred's
249d State Rd.
Edgartown 02539
(508) 627-8004

Two Guys Smoke Shop
423 Broadway
Everett 02149
(617) 387-6691

The Old Firehouse Smoke & Brew Shop
116 Rock St.
Fall River 02720
(508) 678-2185

Tobacco Shed
400 Cochituate Rd.
Framingham 01701
(508) 875-9851

The Wine Vault
2 Fairbanks St.
Framingham 01701
(508) 875-6980

Psych-O-Delic
9 Main St.
Framingham 01701
(508) 626-8004

Franklin News
36 Main St.
Franklin 02038
(508) 528-8263

Liquor World
365 W. Central St.
Franklin 02038
(508) 528-0138

Trotta's Liquors
490 Main St.
Great Barrington 01230
(413) 528-3490

Dad's Cigars
34 Chapman St.
Greenfield 01301
(888) 244-2760

Four Seasons Wines & Liquors
333 Russell St.
Hadley 01035
(413) 584-8174

Tobacco Road
206 Russell St.
Hadley 01035
(413) 585-1159

B & F Tobacco
1775 Washington St.
Hanover 02339
(617) 826-1344

Psych-O-Delic
1012 Washington St.
Hanover 02339
(617) 826-4370

Hopkinton Wine & Spirit
77 W. Main St.
Hopkinton 01748
(508) 435-1292

Cape Cod Mall Liquors
226 Falmouth Rd.,
Rte. 28
Hyannis 02601
(508) 790-4770

Loose Caboose
382 Barnstable Rd.
Hyannis 02601
(508) 775-3558

Summer Hill Smoke Shop
161 Summer St.
Kingston 02364
(617) 585-5588

Najaime's Wine & Liquor
444 Pittsfield
Lenox 01240
(413) 637-1220

Nejaime's Wine Cellar
27 Church St.
Lenox 02140
(413) 637-2221

Wyman's Liquors
30 Pleasant St.
Leominster 01453
(508) 537-5537

The Cigar Emporium At Busa Liquors
55 Bedford St.
Lexington 02173
(617) 862-1400

Pleasant Smoke Shop
428 Main St.
Malden 02148
(617) 321-3593

Dub's Liquor
30 Chauncy St.,
Rte. 106
Mansfield 02048
(508) 339-3454

Rum Runner Wine & Spirit
377 Chancey St.
Mansfield 02048
(508) 399-7447

Tufts Square Tobacco
468 Main St.
Medford 02155
(617) 391-1820

Liquor World
Star Market Plaza, 9
Medway Rd.,
Rte. 109
Milford 02038
(508) 478-1700

Up In Smoke
136 Main St.
Milford 01757
(508) 478-8678

Powers Package Store
4 South Ave.
Natick 01760
(508) 653-6832

The Cigar Emporium At Newton Upper Falls Liquors
Highland Ave.
Newton 02164
(617) 969-9200

Pipe Rack
1247-49 Center St.
Newton Center 02159
(617) 969-3734

GLOUCESTER STREET CIGAR COMPANY

Introducing Boston's newest and most exciting cigar shop.

We pride ourselves in featuring the areas most extensive cigar selection. Over 150 brands and 800 sizes stored with elegance and care in our luxurious walk-in humidor. And of course, a full complement of smoker's accessories.

You will find us under the smoking cigar at
34 Gloucester Street
Boston, MA 02115
617.424.1000

Until recently, the best place to buy cigars was in a tobacco shop.

that was before

The Cigar Emporium

opened in these fine liquor stores

Upper Falls Liquors Highland Ave. Newton, MA
Post Road Liquors Boston PostRoad, Wayland, MA
Auburndale Liquors Rte. 30, Auburndale, MA
Curtis Liquors Bedford St. Weymouth, MA
Curtis Liquors, Rte 3A Cohasset, MA
Busa Liquors, Cambridge St. Burlington, MA
Busa Liquors, Bedford St.Lexington, MA

At the The Cigar Emporium, you will find New England's premier selection of fine cigars. Our luxurious walk-in humidors house some of the finest cigars in the world; with a selection of brands surpassing those found at any tobacconist. And, since we are located within fine retail liquor merchants, there is ample parking, extended store hours 6 days a week (9am-10 pm) and a huge variety of well priced fine wines, single malts or microbrews.

for information please call us at 508.470.0300

Marty's Wine, Gourmet Food & Tobacco
675 Washington St.
Newtonville 02160
(617) 332-1230

NORTH ANDOVER

The Cigar Emporium
800 Turnpike St.,
Ste. 300
North Andover 01845
(508) 470-0300

Den Rock Liquor Mart
North Andover Mall,
Winthrop Ave.
North Andover 01845
(508) 683-2216

The Vineyard
554 Turnpike St.
North Andover 01845
(508) 688-5005

Friendly Discount Liquor
135 Providence Rd.
Northbridge 01588
(508) 234-7951

Aurora Borealis
25 King St.
Northampton 01060
(413) 585-9533

Armeno Coffee Roasters
75 Otis St.
Northborough 01532
(508) 393-2821

Jim's Package Store
Circuit Ave. Ext.
Oakbluff 02557
(508) 693-0236

Kappy's
175 Andover St.
Peabody 01960
(508) 532-2330

Brennan's Smoke Shop
17 Court St.
Plymouth 02360
(508) 746-5711

El Breco Cigar Company
53 Main St.
Plymouth 02360
(508) 746-0496

Richard's Liquor
301 Quincy Ave.
Quincy 02169
(617) 376-0709

The Smoke Shop
618 Hancock St.
Quincy 02169
(617) 472-9997

ABC The Cigar Store
170 Revere St.
Revere 02151
(617) 289-4959

Yankee Spirits
167 Market St.
Rockland 02370
(617) 878-0226

Salty Dog Smoke Shop
23 Whistlestop Mall
Rockport 01966
(508) 546-5162

Jack's Smoke Shop
469 Lincoln Ave.
Sauguss 01906
(617) 233-0604

Yankee Spirits
628 Washington St.
South Attleboro 02703
(508) 399-5860

Doc James Tobacco
420 Rte. 134
South Dennis 02660
(508) 760-1223

South Egermont Spirit Shop
71 Main St.
South Egermont 01258
(413) 528-1490

The Cigar Emporium At Curtis Liquors
486 Columbian St.
South Weymouth 02190
(617) 331-2345

Nicotine's Cigar & Newsstand
260 Worthington St.
Springfield 01103
(413) 781-0386

Phoenix Tobacconist
1676 Main St.
Springfield 01103
(413) 731-8322

Yankee Spirits
376 Main St.
(Rte. 20)
Sturbridge 01566
(508) 347-2231

Harringtown News & Gifts
2 Galleria Mall Dr.
Taunton 02780
(508) 880-9301

Aubut's Liquor
1768 Main St.
Tewksbury 01876
(508) 851-2031

Mark's Smoke Shop
360 Main St.
Wakefield 01880
(617) 245-1211

Gordon's Liquor Store
867 Main St.
Waltham 02154
(617) 893-1900

The Cigar Emporium At Post Rd. Liquors
44 Boston Post Rd.
Wayland 01778
(508) 358-4300

C Garr Importers
437 Cherry St.,
Ste. 106
West Newton 02165
(617) 969-8855

Town & Country
1119 Riverdale St.
West Springfield 01089
(413) 736-4694

Julio's Liquor
140 Boston Turnpike Rd.
Westboro 01581
(508) 366-0569

Cigar Emporium at
Curtis Liquors
Bedford St.
Weymouth 02025
(617) 383-9800

WOBURN

Cigar Landing II
10 Tower Office
Park, Ste. 419
Woburn 01801
(617) 723-0147

The Smoke Shop
461 Main St.
Woburn 01801
(617) 935-2760

Tobacco Shed
Woburn Mall, 300
Mishawum Rd.
Woburn 01801
(617) 933-0231

WORCESTER

Highland Emporium
146 Highland St.
Worcester 01609
(508) 756-1989

The Owl Shop
416 Main St.
Worcester 01608
(508) 753-0423

Palley Cash-n-
Carry
1049 Main St.
Worcester 01603
(508) 752-2811

R A Tiscione's
Cigar Cafe
257 Shrewsbury St.
Worcester 01604
(508) 754-0067

Michigan

Chaloner &
Company
108 W. Maumee St.
Adrian 49221
(517) 263-9803

Smokers Only #7
9095 Allen Rd.
Allen Park 48101
(313) 381-0480

ANN ARBOR

Blue Heron Fine
Foods & Wines
882 W. Eisenhower
Pkwy.
Ann Arbor 48103
(313) 662-2270

Maison Edwards
Tobacconist
11 Nickels Arcade
Ann Arbor 48104
(313) 662-4145

Smoker's Depot
1760 Plymouth Rd.
Ann Arbor 48105
(313) 669-9277

Village Corner
601 S. Forest Ave.
Ann Arbor 48104
(313) 995-1818

Smoky's Cigarette
& Cigars
3029 E. Walton Blvd.
Auburn Hills 48326
(810) 373-7174

Tinder Box
2050 N. Opdyke
Auburn Hills 48326
(810) 377-6840

Smokers Palace II
705 N. Euclid Ave.
Bay City 48706
(810) 667-4410

Smokey's Cigarettes
& Cigars
2727 S. Woodward
Berkley 48072
(810) 546-8431

Churchill's Of
Birmingham
142 S. Woodward
Birmingham 48009
(810) 647-4555

Bloomfield
Gourmet
1081 W. Lons Lake Rd.
Bloomfield Hill
48302
(810) 647-5570

Smokers Depot
10006 E. Grand
River
Brighton 48116
(810) 220-2701

The Cigar Box
124 N. Main St.
Brooklyn 49230
(517) 592-9064

Smoker's Kastle
1235 S. Center Rd.,
Unit 4
Burton 48509
(810) 743-6050

H & I Smokers
42090 Ford Rd.
Canton 48187
(313) 844-3003

Bridge Street Book
Shop Inc.
407 Bridge St.
Charlevoix 49720
(616) 547-7323

Parkway Beverage
37031 Groesbeck Hwy.
Clinton Township
48036
(810) 468-1631

DEARBORN

Churchills
Fairlane Town
Center Mall,
18900 Michigan
Ave.
Dearborn 48126
(313) 240-4112

Dearborn Tobacco
Company
22085 Michigan Ave.
Dearborn 48124
(313) 562-1221

Hill & Hill
Tobacconists
Fairlane Town
Center Mall, 18900
Michigan Ave.
Dearborn 48126
(313) 441-3959

The Ritz Carlton
Gift Shop
Fairlane Plaza, 300
Town Center Dr.
Dearborn 48126
(313) 441-2000

Telegraph Cigarette
Station
3965 Telegraph
Dearborn Heights
48125
(313) 565-9484

DETROIT

New Center Tobacco & Snack
3011 W. Grand
Blvd., Ste. 114
Detroit 48202
(313) 873-7833

Smoker's Bargain
150 Michigan Ave.
Detroit 48226
(313) 964-5283

Walters-Watkins Tobacco
122 W. Lafayette Blvd.
Detroit 48226
(313) 965-5326

Campbells Smoke Shop Inc.
207 Mac Ave.
East Lansing 48823
(517) 332-4269

Smoker's Paradise
20853 Kelly Rd.
Eastport 48120
(810) 445-1818

Farmington Hills Wine & Liquor
24233 Orchard Lake Rd.
Farmington Hills 48336
(810) 476-0682

Smoker's & More
38499 W. 10 Mile Rd.
Farmington Hills 48335
(810) 442-2499

Smokers Only
24275 Middlebelt
Farmington Hills 48336
(810) 476-8013

Paul's Pipe Shop
647 S. Saginaw St.
Flint 48502
(810) 235-0581

Port Of Call
G-4225 Miller Rd.
Flint 48507
(810) 732-2793

Oliver T's
1553 E. Hill Rd.
Grand Blanc 48439
(810) 695-6550

Hostetter's News Agency
135 Washington St.
Grand Haven 49417
(616) 842-3920

GRAND RAPIDS

Buffalo Tobacco Traders
952 E. Fulton St.
Grand Rapids 49503
(616) 451-8090

Elliotts News & Tobacco
21 Ottawa Ave. Nw
Grand Rapids 49503
(616) 235-6400

London Shire Tobacco & Spirits
132 Monroe Center
Grand Rapids 49503
(616) 774-3714

Martha's Vineyard Limited
200 Union NE
Grand Rapids 49503
(616) 459-0911

Smoker's Express #2
3927 28th St. SE
Grand Rapids 49512
(616) 977-0199

Tuttle's
3835 28th St. SE
Grand Rapids 49512
(616) 942-6990

Hill & Hill Tobacconists
19529 Mack Ave.
Grosse Pointe 48236
(313) 259-3388

H S I Cigar
19818 Mack Ave.
Grosse Pointe Woods 48236
(313) 417-1940

Smoker's Landing
1442 S. Milford
Highland 48357
(810) 887-2099

Smoker's World
135 W. Highland Rd.
Highland 48357
(810) 889-3900

Smokers Depot-Howell
1235 E. Grand River
Howell 48843
(517) 546-2646

KALAMAZOO

Kalamazoo Brewing Company
427½ E. Michigan Ave.
Kalamazoo 49007
(616) 382-2338

Tiffany's Spirit Shoppe
1714 W. Main St.
Kalamazoo 49006
(616) 381-1414

Tinder Box
Crossroads Mall,
6650 S. Westnedge
Kalamazoo 49002
(616) 327-3447

The Humidor
117 S. Washington Square
Lansing 49833
(517) 484-3434

Mac's
207 S. Washington Square
Lansing 48933
(517) 487-0670

Smokers Palace-Lapeer
1045 Summit St.
Lapeer 48446
(810) 667-3337

LIVONIA

Smoky's Cigarette & Cigar
16705 Middlebelt Rd.
Livonia 48154
(313) 513-2622

USA Smokers Mart
27548 Schoolcraft St.
Livonia 48154
(313) 425-3260

Wine Barrell Plus
30303 Plymouth Rd.
Livonia 48150
(313) 522-9463

....

**Smokers Outlet Of
Madison Hts.**
160 W. 12 Mile
Madison Heights
48071
(810) 414-7007

Surroundings
423 River St.
Manistee 49660
(616) 723-0637

Tobacco Outlet
Eastlawn Plaza, 971
S. Saginaw Rd.
Midland 48640
(800) 618-7679

**Main Street Wine
Shoppe**
426 N. Main
Milford 48381
(810) 685-7191

**French Town
Liquor Shoppe**
3616 N. Dixie Hwy.
Monroe 48162
(313) 289-9952

**Trader Toms
Tobacco Shop**
43249 W. Seven
Mile Rd.
Northville 48167
(810) 348-8333

**The Beverage
Warehouse &
Market Place**
24150 Novi Rd.
Novi 48375
(810) 349-2034

Dusty's Cellar
1839 Grand River Ave.
Okemos 48864
(517) 349-5150

Vintage Wine Shop
4137 Orchard Lake Rd.
Orchard Lake 48323
(313) 626-3235

Barrel Craft
305 E. Mitchell St.
Petoskey 49770
(616) 347-3322

Tobacco Etc.
7503 South Us 31
Petoskey 49770
(616) 348-5808

PLYMOUTH

Smoker's Ave.
1440 Sheridan Rd.
Plymouth 48170
(313) 922-0339

Smokers Only #15
585 S. Main St.
Plymouth 48170
(313) 453-5644

Wellington Ltd.
14 Forest Pl.
Plymouth 48170
(313) 453-8966

....

Serafino's
8004 N. 32nd St.
Richland 49083
(616) 629-4721

**Smokey's Of
Richmond**
67365 Main St.
Richmond 48062
(810) 727-5834

Smokers Shop
19158 Fort St.
Riverview 48192
(313) 479-0404

Tobacco Town
18080 Fort St.
Riverview 48192
(313) 246-3460

Golden Unicorn
120 W. 4th St.
Rochester 48307
(810) 652-6699

**Red Wagon Wine
Shop**
2940 S. Rochester
Rd.
Rochester 48307
(810) 852-9307

**Embassy Wine &
Cigar**
29010 Beaconsfield
Rd.
Roseville 48066
(810) 771-7880

Smokers Outlet Inc.
18655 E. 10 Mile Rd.
Roseville 48066
(810) 772-3999

Malaga Briar Pipe
1406 E. 11 Mile Rd.
Royal Oak 48067
(810) 542-5000

**Casablanca
Tobacconist**
720 E. 14 Mile Rd.
Royal Oak 48073
(810) 585-9599

**Austin's Fine Pipes
& Tobaccos**
4340 Bay Rd.
Saginaw 48603
(517) 792-4731

Daves Smokin' Post
3986 Bay Rd.
Saginaw 48603
(517) 790-0066

Churchill's
21425 Great Mack
Ave.
St. Clair Shores
48080
(810) 775-3181

Double Corona
406 State St.
St. Joe 49085
(616) 683-2044

**Austin's Pipe &
Tobacco**
539 Ashmun St.
Sault Ste. Marie
49783
(906) 632-1775

Smokers Express
47079 Van Dyke
Shelby Township
48317
(810) 674-1100

SOUTHFIELD

Hayes Market
22580 Telegraph
Southfield 48034
(810) 352-2216

**Humidor
One/Panache**
20000 W. Ten Mile Rd.
Southfield 48075
(810) 356-4600

JR Tobacco
28815 Northwestern
Hwy.
Southfield 48034
(810) 357-2340

**Majestic Market
Inc.**
25877 Lahser
Southfield 48034
(810) 352-8556

**Old Wooden Indian
Tobacco**
13260 Northline St.
Southgate 48195
(313) 282-1379

STERLING
HEIGHTS

**Casablanca
Tobacconist**
33126 Dequindre Rd.
Sterling Heights
48310
(810) 268-5577

Smokers Outlet
43089 Van Dyke
Sterling Heights
48314
(810) 997-4030

Tobacco To Go
11508 15 Mile Rd.
Sterling Heights
48312
(810) 978-9870

**Smokers Outlet Of
Taylor**
7150 Pardee
Taylor 48180
(313) 292-8006

TRAVERSE
CITY

**Folgarelli Import
Market**
424 W. Front St.
Traverse City 49684
(616) 941-7651

Nolan's Tobacco
336 E. Front St.
Traverse City 49684
(616) 946-2640

Smokers Den
1073 S. Airport Rd.
Traverse City 49686
(616) 946-2742

TROY

**Hill & Hill
Tobacconists**
Oakland Mall, 662
W. 14 Mile Rd.
Troy 48083
(810) 585-0621

Hsi Cigar
Northfield Hilton,
5500 Crooks Rd.
Troy 48098
(810) 879-2100

Smoker's Outlet
5086 Rochester Rd.
Troy 48098
(810) 528-8018

Tobacco Emporium
2981 E. Big Beaver
Rd.
Troy 48083
(810) 689-1840

Tobacco Road
341 Pontiac Trail
Walled Lake 48390
(810) 926-9266

Smoker's Oasis
23890 Schoenherr
Warren 48089
(810) 777-1981

**Great American
Trading Post**
7380 Hiland Rd.
Waterford 48327
(810) 666-7935

Smokers Only IX
4646 Walton Blvd.
Waterford 48329
(810) 674-1199

Lil' Havana
6690-A Orchard
Lake Rd.
West Bloomfield
48322
(810) 539-0190

Smoke City Inc.
34873 Ford Rd.
Westland 48185
(313) 326-6770

Smoker's Express
224-C 28th St. SW
Wyoming 49509
(616) 261-9456

Smoker's Express
1799 Washtenaw
Yspilanti 48197
(313) 480-0705

Minnesota

Fulton Warehouse Liquor
160 Bridge Ave.
Albert Lee 56007
(507) 377-0818

L & M Smoke Shop
429 87th Lane
Blaine 55434
(612) 784-1140

BLOOMINGTON

Everything But The Cigar
Mall Of America,
1624 W. Market
Bloomington 55425
(612) 625-1084

Street Corner News
Mall Of America,
119 E. Broadway
Bloomington 55425
(615) 858-9826

Tobacco Warehouse
Valley West Shopping
Center, 10602 B
France Ave.
Bloomington 55431
(612) 703-0366

Smoke Shoppe & Booknook
109 Washington St.
Brainerd 56401
(218) 829-5830

Tobacco Warehouse
2125 Hwy. 13 S.,
Ste. 108
Burnsville 55337
(612) 890-8606

Wine Cellars
600 E. Superior
Duluth 55802
(218) 733-1314

Tobacco Warehouse
2149-C Cliff Rd.
Eagan 55122
(612) 454-8971

Cigar Importers Limited
7029 Amundson
Ave.
Edina 55439
(612) 942-8785

The Smoke Shop
809 Sibley Memorial
Hwy.
Lilydale 55118
(612) 457-4953

Westside Discount Liquor
116 S. Lindberg Dr.
Little Falls 56345
(320) 632-2582

Lakeside Wine & Spirits
1605 W. Wayzata
Blvd.
Long Lake 55356
(612) 404-2500

Tobacco Deals
3000 White Bear N.
Maplewood 55109
(612) 704-9778

MINNEAPOLIS

Depot Liquor
1010 Washington
Ave. S.
Minneapolis 55415
(612) 339-4040

Golden Leaf Limited
Calhoun Square,
3001 Hennepin
Ave. S.
Minneapolis 55408
(612) 824-1867

Lewis Pipe & Tobacco
512 Niccollet Mall
Minneapolis 55402
(612) 332-9129

South Lyndale Liquor
5300 Lyndale Ave. S.
Minneapolis 55419
(612) 827-5811

Surdyk's Liquors
303 E. Hennepin
Minneapolis 55414
(612) 379-3232

Tobacco Road
Foshay Twr., 831
Marquette Ave.
Minneapolis 55402
(612) 333-1315

Tobacco Shop
2900 Hennepin Ave. S.
Minneapolis 55408
(612) 825-3380

Tobacco Warehouse
Parkway Plaza
Shopping Center,
4727 Hiawatha
Ave.
Minneapolis 55406
(612) 724-8142

Haskell's Inc.
12900 Wayzata Blvd.
Minnetonka 55305
(612) 544-4456

Tobacco Deals
2767 Winnetka Ave.
N.
New Hope 55427
(612) 540-9355

Smoker's Haven
1640 Hastings Ave.
Newport 55055
(612) 647-0686

Smokers' Haven #2
2231 11th Ave. E.
North St. Paul 55109
(612) 773-5935

Cap 'n' Cork
40644 W. Five Mile
Rd.
Plymouth 48170
(313) 420-0055

Chundee Smoke Shop
Mistic Lake Casino,
2400 Mistic Lake
Blvd.
Prior Lake 55372
(612) 445-9000

West End Liquors
1430 W. Main
Red Wing 55066
(612) 388-9425

Apollo Smokeshop
1513 12th St. SE
Rochester 55904
(507) 281-0888

G & W Coffee &
Tobacco
21 Wilson Ave. NE
St. Cloud 56304
(320) 654-6111

ST. PAUL

Havana Jack's
1170 Cushing
Circle, #138
St. Paul 55108
(800) 258-9471

JR Fielding
Company
1767 Lexington Ave.
St. Paul 55113
(612) 489-7504

MGM Liquor
Warehouse
1124 Larpenteur
Ave. W.
St. Paul 55113
(612) 487-1006

P R Cigars
1440 Arcade St.
St. Paul 55106
(612) 772-1272

Smoke 'n Gun
634 North Snelling
Ave.
St. Paul 55104
(612) 647-9397

Thomas Liquor
Store
1941 Grand Ave.
St. Paul 55105
(612) 699-1860

Tobak & News Inc.
2140 Ford Pkwy.
St. Paul 55116
(612) 698-3835

Jonathon's
18 Riverside Ave. S.
Sartell 56377
(320) 259-5011

Up In Smoke
333 N. Concord
Exchange
South St. Paul 55075
(612) 552-9559

Central Park
Warehouse
8101 Hwy. 65
Springlake Park 55432
(612) 780-8246

Westside Discount
Liquor
45 N. Waite Ave.
Waite Park 56387
(320) 253-9511

JT Tobacconist
17613 Minnetonka
Blvd.
Wayzata 55391
(612) 475-3131

Island Pearl Gift
Shop
Treasure Island
Casino, 5734
Sturgeon Lake Rd.
Welch 55089
(800) 222-7077

Boozemart Wine &
Spirits
131 E. Wentworth
West St. Paul 55118
(612) 457-6111

Smokers' Haven #3
1981 Whitaker Ave.
White Bear Lake
55110
(612) 426-6400

Summit Liquor &
Cigars
2000 County Rd. E.
White Bear Lake
55110
(612) 770-9622

Westgate Liquor &
Cigars
1429 W.T. Service
Drive
Winona 55987
(507) 454-1111

Mississippi

The Epitomy
Edgewater Mall,
2600 W. Beach
Blvd.
Biloxi 39531
(601) 388-2022

Rez Smoke Shop
115 Village Square,
Ste. J
Brandon 39042
(601) 992-2882

Dyre-Kent Drug
Company
109 1st St.
Grenada 38901
(601) 226-5232

The Country Squire
1855 Lakeland Dr.
Jackson 39216
(800) 222-8976

Smokey's Discount
Tobacco
2961 Bienville Blvd.
Ocean Spring 39564
(601) 872-5322

Missouri

Smoke Shop
1389 Jeffco Blvd.
Arnold 63010
(314) 296-5523

Welcome Smokers
523 Jeffco Blvd.
Arnold 63010
(314) 282-9910

Cigarettes For Less
Metro Plaza, Ste.
102, 7141
Metropolitan
Barnhart 63012
(314) 464-4920

The Wine Company
1447 Hwy. 248,
Ste. G
Branson 65616
(417) 334-4551

Tobacco Lane
265 W. Park Mall
Cape Girardeau
63702
(573) 651-3414

The Discount
Smokes
2430 Grand
Carthrage 64836
(417) 358-3455

Jon's Pipe Shop
42 N. Central Ave.
Clayton 63105
(314) 721-1480

JR Cigars
4 N. Central Ave.
Clayton 63105
(314) 727-5667

Nostalgia Shop
819 E. Walnut
Colombia 65201
(573) 442-6171

Discount Smoke Shop
11754 Manchester Rd.
De Peres 63131
(314) 822-6557

Tinder Box
814 Star Ridge Ct.
Defiance 63341
(314) 798-2224

Tinder Box
147 Jamestown Mall
Florissant 63034
(314) 741-0899

Jaid Tobacco Emporium
113 E. High St.
Jefferson City 65101
(573) 761-5307

Welcome Smokers
2111 Mission Blvd.
Jefferson City 65101
(573) 635-7045

Smokers Outlet Stores
1902 Main
Joplin 64803
(417) 624-2525

TJ Boggs Tobacconist
205 W. 20th St.
Joplin 64804
(417) 623-1804

KANSAS CITY

Berbiglia
1101 E. Banister
Kansas City 64131
(816) 942-0070

Boardwalk Cigar & Coffee
6232 NW Barry Rd.
Kansas City 64154
(816) 587-0560

Diebel's Sportsmens Gallery
Country Club Plaza,
426 Ward Pkwy.
Kansas City 64112
(816) 931-2988

Havana Moon Inc.
1614 W. 39th St.
Kansas City 64111
(816) 756-3367

John Bull
4112 Pennsylvania
Kansas City 64111
(816) 561-3383

Royal Chieftian Cigars
Kansas City Station
Casino, 8201 NE
Birmingham
Kansas City 64161
(816) 414-7418

Grape Vine Wines
114 W. Jefferson
Kirkwood 63122
(314) 909-7044

JJ's Specialty Store
794 Hwy. Hh
Lake Ozark 65049
(573) 365-6989

Barrels Of Fun
1100 S. Jefferson
Lebanon 65536
(417) 532-7700

Welcome Smokers
176 Weldon Pkwy.
Maryland Heights
63043
(314) 569-2265

Welcome Smokers
206 Terra Lane W.
O'Fallon 63366
(314) 978-3714

Welcome Smokers
4 Kings Plaza
Osage 65065
(314) 569-2294

Gomers Northland Fine Wines
8995 NW 45 Hwy.
Parkville 64152
(816) 746-0400

Ron's Amoco & Smoke Shop
1036 S. Westwood
Blvd.
Popular Bluff 63901
(573) 785-3416

Red X General Store
2401 W. Platte Rd.
Riverside 64150
(816) 741-8074

Tinder Box
412 Northwest Plaza
St. Ann 63074
(314) 298-7134

John Dengler, Tobacconist
700 S. Main St.
St. Charles 63301
(314) 946-6899

ST. LOUIS

The Adam's Mark Hotel The Gift Shop
4th And Chestnut
St. Louis 63102
(314) 241-7400

Briars & Blends
6008 Hampton Ave.
St. Louis 63109
(314) 351-1131

Joel's Shell Food Mart
1815 Arsonal St.
St. Louis 63118
(314) 772-1977

J R Cigars
710 Olive St.
St. Louis 63101
(314) 231-4434

Smoke Shop
11086 Midland
St. Louis 63114
(314) 427-5006

Smoke Shop
3134 Telegraph Rd.
St. Louis 63125
(314) 487-9992

Town & Country Tobacco
13933 Manchester Rd.
St. Louis 63011
(314) 227-0707

Welcome Smokers
3524 Lemay Ferry Rd.
St. Louis 63125
(314) 845-3680

Welcome Smokers
10544 Page Blvd.
St. Louis 63132
(314) 423-2264

Welcome Smokers
19 Grasso Plaza
St. Louis 63123
(314) 631-1211

SPRINGFIELD

Brown Derby
2023 S. Glenstone
Springfield 65804
(417) 881-1215

**Don Johnson's
Tobacco World**
1420 S. Glenstone
Springfield 65804
(417) 890-1978

The Humidor Ltd.
Brentwood Center,
2728 S. Glenstone
Springfield 65804
(417) 887-9619

Just For Him
1334 E. Battlefield
Springfield 65804
(417) 886-8380

H S B Tobacconist
6362 Delmar At
Westgate
University City
63130
(314) 721-1483

Welcome Smokers
6301 Weldon
Springs Rd.
Weldon Springs
63304
(314) 939-5539

Montana

BILLINGS

The Cigarette Store
1302 24th St. W.
303
Billings 59102
(406) 238-3327

The Cigarette Store
249 Main St.
Billings 59102
(406) 238-3327

Tobacco Row
2450 King Ave. W.
Billings 59102
(406) 656-1188

Smokers Friendly
1520 3rd St. NW
Great Falls 59404
(406) 771-0806

Cigarette Store
1530 Cedar St.
Helena 59601
(406) 443-3158

Maine News
9 N. Last Chance
Gulch
Helena 59601
(406) 442-6424

**Bill Pipe & Tabacco
Shop**
136 E. Broadway St.
Missoula 59802
(406) 728-2781

Nebraska

**BJ's Tobacco &
Candy Outlet**
3019 23rd St.
Columbus 68601
(402) 562-8086

Cigar Humidor
17 E. 21st St.
Kearney 68847
(308) 236-9945

The Still
5560 S. 48
Lincoln 68516
(402) 423-1875

Ted's Tobacco
2 Gateway Ward's
61st & O St.
Lincoln 68505
(402) 467-3350

OMAHA

Cigarros
13110 Birch Dr.
Omaha 68164
(402) 496-9595

David's Briar Shop
10000 California St.,
Ste. 3337
Omaha 68114
(402) 397-4760

David's Briar Shop
Oak View Mall,
Ste. 1113
Omaha 68144
(402) 697-0771

**Nickleby's Smoke
Ring**
2464 S. 120
Omaha 68144
(402) 330-4556

S. G. Roi
503 S. 11th St.
Omaha 68102
(402) 341-9264

Tobacco Hut
13766 Millard Ave.
Omaha 68137
(402) 895-1016

**Sherm's Smoke
Shop**
100 W. 6th St.
South Sioux City
68776
(402) 494-7952

Hy-Vee Food Store
2501 Corn Husker
Plaza
South Sioux City
68776
(402) 494-4675

Nevada

**Carsons Cigar
Company**
318 N. Carson, Ste. 101
Carson City 89701
(702) 884-4402

Cigarettes Cheaper!
Plaza 50 Center,
2182 Hwy. 50 E.
Carson City 89701
(702) 883-3867

Fallon Smoke Shop
987 Rio Vista
Fallon 89406
(702) 423-5655

Cigarettes Cheaper!
4136 E. Sunset Rd.
Henderson 89014
(702) 433-8388

LAS VEGAS

Churchill's Tobacco Emporium
3144 N. Rainbow Blvd.
Las Vegas 89108
(702) 645-1047

Cigarettes Cheaper!
Charleston Plaza,
1838 E.
Charleston Blvd.
Las Vegas 89104
(702) 384-8434

Cigarettes Cheaper!
Decatur Meadows,
348 S. Decatur Blvd.
Las Vegas 89107
(702) 822-1350

Cigarettes Cheaper!
Lone Mountain
Plaza, 4870 Lone
Mountain Rd.
Las Vegas 89130
(702) 395-0951

Cigarettes Cheaper!
Spring Oaks Center,
4821 W. Spring
Mt. Rd., Ste. E
Las Vegas 89102
(702) 220-8460

Cigarettes Cheaper!
Sahara Pavillion
Center, 4750 W.
Sahara Ave. #16
Las Vegas 89102
(702) 880-9184

Cigarettes Cheaper!
Winterwood Pavil-
lion Center, 2232
S. Nellis Blvd. G-2
Las Vegas 89104
(702) 432-8633

Cigarettes Cheaper!
Pecos Plaza, 3315 E.
Russell Rd.
Las Vegas 89102
(702) 547-3811

Cigarettes Cheaper!
Sahara Towne Sq.,
2620 S. Maryland
Pkwy. #16
Las Vegas 89109
(702) 731-9122

Cigarettes Cheaper!
Cheyenne Plaza,
3266 Las Vegas
Blvd. #7
Las Vegas 89115
(702) 651-9097

Don Pablo Cigar Company
3025 Las Vegas Blvd. S.
Las Vegas 89109
(702) 369-1818

Don Ye Yo
510 E. Fremont
Las Vegas 89101
(702) 384-9262

Ed's Pipes, Tobacco & Gifts
Maryland Sq., 3661
S. Maryland Pkwy.
#12N
Las Vegas 89109
(702) 734-1931

Ed's Pipes, Tobacco & Gifts
7161 S. Easern Ave.,
Ste. C
Las Vegas 89119
(702) 260-9223

Elite Cigars
Riviera Hotel &
Casino, 2901 Las
Vegas Blvd.
Las Vegas 89109
(702) 734-5110

Gourmet Plaza Inc.
8400 W. Sahara Ave.,
8th Fl.
Las Vegas 89117
(702) 869-8400

Hiland's Gift & Tobacco
4300 Meadows
Mall #211
Las Vegas 89107
(702) 878-7720

Las Vegas Cigar Company
3755 S. Las Vegas
Blvd.
Las Vegas 89109
(800) 432-4277

Le Cigar Boutique
500 Fandwood Lane
Las Vegas 89107
(702) 877-6435

Lee's Discount Liquors
1780 S. Rainbow
Las Vegas 89102
(702) 870-6300

Lee's Discount Liquors
4421 N. Rancho Rd.
Las Vegas 89131
(702) 658-2300

Lee's Discount Liquors
3480 E. Flamingo
Las Vegas 89121
(702) 458-5700

Mardi Graw Cigars
Rio Hotel, 3700 W.
Flamingo
Las Vegas 89109
(702) 252-7777

Mr. Bill's Pipe & Tobacco
4632 S. Maryland
Las Vegas 89119
(702) 739-8840

Mr. Bill's Pipe & Tobacco
2550 S. Rainbow Blvd.
Las Vegas 89102
(702) 362-4427

Mr. Bill's Pipe & Tobacco
4510 E. Charleston
Blvd.
Las Vegas 89104
(702) 459-3400

Mr. Bill's Pipe & Tobacco
4441 W. Flamingo Rd.
Las Vegas 89103
(702) 221-9771

Mr. Bill's Pipe & Tobacco
4343 N. Rancho Rd.
Las Vegas 89130
(702) 395-7264

Pheasant Tobacconist
2800 W. Sahara, Ste.
6A
Las Vegas 89102
(702) 368-1700

Royal Cigar Society
3900 Paradise Rd.,
Ste. J
Las Vegas 89109
(702) 732-4411

Scarpe
3200 Las Vegas Blvd. S.
Las Vegas 89109
(702) 369-3500

Smoker's Paradise East
6235 S. Pecos
Las Vegas 89120
(702) 434-6444

Spirits Plus Liquor Store
4880 W. Flamingo Rd.
Las Vegas 89103
(702) 873-6000

Stogie International
4972 S. Maryland
Pkwy., Ste. 12
Las Vegas 89119
(702) 736-1990

Stogies Ltd
4079 S. Industrial Rd.
Las Vegas 89103
(702) 893-0024

Tinder Box
3536 Maryland Pkwy.
Las Vegas 89109
(702) 737-1807

Tobacco Road I
3650 E. Flamingo
Rd.
Las Vegas 89121
(702) 435-8511

Tobacco Road II
1129 S. Rainbow
Rd.
Las Vegas 89102
(702) 254-8511

RENO

Cigarettes Cheaper!
Keystone Center,
975 W. 5th St.
Reno 89503
(702) 348-7077

Cigarettes Cheaper!
Old Town Mall, 180
W. Peckham, Ste.
1030
Reno 89509
(702) 829-0605

Cigarettes Cheaper!
N. Hills Center,
1075 N. Hills Blvd.
#220
Reno 89506
(702) 677-4448

French Quarter
270 Lake St.
Reno 89501
(702) 786-7800

Tinder Box
Park Lane Mall,
186 E. Plumb Lane
Reno 89502
(702) 826-2680

Tinder Box #369
3950 Mayberry Dr.
Reno 89509
(702) 787-2215

Cigarettes Cheaper!
Ironhorse Center,
529 E. Prater St.
Sparks 89431
(702) 331-3599

New Hampshire

The News Shop
Steeple Gate Mall
Concord 03302
(603) 226-2833

Happy Jacks Pipe &
Tobacco
71 Church St.
Laconia 03246
(603) 528-4092

Paugus Variety
1325 Union Ave.
Laconia 03246
(603) 527-1900

The News Shop
1500 S. Willow St.
Manchester 03103
(603) 622-1782

Fermentation
Station
72 Main St.
Meredith 03253
(603) 279-4028

Castro's Back Room
182 Main St.
Nashua 03060
(603) 881-7703

The News Shop
310 Daniel Webster
Hwy., Ste 123
Nashua 03060
(603) 891-1867

News Shop
Fox Run Mall
Newington 03801
(508) 842-6300

Federal Cigar
1 Market Square
Portsmouth 03801
(603) 436-5363

SALEM

The News Shop
99 Rockingham Park
Blvd.
Salem 03079
(603) 890-3699

Post Time Beer &
Smoke
375 S. Broadway
Salem 03079
(603) 898-3704

Two Guy's Smoke
Shop
309 S. Broadway
Salem 03079
(603) 898-5322

The Gold Leaf
Tobacconist
920 Lafayette Rd.,
Unit 3
Seabrook 03874
(603) 474-7744

New Jersey

Trump Plaza
Hotel/Casino
Front Page Gift
Shop, Mississippi
Ave. & Boardwalk
Atlantic City 08401
(609) 441-6751

Barnegat Gourmet
& Gift
690 E. Bay Ave.
Barnegat 08005
(609) 698-1944

Olde Tyme Smoke
Shoppe
213-A Long Beach
Blvd.
Beach Haven 08008
(609) 492-4458

Village Tobacco
41 Clementon Rd.
Berlin 08009
(609) 768-5181

Brookdale Buy-Rite
1057 Broad St.
Bloomfield 07003
(201) 338-7090

Village Tobacco
114 Main St.
Bradley Beach 07720
(908) 774-7055

Cigars Plus
2140-1 Rte. 88
Brick 08724
(908) 295-9795

C B Perkins #75
Bridgewater
Commons Mall,
400 Commons Way
Bridgewater 08807
(908) 707-8787

Brielle Pharmacy
602 Higgins Ave.
Brielle 08730
(908) 528-5400

Delmonte's News
Agency
2999 Mt. Ephraim
Ave.
Camden 08104
(609) 962-6929

Cape May News
Victorian Plaza, #8
Cape May 08204
(609) 884-5511

Grant Regard's
Congress Hall, 251
Beach Drive
Cape May 08204
(609) 884-7917

Super Wines &
Spirits
99 Ridgedale Ave.
Cedar Knolls 07927
(201) 267-1999

The Chatham Wine
Shop
465 Main St.
Chatham 07928
(201) 635-0088

Track Town Smoke Shop
2111 Rte. 70 W.
Cherry Hill 08002
(609) 662-0214

Frederick's Jewelers
1083 Raritan Rd.
Clark 07066
(908) 388-8889

Havana Knight
1063 Raritan Rd.
Clark 07066
(908) 499-7100

Shop Rite Liquors
494 Anderson Ave.
Cliffside Park 07010
(201) 943-2650

Rowe-Manse Emporium
1065 Bloomfield Ave.
Clifton 07012
(201) 472-8170

Clinton Wine & Spirits
57 Laneco Plaza
Clinton 08809
(201) 735-9655

Columbus Discount Smoke Shop
Columbus Farmers Market, 2919 Rte. 206 S.
Columbus 08022
(609) 267-4495

Puff And Stuff
21 E. North Ave.
Cranford 07016
(908) 272-6989

CB Perkins
Deptford Mall
Deptford 08096
(609) 848-3363

Market Place Wines & Spirits
647-G Hwy. 18 S.
East Brunswick 08816
(908) 432-9393

Mr. Pipe
Brunswick Sq. Mall
East Brunswick 08816
(908) 257-0200

Eatontown Smoke Shop
21 Main St.
Eatontown 07724
(908) 542-1855

Azucar Restaurant
10 Dempsey Ave.
Edgewater 07020
(201) 886-0747

John David Ltd.
453 Menlo Park
Edison 08837
(908) 494-8333

Your Cigar Box
263 Barberry Rd.
Egg Harbor
Township 08234
(609) 383-3368

Smokers World
Limited
126 Engle St.
Englewood 07631
(201) 567-1305

Bern Stationers
24-24 Fairlawn Ave.
Fairlawn 07410
(201) 797-1311

Smokey Joe's Inc.
125 Main St.
Flemington 08822
(908) 788-0560

The Cigar Room
200 Main St.
Fort Lee 07024
(201) 947-5835

Smokin'
2450 Lemoine Ave.
Fort Lee 07024
(201) 944-0234

Kingston Wine &
Liquors
3391 State Hwy.,
Ste. 128
Franklin Park 08823
(908) 422-2324

FREEHOLD

County Seat
Tobacco
11 South St.
Freehold 07728
(908) 845-4944

Mr. Pipe
Freehold Raceway
Mall, 3710 Hwy. 9,
Ste. 1212
Freehold 07728
(908) 303-9500

Spirit Unlimited
611 Park Ave.
Freehold 07728
(908) 462-8100

Spirit Unlimited
Rte. 9 & Adelphia Rd.
Freehold 07728
(908) 462-3738

Spirit Unlimited
138 Village Center Dr.
Freehold 07728
(908) 409-3060

The Jigger Shop
190 Main St.
Hackettstown 07840
(908) 852-3080

Groucho's Cigars
3 Kings Hwy E.
Haddenfield 08033
(609) 795-1982

Shoprite Liquors
3161 Quaker Bridge
Rd.
Hamilton 08619
(609) 587-2849

**Pipe & Tobacco
Shop**
797 Rte. 33
Hamilton Square
08619
(609) 587-6375

Trent Jewelers
1750 Whitehorse
Mercerville Rd.
Hamilton Township
08619
(609) 584-8800

JR Tobacco
65 Rte. 17 S.
Hasbrouck Heights
07604
(201) 288-7676

Sasha's Boutique
1 Bay Ave.
Highlands 07732
(908) 872-8788

Garden State News
106 Broadway
Hillsdale 07642
(201) 664-2225

HOBOKEN

Foodtown
614 Clinton St.
Hoboken 07030
(201) 795-1783

The Smoke Shop
235 Hudson St.
Hoboken 07030
(201) 217-1701

**Sparrow Wine &
Liquor**
126 Washington St.
Hoboken 07030
(201) 659-1500

Stoagie's
37 Gillane
Iselin 08830
(908) 283-5535

Shop Rite Liquors
60 Beaver Brook Rd.
Lincoln Park 07035
(201) 694-4420

**Main Tobacco &
Confectionery**
83 Main St.
Little Falls 07824
(201) 812-1382

**Livingston Bottle
King**
19 S. Livingston Ave.
Livingston 07452
(201) 994-4100

Court Liquors
Foodtown Shopping
Center, #1 W. End
Ct.
Long Branch 07740
(908) 870-9859

JJR Cigar Emporium
607 Ridge Rd.
Lyndhurst 07071
(201) 438-8760

**Garden State News
Village**
43 Main St.
Madison 07940
(201) 660-9600

**Shoppers
Liquor/Madison**
121 Main St.
Madison 07940
(201) 822-0200

Goodloe Liquors
119 Taylor Ave.
Manasquan 08736
(908) 223-3180

**Canal's/The Bottle
Shop**
10 W. Rte. 70
Marlton 08053
(609) 983-4991

**Spirits Of The
Valley**
1990 Washington
Valley Rd.
Martinsville 08836
(908) 302-0011

**Havana's Cigar
Emporium**
952 Hwy. 34
Matawan 07747
(908) 583-3433

**Holy Smoke Cigar
Shop**
1 N. Main St.,
Unit 3C
Medford 08055
(609) 654-1233

Flintlock Room
6 Hilltop Rd.
Mendham 07945
(201) 543-1861

**John's Greeting
Center**
356 Rte. 33
Mercerville 08619
(609) 586-7050

**Crestview
Pharmacy**
52 S. Hwy. 35
Middletown 07748
(908) 747-6833

**Wine Cellar Of
Millburn**
279 Millburn Ave.
Millburn 07041
(201) 379-0123

Bliwise Liquors
1267 Rte .22
Mountainside 07092
(908) 233-1133

**Bottom Of The Hill
Newsstand**
3 Easton Ave.
New Brunswick
08901
(908) 745-7983

Sell Rite Liquors
579 Rte. 22 W.
North Plainfield
07060
(908) 756-0400

Northfield News & Tobacco
Rte. 9 & Tilton Rd.
Northfield 08225
(609) 641-9112

Beverage Barn
224 Livingston St.
Northvale 07647
(201) 768-8848

Cavliew Limited
1704 Holbrook St.
Oakhurst 07755
(908) 531-7588

Smoke 'n' More
2005 Rte. 35 N.
Oakhurst 07755
(908) 660-0600

John David Limited #78
Garden State Plaza
Paramus 07652
(201) 368-1975

Hinkle's News Shop
233 N. Broadway
Pennsville 08070
(609) 678-2460

A Little Taste Of Cuba
70 Witherspoon St.
Princeton 08542
(609) 683-8988

The Cigar Box
476 Rte. 17 N.
Ramsey 07446
(201) 236-0111

Tobacco Hut
31 Rte. 206
Raritan 08869
(908) 725-4440

REDBANK

Crates Wine & Liquor
14 N. Bridge Ave.
Redbank 07701
(908) 747-1485

The Red Pipe
39½ Broad St.
Redbank 07701
(908) 842-6633

Tinder Box International #373
68 White St.
Redbank 07701
(908) 530-0006

Scott's Smoke Shop
345 Pennsauken Mart., Rte. 130 & Rte. 73
Rennsauken 08110
(609) 662-6447

Exquisite Wine Liquor
230 Main St.
Ridgefield 07660
(201) 641-1218

Smokers Paradise
577 Bergen Blvd.
Ridgefield 07657
(201) 840-8999

Tobacco Shop Inc.
10 Chestnut St.
Ridgewood 07450
(201) 447-2204

Foodtown
Kinderkamack & Main
River Edge 07661
(201) 342-4020

John David Limited #77
Rockaway Town Sq.
Rockaway 07866
(201) 328-0603

Rumson Buy-Rite
5 W. River Rd.
Rumson 07760
(908) 842-0552

Secaucus Liquors
115 Plaza Center
Secaucus 07094
(201) 867-7428

Brick Church Collection
The Mall At Short Hills
Short Hills 07078
(201) 379-6920

Circle Liquor Store
1 MacArthur Circle
Somers Point 08244
(609) 927-2921

Cedar Grove Wine & Liquor
120 Cedar Grove Lane
Somerset 08873
(908) 560-0009

Big Mikes Cigar Sanctuary
2201 Unit K, S. Clinton Ave.
South Plainfield 07080
(908) 769-7100

Tobacco Barn
Middlesex Mall,
6739 Hadley Rd.
South Plainfield 07080
(908) 753-7855

Finlay's Cigars
207 Hawkin Rd.
Southampton 08088
(609) 268-2489

The Spring Lake Bottle Shop
1400 3rd Ave.
Spring Lake 07762
(908) 449-5525

Shoppers Discount Liquors
8 Millburn Ave.
Springfield 07081
(201) 376-0005

Florez Tobacconist
34 Maple St.
Summit 07901
(908) 598-1600

E Z Liquors
35 Rte. 37 E.
Toms River 08753
(908) 341-3444

Monaghan's Liquors
1617 Rte. 37 E.
Toms River 08753
(908) 270-6060

TRENTON

Friend's Cigar Parlour
401 Elmer Str.
Trenton 08611
(609) 393-3300

Lee's Pharmacy
940 Parkway Ave.
Trenton 08618
(609) 406-1901

**Princeton Ave.
Cigar**
1258 Princeton Ave.
Trenton 08638
(609) 396-9610

**Smoke's Cigar &
Tobacco**
1679 Hamilton Ave.
Trenton 08629
(609) 890-6090

Smokes Delight
1053 Stuyvesant
Ave.
Union 07083
(908) 810-7352

Cuban Aliados
329 48th St.
Union City 07087
(201) 348-0189

Angelbecks
621 Valley Rd.
Upper Montclair
07043
(201) 744-1375

The Tobacco Store
405 Bloomfield Ave.
Verona 07044
(201) 857-2266

**Universal Cigar
Company**
707 Bloomfield Ave.
Verona 07044
(201) 857-9002

**Williams
Continental
Tobacco Shop**
137 S. Delsea Dr
Vineland 08360
(609) 692-8034

Foodtown
315 Pascack Rd.
Washington 07675
(201) 666-2185

Smoker's Delight
5213 Fairview
Terrace
West New York
07093
(201) 865-1399

Westfield Pipe Shop
214 E. Broad St.
Westfield 07090
(908) 232-2627

Stogie's Ltd
50 Madison Ave.
Westwood 07675
(201) 666-1234

JR Tobacco
301 Rte. 10 E.
Whippany 07981
(201) 882-6446

**Mr. Pipe's Smoke
Shop**
320 Woodbridge
Center
Woodbridge 07095
(908) 636-7626

**Churchill Cigar
Parlor**
4327 S. Broad St.
Yardville 08620
(609) 585-7552

New Mexico

ALBUQUERQUE

Cigarettes Cheaper!
4411 San Mateo
Blvd. Ne, Ste. E
Albuquerque 87109
(505) 872-2254

Cigarettes Cheaper!
Glenwood Village
Center, 4710
Tramway Blvd NE
#C-2
Albuquerque 87111
(505) 291-9104

Cigarettes Cheaper!
Coors Central
Center, 111 Coors
Blvd. NW
Albuquerque 87121
(505) 352-2576

Cigarettes Cheaper!
Wyoming Mall,
2268-A Wyoming
Blvd. NE
Albuquerque 87112
(505) 291-1516

Cigarettes Cheaper!
7200 Montgomery
Blvd. NE, Ste. B 5/6
Albuquerque 87110
(505) 872-0410

Kelly Liquors
2621 Tennessee NE
Albuquerque 87110
(505) 293-3270

**Pueblo Pipe Shop &
Men's Gifts**
2685 Louisana Blvd.
NE
Albuquerque 87110
(505) 881-7999

**Sagebrush Gift &
News**
2200 Sunport Blvd. NE
Albuquerque 87106
(505) 243-3100

Smokers Depot
8212 Montgomery NE
Albuquerque 87109
(505) 292-6641

**Stag Tobacconist
Ofalbuquerque**
112000 Montgomery
NE, #27
Albuquerque 87111
(505) 237-9366

**Strollers Palace
Cigar**
San Felipe Plaza, 2103
Mount Rd. NW
Albuquerque 87104
(505) 247-8780

Tinder Box #250
6600 Menaul Blvd.
NE, Ste. 381
Albuquerque 87110
(505) 883-6636

Tobacco Joe's
Cottonwood Mall,
10000 Coors NW
Albuquerque 87114
(505) 898-0237

Smokers Outlet
880 N. Main C-3
Anthony 88021
(505) 882-5208

**Lucas Pipe &
Tobacco**
Holiday Inn De Las
Cruce, 201 E.
University
Las Cruces 88001
(505) 526-3411

Cigarettes Cheaper!
Country Club Plaza.,
3301 Southern
Blvd. #401
Rio Rancho 87124
(505) 896-4103

Siano's
2318 Sudderth Dr.
Ruidoso 88345
(505) 257-9898

SANTA FE

Santa Fe Cigar Co
518 Old Santa Fe
Trail #3
Santa Fe 87501
(505) 982-1044

**Stag Tobacconist Of
New Mexico**
524 N. Guadalupe
Santa Fe 87501
(505) 982-3242

Strollers Palace Cigar
7 Montoya Circle
Santa Fe 87501
(505) 988-3739

**Strollers Palace
Cigar**
Sanbusco Market
Center,
500 Montezuma
Santa Fe 87501
(505) 982-8780

Smoke Shop
1308 Pope St.
Silver City 88061
(505) 388-5575

**Bravo Fine
Wines/Food/Spirits**
1353-A Paseo Del
Pueblo
Taos 87571
(505) 758-8100

New York

ALBANY

**Classico Cigar
Company**
14 Quary Dr., Ste. B
Albany 12205
(518) 496-0397

Coulson's
420 Broadway
Albany 12207
(518) 449-7577

Edleez Tobacco
Stuyvesant Plaza
Albany 12203
(518) 489-6872

297

Habana Premium Cigar Club
Colonie Center
Albany 12205
(518) 482-1351

The Smoker
136 Washington Ave.
Albany 12210
(518) 462-1302

The Village Tobacconist
76 Deer Park Ave.
Babylon 11702
(516) 661-8406

Stan Tobacco Emporium
2169 Grand Ave.
Baldwin 11510
(516) 378-9059

The Great Cove Deli And General Store
139 S. Clinton Ave.
Bayshore 11706
(516) 665-1372

Hamptons Tobacco
2426 Montauk Hwy.
Bridgehampton 11932
(516) 537-8247

Cigars International Limited
7 Park Pl.
Bronxville 10708
(914) 235-6868

Bernstone's Cigar Store
275 Main St.
Buffalo 14203
(716) 852-2135

Sans Souci
1783 Hertel Ave.
Buffalo 14216
(716) 836-3248

Valvano's Central News
185 S. Main St.
Canandaigua 14424
(716) 394-1176

The Party Store
540 N. Main St.
Canandaiqua 14424
(716) 394-2894

Habana Premium Cigar Shop
64-B Dunsbach Rd.
Cliffton Park 12065
(518) 371-0854

Michaelson's News & Variety
222 Guide Board Rd.
Clifton Park 12065
(518) 373-8703

Valvano's Clifton News
22 W. Main St.
Clifton Springs 14432
(716) 462-5297

One Stop Smoke Shop
6214 Jericho Tpke.
Commack 11725
(516) 462-9192

Coram Smoke Shop
337 Middle County Rd.
Coram 11727
(516) 736-1959

W E Brown & Company
6 W. Market St.
Corning 14830
(607) 962-2612

The Tobacco Smiths
297-A Main St.
Cornwall 12518
(914) 534-5317

Kristy's Smoke Shop
1836 Deer Park Ave.
Deer Park 11729
(516) 242-7421

McBurney's
716 Main St.
East Aurora 14052
(716) 652-4011

EAST HAMPTON

The Cigar Box
Parish Mews, 10 Main St.
East Hampton 11937
(516) 324-8844

Dixon Sporting Life
74 Montauk Hwy. #9
East Hampton 11937
(516) 324-7979

London Jewelers
2 Main St.
East Hampton 11937
(516) 329-3939

A & D Tobacco
2031 Jericho Tpke.
East Northport 11731
(516) 499-2330

Alaiddin's Tobacco Shop
260 Main St.
East Setauket 11733
(516) 689-9418

Hamptons Tobacco
55-D Main St.
Easthampton 11939
(516) 329-6601

Wolcott's Beverage & Tobacco
1007 Union Center Hwy.
Endicott 13760
(607) 754-4261

Bahama Bob's
135 Packetts Landing
Fairport 14450
(716) 223-7490

Fishkill Beer & Soda
169 Main St.
Fishkill 12524
(914) 897-5412

Puff-n-Stuff
161-10 Northern Blvd.
Flushing 11358
(718) 321-3908

Edleez Tobacco West
4 W. Main St.
Fredonia 14063
(716) 672-4470

Cigar Haus
31 W. 3rd St.
Freeport 11520
(516) 868-7718

Baroody's Cigar Store
372 Exchange St.
Geneva 14456
(315) 789-3133

Tobacco Plaza
70 Forest Ave.
Glen Cove 11542
(516) 671-9037

Main Street News
14 Ridge St.
Glens Falls 12801
(518) 792-4277

Cigar Shop Limited
215 Middleneck Rd.
Great Neck 11021
(516) 487-4830

Tobacco Plaza Limited
80 Northern Blvd.
Great Neck 11021
(516) 829-7134

Colonial Drugs
100 Front St.
Greenport 11944
(516) 477-1111

Tobacco King, Inc.
69 Glen Cove Rd.
Greenvale 11548
(516) 484-1875

Smoke Stax
240 N. Broadway
Hicksville 11801
(516) 938-8347

Huntington Humidor
8 New St.
Huntington 11743
(516) 423-8599

Marx Brothers Tobacconists
264 Main St.
Huntington 11743
(516) 427-2624

Townhouse Smoke
517-A E. Jericho Tpke.
Huntington Station 11746
(516) 351-7131

Pop's Wine & Spirits
265 Long Beach Rd.
Island Park 11558
(516) 431-0025

Trade Winds Cigar
454 Main St.
Islip 11751
(516) 277-6088

The Fulton County Cigar Company
21 E. Main
Johnstown 12095
(518) 762-5525

Black Dog Cigar & Gift
44 Broad St.
Kinderhook 12106
(518) 758-9150

Circle Beverage
10 Washington Ave.
Kingston 12401
(914) 331-2935

Uptown Cigar Company
42 N. Front St.
Kingston 12401
(914) 340-1142

With Pipe & Book
91 Main St.
Lake Placid 12946
(518) 523-9096

KY's Premium Imported Cigars, Pipes & Cigarettes
470 Hawkins Ave.
Lake Ronkonkoma 11779
(516) 467-8473

Coulson's
Newton Plaza, 594 Loudon Rd.
Latham 12110
(518) 785-6499

Zubair Tobacco
315 Rockaway Tpke.
Lawrence 11559
(516) 371-6213

Lindy's Smoke Shop
260 E. Sunrise Hwy.
Lindenhurst 11757
(516) 957-0287

Lynbrook Smoke Shop
839 Sunrise Hwy.
Lynbrook 11563
(516) 596-1586

Old Time Cigar & Sweets
571 Rte. 6
Mahopac 10541
(914) 621-3541

Boston Rd. Cigars
164 E. Boston Post Rd.
Mamaroneck 10543
(914) 831-4006

Mamaroneck Station Liquors
137 Halstead Ave.
Mamaroneck 10543
(914) 698-1112

Merrick Smoke Shop
3-A Hicksville Rd.
Massapequa 11758
(516) 799-7000

Main Street News
67 Main St.
Massena 13662
(315) 764-7406

S & T Smoke Shoppe
394 Old Walt Whitman Rd.
Melville 11747
(516) 549-3928

Supersale Of Melville
825 Rte. 110
Melville 11746
(516) 385-0190

Fortune Smoke Shop
1701 Merrick Rd.
Merrick 11566
(516) 868-2342

Golden Embers Tobacconists
23 North St.
Middletown 10940
(914) 343-3373

Tobacco Junction
428 Jericho Tpke.
Mineola 11501
(516) 741-3385

Empire Tobacco
Rd. 4, Box 559, Old
    Dutch Hollow Rd.
Monroe 10950
(914) 477-2290

Roth's Cigar Shop
288 Broadway
Monticello 12701
(914) 794-4460

Smokers Harbor
49 S. Moger Ave.
Mount Kisco 10549
(914) 666-2648

Jim Smoke Shop II
331 Rte. 25A
Mount Sinai 11766
(516) 331-4370

Smoke Stax
914 Jericho Tpke.
New Hyde Park 11040
(516) 354-1166

NEW YORK CITY

MANHATTAN

Alfred Dunhill
    Limited
450 Park Ave.
New York 10022
(212) 753-9292

Arnold's Tobacco
    Shop
323 Madison Ave.
New York 10017
(212) 697-1477

Barclay - Rex Inc.
7 Maiden Lane
New York 10038
(212) 962-3355

Barclay - Rex Inc.
70 E. 42nd St.
New York 10165
(212) 962-3355

Barclay - Rex Inc.
570 Lexington Ave.
New York 10022
(212) 888-1015

The Big Cigar
    Company
193-A Grand St.
New York 10013
(212) 966-9122

Cigar Emporium
541 Warren St.
New York 12534
(518) 828-5014

The Cigar Inn
1314 1st Ave.
New York 10021
(212) 717-7403

De La Concha Tobacconists

Over the last hundred years four generations of the Melendi family have been involved in the tobacco industry, from the fields to the factory to the stores in New York City and Hartford. Whether you are a novice or a connoisseur, the expertise and service at both **De La Concha** locations will complement a wide array of premium cigars and accessories.

Featuring:
- Arturo Fuente • Avo XO • Davidoff • De La Concha
- Montecristo • Por Larranaga • Puros Indios • Opus X

And the Humidors of Elie Bleu, Mastro de Paja and Savinelli

**1390 Avenue of
the Americas
New York City
212-757-3167
FAX: 212-333-3162**

**Civic Center
Hartford, CT
860-527-4291
FAX: 860-724-5571**

1-888-CIGAR-04
(2 4 4 2 7)

Member of RTDA and TAA

Visit us at our Web site: www.delaconcha.com

Cigar Landing
South Street
  Seaport, Pier 17
New York 10038
(212) 406-3886

Cigar Stop
Penn Station, Main
  Concourse, 400
  7th Ave.
New York 10001

Club Macanudo
26 E. 63rd St.
New York 10021
(212) 752-8200

Davidoff Of Geneva (NY)
535 Madison Ave.
New York 10022
(212) 751-9060

De La Concha Tobacconist
1390 Ave. of The
  Americas
New York 10019
(212) 757-3167

Eastside Cigars
969 3rd Ave.
New York 10022
(212) 755-3255

Famous Smoke Shop
55 W. 39th St.
New York 10018
(212) 221-1408

Florio
192 Grand St.
New York 10013
(212) 226-7610

Future Card
1 Whitehall St.
New York 10004
(212) 425-0198

Hamptons Tobacco
72nd & Columbus
New York 10023
(212) 279-9138

Hamptons Tobacco
at Angelo & Maxies
  Steakhouse,
  19th & Park Ave. S.
New York 10003
(212) 220-9200

Home Of Tobacco Products
133 8th Ave.
New York 10011
(212) 989-3900

H R Scott
64 Exchange Pl.
New York 10004
(212) 422-3046

Jay Kos
986 Lexington Ave.
New York 10021
(212) 327-2382

JR Tobacco
11 E. 45th St.
New York 10017
(212) 983-4160

JR Tobacco
219 Broadway
New York 10007
(212) 233-6620

Kwik Stop Convenience Store
125 Sullivan St.
New York 10012
(212) 226-2687

La Rosa Cigars
862 6th Ave.
New York 10001
(212) 532-7450

Menash Signatures
213 W. 79th St.
New York 10024
(212) 595-6161

Mom's Cigars
House Of Oxford,
  172 5th Ave.
New York 10010
(212) 243-1996

Nat Sherman
629 W. 54th St.
New York 10019
(212) 246-5500

QC Cigar Company Inc.
1 World Trade Center,
  Concourse Level
New York 10048
(718) 406-3434

Rhyme & Reason
419 Park Ave. S.
New York 10016
(212) 328-2540

Smoker's Choice
1 Beekman
New York 10038
(212) 285-0929

The Smoking Den
150 E. 39th St.
New York 10016
(212) 687-2790

The Smoking Shop
45 Christopher St.
New York 10014
(212) 929-1151

Tinder Box
Internationale
500 Lexington Ave.
New York 10017
(212) 888-5071

Trinity Smoke
160 Pearl St.
New York 10005
(212) 425-0070

Yahoo
171 W. 4th St.
New York 10014
(212) 229-0562

BRONX

La Casa Grande
Tobacco
2344 Arthur Ave.
Bronx 10458
(718) 364-4657

BROOKLYN

Barney's Smoke Shop
76 Court St.
Brooklyn 11201
(718) 875-8355

Bay Ridge Smoke
Shop
7926 5th Ave.
Brooklyn 11209
(718) 491-3608

Cigargoyles
7 Old Fulton St.
Brooklyn 11201
(718) 254-0656

86 Smoke Shop
1953 86th St.
Brooklyn 11214
(718) 714-9289

Good Newsstand
1836 Rockaway
Pkwy.
Brooklyn 11236
(718) 763-1926

JGP Cigars
9212 Third Ave.
Brooklyn 11209
(718) 238-2224

La Rouge Cigar
Society
420 64th St.
Brooklyn 11220
(718) 567-8681

See Gar
404-B 7th Ave.
Brooklyn 11215
(718) 499-8303

QUEENS

The Gift Source
90-15 Queens Blvd.
Elmhurst 11373
(718) 592-0400

45th Street Smoke
Shop
4520 Queens Blvd.
Sunnyside 11104
(718) 437-4427

B & A Newsstand
& Grocery Inc.
55-47 69th St.
Maspeth 11378
(718) 898-0044

Maspeth Express
Minimart
69-28 Grand Ave.
Maspeth 11378
(718) 397-5633

STATEN ISLAND

Carmine's Cigars
1671 Richmond Rd.
Staten Island 10304
(718) 351-6637

Empire Smoke Shop
1398 Forest Ave.
Staten Island 10302
(718) 815-4444

Tobacco & Gift
Emporium
3277 Richmond Ave.
Staten Island 10312
(718) 948-2899

Tommy's Smoke
Shop
768 Broadway
Newburgh 12550
(914) 569-9255

Mario's
2304 Pine Ave.
Niagara Falls 14301
(716) 282-4391

Supersale Of Babylon
1205 Deer Park Ave.
North Babylon 11703
(516) 242-6397

NORTHPORT

Country Tobacco
765 Rte. 25-A
Northport 11768
(516) 261-3165

Doc James Tobacco
1019 Fort Salonga
Northport 11768
(516) 757-9291

Supersales Of Northport
440 Fort Salonga Rd.
Northport 11768
(516) 368-6397

Nyack Tobacco Company
140 Main St.
Nyack 10960
(914) 358-9300

Tobacco Connection
3224 Long Beach Rd.
Oceanside 11572
(516) 763-4300

Jim's Smoke Shop
582 Sunrise Hwy. W.
Patchogue 11772
(516) 331-4370

The Brown Leaf
Kalyto Plaza,
63 E. Main St.
Pawling 12564
(914) 855-0141

Village Smoke Shope
12 E. Central Ave.
Pearl River 10965
(914) 735-2638

The Cigar Store At Jerry's
129 Wolff Lane
Pelham 10803
(914) 738-0792

Hickey's
19 S. Main St.
Pittsford 14534
(716) 385-1780

Pittsford Village Market
57 N. Main St.
Pittsford 14534
(716) 264-1060

Bryant & Friend Tobacconist
218 E. Main St.
Port Jefferson 11777
(516) 331-7478

Lee's Smoke Shop
553 Port Washington Blvd.
Port Washington 11050
(516) 883-3039

The Brewery
11 Market St.
Potsdam 13676
(315) 265-0422

O'Leary's Smoke Shop
Poughkeepsie Plaza Mall, South Rd.
Poughkeepsie 12601
(914) 471-5736

Quogue Country Market
146 Jessup Ave.
Quogue 11959
(516) 653-4191

United Smoke Shop
2 E. Market St.
Rhinebeck 12572
(914) 876-7185

ROCHESTER

Dewey Ave Smoke Shop
820 Dewey Ave.
Rochester 14613
(716) 458-8824

Havana House, Inc.
365 N. Washington St.
Rochester 14625
(716) 586-0620

House Of Bacchus
1050 Ridge Rd. E.
Rochester 14621
(716) 266-6390

J & J Newsstand
231 Irondequoit Mall Dr.
Rochester 14622
(716) 266-1870

J & J Newstand
428 Greece-Ridge Center Mall
Rochester 14626
(716) 227-0270

Park Oxford Cigar Company
365 Park Ave.
Rochester 14607
(716) 271-3850

Poco's Cigars
768 Monroe Ave.
Rochester 14607
(716) 256-1090

The Smoke Shop
149 State St.
Rochester 14614
(716) 454-2180

Twelve Corners Apothecary
1832 Monroe Ave.
Rochester 14618
(716) 244-8600

P & P Smoke Shop
600 Merrick Rd.
Rockville Center 11570
(516) 536-1513

Trinity East Smoke Shop
215 Sunrise Hwy.
Rockville Center 11570
(516) 678-1822

OJ's Coffee & Tobacco Shop
281 E. Dominic St.
Rome 13440
(315) 334-9575

The Cigar Bar
1 Bay St.
Sag Harbor 11963
(516) 725-2575

Yellow Fin @ Amazon Club
Long Warf Marina
Sag Harbor 11963
(516) 725-9000

Saratoga Cigar & Pipe
130 S. Broadway
Saratoga Springs
12866
(518) 584-4716

Saratoga Newsstand
382 Broadway
Saratoga Springs
12866
(518) 581-0133

Cigar Box Of Scarsdale
44 E. Pkwy.
Scarsdale 10583
(914) 722-4300

Mom's Cigars
1119 Central Park Ave.
Scarsdale 10583
(914) 723-3088

Orion Boutique
169 Jay St.
Schenectady 12305
(518) 346-4902

Fortune Tobacco
281 Middle Country Rd.
Selden 11784
(516) 732-1701

Doc James Tobacco
Rte. 132
Shrub Oak 10588
(800) 41SMOKE

Mr. Tobacco Store
126 E. Main St.
Smithtown 11787
(516) 724-7463

Bellezia Tobacco Shop
4549 Main St.
Snyder 14226
(716) 839-5381

Hamptons Tobacco
61 Jobes Lane
Southampton 11968
(516) 287-6653

The Market Place Smoke Shop
31 Spring Valley Market Place
Spring Valley 10977
(914) 356-3717

Maxim Smoke
406 Jericho Tpke.
Syosset 11791
(516) 921-4513

SYRACUSE

Kieffers Cigar Store
851 N. Salinas St.
Syracuse 13208
(315) 475-3988

Mallard Tobacconist
208 Walton St.
Syracuse 13202
(315) 475-5839

Olympic News Gallery
441 S. Salina St.
Syracuse 13202
(315) 424-1336

Rocky's Newsstand
447 N. Salina St.
Syracuse 13203
(315) 422-1997

Mainstreet Cigars
84 Main St.
Tarrytown 10591
(914) 366-4381

Balls Card Shop
2 Lafayette St.
Utica 13502
(315) 733-7005

Pipes Unlimited
19 Auburn Ave.
Utica 13501
(315) 735-2588

Mom's Cigars
126 E. Sunrise Hwy.
Valley Stream 11581
(516) 825-0901

Thruway Shopping Center
78 Oak St.
Walden 12586
(914) 778-3535

Sunrise Tobacco
3300 Sunrise Hwy.
Wantagh 11793
(516) 783-8646

Demar Cigar Company
Salmon Run Mall
Watertown 13601
(315) 788-3605

The Cigar Shop
605 Coffeen St.,
Carbone Plaza
Watertown 13601
(315) 779-8460

Fortune Smoke Stax
485 Hempstead
Tpke.
West Hempstead
11552
(516) 481-0280

Smokers Haven
1167 Union
West Seneca 14224
(716) 675-6195

Fortune Smoke Shop
527 Old Country
Rd.
Westbury 11590
(516) 997-8109

Hampton's Tobacco
121c Main St.
Westhampton 11978
(516) 288-2401

John David Limited
Galleria Mall, 100
Main St.
White Plains 10601
(914) 761-0180

White Plains Tobacconist
148 Mamaroneck
Ave.
White Plains 10601
(914) 761-6105

Tinder Box Store #362
8212 Transit Rd.
Williamsville 14221
(716) 689-2914

J & P Mini Mart
22 Hillside Ave.
Williston Park
11596
(516) 248-4563

Just Alan
11 Millhill Rd.
Woodstock 12498
(914) 679-5676

Ajit K Corporation
944 Central Park Ave.
Yonkers 10704
(914) 963-9826

Cigar World
777 B Central Park
Ave.
Yonkers 10704
(914) 423-0771

A Fine Cigar
Jefferson Valley
Mall, 650 Lee
Blvd.
Yorktown Heights
10598
(914) 243-4848

North Carolina

Asheboro Wholesale Grocery
228 W. Ward St.
Asheboro 27203
(910) 625-5570

Bonnie's Little Corner
1 Park Sq. SW
Asheville 28801
(704) 252-1679

Cigar Box
800 Brevard Rd.
Biltmore Sq. Mall
Asheville 28806
(704) 670-1177

First World
8213 N. Lexington
Ave.
Asheville 28801
(704) 285-9885

Pipes Limited
3 S. Tunnel
Asheville 28805
(704) 298-2392

Carving Tree Gallery
8513 Roxboro Rd.
Bahama 27503
(919) 620-9077

Expressions In Boone
641 W. King St.
Ste. 4
Boone 28607
(704) 262-1816

Highland Newsstand
240 Shadowline Dr.
Boone 28607
(704) 264-5850

International House Limited
108 Holly Hill Mall
Burlington 27215
(910) 228-0024

Pipes By George
15 The Courtyard,
431 W. Franklin St.
Chapel Hill 27516
(919) 967-5707

CHARLOTTE

Arthur's Wine Shop
Belk Department
Store, 4400
Sharon Rd.
Charlotte 28211
(704) 366-8610

Cutters Cigar Bar
Charlotte Marriot
City, 100 W. Trade
St.
Charlotte 28202
(704) 333-9000

The Humidor
316 Overstreet Mall,
200 S. College St.
Charlotte 28202
(704) 334-3449

McCranies Pipe Shop
4143 Park Rd.
Charlotte 28209
(704) 523-8554

Tinder Box
1373 E. Morehead
St., Ste. 4
Charlotte 28204
(704) 334-0480

Tinder Box
South Park Mall
4400 Sharon Rd.
Charlotte 28211
(704) 366-5164

Tinder Box
Eastland Mall, 5521
Central Ave.
Charlotte 28212
(704) 568-8798

Highland Newstand
982 Jakes Mountain
Rd.
Deep Gap 28618
(704) 262-9955

The Tinder Box
242 S. Square Mall
4001 Chapel Hill
Blvd.
Durham 27707
(919) 489-7765

Anstead Tobacco
337 Cross Creek
Mall
Fayetteville 28303
(910) 864-5705

Alpine Tobacco Limited
2A E. Main St. 2a
Franklin 28734
(704) 369-6607

GREENSBORO

GSO Wine Warehouse
2212 Battleground
Ave.
Greensboro 27408
(910) 288-2002

GSO Wine Warehouse
5002-B High Point Rd.
Greensboro 27407
(910) 299-9901

Just One More
3722-G Battleground
Ave.
Greensboro 27410
(910) 282-2900

Pleasures & Treasure
229 Four Seasons
Town Center
Greensboro 27407
(910) 855-1301

Tobacco USA
1305 Coliseum Blvd.
Greensboro 27403
(910) 292-5130

Onix Tobacco Shop
505 S. Evans St.
Greenville 27834
(919) 4130900

Village Vineyard
729 Redbanks Rd.
Greenville 27858
(919) 355-6714

The Tobacco Shop
1315 E. Main St.
Havelock 28532
(919) 447-8282

Sir Tom's Tobacco Emporium
129 W. 4th Ave.
Hendersonville
28792
(704) 697-7753

Pipes Limited
174 Valley Hills
Mall
Hickory 28602
(704) 328-8002

Pleasures And Treasures
Oak Hollow Mall,
921 Eastchester Dr.
High Point 27262
(910) 282-3023

Highlands Emporium
Town Square - Main
St.
Highlands 28741
(704) 526-1660

Highlands Wine
1 Mantian Brook Ctr.
Highlands 28741
(704) 526-5210

Northwoods Tobacco
Northwoods
Shopping Center
Jacksonville 28540
(910) 455-0629

307

Havana Day
Dreaming
2701 N. Croatan
Hwy.
Kill Devil Hill 27948
(919) 480-3934

Tinder Box
Carolina Place,
11025 Carolina
Place Pkwy.
Pineville 28134
(704) 542-6115

RALEIGH

Pipes By George
1209 Hillsborough St.
Raleigh 27603
(919) 829-1167

The Tinder Box
Crabtree Valley
Mall, 4325
Glenwood Ave.
Raleigh 27612
(919) 787-1310

Tobacconists Of
Raleigh
3901 Capitol Blvd.
Ste. 171
Raleigh 27604
(919) 954-0020

The Wine Merchant
1214 Ridge Rd.
Raleigh 27607
(919) 828-6969

Club 329
329 S. Church St.
Salisbury 28144
(704) 637-7174

JR Tobacco
67 Jr Rd.
Selma 27576
(919) 965-5055

Tobacco Road
Smoke Shop
915-1 Old Boiling
Springs Rd.
Shelby 28152
(704) 487-0621

Pinecrest Beverage
31 Pinecrest Pl.
Southern Pines
28387
(910) 695-7293

JR Tobacco
1515 E. Broad St.
Statesville 28677
(704) 872-5300
(800) 572-4427
Smokey Joes Inc.
164 Ebenezer Lane
Statesville 28677
(704) 876-0690

Davis & Sons
Smokers
Emporium
Longleaf
Mall/Shipyard
Blvd.
Wilmington 28403
(910) 791-6688

Harris Teeter
1955 N. Peace
Haven Rd.
Winston 27104
(910) 760-0116

WINSTON SALEM

Garner's Tobacco
Shop
114-E Reynolda
Village

Winston Salem
27106
(910) 725-7611

Harris Teeter #155
420-22 S. Stratford
Rd.
Winston Salem
27103
(910) 723-2305

Pipes Etc.
Thruway Shopping
Center, 385 Lower
Mall Dr.
Winston Salem
27103
(910) 723-1269

Tinder Box # 237
Hanes Mall, 3320
Silas Creek Pkwy.,
Ste. 208
Winston Salem
27103
(910) 945-9068

North Dakota

MVP Sports
114 N. 5th St.
Bismarck 58501
(701) 258-8806

FARGO

Crown Liquors
3051 25th St. S.,
Unit C
Fargo 58103
(701) 298-3260

Empire Liquor
4325 13th Ave. SW
Fargo 58103
(701) 282-2882

Happy Harry's
Bottle Shop
1125 19th Ave. N.
Fargo 58102
(701) 235-4661

Smoke Shop
1525 S. University Dr.
Fargo 58103
(701) 298-7824

Happy Harry's
2051 32nd Ave. S.
Grand Forks 58208
(701) 780-0902

Pipe Land
South Fork Plaza, 1826-P
S. Washington
Grand Forks 58201
(701) 772-2373

Market Place
Liquor
1930 S. Broadway
Minot 58701
(701) 839-7580

Oak Park Liquors
326 16th St. NW
Minot 58703
(701) 838-1529

Ohio

AKRON

The Pipe Rack
2200 Manchester Rd.
Akron 44314
(330) 745-9022

The United Cigar
Company
The Everett Bldg., 3
N. Main St.
Akron 44308
(330) 535-7474

Village Tobacconist
3265 W. Market,
Summit Mall, #202
Akron 44333
(330) 864-3929

Oakway Cigar &
Tobacco
7291 Roberts Rd.
Athens 45701
(614) 593-7169

Sirna And Sons
7307 Aurora Rd.
Aurora 44202
(216) 562-5221

Wine Reserve
16785 Chillicothe
Rd.
Bainbridge 44023
(216) 543-3339

Tinder Box #361
2727 Fairfield
Commons #103
Beaver Creek 45431
(513) 429-1172

Tobacco Wharf
3464-A New
Germany Trebein
Rd.
Beaver Creek 45431
(513) 426-0633

The Belpre News
Stand
1009 Washington
Blvd.
Belpre 45714
(614) 423-6872

BOARDMAN

Cigarette Express #1
4605 Market St.
Boardman 44512
(216) 782-0700

Cigarette World
110 Boardman -
Poland
Boardman 44512
(330) 629-9295

Plaza Book &
Smoke Shop
Boardman Plaza,
Boardman
Canfield Rd.
Boardman 44512
(330) 726-9493

Briarpatch
2880 Whipple Ave.
NW
Canton 44708
(330) 477-2511

Carey's Smokeshop
4450 Belden Village St.
Canton 44718
(330) 494-2323

Boston Stoker
Washington Square,
14 W. Whipp Rd.
Centerville 45459
(513) 439-2400

Tobacco Pouch
26 N. Main St.
Chagrin Falls 44022
(216) 247-5365

Cheese & Wine
Etc.
12613 Chillicotte Rd.
Chesterland 44126
(216) 729-7026

CINCINNATI

Burning Desires
7833 Cooper Rd.
Cincinnati 45242
(513) 984-2876

Carousel Tobacco
Shoppe
8001 Reading Rd.
Cincinnati 45237
(513) 821-5350

Cincinnati
Tobacconist
61-D Vine St.
Cincinnati 45202 .
(513) 621-9932

Kroger Company
#248
6150 Glenway Ave.
Cincinnati 45211
(513) 662-2460

The Smoke Store
2034 Madison Rd.
Cincinnati 45208
(513) 871-4367

Straus Tobacconist
410 Walnut St.
Cincinnati 45202
(513) 621-3388

Tinder Box
Tri County Mall,
11700 Princeton
Pike
Cincinnati 45246
(513) 671-8966

Tinder Box #293
4601-B 316 Eastgate
Blvd.
Cincinnati 45245
(513) 752-7359

Tinder Box #356
7875 Montgomery
Rd. #1109
Cincinnati 45236
(513) 891-3380

CLEVELAND

Back Door
Beverage
658 E. 185th St.
Cleveland 44119
(216) 383-0900

Cousin Cigar Co.
1828 Euclid Ave.
Cleveland 44115
(216) 781-9390

Dad's Smoke Shop
17112 Lorain Ave.
Cleveland 44111
(216) 671-3663

Huntington Bldg.
Cigar Store
Huntington Bank
Bldg., 925 Euclid
Ave.
Cleveland 44115
(216) 621-5420

McBill Beverages
Inc.
1015 E. 185th St.
Cleveland 44119
(216) 531-1299

Old Erie Tobacco Co.
150 The Arcade,
401 Euclid Ave.
Cleveland 44114
(216) 861-0487

Sam Klein Cigar Co.
1834 E. 6th St.
Cleveland 44114
(216) 621-2673

COLUMBUS

Barclay Pipe & Tobacco
1677 W. Lane Ave., M-12
Columbus 43221
(614) 486-4243

Barclay Tobacco & Cigar
2673 Federated Blvd.
Columbus 43235
(614) 764-0300

Beer & Wine Shop
6157 Cleveland Ave.
Columbus 43231
(614) 891-9463

The Hoster Brewing Company
550 S. High St.
Columbus 43215
(614) 228-6066

Humidor Plus
6157 Cleveland Ave.
Columbus 43231
(614) 891-9463

The Original Smokers' Haven
1097 Bethel Rd.
Columbus 43220
(614) 538-9534

Pace-Hi Carry Out
3179 N. High St.
Columbus 43202
(614) 267-1918

Pipes & Pleasures
4244 E. Main St.
Columbus 43213
(614) 235-6422

Premium Cigar Company
400 N. High St.
Columbus 43215
(614) 221-4555

Tinder Box
4236 Westland Mall
Columbus 43228
(614) 276-2904

Tobacco Discounters #6
5425 Roberts Rd.
Columbus 43026
(614) 527-0505

Vino's
6072 Busch Blvd.
Columbus 43229
(614) 431-9463

DAYTON

Bernardo's Cigar & Martini Bar
2801 S. Dixie Dr.
Dayton 45409
(937) 643-2739

Boston Stoker
8341 N. Main St.
Dayton 45415
(513) 836-2200

Smoker's Paradise/Coffee
3200 N. Main St.
Dayton 45405
(513) 277-8556

Tinder Box
2700 Miamisburg Centerville Rd.
Dayton 45459
(513) 433-2841

Tobacco Man
4958 Springboro Rd.
Dayton 45439
(513) 298-6751

Boston Stoker
University Shoppes, 2624 Colonel Glenn Hwy.
Fairborn 45324
(513) 426-1005

Jungle Jim's Markets
5440 Dixie Hwy.
Fairfield 45014
(513) 829-1918

Moniti Inc.
20550 Lorraine Rd.
Fairview Park 44126
(216) 333-0057

Girard Book & News
101 N. State St.
Girard 44420
(330) 799-1050

Tom's Cigar Store
135 Main St.
Hamilton 45013
(513) 896-1724

Oakward Kettering Smoke Shop
2970 Far Hills Ave.
Kettering 45429
(513) 294-2100

Emporium Downtown
154 W. Main St.
Lancaster 43130
(614) 653-5717

Doc's Smoke Shop
12 W. Mulberry St.
Lebanon 45036
(513) 932-5376

City News
738 Broadway
Lorain 44052
(216) 246-9097

Cigar Affair
101 E. Wayne St.
Maumee 43537
(419) 891-0109

Jo Vann's Tobacco Shop
6260 May Field Rd.
Mayfield Heights 44124
(216) 442-4775

Downtown Tobacco
44 Public Square
Medina 44256
(330) 722-9096

Molinari's Food & Wine
8900 Mentor Ave.
Mentor 44060
(216) 974-2750

Vintage & Cheese
7545 Pearl Rd.
Middleburg 44130
(216) 826-0781

Alberini's
1201 Youngstown Rd.
Niles 44446
(216) 652-5895

Ohio Cigar
410 Robbins Ave.
Niles 44446
(330) 544-7900

Tinder Box
434 Great Northern
Mall
North Olmsted
44070
(216) 572-3668

Wine World
27600 Lorain Rd.
North Olmsted
44070
(216) 779-7571

Olde Loyal Oak
Tavern & Rest.
3044 Wadsworth Rd.
Norton 44203
(330) 825-8280

Magazines & More
6436 Pearl Rd.
Parma Heights
44130
(216) 734-7637

Parma Heights
Smoke Shop
6647 Pearl Rd.
Parma Heights
44130
(216) 886-3449

La Luna
Tobacconist
1767 Hill Rd. N.
Pickerington 43147
(614) 864-6254

Revanna Cigar
Company
135 E. Main
Revanna 44266
(330) 981-0068

Minoti Inc.
198-55 Detroit
Rocky River 44140
(216) 333-4195

Cheese And Wine
Etc.
20140 Van Aken Blvd.
Shaker Heights
44122
(216) 283-7260

Arisen Merchandise
145 W. Main St.
Springfield 45502
(513) 323-1791

Paragon Cigar
Company
19016 Quail Hollow
Dr.
Strongsville 44136
(216) 572-1339

King's Rook 4 Pipe
Shop
110 E. Main St.
Tipp City 45371
(513) 667-6821

El Fumador
3065 W. Bancrost,
Ste. B
Toledo 43606
(419) 535-9990

Port Royale
3301 W. Central
Toledo 43606
(419) 537-1491

Amter Bors
Company
7825 Hub Pkwy.
Valley View 44125
(216) 642-0070

Boston Stoker
10855 Eagle Rd.
Vandalia 45377
(513) 890-6401

Low Joes Discount
Tobacco
1334 Rombach Ave.
Wilmington 45177
(937) 382-7383

Cousins Cigar
28400 Chagrin
Woodmere 44122
(216) 464-9396

City News
135 S. Market St.
Wooster 44691
(330) 262-5151

Cigarette Express #2
3814 Belmont Ave.
Youngstown 44505
(330) 759-0034

Plaza Book &
Smoke Shop
6000 Mahoning
Ave.
Youngstown 44515
(330) 799-1050

Oklahoma

Havana Leaf
Tobacco
3322 S. Broadway
Edmond 73013
(405) 330-9478

Dave's Pipe &
  Tobacco Shop
216 W. Maple St.,
  #216
Enid 73701
(405) 237-1666

Plantations
3335 W. Main
Norman 73072
(405) 364-5152

Royal Pipe &
  Tobacco
105 E. Boyd St.
Norman 73069
(405) 364-5151

OKLAHOMA
CITY

ABC Tobacco
4508 S. May
Oklahoma City
  73119
(405) 685-1716

Jose's Party Stand
10902 N. Penn Ave.
Oklahoma City
  73120
(405) 752-7380

Plantations
7000 Crossroads
  Blvd., Ste. 1128
Oklahoma City
  73149
(405) 631-2511

R & K Cigars
Quail Plaza
  Shopping Center,
  10904-J N. May
  Ave.
Oklahoma City
  73120
(405) 752-2772

Tobacco Exchange
French Market Mall,
  2828 NW 63rd
Oklahoma City
  73116
(405) 843-1688

The Tobacco Room
7400 N. May Ave.
Oklahoma City
  73116
(405) 843-1010

TULSA

Fogue & Bates Inc.
6929 E. 71st St.
Tulsa 74133
(918) 488-0818

Mecca Coffee
  Company
1143 E. 33rd Place
Tulsa 74105
(918) 749-3509

Park Hill And
  Villines Cigars
5111-A S. Lewis
Tulsa 74105
(918) 749-2229

Ric's Fine Cigars
3148 E. 11th St.
Tulsa 74104
(918) 584-1090

Ted's Pipe Shop
2002 Utica Square
Tulsa 74114
(918) 742-4996

Tobacco Pouch
5800 S. Lewis,
  Ste. 117
Tulsa 74105
(918) 742-1660

Vintage Cigar
  Company
8929 S. Memorial
  Ste. 250
Tulsa 74133
(918) 250-8999

Oregon

Cigarettes Cheaper!
Albany Plaza, 1321
  Waverly Dr. SE
Albany 97321
(541) 924-2445

Cigarettes Cheaper!
Aloha Market
  Centre, 20431 SW
  Tualatin Hwy.
Aloha 97006
(503) 642-1911

Timber Valley
  Tobaccos
3355 SW Cedar
  Hills Blvd.
Beaverton 97005
(503) 644-3837

BEND

Newport Ave.
  Market
1121 NW Newport
  Ave.
Bend 97701
(541) 382-3940

News & Smokes
3310 N. Hwy. 97
Bend 97701
(541) 330-6102

Specialty Cigar
906 NW Harrison St.
Bend 97701
(541) 389-1001

Domestic Gourmet
12044 SE Sunnyside
  Rd.
Clackamas 97015
(503) 698-3176

The Briar Shoppe
278 Valley River
  Center
Eugene 97401
(541) 343-4738

Cigarettes Cheaper!
Oregon Trail Center,
  2025 E. Burnside
Gresham 97030
(503) 666-4111

Cigarettes Cheaper!
Schoolhouse Square,
  5085 River Rd. N.
Keizer 97303
(503) 393-5436

Rick Smoke Shop
124 S. 11th St.
Klamath Falls 97601
(541) 884-0313

News & Smokes
259-C Barnett Rd.
Medford 97501
(541) 779-3900

Cascade Cigar &
  Tobacco
11103 SE Main St.
Milwaukee 97222
(503) 786-3607

Pappy's Tobacco
  Road
910-A N. Coast Hwy.
Newport 97635
(541) 265-8384

Cigarettes Cheaper!
Berry Hill Center,
19057 S. Beaver
Creek Rd.
Oregon City 97045
(503) 657-8441

PORTLAND

Burlingame Grocery
8502 SW Terwillger
Blvd.
Portland 97219
(503) 246-0711

Cascade Cigar &
Wine
528 SW Madison
Portland 97204
(503) 790-9045

Cigarettes Cheaper!
Meadowland Center,
17112 SE Powell
Blvd. #8
Portland 97236
(503) 618-7877

Cigarettes Cheaper!
7901 SE Powell Blvd.
Portland 97206
(503) 771-4849

82nd Ave. Tobacco
& Pipe
400 SE 82nd Ave.
Portland 97216
(503) 255-9987

KC's Tobacco Town
8200 SW Barber
Blvd.
Portland 97219
(503) 774-0858

Paul's Trading Co.
1409 Jantzen Beach
Center
Portland 97217
(503) 283-4924

Paul's Trading Co.
9986 SE Washington
St.
Portland 97216
(503) 255-4471

Rich Cigar Store
801 SW Alder St.
Portland 97205
(503) 228-1700

T Whittaker
Tobacco's
1123 Lloyd Center
Portland 97232
(503) 654-4812

The Tobacco Shack
6835 N. Fessenden
Portland 97203
(503) 286-4527

Redmond Smoke &
Gift
245 SW 6th
Redmond 97756
(541) 923-6307

News & Smokes
457 NW Garden
Valley
Roseburg 97470
(541) 673-1601

Ray's Food Place
500 W. Hwy. 20
Sisters 97759
(541) 549-2222

Sun River Country
Store
Sun River Village
Mall
Sun River 97707
(541) 593-8113

Tinder Box Of
Oregon
9614 SW
Washington Sq. Rd.
Tigard 97223
(503) 639-8776

Cigarettes Cheaper!
7965 Nyberg Rd.,
Tualatin
Convenience
Center
Tualatin 97062
(503) 691-7820

Pennsylvania

Johnny Montano's
3114 William Flynn
Hwy
Allison Park 15101
(412) 492-7022

Tinder Box
International
3 Bala Plaza E.,
Ste. 102
Bala Cynwyd 19004
(610) 668-4220

Tobacco World
638 B Rostraver Rd.
Belle Vernon 15012
(412) 930-0112

Keystone News
2854 Street Rd.
Bensalem 19020
(215) 638-3605

Tobacco Country
107 Neshaminy Mall
Bensalem 19020
(215) 357-6615

Tinder Box
1021 Blake St.
Bethleham 18017
(616) 882-9884

Tinder Box #371
3926 Linden St.
Bethleham 18017
(610) 882-9195

Pat's News
327 S. New St.
Bethlehem 18015
(215) 865-6233

Johnsons Pipe Shop
151 S. Hanover St.
Carlisle 17013
(717) 243-8260

JM Boswell's Pipe
& Tobacco
170 S. Main St.
Chambersburg
17201
(717) 264-1711

Smokin Joe's
Rte. 67
Choconut
(717) 553-2990

Cigarette Express
20734 Rte. 19
Cranberry Township
16066
(412) 772-7810

Classic Cigar Parlor
12 N. Main St.
Doylestown 18901
(215) 348-2880

Country Food
Market
203 W. State St.
Doylestown 18901
(215) 348-8845

Smokin Joe's
Rte. 209 N.
E. Stroudsburg
(717) 476-1123

Lu-Co
247 N. Hampton St.
Easton 18042
(610) 258-3561

Silicone Indian
Cigars
1213 Washington St.
Easton 18042
(610) 515-9991

J & S Tobacco
Emporium
211 5th St.
Ellwood City 16117
(412) 752-4929

ERIE

The Cigar Box
2661 W. 8th St.
Erie 16505
(814) 866-8018

Red Apple Smoke
Shop
Rte I-90 & Peach St.
Erie 16509
(814) 864-2641

Red Apple Store
3360 W. 38th St.
Erie 16506
(814) 833-8077

Tobaccoland
330 Mill Creek Mall
Erie 16565
(814) 868-8413

J M Cigars
27 Marchwood Rd.
Exton 19341
(610) 363-3063

Flourtown Beverage
1114 Bethlehem Pike
Flourtown 19031
(215) 233-4717

Cigar Express
5325 Rte. 8
Gibsonia 15044
(412) 449-9070

Smoke Shop
114 S Easton Rd.
Glenside 19038
(215) 886-7415

Jernigan's Tobacco
Village
Westmoreland Mall,
Rte. 30
Greensburg 15601
(412) 838-1090

Smokin Joe's
Rte. 11
Hallsted
(717) 879-8059

Pipe Den
Harrisburg East Mall
Harrisburg 17111
(717) 564-8425

Tinder Box
219 N. 2nd St.
Harrisburg 17101
(717) 232-7166

Burdick's Hatboro
News
206 S. York Rd.
Hatboro 19040
(215) 675-9960

Hatboro Beverages
201 Jacksonville Rd.
Hatboro 19040
(215) 675-1078

Tinder Box #364
391 W. Lancaster Ave.
Haverford 19041
(610) 896-511

Quik Picks & Paks
218 Laurel Mall
Hazleton 18254
(717) 459-3099

Ken's Cigar &
Tobacco
517 Allegheny St.
Hollidaysburg 16648
(814) 695-6650

Widmer's Tobacco
Shop
Macdade Mall
Holmes 19043
(610) 586-3857

Pavilion News
Bent Fox Pavilion
Jenkintown 19046
(215) 885-1881

Ye Olde Tobacco
Barrell #60
King Of Prussia Plaza
King Of Prussia
19406
(610) 265-4544

Tobacco Palace Inc.
311 Park City
Center
Lancaster 17601
(717) 397-7569

Tobacco Road
154 N. Prince St.
Lancaster 17603
(717) 293-8688

CB Perkins #119
Oxford Valley Mall,
2300 E. Lincoln
Hwy.
Langhorne 19047
(215) 750-1775

Wingenroth Pipe
Shop
638 Cumberland St.
Lebanon 17042
(717) 273-7727

The General Store
II
5323 New Falls Rd.
Levittown 19056
(215) 547-7762

Wholly Smokes
1576 Haines Rd.
Levittown 19055
(215) 946-0330

Tobacco Mart
900 Market St.
Lemoyre 17043
(717) 975-0994

Mainly Cigars
4335 Main St.
Manayonk 19127
(215) 508-1111

Rose's Newstand
117 S. Olive
Media 19063
(610) 565-9015

Migliore's Hardware
627 Midland Ave.
Midland 15059
(412) 643-8122

The Country Boys
624 W. Harford
Milford 18337
(717) 296-5000

Cigar Cellar
935 Beaver Grade Rd.
Moon Township
15108
(412) 262-7616

Pennsylvania News & Tobacco
Mill Pond Shopping
Center
Morrisville 19067
(215) 295-4004

United Cut Rate
19 E. Bridge St.
Morrisville 19067
(215) 295-3835

Tobacco World
Crossroads Plaza
Mount Pleasant
15666
(412) 547-7166

Prime Cigars
822 Montgomery Ave.
Narberth 19072
(888) PRIME 79

Klafters
216 N. Beaver St.
New Castle 16101
(412) 658-6561

A Little Taste Of Cuba
102-A S. Main St.
New Hope 18938
(215) 862-1122

Ned's Cigar Store
4 S. State St.
Newtown 18940
(215) 968-6337

Black Horse Cigars
1515 Ridge Pike
Norristown 19401
(610) 279-7676

Hill Crest Tobacco
120 W. Germantown
Pike
Norristown 19401
(610) 279-8610

Plaza News Plus
1901 Lincoln Hwy.
North Versailes
15137
(412) 824-6999

Raven Trading Company
37 S. 3rd St.
Oxford 19363
(610) 932-3100

Discount Tobacco Shop
1129 Main St.
Peckville 18452
(717) 383-6944

PHILADELPHIA

Artifax
2446 Cottman Ave.
Philadelphia 19149
(215) 331-0306

Black Cat Cigar Company
1518 Sansom St.
Philadelphia 19102
(215) 563-9850

Chestnut Smoke Shop
27 S. 8th St.
Philadelphia 19106
(215) 923-1699

Harry's Smoke Shop
15 N. 3rd St.
Philadelphia 19106
(215) 925-4770

Holts Cigar
1522 Walnut St.
Philadelphia 19102
(215) 676-8778

Mami's Pharmacy
2506 Welsh Rd.
Philadelphia 19152
(215) 464-1810

Max's Tobacconists
The Pipe Rack,
8433-C Germ-
antown Ave.
Philadelphia 19118
(215) 242-3625

Philadelphia Cigar Company
2506 Welsh Rd.
Philadelphia 19152
(215) 464-1810

Smokin-Java
524 S. 3rd St.
Philadelphia 19147
(215) 440-0776

Tobacco Junction
9961 Bustleton Ave.
Philadelphia 19115
(215) 464-2484

Tobacco Village
NE Plaza #231, 7300
Bustleton Ave.
Philadelphia 19152
(215) 745-7040

PITTSBURGH

**Bloom Cigar
Company**
54 S 12th St.
Pittsburgh 15203
(412) 431-4277

**Continental Smoke
Shop**
2210 Murray Ave.
Pittsburgh 15217
(412) 422-4444

Darla's Coffee House
8501 Perry Hwy.
Pittsburg 15237
(412) 367-8151

**Jernigan's Tobacco
Village**
2501 The Galleria,
1500 Washington
Rd.
Pittsburgh 15228
(412) 531-5881

**Market Street Cigar
Shoppe**
107 Market St.
Pittsburgh 15222
(412) 338-CGAR

**Pittsburgh Cigar
Company**
8623 Old Perry Hwy.
Pittsburgh 15237
(412) 635-7784

Poor Richard's
Freight House Shops
Station Square
Pittsburgh 15219
(412) 281-1133

Ross Park News
1000 Ross Park
Mall Dr.
Pittsburgh 15237
(412) 366-0160

**Save-more Beer &
Pop Warehouse**
4516 Browns Hill Rd.
Pittsburgh 15217
(412) 421-8550

Smoke Signals
120 S. River St.
Plains 18705
(717) 822-5058

Cole Tobaccoland
213 High St.
Pottstown 19464
(610) 323-6060

Tobacco Outlet II
201 Station Rd.
Quakertown 18951
(215) 538-3665

SCRANTON

Markowitz Brothers
256 Wyoming Ave.
Scranton 18503
(717) 342-0315

Montage Tobacco
632 Davis St.
Scranton 18505
(717) 342-3388

Sunshine News
546 Spruce St.
Scranton 18503
(717) 347-4337

El Fumador Cigars
412 Beaver St.
Sewickley 15143
(412) 741-1300

The Cigar Shop
231 E. Beaver Ave.
State College 16801
(814) 231-0828

**Kwik Fill Smokers
Outlet**
302 E. Central Ave.
Titusville 16354
(814) 726-4825

Smokers Outlet
302 E. Central Ave.
Titusville 16354
(814) 827-1104

Pete's News
Rte. 59 E., Tinga St.
Tunkhannock 18657
(717) 836-7001

Tobacco World
72 Lebanon Ave.
Uniontown 15401
(412) 438-3534

The Smoke Shop
Franklin Mall
Washington 15301
(412) 228-3266

**Smokin Joes
  Tobacco Inc.**
270 West Roosevelt
  Hwy.
Waymart 18472
(717) 282-9085

**The Tinder Box
  #286**
Century III Mall,
  3075 Clairton Rd.
West Mifflin 15122
(412) 653-1177

**Kensington
  Tobacconist**
600 Penn Ave.
West Reading 19611
(610) 373-5001

La Habana Cabana
1985 Lincoln Way
White Oak 15131
(412) 664-6002

Collins Tobacco
205 Lehigh Valley
  Mall
Whitehall 18052
(610) 264-7911

Tobacco Village
598 Whitehall Mall
Whitehall 18052
(610) 264-5371

WILKES-BARRE

El Humidor
525 Scott St.
Wilkes-Barre 18702
(717) 822-3544

Leo Matus
46 Public Square
Wilkes-Barre 18701
(717) 822-3613

Thrifty Beverage
734 San Souci Pkwy.
Wilkes-Barre 18702
(717) 823-2117

**Newberry Tobacco
  & Speciality**
2326 W. 4th St.
Williamsport 17701
(717) 322-454

Tobacco Center
21 W. Church St.
Williamsport 17701
(717) 322-7766

**Thomas & Fisk
  Speciality Shop**
204 N. Front St.
Wormleysburg
  17043
(717) 561-1969

Tobacco Land
Berkshire Mall
Wyomissing 19610
(610) 372-6571

YORK

Cigar World
3400 Eastern Blvd.,
  5-E
York 17402
(717) 840-1716

Custom Blends
2559 S. Queen St.
York 17402
(717) 741-4972

Hains Pipe Shop
225 S. George St.
York 17403
(717) 843-2237

Rhode Island

Humidor
1500 Oaklawn Ave.
Cranston 02920
(401) 463-5949

**Barbato & Sons
  Candy Co.**
65 Newport Ave.
East Providence
  02916
(401) 434-3004

Liquor Depot
1235 Wampanoag
  Trail
East Providence
  02915
(401) 433-0231

**Dapper Dave's
  Smoke Shop**
1465 Atwood Ave.
Johnston 02919
(401) 751-8499

**Bag Piper Smoke
  Shoppe**
8-A Pier Market
  Plaza
Nargansett 02882
(401) 783-0555

NEWPORT

Bridge Liquors
23 Connel Hwy.
Newport 02840
(401) 848-9200

Humidor
182 Thames St.
Newport 02840
(401) 842-0270

**Wellington Square
  Liquor**
580 Thames St.
Newport 02840
(800) 898-WINE

**Cooper's Smoke
  Shop**
742 Broadway
Pawtucket 02860
(401) 727-3198

**Moriarty Liquor
  Locker**
624 Park Ave.
Portsmouth 02871
(401) 683-4441

PROVIDENCE

Headlines
270 Wickenden St.
Providence 02903
(401) 274-6397

Olde Smoke Shoppe
130 Westminster St.
Providence 02903
(401) 272-4699

**Red Carpet Smoke
  Shop**
108½ Waterman St.
Providence 02906
(401) 421-4499

**Sir Winston's
  Tobacco
  Emporium**
341 S. Main St.
Providence 02903
(401) 861-5700

Town Wine &
   Spirits
179 Newport Ave.
Rumford 02916
(401) 434-4563

Joyal's Liquors
90 W. Warwick Ave.
West Warwick
   02893
(401) 822-0536

Up In Smoke
116 Granite Center
Westerly 02891
(401) 348-0534

South Carolina

Mud & Stogies
231 The Alley
Aiken 29801
(803) 648-9777

Pipe Dreams
Aiken Mall, 2441
   Whiskey Rd. S.
Aiken 29803
(803) 642-0080

Tobacco Corner
510 E. Dekalb St.
Camden 29020
(803) 432-4735

CHARLESTON

Harris Teeter #277
E. Bay St.
Charleston 29401
(803) 722-6821

The Smoking Lamp
197 E. Bay St.
Charleston 29401
(803) 577-7339

Tinder Box
   International
177 Meeting St.
Charleston 29401
(803) 853-3720

Tobaccos, Teas &
   Spirits
364 King St.
Charleston 29401
(803) 853-3513

COLUMBIA

4 Morganelli's Inc.
3155 Forest Dr.
Columbia 29204
(803) 787-5651

Groff Jewelers
107 Harbison Blvd.
Columbia 29212
(803) 781-6905

Palmetto Reserve
9940 Two Notch Rd.
Columbia 29223
(803) 865-0013

GREENVILLE

Boda Pipes
McAllister Square
   Mall, 225 S.
   Pleasantburg
Greenville 29607
(864) 242-1545

Harris Teeter #260
Roper Mountain Rd.
Greenville 29615
(864) 987-9103

Leaf N Match
233 N. Main St. #5
Greenville 29601
(864) 271- 9080

HILTON HEAD

The Lodge
7-C Hilton Head Plaza,
   Greenwood Dr.
Hilton Head 29928
(803) 842-8966

Low Country
   Outfitters
1533 Fording Island
   Rd., Ste. 316
Hilton Head 29926
(803) 837-6100

Stogie Express
200 Professional
   Bldg., New
   Orleans Rd.
Hilton Head 29928
(803) 341-2930

Harris Teeter #19
920 Houston N.
   Cutt Blvd.
Mount Pleasant
   29464
(803) 881-1983

MYRTLE BEACH

Dune's Wine Club
7829 N. Kings Hwy.
Myrtle Beach 29572
(803) 449-5835

Owen's Liquors Inc.
8000 N. Kings Hwy.
Myrtle Beach 29572
(803) 449-6835

Tinder Box
2501 N. Kings Hwy.
Myrtle Beach 29577
(803) 272-2336

Tinder Box
Broadway At The
   Beach, Space F-126
Myrtle Beach 29577
(803) 444-5690

Tinder Box #325
10177 N. Kings
   Hwy., Space F-126
Myrtle Beach 29577
(803) 272-2336

Smoky's Tobacco
   Shop
5720 Northwoods Mall
North Charleston
   29418
(803) 553-4447

General Store
1985 E. Main
Spartanburg 29307
(864) 585-6328

The Tobacco
   Merchant
1600 Reidville Rd.
Spartanburg 29301
(864) 587-1566

South Dakota

Doc James Tobacco
668 Main St.
Deadwood 57732
(605) 578-1969

Miller Liquors
101 Military Rd.
North Sioux City
   57049
(605) 232-4616

Hy-Ve Smoke Shop
1601 S. Sycamore Ave.
Sioux Falls 57103
(605) 334-4570

**Tobacco Road
Smoke Shop**
901 Broadway
Yankton 57078
(605) 665-7057

Tennessee

Tobacco Harbor
3051 Kirby Whitten,
Ste. 10
Bartlette 38134
(901) 382-8266

**Chattanooga
Billards Club**
110 Jordan Dr.
Chattanooga 37421
(423) 499-3883

Tobacco Mart
4011 C-3 Brainerd Rd.
Chattanooga 37411
(615) 493-9056

Briar & Bean
2801 Wilma
Rudolph Blvd.,
Governors Sq.,
Ste. 280
Clarksville 37040
(615) 552-6465

Smokin Joes
6501 Ring Gold Rd.
East Ridge 37412
(423) 490-0344

**Uptown's Smoke
Shop**
1745 Galleria Blvd.
Franklin 37064
(615) 771-7027

**The Gatlin-Burlier
Tobacconist**
603 Skyline Dr.
Gatlinburg 37738
(615) 436-9177

Cigar Depot
3133 Forest Hill,
Irene Rd., Ste. 106
Germantown 38138
(901) 755-7279

**Shamrock Beverage
& Tobacco**
300 W. Walnut St.
Johnson City 37604
(423) 926-8511

KNOXVILLE

The CEO Agenda
602 S. Gay St.
Knoxville 37902
(423) 637-0456

Imperial Smoker
111 N. Central Ave.
Knoxville 37902
(423) 546-6372

Jim's Pipes & Gifts
6925-B Maynard-
ville Hwy.
Knoxville 37918
(615) 922-3914

Smokin Joes
5236 Broadway
Knoxville 37918
(423) 281-2002

Smokin Joes
6110 Papermill Rd.
Knoxville 37919
(423) 584-9010

**Smokys Pipe &
Tobacco & Cigars**
143 Montvue Center
Knoxville 37919
(423) 693-8371

The Tobacco Box
930 Mulberry St.
Loudon 37774
(423) 458-0453

The Smoke Shop
1011 S. Galitin Pike
Madison 37115
(615) 860-8253

MEMPHIS

Lansky Brothers
92 S. Front St.
Memphis 38103
(901) 525-5401

Select Smoke Shop
5100 Poplar Ave.,
Ste. 163
Memphis 38137
(905) 685-7788

The Tobacco Bowl
152 Madison Ave.
Memphis 38103
(901) 525-2310

**Tobacco Corner
Limited**
669 S. Mendenhall
Memphis 38117
(901) 682-3326

**Tobacco Super
Store**
6063 Mt. Moriah
Rd., Ste. # 3
Memphis 38115
(901) 367-0354

Panther Pipe Shop
1937 S. Economy Rd.
Morristown 37813
(423) 581-7473

**Three Ten Pipe
Shop**
109 E. Main St.
Murfreesboro 37130
(615) 893-3100

NASHVILLE

Arcade Smoke Shop
11 Arcade
Nashville 37219
(615) 726-8031

**Elliston Place Pipe
& Tobacco**
2204 H Elliston Pl.
Nashville 37203
(615) 320-7624

Mosko's Inc.
2204 Elliston Pl.
Nashville 37203
(615) 321-3377

Smoke Depot
563 Stewart Ferry
Pike
Nashville 37214
(615) 391-4171

**Tobacco Road
Smoke Shop**
Harding Mall, 4050
Nolansville Rd.
Nashville 37211
(615) 331-7139

Uptowns Smoke Shop
3900 Hillsboro Rd.
Nashville 37215
(615) 292-6866

Texas

Bradley's Pipe & Gift
202 Cypress
Abalene 79601
(915) 673-9215

Cigar Shop & More
4285 Beltline Rd.
Addison 75244
(972) 661-9136

Red Coleman's
14733 Inwood Rd.
Addison 75240
(214) 233-8967

AMARILLO

Cowan Pipe & Tobacco
Wolftin Square N.,
2497 I-40 W.
Amarillo 79109
(806) 355-2821

The Smoke Shop
30 Western Plaza
Amarillo 79109
(806) 353-6331

Summit Wine & Spirits
3300-1 S. Coulter
Amarillo 79106
(806) 355-3072

ARLINGTON

Legacy
2203 Park Springs Ct.
Arlington 76013
(817) 469-9801

Majestic Markets
3000 Meadowbrook
Arlington 76103
(817) 275-1811

Pipe Dream Cigar/Tobacco
1308 S. Cooper St.
Arlington 76013
(817) 469-8986

Pipeline Tobacco
839 NE Green Oaks
Blvd.
Arlington 76006
(817) 461-7473

Tobacco Lane #1
2911 E. Division St.
#318
Arlington 76011
(817) 640-3210

Tobacco Lane #9
3811 S. Cooper, Ste.
2136, Parks Mall
Arlington 76015
(817) 784-0022

Smoke Signals
414 E. Maine St.
Atlanta 75551
(903) 796-8873

AUSTIN

Austin Wine & Spirits
5505 Balconies
Austin 78731
(512) 458-2244

BR News
3208 Guadalupe
Austin 78705
(512) 454-9110

Cedar Valley Liquor
12009 Hwy. 290 W. 2
Austin 78737
(512) 288-4937

Cigar Palace
121 W. 8th St.
Austin 78701
(512) 472-2277

Hansen Wine & Spirits
2300 Lohman's
Shopping Center,
#122
Austin 78734
(512) 263-7130

Heroes & Legacies
3663 Bee Caves Rd.,
Ste. 411
Austin 78746
(512) 306-8200

Heroes & Legacies
10000 Research
Blvd., Ste. 123
Austin 78759
(512) 343-6600

Pipe World
2160 Highland Mall
Austin 78752
(512) 451-3713

Pipe World
2525 W. Anderson
Lane, Ste. #501-A
Austin 78758
(512) 451-5347

Ruta-Maya Coffee Co., Inc.
218 W. 4th St.
Austin 78701
(512) 472-9637

Texas Tobacconist
115-T E. 6th
Austin 78701
(512) 479-8741

Twin Liquors
8030 Mesa Dr.
Austin 78731
(512) 346-1861

Wiggy's
1130 W. 6th
Austin 78703
(512) 474-9463

Discount Cigs & Cigars #25
9433 State Hwy. 377
Ban Brook 76126
(817) 249-0656

Butch Hoffer
136 Parkdale
Beaumont 77706
(409) 892-9311

Lucky Liquor
5820 Hwy. 105
Beaumont 77708
(409) 892-4784

C & C Beverage Center
302 S. Cedar
Borger 79007
(806) 274-2781

J.J.'s Package Stores
1219 N. Texas Ave.
Bryan 77803
(409) 822-1042

Smoker's Discount #20
605 South Bell
Blvd., Ste. F
Cedar Park 78613
(512) 331-9474

Mr. Smokes
114 Truly Plaza
Cleveland 77327
(713) 592-8586

J.J.'s Package Stores
1600 Texas Ave. S.
College Station
77840
(409) 260-2068

Cigar Specialist
10123 Stidham
Conroe 77302
(800) 244-2766

Mr. Smoke's
1029 N. Loop,
336-W
Conroe 77301
(409) 760-2727

Tobacco World
1220 Airline Rd.,
Ste. 270
Corpus Christi
78412
(512) 992-4427

D's Pipes Etc.
200N 15th St.
Corsicana 75110
(903) 874-8661

Senor Smoke II
105 Kenning Rd., #14
Crosby 77532
(713) 328-7561

DALLAS

Centennial Liquor
1827 W.
Mockingbird Lane
Dallas 75235
(214) 630-5004

**Discount Cigs &
Cigars #16**
13527 Monfort
Dallas 75240
(214) 726-9613

**Discount Cigs &
Cigars #20**
5214 E. Mockingbird
Dallas 75205
(214) 559-2221

**Edward's Pipe &
Cigar**
3307 Oak Lawn
Ave.
Dallas 75219
(214) 522-1880

**Edward's Pipe &
Cigar**
15757 Coit Rd.,
Ste. 338
Dallas 75248
(214) 774-1655

Lone Star Cigars Inc.
13305 Montfort Dr.
Dallas 75240
(972) 392-4427

Marty's
3316 Oak Lawn
Dallas 75219
(214) 520-3767

Perry's Wine Shop
9669 N. Central
Exp., Ste. 190
Dallas 75231
(214) 373-7646

**Pipe Dream Cigar
& Tobacco**
7728 S. Loop 12 #6
Dallas 75217
(214) 398-8056

**Pipe Dream Cigar
& Tobacco**
4706 Maple Ave.
Dallas 75219
(214) 520-8000

**Pipe Dream Cigar
& Tobacco**
2416 W. Ledbetter
Dallas 75233
(214) 339-7977

Pogo's Wine & Spirits
Inwood Village
Shopping Center,
5360 W. Lovers
Lane., Ste. 20
Dallas 75209
(214) 350-8989

Red Coleman's
2030 Empire Central
Dallas 75235
(214) 350-4300

Red Coleman's
7560 Greenville Ave.
Dallas 75231
(214) 363-0201

Red Coleman's
2131 W. Northwest
Hwy.
Dallas 75220
(214) 556-1611

Servi Cigar Inc.
3840 W. Northwest
 Hwy., Ste. 430
Dallas 75220
(214) 350-1496

Sigel's Beverages
2960 Anode Lane
Dallas 75220
(214) 350-1271

Sir Elliot's Tobacco
18101 Preston Rd.,
 Ste. 203
Dallas 75252
(214) 250-4650

Smokers Shoppe
1704 Commerce St.
Dallas 75201
(214) 747-6786

Tiecoon Trading
4015 Villanova
Dallas 75225
(214) 369-8437

Tobacco Club Inc.
4043 Trinity Mills
 Rd., Ste. 112
Dallas 75287
(972) 306-2880

Tobacco Gallery #2
8453 Kate St.
Dallas 75225
(214) 692-9214

Tobacco Lane
Preston Wood Mall,
 5301 Belt Line
 Rd., #2087
Dallas 75240
(972) 239-1521

The Royal Habana
 Cigar Shop
806 S. 9th St.
Edinburg 78539
(210) 318-0120

EL PASO

Airline
 International
 Luggage & Gifts
8701 Montana Ave.
El Paso 79925
(915) 778-1234

Cigar Gallery
6310 N. Mesa A-3
El Paso 79912
(915) 587-7657

Cigarette Outlet
1090 Country Club Rd.
El Paso 79932
(505) 589-9805

Pipes & Gifts
6254 Edgemere
El Paso 79925
(915) 778-5950

Tobacco Tin
Sunland Park Mall,
 750 Sunland Park Dr.
El Paso 79912
(915) 584-0945

FORT WORTH

Majestic Liquors
4520 Camp Bowie
Fort Worth 76107
(817) 731-0634

Majestic Liquors
6801 Randol Mill Rd.
Fort Worth 76112
(817) 451-8011

Majestic Liquors
5400 Mansfield Hwy.
Fort Worth 76140
(817) 478-2661

Majestic Liquors
111 Jacksboro Hwy.
Fort Worth 76147
(817) 335-5252

Smokes Etc.!
3014 Alta-Mere Dr.
Fort Worth 79116
(817) 244-9394

Tobacco Lane #8
Ridegmar Mall, 2090
 Green Oaks Rd.
Fort Worth 76116
(817) 738-6806

Tobacco Lane On
 The Square
512 Main St.,
 Ste. 110
Fort Worth 76102
(817) 284-7251

Lincoln Street Wine
 Market
111 S. Lincoln St.
Fredericksburg
 78624
(210) 997-VINE

Carol's Pipe Pub
19020 Gulf Freeway
Friendswood 77546
(713) 488-7300

Strand Market
215 Tremont
Galvaston 77550
(409) 763-5177

Hollywood Tobacco
1660 Westheimer St.
Hollywood 77006
(713) 528-0456

HOUSTON

Alfred Dunhill
 Limited
Galleria II , 5085
 Westheimer Rd.
Houston 77056
(713) 961-4661

Antique Pipe
 Shoppe
6366 Richmond
 Ave.
Houston 77057
(713) 667-1812

Avalon Discount
 Liquors & Cigars
3135 W. Holcombe
Houston 77025
(713) 662-3800

Avalon Liquors
12514 Memorial
Houston 77024
(713) 932-8000

Bobalu's Cigar
 Company
2146 Portsmouth
Houston 77098
(713) 520-8373

The Briar Shoppe
2412 Times Blvd.
Houston 77005
(713) 529-6347

Carol's Pipe Pub
13236-A NW
Freeway
Houston 77040
(713) 690-9346

Churchill &
Company
2727 Kirby Dr.
Houston 77098
(713) 523-4574

Cigars Pipes &
More
14520 Memorial Dr.,
Ste. 22
Houston 77079
(713) 493-9196

Greenway Pipe &
Tobacco
5 Greenway Plaza E.,
Ste. C-4
Houston 77046
(713) 626-1613

Hammerly Spirits
9476 Hammerly
Houston 77080
(713) 984-8210

Hearthstone
Tobacco Mart
6176 N. Hwy. 6
Houston 77084
(713) 345-9199

Houston Discount
8548 Hwy. 6 N.
Houston 77095
(713) 550-5400

Jeffery Stone
Limited
5000 Westheimer
Rd., Ste. 610
Houston 77056
(713) 621-2812

Jeffrey Stone
Limited
9694 Westheimer Rd.
Houston 77063
(713) 783-3555

Lone Star Tobacco
3741 FM 1960 W.
Houston 77068
(713) 444-2464

Mandalas
Warehouse
Liquors
4310 Richmond
Houston 77027
(713) 621-5314

McCoy's Fine
Cigars & Tobacco
1201 Louisiana,
#B-204
Houston 77002
(713) 739-8110

Paradise Gift Store
1200 McKinney, Ste.
481
Houston 77010
(713) 650-8708

Paradise Gift Store II
600 Travis, Level A
Houston 77002
(713) 228-7818

Pro Liquor
Warehouse
9442 Highway 6 S.
Houston 77083
(713) 879-8383

Richards Liquor &
Fine Wines
1701 Brun, Ste. 200
Houston 77019
(713) 529-6266

Richmond Ave.
Cigar
3301 Fondren Rd.
Houston 77063
(713) 975-9057

Smoker's Gallery
1864 Fountain View
Dr.
Houston 77057
(713) 780-9993

Spec's Warehouse
2410 Smith St.
Houston 77006
(713) 526-8787

Tobacco Center
14045 Memorial Dr.
Houston 77079
(713) 293-9211

Tobacco Habana
6513-B Westheimer
Houston 77057
(713) 266-5508

Whole Foods
Market
6401 Woodway
Houston 77057
(713) 789-4477

Wines Of America
6530 Woodway
Houston 77057
(713) 461-4497

Wines Of America
2055 Westheimer, #155
Houston 77098
(713) 524-3397

Atascocita Liquors
5311 FM 1960 E.
Humble 77346
(713) 852-4845

Tobacco Lane #2
2220 NE Mall
Hurst 76053
(817) 284-7251

Up In Smoke/
Tobacco Lane
3621 Irving Mall
Irving 75062
(972) 255-8812

Cigar Box
2501 Sw Young Dr.,
Ste. 309
Killeen 76542
(817) 526-6811

Clubs Are Us
22704 Loop 494,
Ste. F
Kingwood 77339
(713) 358-5040

Tobacco Tin
Brazos Mall, #1070
Lake Jackson 77566
(409) 297-5771

LUBBOCK

Clousseau's
1802 Buddy Holly
Ave.
Lubbock 79401
(806) 749-5282

Elwood Cigars
1113-A University
Ave.
Lubbock 79401
(806) 762-2442

Smokers Haven
1915 19th St.
Lubbock 79405
(806) 744-0017

Smokers Haven
S. Plains Mall, 6002
Slide Rd.
Lubbock 79414
(806) 799-2489

Magnolia Foods
619 Magnolia Blvd.
Magnolia 77355
(409) 356-2700

Casa Petrides
306 S. Broadway
McCallen 78501
(210) 631-5219

Tobacco Club
1705 W. University,
#115
Mckinney 75069
(972) 562-2500

Sir Elliot's Tobacco
2176 Town East
Mall
Mesquite 75150
(972) 681-4959

**Old Town
Mercantile**
201 W. Ave. G
Midlothian 76065
(972) 775-4663

Smoker's Choice
837 N. University
Nacogdoches 75963
(409) 560-5916

**Seazars Fine Wine
& Spirits**
651 S. Walnut,
Ste. A
New Braunfels
78130
(210) 829-7151

Tobacco Haus
180 W. San
Antonio St.
New Braunfels
78130
(210) 620-7473

Mr. Smokes
Lot 4 FM 1485 W.
New Caney 77357
(713) 689-7094

Tobacco House
Santa Fe Square,
3952 E. 42nd St.
Odessa 79762
(915) 367-7314

J Morgan's Tobacco
2407-A W. Arkansas
Lane
Pantego 76013
(817) 860-2343

Puff 'n' Stuff
311 Pasadena Plaza
Center
Pasadena 77504
(713) 943-0170

PLANO

Beverage City #2
1100 Preston Rd.
Plano 75093
(972) 964-8660

Black Tack
3115 Parker Rd.,
Ste. 420
Plano 75023
(972) 596-2505

Mr. G's Beverage
1453 Coit Rd.
Plano 75075
(214) 867-2821

**Smart Mart & Fine
Cigars**
3304 Coit Rd.,
Ste. 400
Plano 75023
(972) 985-6147

**Discount Cigs &
Cigars #2**
806 University
Village
Richardson 75081
(972) 235-8870

**Discount Smoke
Shop & More**
2-A Arapaho Village E.
Richardson 75080
(972) 238-8806

Colonel's Pipe Shop
3544 Knickerbocker Rd.
San Angelo 76904
(915) 944-3322

SAN
ANTONIO

The Cigar Club
17115 Fawn Brook
Dr.
San Antonio 78248
(210) 805-8580

**Cigars Solamente
Club**
205 N. Presa,
Ste. C-100
San Antonio 78205
(210) 227-3377

The Humidor
6900 San Pedro
San Antonio 78216
(210) 824-1209

The Humidor
112 N. Star Mall
San Antonio 78216
(210) 308-8545

The Humidor
204-J Alamo Plaza
San Antonio 78205
(210) 472-2875

**Joe Saglimbeni Fine
Wine**
638 W. Rhapsody #1
San Antonio 78216
(210) 349-5149

**Seazars Fine Wine
& Spirits**
14906 Jones-
Maltberger
San Antonio 78247
(210) 829-7151

**Seazars Fine Wines
& Spirits**
6422 N. New
Braunfels
San Antonio 78209
(210) 822-6094

**Hill Country
Humidor**
122 N. LBJ
San Marcos 78666
(512) 396-7473

Tobacco Gallery
4800 North Pkwy.,
Ste. 722
Sherman 75090
(903) 892-8854

**Market Wine &
Spirit**
110 N. IH 35, Ste. 175
Sound Rock 78681
(512) 310-0486

**Avalon Discount
  Liquors & Cigars**
11721 W. Bellford
Stafford 77477
(713) 495-0663

**Cynthia's Rose
  Garden**
1918 W. Ave. H
Temple 76504
(817) 771-3388

**The Beverage
  Shoppe**
The Woodlands,
  4775 W. Panther
  Creek, C-300
77381
(713) 363-9463

Don's Humidor
1412 N. Valley Mills
  Dr.
Waco 76710
(817) 772-3919

The Smoke Ring
17050 Hwy. 3
Webster 77598
(713) 332-9871

Cigars Tobacco Etc...
4208 Kemp Blvd.
Wichita Falls 76308
(817) 691-2347

Aroma's
4936 Windsor Hill
Windcrest 78239
(210) 590-1802

Utah

**Tobacco Products
  International**
4227 S. Highland
  Dr. #8
Holladay 84124
(801) 278-8508

**The Tinder Box
  #124**
Fashion Place Mall,
  6191 S. State #381
Murray 84107
(801) 268-1321

**Crawford-Bennett
  Trading**
419 Main St.
Park City 84060
(801) 649-0101

SALT LAKE
CITY

**Jeanie's Smoke
  Shop**
156 S. State St.
Salt Lake City 84111
(801) 322-2817

**Knuckleheads
  Tobacco & Gifts**
443 E. 4th S.
Salt Lake City 84111
(801) 533-0199

Tinder Box
2A26 Crossroads Plaza,
  50 S. Main St.
Salt Lake City 84144
(801) 355-7336

Vermont

**Smoker's Den and
Discount Beverage
  Center**
214 Hunt St.
Bennington 05201
(802) 442-2861

**Garcia Tobacco
  Shop**
Burlington Square
  Mall
Burlington 05401
(802) 658-5737

Orvis
Historic Rte. 7A
Manchester 05254
(802) 362-3750

Sam Frank Inc.
15 Center St.
Rutland 05701
(802) 773-7770

Lilydale Inc.
1350 Shelburne Rd.,
  Ste. 270
South Burlington
  05403
(802) 658-5896

**Queen City Coins
  Inc.**
1174 Williston Rd.
South Burlington
  05403
(802) 864-7840

Discount Beverage
157 Marlboro Rd.
West Brattleboro
  05301
(802) 254-950

The Hermitage
457-B Cold Brook Rd.
Wilmington 05363
(802) 464-3511

Virginia

ALEXANDRIA

**Cigar Club
International**
2869 Duke St.
Alexandria 22314
(703) 823-2234

**John Crouch
  Tobacconist**
215 King St.
Alexandria 22314
(703) 548-2900

Total Beverage
Landmark Plaza,
  6240 Little River
  Tpke.
Alexandria 22312
(703) 941-1133

ARLINGTON

The Cigar Vault
1500 Wilson Blvd.
Arlington 22209
(703) 276-7225

**The Cigar Vault
  (crystal City)**
Century Mall, Ste.
  109, 2341 Jefferson
  Davis Hwy.
Arlington 22202
(703) 413-8727

Tobacco Barns
Fashion Centre
Pentagon City,
  1200 S. Hayes St.
Arlington 22202
(703) 415-5554

**Silk Leaf
  Connection**
106 S. Center St.
Ashland 23005
(804) 798-4667

Tobacco Alley
120 Wilson St.
Blacksburg 24060
(540) 951-3154

**Side Track Tobacco
Shop**
300 Randall St.
Expy.
Bristol 24201
(540) 466-8450

The Cigar Vault
Centreville Square
Shopping Center,
14011-B St.
Germain Dr.
Centreville 22020
(703) 968-9102

Total Beverage
Greenbriar Twin
Center, #13055-C
Lee Jackson Hwy.
Chantilly 22035
(703) 817-1177

CHARLOTTESVILLE

**Artesanias
Mexicanas**
Carmelita's, 316 E.
Main St.
Charlottesville
22902
(804) 979-0936

Cavalier Pipe Shop
1100 Emmet St.
Charlottesville
22901
(804) 293-6643

Tobacconist & Gift
214 Zan Rd.
Charlottesville
22905
(804) 973-9065

Harris Teeter #176
Greenbriar Mkt.,
1216 Greenbriar
Pkwy.
Chesapeake 23320
(757) 382-7300

The Mug & Chalice
6523 Centralia Rd.
Chesterfield 23832
(804) 796-5552

Cigarette City
595 S. Park Blvd.
Colonial Heights
23834
(804) 520-4426

Tobacco Barn
2626 Riverside Dr.
Danville 24541
(804) 797-9055

**John B. Hayes
Tobacconist**
11755-L Fair Oaks
Mall
Fairfax 22033
(703) 385-3033

Tobacco Barns
6208-K Leesburg
Pike
Falls Church 22044
(703) 536-5588

**Fredericksburg
News & Tobacco**
719-A Caroline St.
Fredericksburg
22401
(540) 373-3727

The Tobacco Bar
Westwood Center,
1915 Plank Rd.
Fredericksburg
22401
(540) 373-4533

Stogies
4040-F Cox Rd.
Glen Allen 23060
(804) 527-1919

The Wine Seller
9912-C Georgetown
Pike
Great Falls 22066
(703) 759-0430

The Smoke House
47 E. Queensway
Hampton 23430
(757) 722-4185

Peace Pipe Inc.
2193 S. Main St.,
Dukes Plaza
Harrisonburg 22801
(540) 433-7473

**Leesburg Emporium
& Smoke Shop**
205 Harrison St. SE
Leesburg 20175
(703) 777-5557

**Washington Street
Purveyors**
9 E. Washington St.
Lexington 24450
(540) 464-9463

Special Somethings
6536 Richmond Rd.
Lightfoot 23090
(804) 564-8346

Cafe France
3225 Old Forest Rd.
Lynchburg 24501
(804) 385-8989

**Opera House
Gourmet**
9084 Center St.
Manassas 20110
(703) 330-9636

Tobacco Barns
Manassas Mall, 8300
Sudley Rd.
Manassas 20109
(703) 330-9753

MCLEAN

The Cigar Club
1774-U Int'l. Dr.
McLean 22102
(703) 734-4303

**Georgetown
Tobacco**
Tysons Corner
Center
McLean 22102
(703) 893-3366

**The Ritz Carlton
Gift Shop**
1700 Tysons Blvd.
McLean 22102
(703) 506-4300

NORFOLK

**Emerson's Fine
Tobacco**
880 N. Military Hwy.
Norfolk 23502
(757) 461-6848

**Emerson's Fine
Tobacco**
116 Granby St.
Norfolk 23510
(757) 624-1520

West Side Wine
Shop
4702 Hampton Blvd.
Norfolk 23508
(804) 440-7600

RICHMOND

The Cigarette Store
6841 Forrest Hill
Ave.
Richmond 23225
(804) 323-6413

Island Tobacco &
Gifts
1601 Willow Lawn
Dr., Ste. 229
Richmond 23230
(804) 285-5604

Tinder Box #224
3 James Center,
1051 E. Cary St.
Richmond 23219
(804) 343-1827

Tobacco House
Limited
3138 W. Cary St.
Richmond 23221
(804) 353-4675

Tobacconist Of
Richmond
11521 H Midlothian
Tpke.
Richmond 23235
(804) 378-7756

Harris Teeter #95
Towers Shopping
Center, 2121
Colonial Ave. SW
Roanoke 24015
(703) 342-1017

Milan Brothers
106 S. Jefferson St.
Roanoke 24011
(540) 344-5191

The Cigar Vault
Concord Shopping
Center, 6127-D
Backlick Rd.
Springfield 22150
(703) 644-9442

Tobacco Barns
6568 Springfield
Mall
Springfield 22150
(703) 971-1933

J.B. Sims Fine
Tobaccos III
20789 Great Falls
Plaza #170
Sterling 20165
(703) 450-4055

Baskets By Design
800 W. Washington
Suffolk 23434
(757) 934-8550

VIRGINIA
BEACH

Atlantic Dominion
5400 Virginia Beach
Blvd.
Virginia Beach
23462
(804) 497-1001

J & M Imports
2973 Shore Dr., Unit
#104
Virginia Beach
23451
(804) 496-5500

P J Baggan Wine
960 Laskin Rd.
Virginia Beach
23451
(804) 491-8900

Ophelia's
28½ E. Piccadilly St.
Windchester 22602
(540) 722-2756

York Tobacco
Company
2231 Rte. 17
Yorktown 23693
(757) 596-2120

Washington

Hands Of Time
Cigar Company
E. 261 Rangier Ct.
Allyn 98524
(360) 275-9615

Trading Post @
March Point
823 S March Point
Rd.
Anacortes 98221
(360) 293-5632

Irby's Fine Cigars
713 W. Main St.,
Ste. 107
Battleground 98604
(360) 666-4877

BELLEVUE

Pete's Eastside
134 105th Ave. NE
Bellevue 98004
(206) 454--1100

Seattle Cigar
10116 NE 8th
Bellevue 98004
(206) 455-0870

Seattle Cigar
3550 128th SE
Bellevue 98006
(206) 643-7110

Seattle Cigar
15600 NE 8th
Bellevue 98008
(206) 865-0282

Tinder Box #316
10150 Main St.
Bellevue 98004
(206) 451-8544

Cigarettes Cheaper!
Sunset Square
Center, 1155 E.
Sunset Dr. #110
Bellingham 98226
(360) 671-9940

Fairhaven Smoke
Shop
1213 Harris Ave.
Bellingham 98225
(360) 647-2379

Seattle Cigar
14130 Juanita Dr. NE
Bothel 98011
(206) 821-4885

Seattle Cigar
22833 Bothel-
Everett Hwy.
Bothel 98021
(206) 485-1991

Cigarettes Cheaper!
Bothell Center.,
18827 Bothell
Way NE #104
Bothell 98011
(206) 806-9560

M & R Tobacco
202 S. Tower St.
Centralia 98531
(360) 736-4933

**G & W Cigar &
Tobacco**
950 Post Lane
Clarkston 99403
(509) 758-6247

Seattle Cigar
22828 100th W.
Edmonds 98020
(206) 775-0542

Seattle Cigar
1009 Monroe St.
Enumclaw 98022
(360) 825-5155

**The Great Northwest
Trading Company**
2908 Wetmore Ave.
Everett 98201
(206) 339-2614

Smokin' Sams
12811 8th Ave. W. E-101
Everett 98204
(206) 347-1971

FEDERAL WAY

Cigarettes Cheaper!
Hillside Plaza, 2106
S. 314th St.
Federal Way 98003
(206) 529-4768

**International Cigar
Store**
31840 Pacific Hwy.
S., Ste. A
Federal Way 98003
(206) 946-5016

Seattle Cigar
31217 Pacific Hwy. S.
Federal Way 98003
(206) 941-0818

Seattle Cigar
5010 Pt. Fosdick Dr.
NW
Gig Harbor 98335
(206) 851-3900

ISSAQUAH

Fine Wines Limited
710 NW Gilman
Blvd., Ste. D-112
Issaquah 98027
(206) 392-6242

Seattle Cigar
1540 Gilman Blvd.
Issaquah 98027
(206) 392-4475

Seattle Cigar
2902 228th Ave. SE
Issaquah 98029
(206) 391-4680

The Briar Shop
313 Columbia
Center
Kennewick 99336
(509) 783-6928

Cigarettes Cheaper!
Panther Lake
Center, 20512
108th Ave. SE
Kent 98031
(206) 859-7110

Smoker's Choice
24817 Pacific Hwy.
S., Ste. 203
Kent 98032
(206) 641-8421

KIRKLAND

The Grape Choice
220 Kirkland Ave.
Kirkland 98033
(206) 827-7551

Seattle Cigar
211 Park Place
Center
Kirkland 98033
(206) 827-2205

Seattle Cigar
11224 NE 124th St.
Kirkland 98034
(206) 821-8502

Smoke 'n' Cigar
12443-116th Ave. NE
Kirkland 98034
(206) 814-8149

Smoker's Choice
13520 100th Ave.
NE #40
Kirkland 98034
(206) 823-9232

Le Bon Vie
5826 Pacific Ave. S.,
Ste. A
Lacey 98503
(360) 493-1454

**H G Tobacco &
Snuff**
5800 198th St., #J
Lynnwood 98036
(206) 774-4002

Tinder Box
222 Alderwood
Mall, 3000 184th
St. SW
Lynnwood 98037
(206) 771-8418

Seattle Cigar
22131 SE 237th
Maple Valley 98038
(206) 432-9961

Smokin' Deal #1
1227-A State Ave.
Marysville 98270
(360) 653-0182

Seattle Cigar
8421 SE 48th
Mercer Island 98040
(206) 232-0102

Seattle Cigar
7823 SE 28th
Mercer Island 98040
(206) 230-0745

Seattle Cigar
926 164th SE
Mill Creek 98012
(206) 742-3240

Valley Blends
1722 Riverside Dr.
Mount Vernon 98273
(360) 424-6365

Seattle Cigar
11700 Mukilteo
Speedway
Mukilteo 98275
(206) 290-6166

Seattle Cigar
6940 Coal Creek
Pkwy. SE
Newcastle 98059
(206) 747-9599

Cigarettes Cheaper!
Olympia Square,
3530 Pacific Ave.
SE #F2
Olympia 98502
(360) 413-3914

The Spar Cafe Bar
& Tobacco
Merchant
114 E. 4th Ave.
Olympia 98501
(360) 357-6444

REDMOND

Seattle Cigar
15800 Redmond
Way NE
Redmond 98052
(206) 885-2311

Seattle Cigar
8867 161st Ave. NE
Redmond 98052

Smoker's Choice
15161 NE 24th St.
Redmond 98052
(206) 641-8421

Seattle Cigar
14030 SE Petrovitsky
Renton 98058
(206) 235-5118

SEATTLE

Arcade Smoke Shop
1522 5th Ave.,
Ste. 101
Seattle 98101
(206) 587-0159

Cigars To Go
7710 18th Ave. NW
Seattle 98117
(206) 784-4494

Downtown Cigar
Store
310 Columbia St.
Seattle 98104
(206) 624-2794

G & G Cigar Store
Inc.
Smith Tower, 504
2nd Ave.
Seattle 98104
(206) 623-6721

International Cigars
& News
1522 3rd Ave.
Seattle 98101
(206) 382-9284

Kirsten Limited
1900 W. Knickerson,
Ste. 112
Seattle 98119
(206) 286-0851

Larry's Market
100 Mercer St.
Seattle 98109
(206) 213-0778

Market Tobacco
Patch & Games
1906 #6 Pike Place
Seattle 98101
(206) 728-7291

Nickel Cigar
89 Yesler Way
Seattle 98104
(206) 622-3204

Pete's Supermarket
58 E. Lynn
Seattle 98102
(206) 322-2660

Seattle Cigar
523 Broadway E.
Seattle 98102
(206) 322-8200

Seattle Cigar
8532 15th Ave. NW
Seattle 98117
(206) 783-0770

Seattle Cigar
1600 W. Dravus
Seattle 98119
(206) 283-3600

Seattle Cigar
11100 Roosevelt
Way NE
Seattle 98125
(206) 361-4849

Seattle Cigar
100 Republican
Seattle 98109
(206) 285-5491

Seattle Cigar
2746 NE 45th
Seattle 98105
(206) 523-5160

Seattle Cigar
2500 SW Barton
Seattle 98126
(206) 935-0585

Smoke Plus
1432 4th Ave.,
Ste. 622
Seattle 98101
(206) 622-1521

Tom's University
Smoke Shop
4140 University
Way NE
Seattle 98105
(206) 632-9260

Seattle Cigar
990 E. Washington
Ave.
Sequim 98382
(360) 683-1151

Thomas D's
Kitsap Mall, Box
3203
Silverdale 98383
(206) 692-0681

Tobacco World
W. #621 Mallon Ave.
Spokane 99201
(509) 326-4665

University Pipe
Square
703 University City
Mall
Spokane 99206
(508) 928-9531

TACOMA

Cigarettes Cheaper!
Discovery Place
Center., 6409 6th
Ave., Ste. H
Tacoma 98406
(206) 566-3733

Mike's Smoke Shop
101 Pioneer Way E.
Tacoma 98404
(206) 627-8959

Puro Mundo
763 Broadway
Tacoma 98402
(206) 272-0565

Seattle Cigar
4101 49th Ave. NE
Tacoma 98422
(206) 925-5040

Tinder Box #168
Tacoma Mall #1131,
4502 S. Steele St.
Tacoma 98409
(206) 472-9993

The Tinder Box #141
751 S. Center
Tukwila 98188
(206) 243-3443

Kev's Cigars & Tobacco
16420 W.
McGillivray, Ste. 103-132
Vancouver 98683
(360) 883-4966

Vashon Thriftway
9740 SW Bark Rd.
Vashon Island 98070
(206) 463-2100

Little Brown Smoke Shack
3201 Goodman Rd.
Yakima 98903
(509) 457-6404

Wisconsin

The Cigar Vault
10 Cottage Ave.,
Ste. 206
Appleton 54911
(414) 954-8984

Jack's Tobacco And Mcs
Brookfield Plaza
Shopping Center.,
13640-A W.
Capitol Dr.
Brookfield 53005
(414) 783-7473

V Richards
17165 W.
Bluemound Rd.
Brookfield 53005
(414) 784-8303

Otto's Wine Cask Inc.
4600 W. Brown Deer
Rd.
Brown Deer 53223
(414) 354-5831

The Coffee Grounds
3460 Mall Dr.
Eau Claire 54701
(715) 834-1733

Elm Grove Liquor
15380 Watertown
Plank
Elm Grove 53122
(414) 784-3545

Bosse's News & Tobacco
220 Cherry St.
Green Bay 54301
(414) 432-8647

Tobacco World
4818 S. 76th St.
Greenfield 53220
(414) 281-1935

Andrea's Tobacconist
2401 60th St.
Kenosha 53140
(414) 657-7732

Briar Patch
519 Main St.
La Crosse 54601
(608) 784-8839

MADISON

Aficionado
702 N. Midvale
Blvd.
Madison 53075
(608) 236-0555

Capital First Cigars
20 S. Carroll St.
Madison 53703
(608) 259-9959

Gerhardt Drugs
4620 Cottage
Grove Rd.
Madison 53716
(608) 221-3688

Knucklehead's
254-A W. Gilman St.
Madison 53703
(608) 284-0151

The Tobacco Bar
6613 Seybold Rd.
Madison 53719
(608) 276-7668

MILWAUKEE

Bert's In Bay View
2523 E. Oklahoma
Ave.
Milwaukee 53207
(414) 744-8478

Downer Wine Shop
2638 N. Downer Ave.
Milwaukee 53211
(414) 332-0880

East Town
Pharmacy
788 N. Jefferson St.,
Ste. 103
Milwaukee 53202
(414) 271-4441

Edward's Pipe &
Tobacco
400 W. Silver Spring
Dr.
Milwaukee 53217
(414) 964-8212

Green Tree Liquors
6945 N. Point
Washington Rd.
Milwaukee 53217
(414) 352-8282

Metropolitan Liquor
5350 N. Sherman
Blvd.
Milwaukee 53209
(414) 463-9710

Uhle's Pipe Shop
114 W. Wisconsin
Ave.
Milwaukee 53203
(414) 273-665

Fox River Brewing
& Cigar
1501 Arboretum Dr.
Oshkosh 54901
(414) 232-2334

Kwik Spirits Liquor
Store & Smoke
Shop
1903 S. Main St.
Rice Lake 54868
(715) 234-6116

Country
Gentlemans
Smoke Shop
216 S. Main St.
River Falls 54022
(715) 425-7478

The Ambassador
327 W. Main St.
Waukesha 53186
(414) 547-9009

Swan-Serv U
Pharmacy
9130 W. North Ave.
Wauwatosa 53226
(414) 258-9550

West Virginia

Budget Tapes &
Records
3708 McCorkle
Charleston 25304
(304) 925-8273

Grandma Treasures
615½ E. Washington St.
Charleston 25414
(304) 728-2199

The Squire Tobacco
Unlimited
30 Capitol St.
Charleston 25301
(304) 345-0366

La Fontaine's
Tobacco
Frederick Bldg.
Lobby, 940 4th
Ave., Ste. 102
Huntington 25701
(304) 523-7879

Stephen Street
Emporium
306 W. Stephen St.
Martinsburg 25401
(800) 249-9130

East Gate Mini
Mart
55½ S. University
Ave.
Morgantown 26505
(304) 291-6930

Crumbakers
232 Grand Central
Mall
Parkersburg 26101
(304) 422-3393

Gumby's Cigarettes
95 Edgington Lane
Wheeling 26003
(304) 242-0002

Wyoming

Lane's Tobacco &
Gifts
Eastridge Mall, 601
SE Wyoming Blvd.
Casper 82609
(307) 577-5209

Tobacco Row
120 N. Cache
Jackson 83001
(307) 733-4385

INTERNATIONAL

Andorra

La Casa del Habano
Plaça Co-Princeps
Escaldes-Ergordany
Andorra La Vella
376 869 225

Argentina

La Casa del Habano
Viamontes No. 524
1st Floor, Apt. 1
Buenos Aires
54 1 315 4085

RC Gift Shop &
Drug Store
Windham Aruba
Resort-Lower
Lobby Shopping
Arcade
Oranjestaad
297 825 699

Aruba

La Bonbonniere
Holland Aruba Mall,
Havenstraat No. 6
Oranjestaad
297 8 20297

La Casa del Habano
Royal Plaza
Oranjestaad
297 8 25355

Australia

Benjamin's &
Daniel's Fine
Shop
10 Strand Central,
250 Elizabeth St.
Melbourne
61 3 966 3289

J & D Of
Alexander's
7A-459 Toorak Rd.,
Toorak 3142
Melbourne
61 9827 1477

Austria

Christian Kozlik
C.A.C. St Veit-
Gasse 22
Vienna 1130
43 1 876 6449

FOR THOSE WHO ENJOY THE FINER THINGS IN LIFE

• The finest hand-made cigars from around the world are available in our walk-in humidor.
  (Cuban, Dominican, Jamaican, etc.)
• A wide selection of desk and travel humidors, cigar cases, cutters,lighters, and accessories to
  compliment them.
• An extensive selection of pipes and smoking goods from the finest manufacturers worldwide.
• Exclusive Gentlemenís Gifts and Board Games

WHY NOT COME IN AND SEE OUR RANGE OF PRODUCTS

J&D of ALEXANDERS

SHOP 7A, TOK H CENTRE • 459 TOORAK ROAD • TOORAK 3142
PHONE: (613) 9827- 1477 • FAX: (613) 9827- 0266
Free call in Australia 1-800-635-505

Unternehmens-bereich Wein
Ikera Warenhandels Gmbh,
Maculangasse 6
Vienna A1220
43 1 250 55 630

Bahamas

La Casa del Habano
Hotel Graycliff
Nassau
(809) 322-2796

Pink Flaimingo Trading Company
Bay & Charlotte Sts.
Nassau
(809) 322-7891

Tropique International Smoke Shop
Marriot Crystal Palace Casino
Shopping Arcade,
W. Bay St.
Nassau
(809) 327-7292

Bahrein

La Casa del Habano
Le Royal Meridiem,
Shop #8
Manama
973 580 400

Bermuda

Chatham House
63 Front St.
Hamilton HM11
(441) 292-8422

The Dockyard Humidor
Hamilton HMPX
(441) 295-3961

La Tienda De Tabaco
The Emporium Building, 69 Front St.
Hamilton
(441) 292-4411

Tobacco Associates, Ltd.
Corner of Victoria & Parliament Sts.
Hamilton
(441) 292-4411

Brazil

La Casa del Habano
Alameda Lorena
1821
Sao Paulo
01424-002
55 11 883 7344

Ranieri Pipes
Alameda Lorena
1221
Sao Paulo CEP 0142
55 11 577 5420

British Virgin Islands

Fort Wine & Spirits
1 Chalwell St.
Road Town, Tortola
(809) 494-2388

Canada

ALBERTA

Shefield & Sons Tobacconist
West Edmonton Mall, Unit 1842,
8770 170 NW
Edmonton T5T 3J7
(403) 444-1104

BRITISH COLUMBIA

Casa De Malahato
@ Malahat Chalet,
265 Malahat Dr.
Malahat V0R 2L0
(604) 478-0812

Shefield & Sons Tobacconist
320-A 4741 Lakelse Ave.
Terrace V8G 1R5
(604) 635-9661

VANCOUVER

Alpha Tobacco
927 Denman St.
Vancouver V6G 2L9
(604) 688-1555

B & J's Daily Stop
925 Davie St.
Vancouver V6Z 1B9
(604) 687- 5954

R.J. Clarke Tobacconist
3 Alexander St.
Vancouver V6A 1B2
(604) 681-8021

Vancouver Cigar Company
1938 W. Broadway.
Vancouver V6J 1Z2
(604) 737-1313

Shefield & Sons Tobacconist
712 Park Royal N.
West Vancouver
V7T 1H9
(604) 926-7011

Memories
4249 Village Stroll
Whistler V0N 1B0
(604) 932-6439

MANITOBA

Thomas Hinds Tobacconist
96-185 Carlton St.
Winnipeg R3C 3JI
(204) 942-0203

NOVA SCOTIA

MacDonald Tobacco & Gifts
Barrington Mall,
1903 Barrington St.
Halifax B3J 3L7
(902) 429-6872

ONTARIO

Smalley's Cigar Store
132 Hurontario St.
Collingwood L9Y 2L8
(705) 445-1666

Havana Tobacconist
Stone Road Mall,
435 Stone Rd.
Guelph N1G 2X6
(519) 837-9193

The King City Outpost
Hwy. 400 N.
King City L0G 1KO
(905) 832-2305

Thomas Hinds
 Tobacconist
8 King St.
Kitchener N2G 2K6
(519) 744-3556

LONDON

Cuban Pete Cigar
 Company
609 Richmond St.
London N6A 3G3
(519) 641-8919

Smoker's Factory
 Outlet
38 Adelaide St. N.
London N6B 4N0
(519) 679-8445

Wiff N Puff
Westmount
 Shopping Center,
 785 Wonderland
 Rd.
London N6K 1M6
(519) 472-1244

Copa-Habana
 Cuban & World
 Cigars
5930 Victoria Ave.,
 Unit #4
Niagara Falls L2G
 3L8
(905) 354-4530

Copa-Habana
 Cuban & World
 Cigars/Cigar Bar
6580 Lundys Lane
Niagara Falls L2J
 3X1
(905) 374-1103

Real Fakes
14402 Niagara Pkwy.
Queenstown L0S
 1L0
(905) 262-5904

Havana Tobacconist
Stone Rd. Mall, 435
 Stone Rd.
Quelph N1Q 2X6
(519) 837-9193

TORONTO

Groucho &
 Company
150 Bloor St. W.
Toronto M5S 2X9
(416) 922-4817

Havana House
87 Avenue Rd.
Toronto M5R 3R9
(416) 927-9070

Thomas Hinds
 Tobacconist
8 Cumberland St.
Toronto M4W IJ5
(416) 927-7703

Thomas Hinds
 Tobacconist
392 Eglinton Ave. W.
Toronto M5N 1A2
(416) 481-6909

Tobacco Haven
595 Bay St.
Toronto M5C 2C2
(416) 593-6655

Touch Of Class
630 Mt. Pleasant
Toronto M4S 2N1
(416) 487-5535

The Wine
 Establishment
250 The Esplanade
 #104
Toronto M5A 1J2
(416) 861-1462

Havana Tobacconist
Bayview Village
 Shopping Center,
 2901 Bayview Ave.
Willowdale M2K 1E6
(416) 733-9736

La Casa del Habano
473 Ouelette Ave.
Windsor
(519) 254-1482

QUEBEC

Davidoff
1452 rue
 Sherbrooke W.
Montreal H3G 1K4
(514) 289-9118

La Casa del Habano
1434 rue
 Sherbrooke W.
Montreal H3G 1K4
(514) 849-0037

Vinum Design
1480 City Councilor
Montreal H3A 2E5
(514) 985-3200

SASKATCHEWAN

**Cigar Venue On
Louise Ave.**
1038 Louise Ave.
Saskatoon S7H 2P6
(306) 249-4321

Cuba

La Casa del Habano
Fábrica Partagás,
Industria No. 520
Habano Vieja
537 33 8060

La Casa del Habano
Museo del Tabaco,
Mercaderes No.
120
Habano Vieja

La Casa del Habano
Ave 1ra. ESQ. 64
Varadero, Matanzas
537 5 66 7843

Cyprus

La Casa del Habano
Riga Fereou, Str. #4
Limassol
357 5 747 341

Czech Republic

La Casa del Habano
Hotel
Intercontinental,
Nam Curieovych
43/5
11000 Prague 1
42 2 488 1544

Denmark

**Alfred & Christian
Petersen A/S**
Norgesvej 10
Horsens DK-8700
45 7 561 2000

W.O. Larsen A/S
9 Amagertorv
Copenhagen DK-
1160
45 3 312 2050

Egypt

La Casa del Habano
Hotel Semiramis
Intercontinentale
Cairo
20 2 354 9608

France

La Casa del Habano
169 Blvd. St. Germain
75006 Paris
33 1 45 49 2430

La Cave à Cigares
14 Blvd. Haussmann
75009 Paris

**La Civette des
Quatre Temps**
Centre Commercial
Des 4, Casier 102,
Cedex 25
92092 Paris
33 1 47 747 528

Germany

Dachauer Str. 7
Filiale Bauerstr 1-U,
Turkenstr.
Munich 43 80335
49 89 550 4448

Pfeifen Archiv
Cal Wer Passage
Stuttgart
49 711 2991555

Alte Tabakstube
Schillerplatz 4
Stuttgart
49 711 292729

Greece

**La Casa Del
Habano**
1-3 Spyromiliov St.
Athens 10564
30 1 32 35 325

Hong Kong

Cohiba Cigar Divan
The Mandarin
Oriental Hotel
Hong Kong
852 2522 0111, ext.
4074

Hungary

**Magyar
Szivarforgalmazas**
Tuzer Ut Ca 43
Budapest 4-1134
36 3055 2551

Ireland

The Decent Cigar
Ballsbridge
Dublin 4
353 1 549 363

J J Fox
119 Grafton St.
Dublin 2
353 1 677 0533

Terroiris Limited
103 Morehampton
Rd., Donnybrook
Dublin 4
353 1 667 1311

Italy

Achille Savinelli Srl
Via Dogana 3
Milano 20123
39 2 875 900

Lebanon

La Casa del Habano
Achrafieh Cassine
Square - Notre
Dame Center
Beirut
961 1 328 568

La Casa del Habano
Zalka Hwy., ARZ
Center - ABU
Jawde Bldg.
Beirut
961 3 741 503

Luxembourg

La Civette
22B Ave. Porte-
Neuve, L-2227
352 221 321

Malaysia

Havana Club
Level 4, Lt. 10
Jalan Sultan Ismail
Kuala Lumpor 50250
60 3 245 5996

Mexico

La Casa del Habano
Plaza Flamingo 233,
Zona Hotelera
Cancun, Quintana
Roo
52 988 52929

MEXICO CITY

La Casa del Habano
Plaza Loreto
Altamirano #46,
Local 119
Col. Tizapan San
Angel
01090 Mexico City,
D.F.
52 5 616 1430

La Casa del Habano
Plaza Masaryk,
Presidente
Masaryk 393,
Local 28
Col. Polancio
11560 Mexico City,
D.F.
52 5 282 1046

**Amigos Smoke
Shop**
Calle M Doblado Y
Morelos
San Jose Del Cabo
52 11421138

La Villa Del Tabaco
Calle 3ra 2015 Ent
Revolucion Y
Madero Zona
Centro
Tijuana
52 668 58 558

Netherlands Antilles

**The New
Amsterdam Store**
66 Front St.,
Philipsburg
St. Maarten
599 5 22787

New Zealand

**Havana House
Cigars Limited**
11-19 Customs St. W.
Auckland
64 9 357 0037

Imperial Tobacco
295-A The Terrace
Wellington
64 4 801 9002

Phillippines

**Tabac at The
Peninsula Manila**
Shop 12 Makati
Tower, Ayala &
Makati Aves.
Makati
63 2 867 1597

**Tabac at The Hotel
Sofitel**
Grand Blvd. Manila,
1990 Roxas Blvd.
Manila
63 2 526 8588

Portugal

**Empor-Importacao e
Export**
Rua Joao Dos Santos,
Lote 2 1300
Lisboa
fax: 351 1 364 6820

Puerto Rico

Tobacco Shop
Isla Verde Mall, 2nd
Level
Carolina
(787) 253-0865

Fun Times
152 Barbosa Ave.
Catano 00962
(809) 788-3588

**International
House Of Cigars**
B-2 Tabonuco St.
Guaynabo 00968
(787) 782-6871

The Smoker's Suite
Pisa de Capassa Ste.
Guaynabo 00966
(809) 720-1200

Tobacco Shop
Plaza Las Americas,
1st Level
Hato Rey
(787) 759-8062

Luigi's Cigar Box
120 Monte Carlo
Humacao 00791
(787) 850-3500

**Good Times Smoke
Shop**
McKinley #74 -
Oeste
Mayaguez 00680
(809) 265-2380

Tobacco Shop
Plaza Del Caribe
Mall, 2nd Level
Ponce
(787) 842-6881

SAN JUAN

Cigar Shop
Plaza Los
Muchachos, 201
Fortaleza
San Juan 00902
(787) 725-4977

El Barco
Borinquen Towers
San Juan 00920-271
(787) 781-5525

**International House
of Cigars**
1203 Americo
Miranda Ave.
Reparto
Metropolitano
San Juan
(809) 782-6871

The Smoker's Suite
El San Juan Hotel &
Casino, La Galeria
6073 Isla Verde Ave.
San Juan 00979
(809) 791-6002

Saudi Arabia

La Casa del Habano
Palestine Rd.
Al Hamra, Jeddah
966 2 665 8227

La Casa del Habano
Saladin St.
Al Malaz, Riyadh
966 1 476 3114

La Casa del Habano
Prince Sultan St.
Olaya, Riyadh
966 1 465 037

South Africa

Wesley's-The Cock 'n Bull
20 Tyger Valley Centre
Bellville Cape
27 21 948 2400

Wesley's
Sanlam Plaza, #14
Bloemfontein
27 51 484 658

CAPE TOWN

Wesley's
Garden's Shopping
 Centre, 5-A
 (Upper Level)
Cape Town
27 21 45 1890

Wesley's
Golden Acre Plaza,
 Level 7, Cape Town
27 21 21 5090

Wesley's-The Cock 'n Bull
Covendish Square,
G-40, Cape Town
27 21 61 14 32

Wesley's-The Cock 'n Bull
143 V & A
 Waterfront
Cape Town
27 21 21 1860

Wesley's-Zoggy's Durban
87 Gardiner St.
Durban
27 31 304 0866

Wesley's
Vincent Park
 Centre, 40-A
East London
27 431 57873

JOHANNESBURG

Wesley's
Garden Pavillion,
 Carlton Centre
 G-39
Johannesburg
27 11 331 1050

Wesley's
The Rosebank Mall,
 #170
Johannesburg
27 11 880 1150

Wesley's
Bank City, Pritchard
St.
Johannesburg
27 11 633 2510

Wesley's Pipe & Tobacco-Swaziland Jewellers
The Mall
Mbabane
27 9268 42460

Wesley's
Buster Brown
 Centre, 22-C
Nelspruit
27 1311 53308

Wesley's-The Cock 'n Bull
The Square, #8
Plettenberg Bay
27 4457 30335

Wesley's
24 Shoprito
 Chockers Mall,
 Greenacres
Port Elizabeth
27 41 34 2036

Sweden

Broberg's Tobakshandel AB
Arkaden Box 111 10
Goteborg S-40423
46 31 153 614

Broberg's Tobakshandel AB
Sturegallerian 39
Stockholm 114 46
46 31 611 69 00

Switzerland

Eden Tabac Cigares
rue du Grand Lancy 6
Acacias 1227
41 22 342 27 57

Davidoff
Steinenvorstadt 2
Basel 4051
41 61 22 87 37

Davidoff
Centralbahnplatz 9
Basel 4052
41 61 23 11 52

Kagi
2 place du Theatre
Berne
41 22 31 37 03

GENEVA

Alfred Dunhill
rue de Rhône 59
Geneva 1204
41 22 312 42 60

Comptoirs du Rhône
rue de Rhône 59
Geneva 1204
41 22 312 14 22

Davidoff
2 rue de Rive
Geneva 1204
41 22 310 90 41

Eden Confederation Emile SA
rue de la
 Confederation 8
Geneva 1204
41 22 311 96 41

Fradkoff Cigares
Quai des Berques 29
Geneva 1201
41 22 342 27 57

Raffi's
2-4 place
 Longemalle
Geneva 1204
41 22 31 97 40

Tabac Rhein
1 rue du Mont-Blanc
Geneva 1204
41 22 32 97 64

ZÜRICH

Davidoff
Hotel Savoy,
 Poststrasse 12
Zürich
41 1 211 48 00

Durr
Bahnhofplatz 6
Zürich
41 1 211 63 23

La Casa del Habano
Bleicherweg 18
Zürich
41 1 202 1211

Tabak
  Schwarzenbach
Hauptbahnof
Zürich
41 1 211 63 25

Thailand

The Davidoff Shop
Hilton International
  Hotel
Bangkok
66 2 253 0123

Turkey

Pogep Inc.
Sulunlu Sok No. 3,
  80620-1 Levent
Istanbul
90 1 212 264 1929

United Kingdom

Berry Brothers &
  Rudd
Heathrow Airport,
  Unit Ru-4,
  Terminal 3 Airside
Hounslow,
  Middlesex TW6
  1JH
44 181 564 8363

LONDON

Alfred Dunhill
  Limited
30 Duke St., St.
  James
London SW1 Y6DL
44 171 4999566

Benson & Hedges
13 Old Bond St.
London W1A 4QP
44 171 4931 85

Davidoff Of London
35 St. James St.
London SW1A 1HB
44 171 930 3079

Desmond Sautter
106 Mount St.
London W1Y 5HE
44 171 4994866

Dunhill
32 St. Andrews Rd.
London E17 6BQ
44 181 498 4000

Harvey Nichols
Knightsbridge
London SW1 7RJ
44 171 235 5000

J.J. Fox London
19 St. James St.
London SW1A 1ES
44 171 493 9009

Monte's
164 Sloane St.
London SW1
44 171 245 0892

Sautter of Mayfair
106 Mount St.
London W1Y 5HE
44 171 499 4866

U.S. Virgin Islands

Baci Duty Free
55 Company St.,
  Christiansted
St Croix 00820
(888) SEE BACI

Steeles Smokes &
  Sweets
1102 Strand St.,
  Christiansted
St. Croix 00820
(809) 773-3366

Shady Days
13-B Wharfside
  Village
St. John 00831
(809) 693-7625

ST. THOMAS

Ah Riise
37 Main St.
St. Thomas
(809) 776-2303

Gregory's
PO Box 9071
St. Thomas
(809) 777-5480

Virgin Islands Cigar
  Society
St. Thomas 0080
(809) 777-5480

West Indies

La Casa del Habano
Heritage Quay No.
  45
St. Johns, Antigua
(809) 462-2677

La Casa del Habano
Centre St. John
  Perse #54
Pointe-a-Pitre,
  Guadeloupe 97110
590 894 216

ST. BARTHELEMY

P & G Associates
Gustavia
St. Barthelemy
  97133
596 275 062

La Casa del Habano
Villa Creole
St. Jean, St.
  Barthelemy 97133
590 276 689

Le Comptoir du
  Cigare
6 General de Gaulle
Gustavia, St.
  Barthelemy 97133
590 275 062

ST. MARTIN

La Casa del Cigarro
Marina Port La
  Royale, BP 445
Marigot, St. Martin
  97150
590 879 048

La Casa del Habano
Port La Royal, Rue
  de La Liberté 71
Marigot, St. Martin
  97105
590 877 910

Le Cigare
rue de la Liberté, BP
  1020
Marigot, St. Martin
  97150
590 877 910

CHAPTER 15

Cigar-Friendly Restaurants

The cigar-friendly restaurants that follow are divided into two sections: United States and International. Restaurants in the United States are listed by state, and then alphabetically by city. International restaurants are listed by country, and then alphabetically by city.

Each listing details where cigar-smoking is allowed inside the restaurant and what type of cuisine is served, if any. A listing that contains "Humidor" indicates that cigars are available at the restaurant.

If the primary role of the establishment is not that of a public, full-service restaurant—for example, if it's a coffee bar, nightclub or private club—that fact is noted in bold at the end of the listing.

The restaurant information was provided by the restaurants themselves in a questionnaire prepared by Cigar Aficionado. Each listing was checked as close to the publication date as possible, but changes occur all the time, so it's best to call ahead.

UNITED STATES

Alabama

Basil's Grill & Wine Bar
1318 20th St. S.
Birmingham
(205) 933-9222
•Bar/lounge and, after 10pm, in smoking section. Cuisine: Bistro.

Montgomery Brewing Co. & Cafe
12 W. Jefferson St.
Montgomery
(334) 834-2739
•Smoking section. Cuisine: features steak, seafood, pasta.

North River Yacht Club
New Watermelon Rd.
Tuscaloosa
(205) 345-0202
•All areas. Cuisine: international.
Private club.

Alaska

Bernie's Bar & Grill
600 E. Northern Lights Blvd.
Anchorage
(907) 272-3223
•Lounge. Cuisine: Continental.

Chilkoot Charlie's
2435 Spenard Rd.
Anchorage
(907) 272-1010
•All areas. Humidor. Cuisine: appetizers only. **Nightclub.**

Chena Hot Springs Resort
206 Driveway

Fairbanks
(907) 369-4111
•Bar. Cuisine: Continental, featuring seafood and steak.

Arizona

The Discovery Lounge at Boulders
34631 N. Tom Darlington Dr.
Carefree
(602) 488-9009
•Lounge. Humidor. Cuisine: hors d'oeuvres only.
Bar/lounge.

Johnny's
3413 Central Ave.
Hot Springs
(501) 623-9788
•Bar. Cuisine: steak and seafood.

Wigwam Resort
300 E. Indian Pool
Litchfield Park
(602) 935-3811
•Bar, lounge and patio. Humidor. Cuisine: three restaurants serve Southwestern, American and Continental.

Loggia Lobby Bar at the Doubletree Paradise Valley Resort
5401 N. Scottsdale Rd.
Paradise Valley
(602) 947-5400
•Smoking section and patio. Humidor. Cuisine: Southwestern.
Bar.

PHOENIX

Another Pointe in Tyme at the South Mountain Hilton
7777 S. Pointe Pkwy.
Phoenix
(602) 431-6472
• Bar, private rooms and patio. Humidor. Cuisine: American.

Christopher's/ Christopher's Bistro
2398 E. Camelback Rd., Phoenix
(602) 957-3214
• Smoking section, private room and patio. Humidor. Cuisine: French at Christopher's; Continental at the Bistro.

Different Pointe of View at the Pointe Hilton Tapatio Cliff
11111 N. 7th St.
Phoenix
(602) 863-0912
• Bar. Humidor. Cuisine: French and regional American. **Nightclub.**

Morton's of Chicago
Shops at the Esplanade/2501 E. Camelback Rd., Ste. 1
Phoenix
(602) 955-9577
• Bar/lounge, smoking section and patio. Humidor. Cuisine: steakhouse.

Pointe in Tyme at the Pointe Hilton Tapatio Cliff
11111 N. 7th St.
Phoenix
(602) 866-6348
• Bar/lounge and smoking section. Humidor. Cuisine: American charbroiler.

The Grill Bar at the Ritz-Carlton
2401 E. Camelback Rd., Phoenix
(602) 468-0700
• Bar before 6pm and after 9pm only. Humidor. Cuisine: classic grill.

Tarbell's
3213 E. Camelback Rd., Phoenix
(602) 955-8100
• Private room. Humidor. Cuisine: American bistro.

Wrong Number Lounge
4041 N. 40th St.
Phoenix
(602) 955-9886
• All areas. **Bar.**

SCOTTSDALE

Marco Polo's Supper Club
8606 E. Shea Blvd.
Scottsdale
(602) 483-1900
• Bar and patio. Humidor. Cuisine: Northern Italian with Oriental flair.

Marquessa at the Scottsdale Princess Hotel
757 E. Princess Dr.
Scottsdale
(602) 585-4848
• Dining room and lounge. Humidor. Cuisine: refined Catalan (Spanish).

Remington's at The Scottsdale Plaza Resort
7200 N. Scottsdale Rd.
Scottsdale
(602) 951-5101
• Lounge and patio. Humidor. Cuisine: regional American.

Thirsty Camel Bar at the Phoenician Resort
6000 E. Camelback Rd.
Scottsdale
(602) 941-8200
• Private rooms and patio. Humidor. Cuisine: Mediterranean.

Lakes Club
10484 W. Thunderbird Blvd.
Sun City
(602) 974-6041
• Bar, lounge, private rooms and patio. Cuisine: American.
Private club/banquet hall.

TUCSON

Anthony's in the Catalinas
6440 N. Campbell
Tucson
(520) 299-1771
• Bar/lounge and patio. Humidor. Cuisine: Continental.

Box Seats Grill & Pub
8848 E. Tanque Verde, Tucson
(520) 760-6699
• Bar and smoking section. Humidor. Cuisine: American.

Charles Restaurant
6400 E. El Dorado Circle, Tucson
(520) 296-7173
• Smoking section. Humidor. Cuisine: Continental.

Daniel's Restaurant
4340 N. Campbell
Tucson
(520) 742-3200
• Bar/lounge, smoking section, private room and patio. Humidor. Cuisine: northern Italian.

El Charro Cafe
311 N. Court Ave.
Tucson
(520) 622-1922
• Bar/lounge, patio and cigar bar. Humidor. Cuisine: Mexican/Tucson.

Suite 102
5350 E. Broadway
Tucson
(520) 745-9555
•*Bar, patio and private room. Humidor.*

Arkansas

James at the Mill at the Inn at the Mill
3906 Greathouse
Springs Rd.
Johnson
(501) 443-1400
•*Smoking section, patio and private room. Humidor. Cuisine: Ozark Plateau.*

Cafe Saint Moritz
225 E. Markham
Little Rock
(501) 372-0411
•*Smoking section and bar. Humidor. Cuisine: Continental.*

Capital Bar & Grill at The Capital Hotel
111 W. Markham
Little Rock
(501) 374-7474
•*Bar/lounge. Humidor. Cuisine: American.*

California

Mama Cozza's
2170 W. Ball Rd.
Anaheim
(714) 635-0063
•*Bar. Cuisine: Italian.*

Mr. Stox
1105 E. Katella Ave.
Anaheim
(714) 634-2994
•*Bar/lounge and patio. Humidor. Cuisine: Continental.*

The Ballard Store Restaurant & Bar
2449 Baseline Ave.
Ballard
(805) 688-5319
•*Wine cellar. Humidor. Cuisine: American and French.*

Marvin Gardens
1160 Old Country
Rd.
Belmont
(415) 592-6154
•*Outdoor garden. Humidor. Cuisine: pub fare.*

BEVERLY
HILLS

Armani Cafe
9533 Brighton Way
Beverly Hills
(310) 271-9940
•*After dinner only. Cuisine: Italian.*

Beverly Hilton Hotel
9876 Wilshire Blvd.
Beverly Hills
(310) 274-7777
•*Bar/lounge only (separate from restaurant). Humidor. Cuisine: Continental and French.*

Grand Havana Room
301 N. Canon Dr.
Beverly Hills
(310) 446-4925
•*Bar/lounge. Humidor. Cuisine: American.* **Private club.**

Hamiltons at The Wine Merchant
9701 Santa Monica
Blvd.
Beverly Hills
(310) 278-0347
•*All areas. Humidor. Cuisine: appetizer menu only.* **Bar/cigar bar/entertainment.**

Lawry's The Prime Rib
100 N. La Cienega
Blvd.
Beverly Hills
(310) 652-2827
•*Lounge. Cuisine: American.*

Maple Drive
345 N. Maple Drive
Beverly Hills
(310) 274-9800
•*Bar/lounge. Humidor. Cuisine: California.*

McCormick & Schmick's Seafood Restaurant
206 N. Rodeo Dr.
Beverly Hills
(310) 859-0434
•*Bar/lounge and patio. Humidor. Cuisine: seafood and steak.*

The Peninsula Beverly Hills
9882 Santa Monica
Blvd. S.
Beverly Hills
(310) 551-2888
•*Bar. Humidor. Cuisine: Continental.*

Philip Dane's Cigar Lounge
9669 S. Santa
Monica Blvd.
Beverly Hills
(310) 285-9945
•*All areas. Humidor.* **Cigar lounge.**

The Regent Beverly Wilshire
9500 Wilshire Blvd.
Beverly Hills
(310) 275-5200
•*Cigar lounge. Humidor. Cuisine: Continental.* **Cigar bar.**

The Stinking Rose— A Garlic Restaurant
55 N. La Cienega
Beverly Hills
(310) N-LA-ROSE
•*Cigar lounge "Tobacco Road." Humidor. Cuisine: California/Italian.*

The Wine Merchant
9701 Santa Monica
Blvd.
Beverly Hills
(310) 278-7322
•*Cigar bar. Humidor. Cuisine: appetizers and desserts only.* **Cigar lounge/bar (also retails wine and cigars).**

La Vie en Rose
240 S. State College
Blvd.
Brea
(714) 529-8333
•*Bar/lounge and private rooms. Humidor. Cuisine: French.*

Havana Studios
245 E. Olive Ave.,
Ste. 100
Burbank
(818) 557-7600
•*All areas. Humidor.*
Private club.

**Pacific's Edge
Restaurant at the
Highlands Inn**
Hwy. 1 (3.8 miles
south)
Carmel
(408) 624-3801
•*Bar/lounge. Humidor. Cuisine: Californian with French influence.*

Rio Grill
101 Crossroads
Carmel
(408) 625-5436
•*Patio. Humidor. Cuisine: American grill with a southwest twist.*

Pepper's Restaurant
13101 Crossroads
Pkwy. S.
City of Industry
(310) 692-4445
•*Bar/lounge, smoking section and patio. Humidor. Cuisine:*
Mexican. **Nightclub.**

COSTA MESA
Amici Trattoria
655 Anton Blvd.,
Ste. C
Costa Mesa
(714) 850-9399
•*Patio. Cuisine: Mediterranean.*

The Golden Truffle
1767 Newport Blvd.
Costa Mesa
(714) 645-9858
•*Patio. Cuisine: French/Caribbean.*

**Habana Restaurant
& Bar**
2930 Bristol St.
Costa Mesa
(714) 556-0176
•*Bar/lounge and patio. Humidor. Cuisine: Cuban.*

Johnny Z's
1655 Saratoga-
Sunnyvale Rd.
Cupertino
(408) 257-1120
•*Bar/lounge, cigar bar and private room. Humidor. Cuisine: Continental.*

**The Library at the
Ritz-Carlton,
Laguna Niquel**
One Ritz Carlton Dr.
Dana Point
(714) 240-2000
•*Cigar bar "The Library." Humidor. Cuisine: Dinner is available in any of the hotel's three restaurants.* **Cigar bar.**

**Brix Dining Cafe
and Bar**
6763 N. Palm Ave.
Fresno
(209) 435-5441
•*Bar and heated patio. Humidor. Cuisine: American and California.*

Il Vesuvio
7089 N. Marks
Fresno
(209) 446-1443
•*Patio. Humidor. Cuisine: Italian.*

The Cellar
305 N. Harbor Blvd.
Fullerton
(714) 525-5682
•*Bar/lounge. Humidor. Cuisine: classic French.*

**Ceegar Gallery &
Lounge**
109 E. Broadway
Glendale
(818) 507-0500
•*Lounge. Humidor.*
Coffee bar.

**Main Street Cafe &
Bar**
213 W. Main St.
Grass Valley
(916) 477-6000
•*Bar/lounge and patio. Humidor. Cuisine: American.*

**Papa Georges
Restaurant and Bar**
2320 S. Cabrillo Hwy.
Half Moon Bay
(415) 726-9417

•*Bar/lounge and patio. Humidor. Cuisine: Continental.*

Bistango
19100 Von Karman
Ave.
Irvine
(714) 752-5222
•*Bar/lounge.*
Cuisine: contemporary California.

Chanteclair
18912 MacArthur
Blvd.
Irvine
(714) 752-8001
•*Bar and grill room. Humidor. Cuisine: French.*

Top O' The Cove
1216 Prospect St.
La Jolla
(619) 454-7779
•*Front patio. Humidor. Cuisine: Continental.*

**Wente Vineyards
Restaurant**
5050 Arroyo Rd.
Livermore
(510) 447-3696
•*Private rooms and veranda. Humidor. Cuisine: American.*

LONG BEACH
Blue Cafe
210 The Promenade
Long Beach
(310) 983-7111
•*All areas. Humidor. Cuisine: deli sandwiches.* **Bar.**

**Moose
McGillycuddy's
Pub & Cafe**
190 Marina Dr.
Long Beach
(310) 596-8108
•*Lounge and patio.
Cuisine: American.*

**Mum's Restaurant
& Club Cohiba**
144 Pine Ave.
Long Beach
(310) 437-7700
•*Cigar bar/patio/
rooftop. Humidor.
Cuisine: Continental.*

**Nino's Ristorante
Italiano**
3853 Atlantic Ave.
Long Beach
(310) 427-1003
•*Smoking dining
room, patio and pri-
vate parties. Cuisine:
Italian.*

Phil Trani's
3490 Long Beach
Blvd.
Long Beach
(310) 426-3668
•*Bar. Humidor. Cui-
sine: creative.*

LOS ANGELES
**Bel-Air Hotel
Dining Room**
701 Stone Canyon
Rd.
Los Angeles
(310) 472-1211
•*Lounge and terrace.
Humidor. Cuisine:
French and
California.*

**Bernard's
Restaurant at
The Regal
Biltmore**
506 S. Grand Ave.
Los Angeles
(213) 612-1580
•*Bar/lounge and patio
(Fountain Court).
Humidor. Cuisine:
Continental.*

Cafe Pinot
700 W. 5th St.
Los Angeles
(213) 239-6500
•*Patio. Humidor.
Cuisine: French
bistro.*

Campanile
624 S. La Brea Ave.
Los Angeles
(213) 938-1447
•*Bar/lounge. Humi-
dor. Cuisine:
Mediterranean.*

Checkers
535 S. Grand Ave.
Los Angeles
(213) 624-0000
•*Bar/lounge. Cuisine:
California.*

Fénix at the Argyle
8358 Sunset Blvd.
Los Angeles
(213) 848-6677
•*Patio. Humidor.
Cuisine: French/
California.*

**Friars Club of
California**
9900 Santa Monica
Blvd.
Los Angeles

(310) 553-0850
•*Bar/lounge. Humi-
dor. Cuisine: Conti-
nental.* **Private club.**

**Gardens
Restaurant,
Window's Bar &
Lounge at the
Four Seasons**
300 S. Doheny Dr.
Los Angeles
(310) 273-2222
•*Smoking area of
Window's Bar &
Lounge, Gardens bar
and patio. Humidor.
Cuisine: California.*

Georgia Restaurant
7250 Melrose Ave.
Los Angeles
(213) 933-8420
•*Patio. Cuisine:
Southern.*

Il Ristorante Rex
617 S. Olive St.
Los Angeles
(213) 627-2300
•*Bar. Humidor. Cui-
sine: American and
Italian.*

L'Orangerie
903 N. La Cienega
Blvd.
Los Angeles
(310) 652-9770
•*Bar/lounge. Humi-
dor. Cuisine: French.*

**McCormick &
Schmick's
Seafood
Restaurant**
633 W. 5th St.
Los Angeles

(213) 629-1929
•*Bar/lounge (after
8pm) and patio. Cui-
sine: seafood.*

**Monty's Steak
House**
1100 Glendon Ave.
Los Angeles
(310) 208-8787
•*Bar/lounge.
Humidor. Cuisine:
California.*

**Morton's of
Chicago**
435 S. LaCienega
Blvd.
Los Angeles
(310) 246-1501
•*Bar. Humidor. Cui-
sine: steakhouse.*

Pinot Hollywood
1448 N. Gower St.
Los Angeles
(213) 461-8800
•*Bar/lounge, cigar
bar, private room and
patio. Humidor. Cui-
sine: French bistro.*

Revival Cafe
7149 Beverly Blvd.
Los Angeles
(213) 930-1210
•*Patio. Humidor.
Cuisine: California.*

**Taix French
Restaurant**
1911 Sunset Blvd.
Los Angeles
(213) 484-1265
•*Bar/lounge. Humi-
dor. Cuisine: French.*

The Tower
1150 S. Olive St.
atop the Trans-
America Center
Los Angeles
(213) 746-1554
•*Bar/lounge and private room. Cuisine: Continental/French.*

Bambu
3835 Cross Creek Rd.
Malibu
(310) 456-5464
•*Patio. Humidor. Cuisine: eclectic California and sushi bar.*

Lobby Lounge at the Ritz-Carlton
4375 Admiralty Way
Marina del Rey
(310) 823-1700
•*Restaurant smoking section and bar. Humidor. Cuisine: Mediterranean.*

Dal Baffo Restaurant
878 Santa Cruz Ave.
Menlo Park
(415) 325-1588
•*Bar/lounge and cigar bar. Humidor. Cuisine: Continental.*

Garden Grill and Red Terrier Pub
1626 Elma St.
Menlo Park
(415) 325-8981
•*Pub and patio. Humidor. Cuisine: British and California.*

Terrace Cafe
1100 El Camino Real
Millbrae
(415) 742-5588
•*Bar, lounge and patio. Cuisine: American.*

Brio Bistro
24050 Camino del Avion
Monarch Beach
(714) 443-1476
•*Patio. Humidor. Cuisine: Italian.*

Casa Munras Garden Hotel
700 Munras Ave.
Monterey
(408) 375-2411
•*Private rooms. Humidor. Cuisine: American.*

The Whaling Station Inn
763 Wave St.
Monterey
(408) 373-3778
•*Bar/lounge. Humidor. Cuisine: American, Continental and Italian.*

Bistro Don Giovanni
4110 St. Helena Hwy.
Napa
(707) 224-3300
•*Outside seating. Cuisine: French/Italian.*

Mustards Grill
7399 St. Helena Hwy.
Napa
(707) 944-2424
•*Patio. Humidor. Cuisine: American.*

NEWPORT BEACH

Accents at The Sutton Place Hotel
4500 MacArthur Blvd.
Newport Beach
(714) 476-2001
•*Bar and cigar bar. Humidor. Cuisine: French and Continental.*

John Dominis Restaurant
2901 W. Coast Hwy.
Newport Beach
(714) 650-5112
•*Patio and private rooms. Humidor. Cuisine: Pacific Rim.*

The Ritz
880 Newport Center Dr.
Newport Beach
(714) 720-1800
•*Bar/lounge. Humidor. Cuisine: Continental/French.*

Twin Palms Newport Beach
630 Newport Center Dr.
Newport Beach
(714) 721-8288

•*Bar/lounge and cigar bar. Cuisine: French country.*

Orsi's (Ristorante Orsi)
340 Ignacio Blvd.
Novato
(415) 883-0960
•*Bar. Cuisine: Italian.*

Aroma Italiano Coffee House & Fine Cigars
1948 N. Tustin
Orange
(714) 282-2382
•*Heated patio. Humidor. Cuisine: lunch menu only. **Coffee bar/cigar bar.***

The Hobbit
2932 E. Chapman Ave.
Orange
(714) 997-1972
•*Cigar lounge and patio. Humidor. Cuisine: Continental.*

Il Sogno
863 Swarthmore Ave.
Pacific Palisades
(310) 454-6522
•*Patio. Cuisine: French/Italian.*

Morton's of Chicago
74-880 Country Club Dr.
Palm Desert
(619) 340-6865
•*Bar. Humidor. Cuisine: steakhouse.*

Empire Grill & Tap Room
651 Emerson St.
Palo Alto
(415) 321-3030
•*Patio. Humidor. Cuisine: French- and Italian-influenced American.*

PASADENA

Bistro 45
45 S. Mentor Ave.
Pasadena
(818) 795-2478
•*Patio (terrace). Humidor. Cuisine: California and French.*

The Humidor
70 N. Raymond Ave.
Pasadena
(818) 584-6383
•*All areas. Humidor. Private cigar lounge.*

The Maryland Bar at the Doubletree Hotel-Pasadena
191 N. Los Robles Ave., Pasadena
(818) 792-2727
•*Bar/lounge, private room and patio. Humidor. Cuisine: American and Northern Italian.*

McCormick & Schmick's Seafood Restaurant
111 N. Los Robles
Pasadena
(818) 405-0064
•*Bar and patio. Humidor. Cuisine: seafood.*

Twin Palms Pasadena
101 W. Green St.
Pasadena
(818) 577-2567
•*Bar and patio. Cuisine: French country.*

Zona Rosa Caffe
15 S. El Molino Ave.
Pasadena
(818) 793-2334
•*Patio. Humidor.*
Coffee bar.

- -

The Bay Club/Inn at Spanish Bay at the Pebble Beach Resort
2700 17 Mile Dr.
Pebble Beach
(408) 647-7433
•*Bar/lounge, private rooms and patio. Humidor. Cuisine: Northern Italian.*

Magic Lamp Inn
8189 Foothill Blvd.
Rancho Cucamonga
(909) 981-8659
•*Bar, lounge and private rooms. Humidor. Cuisine: American and Continental.*

The Bar at the Ritz-Carlton
68900 Frank Sinatra Dr.
Rancho Mirage
(619) 321-8282
•*Bar. Humidor. Cuisine: Mediterranean.*
Cigar bar.

Auberge du Soleil
180 Rutherford Hill Rd.
Rutherford
(707) 963-1211
•*Bar. Cuisine: wine country.*

SACRAMENTO

A Tabola
2627 Town & Country Place
Sacramento
(916) 973-1800
•*Patio. Humidor. Cuisine: Tuscan-Italian.*

Ciao Yama and Dawson's at the Hyatt Regency Sacramento
1209 L St.
Sacramento
(916) 443-1234
•*Patio and other designated areas. Humidor. Cuisine: Japanese (Ciao Yama); upscale chophouse (Dawson's).* **Nightclub.**

Harlows Restaurant & Nightclub
2708 J St.
Sacramento
(916) 441-4693
•*Cigar lounge over the bar. Humidor. Cuisine: modern American.*

Mace's
501 Pavillion Lane
Sacramento
(916) 922-0222

•*Bar/lounge and patio. Humidor. Cuisine: American.*

Morton's of Chicago
521 L St.
Sacramento
(916) 442-5091
•*Bar. Humidor. Cuisine: steakhouse.*

- -

The Pig's Ear Pub
1987 S. Diners Court
San Bernardino
(909) 889-1442
•*Bar and smoking restaurant (where drinks are primary and food is secondary). Humidor. Cuisine: British—fish and chips, roast beef and other pub food.*

SAN DIEGO

Baci's
1955 W. Morena Blvd.
San Diego
(619) 275-2094
•*Bar/lounge. Humidor. Cuisine: Italian.*

El Bizcocho
17550 Bernardo Oaks Dr.
San Diego
(619) 487-1611
•*Bar/lounge. Humidor. Cuisine: French/California.*

Grant Grill
326 Broadway
San Diego
(619) 239-6806
•Bar/lounge and patio. Humidor. Cuisine: Continental.

Osteria Panevino
722 5th Ave.
San Diego
(619) 595-7959
•Patio. Humidor. Cuisine: Tuscan.

Prego Ristorante
1370 Frazee Rd.
San Diego
(619) 294-4700
•Heated courtyard. Humidor. Cuisine: regional Italian.

Trattoria Portobello
715 4th Ave.
San Diego
(619) 232-4440
•Bar and patio. Humidor. Cuisine: contemporary Italian.

SAN FRANCISCO

The Big Four Restaurant at the Huntington Hotel
1075 California St.
San Francisco
(415) 771-1140
•Bar. Humidor. Cuisine: contemporary/American.

Cafe Tiramisu
28 Belden Lane
San Francisco
(415) 421-7044

•Private room. Humidor. Cuisine: Northern Italian.

Cypress Club
500 Jackson St.
San Francisco
(415) 296-8555
•Bar, lounge, private rooms and patio. Cuisine: American.

Essex Supper Club
847 Montgomery St.
San Francisco
(415) 397-5969
• "Bacchus Wine Cellar"—floor devoted to cigar smoking. Humidor. Cuisine: French. **Jazz supper club.**

Fournou's Ovens
905 California St.
San Francisco
(415) 989-3500
•Lounge. Humidor. Cuisine: Mediterranean.

Fumé Restaurant
101 Cyril Magnin
San Francisco
(415) 788-3803
•Cigar bar. Humidor. Cuisine: French-Japanese.

George's Global Kitchen & Take-Out Cafe
340 Division St.
San Francisco
(415) 864-4224
•Dining room during smoker nights only and patio. Humidor. Cuisine: American (on

smoker nights California & French is served).

The Gold Club
650 Howard
San Francisco
(415) 536-0300
•All areas. Humidor. Cuisine: features salmon, pasta, steak. **Upscale gentleman's club.**

Harrington's Bar & Grill
245 Front St.
San Francisco
(415) 392-7595
•Bar. Cuisine: American.

Harry Denton's Starlight Room
450 Powell St.
San Francisco
(415) 395-8595
•Bar/lounge area. Humidor. Cuisine: light fare featuring caviar, caesar salads, shrimp and crabcakes. **Nightclub.**

J.T.'s
555 Golden Gate Ave.
San Francisco
(415) 861-7827
•Special facility, the "Stellar Cigar Society Smoke Room." Humidor. Cuisine: Continental and exotic.

Lehr Brothers Bistro & Grill
740 Sutter St.
San Francisco

(415) 474-6478
•Cigar room. Humidor. Cuisine: American featuring "Towering" appetizers, an oyster bar, certified dry-aged steaks and fresh grilled & house-smoked seafood.

Morton's of Chicago
400 Post St.
San Francisco
(415) 986-5830
•Bar/lounge. Humidor. Cuisine: steakhouse.

The Occidental Grill
453 Pine St.
San Francisco
(415) 834-0484
•Bar/lounge. Humidor. Cuisine: American.

The Park Grill at the Park Hyatt Hotel
333 Battery St.
San Francisco
(415) 296-2933
•Bars only. Humidor. Cuisine: California/Pacific Rim and Continental.

Redwood Room at the Clift Hotel
495 Gedry St.
San Francisco
(415) 775-4700
•Lounge. Humidor. Cuisine: appetizers in lounge.

The Ritz-Carlton
600 Stockton St.
San Francisco
(415) 296-7465
•*Ritz-Carlton Bar
from 6 pm until closing. Humidor. Cuisine: California and American.*

Stars
150 Redwood Alley
San Francisco
(415) 861-7827
•*Special facility, the
"Stellar Cigar Society
Smoke Room," which
Stars shares with
J.T.'s. Humidor. Cuisine: American.*

Timo's
842 Valencia St.
San Francisco
(415) 647-0558
•*Smoking room and
patio. Humidor. Cuisine: Spanish tapas.*

Timo's Norte
900 N. Point St.
San Francisco
(415) 440-1200
•*Smoking room.
Humidor. Cuisine:
Spanish tapas.*

Vendetta
12 Tillman Place
San Francisco
(415) 397-7755
•*Cigar smoking
room—members only.
Humidor. **Smoking
club and men's
retail apparel and
cigars**.*

Cafe Roma
1819 Osos St.
San Luis Obispo
(805) 541-6800
•*Patio. Humidor.
Cuisine: Italian.*

Barley & Hopps
201 S. B St.
San Mateo
(415) 348-7808
•*Billiards parlor. Humidor. Cuisine: steakhouse. **Blues club/
billiards parlor/microbrewery**.*

**Ports O'Call
Restaurant**
Berth 76, Worldport
Lane
San Pedro
(310) 833-3553
•*Bar/lounge and patio. Humidor. Cuisine: California-casual
cuisine featuring fresh
seafood.*

**Morton's of
Chicago**
1661 W. Sunflower
Ave., Ste. C-5
Santa Ana
(714) 444-4834
•*Bar/lounge and private room. Humidor.
Cuisine: steakhouse.*

Wine Cask
813 Anacapa St.
Santa Barbara
(805) 966-9463
•*Heated patio.
Humidor. Cuisine:
California.*

**Wine Cask
Intermezzo**
813 Anacapa St.
Santa Barbara
(805) 966-9463
•*Front patio. Humidor. Cuisine: light
bistro featuring breakfast, lunch, and a light
dinner menu.
Cafe/bar/cigar bar.*

**SANTA
MONICA**

Drago Ristorante
2628 Wilshire Blvd.
Santa Monica
(310) 828-1585
•*Bar and private
rooms. Cuisine:
Italian.*

Michael's
1147 3rd St.
Santa Monica
(310) 451-0843
•*Bar/lounge and patio. Humidor. Cuisine: California/
French.*

Remi
1451 3rd St.
Promenade
Santa Monica
(310) 393-6545
•*Private rooms and
patio. Humidor.
Cuisine: Italian.*

Röckenwagner
2435 Main St.
Santa Monica
(310) 399-6504
•*Patio. Humidor.
Cuisine: French.*

Schatzi on Main
3110 Main St.
Santa Monica
(310) 399-4800
•*Bar and patio. Humidor. Cuisine:
Californian.*

Valentino
3115 Pico Blvd.
Santa Monica
(310) 829-4313
•*Smoking section and
patio. Cuisine:
Italian.*

World Cafe
2820 Main St.
Santa Monica
(310) 392-1661
•*Bar. Cuisine: California with a Continental flair.*

**The Restaurant at
the Meadowood
Resort**
900 Meadowood
Lane
St. Helena
(707) 963-3646
•*Bar and private
rooms. Humidor.
Cuisine: Napa Valley
Provençal.*

**Showley's at
Miramonte**
1327 Railroad Ave.
St. Helena
(707) 963-1200
•*Outdoor patio and
private rooms (please
call). Humidor.
Cuisine: California.*

Romeo et Juliette
1198 Pacific Coast
Hwy., Ste. E
Seal Beach
(310) 430-2331
•*Outdoor patio. Humidor. Cuisine: cafe-style.* **Coffee bar.**

**Spaghettini
Rotisserie &
Grill**
3005 Old Ranch
Pkwy.
Seal Beach
(310) 596-2199
•*Cigar bar, private
room and patio.
Humidor. Cuisine:
Italian.*

**The Bistro Garden
at Coldwater**
12950 Ventura Blvd.
Studio City
(818) 501-0202
•*Bar/lounge. Humidor. Cuisine: Continental/French.*

Pinot Bistro
12969 Ventura Blvd.
Studio City
(818) 990-0500
•*Patio. Humidor.
Cuisine: French
bistro.*

Aioli Restaurant
1261 Cabrillo Ave.
Torrance
(310) 320-9200
•*Tapas Bar and banquet facility. Humidor. Cuisine:
Mediterranean.*

**Vintage Press
Restaurant**
216 N. Willis St.
Visalia
(209) 733-3033
•*Bar, lounge, private
rooms and patio. Humidor. Cuisine:
American.*

Eclipse
8800 Melrose Ave.
West Hollywood
(310) 724-5959
•*Smoking section.
Humidor. Cuisine:
California with French
accents.*

The Viper Room
8852 Sunset Blvd.
West Hollywood
(310) 358-1880
•*All areas.* **Nightclub.**

The Cigar Cafe
21550-A Yorba
Linda Blvd.
Yorba Linda
(714) 693-2427
•*Cigar bar. Humidor.
Cuisine: Japanese featuring a sushi bar and
microbrewery.*

Colorado

Marie's Inn
400 Mountain Ave.
Berthoud
(970) 532-2648
•*Smoking room. Cuisine: Czech-German
and American.*

The Greenbriar
Lefthand Cyn & 36
Boulder
(303) 440-7979
•*Bar. Humidor. Cuisine: Continental European with a Pacific
Rim influence.*

Laudisio
2785 Iris Ave.
Boulder
(303) 442-1300
•*Private cigar room.
Humidor. Cuisine:
Italian.*

DENVER
Avenue Grill
630 E. 17th Ave.
Denver
(303) 861-2820
•*Bar, private rooms
and late night in the
dining room. Humidor. Cuisine: traditional grilled cuisine in
the manner of a San
Francisco-style bar
and grill.*

**Churchill Cigar Bar
at the Brown
Palace Hotel**
321 17th St.
Denver
(303) 297-3111
•*All areas. Humidor.
Cuisine: American.*
Cigar bar.

Enoteca
1730 Wynkoop St.
Denver
(303) 293-2887

•*Bar/lounge and
smoking section (all
areas after hours).
Humidor. Cuisine:
light Italian.*

**Morton's of
Chicago**
1710 Wynkoop St.
Denver
(303) 825-3353
•*Smoking section.
Humidor. Cuisine:
steakhouse.*

The Parlour
846 Broadway
Denver
(303) 837-0660
•*Bar area downstairs.
Cuisine: Italian, Mexican and American.*

Shakespeare's
2375 15th St.
Denver
(303) 433-6000
•*All areas. Humidor.
Cuisine: American
bistro.* **Billiard hall.**

Tante Louise
4900 E. Colfax Ave.
Denver
(303) 355-4488
•*Select areas of the
dining room and
lounge. Humidor.
Cuisine: contemporary French.*

Trinity Grille
1801 Broadway
Denver
(303) 293-2288
•*Bar area. Humidor.
Cuisine: American.*

349

Nico's Catacombs
115 S. College Ave.
Fort Collins
(970) 484-6029
• *Bar, lounge and private rooms after 9:30 pm. Cuisine: American and Continental.*

Club Chelsea
304 Bridge
Vail
(970) 476-5600
• *Smoking section. Humidor.* **Nightclub/bar.**

The Divide Grill Atop Cooper Creek Square
Main St. - Hwy. 40
Winter Park
(970) 726-4900
• *Bar area. Humidor. Cuisine: Black Angus steaks, fresh seafood and pasta.*

Smokin' Moe's Ribhouse & Saloon Courtyard at Cooper Creek Square
Downtown Winter Park - Hwy. 40
Winter Park
(970) 726-4600
• *Bar area and specified section of the restaurant. Humidor. Cuisine: Oklahoma-Texas featuring hickory ribs, chicken, brisket and chops.*

Connecticut

Callahan's Restaurant
1027 S. Main St.
Cheshire
(203) 271-1993
• *All areas. Humidor. Cuisine: American.*

Peppercorn's Grill
357 Main St.
Hartford
(860) 547-1714
• *Lounge after dinner and bar. Humidor. Cuisine: Italian.*

Tollgate Hill Inn
Rte. 202 & Tollgate Rd.
Litchfield
(860) 567-4545
• *Bar, smoking section and patio. Humidor. Cuisine: American.*

Eli Cannon's Tap Room
695 Main St.
Middletown
(860) 347-3547
• *Tap room and outdoor courtyard. Cuisine: American.*

Scribner's
31 Village Rd.
Milford
(203) 878-7019
• *Bar/lounge. Cuisine: seafood.*

Flood Tide
Junction Rtes. 1 & 27
Mystic
(860) 536-8140

• *Bar, lounge and private rooms. Humidor. Cuisine: Continental.*

NEW HAVEN

Barkies Grill and Rotisserie
220 College St.
New Haven
(203) 752-1000
• *Lounge area. Humidor. Cuisine: steaks, pastas, grilled fish.*

The Brewery
458 Grand Ave.
New Haven
(203) 773-5297
• *Bar and smoking section. Humidor. Cuisine: American Grill.*

Scoozzi Trattoria & Wine Bar
1104 Chapel St.
New Haven
(203) 776-8268
• *Bar, lounge and patio. Humidor. Cuisine: innovative Italian.*

Le Bon Coin
223 Litchfield Tpke.
New Preston
(203) 868-7763
• *Bar/lounge. Cuisine: French.*

Old Lyme Inn
85 Lyme St.
Old Lyme
(860) 434-2600
• *Bar. Cuisine: classic American.*

La Bretagne Restaurant
2010 W. Main St.
Stamford
(203) 324-9539
• *Bar/lounge. Cuisine: French.*

WATERBURY

Bacco's Restaurant
1230 Thomaston Ave., Waterbury
(203) 755-0635
• *Bar. Humidor. Cuisine: Italian.*

Cafe 4 Fifty 7
457 W. Main St.
Waterbury
(203) 574-4507
• *All areas. Cuisine: Italian specializing in fish and pasta.*

Carmen Anthony's Steakhouse
496 Chase Ave.
Waterbury
(203) 757-3040
• *Bar. Humidor. Cuisine: steakhouse.*

Restaurant Promis/ Club Boca Chica
1563 Post Rd. E.
Westport
(203) 256-3309
• *Bar/lounge and Club Boca Chica. Humidor. Cuisine: Continental.*

Madeleines Restaurant
1530 Palisado Ave.
Windsor
(860) 688-0150

•*Private room and bar. Humidor. Cuisine: French.*

Delaware

Blue Coat Inn
800 N. State St.
Dover
(302) 674-1776
•*Designated smoking sections. Cuisine: American.*

Paradiso Restaurant
1151 E. Lebanon Rd./Rte. 10 Plaza
Dover
(302) 697-3055
•*Smoking section and cappacino bar. Humidor. Cuisine: Northern Italian.*

Rose & Crown
108 Second St.
Lewes
(302) 645-2373
•*Bar and smoking section after 9:00pm or in the afternoon. Humidor. Cuisine: seafood, steaks and pastas.*

Columbus Inn
2216 Pennsylvania Ave.
Wilmington
(302) 571-1492
•*Bar, adjoining club room and 3 private dining rooms. Humidor. Cuisine: American and Continental, specializing in certified angus beef.*

Harry's Savoy Grill
2020 Naaman's Rd.
Wilmington
(302) 475-3000
•*Bar/lounge, smoking section, private room and patio. Humidor. Cuisine: American.*

District of Columbia

Café Atlantico
405 8th St. NW
Washington, D.C.
(202) 393-0812
•*Bar/lounge and smoking section. Humidor. Cuisine: Nuevo Latino.*

The Capital Grille
601 Pennsylvania Ave.
Washington, D.C.
(202) 737-6200
•*Bar/lounge, smoking sections and private room. Humidor. Cuisine: steakhouse specializing in dry-aged steak.*

The City Club of Washington, D.C.
555 13th St. NW
Washington, D.C.
(202) 347-0818
•*Lounge area. Humidor. Cuisine: American and Continental.*
Private club.

i Ricchi
1220 19th St. NW
Washington, D.C.
(202) 835-0459
•*Smoking areas. Cuisine: Tuscan Trattoria.*

J. Paul's
3218 M St. NW
Washington, D.C.
(202) 333-3450
•*Bar/lounge and smoking section. Humidor. Cuisine: American saloon.*

Jockey Club at the Ritz-Carlton
2100 Massachusetts Ave. NW
Washington, D.C.
(202) 293-2100
•*Fairfax Bar. Humidor. Cuisine: French/ Continental.*

John Hay Room at the Hay Adams Hotel
800 16th St. NW
Washington, D.C.
(202) 638-6600
•*Lounge. Humidor. Cuisine: American.*

La Brasserie
239 Massachusetts Ave. NE
Washington, D.C.
(202) 546-9154
•*Bar and private rooms (must be reserved in advance). Cuisine: French.*

La Colline
400 N. Capitol St. NW
Washington, D.C.
(202) 737-0400
•*Smoking area. Humidor. Cuisine: French.*

Les Halles Restaurant
1201 Pennsylvania Ave. NW
Washington, D.C.
(202) 347-6848
•*3rd level dining room and bar/lounge. Humidor. Cuisine: French/American steakhouse.*

Les Pinasse at the Sheraton Carlton
923 16th St. NW & K St.
Washington, D.C.
(202) 638-2626
•*Library lounge. Humidor. Cuisine: Continental.*

The Monocle on Capitol Hill
107 D St. NE
Washington, D.C.
(202) 546-4488
•*Dining room and bar. Humidor. Cuisine: American.*

Morton's of Chicago
3251 Prospect St. NW
Washington, D.C.
(202) 342-6258
•*Smoking section. Humidor. Cuisine: steakhouse.*

Nathan's
3150 M St. NW
Washington, D.C.
(202) 338-2000
•Bar. Cuisine:
Northern Italian.

Ozio
1835 K St. NW
Washington, D.C.
(202) 822-6000
•All areas. Humidor.
Cuisine: American
Tapas. **Martini bar/
cigar bar.**

Roma Restaurant
3419 Connecticut
Ave. NW
Washington, D.C.
(202) 363-6611
•Bar, private rooms
and patio. Humidor.
Cuisine: American
and Italian.

Sam & Harry's
1200 19th St. NW
Washington, D.C.
(202) 296-4333
•Smoking section.
Humidor. Cuisine:
American.

**Seasons Restaurant
at the Four
Seasons Hotel**
2800 Pennsylvania
Ave. NW
Washington, D.C.
(202) 342-0810
•Bar/lounge, smoking
section, private room
and patio. Humidor.
Cuisine: contempo-
rary American.

Sesto Senso
1214 18th St. NW
Washington, D.C.
(202) 785-9525
•Bar/lounge, smoking
section and cigar bar.
Humidor. Cuisine:
Italian.

**Tunnicliff's
Restaurant**
222 7th St. SE
Washington, D.C.
(202) 546-3663
•Bar, living room, pa-
tio and front tables in
the restaurant. Humi-
dor. Cuisine: Cajun
and American.

Washington Grill
1143 New
Hampshire Ave.
NW
Washington, D.C.
(202) 775-0800
•Dining room, bar
and private rooms.
Humidor. Cuisine:
American.

Florida

Maison & Jardin
430 S. Wymore Rd.
Altamonte Springs
(407) 862-4410
•Lounge, patio and
private dining rooms.
Humidor. Cuisine:
Continental.

**The Grill & Cafe
at the Ritz-
Carlton**
4750 Amelia Island
Pkwy.
Amelia Island
(904) 277-1100

•Bar/lounge, private
room and patio. Hu-
midor. Cuisine: Grill
is fine dining; Cafe
serves Continental.

Sheldon's
9501 Harding Ave.
Bal Harbour
(305) 866-6251
•Bar. Humidor. Cui-
sine: American.

BOCA RATON
**Boca Raton Hotel
& Club**
501 E. Camino Real
Boca Raton
(407) 395-3000
•Bar/lounge, lobby
and smoking section.
Humidor. Cuisine:
Continental, Italian
and seafood.

The Cigar Bar
51 SE 1st Ave.
Boca Raton
(561) 416-9444
•All areas. Humidor.
Cuisine: appetizers
only. **Bar/cigar bar/
nightclub.**

**Maxwell's
Chophouse**
501 E. Palmetto Park
Rd., Boca Raton
(561) 347-7077
•Bar and Club Room.
Humidor. Cuisine:
steak and seafood.

**Bobby's Bistro &
Wine Bar**
447 Mandalay Ave.
Clearwater Beach

(813) 446-WINE
•Smoking section, bar
and patio. Humidor.
Cuisine: diverse menu
features such items as
elk, buffalo and
snook.

Cafe Tu Tu Tango
Cocowalk
3015 Grand Ave.
Ste. 2510
Coconut Grove
(305) 529-2222
•Patio. Humidor.
Cuisine: appetizers
only. **Nightclub/bar.**

**Churchill's
Restaurant &
Pub**
Pine Lake Plaza/
10076 Griffin Rd.
Cooper City
(954) 680-0226
•Pub and private din-
ing room. Humidor.
Cuisine: Euro-
American.

Caffe Abbracci
318 Aragon Ave.
Coral Gables
(305) 441-0700
•Bar. Humidor. Cui-
sine: Italian.

**Huddleston's Blind
Pig Pub**
431 East New York
Ave.
DeLand
(904) 736-3450
•All areas. Humidor.
Cuisine: pub fare.

Destin Chops
320 Hwy. 98 E.
Destin
(904) 654-4944
•*Bar/lounge, cigar bar and smoking area. Humidor. Cuisine: steakhouse.*

FORT LAUDERDALE

Burt & Jack's
Berth 23, Port
  Everglades
Fort Lauderdale
(954) 522-5225
•*Cocktail lounge and patio. Humidor. Cuisine: sophisticated American.* ˈ

Canyon
1818 E. Sunrise
  Blvd.
Fort Lauderdale
(954) 765-1950
•*All areas after 10:00pm. Cuisine: gourmet American/ Southwestern.* **Martini & cigar club.**

Harbor Beach at the Marriott Hotel
3030 Holiday Dr.
Fort Lauderdale
(954) 525-4000
•*Bar. Cuisine: eclectic.*

Playoffs Sports Grill
3001 E. Commercial
  Blvd.
Fort Lauderdale
(954) 772-7890

•*Skybox area. Humidor. Cuisine: steaks and chops.*

Smoke Chophouse and Cigar Emporium
2863 E. Commercial
  Blvd.
Fort Lauderdale
(954) 489-1122
•*All areas. Humidor. Cuisine: steak, chops and seafood.*

Smugglers of Las Olas, Martini & Cigar Club
609 E. Las Olas
  Blvd.
Fort Lauderdale
(954) 728-9282
•*Cigar bar. Humidor. Cuisine: American.*

Studio One Cafe
2447 E. Sunrise
  Blvd.
Fort Lauderdale
(954) 565-2052
•*Dining room after 9:00pm and patio. Cuisine: American, French and Mediterranean.*

Up-In-Smoke
2863 E. Commercial
  Blvd.
Fort Lauderdale
(954) 489-1122
•*All areas. Humidor. Cuisine: Continental cuisine at the Smoke Chophouse downstairs.* **Cocktail lounge/bar.**

Veranda
2122 Second St.
Fort Myers
(941) 332-2065
•*Piano lounge. Humidor. Cuisine: elegant southern.*

Uncle's Restaurant
M.M. 80
Islamorada
(305) 664-4402
•*Smoking area and patio. Humidor. Cuisine: fresh pasta, steak, chicken, Italian seafood and wild game.*

The Blue Anchor Pub
10550 Old St.
  Augustine Rd.
Jacksonville
(904) 262-1592
•*All areas. Humidor. Cuisine: pub fare.*

Rusty Pelican Restaurant
3201 Rickenbacker
  Causeway
Key Biscayne
(305) 361-3818
•*Bar/lounge, smoking section and patio. Humidor. Cuisine: seafood.*

Snook's Bayside Restaurant and Patrick's Waterfront Bar
M.M. 99.9 (behind
  Largo Honda)
Key Largo
(305) 453-3799

•*Bar/lounge and patio. Humidor. Cuisine: features seafood, certified beef, veal and chicken.*

KEY WEST

Flagler's Restaurant at The Marriot's Casa Marina Hotel
1500 Reynold's St.
Key West
(305) 296-3535
•*Dining room smoking section and lounge. Humidor. Cuisine: upscale dining featuring fresh local seafood and aged meats.*

Louie's Backyard
700 Weddell Ave.
Key West
(305) 294-1061
•*Bar/lounge. Humidor. Cuisine: International.*

The Ocean View
1435 Simonton St.
Key West
(305) 296-5000
•*Bar/lounge. Humidor. Cuisine: Continental, featuring fresh seafood.*

Pleasure Island Jazz Company
PO Box 10,150
Lake Buena Vista
(407) 828-5665
•*In the cigar area. Humidor.* **Nightclub.**

The Colony Restaurant at the Colony Beach Hotel & Tennis Resort
1620 Gulf of Mexico Dr.
Longboat Key
(941) 383-5558
•*Lounge. Humidor. Cuisine: regional American.*

The Ritz-Carlton
100 Ocean Blvd.
Manalapan
(407) 533-6000
•*Bar/lounge and terrace. Humidor. Cuisine: Mediterranean and Continental.*

Blue Water Bay
State Road 26
Melrose
(352) 475-1928
•*Bar and smoking section. Humidor. Cuisine: seafood and steak.*

MIAMI

Casa Juancho Restaurant
2436 SW 8th St.
Miami
(305) 642-2452
•*Dining room, bar, lounge and private rooms. Humidor. Cuisine: Spanish, specializing in seafood.*

Grand Cafe at the Grand Bay Hotel
2669 S. Bayshore Dr.
Miami
(305) 858-9600

•*Bar, lounge, private rooms and patio. Humidor. Cuisine: Continental.*

Hotel Casa de Campo
2600 SW 3rd Ave., #300, Miami
(809) 523-3333
•*Lounge. Humidor. Cuisine: American, Caribbean, Mexican and Dominican, specializing in seafood and steak.*

La Casona
6355 SW 8th St.
Miami
(305) 262-2828
•*Smoking section. Humidor. Cuisine: Cuban International.*

Le Pavillon Restaurant at the Hotel Intercontinental
100 Chopin Plaza
Miami
(305) 577-1000
•*Salon and after dinner only. Humidor. Cuisine: Continental and French.*

Speakeasy-Les Deux Foutaines
1238 Ocean Dr.
Miami
(305) 672-7878
•*Bar and outdoors. Humidor. Cuisine: French/Mediterranean.* **Bar/cigar bar.**

Victor's Cafe
2340 SW 32nd Ave.
Miami
(305) 445-1313
•*Bar/lounge and smoking section. Humidor. Cuisine: Cuban & Spanish. Cabaret.*

MIAMI BEACH

Alfredo the Original of Rome Doral Ocean
4833 Collins Ave.
Miami
(305) 532-3600
•*Bar/lounge. Humidor. Cuisine: Italian.*

Cafe Royal at the Hotel Sofitel Miami
5800 Blue Lagoon Dr., Miami Beach
(305) 264-4888
• *"Le Fumoir" cigar lounge and bar; private parties in the Limoges room. Humidor. Cuisine: French Classical.*

Cuba Club
432 Arthur Godfrey Rd., Miami Beach
(305) 604-9798
•*All areas. Humidor. Cuisine: American and Continental.* **Private club.**

The Forge
432 Arthur Godfrey Rd.
Miami Beach
(305) 538-8533

•*Smoking section. Humidor. Cuisine: American and Continental.*

i Paparazzi
940 Ocean Dr.
Miami Beach
(305) 531-3500
•*Patio. Humidor. Cuisine: Italian.*

Joe's Stone Crab
227 Biscayne St.
Miami Beach
(305) 673-0365
•*Bar and smoking area. Cuisine: seafood, specializing in stone crabs.*

Le Festival
2120 Salzedo St.
Miami Beach
(305) 442-8545
•*Private room. Cuisine: French.*

The Living Room at the Strand
671 Washington St.
Miami Beach
(305) 532-2340
•*All areas. Humidor. Cuisine: American with a twist of French.*

Yuca
501 Lincoln
Miami Beach
(305) 532-9822
•*Smoking section, bar and lounge. Humidor. Cuisine: innovative new world.*

NAPLES

Heaven
The Hibiscus
Center/2950 N.
Tamiami Trail
Naples
(941) 649-6373
•*All areas. Humidor.
Cuisine: nouveau.*
Cigar bar.

Terra
1300 3rd St. S.
Naples
(941) 262-5500
•*Smoking area. Cuisine: Mediterranean.*

Villa Pescatore
8920 N. Tamiami
Trail, Naples
(941) 597-8119
•*Bar/lounge. Cuisine: Italian.*

....

Chef Allen's
19088 NE 29th Ave.
North Miami Beach
(305) 935-2900
•*Bar and smoking
section. Humidor.
Cuisine: New World.*

**Art's Premium
Cigars & Exquisite
Accessories**
1235 N. Orange Ave.

Orlando
(407) 895-9772
•*Private club.* **Retail
store and private
smoking club** *with
full service bar.*

**Morton's of
Chicago**
7600 Dr. Philips
Blvd.
Orlando
(407) 248-3485
•*All areas. Humidor.
Cuisine: steakhouse.*

**The Living Room
at the Four Seasons Restaurant**
2800 S. Ocean Blvd.
Palm Beach
(561) 582-2800
•*Bar/lounge. Humidor. Cuisine: Southeastern regional.*

**The Leopard Room
Restaurant &
Supper Club at
the Chesterfield
Hotel**
363 Cocoanut Row
Palm Beach
(407) 659-5800
•*All areas. Humidor.
Cuisine: Continental.*

Fisherman's Wharf
222 Pompano Beach
Blvd.
Pompano Beach
(954) 941-5522
•*Smoking section.
Cuisine: American,
specializing in seafood.*

**TPC (Tournament
Players Club) at
Sawgrass**
110 TPC Blvd.
Ponte Vedra
(904) 273-3242

•*Throughout the club-
house. Humidor. Cuisine: American,
Caribbean and Continental, specializing in
seafood.* **Private
club.**

SARASOTA

Cafe L'Europe
431 St. Armand
Circle, Sarasota
(941) 388-4415
•*Front dining room
and private rooms.
Cuisine: Continental.*

**Gecko's Grill &
Pub**
4870 S. Tamiami
Trail, Sarasota
(941) 923-8896
•*All areas. Humidor.
Cuisine: American
pub.*

**Tabacchino (at
Caragiulos)**
69 S. Palm Ave.
Sarasota
(813) 951-0866
•*Cigar bar. Humidor.
Cuisine: Italian.*

....

**Barrancotto's Roma
Restaurant**
165 Vilano Rd.
St. Augustine
(904) 829-5719
•*Private room and
cigar room. Humidor.
Cuisine: Italian-
American.*

**Zeno's Italian
Restaurant**
267 U.S. Hwy. 27 N.
Sebring
(941) 471-9844
•*Outside. Humidor.
Cuisine: Italian.*

**Vecchia Brera i
Ristorante**
1440 Ocean Dr.
South Beach
(305) 535-9995
•*Special designated
dining area for cigar
smokers. Humidor.
Cuisine: Northern
Italian with "a touch
of the new world."*

TAMPA

**Armani's at the
Hyatt Regency
Westshore**
6200 Courtney
Campbell
Causeway
Tampa
(813) 281-9165
•*Lounge and terrace.
Humidor. Cuisine:
Italian.*

Bern's Steakhouse
1208 S. Howard
Ave., Tampa
(813) 251-2421
•*Bar/lounge and the
Dessert Room. Humidor. Cuisine: American, specializing in
steak.*

Columbia Restaurant & Cafe Cigar Bar
2117 E. 7th Ave.
Tampa
(813) 248-4961
•*Cafe cigar bar. Humidor. Cuisine: Spanish.*

Floyd's Stone Crabs
10438 N. Dale Mabry Hwy.
Tampa
(813) 969-0333
•*All areas. Humidor. Cuisine: stone crabs and seafood at a long bar.*

Le Bordeaux
1502 S. Howard Ave., Tampa
(813) 254-4387
•*Bistro (bar) only. Humidor. Cuisine: French.*

- -

O'Keefe's Irish Pub Restaurant
115 S. Rockingham Ave., Tavares
(352) 343-2157
•*Smoking area. Humidor. Cuisine: Irish and Continental.*

Morton's of Chicago
777 S. Flagler
West Palm Beach
(407) 835-9664
•*Smoking section, lounge and private rooms. Humidor. Cuisine: steakhouse.*

Georgia

ATLANTA
103 West
103 W. Paces Ferry Rd., Atlanta
(404) 233-5993
•*Bar/lounge. Humidor. Cuisine: new American with a French influence.*

The Abbey
163 Ponce de Leon Ave., Atlanta
(404) 876-8532
•*Bar, lounge and private rooms. Humidor. Cuisine: Continental.*

Bone's Restaurant
3130 Piedmont Rd.
Atlanta
(404) 237-2663
•*Bar/lounge and smoking section. Humidor. Cuisine: steak and seafood.*

Bugatti Restaurant
100 CNN Center
Atlanta
(404) 818-4450
•*Smoking area of dining room and lounge. Humidor. Cuisine: northern Italian.*

Cafe Intermezzo
1845 Peachtree Rd.
Atlanta
(404) 355-0411
•*In Loggia (special smoking room—dining available), bar and patio. Humidor. Cuisine: international*

bistro and European coffeehouse items. ***Coffee bar.***

Cheyene Grill & Martini Club
2391 Peachtree Rd.
Atlanta
(404) 842-1010
•*Martini room. Humidor. Cuisine: American grill.*

Chops
70 W. Paces Ferry Rd., Atlanta
(404) 262-2675
•*Bar/lounge and smoking area. Humidor. Cuisine: American.*

Filibuster's
1049 Juniper St.
Atlanta
(404) 875-6634
•*Smoking section and bar area. Humidor. Cuisine: traditional American.*

Florencia
75 14th St.
Atlanta
(404) 881-9898
•*Bar/lounge. Humidor. Cuisine: Continental.*

The Mansion
179 Ponce de Leon Ave., Atlanta
(404) 876-0727
•*Smoking section. Humidor. Cuisine: American and Continental.*

The Martini Club
1140 Crescent Ave.
Atlanta
(404) 873-0794
•*All areas. Humidor.* ***Nightclub/piano bar.***

Morton's of Chicago
303 Peachtree St. NE
Atlanta
(404) 577-4366
•*Smoking section, bar and lounge. Humidor. Cuisine: steakhouse.*

Morton's of Chicago, Buckhead
Peachtree Lenox Building/3379 Peachtree Rd. NE
Atlanta
(404) 816-6535
•*Smoking area, bar and boardrooms. Humidor. Cuisine: steakhouse.*

The Restaurant at the Ritz-Carlton, Atlanta
181 Peachtree St. NE, Atlanta
(404) 659-0400
•*Bar. Humidor. Cuisine: haute-fusion French.*

The Dining Room & Cafe at the Ritz-Carlton, Buckhead
3434 Peachtree Rd.
Atlanta
(404) 237-2700

•*Lobby lounge. Humidor. Cuisine: Continental.*

Tongue & Groove
3055 Peachtree Rd.
Atlanta
(404) 261-2325
•*All areas. Humidor. Cuisine: Pan-Pacific.* **Nightclub.**

Veni Vidi Vici
41 14th St.
Atlanta
(404) 875-8424
•*Bar. Humidor. Cuisine: Italian.*

Winfield's at the Galleria Mall
1 Galleria Pkwy.
Atlanta
(770) 955-5300
•*Bar/lounge. Cuisine: American and Continental.*

Havana Club
247 Buckhead Ave.
Buckhead
(404) 869-8484
•*All areas. Humidor. Cuisine: Cuban.* **Nightclub.**

Marra's Seafood Grill
1782 Cheshire Bridge Rd.
Northeast Atlanta
(404) 874-7347
•*Lounge, patio and private room. Humidor. Cuisine: Italian.*

Hackett's at the Holiday Inn Skytop Convention
20 U.S. 411 E.
Rome
(706) 295-1100
•*Smoking area. Cuisine: American and Continental, specializing in steak and seafood.*

45 South at the Pirate's House
20 E. Broad St.
Savannah
(912) 233-1881
•*Lobby lounge, private parties and late night after dinner. Cuisine: contemporary American.*

Hawaii

HONOLULU
Caffe Pronto
131 Kaiulani Ave.
Honolulu
(808) 923-0111
•*Patio. Humidor. Coffee bar.*

Gordon Biersch
1 Aloha Tower
    Marketplace #108
Honolulu
(808) 599-4877
•*Bar/lounge, smoking section and patio. Humidor. Cuisine: Pacific Rim.*

Kapalua Bay Club
1 Kapalua Bay Dr.
Honolulu
(808) 669-8008
•*Poolside. Humidor. Cuisine: American and Mediterranean.*

Murphy's Bar & Grill
2 Merchant St.
Honolulu
(808) 531-0422
•*Smoking section. Cuisine: American.*

O'Tooles Irish Pub
902 Nuuanu St.
Honolulu
(808) 536-6360
•*All areas. Humidor. Bar.*

Friends Espresso and Dessert Cafe
151 Hekili St.
Kailua
(808) 263-2233
•*Patio. Humidor. Cuisine: light lunches and desserts.* **Coffee bar.**

Fish and Games Sports Grill
4405 Honoapiilani Hwy.
Lahaina, Maui
(808) 669-3474
•*All areas after 10pm. Humidor. Cuisine: Continental, Classical French.*

Reilley's Steaks & Seafood
2290 Kaanapali Pkwy.
Lahaina, Maui
(808) 667-7477
•*Bar/lounge. Humidor. Cuisine: steak and fresh fish.*

Idaho

Mugger's Brewpub
516 2nd St. S.
Twin Falls
(208) 733-2322
•*All areas (except Bistro). Humidor. Cuisine: pub fare.*

Illinois

CHICAGO
Bice Ristorante
158 E. Ontario St.
Chicago
(312) 664-1474
•*Bar, private rooms and patio. Humidor. Cuisine: Northern Italian.*

B.L.U.E.S. Etc..
1124 W. Belmont
Chicago
(312) 549-9416
•*All areas. Humidor.* **Blues club.**

Cafe Ba Ba Reeba!
2024 N. Halsted St.
Chicago
(312) 935-5000
•*Cigar Lounge, bar and private rooms only. Humidor. Cuisine: Spanish.*

Chicago Chop House
60 W. Ontario St.
Chicago
(800) 229-2356,
   (312) 787-7100
•*Bar. Humidor. Cuisine: steakhouse.*

Coco Pazzo
300 W. Hubbard
Chicago
(312) 836-0900
•*Bar and limited tables in dining room. Humidor. Cuisine: Italian.*

Como Inn
546 N. Milwaukee
Chicago
(312) 421-5222
•*Bar. Humidor. Cuisine: Northern Italian.*

Cuisine's at the Stouffer Riviere Hotel
1 W. Wacker
Chicago
(312) 372-7200
•*Court area. Cuisine: Mediterranean.*

Danilo's
464 N. Halsted St.
Chicago
(312) 421-0218
•*Two rooms and outdoors. Humidor. Cuisine: Italian steakhouse.*

Distant Mirror Cafe
7007 N. Sheridan Rd.
Chicago
(312) 761-3776

•*All areas. Humidor. Cuisine: Spanish-style tapas cooked on "Hot Rocks" at the table.*

Drink & Eat, Too!
702 W. Fulton
Chicago
(312) 441-0818
•*All areas. Humidor. Cuisine: Italian and American.*

Erie Cafe
536 W. Erie St.
Chicago
(312) 266-2300
•*Bar/lounge, smoking section and private room. Humidor. Cuisine: steak and chops.*

Four Seasons Hotel
120 E. Delaware
Chicago
(312) 280-8800
•*Bar/lounge and private rooms. Humidor. Cuisine: American.*

Frontera Grill
445 N. Clark St.
Chicago
(312) 661-1434
•*Bar. Cuisine: Mexican.*

Fumatore Club
1723 N. Halstead
Chicago
(312) 266-8900
•*All areas. Humidor. Cuisine: Continental and Cuban.* **Cigar bar.**

Gene & Georgetti
500 N. Franklin St.
Chicago
(312) 527-3718
•*Bar. Cuisine: American steakhouse.*

Gibsons
1028 N. Rush St.
Chicago
(312) 266-8999
•*Bar/lounge and private rooms. Humidor. Cuisine: steakhouse.*

Green Dolphin St.
2200 N. Ashland
Chicago
(312) 395-0066
•*Bar, jazz club and patio. Humidor. Cuisine: fine dining.*

Harry's Velvet Room
534 N. Clark St.
Chicago
(312) 828-0770
•*All areas. Humidor. Cuisine: American.*

Havana
2320 W. Kinzle
Chicago
(312) 595-0101
•*Bar, cigar bar and private room. Humidor. Cuisine: Cuban.*

Iron Mike's Grille at the Tremont Hotel
100 E. Chestnut
Chicago
(312) 587-8989
•*Smoking parlour and bar. Humidor. Cuisine: regional Italian.*

Jesse Livermore's
401 S. LaSalle St.
Chicago
(312) 786-5272
•*All areas.* **Bar.**

Jilly's Bistro/Jilly's Retro Club
1007 N. Rush
Chicago
(312) 664-1001
•*All areas. Humidor.* **Bar/cigar bar/nightclub.**

Kirzie Street Chophouse
400 North Wells St.
Chicago
(312) 822-0191
•*Bar. Humidor. Cuisine: classic American steakhouse.*

Magnum's Steak & Lobster
225 W. Ontario St.
Chicago
(312) 337-8080
•*Dining room after 9:00pm and in the piano bar. Humidor. Cuisine: steaks, chops and seafood.*

Morton's of Chicago
1050 N. State St.
Chicago
(312) 266-4820
•*Smoking section, bar, lounge and private rooms. Humidor. Cuisine: steakhouse.*

Nick's Fishmarket
1 First National
   Plaza
Chicago
(312) 621-0200
•*Cocktail lounge.*
Humidor. Cuisine:
Continental and
Mediterranean
seafood.

O'Brien's
   Restaurant & Bar
1528 N. Wells St.
Chicago
(312) 787-3131
•*Bar/lounge and pri-*
vate rooms. Humidor.
Cuisine: steak and
seafood.

P.J. Clarke's-
   Chicago
1204 N. State Pkwy.
Chicago
(312) 664-1650
•*Bar/lounge and pri-*
vate room. Humidor.
Cuisine: American.

Printer's Row
   Restaurant
550 S. Dearborn St.
Chicago
(312) 461-0780
•*Lounge and private*
dining room. Humidor.
Cuisine: American.

The Pump Room at
   The Ambassador
   East Hotel
1301 N. State Pkwy.
Chicago
(312) 266-0360
•*Bar/lounge. Humi-*
dor. Cuisine: Ameri-
can and Continental.

Reminiscent Bar &
   Grill
3614 N. Damen
   Ave., Chicago
(312) 281-2118
•*Bar/lounge, smoking*
section and private
room. Humidor. Cui-
sine: steak and
seafood.

Rigoletto
2478 N. Lincoln
Chicago
(847) 234-7675
•*Dining area in the*
bar. Humidor.
Cuisine: Italian.

The Dining Room
   at the Ritz-
   Carlton
160 E. Pearson St.
Chicago
(312) 266-1000
•*Cigar bar (Trianon)*
and Terrace Green-
house. Humidor. Cui-
sine: contemporary
French.

Saloon Steakhouse
200 E. Chestnut
Chicago
(312) 280-5454
•*Bar. Humidor. Cui-*
sine: classic American
steakhouse.

Scoozi!
410 W. Huron St.
Chicago
(312) 943-5900
•*Bar. Cuisine:*
Italian.

Seasons Bar
120 E. Delaware
Chicago
(312) 280-8800
•*All areas. Humidor.*
Cuisine: Asian-style
hors d'oeuvres. **Cigar**
bar.

Shaw's Crab House
21 E. Hubbard St.
Chicago
(312) 527-2722
•*Bar. Cuisine:*
seafood.

Sorriso
321 N. Clark
Chicago
(312) 644-0283
•*Dining room and*
bar. Humidor. Cui-
sine: American and
Italian.

Spago Chicago
520 N. Dearborn St.
Chicago
(312) 527-3700
•*Cigar bar and pri-*
vate room. Humidor.
Cuisine: American.

Tailgators Sports
   Bar
2263 N. Lincoln
Chicago
(312) 348-7200
•*All areas. Humidor.*
Cuisine: American.

Tania's Restaurant
2659 N. Milwaukee
   Ave., Chicago
(312) 235-7120
•*Dining room, bar,*
lounge and private
rooms. Humidor.

Cuisine: Cuban,
Spanish and Puerto
Rican and Mexican.

Mitchell's
9932 W. 55th St.
Countryside
(708) 352-6840
•*Bar. Cuisine: fea-*
tures seafood, steak
and ribs.

Pete Miller's
   Steakhouse
1557 Sherman Ave.
Evanston
(847) 328-0399
•*Smoking area, bar,*
jazz lounge and billiard
room. Humidor.
Cuisine: steakhouse.

Benjamin's
103 N. Main St.
Galena
(815) 777-0467
•*Bar area. Humidor.*
Cuisine: American.

Maurie's Table
2360 Glenwood Ave.
Joliet
(815) 744-2619
•*Dining room and*
bar. Cuisine: Ameri-
can, Italian, pizza.

Uptown Bar &
   Grill
613 1st St.
LaSalle
(815) 224-4545
•*Bar/lounge and*
smoking section. Hu-
midor. Cuisine:
American bistro.

The Living Room
801 E. Butterfield Rd.
Lombard
(630) 368-0069
•2/3 of area. Humi-
dor. Cuisine: tapas
and eclectic appetizers.
Upscale nightclub.

Cypress Inn
1352 Shermer Rd.
Northbrook
(847) 272-8787
•All areas. Cuisine:
pub fare. **Pub.**

Ken's Guest House
9848 SW Hwy.
Oaklawn
(708) 422-4014
•Bar, lounge and pri-
vate rooms. Cuisine:
American, specializing
in seafood and steak.

ROCKFORD
Cafe Patou
3929 Broadway
Rockford
(815) 227-4100
•Bar/lounge. Cuisine:
French.

**The City Club of
Rockford**
555 N. Court St.
Rockford
(815) 966-6966
•Bar and "Blue
Smoke Cigar
Lounge." Humidor.
Cuisine: American.

**Giovanni's
Restaurant**
610 N. Bell School
Rd., Rockford
(815) 398-6411
•Bar/lounge, smoking
section, private room
and banquet rooms.
Humidor. Cuisine:
Continental.

**Morton's of
Chicago**
9525 W. Bryn Mawr
Rosemont
(847) 678-5155
•All areas. Humidor.
Cuisine: steakhouse.

Baur's Restaurant
620 S. 1st St.
Springfield
(217) 789-4311
•Dining room and
lounge. Humidor.
Cuisine: Continental
featuring German
specialities.

Scalawag's
313 W. State
Sycamore
(815) 895-4333
•Bar/lounge. Cuisine:
American.

**Morton's of
Chicago**
1 Westbrook
Corporate Center,
22nd & Wolf Rds.
Westchester
(708) 562-7000

•Bar/lounge, smoking
section and private
dining rooms.
Humidor. Cuisine:
steakhouse.

Indiana

**The Jungle and Fat
Cats Bar & Cigar
Lounge**
415 Main St.
Evansville
(812) 425-5282
•All areas of Fat Cats
on the lower level.
Humidor. Cuisine:
American Bistro
featuring steaks,
chops and seafood.

INDIANAPOLIS
**The Restaurant at
the Canterbury**
123 S. Illinois St.
Indianapolis
(317) 634-3000
•Bar area. Humidor.
Cuisine: Continental.

Henry Gratton Pub
745 Broad Ripple
Ave.
Indianapolis
(317) 257-6030
•All areas. Cuisine:
American/Irish.

Keystone Grill
8650 Keystone
Crossing
Indianapolis
(317) 848-5202
•Bar/lounge and
smoking section of din-
ing room. Humidor.
Cuisine: American.

**The Marker
Restaurant at the
Adam's Mark
Hotel**
2544 Executive Dr.
Indianapolis
(317) 248-2481
•Smoking section.
Cuisine: fine dining.

Philabuster's
50 S. Capital
Indianapolis
(317) 231-3970
•All areas. Humidor.
Cuisine: American.

**Ruth's Chris Steak
House**
9445 Three L Rd.
Indianapolis
(317) 844-1155
•Lounge/bar area and
in private rooms.
Humidor. Cuisine:
steakhouse.

**St. Elmo Steak
House**
127 S. Illinois St.
Indianapolis
(317) 635-0636
•Bar and private
rooms. Humidor.
Cuisine: steakhouse.

**Rich O's Public
House**
3312 Plaza Dr.
New Albany
(812) 949-2804
•All areas. Humidor.
Cuisine: casual cuisine
featuring BBQ and
Pizzas.

La Salle Grill
115 W. Colfax
South Bend
(800) 382-9323,
(219) 288-1155
•*Smoking section, private room and cigar bar. Humidor. Cuisine: steakhouse and seafood.*

Orion's Restaurant
1700 Rozella Rd.
Warsaw
(219) 269-9100
•*Bar/lounge. Humidor. Cuisine: regional American.*

Up For Grabs Restaurant & Bar
1923 Calumet Ave.
Whiting
(219) 659-4508
•*All areas. Humidor. Cuisine: sandwiches to seafood.*

Iowa

Eight Hundred One Steak & Chop House
801 Grand Ave.
Des Moines
(515) 288-6000
•*Bar and special cigar and wine room (seats 35). Humidor. Cuisine: steakhouse.*

Embassy Club
801 Grand Ave.
Des Moines
(515) 244-2582
•*Bar/lounge. Humidor. Cuisine: American and French.*
Private club.

The Tobacco Bowl
111 S. Dubuque
Iowa City
(319) 338-5885
•*All areas. Humidor. Cuisine: pastries.*
Coffee bar.

Kansas

Grain Bin Supper Club
1301 E. Fulton
Garden City
(316) 275-5954
•*All areas. Humidor. Cuisine: American.*

Auntie Mae's Parlor
616 N. 12th St.
Manhattan
(913) 539-8508
•*All areas. Humidor. Bar.*

Lucky Bar & Grille
710 N. Manhattan Ave.
Manhattan
(913) 776-9090
•*Bar/lounge and smoking area. Humidor. Cuisine: pizzas, pastas and sandwiches.*

Pinestone Restaurant & Lounge
126 S. First St.
Norton
(913) 877-2111
•*Bar. Humidor. Cuisine: steak, prime rib and seafood.*

La Mediterranee
9058 B Metcalf Ave.
Overland Park
(913) 341-9595
•*Bar. Humidor. Cuisine: classical French.*

Mort's
923 E. 1st St.
Wichita
(316) 262-1785
•*All areas. Humidor. Cuisine: sandwiches.*
Cigar bar.

Kentucky

Coach House Restaurant
855 S. Broadway
Lexington
(606) 252-7777
•*Bar. Humidor. Cuisine: Continental and French.*

LOUISVILLE

Azalea
3612 Brownsboro Rd.
Louisville
(502) 895-5493
•*Private room. Humidor. Cuisine: new American fusion.*

Bobby J's
1314 Bardstown Rd.
Louisville
(502) 452-2665
•*Bar/lounge and cigar dining room. Humidor. Cuisine: American and Italian.*
Nightclub.

Brasserie Deitrich
2862 Frankfort Ave.
Louisville
(502) 897-6076
•*Lounge. Humidor. Cuisine: French.*

Illusions Nightclub
1506 Lake Shore Court
Louisville
(502) 425-7339
•*All areas. Humidor.*
Nightclub.

Louisiana Jack's
630 Barret Ave.
Louisville
(502) 589-2739
•*Bar, patio and patio room. Humidor. Cuisine: regional American.*

The Oakroom at the Seelbach Hotel
500 4th Ave.
Louisville
(502) 585-3200
•*"Oakroom Anteroom," The Old Seelbach Bar and Jazz Club. Humidor. Cuisine: American regional, specializing in rack of lamb, Angus beef and fresh fish.*

Porcini
2730 Frankfort Ave.
Louisville
(502) 894-8686
•*Bar. Cuisine: Italian featuring fresh pastas, hand-tossed gourmet pizzas and veal specialties.*

Louisiana

Juban's Restaurant
3739 Perkins Rd.
Baton Rouge
(504) 346-8422
•*Bar. Humidor. Cuisine: Creole.*

Charley G's Seafood Grill
111 Veterans Blvd.
Metairie
(504) 837-6408
•*Dining room, bar and private rooms. Humidor. Cuisine: contemporary South Louisiana, specializing in grilled seafood.*

Crozier's Restaurant
3216 W. Esplanade Ave. N.
Metairie
(504) 833-8108
•*After late dinners and on cigar nights. Humidor. Cuisine: French.*

NEW ORLEANS

Antoine's
713 St. Louis St.
New Orleans
(504) 581-4422
•*Main dining room and private banquet rooms. Cuisine: French/Creole.*

Arnaud's Restaurant
813 Bienville St.
New Orleans
(504) 523-5433
•*Cigar Bar and private rooms. Humidor. Cuisine: Creole.*

Brennan's
417 Royal St.
New Orleans
(504) 525-9711
•*Smoking areas. Humidor. Cuisine: French/Creole.*

Brossard's Restaurant
819 Conti St.
New Orleans
(504) 581-3866
•*Bar, courtyard and banquet rooms at all times; main dining room late in the evening. Humidor. Cuisine: Nouvelle Creole.*

Cafe Rue Bourbon Restaurant
241 Rue Bourbon at Bienville
New Orleans
(504) 524-0114
•*Smoking section, private room and wine room. Cuisine: New Orleans Style.*

The Court of Two Sisters
613 Royal St.
New Orleans
(504) 522-7261
•*Smoking area. Humidor. Cuisine: Cajun, Creole and French.*

Dos Jefes Uptown Cigar Bar
5535 Tchoupitoulas St., New Orleans
(504) 891-8500
•*All areas. Humidor.*
Cigar bar/jazz bar.

Emeril's Restaurant
800 Tchoupitoulas
New Orleans
(504) 528-9393
•*Bar and dining room. Humidor. Cuisine: American and Creole.*

Galatoire's
209 Bourbon St.
New Orleans
(504) 525-2021
•*Dining room. Cuisine: French.*

The Grill Room
300 Gravier St.
New Orleans
(504) 522-1992
•*Bar/lounge. Humidor. Cuisine: Continental.*

Hyttops Sports Bar & Grill
500 Poydras Plaza
New Orleans
(504) 561-1234
•*All areas. Humidor. Cuisine: pub fare.*
Sports bar.

Louis XVI Restaurant
730 Rue Bienville
New Orleans
(504) 581-7000
•*Bar/lounge, private room and patio. Humidor. Cuisine: classic French.*

Maximo's Italian Grill
1117 Decatur St.
New Orleans
(504) 586-8883
•*Bar/lounge and smoking section. Humidor. Cuisine: modern, innovative and Italian.*

Mint Julep Lounge at the Hyatt Regency New Orleans
500 Poydras Plaza
New Orleans
(504) 561-1234
•*All areas. Humidor. Cuisine: appetizers only.* **Piano bar/lounge.**

The Rib Room at the Omni Royal Orleans Hotel
621 St. Louis St.
New Orleans
(504) 529-5333
•*Smoking room "Escoffier" adjacent to restaurant. Humidor. Cuisine: American, Continental and New Orleans Creole.*

Sazerac Bar at The Fairmont Hotel
123 Barrone St.
New Orleans
(504) 529-7111
•*Bar. Humidor. Cuisine: elegant French and Continental.*

Top of the Dome Steakhouse at the Hyatt Regency New Orleans
500 Poydras Plaza
New Orleans
(504) 561-1234
ext. 2755
•*Smoking section. Humidor. Cuisine: steakhouse.*

Windsor Court Hotel
300 Gravier St.
New Orleans
(504) 523-6000
•*Polo Lounge/Bar. Humidor. Cuisine: Continental.*

Maine

The Greenhouse Restaurant
193 Broad St.
Bangor
(207) 945-4040
•*Dining room, lounge and private rooms. Cuisine: American.*

Wine & Espresso Cafe
37 Bay View St. 2nd Fl., Camden
(207) 230-0533
•*Cafe/wine and cigar bar.*

La Conque at The Manor Inn
Battle Ave., Box 276
Castine
(207) 326-4335

•*Smoking section. Humidor. Cuisine: American, French and Mediterranean.*

Seasons Cafe
157 Main St.
Lewiston
(207) 782-5054
•*All areas. Humidor. Cuisine: eclectic American featuring fish and duck.*

Maryland

BALTIMORE

Baltimore Brewing Company
104 Albemarle St.
Baltimore
(410) 837-5000
•*Bar/lounge and patio. Humidor. Cuisine: American.*

The Brass Elephant
924 N. Charles St.
Baltimore
(410) 547-8480
•*Lounge. Cuisine: northern Italian.*

Da Mimmo Finest Italian Cuisine
217 S. High St.
Baltimore
(410) 727-6876
•*Bar, lounge, private rooms and patio. Humidor. Cuisine: Italian.*

Daniel's Restaurant
1026 S. Charles St.
Baltimore
(410) 752-3810

•*Smoking section. Humidor. Cuisine: seafood and steak.*

Edgar's Billiard Club
1 E. Pratt St.
Baltimore
(410) 752-8080
•*All areas except non-smoking. Humidor. Cuisine: light fare/ Continental cuisine.*
Upscale billiard hall/bar.

Explorer's Lounge at the Harbour Court Hotel
550 Light St.
Baltimore
(410) 234-0550
•*Bar/lounge area. Humidor. Cuisine: nouvelle American.*

The Fishery Restaurant
1717 Eastern Ave.
Baltimore
(410) 327-9340
•*Bar/lounge, smoking section and private room. Humidor. Cuisine: Spanish and Italian, featuring Maryland seafood.*

La Scala Italian Restaurant
411 S. High St.
Baltimore
(410) 783-9209
•*Godfather Lounge. Humidor. Cuisine: Italian.*

Max's on Broadway
737 S. Broadway
Baltimore
(410) 276-2850
•*All areas. Humidor. Cuisine: pub fare.*
Bar.

Pickles Pub
520 Washington Blvd.
Baltimore
(410) 752-1784
•*All areas. Humidor. Cuisine: pub fare.*
Bar.

The Prime Rib
1101 N. Calvert St.
Baltimore
(410) 539-1804
•*Bar. Humidor. Cuisine: features prime aged beef and fresh seafood.*

Ropewalk Tavern
1209 S. Charles St.
Baltimore
(410) 727-1298
•*All areas. Humidor.*
Cigar bar.

Ruth's Chris Steak House
600 Water St.
Baltimore
(410) 783-0033
•*Dining room and lounge/cigar room (seats 50). Humidor. Cuisine: steakhouse.*

Savannah at the Admiral Fell Inn
888 S. Broadway
Baltimore
(410) 522-2195
•Bar/lounge, wine cellar and English Pub. Humidor. Cuisine: modern American with southern accents.

Windows
202 E. Pratt St.
Baltimore
(410) 547-1200
•Lounge. Humidor. Cuisine: contemporary American.

Windsor Club
7 N. Calvert St.
Baltimore
(410) 332-0700
•All areas. Humidor. Private cigar club with bar & billiards—new members are always welcome.

Patrick's Pub & Restaurant
550 Cranbrook Rd.
Cockeysville
(410) 683-0604
•Bar/lounge. Humidor. Cuisine: Continental.

Nick's Airport Inn
Rte. 11 N.
Hagerstown
(301) 733-8560
•Lounge. Humidor. Cuisine: Continental.

Old Angler's Inn
10801 McArthur Blvd.
Potomac
(301) 365-2425
•Bar, lounge, private rooms and patio. Humidor. Cuisine: contemporary American.

Shelly's Back Room at the Shelly's Woodroast
1699 Rockville Pike
Rockville
(301) 984-3300
•Bar/lounge area. Humidor. Cuisine: American.

The Inn at Perry Cabin
308 Watkins Lane
St. Michael's
(800) 722-2949,
   (410) 745-2200
•All areas. Humidor. Cuisine: Continental.

St. Michael's Crab House
305 Mulberry St.
St. Michael's
(410) 745-3737
•Bar/lounge and smoking section. Humidor. Cuisine: seafood.

Antrim 1844 Country Inn
30 Treventon Rd.
Taneytown
(410) 756-6812
•Tavern and patio. Humidor. Cuisine: regional American.

Hersh's Orchard Inn
1528 E. Joppa Rd.
Towson
(410) 823-0384
•Bar/lounge. Cuisine: Continental.

Westminster Inn
5 S. Center St.
Westminster
(410) 857-4445
•Cigar lounge/shop and Courtyard Restaurant (when lounge/shop is closed). Humidor. Cuisine: American.

Massachusetts

BOSTON

Anthony's Pier 4
140 Northern Ave.
Boston
(617) 682-6262
•Smoking areas. Humidor. Cuisine: American, specializing in seafood.

Biba Restaurant
272 Boylston St.
Boston
(617) 426-7878
•Bar/lounge. Humidor. Cuisine: eclectic American.

The Capital Grille
359 Newbury St.
Boston
(617) 262-8900
•Dining rooms, bar and private rooms. Humidor. Cuisine: steak.

Bristol Lounge at the Four Seasons Hotel, Boston
200 Boylston St.
Boston
(617) 338-4400
•Smoking area. Humidor. Cuisine: Continental.

Grill 23 & Bar
161 Berkeley St.
Boston
(617) 542-2255
•Dining room, bar and lounge. Humidor. Cuisine: American, specializing in prime aged beef, seafood and rotisserie cooking.

Jimmy's Harborside
242 Northern Ave.
Boston
(617) 423-1000
•Bar and cocktail lounge. Humidor. Cuisine: American seafood.

Julien Restaurant
250 Franklin St.
Boston
(617) 451-1900
•Bar/lounge area. Humidor. Cuisine: French.

Locke-Ober
3 Winter Place
Boston
(617) 542-1340
•Dining room, lounge and Yvonne's (a private club). Humidor. Cuisine: Continental.

Morton's of Chicago
1 Exeter Plaza
Boston
(617) 266-5858
•Smoking section. Humidor. Cuisine: steakhouse.

Oliver Tavern
33 Batterymarch St.
Boston
(617) 350-7975
•All areas. Humidor. Cuisine: American.

Oskar's
107 South St.
Boston
(617) 542-6756
•Bar/lounge, smoking section and private room. Humidor. Cuisine: American.

The Ritz-Carlton
15 Arlington St.
Boston
(617) 536-5700
•Bar/lounge and private rooms. Humidor. Cuisine: French.

Ron's Grill and Cue Club
256 Commercial St.
Boston
(617) 227-4545
•Bar and billiards room (after hours in the dining area). Humidor. Cuisine: American with a Southwestern flair.
Billiard hall.

Seasons at The Bostonian Hotel
Faneuil Hall Market Place, Boston
(617) 523-3600
•Atrium lounge and smoking area after 9:30pm. Humidor. Cuisine: New England.

The Trowbridge Tavern & Ale House
100 Trowbridge Rd.
Bourne
(508) 759-1776
•Bar. Humidor. Cuisine: American.

Chez Henri
1 Shepard St.
Cambridge
(617) 354-8980
•Bar. Humidor. Cuisine: French/Cuban.

Upstairs at the Pudding
10 Holyoke St.
Cambridge
(617) 864-1933
•Bar, herb garden terrace and waiting area only. Cuisine: hand-crafted with Italian influences.

Sun Tavern
500 Congress St.
Duxbury
(617) 837-4100
•Bar. Cuisine: country Continental.

The Barley Neck Inn & Lodge
5 Beach Rd.
East Orleans
(508) 255-0212
•Bar/lounge. Humidor. Cuisine: French and traditional New England.

Joe's Beach Road Bar & Grille
5 Beach Rd.
East Orleans 02643
(508) 255-0212
•Bar/lounge. Humidor. Cuisine: bistro fare.

Down Under Restaurant
91 Purchase St.
Fall River
(508) 672-6951
•All areas. Humidor. Cuisine: pub fare.
Pub.

Castle Restaurant
1230 Main St.
Leicester
(508) 892-9090
•Bar/lounge. Humidor. Cuisine: American and Continental.

Blantyre Hotel
16 Blantyre Rd.
Lenox
(413) 637-3556
•Lounge, music room and patio. Humidor. Cuisine: American/French.

Cobblestones
91 Dutton St.
Lowell
(508) 970-2282
•Bar. Humidor. Cuisine: Eclectic American.

The Chanticleer
9 New St.
Siaconset, Nantucket
(508) 257-6231
•Bar and patio. Humidor. Cuisine: traditional French.

Silks at the Stonehedge Inn
160 Pawtucket Blvd.
Tyngsboro
(508) 649-4400
•Bar and Library. Humidor. Cuisine: French Continental/ Nouvelle American.

Union Market Station
17 Nichols Ave.
Watertown
(617) 923-0480
•Dining room and bar. Cuisine: American and Mediterranean.

Moby Dick Wharf Restaurant & Marina
1 Bridge Rd.
Westport Point
(508) 636-6500
•West deck. Humidor. Cuisine: French-style seafood.

Michigan

Dick O'Dow's Irish Pub & Restaurant
160 W. Maple St.
Birmingham
(810) 642-1135
•*Pub area. Humidor. Cuisine: Irish American.*

Fox & Hounds
1560 N. Woodward
Bloomfield Hills
(810) 644-4800
•*Pub only. Humidor. Cuisine: classic American and seafood.* **Pub/oyster bar.**

DETROIT

Carl's Chop House
320 Grand River
Detroit
(313) 833-0700
•*Bar/lounge and smoking section. Cuisine: American.*

Caucus Club
150 W. Congress
Detroit
(313) 965-4970
•*Bar/lounge and smoking section. Humidor. Cuisine: American and Continental.*

Joe Meur's
2000 Gratiot Ave.
Detroit
(313) 567-1088
•*2 of 5 dining rooms are smoking. Humidor. Cuisine: seafood.*

Opus One
565 E. Larned
Detroit
(313) 961-7766
•*Bar/lounge. Humidor. Cuisine: American with a French flair.*

The Rattlesnake Club
300 River Place
Detroit
(313) 567-4400
•*Bar/lounge. Humidor. Cuisine: contemporary American.*

Vivio's
2460 Market St.
Detroit
(313) 393-1711
•*Bar and bar room. Cuisine: American.*

The Whitney
4421 Woodland Ave.
Detroit
(313) 832-5700
•*Third floor. Humidor. Cuisine: American.*

Rowe Inn
6303 C-48
Ellsworth, E. Jordan Rd.
Ellsworth
(616) 588-7351
•*Wine cellar. Humidor. Cuisine: regional Michigan.*

Ginopolis' on the Grill
27815 Middlebelt Rd.
Farmington Hills

(810) 851-8222
•*Bar/lounge. Humidor. Cuisine: American.*

Glen Oaks Golf Club
30500 W. 13 Mile Rd.
Farmington Hills
(810) 626-2600
•*Dining room and bar. Cuisine: American.* **Golf club.**

Laredo Steak House
2324 S. Ballenger
Flint
(810) 234-1271
•*Smoking section of the dining room and bar. Cuisine: steak featuring baby back ribs and large cuts of USDA choice beef.*

Lakos Downtown
188 Monroe NW
Grand Rapids
(616) 459-4135
•*Bar/lounge. Humidor. Cuisine: American and French.*

Arboretum
7075 S. Lakeshore Dr.
Harbor Springs
(616) 526-6291
•*Bar, lounge and private rooms. Humidor. Cuisine: American.*

Bar Harbor
100 State St.
Harbor Springs
(616) 526-2671
•*All areas. Humidor.* **Tavern.**

Whirligig
2000 Holiday Inn Dr.
Jackson
(517) 783-2681
•*All areas. Cuisine: American.*

Corner Bar
1030 E. Vine
Kalamazoo
(616) 385-2028
•*All areas except nonsmoking. Humidor. Cuisine: grill and pub fare.*

Vannelli Steak House
801 S. Lapeer, M-24
Lake Orion
(810) 693-8882
•*Smoking areas. Humidor. Cuisine: steakhouse.*

Knight Cap
320 E. Michigan Ave.
Lansing
(517) 484-7676
•*All areas. Cuisine: steak and seafood.*

Herman's Garland Resort
Rte. 1, Box 364 M
Lewiston
(517) 786-2211
•*Lounge. Humidor. Cuisine: American.*

Fonte d'Amore
32030 Plymouth Rd.
Livonia
(313) 422-0770
•*All areas. Humidor. Cuisine: Abruzzo-style Italian.*

The Pink Pony
PO Box 250
Mackinac Island
(906) 847-3341
•*All areas. Humidor.
Cuisine: bar & grill.*

**Laredo Steak
House**
350 E. 14 Mile Rd.
Madison Heights
(810) 583-1077
•*Smoking section of
the dining room and in
the bar. Cuisine: steak
featuring baby back
ribs and large cuts of
USDA choice beef.*

**Muskegon Country
Club**
2801 Lakeshore Dr.
Muskegon
(616) 755-3737
•*Bar/lounge. Humidor. Cuisine: Continental.* **Private club**.

**MacKinnon's
Restaurant**
126 E. Main St.
Northville
(810) 348-1991
•*Bar/lounge and cigar
bar. Humidor. Cuisine: French.*

**Cheers on the
Channel**
6211 Point Tremble
Pearl Beach
(810) 794-9017
•*Lounge area where
food is available (seats
20). Humidor.
Cuisine: French/
American.*

Park Garden Cafe
432 E. Lake St.
Petoskey
(616) 347-0101
•*Bar/lounge.
Humidor. Cuisine:
American.*

**Pike Street
Restaurant**
18 W. Pike
Pontiac
(810) 334-7878
•*Bar, lounge and private rooms. Humidor.
Cuisine: American
and French.*

**Rochester Chop
House**
306 Main St.
Rochester
(810) 651-2266
•*Special room. Humidor. Cuisine: steak,
veal and seafood.*

**D'Amato's
Neighborhood
Restaurant**
222 Sherman Dr.
Royal Oak
(810) 544-7400
•*Bar/lounge. Humidor. Cuisine: Italian.*

Goodnite Gracie
224 Sherman Dr.
Royal Oak
(810) 544-7490
•*All areas. Humidor.*
**Cocktail & cigar
lounge.**

Treasure Island
924 N. Niagara St.
Saginaw
(517) 755-6577

•*Bar/lounge. Humidor. Cuisine: Continental, features regional fresh fish.*
**Nightclub/banquet
& conference facility.**

SOUTHFIELD

**Chianti Villa
Italiana**
28565 Northwestern
Hwy., Southfield
(810) 350-0055
•*Bar/lounge. Cuisine:
Italian.*

**Excalibur
Restaurant**
28875 Franklin Rd.
Southfield
(810) 358-3355
•*All areas. Humidor.
Cuisine: American
and Continental, specializing in seafood
and steak.* **Nightclub.**

Golden Mushroom
18100 W. 10 Mile
Rd., Southfield
(810) 559-4230
•*Bar/lounge.
Humidor. Cuisine:
Continental.*

**Morton's of
Chicago**
One Towne Square
Southfield
(810) 354-6006
•*Bar/lounge, smoking
section and private
room. Humidor. Cuisine: steakhouse.*

**Andiamo Lakefront
Bistro**
24026 Jefferson Ave.
St. Clair Shores
(810) 773-7770
•*Bar, lounge and patio. Humidor. Cuisine: Italian and
American.*

Grub Street Hermit
2865 W. Maple
Troy
(810) 435-5858
•*Dining room, bar
and patio. Cuisine:
American.*

Spectadium
2511 Livernois
Troy
(810) 362-4030
•*All areas. Humidor.
Cuisine: American
classic pub fare.*
Bar/nightclub.

Cass Avenue Cafe
45199 Cass Ave.
Utica
(810) 726-0770
•*2 of 4 rooms. Humidor. Cuisine: French.*

Minnesota

Shorewood
6161 Hwy. 65 NE
Fridley
(612) 571-3444
•*Smoking section and
lounge. Humidor.
Cuisine: Grecian and
American.*

MINNEAPOLIS

Brit's Pub & Eating Establishment
1110 Nicollet Mall
Minneapolis
(612) 332-3908
•*Upstairs dining area, bar, lounge and near fireplaces. Humidor. Cuisine: British.*

Crowne Plaza North South
618 2nd Ave. S.
Minneapolis
(612) 338-2288
•*Smoking section and lounge. Cuisine: gourmet Continental and classic American.*

D'Amico Cucina
100 N. 6th St.
Minneapolis
(612) 338-2401
•*Lounge. Humidor. Cuisine: modern Italian.*

Huberts
601 Chicago Ave.
Minneapolis
(612) 332-6062
•*Bar/lounge, private room and patio. Cuisine: American.*

Jimmy's Steak & Spirits
3675 Minnehaha Ave. S.
Minneapolis
(612) 729-9635
•*All areas. Humidor. Cuisine: steaks and pub fare.*

Manny's Steak House at the Hyatt Regency
1300 Nicolett Mall
Minneapolis
(612) 339-9900
•*Bar. Humidor. Cuisine: American steakhouse.*

Minneapolis Cafe
2730 W. Lake St.
Minneapolis
(612) 920-1401
•*Bar area and on the patio in the summer. Humidor. Cuisine: French/Northern Italian fusion.*

Morton's of Chicago
555 Nicollet Mall
Minneapolis
(612) 673-9700
•*Bar/lounge and smoking section. Humidor. Cuisine: steakhouse.*

Murray's
26 S. 6th St.
Minneapolis
(612) 339-0909
•*Bar/lounge. Humidor. Cuisine: American.*

Nye's Polonaise Room
112 E. Hennepin
Minneapolis
(612) 379-2021
•*Bar/lounge. Humidor. Cuisine: Polish/American.*

Schiek's Palace Royale
115 S. 4th St.
Minneapolis
(612) 341-0054
•*All areas. Humidor. Cuisine: American.*
Nightclub.

ST. PAUL

Chang O'Hara's Bistro
498 Selby
St. Paul
(612) 290-2338
•*All smoking areas. Humidor. Cuisine: American bistro fare influenced by spices from around the world.*

Forepaugh's
276 S. Exchange St.
St. Paul
(612) 224-5606
•*Bar/lounge. Cuisine: French.*

The St. Paul Grill at the St. Paul Hotel
350 Market St.
St. Paul
(612) 22 GRILL
•*Bar/lounge. Humidor. Cuisine: American.*

Sweeney's Saloon
96 N. Dale St.
St. Paul
(612) 221-9157
•*All areas. Humidor. Cuisine: American. Bar.*

Town & Country Club
300 Mississippi River Blvd. N.
St. Paul
(612) 646-7121
•*Bar/lounge, smoking section, patio and private rooms. Humidor. Cuisine: American.*
Private club.

Slippery's
10 Church Ave.
Wabasha
(612) 565-2752
•*Smoking section and bar. Cuisine: American, featuring steak, pasta, seafood.*

Missouri

Annie Gunn's
16806 Chesterfield Airport Rd.
Chesterfield
(314) 532-7684
•*All areas. Humidor. Cuisine: American.*

CLAYTON

Bernard's Bar & Bistro
26 N. Meramec
Clayton
(314) 727-7004
•*Bar. Humidor. Cuisine: American/Continental.*

John P. Fields
26 N. Central
Clayton
(314) 862-1886

•Smoking section, patio and cigar bar. Humidor. Cuisine: American/Continental.

Morton's of Chicago
7822 Bonhomme Ave., Clayton
(314) 725-4008
•Dining room and bar. Humidor. Cuisine: steakhouse.

Seven Gables Inn
26 Meramec
Clayton
(314) 863-8400
•Bar and patio. Humidor. Cuisine: American.

....

Gerard's
1153 Colonnade Center
Des Peres
(314) 821-0458
•Smoking section. Humidor. Cuisine: Continental.

KANSAS CITY

American Restaurant
25th & Grand
Kansas City
(816) 426-1133
•Lounge. Cuisine: American.

Cafe Allegro
1815 W. 39th St.
Kansas City
(816) 561-3663

•Bar/lounge. Humidor. Cuisine: Continental.

Fedora Cafe & Bar
210 W. 47th St.
Kansas City
(816) 561-6565
•Bar/lounge. Cuisine: Continental.

Harry's Bar & Tables
501 Westport Rd.
Kansas City
(816) 561-3950
•All areas. Humidor. Cuisine: upscale casual.

Il Caffe
7510 Wornall Rd.
Kansas City
(816) 361-0900
•Bar/lounge. Humidor. Cuisine: Coffee shop.

Jasper's
405 W. 75th St.
Kansas City
(816) 363-3003
•Bar, lounge and private rooms. Humidor. Cuisine: Northern Italian.

Majestic Steakhouse
931 Broadway
Kansas City
(816) 471-8484
•Main dining room, jazz club and private dining room. Humidor. Cuisine: American, featuring steaks.

Marco Polo's
7514 Wornall
Kansas City
(816) 361-0900
•Bar, private rooms and coffee shop. Humidor. Cuisine: Italian.

Plaza III Jazz Club
4749 Pennsylvania Ave.
Kansas City
(816) 753-0000
•Bar and jazz club. Cuisine: steakhouse.

Savoy Grill
219 W. 9th St.
Kansas City
(816) 842-3890
•All areas. Humidor. Cuisine: lobster and steak.

The Woodlands
9700 Leavenworth Rd.
Kansas City
(913) 299-9797
•Smoking areas. Cuisine: American.

Zola
4113 Pennsylvania
Kansas City
(816) 561-9191
•All areas. Cuisine: European Peasant Dishes.

....

Nearly Famous Deli & Pasta House
1828 S. Kentwood
Springfield
(417) 883-3403

•Smoking section and patio. Cuisine: American, French and Italian. Restaurant/catering services.

ST. LOUIS

Cardwell's
8100 Maryland
St. Louis
(314) 726-5055
•Bar and patio. Cuisine: American.

Cheshire Inn
7036 Clayton Ave.
St. Louis
(314) 647-7300 ext. 601
•Private room, bar and cigar bar. Humidor. Cuisine: American.

Dierdorf & Harts Steakhouse
734 Westport Plaza, #262, St. Louis
(314) 878-1801
•Bar and private room. Humidor. Cuisine: American, specializing in seafood and steak.

Jake's Steaks
707 Clamorgan Alley, St. Louis
(314) 621-8184
•Smoking area of dining room and bar. Humidor. Cuisine: Southwestern.

Kemoll's of Saint Louis
211 N. Broadway
St. Louis
(314) 421-0555
•*Lounge. Cuisine: gourmet Italian.*

LoRusso's Cucina
3121 Watson
St. Louis
(314) 647-6222
•*Piano lounge. Humidor. Cuisine: Italian.*

Noonday Club
1 Metropolitan Square
St. Louis
(314) 231-8452
•*All areas. Humidor. Cuisine: Continental.* **Private club.**

The Ritz-Carlton
100 Carondelet Plaza
St. Louis
(314) 863-6300
•*Lounge, private room and cigar bar. Humidor. Cuisine: American and Continental.*

Station Grill at the Hyatt Regency
1 St. Louis Union Station, St. Louis
(314) 231-1234
•*Bar/lounge and private room. Humidor. Cuisine: seafood and steakhouse.*

Tony's
410 Market St.
St. Louis
(314) 231-7007
•*Bar/lounge. Humidor. Cuisine: Italian.*

Wilbur & Gil's
639 Westport Plaza Dr., St. Louis
(314) 514-0466
•*Bar and cigar bar area. Humidor. Cuisine: upscale American.*

Montana

The Grand Hotel
139 McLeod St.
Big Timber
(406) 932-4459
•*Bar. Cuisine: American and Continental.*

BILLINGS

Jake's
2701 1st Ave. N.
Billings
(406) 259-9375
•*Bar, smoking section and casino. Humidor. Cuisine: steaks, ribs and chops.*

Lamplighter
75 27th St. W.
Billings
(406) 652-6773
•*Bar/lounge. Humidor. Cuisine: Pub fare.*

Montana Brewing Co.
113 N. Broadway
Billings
(406) 252-9200

•*Bar. Humidor. Cuisine: American featuring wood-fired pizzas, burgers and pastas.*

Nebraska

Misty's Restaurant & Lounge
6235 Havelock Ave.
Lincoln
(402) 466-8424
•*Bar, lounge and private rooms. Humidor. Cuisine: steakhouse.*

Top Hat
736 W. Cornhusker
Lincoln
(402) 479-9935
•*All areas. Humidor. Cuisine: American.*

OMAHA

The Aquarium
1830 S. 72nd St.
Omaha
(402) 392-0777
•*Lounge (piano bar). Humidor. Cuisine: fresh seafood.*

Le Cafe de Paris
1228 S. 6th St.
Omaha
(402) 344-0227
•*Smoking area. Cuisine: French.*

Omaha Prime
415 S. 11th St.
Omaha
(402) 341-7040
•*Cigar bar and private dining room. Humidor. Cuisine: steak and seafood.*

Passport
1101 Jackson St.
Omaha
(402) 344-3200
•*Bar/lounge and cigar room. Humidor. Cuisine: steakhouse.*

Vivace
1108 Howard St.
Omaha
(402) 342-2050
•*Bar. Humidor. Cuisine: contemporary Italian with a Mediterranean influence.*

Nevada

LAS VEGAS

Caesar's Palace Hotel
3570 Las Vegas Blvd.
Las Vegas
(702) 731-7502
•*All areas. Humidor. Cuisine: American, Chinese, French, Japanese and Italian.* **24-hour restaurants/ hotel/casino.**

Carver's
2061 Sunset
Las Vegas
(702) 433-5801
•*Bar area. Cuisine: steakhouse.*

The Fiore at the Rio Hotel
3700 W. Flamingo
Las Vegas
(702) 252-7777
•*Cigar terrace. Humidor. Cuisine: European cuisine prepared in a new American style.*

Morton's of Chicago
3200 Las Vegas Blvd. S., Las Vegas
(702) 893-0703
• *All areas. Humidor. Cuisine: steakhouse.*

Ruth's Chris Steak House
3900 Paradise Rd.
Las Vegas
(702) 791-7011
• *Bar/lounge. Humidor. Cuisine: steakhouse.*

Ruth's Chris Steak House
4561 W. Flamingo Rd., Las Vegas
(702) 248-7011
• *Smoking section. Humidor. Cuisine: steakhouse.*

Sfuzzi
3200 S. Las Vegas Blvd., B-11
Las Vegas
(702) 699-5777
• *Private rooms, bar and patio. Humidor. Cuisine: Italian.*

Spago Las Vegas at Caesar's Palace
3500 Las Vegas Blvd. S., Las Vegas
(702) 369-0360
• *Private rooms and patio. Humidor. Cuisine: Californian.*

The Tillerman
2245 E. Flamingo Rd., Las Vegas
(702) 731-4036
• *Bar, lounge and patio. Cuisine: seafood and steak.*

Tommy Rocker's Cantina & Grill
4275 S. Industrial
Las Vegas
(702) 261-6688
• *All areas. Humidor. Cuisine: American, Mexican, BBQ.*

Harrah's Steak House
219 S. Center St.
Reno
(702) 788-2929
• *Lounge and cigar bar. Cuisine: steak.*

Rapscallion
1555 S. Wells
Reno
(702) 323-1211
• *Bar/lounge and private room. Humidor. Cuisine: seafood.*

Harvey's Resort, Hotel & Casino
Hwy. 50
Stateline
(702) 588-2411
• *Bar/lounge. Humidor. Cuisine: international.*

New Hampshire

Stark Mill Brewery & Restaurant
500 Commercial St.
Manchester
(603) 622-0000
• *Large lounge area and bar. Humidor. Cuisine: steaks, seafood, pizza, salads and sandwiches.*

Wild Rover
21 Kosciuszko St.
Manchester
(603) 669-7722
• *All areas. Cuisine: variety of dishes.*

Waterworks
1 Nashua Dr.
Nashua
(603) 882-4433
• *Cigar bar. Humidor. Cuisine: eclectic American.* **Nightclub.**

Scottish Lion Inn & Restaurant
Rte. 16
North Conway
(888) 356-4345
• *Blackwatch Pub (special room for cigars & pipes). Humidor. Cuisine: Continental.*

Barnstormers Restaurant
27 International Dr., Pease Int'l. Trade Port
Portsmouth
(603) 433-6700
• *Sports and piano bars. Cuisine: steak and seafood.*

Legends 1291
Town Square
Waterville Valley
(603) 236-4678
• *All areas. Humidor. Cuisine: American.*

The Seven Barrel Brewey Pub
Rte. 12-A at I-89, exit 20
West Lebanon
(603) 298-5566
• *Smoking section. Cuisine: British pub fare.* **Pub.**

New Jersey

The Ram's Head Inn
9 W. White Horse Pike
Absecon
(609) 652-1700
• *Bar, lounge, private rooms, gallery and patio. Humidor. Cuisine: Continental.*

Trump Plaza Hotel & Casino
Boardwalk at Mississippi
Atlantic City
(609) 441-6000
• *All smoking areas of Ivana's, Max's, Fortune's and Roberto's. Humidor. Cuisine: variety in the four gourmet restaurants.* **Casino/hotel.**

Seven Hills Restaurant
88 Washington St.
Bloomfield
(201) 743-5331
•*Bar/lounge and private rooms. Humidor. Cuisine: Italian-American.*

Azúcar
10 Dempsey Ave.
Edgewater
(201) 886-0747
•*All areas. Humidor. Cuisine: Cuban.*

Pronto Cena Ristorante
87 Sussex St.
Jersey City
(201) 435-0004
•*All areas. Humidor. Cuisine: authentic Tuscan-Italian.*

Conservatory at the Madison Hotel
1 Convent Rd.
Morristown
(201) 285-1800
•*Bar/lounge. Humidor. Cuisine: French and Continental.*

The Park Steakhouse
151 Kinderkamack Rd.
Park Ridge
(201) 930-1300
•*Private dining room for smokers only and bar. Humidor. Cuisine: steakhouse.*

Basil T's Brewpub & Italian Grill
183 Riverside Ave.
Redbank
(909) 842-5990
•*Bar and dining room. Humidor. Cuisine: Italian and pizza.*

Stage House Inn
366 Park Ave.
Scotch Plains
(908) 322-4224
•*Cocktail lounge and bar. Cuisine: French/American.*

Verve American Bar & Restaurant
18 E. Main St.
Somerville
(908) 707-8655
•*Bar (dining room on smoker nights). Humidor. Cuisine: new American.*

Luigi's Restaurant
Roxbury Mall/275-230 Rte. 10
Succasunna
(201) 584-2881
•*Bar/lounge. Cuisine: Italian.*

Diamond's
132 Kent St.
Trenton
(609) 393-1000
•*All areas. Humidor. Cuisine: Italian, prime aged steak, Maine lobsters and fresh seafood.*

Season's Restaurant
644 Pascack Rd.
Washington Township
(201) 664-6141
•*Lounge area. Humidor. Cuisine: Continental.*

The Taco Maker
61 Berdan Ave.
Wayne
(201) 305-8226
•*Dining room. Humidor. Cuisine: Mexican.*

El Rey del Mundo
301 Rte. 10-E
Whippany
(201) 887-0800
•*All areas. Humidor. Cuisine: light snacks. Bar.*

The Ryland Inn
Rte. 22 W.
Whitehouse
(908) 534-4011
•*In the special cigar & brandy room and the bar/lounge; entire restaurant during cigar dinners only. Humidor. Cuisine: modern regional French.*

New Mexico

Ranchers Club at the Albuquerque Hilton
1901 University Blvd. NE
Albuquerque
(505) 884-2500

•*Lounge. Humidor. Cuisine: American, specializing in seafood and steak.*

The A Bar
331 Sandoval St.
Santa Fe
(505) 982-8999
•*Bar/lounge. Humidor. Cuisine: Western American.* **Nightclub/restaurant.**

Billy Crews
1200 Country Club Rd.
Santa Teresa
(505) 589-2071
•*Dining room and lounge. Humidor. Cuisine: American.*

New York

Mansion Hill Inn
115 Philip St.
Albany
(518) 465-2038
•*All areas. Humidor. Cuisine: regional American.*

Riveredge Resort Hotel
17 Holland St.
Alexandria Bay
(305) 482-9917
•*Bar and front deck. Humidor. Cuisine: French.*

The Dakota Grill & Cigar Bar and Ciao
4224 Maple Rd./
Maple Ridge Plaza
Amherst
(716) 834-6600
•Cigar bar. Humidor. Cuisine: steaks, fresh fish and chicken at The Grill and Italian trattoria at Ciao.

Lock, Stock & Barrel
35 Bardonia Rd.
Bardonia
(914) 623-6323
•Bar/lounge, smoking section and patio. Humidor. Cuisine: American.

Hoppfields Restaurant
954 Old Post Rd.,
Rte. 121
Bedford
(914) 234-3374
•Bar/lounge, smoking section, patio, private room and cigar bar. Humidor. Cuisine: American.

Tomaso's at the Bedford Village Inn
Rte. 22
Bedford Village
(914) 234-6739
•Bar area. Cuisine: Italian.

E.T. Quigg's
2807 Merrick Rd.
Bellmore
(516) 785-9559

•All areas. Cuisine: pub fare. **Bar/pub.**

Cavanaugh's
255 Blue Point Ave.
Blue Point
(516) 363-2666
•All areas. Humidor. Cuisine: pub fare.

Arch Restaurant
Rte. 22
Brewster
(914) 279-5011
•Bar. Humidor. Cuisine: Continental.

Adam's Steak & Seafood
204 Como Park Blvd.
Buffalo
(716) 683-3784
•Bar/lounge. Cuisine: American, specializing in seafood and steak.

Crabtree's Kittle House
11 Kittle Rd.
Chappaqua
(914) 666-8044
•Bar. Humidor. Cuisine: progressive American.

Alexander Hamilton Inn & Alexander's Cigar Bar
21 W. Park Row
Clinton
(315) 853-5555
•Smoking section, bar and cigar bar. Humidor. Cuisine: International/Continental.

Louisiana Cajun Cafe
25 Cedar St.
Dobbs Ferry
(914) 693-9762
•Bar. Humidor. Cuisine: Cajun/Creole.

Old Drovers Inn
Old Rte. 22
Dover Plains
(914) 832-9311
•Private room. Humidor. Cuisine: traditional and contemporary American.

The Palm
94 Main St.
East Hampton
(516) 324-0411
•Bar/lounge. Cuisine: steakhouse.

The White Inn
52 E. Main St.
Fredonia
(716) 672-2103
•Bar, lounge and patio. Cuisine: American.

Jonathan's American Grill
3000 Jericho Tpke.
Garden City Park
(516) 742-7300
•Lounge. Humidor. Cuisine: American and International.

Nassau Country Club
St. Andrews Lane
Glen Cove
(516) 676-0554

•Main bar and adjoining lounge areas. Humidor. Cuisine: Continental. **Private club.**

Depuy Canal House
Rte. 213
High Falls
(914) 687-7700
•Bar. Humidor. Cuisine: American.

Broadway Bar & Grill
8 S. Broadway
Irvington
(914) 591-9861
•All areas. Humidor. Cuisine: American, steak and seafood.

John Thomas Steakhouse
1152 Danby Rd.
Ithaca
(607) 273-3464
•Lounge and deck (weather permitting) where food and drink are available. Humidor. Cuisine: steakhouse.

Wiltwyck Golf Club
404 Stewart Lane
Kingston
(914) 331-0700
•Bar/lounge. Humidor. **Private golf club.**

Marco
Rte. 6
Lake Mahopac
(914) 621-1648
•*Lounge. Humidor.
Cuisine: nouvelle
cuisine.*

**The Riverside Inn-
"On the water"**
115 S. Water St.
Lewiston
(716) 754-8206
•*Bar/lounge, smoking
area and patio. Humidor. Cuisine: American with a California
flair.*

Beardslee Castle
Rte. 5
Little Falls
(315) 823-3000
•*Bar, grill and smoking section. Humidor.
Cuisine: creative
American.*

Brick Cafe
157 Lakeview Ave.
Lynbrook
(516) 599-9669
•*Dining room and
bar. Cuisine:
American.*

Eleanor Rigby's
133 Mineola Blvd.
Mineola
(516) 739-6622
•*Bar and designated
tables in smoking section. Humidor. Cuisine: Continental.*

NEW YORK CITY

MANHATTAN

1st Ave.
361 1st Ave. (corner
of 21st & 1st)
New York
(212) 475-9068
•*All areas. Humidor.
Cuisine: American.*

21 Club
21 W. 52nd St.
New York
(212) 582-7200
•*Bar/lounge, private
room and wine cellar
dining room.
Humidor. Cuisine:
American.*

53rd St. Cigar Bar
53rd St. & 7th Ave.
New York
(212) 581-1000
•*Cigar bar. Humidor.
Cuisine: Continental.*

The Alamo
304 E. 48th St.
New York
(212) 759-0590
•*Bar. Cuisine:
Mexican/Texas.*

Alva
36 E. 22nd St.
New York
(212) 228-4399
•*Bar/lounge. Humidor. Cuisine: contemporary American
bistro.*

An American Place
2 Park Ave.
New York
(212) 684-2122
•*Bar. Cuisine: regional American.*

**Angelo & Maxie's
Steakhouse**
233 Park Ave. S.
New York
(212) 220-9200
•*Cigar bar. Humidor.
Cuisine: steakhouse.*

Armstrong's
876 10th Ave.
New York
(212) 581-0606
•*Bar area. Humidor.
Cuisine: eclectic.*

Bambou
243 E. 14th St.
New York
(212) 505-1180
•*Bar/lounge. Cuisine:
Caribbean/French.*

Beefsteak Charlie's
2 Penn Plaza
New York
(212) 630-0301
•*Bar area. Cuisine:
steakhouse.*

**Beekman Bar and
Books featuring
The Cigar Bar**
889 1st Ave.
New York
(212) 980-9314
•*All areas. Humidor.
Cuisine: hors d'oeuvres only. **Bar/cigar
lounge.***

**Béla Restaurant &
Go Go Room**
316 Bowery
New York
(212) 475-0550
•*Cigar room. Humidor. Cuisine: New
York.*

**Ben Benson's
Steakhouse**
123 W. 52nd St.
New York
(212) 581-8888
•*Bar/lounge. Humidor. Cuisine:
steakhouse.*

Bice
7 E. 54th St.
New York
(212) 688-1999
•*Bar and lounge area.
Humidor. Cuisine:
Italian.*

**BlackFinn Bar and
Restaurant**
994 2nd Ave.
New York
(212) 355-6993
•*All areas. Humidor.
Cuisine: Cajun.*

**The Box Tree
Restaurant**
250 E. 49th St.
New York
(212) 758-8320
•*Bar, smoking section
and private rooms.
Humidor. Cuisine:
steakhouse and
French.*

Boxers
190 W. 4th St.
New York
(212) 633-BARK
•*Bar. Cuisine: American bar & grill.*

374

Brew's
156 E. 34th St.
New York
(212) 889-3369
•Bar. Humidor. Cuisine: American, specializing in steak.

The Bubble Lounge
228 W. Broadway
New York
(212) 431-3433
•All areas. Humidor. Cuisine: hors d'oeuvres only. **Champagne bar.**

Bull & Bear Restaurant at the Waldorf Astoria
301 Park Ave.
New York
(212) 872-4900
•Bar. Humidor. Cuisine: American, specializing in steak.

Butlers Restaurant
1407 Broadway
New York
(212) 575-1407
•Upstairs. Humidor. Cuisine: American.

Cafe Aubette
119 E. 27th St.
New York
(212) 686-5500
•All areas, but encouraged in the back room. Humidor. Cuisine: innovative American appetizers and dessert at night; European espresso bar in the afternoon. **Cafe and bar.**

Café des Artistes
1 W. 67th St.
New York
(212) 877-3500
•Bar/lounge and private room. Humidor. Cuisine: country French.

Cafe Pierre at The Pierre Hotel
2 E. 61st St.
New York
(212) 940-8185
•Bar/lounge. Cuisine: American, Continental, French.

Cal's
22 W. 21st St.
New York
(212) 929-0740
•Bar. Cuisine: Mediterranean.

Campagna
24 E. 21st St.
New York
(212) 460-0900
•Bar, lounge and patio. Humidor. Cuisine: Italian.

Carnegie Bar and Books
156 W. 56th St.
New York
(212) 957-9676
•All areas. Humidor. Cuisine: hors d'oeuvres only. **Bar/cigar lounge.**

Cellini
65 E. 54th St.
New York
(212) 751-1555
•Private room. Humidor. Cuisine: Tuscan.

Central Park South
150 Central Park South
New York
(212) 765-1444
•Cigar bar. Humidor. Cuisine: American fusion. **Cigar, champagne & espresso bar.**

Charltons
922 3rd Ave.
New York
(212) 688-4646
•Bar. Humidor. Cuisine: steakhouse.

Chiam
160 E. 48th St.
New York
(212) 371-2323
•Bar and wine cellar. Humidor. Cuisine: Chinese.

Christo's Steakhouse & Grill
541 Lexington Ave.
New York
(212) 355-2695
•Bars and in semi-private room. Humidor. Cuisine: Italian/steakhouse.

The Cigar Room at Trumpets at the Grand Hyatt Hotel
Grand Central Station, New York
(212) 850-5999
•All areas. Humidor. Cuisine: Continental. **Cigar restaurant & bar.**

Cinquanta
50 E. 50th St.
New York
(212) 759-5050
•One floor for smokers. Cuisine: Italian.

Cité
120 W. 51st St.
New York
(212) 956-7100
•Bar. Cuisine: American.

City Crab & Seafood Co.
235 Park Ave. S.
New York
(212) 529-3800
•Private dining room and bar. Humidor. Cuisine: seafood.

City Wine & Cigar Co.
62 Laight St.
New York
(212) 334-2274
•Bar. Humidor. Cuisine: food from cigar producing regions. **Bar/cigar bar.**

Club Macanudo
26 E. 63rd St.
New York
(212) 752-8200
•All areas. Humidor. **Cigar bar.**

Coco Pazzo
23 E. 74th St.
New York
(212) 794-0205
•Bar/lounge and smoking section. Humidor. Cuisine: Italian.

The Conservatory at the Mayflower Hotel
15 Central Park W.
New York
(212) 641-1173
•*Bar/lounge. Cuisine: American.*

Dakota Bar & Grill
1576 3rd Ave.
New York
(212) 427-8889
•*Bar area. Cuisine: American.*

Delano Drive Restaurant
E. 25th St. & the East River (FDR Dr.)
New York
(212) 683-3001
•*Bar, lounge and patio. Humidor. Cuisine: steaks, fresh fish and pasta.*

Divine Bar
244 E. 51st. St.
New York
(212) 319-9463
•*All areas. Humidor. Cuisine: Spanish (tapas).* **Lounge/wine bar.**

Dix et Sept
181 W. 10th St.
New York
(212) 645-8023
•*Bar. Cuisine: French.*

Drake Bar & Restaurant at the Drake Swiss Hotel
440 Park Ave.
New York
(212) 756-3925
•*Bar/lounge. Humidor. Cuisine: American, Continental, French and Mediterranean.*

Eight and One Half Restaurant
208 E. 52nd St.
New York
(212) 759-7373
•*Bar/lounge. Humidor. Cuisine: Italian and Colombian.*

Elaine's Restaurant
1703 2nd Ave.
New York
(212) 534-8114
•*Dining room and bar. Humidor. Cuisine: Italian.*

Ferrier
29 E. 65th St.
New York
(212) 772-9000
•*Bar. Cuisine: French.*

Filli Ponte Ristorante
39 Debrosses St.
New York
(212) 226-4621
•*Cigar lounge and bar. Humidor. Cuisine: Italian.*

Florio's of Little Italy
192 Grand St.
New York
(212) 226-7610
•*Bar/lounge, cigar bar and smoking area. Humidor. Cuisine: Italian.*

Flowers
21 W. 17th St.
New York
(212) 691-8888
•*Bar area. Humidor. Cuisine: exotic Continental.*

Fifty Seven Fifty Seven, Four Seasons Hotel
57 E. 57th St.
New York
(212) 758-5700
•*Bar, lounge and private rooms. Humidor. Cuisine: American.* **Bar.**

Frank's Restaurant
85 10th Ave.
New York
(212) 243-1349
•*Bar/lounge, smoking section and private room. Humidor. Cuisine: steakhouse.*

Frankie & Johnnie's
269 W. 45th St.
New York
(212) 997-9494
•*Cigar bar. Cuisine: steakhouse.*

Fresco by Scotto
34 E. 52nd St.
New York
(212) 935-3434
•*Bar and lounge area. Humidor. Cuisine: modern Tuscan.*

Frontiere
199 Prince St.
New York
(212) 387-0898
•*Bar. Cuisine: Southern French provincial/ Northern Italian.*

Gallagher's Steak House
228 W. 52nd St.
New York
(212) 245-5336
•*Bar/lounge and smoking section. Humidor. Cuisine: steakhouse.*

The Ginger Man
11 E. 36th St.
New York
(212) 532-3740
•*All areas. Humidor. Cuisine: light bar fare.* **Beer bar.**

Giovanni
47 W. 55th St.
New York
(212) 262-2828
•*Cigar room. Humidor. Cuisine: northern Italian (Venetian).*

Granville
40 E. 20th St.
New York
(212) 253-9088
•*Smoking section, bar and upstairs. Humidor. Cuisine: classic American.*

**Greatest Bar on
 Earth & The
 Skybox**
One World Trade
Center, 107th
Floor
New York
(212) 524-7107
•*Skybox cigar lounge
after 7pm and at 3
bars. Humidor. Cuisine: world view
theme, international.*

**The Grotto Lounge
 at Limoncello
 Restaurant**
777 Seventh Ave.
New York
(212) 582-7932
•*All areas. Humidor.
Cuisine: Italian.*
Cigar bar.

Halcyon
151 W. 54th St.
New York
(212) 468-8736
•*Bar/lounge. Cuisine:
American.*

Harbour Lights
South Street
 Seaport, Pier 17
New York
(212) 227-2800
•*Separate room for
smokers. Humidor.
Cuisine: American
and seafood.*

**Harry's at Hanover
 Square**
1 Hanover Square
New York
(212) 425-3412
•*Bar. Cuisine:
Continental.*

**Havana Tea Room
 & Cigar House**
265 E. 78th St.
New York
(212) 327-2012
•*All areas. Humidor.
Cuisine: English tea,
Cuban sandwiches.*
**English tea service
and cigar house.**

Heartland Brewery
35 Union Square N.
New York
(212) 645-3400
•*Smoking section and
bar. Humidor.
Cuisine: American
Continental.*

**Hudson Bar and
 Books**
636 Hudson St.
New York
(212) 229-2642
•*All areas. Humidor.
Cuisine: elegant light
fare.* **Bar/cigar
lounge.**

Il Monello
1460 2nd Ave.
New York
(212) 535-9310
•*Bar/lounge and private room. Humidor.
Cuisine: Italian.*

**Il Valentino
 Restaurant**
330 E. 56th St.
New York
(212) 355-0001
•*Bar/lounge and outdoor dining room.
Cuisine: Tuscan.*

Jake's Steakhouse
1155 Third Ave.
New York
(212) 879-9888
•*Bar. Humidor. Cuisine: steak.*

**John Street Bar &
 Grill**
17 John St.
New York
(212) 349-3278
•*All smoking areas
and private rooms.
Humidor. Cuisine:
American pub fare.*

Jubilee
347 E. 54th St.
New York
(212) 888-3569
•*Smoking area near
the bar. Humidor.
Cuisine: French.*

Keens Steakhouse
72 W. 36th St.
New York
(212) 947-3636
•*Bar. Humidor.
Cuisine: steakhouse.*

L'Auberge du Midi
310 W. 4th St.
New York
(212) 242-4705
•*Bar. Humidor.
Cuisine: Provençal.*

La Granita
1470 2nd Ave.
New York
(212) 717-5500
•*Special separate
room. Cuisine: Italian/Tuscan.*

Le Bar Bat
311 W. 57th St.
New York
(212) 307-7228
•*All three levels. Humidor. Cuisine:
American Grill.*
Nightclub.

Le Cirque 2000
455 Madison Ave.
New York
(212) 794-9292
•*Bar and private
rooms.Humidor.
Cuisine: French.*

Le Colonial
149 E. 57th St.
New York
(212) 752-0808
•*Bar/lounge area.
Humidor. Cuisine:
Vietnamese.*

Le Madri
168 W. 18th St.
New York
(212) 727-8022
•*Bar and patio.
Humidor. Cuisine:
Italian.*

Le Marais
150 W. 46th St.
New York
(212) 869-0900
•*Bar and upstairs
area. Humidor.
Cuisine: French
steakhouse.*

Le Veau d' Or
129 E. 60th St.
New York
(212) 838-8133
•*All areas. Humidor.
Cuisine: French.*

Les Célébrités at the Hotel Nikko
155 W. 58th St.
New York
(212) 484-5113
•*Bar/lounge and private room. Humidor. Cuisine: French.*

Lexington Bar and Books featuring The Cigar Bar
1020 Lexington Ave.
New York
(212) 717-3902
•*All areas. Humidor. Cuisine: elegant light fare.* **Bar/cigar lounge.**

Maggie's Place Restaurant & Bar
21 E. 47th St.
New York
(212) 753-5757
•*Bar/lounge (evenings, only). Humidor. Cuisine: Nouvelle American.*

Manhattan Cafe
1161 1st Ave.
New York
(212) 888-6556
•*Separate cigar smoking dining room (seats 60-70). Humidor. Cuisine: American/Continental.*

Mark's Restaurant and Bar
25 E. 77th St.
New York
(212) 879-1864
•*Bar and private rooms. Humidor. Cuisine: French Continental.*

Marti Kebab
1269 1st Ave.
New York
(212) 737-6104
•*Private room. Cuisine: Turkish.*

Merchant NY
1125 1st Ave.
New York
(212) 832-1551
•*Downstairs. Humidor. Cuisine: Noveau.*

Michael's
24 W. 55th St.
New York
(212) 767-0555
•*Bar/lounge. Humidor. Cuisine: American.*

Minetta Tavern
113 MacDougal St.
New York
(212) 475-3850
•*Bar. Humidor. Cuisine: Northern Italian.*

Monkey Bar
60 E. 54th St.
New York
(212) 838-2600
•*Bar. Humidor. Cuisine: American.*

Moran's Restaurant
146 10th Ave.
New York
(212) 627-3030
•*Bar and private rooms. Humidor. Cuisine: American, specializing in seafood and steak.*

Morton's of Chicago
551 5th Ave.
New York
(212) 972-3315
•*Bar/lounge. Humidor. Cuisine: steakhouse.*

North Star Pub
93 South St.
New York
(212) 509-6757
•*All areas. Cuisine: British.*

O'Flaherty's Ale House
334-336 W. 46th St.
New York
(212) 246-8928
•*Bar and in dining room when the kitchen closes. Cuisine: international Irish pub fare.*

O'Nieal's Grand St.
174 Grand St.
New York
(212) 941-9119
•*Bar/lounge and after dinner in the dining area. Humidor. Cuisine: upscale American with French influences.*

Oak Bar at the Plaza Hotel
768 5th Ave.
New York
(212) 546-5330
•*Bar. Humidor. Cuisine: sandwiches and appetizers.*

Oceana
55 E. 54th St.
New York
(212) 759-5941
•*Bar/lounge. Humidor. Cuisine: seafood.*

The Odeon
145 W. Broadway
New York
(212) 233-0507
•*Bar. Cuisine: European/American.*

Old Homestead
56 9th Ave.
New York
(212) 242-9040
•*Bar and cocktail area. Humidor. Cuisine: steak and seafood.*

Oyster Bar
Grand Central Station
New York
(212) 490-6650
•*Bar, cigar bar and smoking section of restaurant. Humidor. Cuisine: seafood.*

Palio
151 W. 51st St.
New York
(212) 245-4850
•*Bar. Humidor. Cuisine: Italian.*

Palm
837 2nd Ave.
New York
(212) 687-2953
•*Bar. Humidor. Cuisine: American— steak and lobster.*

Park Avenue Cafe
100 E. 63rd St.
New York
(212) 644-1900
•*Bar and private room. Humidor. Cuisine: American.*

Patroon
160 E. 46th St.
New York
(212) 883-7373
•*Cigar lounge. Humidor. Cuisine: American/Continental.*

Pen & Pencil
205 E. 45th St.
New York
(212) 682-8660
•*Smoking areas. Humidor. Cuisine: steakhouse.*

The Post House
28 E. 63rd St.
New York
(212) 935-2888
•*Bar. Humidor. Cuisine: American, specializing in steak.*

Pravda
281 Lafayette St.
New York
(212) 226-4696
•*All areas. Humidor. Cuisine: Russian inspired.*

Rainbow Room
30 Rockefeller Plaza
New York
(212) 632-5000
•*The Rainbow Promenade bar. Humidor. Cuisine: French/Continental.* **Nightclub.**

Raoul's
180 Prince St.
New York
(212) 966-3518
•*Garden room and bar. Cuisine: French.*

Remi
145 W. 53rd St.
New York
(212) 581-4242
•*Bar, private room, atrium and garden. Humidor. Cuisine: Venetian.*

Runyon's
932 2nd Ave.
New York
(212) 223-9592
•*Bar and some tables. Cuisine: American steakhouse.*

Russian Samovar
256 W. 52nd St.
New York
(212) 757-0168
•*Bar/lounge and upstairs cigar bar. Humidor. Cuisine: Russian.*

Ruth's Chris Steak House
148 W. 51st St.
New York
(212) 245-9600
•*Bar/lounge and private rooms. Humidor. Cuisine: steakhouse.*

St. Regis Hotel-King Cole Bar & Astor Court
2 E. 55th St.
New York
(212) 753-4500
•*Bar and Cognac Room. Humidor. Cuisine: upscale bistro.* **Bar.**

San Domenico
240 Central Park S.
New York
(212) 459-9016
•*Bar/lounge. Humidor. Cuisine: Italian.*

SettaMoMA at the Museum of Modern Art
12 W. 54th St.
New York
(212) 708-9710
•*Bar/lounge and smoking section. Humidor. Cuisine: Italian.*

Slaughtered Lamb Pub
182 W. 4th St.
New York
(212) 727-3350
•*Smoking section. Cuisine: Old English Tavern/American.*

Smith & Wollensky
201 E. 49th St.
New York
(212) 753-1530
•*Bar/lounge. Humidor. Cuisine: steakhouse.*

Spy
101 Greene St.
New York
(212) 343-9000
•*All areas. Humidor.* **Nightclub/bar.**

Tatou
151 E. 50th St.
New York
(212) 753-1144
•*Cigar bar and near the bar in main dining room. Humidor. Cuisine: French/American.*

Ten's World Class Cabaret
35 E. 21st St.
New York
(212) 254-2444
•*Dining room, bar and lounge. Humidor. Cuisine: American and Continental.* **Gentleman's club.**

Third Floor Cafe
315 5th Ave.
New York
(212) 481-3669
•*Smoking section. Humidor. Cuisine: international.* **Cafe.**

Torre di Pisa
19 W. 44th St.
New York
(212) 398-4400
•*Bar/lounge and smoking area. Humidor. Cuisine: Italian.*

Torremolino's Restaurant
230 E. 51st St.
New York
(212) 755-1862
•*Bar. Cuisine: Spanish and Continental.*

Tse Yang
34 E. 51st St.
New York
(212) 688-5588
•*Bar/lounge and private rooms. Humidor. Cuisine: Gourmet Peking- and Shanghai-style Chinese.*

Twins Restaurant
1712 2nd. Ave. (at 89th St.)
New York
(212) 987-1111
•*Bar and at private parties. Humidor. Cuisine: American with a Mediterranean influence.*

Typhoon Brewery
22 E. 54th St.
New York
(212) 754-9006
•*Bar. Humidor. Cuisine: upscale Thai.*

Victor's Cafe 52
236 W. 52nd St.
New York
(212) 586-7714
•*Bar. Humidor. Cuisine: Cuban.*

Wall Street Kitchen & Bar
70 Broad St.
New York
(212) 797-7070
•*Bar/lounge. Humidor. Cuisine: eclectic American.*

The Water Club
500 E. 30th St.
New York
(212) 683-3333
•*Bar/lounge, smoking section, patio and private rooms. Humidor. Cuisine: American, specializing in seafood.*

The Havana Lounge at Webster Hall
125 E. 11th St.
New York
(212) 606-4202
•*Cigar bar. Humidor.* **Cigar bar/nightclub.**

West 63rd Street Steakhouse
44 W. 63rd St.
New York
(212) 246-6363
•*Bar, lounge and private rooms. Humidor. Cuisine: steakhouse.*

BROOKLYN

Cigargoyles
7 Old Fulton St.
Brooklyn
(718) 254-0656
•*All areas. Humidor. Cuisine: Continental.*

La Rouge Cigar Club & Salon
420 64th St.
Brooklyn
(718) 567-8681
•*All areas. Humidor.* **Cigar club/salon.**

Lundy Bros. Restaurant
1901 Emmons Ave.
Brooklyn
(718) 743-0022
•*Bar/lounge, smoking section, patio and cigar bar. Humidor. Cuisine: features seafood and steakhouse.*

Mike & Tony's Bar & Grill
239 5th Ave.
Brooklyn
(718) 857-2800
•*Bar, lounge and cigar bar. Humidor. Cuisine: steak and seafood featuring large lobsters.*

The River Cafe
1 Water St.
Brooklyn
(718) 522-5200
•*Bar/lounge and private room. Humidor. Cuisine: American and Continental.*

QUEENS

Caffe on the Green
201-10 Cross Island Pkwy.
Bayside
(718) 423-7272
•*Bar/lounge and smoking section. Humidor. Cuisine: Italian.*

Calla Larga
247-63 Jamaica Ave./Jericho Tpke.
Bellrose
(718) 343-2185
•*Bar/lounge area. Humidor. Cuisine: Northern Italian.*

Piccola Venezia Ristorante
42-01 28 Ave.
Astoria
(718) 721-8470
•*Bar/lounge, smoking section and private room. Humidor. Cuisine: Italian.*

Jerry's Restaurant & Tap Room
1575 Montauk Hwy.
Oakdale
(516) 567-0055
•*Bar. Humidor. Cuisine: American.*

Maxfield's Restaurant
5 Market St.
Potsdam
(315) 265-3796
•*Bar. Cuisine: pasta, steaks and seafood.*

La Pavillon
230 Salt Point Tpke.
Poughkeepsie
(914) 473-2525
•*Bar/lounge and private rooms. Humidor. Cuisine: French.*

Thendara Inn & Restaurant
4356 E. Lake Rd.
Rochester
(716) 394-4868
•*Bar/lounge and patio. Humidor. Cuisine: American, Continental and French.*

Water Street Grill
175 Water St.
Rochester
(716) 546-4980
•*Bar, lounge and patio/sidewalk. Humidor. Cuisine: American and Mediterranean, specializing in seafood and steak.*

Bryant & Cooper Steakhouse
2 Middleneck Rd.
Roslyn
(516) 627-7270
•*Large bar area.
Humidor. Cuisine:
steakhouse.*

The Black Bass Grille
2 Central Ave.
Rye
(914) 967-6700
•*Bar area. Humidor.
Cuisine: American.*

American Hotel
25 Main St.
Sag Harbor
(516) 725-3535
•*Bar/lounge. Humidor. Cuisine: French.*

Forty Three Phila Bistro
43 Phila. St.
Saratoga Springs
(518) 584-2720
•*Smoking section and bar. Cuisine: upscale American bistro.*

The Inn at Speculator
Rte. 163
Speculator
(518) 548-3811
•*Bar, lounge and private rooms. Humidor.
Cuisine: American,
Continental, French,
Mediterranean and
Mexican, specializing
in seafood and steak.*

Moretti's of San Francisco
3300 Monroe Ave.
Spencerport
(716) 352-4000
•*Smoking lounge, private rooms and patio.
Humidor. Cuisine:
Italian.*

SYRACUSE
Clark's Ale House
122 W. Jefferson St.
Syracuse
(315) 479-9859
•*All areas. Humidor.
Cuisine: pub fare.
Bar.*

Danzer's Restaurant
153 Ainsley Dr.
Syracuse
(315) 422-0089
•*Smoking section.
Cuisine: German.*

Riley's For the Fun of It
312 Park St.
Syracuse
(315) 471-7111
•*Bar. Humidor. Cuisine: American.*

Pascale Restaurant
204 W. Fayette St.
Syracuse
(315) 471-3040
•*Bar and private
room. Humidor. Cuisine: American and
Mediterranean.*

Jack Appleseed's Tavern
147 N. Genesee
Utica
(315) 797-7979
•*Smoking section
and bar. Cuisine:
American.*

Yesterday's
907 Vestal Pkwy. E.
Vestal
(607) 785-3313
•*Bar/lounge. Cuisine:
American.*

Hemingway's American Bar & Grill
1885 Wantagh Ave.
Wantagh
(516) 781-2700
•*Bar and smoking
area. Humidor.
Cuisine: American/
Continental.*

Gregory's Steak Pub
324 Central Ave.
White Plains
(914) 684-8855
•*Bar. Humidor. Cuisine: Italian.*

The Lazy Boy Saloon & Ale House
154 Mamaroneck
Ave.
White Plains
(914) 761-0272
•*Cigar bar. Humidor.
Cuisine: American.*

North Carolina

Prestonwood Country Club
300 Prestonwood
Pkwy.
Cary
(919) 467-2566
•*Bar/lounge, private
room and patio. Humidor. Cuisine:
American. **Private
country club.***

Southend Brewery & Smokehouse, Charleston
161 E. Bay St.
Charleston
(803) 853-4677
•*Bar on the 1st floor
and also in the 3rd
floor lounge (with billiards). Humidor.
Cuisine: American
smokehouse featuring
wood-oven pizzas.*

CHARLOTTE
H. Dundee's Steakhouse
8128 Providence Rd. &
4508 Independence
Blvd. (2 Locations)
Charlotte
(704) 543-6299,
536-5003
•*Dining room, bar
and lounge. Humidor.
Cuisine: steakhouse.*

The Lamplighter Restaurant
1065 E. Moorehead St.
Charlotte
(704) 372-5343
•Bar/lounge and private rooms. Humidor. Cuisine: American, French and Continental.

Morton's of Chicago
227 W. Trade St.
Charlotte
(704) 333-2602
•All areas. Humidor. Cuisine: steakhouse.

Pewter Rose
1820 South Blvd.
Charlotte
(704) 332-8149
•Cigar bar. Humidor. Cuisine: International featuring steak, seafood and pastas.

Southend Brewery & Smokehouse
2100 South Blvd.
Charlotte
(704) 358-4677
•Bar and patio. Humidor. Cuisine: American smokehouse featuring wood-oven pizzas.

Nana's Restaurant
2514 University Dr.
Durham
(919) 493-8469
•Bar/lounge. Humidor. Cuisine: American.

Vinnie's Steak House & Tavern
4015 University Dr.
Durham
(919) 493-0004
•All areas. Humidor. Cuisine: steakhouse.

The City Club of Gastonia
532 S. New Hope Rd.
Gastonia
(704) 865-1980
•All areas. Humidor. Cuisine: American.
Private club.

Lucky 32
1421 Westover Terrace
Greensboro
(910) 370-0707
•Grill Room & Bar and outside patio. Cuisine: American.

... On the Verandah
1536 Franklin Rd. (overlooking Lake Sequoyah on U.S. 64)
Highlands
(704) 526-2338
•Wine and cigar bar. Humidor. Cuisine: contemporary American.

House of Wang
710 W. Vernon Ave.
Kinston
(919) 527-7897
•Lounge. Humidor. Cuisine: Chinese.

Angus Barn
U.S. 70 W. at Aviation Pkwy.
Raleigh
(919) 787-3505
•Bar/lounge. Humidor. Cuisine: steak and seafood; wine cellar offers French.

The Capital City Club
411 Fayetteville Street Mall
Raleigh
(919) 832-5526
•Lounge and private rooms. Humidor. Cuisine: American and Continental.
Private club.

It's Prime Only
5509 Edwards Mill Rd.
Raleigh
(919) 420-0224
•All areas. Humidor. Cuisine: steakhouse.

Lucky 32
832 Spring Forest Rd.
Raleigh
(919) 876-9932
•Grill Room & Bar. Cuisine: American-style.

Vinnie's Steak House & Tavern
7440 Six Forks Rd.
Raleigh
(919) 847-7319
•All areas. Humidor. Cuisine: steakhouse.

Lucky 32
109 S. Stratford Rd.
Winston-Salem
(910) 777-0032
•Grill Room & Bar and outside patio. Cuisine: American-style.

New Town Bistro & Bar
421 Jonestown Rd.
Winston-Salem
(910) 659-8062
•Bar/lounge and smoking section. Humidor. Cuisine: bistro.

Vinnie's Steak House & Tavern
1900 Ste. Z, Cumina Station/Eastwood Rd.
Wrightsville Beach
(910) 256-0995
•All areas. Humidor. Cuisine: steakhouse.

Ohio

Natalie's Restaurant
25 Ghent Rd.
Akron
(330) 869-9697
•Bar/lounge, smoking section, patio and cigar bar. Humidor. Cuisine: American.

Ristoranti Giovanni's
25550 Chagrin Blvd.
Beachwood
(216) 831-8625
•Lounge. Humidor. Cuisine: Northern Italian.

Springfield Grille
7413 S. Tiffany
Boardman
(330) 726-0895
• *Bar. Humidor. Cuisine: American, featuring fire-grilled steaks and seafood.*

CINCINNATI

The Boathouse at the Montgomery Inn
925 Eastern Ave.
Cincinnati
(513) 721-7427
• *All areas. Humidor. Cuisine: American.*

Celestial Restaurant
1071 Celestial St.
Cincinnati
(513) 241-4455
• *Bar/lounge. Humidor. Cuisine: Continental and French.*

Cricket Lounge
601 Vine St.
Cincinnati
(513) 381-3000
• *All areas. Humidor. Cuisine: American.*

The International Bar & Grill
11911 Sheraton Lane
Cincinnati
(513) 671-6600
• *Smoking section, bar and lounge. Cuisine: American, Chinese, Continental, French, Mexican and Spanish.*

Morton's of Chicago
Tower Place, 28 W. 4th St.
Cincinnati
(513) 241-4104
• *Bar/lounge, smoking section and private rooms. Humidor. Cuisine: steakhouse.*

Orchids
35 W. 5th St.
Cincinnati
(513) 564-6465
• *Bar, lounge and private rooms. Humidor. Cuisine: American.*

CLEVELAND

Baricelli Inn
2203 Cornell Rd.
Cleveland
(216) 791-6500
• *Lobby and Inn sitting area. Humidor. Cuisine: Continental.*

John Q's Steakhouse
55 Public Square
Cleveland
(216) 861-0900
• *Bar/lounge. Humidor. Cuisine: steakhouse.*

The Lincoln Inn
75 Public Square
Cleveland
(216) 621-9085
• *Bar, lounge and private rooms. Humidor. Cuisine: Continental and Sicilian specialities.*

The Lobby Lounge
1515 W. 3rd St.
Cleveland
(216) 623-1300
• *Lounge. Humidor. Cuisine: Continental.*

Morton's of Chicago
230 Huron Rd. NW
Cleveland
(216) 621-6200
• *Bar/lounge and smoking section. Humidor. Cuisine: steakhouse.*

Ninth Street Grill
100 Erieview Plaza
Cleveland
(216) 579-9919
• *Bar/lounge. Cuisine: Continental and Italian.*

COLUMBUS

Bravo! Cucina
3000 Hayden Rd.
Columbus
(614) 791-1245
• *Bar. Humidor. Cuisine: Italian.*

Morton's of Chicago
2 Nationwide Plaza
Columbus
(614) 464-4442
• *Bar/lounge and smoking section. Humidor. Cuisine: steakhouse.*

The Refectory
1092 Bethel Rd.
Columbus
(614) 451-9774

• *Lounge, private rooms and patio. Cuisine: French.*

Miss Kitty's Steakhouse and Grand Saloon
4336 Medina Rd.
Copley
(330) 666-7429
• *Bar and patio. Cuisine: steakhouse.*

Mad Anthony's at the Greenville Inn
851 E. Martin St.
Greenville
(513) 548-3613
• *Smoking section and lounge. Humidor. Cuisine: American.*

The White House Inn
4940 Muhlhausern Rd.
Hamilton
(513) 860-1110
• *Tavern. Cuisine: American.*

Courthouse Cafe
110 S. Broadway
New Philadelphia
(330) 343-7896
• *All areas. Cuisine: seafood and pasta.*

Alberini's
1201 Youngstown Rd.
Niles
(216) 652-5895
• *Private cigar smoking room, bar and lounge. Humidor. Cuisine: Italian.*

**The Olde Loyal
Oak Tavern &
Restaurant**
3044 Wadsworth Rd.
Norton
(330) 825-8280
•*Specified area of the
main dining room,
bar, lounge and pri-
vate rooms. Humidor.
Cuisine: American
and Continental.*

**Town Crier
Restaurant**
2293 Wadsworth Rd.
Norton
(216) 745-8110
•*Bar. Humidor. Cui-
sine: American.*

Rider's Inn
792 Mentor Ave.
Painesville
(216) 354-8200
•*Pub only. Cuisine:
American.*

Citi Lounge
114 Louisiana Ave.
Perrysburg
(419) 872-6437
•*All areas after
10:30pm, and in the
loft "Exhale Room".
Humidor. Cuisine:
Italian.*

**The Bogey Inn
Restaurant &
Sports Site**
6013 Glick Rd.
Powell
(614) 889-0150
•*Bar/lounge, private
room and patio. Hu-
midor. Cuisine:
American.*

Chez Francois
555 Main St.
Vermilion
(216) 967-0630
•*Bar/lounge and din-
ing room after
9:30pm. Humidor.
Cuisine: French.*

Eddie's Place
28601 Chagrin Blvd.
Woodmere
(216) 591-1545
•*Bar. Humidor. Cui-
sine: Southern Italian.*

Boat Yard Ltd.
3163 Belmont Ave.
Youngstown
(216) 759-7892
•*Bar and patio. Hu-
midor. Cuisine: Ital-
ian, specializing in
seafood.*

Oklahoma

**Old Germany
Restaurant**
15920 SE 29th
Choctaw
(405) 390-8647
•*Wine cellar.
Humidor. Cuisine:
German.*

Nikz At The Top
United Founders
Tower /5900
Mosteller Dr.
Oklahoma City
(405) 843-7875
•*All smoking areas
and in the cigar room.
Humidor. Cuisine:
American Continental
with a French
influence.*

Oregon

**Crossings at the
Riverhouse**
3075 N. Hwy. 97
Bend
(541) 389-8810
•*Bar. Humidor. Cui-
sine: USDA prime
beef.*

PORTLAND
The Brazen Bean
2075 NW Glisan
Portland
(503) 294-0636
•*All areas. Humidor.*
Cigar bar.

**The Heathman
Hotel**
1001 SW Broadway
at Salmon
Portland
(503) 241-4100
•*Cigar bar, private
room and patio. Hu-
midor. Cuisine: Pacif-
ic Northwest and
French.*

**Jake's Grill at the
Governor Hotel**
611 SW 10th St.
Portland
(503) 220-1850
•*Bar. Humidor. Cui-
sine: steak, pasta, sal-
ads and seafood.*

**McCormick &
Schmick's
Seafood
Restaurant**
235 SW 1st Ave.
Portland
(503) 224-7522
•*Bar/lounge. Humi-
dor. Cuisine: seafood.*

**The Sports Den at
the Shilo Inn**
9900 SW Canyon
Rd., Portland
(503) 297-6125
•*Cigar bar. Humidor.
Cuisine: Pacific
Northwest.*

Pennsylvania

Hartefeld National
1 Hartefeld Dr.
Avondale
(800) 240-7373,
(610) 268-8800
•*Irish Pub and Walk-
ing Cup dining room.
Humidor. Cuisine:
traditional American.*

**Wooden Angel
Restaurant &
Casual Cafe**
Sharon Rd./Leopard
Lane, Bridgewater
Beaver
(412) 774-7880
•*Smoking section and
bar/lounge. Humidor.
Cuisine: American.*

King George II Inn
102 Radcliff St.
Bristol
(215) 788-5536
•*Tavern. Humidor.
Cuisine: regional
American.*

**Country Squire
Diner/Restaurant**
2560 W. Chester
Pike
Broomall
(610) 356-3030
•*Smoking section.
Humidor. Cuisine:
American.*

Central Bar & Grille
39 Morris Ave.
Bryn Mawr
(610) 527-1400
•Bar. Cuisine: American.

Log Cabin Inn
430 Perry Hwy.
Harmony
(412) 452-4155
•Bar. Humidor. Cuisine: American, specializing in seafood and steak.

Nick's 1014 Cafe
1014 N. 3rd St.
Harrisburg
(717) 238-8844
•All areas. Humidor. Cuisine: seafood and steakhouse.

Scotts' Bar & Grille
212 Locust St.
Harrisburg
(717) 234-7599
•Dining room and bar. Humidor. Cuisine: American and Continental.

The Park Ridge at Valley Forge
480 N. Gulph Rd.
King of Prussia
(610) 337-1800
•Bar/lounge. Humidor. Cuisine: American.

The General Layfayette Inn & Brewery
646 Germantown Pike
Lafayette Hill
(610) 941-0600
•Two cigar lounges. Humidor. Cuisine: fine dining.

LANCASTER

Gallo Rosso
337 N. Queen St.
Lancaster
(717) 392-5616
•Bar. Humidor. Cuisine: upscale Northern Italian.

Market Fare Restaurant
50 W. Grant St.
Lancaster
(717) 299-7090
•Bar/lounge. Humidor. Cuisine: New American.

Roadhouse Cafe
700 E. Chestnut St.
Lancaster
(717) 393-5555
•All areas but nonsmoking. Humidor. Cuisine: American with southwestern flair.

Strawberry Hill
128 W. Strawberry St.
Lancaster
(717) 393-5544
•Bar and private rooms. Humidor. Cuisine: American, Continental, French and Mediterranean.

D'Ignazio's Town House Restaurant
117 Veterans' Square
Media
(610) 566-6141
•Bar. Humidor. Cuisine: steaks, seafood and pasta.

Springfield Grille
1553 Perry Hwy.
Mercer
(412) 748-3589
•Bar. Humidor. Cuisine: American, featuring fire-grilled steaks and seafood.

Alfred's Victorian
38 N. Union St.
Middletown
(717) 944-4929
•Bar/lounge and patio. Cuisine: Continental and Northern Italian.

Italian Village Restaurant
902 MacDade Blvd.
Milmont Park
(610) 237-0200
•Adjoining cigar lounge. Humidor. Cuisine: Italian.

The Watering Trough
905 W. Main St.
Mount Joy
(717) 653-6181
•Lounge. Humidor. Cuisine: Continental, salads and sandwiches.

East Wind
1418 Butler Ave.
New Castle

(412) 658-7175
•Dining room, bar and private rooms. Cuisine: American and Italian.

Charlotte's Restaurant
3207 W. Chester Pike
Newtown Square
(610) 356-7100
•Lounge seating. Humidor. Cuisine: features seafood, veal and beef.

D'Ignazio's Nottingham Inn
Old U.S. 1 & Rte. 272
Nottingham
(610) 932-4050
•Back of dining room and bar area. Humidor. Cuisine: American/Italian.

PHILADELPHIA

Chris's Cafe
1421 Sansom St.
Philadelphia
(215) 568-3131
•All areas. Humidor. Cuisine: seafood. *Jazz club.*

Ciboulette at The Bellevue Building
200 S. Broad St.
Philadelphia
(215) 790-1210
•Bar/lounge, cigar bar and private room. Humidor. Cuisine: French.

Dickens Inn
421 S. 2nd St.
Philadelphia
(215) 928-9307
•*All bar areas. Humidor. Cuisine: English and Continental.*

Dilullo Centro
1407 Locust St.
Philadelphia
(215) 546-2000
•*Bar/lounge. Cuisine: Northern Italian.*

Founders Restaurant/ Library Lounge/ The Bellevue
1415 Chancellor Ct.
Philadelphia
(215) 893-1776
•*Library lounge. Humidor. Cuisine: Continental with a French flair.*

The Happy Rooster
119 S. 16th St.
Philadelphia
(215) 563-1481
•*All areas. Humidor. Cuisine: American and Continental.*

Jack's Firehouse
2130 Fairmount Ave.
Philadelphia
(215) 232-9000
•*Bar area. Cuisine: American regional.*

Le Bar Lyonnais at Le Bec Fin
1523 Walnut St.
Philadelphia
(215) 496-9606

•*Bar Lyonnais after 9:30pm. Humidor. Cuisine: classic French with nouvelle influences.*

London Grill
2301 Fairmount Ave.
Philadelphia
(215) 978-4545
•*Bar/lounge and private room. Humidor. Cuisine: New American.*

McGillin's Olde Ale House
1310 Drury Lane
Philadelphia
(215) 735-5562
•*Dining room, bar and lounge. Cuisine: American.*

Mia's Restaurant and Wine Bar at The Warwick Hotel
1701 Locust St.
Philadelphia
(215) 545-4655
•*Lounge. Humidor. Cuisine: Italian, French and Spanish.*

Morton's of Chicago
1 Logan Square
Philadelphia
(215) 557-0724
•*Bar/lounge, smoking section and private room. Humidor. Cuisine: steakhouse.*

Old Original Bookbinder's Restaurant
125 Walnut St.
Philadelphia
(215) 925-7027
•*Bar and smoking section. Humidor. Cuisine: seafood and steak.*

Palm Restaurant
200 S. Broad St.
Philadelphia
(215) 546-7256
•*Dining room and bar. Cuisine: American, specializing in steak.*

Philip's Italian Restaurant
1145 S. Broad St.
Philadelphia
(215) 334-0882
•*All areas. Humidor. Cuisine: Italian and American.*

The Ritz-Carlton
Liberty Plaza
17th & Chestnut
Philadelphia
(215) 563-1600
• *"The Grill Bar." Humidor. Cuisine: contemporary American.*

Seven Stars Inn
Rte. 23 & Hoffecker Rd.
Phoenixville
(610) 495-5205

•*Bar/lounge and special dining room (seats 12-18 people). Humidor. Cuisine: seafood and steak.*

PITTSBURGH

The Carlton
One Mellon Bank Center
Pittsburgh
(412) 391-4099
•*Smoking section, bar and lounge. Humidor. Cuisine: steaks, fresh seafood, veal and pasta.*

Cliffside
1208 Grandview Ave., Pittsburgh
(412) 431-6996
•*Bar.*

Heaven
107 6th St.
Pittsburgh
(412) 338-2720
•*Bar/lounge, smoking section and cigar bar. Humidor. Cuisine: steak and seafood.*

Le Mont
1114 Grandview Ave., Pittsburgh
(412) 431-3100
•*Front dining room, lounge and private rooms. Humidor. Cuisine: contemporary American.*

Louis Tambellini Restaurant
860 Sawmill Run Blvd., Pittsburgh
(412) 481-1118

•*Bar. Humidor. Cuisine: seafood and Italian specialties.*

Morton's of Chicago
625 Liberty Ave.
Pittsburgh
(412) 261-7141
•*Bar, private rooms and patio. Humidor. Cuisine: steakhouse.*

Roland's Seafood Grill
1904 Pennsylvania Ave., Pittsburgh
(412) 261-3401
•*All areas. Humidor. Cuisine: seafood.*

Siena
430 Market Square
Pittsburgh
(412) 338-0945
•*Bar/lounge. Humidor. Cuisine: modern American.*

....

Tink's Cafe
519 Linden St.
Scranton
(717) 346-8465
•*Bar and patio. Humidor. Cuisine: American.* **Nightclub.**

The Washington House at the Historic Strasburg Inn
1 Historic Dr.
Strasburg
(717) 687-7691
•*Tavern. Humidor. Cuisine: French colonial.*

Catalanos
461 S. Front St.
Wormleysburg
(717) 763-7905
•*Bar. Cuisine: gourmet.*

Rhode Island

The Clarke Cooke House
Bannister's Wharf
Newport
(401) 849-2900
•*In the three bars and in one dining room. Humidor. Cuisine: Continental.*

PROVIDENCE

Atomic Grill
99 Chestnut St.
Providence
(401) 621-8888
•*Smoking area, bars and nightclub. Humidor. Cuisine: nouvelle cuisine.*

The Capital Grille
1 Cookson Place
Providence
(401) 521-5600
•*Dining room, bar and lounge. Humidor. Cuisine: American, specializing in steak.*

Capriccio
2 Pine St.
Providence
(401) 421-1320
•*Lounge and smoking section. Humidor. Cuisine: European.*

Sikar Cafe and Smoking Lounge
190 Atwells Ave.
Providence
(401) 273-SIKAR
•*Cigar areas. Humidor.* **Coffee bar.**

South Carolina

Restaurant Million
2 Unity Alley
Charleston
(803) 577-3141
•*Lounge and atrium. Humidor. Cuisine: French.*

Austin's and Beau's at the Greenville Marriott
1 Parkway E.
Greenville
(803) 297-0300
•*Dining room, bar and private rooms (Beau's open after 5pm). Cuisine: American.*

Commons Bar at the Hyatt Regency Greenville
210 N. Main St.
Greenville
(864) 258-2470
•*All areas. Humidor. Cuisine: appetizers only.*

Inn on the Square
104 Court St.
Greenwood
(864) 223-4488
•*Pub and private rooms. Humidor. Cuisine: French.*

The Gentleman's Club
1 Dunnigan's Alley
Hilton Head
(803) 842-3340
•*All areas. Humidor.* **Gentleman's club.**

New York Prime
405 28th Ave. N.
Myrtle Beach
(803) 448-8081
•*Smoking section and bar area. Humidor. Cuisine: New York-style prime steaks.*

H. Dundee's Steakhouse
2455 Cherry Rd.
Rock Hill
(803) 325-7661
•*Dining room, bar and lounge. Humidor. Cuisine: steak.*

South Dakota

Alcester Steakhouse
Junction of Hwys. 11 & 13
Alcester
(605) 934-2974
•*Bar/lounge. Humidor. Cuisine: steakhouse.*

Sioux Falls Brewing Co.
431 N. Phillips Ave.
Sioux Falls
(605) 332-4847
•*Pub only. Humidor. Cuisine: handcrafted cuisine.*

Theo's Great Food
601 W. 33rd St.
Sioux Falls
(605) 338-6801
•*Smoking section, bar and lounge. Humidor. Cuisine: American, Continental, French and Mediterranean.*

Tennessee

Chattanooga Billiard Club
110 Jordan Dr.
Chattanooga
(423) 499-3883
•*All areas of club. Humidor. Cuisine: traditional American.* **Upscale billiards lounge.**

Chattanooga Billiard Club
725½ Cherry St.
Chattanooga
(423) 267-7740
•*All areas of club. Humidor. Cuisine: traditional American.* **Upscale billiards lounge.**

Regas
318 N. Gay St.
Knoxville
(423) 637-9805
•*Bar/lounge area. Cuisine: steak and seafood.*

NASHVILLE
Arthur's at the Grand Heritage Hotel
1001 Broadway
Nashville

(615) 255-1494
•*Smoking section. Humidor. Cuisine: Continental.*

Belle Meade Brasserie
101 Page Rd.
Nashville
(615) 356-5450
•*Bar/lounge and smoking area. Humidor. Cuisine: new American.*

Black Stone Restaurant & Brewery
1918 West End Ave.
Nashville
(615) 327-9969
•*Bar/lounge. Humidor. Cuisine: American.*

The Bound'ry
711 20th Ave. S.
Nashville
(615) 321-3043
•*Bar/lounge and patio. Humidor. Cuisine: upscale international.*

Cafe Coco Coffee House
210 Louise Ave.
Nashville
(615) 329-0024
•*Humidor room, front and back patios. Humidor. Cuisine: pizza/pasta.* **Bar/coffee bar.**

F. Scott's
2210 Crestmoore Rd.
Nashville

(615) 269-5861
•*Bar. Humidor. Cuisine: American with southwestern & Pacific influences.*

Ivory's Lounge
2200 Elm Hill Pike
Nashville
(615) 883-9770
•*All areas. Humidor. Cuisine: mixed variety.* **Nightclub.**

Mario's
2005 Broadway
Nashville
(615) 327-3232
•*Bar/lounge. Humidor. Cuisine: Northern Italian.*

The Merchants Restaurant
401 Broadway
Nashville
(615) 254-1892
•*Bar/lounge. Humidor. Cuisine: American.*

Mere Bulles
152 2nd Ave. N.
Nashville
(615) 256-1946
•*Bar/lounge. Humidor. Cuisine: Continental and seafood.*

Morton's of Chicago
641 Church St.
Nashville
(615) 259-4558
•*Smoking section, bar area and private rooms. Humidor. Cuisine: steakhouse.*

Ruth's Chris Steak House
2100 W. End Ave.
Nashville
(615) 320-0163
•*Bar/lounge. Humidor. Cuisine: steakhouse.*

Sunset Grill
2001-A Belcourt Ave., Nashville
(615) 386-3663
•*Bar, lounge and patio. Humidor. Cuisine: American.*

Valentino's
1907 W. End Ave.
Nashville
(615) 327-0148
•*Smoking section and bar. Humidor. Cuisine: Northern Italian.*

Wild Boar
2014 Broadway
Nashville
(615) 329-1313
•*Cocktail lounge. Humidor. Cuisine: Continental.*

Texas

ADDISON
Flying Saucer
14999 Montfort
Addison
(972) 934-2537
•*Indoor beer garden. Humidor. Cuisine: pub fare.* **Specialty beer house.**

Morton's of Chicago
14831 Midway Rd.
Addison
(214) 233-5858
•*Bar/lounge and smoking section. Humidor. Cuisine: steakhouse.*

Old Chicago
4060 Beltline Rd.
Addison
(972) 490-3900
•*Bar, lounge and patio. Humidor. Cuisine: pizza/pasta.*

AUSTIN

Louie's 106 Grill & Tapas Bar
106 E. 6th St.
Austin
(512) 476-1997
•*Private room. Humidor. Cuisine: Spanish and Mediterranean.*

Sfuzzi
311 W. 6th St.
Austin
(512) 476-8100
•*Bar. Humidor. Cuisine: Northern Italian.*

The Yellow Rose
6528 N. Lamar
Austin
(512) 458-2106
•*All areas. Humidor. Cuisine: American.*
Nightclub/cabaret.

Hoffbrau Steaks
2310 N. 11th St.
Beaumont

(409) 892-6911
•*Bar/lounge, smoking section, private room and outdoor beer garden. Humidor. Cuisine: steakhouse and seafood.*

Steak & Ale
315 I H-10
Beaumont
(409) 832-3441
•*Smoking section. Cuisine: American.*

Monet's Restaurant & Catering
5005 Colleyville Blvd., Ste. 240
Colleyville
(817) 498-5525
•*Bar. Cuisine: French Continental.*

DALLAS

Addison Point
4578 Belt Line Rd.
Dallas
(214) 661-2230
•*All areas. Cuisine: American burger joint.*
Sports bar.

Bob's Steak & Chop House
4300 Lemmon Ave.
Dallas
(214) 528-9446
•*Bar, smoking section and private room. Humidor. Cuisine: American, specializing in steak.*

Bugatti
3802 W. Northwest Hwy., Dallas
(214) 350-2470

•*Cigar room. Humidor. Cuisine: Italian.*

Cabaret Royale
10723 Composite Dr.
Dallas
(214) 350-0303
•*All areas. Humidor. Cuisine: American and Southwestern.*

Del Frisco's Double Eagle Steakhouse
5251 Spring Valley Rd., Dallas
(214) 490-9000
•*Dining room and bar. Humidor. Cuisine: steak.*

Dick's Last Resort
West End Market Place, Dallas
(214) 747-0001
•*All areas. Cuisine: ribs, steak and shrimp.*

Four Seasons Resort & Club
4150 N. MacArthur Blvd., Dallas
(214) 717-0700
•*Smoking section in bar and lounge. Humidor. Cuisine: new American.*

Javier's Gourmet Mexicano Restaurant
4912 Cole Ave.
Dallas
(214) 521-4211
•*Cigar-smoking room with a hunting lodge theme, overstuffed chairs, and great ventilation. Humidor.*

Cuisine: upscale Mexican (Mexico City-style) and seafood.

Les Saisons
165 Turtle Creek Village, Dallas
(214) 528-1102
•*Bar area. Humidor. Cuisine: French.*

The Lodge
10530 Spangler Rd.
Dallas
(972) 506-9229
•*All areas. Humidor. Cuisine: American.*
Gentleman's club.

Mansion on Turtle Creek
2821 Turtle Creek Blvd., Dallas
(214) 559-2100
•*Bar and lounge area. Cuisine: southwestern.*

Matt's No Place
6310 La Vista Dr.
Dallas
(214) 823-9077
•*Smoking section and bar area. Humidor. Cuisine: steaks, wild game and seafood.*

Morton's of Chicago
50l Elm St.
Dallas
(214) 741-2277
•*Smoking section, bar and private rooms. Humidor. Cuisine: steakhouse.*

Mr. G's at the Hyatt Regency DFW
DFW International Pkwy., DFW Airport, Dallas
(972) 453-1234
•Smoking section. Humidor. Cuisine: steak and seafood.

Nana Grill
2201 Stemmons Fwy. Dallas
(214) 761-7459
•Bar and private dining rooms. Humidor. Cuisine: American.

Newport's Seafood Restaurant
703 McKinney Ave. Dallas
(214) 954-0220
•Bar and private room. Cuisine: seafood.

The Palm
701 Ross Ave. Dallas
(214) 698-0470
•Bar/lounge and private room. Cuisine: steakhouse.

Pyramid Room at the Fairmont Hotel
1717 N. Akard St. Dallas
(214) 720-5249
•Bar. Humidor. Cuisine: classical & New American.

Trail Dust Steak House
10841 Composite Dr. Dallas
(214) 357-3862
•Only private cigar dinners or reservations for cigar dinners. Cuisine: steak.

Watel's
1923 McKinney Ave. Dallas
(214) 720-0323
•Patio and after dinner in the main dining room. Humidor. Cuisine: French.

West End Pub
211 N. Record Dallas
(214) 748-5711
•All areas. Humidor. Cuisine: pub fare. **Bar.**
- -

Carmen's at the Radisson Hotel
2211 I-35E N. Denton
(817) 381-0263
•Smoking section. Cuisine: Italian.

Cafe Central
109 N. Oregon El Paso
(915) 545-CAFE
•Bar/lounge. Humidor. Cuisine: eclectic contemporary including fresh seafood, prime steaks, lamb and pasta.

Flying Saucer
111 E. 4th Street Fort Worth
(817) 336-7470
•Indoor beer garden, "Half-Acre" gaming parlor. Humidor. Cuisine: pub fare. **Specialty beer house.**

Michaels
3413 W. 7th St. Fort Worth
(817) 877-3413
•Dining room after hours, bar/lounge and private room. Humidor. Cuisine: contemporary ranch.

Gaido's Restaurant
3800 Seawall Galveston
(409) 762-9625
•Smoking section. Cuisine: seafood.

Grey Moss Inn
19010 Scenic Loop Rd. Grey Forest
(210) 695-8301
•Patio. Cuisine: steakhouse.

HOUSTON

Big John's Neighborhood Bar
6150 Wilcrest Houston
(281) 498-3499
•All areas of bar. Humidor. Cuisine: pub fare. **Bar.**

Brennan's
3300 Smith St. Houston
(713) 522-9711
•Bar. Humidor. Cuisine: Southwestern/American.

The Brownstone
2736 Virginia Houston
(713) 520-5666
•Terrace. Humidor. Cuisine: Continental.

Cent'anni Gran Ristorante
2128 Portsmouth Houston
(713) 529-4199
•Smoking section and bar. Cuisine: Italian.

Charley's 517
517 Louisiana St. Houston
(713) 224-8712
•Lounge. Humidor. Cuisine: American and Continental.

Colorado Bar & Grill
6710 SW Fwy. Houston
(713) 781-1122
•All areas. Humidor. Cuisine: steaks, pizza and sandwiches. **Upscale gentlemen's club.**

DeVille, Terrace Cafe, Lobby Lounge at the Four Seasons Hotel
1300 Lamar St.

Houston
(713) 650-1300
•*Bar. Humidor.*
Cuisine: American
with an Italian flair;
Terrace Cafe: light
American.

8.0 Restaurant &
   Bar
3745 Greenbriar
Houston
(713) 523-0880
•*All areas after*
10:00pm. Humidor.
Cuisine: contempo-
rary American.

The Ginger Man
5607 Morningside
Houston
(713) 526-2770
•*All areas. Humidor.*
Bar.

La Colombe d'Or
3410 Montrose Blvd.
Houston
(713) 524-7999
•*Bar and library.*
Humidor. Cuisine:
Continental.

La Reserve at the
   Omni Houston
4 Riverway
Houston
(713) 871-8177
•*Bar, lounge and*
private rooms. Humi-
dor. Cuisine: creative
Continental.

Matthias'
   Restaurant &
   Pub
3755 FM 1960 W.
Houston

(281) 537-5837
•*All areas. Humidor.*
Cuisine: American.

Montesano
   Ristorante
   Italiano
6009 Beverly Hill
   Lane, Houston
(713) 977-4565
•*Smoking section,*
bar/lounge and fire-
place room. Humidor.
Cuisine: Italian.

Morton's of
   Chicago
Centre at Post Oak,
   5000 Westheimer
Houston
(713) 629-1946
•*Bar/lounge, smoking*
section and private
room. Humidor. Cui-
sine: steakhouse.

Pappas Bros.
   Steakhouse
5839 Westheimer
Houston
(713) 780-7352
•*Bar/lounge and*
smoking section.
Humidor. Cuisine:
steakhouse.

Rainbow Lodge
1 Birdsall
Houston
(713) 861-8666
•*Bar, lounge and pri-*
vate rooms. Humidor.
Cuisine: American.

Bar & Grill at the
   Ritz-Carlton
1919 Briar Oaks
   Lane, Houston

(713) 840-7600
•*Dining room, bar,*
lounge and private
rooms. Humidor.
Cuisine: American
with a southwest
influence.

The Roxy
5351 W. Alabama
Houston
(713) 850-ROXY
•*All areas. Humidor.*

Ruggles
903 Westheimer
Houston
(713) 524-3839
•*Nightclub. Cuisine:*
American with a
southwestern flair.
Nightclub.

Ruth's Chris Steak
   House
6213 Richmond Ave.
Houston
(713) 789-2333
•*Lounge. Humidor.*
Cuisine: steakhouse.

Shooters Billiards
   & Sports Cafe
6306 Richmond Ave.
Houston
(713) 952-9628
•*Pool hall. Humidor.*
Cuisine: appetizers
only.

The Velvet Elvis
3303 Richmond Ave.
Houston
(713) 520-0434
•*All areas. Humidor.*
Cuisine: American.

Blank & Company
203½ E. Main
Nacogdoches
(409) 560-0776
•*Anywhere, anytime.*
Cuisine: steakhouse.

Marcello's Italian
   Restaurant
110 N. Tarmada
Port Isabel
(210) 943-7611
•*Smoking section.*
Humidor. Cuisine:
Italian.

Wizard's Sports
   Cafe
747 S. Central Expy.
Richardson
(214) 235-0371
•*All areas. Humidor.*
Cuisine: steaks, salad,
brisket.

SAN
ANTONIO
Barcelona Cafe
Broadway Ave.
San Antonio
(210) 822-6129
•*Cigar bar.*
Humidor. Cuisine:
Mediterranean.

Morton's of
   Chicago
300 Crockett St.
San Antonio
(210) 228-0700
•*Smoking section, bar*
and private rooms.
Humidor. Cuisine:
steakhouse.

**Polo's at the
Fairmont Hotel**
401 S. Alamo
San Antonio
(210) 224-8800
•*Bar. Humidor. Cuisine: Southwestern with an Asian flair.*

Louie's Backyard
2305 Laguna Blvd.
South Padre Island
(210) 761-4282
•*All areas outside and 80% of indoors. Humidor. Cuisine: ribs and crabcakes.*
Nightclub.

**Rock Bottom
Brewery**
4050 Beltline Rd.
West Addison
(972) 404-7456
•*Cigar bar, private room and patio. Humidor. Cuisine: pub fare.*

Vermont

**Main Street Grill &
Bar**
118 Main St.
Montpelier
(802) 229-9202
•*Smoking room off of pub. Cuisine: American.*

La Poule a Dents
Main St.
Norwich
(802) 649-2922
•*Patio (summer only). Humidor. Cuisine: French.*

**Ye Olde England
Inne**
433 Mountain Rd.
Stowe
(802) 253-7064
•*Private dining rooms. Cuisine: American and English.*

Hermitage Inn
Coldbrook Rd.
Wilmington
(802) 464-3511
•*Bar/lounge and smoking section. Humidor. Cuisine: Continental.*

Virginia

Bullfeathers
112 King St.
Alexandria
(703) 836-8088
•*Bar area. Humidor. Cuisine: American steakhouse.*

Morrison House
116 S. Alfred St.
Alexandria
(703) 838-8000
•*Grille and library. Humidor. Cuisine: contemporary American.*

ARLINGTON

**Blue'n'Gold
Brewing
Company**
3100 Clarendon
Blvd., Arlington
(703) 908-4995
•*Bar. Humidor. Cuisine: French Creole.*

**Coco's Casa Mia
Ristorante**
3111 Columbia Pike
Arlington
(703) 920-5450
•*Bar, lounge and smoking section. Humidor. Cuisine: American and Italian.*
Nightclub.

The Ritz-Carlton
1250 S. Hayes St.
Arlington
(703) 412-2760
•*Bar/lounge. Humidor. Cuisine: Continental.*

**Michael's Bistro &
Taphouse**
1427 University Ave.
Charlottesville
(804) 977-3697
•*Bar during dinner and all areas after 10pm. Humidor. Cuisine: regional American bistro.*

**Tavern at Boar's
Head Inn &
Sports Club**
Rte. 250 W.
Charlottesville
(804) 296-2181
•*After 9pm in the lounge and restaurant. Humidor. Cuisine: American and Continental.*

AJ's on the Creek
6585 Maddox Blvd.
Chincoteague
(804) 336-5888

•*Bar. Cuisine: seafood, seafood pastas, steaks, lamb and veal.*

**The Riverview—A
Steak & Seafood
Restaurant**
1101 Sophia St.
Fredericksburg
(540) 373-6500
•*Captain Irvin's lounge. Cuisine: steak (featuring Black Angus), seafood, chicken and pastas.*

**The Cigar Lounge
at Oasis Winery**
14141 Hume Rd.
Hume
(540) 635-3103
•*Back patio. Humidor.* **Winery.**

Cafe France
3225 Old Forest Rd.
Lynchburg
(804) 385-8989
•*Dining room after 9:45pm. Humidor. Cuisine: Nouvelle American.*

**Evans Farm Inn
and The Sitting
Duck Pub**
1696 Chain Bridge
Rd.
McLean
(703) 356-8000
•*Sitting Duck Pub and smoking section of dining room. Humidor. Cuisine: American and Continental.*

RICHMOND

Havana '59
16 N. 17th St.
Richmond
(804) 649-2822
•*Bar/lounge and smoking section. Humidor. Cuisine: Cuban.*

Rare Old Times
10602 Patterson Ave., Richmond
(804) 750-1346
•*All areas. Humidor. Cuisine: Irish pub fare.*

The Tobacco Co. Restaurant
1201 E. Cary St.
Richmond
(804) 782-9431
•*Dining room, bar and lounge. Humidor. Cuisine: American.*

- - - - - - - - - - - - - - - - - - - -

Morton's of Chicago
8075 Leesburg Pike
Vienna
(703) 883-0800
•*Bar/lounge and smoking section. Humidor. Cuisine: steakhouse.*

Coyote Cafe & Cantina
972 Laskin Rd.
Virginia Beach
(757) 425-5568
•*Bar. Humidor. Cuisine: southwestern.*

Croc's
620 19th St.
Virginia Beach
(804) 428-5444
•*Bar and patio at all times; all areas after 11:00pm. Humidor. Cuisine: Caribbean-inspired, featuring steak, pasta, seafood and gator bites.*

Ford's Colony Williamsburg
240 Ford's Colony Dr.
Williamsburg
(804) 258-4107,
•*Bar/lounge. Humidor. Cuisine: Dining room offers upscale American; Grill Room, American bistro.*

Piper's
136 Creekside Lane
Winchester
(540) 662-2900
•*Special area of dining room for cigar smoking. Humidor. Cuisine: American.*

Washington

The Spar Cafe & Bar
114 4th Ave. E.
Olympia
(360) 357-6444
•*Bar/lounge, smoking section and cigar bar. Humidor. Cuisine: American.*

SEATTLE

Bandoleone
2241 Eastlake Ave. E.
Seattle
(206) 329-7559
•*Lounge area T-Su, all areas on M. Humidor. Cuisine: Cubano/ Latino with a gourmet twist.*

Bookstore Bar at the The Alexis Hotel
1007 1st Ave.
Seattle
(206) 382-1506
•*All areas. Humidor. Cuisine: new American.*

F.X. McRory's Steak, Chop & Oyster House
419 Occidental Ave. S., 501
Seattle
(206) 623-4800
•*Bar. Humidor. Cuisine: seafood and steak.*

Georgian Room at the Four Seasons Hotel
411 University St.
Seattle
(206) 621-7889
•*Terrace Lounge and private rooms. Humidor. Cuisine: regional Northwest.*

McCormick's Fish House & Bar
722 4th Ave.
Seattle
(206) 682-3900

•*Bar and patio. Humidor. Cuisine: fresh seafood.*

Metropolitan Grill
820 2nd Ave.
Seattle
(206) 624-3287
•*Lounge and private dining rooms. Humidor. Cuisine: American steakhouse.*

Ray's Boathouse
6049 Seaview NW
Seattle
(206) 789-3770
•*Smoking section. Cuisine: Pacific Northwest and seafood.*

- - - - - - - - - - - - - - - - - - - -

John Horan House
2 Horan Rd.
Wenatchee
(509) 663-0018
•*Outside dining area. Humidor. Cuisine: American, specializing in seafood and steak.*

West Virginia

The Anvil Restaurant
1270 Washington St.
Harpers Ferry
(304) 535-2582
•*Bar/lounge. Cuisine: seafood and steak.*

The Red Fox Inn
Snowshoe Rd.
Snowshoe
(304) 572-1111
•*Bar/lounge. Cuisine: wild game.*

Greenbrier Hotel
Main St.
White Sulphur
Springs
(304) 536-1110
•*Bar, lounge, private rooms and patio. Humidor. Cuisine: American.*

Wisconsin

Jimmie's White House Inn
5776 Main St.
Butte des Morts
(414) 582-7211
•*Old Antique bar and private rooms. Cuisine: American, specializing in steak.* **Supper club.**

Fountain Blue
5133 S. Lake Dr.
Cudahy
(414) 481-1482
•*Bar/lounge and smoking section. Cuisine: American and Polish.*

Studio Grille
1318 Racine St.
Delavan
(414) 728-0456
•*Bar/lounge and smoking section. Humidor. Cuisine: American.*

Alfred's Supper Club
506 Hill St.
Green Lake
(800) 664-3631,
(414) 294-3631

•*Dining room, bar and private rooms. Humidor. Cuisine: American and Mediterranean.*

The Fox & Hounds
1298 Friess Lake Rd.
Hubertus
(414) 251-4100
•*Bar and private rooms. Humidor. Cuisine: Continental.*

Horse & Plow at The American Club
Highland Dr.
Kohler
(414) 457-8000
•*Bar. Humidor. Cuisine: American and Mexican/Tex-Mex.*

Kirsch's Restaurant at the French Country Inn
Hwy. 50 W.
Lake Geneva
(414) 245-5756
•*Bar, lounge, private rooms and patio. Humidor. Cuisine: American, Continental and French.*

The Bistro at the Madison Concourse Hotel
1 W. Dayton St.
Madison
(608) 257-6000
•*Bar and Solitaire Room. Humidor. Cuisine: Continental.* **Bar.**

The Cardinal Bar & Dance Club
418 E. Wilson St.

Madison
(608) 251-0080
•*All areas. Humidor.* **Bar/dance club.**

Inn on Maritime Bay
101 Maritime Dr.
Manitowoc
(414) 682-7000
•*Smoking section. Humidor. Cuisine: American/Continental, specializing in seafood and steak.*

Johnny's Bar & Grill
3161 Hwy. 51
Mercer
(715) 476-2516
•*All areas. Humidor. Cuisine: pub fare.*

Grenadier's
747 N. Broadway
Milwaukee
(414) 276-0747
•*Bar/lounge. Cuisine: Continental.*

Shaker's Cigar Bar
422 S. 2nd St.
Milwaukee
(414) 272-4222
•*All areas. Humidor. Cuisine: Caribbean, Cuban and Japanese.*

Fox River Brewing Co. & Fratello's Italian Cafe
1501 Arboretum Dr.
Oshkosh
(414) 232-2337
•*Bar area. Humidor. Cuisine: Italian and American.*

Fifty Two Stafford, An Irish Guest House
52 Stafford St.
Plymouth
(414) 893-0552
•*Smoking section and bar. Humidor. Cuisine: American and Continental, specializing in seafood.*

Cavalier Room Restaurant & Lounge
70 N. Stevens St.
Rhinelander
(715) 362-7100
•*Lounge and private rooms. Cuisine: American.*

Ambassador Club
327 W. Main St.
Waukesha
(414) 547-9009
•*All areas. Humidor.* **Jazz and cigar bar.**

Wausau Club
309 McClellan St.
Wausau
(715) 845-2131
•*Private dining club. Humidor. Cuisine: Continental.* **Private dining club.**

Steakhouse 100
10725 W. Greenfield Ave.
West Allis
(414) 771-2223
•*Bar/lounge. Humidor. Cuisine: steakhouse.*

INTERNATIONAL

Austria

VIENNA

Gottfried
Untere Viaduktgasse
45, Vienna
43 1 71 38 256
•*All areas. Humidor.
Cuisine: French.*

**Korso at the Bristol
Hotel**
Karntner Ring 1
Vienna
43 1 51 51 60
•*All areas. Humidor.
Cuisine: Austrian and
French.*

**La Scala at The
Vienna Plaza**
Schottenring 11
Vienna
43 1 31 39 00
•*Smoking section.
Humidor. Cuisine:
Austrian.*

**Restaurant
Steirereck**
Rasumofskygasse 2
Vienna
43 1 71 33 168
•*Bar/lounge and
smoking section.
Humidor. Cuisine:
new Austrian.*

Belgium

'T Fornuis
Reyndersstraat 24
Antwerp
32 3 23 36 270

•*Bar and after dinner.
Humidor. Cuisine:
French.*

BRUSSELS

Bruneau
ave. Broustin 75
Brussels
32 2 42 76 978
•*All areas. Humidor.
Cuisine: French.*

Comme Chez Soi
23 place Rouppe
Brussels
32 2 51 22 921
•*Dining room and pri-
vate rooms. Humidor.
Cuisine: French.*

**La Maison du
Cygne**
Grand Place 9
Brussels
32 2 51 18 244
•*All areas. Humidor.
Cuisine: French.*

La Truffe Noire
12 blvd. de La
Cambre
Brussels
32 2 64 04 422
•*All areas. Humidor.
Cuisine: French and
Italian.*

**Les 4 Saisons at the
Royal Windsor**
rue Duquesnoy 5
Brussels
32 2 50 55 100
•*Smoking section.
Humidor. Cuisine:
classic French.*

Maison du Boeuf
blvd. du Waterloo 38
Brussels
32 2 50 41 111
•*All areas. Humidor.
Cuisine: Continental.*

Sea Grill
J. Le Divellec, rue
Fossé-aux-Loups
47, Brussels
32 2 22 73 120
•*Smoking section, bar
and atrium lounge.
Humidor. Cuisine:
French/seafood.*

Villa Lorraine
ave. du Vivier d'Oie
75, Brussels
32 2 37 43 163
•*Smoking section.
Humidor. Cuisine:
French.*

Carême
Koningin Astridlaan
114
Kontich
32 3 45 76 304
•*All areas. Humidor.
Cuisine: Belgium.*

**Rudy's
Fonduehuisje**
St. Maartenstraat
12-C
Leuven
32 16 20 44 20
•*All areas. Humidor.
Cuisine: Swiss.*

Canada

ALBERTA

Osteria de Medici
201 Lost Plaza NW
Calgary
(403) 283-5553
•*Private room.
Humidor. Cuisine:
Italian.*

**Tasmanian
Ballroom &
Havana's Cigar
Lounge**
1215 1st St. SW
Calgary
(403) 266-1824
•*All areas. Humidor.*
**Nightclub/private
club (guests are
welcome).**

BRITISH
COLUMBIA

Deep Cove Chalet
11190 Chalet Rd.,
Vancouver Island
Sidney
(604) 656-3541
•*All areas. Humidor.
Cuisine: French.*

La Gavroche
1616 Alberni St.
Vancouver
(604) 685-3924
•*Private rooms. Cui-
sine: contemporary
French.*

Bearfoot Bistro
4121 Village Green
Whistler
(604) 932-3433
•*Cigar room. Humidor. Cuisine: fusion.*

NOVA SCOTIA

**Joe's Warehouse &
Food Emporium**
424 Charlotte St.
Sydney
(902) 539-6686
•*Smoking section, bar and private dining room. Cuisine: steak and seafood.*

ONTARIO

**Calhoon's
Steakhouse**
135 Bayfield St.
Barrie
(705) 727-1520
•*Bar and smoking area. Humidor. Cuisine: steakhouse.*

Hennepin's
1486 Niagara Stone Rd.
Niagara on the Lake
(905) 468-1555
•*Smoking section. Cuisine: tapas and a combination of traditional and contemporary fare.*

**Lake Obabika
Lodge**
P.O. Box 10
River Valley
(705) 858-1056
•*Bar, smoking section, patio and balcony. Humidor.*

TORONTO

**Barberian's Steak
House Tavern**
7 Elm St.
Toronto
(416) 597-0335
•*Bar/lounge, smoking section and private room. Humidor. Cuisine: steakhouse.*

George Bigliardi's
463 Church St.
Toronto
(416) 922-9594
•*Dining room, bar and private rooms. Humidor. Cuisine: Italian, specializing in seafood and steak.*

**Mary Johns
Restaurant**
91 Gerard St. W.
Toronto
(416) 595-1475
•*Smoking section. Cuisine: Continental.*

Opus Restaurant
37 Prince Arthur Ave.
Toronto
(416) 921-3105
•*Bar. Humidor. Cuisine: European and Mediterranean.*

Prego della Piazza
150 Bloor St. W.
Toronto
(416) 920-9900
•*Wine bar "Enoteca" at all times; Cigar bar "Black and Blue Le Cigar Lounge;" dining room after 10:30 pm. Humidor. Cuisine: Italian.*

The Senator
249 Victoria St.
Toronto
(416) 364-7517
•*Cigar bar, private room and patio. Humidor. Cuisine: steakhouse.* **Nightclub.**

**Shark City Bar &
Grill**
117 Eglinton Ave. E.
Toronto
(416) 488-7899
•*Bar/lounge, smoking section, private room and patio. Humidor. Cuisine: Eurasian.*

**The School of Fine
Dining**
4121 14th Ave.
Unionville
(905) 477-1161
•*Lounge. Humidor. Cuisine: steak and seafood.*

QUEBEC

MONTREAL

**Piano Bar at the
Four Seasons
Hotel**
1050 Scherook St.
Montreal
(514) 284-1110
•*Smoking section. Cuisine: breakfast buffet, lunch; hors d'oeuvres only after lunch.* **Bar.**

Le Lutetia
1430 rue de La Montagne
Montreal
(514) 288-5656
•*Special smoking area in lobby. Humidor. Cuisine: French.*

**Les Caprices de
Nicolas**
2072 Drummond
Montreal
(514) 282-9790
•*Smoking section and patio. Humidor. Cuisine: French.*

Pub St.-Alexandre
1087 St.-Jean
Quebec G1R 1S3
(418) 694-0015
•*Bar and second floor. Cuisine: pub fare.*

L'Inox
37 St. André
Quebec City
(418) 692-2877
•*All areas. Cuisine: pub fare.*

Bistro à Champlain
75 Chemin Masson
Sainte-Marguerite du Lac Masson
(514) 228-4988
•*Special cigar room. Humidor. Cuisine: French.*

Denmark

COPENHAGEN

Restaurant Kanalen
Wilders Plads
Copenhagen
45 3295 1330
•All areas. Humidor.
Cuisine: Danish and
French.

Kommandanten
NY Adelgade 7
Copenhagen
45 3 312 0990
•All areas. Cuisine:
Danish and French.

Nouvelle
Gammel Strand 34
Copenhagen
45 3 313 5018
•All areas. Humidor.
Cuisine: French.

Finland

Lord a la Carte
Lönnrotinkatu 29
Helsinki
358 9 68 01 680
•All areas. Humidor.
Cuisine: Finnish and
French.

France

**Restaurant La Belle
Otéro & Carlton
Casino Club at
the Hôtel Carlton
International**
58 blvd. Croisette
Cannes
33 4 93 68 00 33
•Dining room

and near the piano
bar. Humidor.
Cuisine: French
Mediterranean.

**La Côte at the
Hôtel Carlton
International**
58 blvd. Croisette
Cannes
33 4 93 06 40 06
•Private room.
Humidor. Cuisine:
French Gastronomique.

Léon de Lyon
1 rue Pleney
Lyons
33 4 7 828 1133
•Bar. Humidor. Cui-
sine: regional French.

Paul Bocuse
Collonges-au-Mont-
d'Or
Lyons
33 4 7 24 29 090
•All areas. Humidor.
Cuisine: traditional
French.

**Restaurant
Chantecler at the
Hôtel Négresco**
37 Promenade des
Anglais
Nice Cedex 1
33 4 93 16 64 00
•Dining room, bar
and private rooms.
Humidor. Cuisine:
French.

PARIS

Alain Ducasse
59 ave. Raymond
Poincaré

Paris
33 1 47 27 12 27
•Cigar bar. Humidor.
Cuisine: French.

Amphyclés
78 ave. Ternes
Paris
33 04 1 40 68 01 01
•All areas. Humidor.
Cuisine: French.

Apicius
122 ave. Villiers
Paris
33 1 43 80 19 66
•All areas. Humidor.
Cuisine: French.

Arpäge
84 rue Varenne
Paris
33 1 45 51 47 33
•All areas. Humidor.
Cuisine: spicy French.

Au Trou Gascon
40 rue Taine
Paris
33 1 43 44 34 26
•Bar. Humidor.
Cuisine: French.

**Bristol at the Hôtel
Bristol**
112 rue Faubourg St-
Honoré, Paris
33 1 53 43 43 00
•Bar/lounge and pri-
vate room. Humidor.
Cuisine: Gastrono-
mique French.

Carré des Feuillants
14 rue de Castiglione
Paris
33 1 42 86 82 82

•Smoking section.
Humidor. Cuisine:
French.

Chez Pauline
5 rue Villédo
Paris
33 1 42 96 20 70
•All areas. Humidor.
Cuisine: contempo-
rary/classic French.

Chiberta
3 rue Arsène-
Houssaye
Paris
33 1 45 63 77 90
•All areas. Humidor.
Cuisine: Gastrono-
mique French.

Drouant
18 place Gaillon
Paris
33 1 42 65 15 16
•All areas. Humidor.
Cuisine: Gas-
tronomique French.

**Espadon at the
Hotel Ritz**
15 place Vendôme
Paris
33 1 43 16 30 80
•Smoking areas.
Humidor. Cuisine:
traditional French.

Faucher
123 ave. de Wagram
Paris
33 1 42 27 61 50
•All areas. Humidor.
Cuisine: grand
French.

Fifteen Montaigne Maison Blanche
15 ave. Montaigne
Paris
33 1 47 23 55 99
•*All areas. Humidor. Cuisine: Gastronomique French.*

Gérard Besson
5 rue Coq Héron
Paris
33 1 42 33 14 74
•*All areas. Humidor. Cuisine: French.*

Goumard-Prunier
9 rue Duphot
Paris
33 1 42 60 36 07
•*All areas. Humidor. Cuisine: seafood.*

Guy Savoy
18 rue Troyon
Paris
33 1 43 80 40 61
•*All areas. Humidor. Cuisine: French.*

Hemingway Bar at the Hotel Ritz
15 Place Vendôme
Paris
33 43 16 33 65
•*All areas of bar. Humidor. Cuisine: tapas.*

Jacques Cagna
14 rue Grands Augustins
Paris
33 1 43 26 49 39
•*Dining room. Humidor. Cuisine: French.*

Joséphine
117 rue Cherche-Midi, Paris
33 1 45 48 52 40
•*Lounge. Cuisine: traditional French.*

Jules Verne
Eiffel Tower, 2nd Platform, Paris
33 1 45 55 61 44
•*Bar. Humidor. Cuisine: French.*

L'Ambroisie
9 place des Vosges
Paris
33 1 42 78 51 45
•*All areas. Humidor. Cuisine: traditional French.*

La Cagouille
10 place Constantin Brancusi, Paris
33 1 43 22 09 01
•*All areas. Humidor. Cuisine: seafood.*

La Couronne at the Hôtel Warwick
5 rue Berri, Paris
33 1 45 63 78 49
•*Smoking section. Humidor. Cuisine: gourmet.*

La Mare
1 rue Daru, Paris
33 1 43 80 20 00
•*Dining room. Humidor. Cuisine: French, specializing in seafood.*

La Table d'Anvers
2 place d'Anvers
Paris
33 1 48 78 35 21
•*All areas. Humidor. Cuisine: new French.*

La Table du Gouverneur
Pavillon Elysée 10 ave. des Champs Elysées
Paris
33 1 42 65 85 10
•*Smoking areas. Humidor. Cuisine: Asiatique and English.*

Lasserre
17 ave. Franklin D. Roosevelt
Paris
33 1 43 59 53 43
•*Smoking section. Humidor. Cuisine: traditional French.*

Laurent
41 ave. Gabriel
Paris
33 1 42 25 00 39
•*Dining room, bar and lounge. Humidor. Cuisine: Bourgeoise Allégée.*

Le Bellecour
22 rue Surcouf
Paris
33 1 45 51 46 93
•*Throughout the restaurant. Humidor. Cuisine: French.*

Le Clos Longchamp
81 blvd. Gouvion-St-Cyr, Paris
33 1 40 68 00 70
•*Smoking areas. Humidor. Cuisine: classical French.*

Le Divellec
107 rue Université, Invalide Esplanade
Paris
33 1 45 51 91 96
•*All areas. Humidor. Cuisine: French, specializing in seafood.*

Le Grand V'efour
17 rue de Beaujolais
Paris
33 1 42 96 56 27
•*All areas. Humidor. Cuisine: contemporary French.*

Le Meurice at the Hôtel Meurice
228 rue Rivoli
Paris
33 1 44 58 10 50
•*All areas. Humidor. Cuisine: traditional French.*

Le Petit Colombier
42 rue Acacias
Paris
33 1 43 80 28 54
•*Fireplace salon. Humidor. Cuisine: traditional French.*

Le Sormani
4 rue Gén-Lanrezac
Paris
33 1 43 80 13 91
•*Dining room. Humidor. Cuisine: Italian.*

Ledoyen
Carré Champs-
Elysées, Paris
33 1 47 42 23 23
•*All areas. Humidor. Cuisine: French.*

**Les Ambassadeurs
at the Hôtel
Crillon**
10 place Concorde
Paris
33 1 44 71 16 16
•*All areas. Humidor. Cuisine: French.*

**Les Elysées at the
Hôtel Vernet**
25 rue Vernet
Paris
33 1 44 31 98 98
•*All areas. Humidor. Cuisine: Provençal.*

Lucas-Carton
9 place Madeleine
Paris
33 1 42 65 22 90
•*Smoking section. Humidor. Cuisine: French.*

Manoir de Paris
6 rue Pierre Demours
Paris
33 1 45 72 25 25
•*Bar. Humidor. Cuisine: French.*

Mercure Galant
15 rue Petits-
Champs, Paris
33 1 42 96 98 89
•*All areas. Humidor. Cuisine: French.*

Michel Rostang
20 rue Rennequin
Paris
33 1 47 63 40 77
•*Smoking area. Humidor. Cuisine: French.*

**Restaurant Morot-
Gaudry**
8 rue de la Cavalerie
Paris
33 1 45 67 06 85
•*All areas. Humidor. Cuisine: classic French.*

**Restaurant Opéra-
Café de la Paix at
the Grand Hôtel
Inter-Continental**
5 place Opéra
Paris
33 1 40 07 30 10
•*Smoking section. Humidor. Cuisine: Gastronomique French.*

Pharamond
24 rue Grande-
Truanderie
Paris
33 1 42 33 06 72
•*Smoking section and private room. Humidor. Cuisine: French.*

Pile ou Face
52 bis rue Notre-
Dames-des-
Victoires
Paris
33 1 42 33 64 33
•*Dining room. Humidor. Cuisine: French.*

Port Alma
10 ave. New York
Paris
33 1 47 23 75 11
•*All areas. Humidor. Cuisine: French.*

Pré Catelan
Route de Suresnes
Paris
33 1 45 24 55 58
•*One dining room. Humidor. Cuisine: international and classical French.*

Récamier
4 rue Récamier
Paris
33 1 45 48 86 58
•*All areas. Humidor. Cuisine: French.*

Relais Louis XIII
1 rue Pont de Lodi
Paris
33 1 43 26 75 96
•*Dining room. Humidor. Cuisine: Continental and French.*

Taillevent
15 rue Lamennais
Paris
33 1 45 61 12 90
•*All areas. Humidor. Cuisine: French.*

Tour d'Argent
15 quai Tournelle
Paris
33 1 43 54 23 31
•*Special cigar smoking section. Humidor. Cuisine: French.*

Vivarois
192 ave. Victor
Hugo, Paris
33 1 45 04 04 31
•*All areas. Humidor. Cuisine: Gastronomique French.*

Les Crayéres
64 blvd. Henry-
Vasnier
Rheims
33 26 82 80 80
•*Bar. Humidor. Cuisine: Gastronomique French.*

Troisgros
22 cour Républíque
Roanne
33 4 77 71 66 97
•*Bar. Humidor. Cuisine: contemporary French.*

Côte d'Or
2 rue Argentine
Saulieu
33 3 80 90 53 53
•*Dining room (except on Saturdays). Humidor. Cuisine: traditional French.*

Au Crocodile
10 rue Outre
Strasbourg
33 3 88 32 13 02
• *Smoking section.*
Humidor. Cuisine:
Continental.

Buerehiesel
4 parc de
L'Orangerie
Strasbourg
33 3 88 47 56 65
• *All areas. Humidor.*
Cuisine: classic
French.

Germany

Brenner's Park
Restaurant &
Oleander Bar at
the Schwarzwald
Schillerstrasse 6,
Lichtenthaler
Allee
Baden Baden
49 7 221 9000
• *All areas. Humidor.*
Cuisine: Continental.

Schloss Thiergarten
Hotel &
Restaurant
Oberthiergärtnerstr.
36
Bayreuth
49 9 209 9840
• *All areas. Humidor.*
Cuisine: German.

DÜSSELDORF

Hotel &
Restaurant
Landsknecht
Poststr. 70,
Meerbusch
Düsseldorf

49 21 325 947
• *All areas. Humidor.*
Cuisine: International.

Restaurant
Schiffchen
Kaiserswerther
Markt 9
Düsseldorf
49 21 140 1050
• *All areas. Humidor.*
Cuisine: French.

Victorian
Königstrasse 3-A
Düsseldorf
49 21 186 550 20
• *All areas. Humidor.*
Cuisine: French.

Schassberger
Ebnisee Spa &
Resort Hotel
Winnender 10
Ebnisee
49 7 184 2920
• *Bar, lounge, private*
rooms and patio. Hu-
midor. Cuisine:
French and Mexican.

La Grappa
Rellinghauserstrasse 4
Essen 0201
49 20 123 1766
• *All areas. Humidor.*
Cuisine: French and
Italian.

Restaurant Français
Bethmannstrasse 33
Frankfurt
49 69 215 118
• *All areas. Humidor.*
Cuisine: French.

Weinhaus
Brückenkeller
Schützenstrasse 6
Frankfurt
49 69 29 80 070
• *Bar/lounge. Humi-*
dor. Cuisine: German
and Continental.

Wald-und
Schlosshotel
Friedrichsruhe
Friedrichsruhe
49 79 41 608 70
• *Bar/lounge, private*
room and lobby. Hu-
midor. Cuisine:
French.

Le Canard
Elbchaussee 139
Hamburg
49 40 88 05 057
• *All areas. Humidor.*
Cuisine: French.

MUNICH

Boettner
Theatinerstrasse 8
Munich
49 89 221 210
• *All areas. Humidor.*
Cuisine: German.

Hilton Grill at The
Hotel Park
Hilton
Am Tucherpark 7
Munich
49 89 384 5261
• *Bar/lounge and cigar*
bar. Humidor. Cui-
sine: Continental.

Königshof at the
Hotel Königshof
Karlsplatz 25
Munich

49 89 551 360
• *All areas. Humidor.*
Cuisine: Continental.

Tantris
Johann-Fichtestrasse
7, Munich
49 89 362 061
• *All areas. Humidor.*
Cuisine: international.

Hotel Wilder Mann
Hauptstrasse 37
Rückersdorf
49 911 9501 0
• *All areas. Cuisine:*
German.

Rüdesheimer
Schloss
Drosselgasse
Rüdesheim am
Rhein
49 6 722 90500
• *All areas. Humidor.*
Cuisine: regional
German.

Restaurant
Backmulde
Karmeliterstrasse 11-
13
Speyer
49 62 32 715 77
• *Bar and after dinner.*
Humidor. Cuisine:
French and
Mediterranean.

Die Ente vom Lehel
Kaiser-Friedrichplatz
3/4
Wiesbaden
49 61 113 3666
• *All areas. Humidor.*
Cuisine: French and
German.

Hotel Waldhaus
Kiefernweg 12
Winterberg
49 2 981 2042
•*All areas. Humidor.
Cuisine: New
German.*

Hong Kong

**Brown's Restaurant
& Wine Bar**
Exchange Square
Tower II
Central Hong Kong
852 2523 7003
•*All areas. Humidor.
Cuisine: American
and Continental.*

**Panorama Western
Fine Dining
Room at the New
World Hotel**
4/F New World
Hotel/22 Salisbury
Rd.
Tsimshatsui,
Kowloon
852 2369 4111
•*Bar/lounge and
smoking section.
Humidor. Cuisine:
Continental.*

**The Peninsula
Hotel**
Salisbury Rd.
Tsimshatsui,
Kowloon
852 2366 6251
•*Smoking section.
Humidor. Cuisine:
French, Chinese,
Mediterranean and
Euro-Asian.*

Ireland

Le Coq Hardi
35 Pembroke Rd.,
Pallsbridge
Dublin
353 1 668 4130
•*Dining room, bar,
lounge and private
rooms. Humidor.
Cuisine: French, spe-
cializing in seafood.*

Israel

**Coffee Bar
Emporium**
13 Yad-Harutsim
Tel-Aviv
972 3 688-9696
•*All areas. Humidor.
Cuisine: French and
Italian.*

Italy

La Taverna
Piazza Castello 2
Colloredo
39 43 28 89 045
•*All areas. Humidor.
Cuisine: Mediterranean.*

Enoteca Pinchiorri
Via Ghibellina 87
Florence
39 55 24 27 77/2
•*Private room. Humi-
dor. Cuisine: tradition-
al, yet creative, Italian.*

MILAN
A Riccione
Via Taramelli 70
Milan
39 2 66 86 807
•*All areas. Cuisine:
seafood.*

Ristorante Sadler
Troilo 14
Milan
39 2 58 10 44 51
•*All areas. Cuisine:
original Italian.*

Scaletta
Piazza Porta Genova
3, Milan
39 2 58 10 02 90
•*All areas. Cuisine:
Italian.*

ROME
**Checchino dal
1887**
Via Monte Testaccio
30, Rome
39 6 57 46 318
•*All areas. Cuisine:
Roman.*

**Relais le Jardin at
the Hotel Lord
Byron**
Via G. De Notaris 5
Rome
39 6 32 20 404
•*Bar/lounge. Cuisine:
Mediterranean and
traditional Italian.*

**Restaurant Sans
Souci**
Via Sicilia 20/24
Rome
39 6 48 21 814
•*Bar/lounge and
smoking section. Hu-
midor. Cuisine:
French and Italian.*

Luxembourg

Patin d'Or
40 route de
Bettembourg
Luxembourg
352 226 499
•*All areas. Humidor.
Cuisine: Continental/
French.*

St-Michel
rue Eau 32
Luxembourg
352 223 215
•*All areas. Humidor.
Cuisine: French.*

Mexico

El Sombrero
Centro Comercial
Los Patios
Ixtapa
52 755 30439
•*All areas. Humidor.
Cuisine: Mexican.*

MEXICO CITY
Champs Elysees
Reforma 316
Mexico City
52 5 514 0450
•*Bar/lounge and
smoking section.
Humidor. Cuisine:
French.*

Circulo del Sureste
Lucerna 12 Col.
Juárez
Mexico City
52 5 535 2704
•*Smoking section.
Humidor. Cuisine:
Yucateca and
international.*

Delmonico's
Londres 91
Mexico City
52 5 207 4949
• *Smoking section.*
Cuisine: international.

Fonda del Recuerdo
Bahia de las Palmas
37
Mexico City
52 5 260 1292
• *Smoking section.*
Cuisine: Mexican.

Fonda del Refugio
Liverpool 166
Mexico City
52 5 207 2732
• *All smoking rooms.*
Cuisine: traditional
Mexican.

El Dorado Bar &
Grill
Belden and Ocampo
401
Nuevo Laredo
Tamaulipas
52 87 120 015
• *All areas. Humidor.*
Cuisine: International.

Monaco

MONTE
CARLO
Grill de l'Hôtel de
Paris
Place du Casino
Monte Carlo
377 92 16 3002
• *Bar/lounge. Humi-*
dor. Cuisine: Mediter-
ranean and Provençal.

La Coupole at the
Hôtel Mirabeau
1 Ave. Princesse
Grace
Monte Carlo
377 92 16 6565
• *Smoking area.*
Humidor. Cuisine:
nouvelle French.

Restaurant Louis
XV at the Hôtel
de Paris
Place du Casino
Monte Carlo
377 92 16 30 01
• *Dining room, bar*
and lounge. Humidor.
Cuisine: French and
Mediterranean.

Netherlands

AMSTERDAM
Christophe
Leliegracht 46
Amsterdam
31 20 625 0807
• *All areas. Humidor.*
Cuisine: French.

Halvemaan
van Leyenberghlaan
320
Amsterdam
31 20 644 0348
• *All areas. Humidor.*
Cuisine: International.

Le Restaurant Tout
Court
Runstraat 13
Amsterdam
31 20 625 8637
• *All areas. Humidor.*
Cuisine: French and
Mediterranean.

Vermeer
Prins Hendrikkade
59-72
Amsterdam
31 20 556 4885
• *All areas. Humidor.*
Cuisine: French.

Kaatje bij de Sluis
Browerstraat 20
Blokzijl
31 527 291833
• *All areas. Humidor.*
Cuisine: French.

Restaurant/Hotel
Savelberg
Oosteinde 14
Eh Voorburg
31 70 387 2081
• *All areas. Humidor.*
Cuisine: French.

De Oude Rosmolen
Duinsteeg 1
Hoorn
31 229 214752
• *All areas. Humidor.*
Cuisine: French.

Netherlands Antilles

Shivsagar
20 Frontstreet
Phillipsburg
599 5 222 99
• *All areas. Cuisine:*
Indian.

Pelican Reef Steak
& Seafood House
Pelican Resort,
Simpson Bay
St. Martin
599 5 43021

• *All areas. Humidor.*
Cuisine: steak and
seafood.

Norway

Bagatelle
Bygdy Alle 3
Oslo
47 2 244 0990
• *Bar/lounge and*
smoking section. Hu-
midor. Cuisine:
French.

Portugal

LISBON
Casa da Comida
Travessa das
Amoreiras 1
Lisbon
351 1 388 5376
• *All areas. Humidor.*
Cuisine: Portugese.

Coventual
Praça das Flores 45
Lisbon
351 1 609 196
• *All areas. Cuisine:*
Portugese.

Tagide
Largo da Academia
Nacional de Belas
Artes
Lisbon 1200
351 1 342 0720
• *Dining room, bar,*
lounge and private
rooms. Cuisine: Con-
tinental and French.

Puerto Rico

**Perichi's at the
Hotel Parador**
Carr 102, KN 14.3,
HC01 Box 16310
Cabo Rojo
(787) 851-0620
•*Bar/lounge. Humidor. Cuisine: American, Caribbean, Continental and Spanish.*

**Pito's Seafood
Restaurant**
Sector Las Cucharas
Ponce Carr. Num. 2
(787) 841-4977
•*Smoking area, terrace and bar. Humidor. Cuisine: creative cuisine featuring seafood.*

SAN JUAN

**The Cigar Bar
El San Juan Hotel
& Casino**
6073 Isla Verde Ave.
San Juan
(809) 791-1000
•*All Areas. Humidor. Cuisine: American, Chinese, Italian, Japanese and Mexican.*

**Johnny's
Restaurant**
208 Domenech Ave.
San Juan
(787) 763-2793
•*Bar/lounge and smoking section. Humidor. Cuisine: International, Cuban and Puerto Rican.*

Pikayo Restaurant
Calle Joffre #1
Condado, San Juan
(787) 721-6194
•*Room adjacent to Bar. Humidor. Cuisine: Puerto Rican w/ Asian & European accents.*

**Shannan's at
Centro Comercial
Caribe**
496 Bori, Box 78
San Juan
(809) 281-8466
•*Bar/lounge area. Cuisine: American (appetizers, burgers, etc.)* **Sports bar.**

Spain

BARCELONA

Botafumeiro
Grand de Gràcia 81
Barcelona
34 3 218 4230
•*All areas. Humidor. Cuisine: Northern Spanish.*

Ca L'Isidre
Les Flors 12
Barcelona
34 3 441 1139
•*All areas. Humidor. Cuisine: Continental.*

La Dama
Ave. Diagonal 423
Barcelona
34 3 202 0686
•*All areas. Humidor. Cuisine: International.*

Neichel
Ave. de Pedralbes 16
bis., Barcelona
34 3 203 8408
•*All areas. Humidor. Cuisine: Mediterranean.*

Via Veneto
Ganduxer 10-12
Barcelona
34 3 200 7244
•*All areas. Humidor. Cuisine: Catalan.*

MADRID

Cabo Mayor
37 Ramón Jiménez
Madrid
34 3 350 8776
•*Bar/lounge, smoking section and private room. Humidor. Cuisine: Spanish, specializing in seafood.*

Casa d'a Troya
Emiliano Barral 14
Madrid
34 1 416 4455
•*All areas. Humidor. Cuisine: seafood.*

El Olivo
General Gallegos 1
Madrid
34 1 359 1535
•*All areas. Humidor. Cuisine: Mediterranean.*

Jockey
Amador de Los Ríos 6
Madrid
34 1 319 2435
•*All areas. Humidor. Cuisine: Continental.*

La Mission
Comandante Zorita 6
Madrid
34 1 533 2757
•*All areas. Humidor. Cuisine: Spanish.*

La Trainera
Lagasca 60
Madrid
34 1 576 0575
•*All areas. Humidor. Cuisine: seafood.*

**Las Cuatro
Estaciones**
General Ibañez Ibero
SA, Madrid
34 1 553 6305
•*All areas. Humidor. Cuisine: Spanish.*

Luculo
Génova 19
Madrid
34 1 319 4029
•*All areas. Humidor. Cuisine: Mediterranean.*

Viridiana
Juan de Mena 14
Madrid
34 1 523 4478
•*All areas. Humidor. Cuisine: Spanish.*

Zalacain
Alvarex de Boena
Madrid
34 1 561 4840
•*All areas. Humidor. Cuisine: Spanish.*

Switzerland

GENEVA

The Griffins Club
36 blvd. Helvetique
Geneva
41 22 735 12 18
•*All areas. Humidor.
Cuisine: French.*
Nightclub.

**La Cigogne at the
Hôtel de la
Cigogne**
17 place Longemalle
Geneva
41 22 818 40 40
•*All areas. Humidor.
Cuisine: French.*

Le Cygne
19 Quai Mont-Blanc
Geneva
41 22 908 90 81
•*All areas. Humidor.
Cuisine: Gastronomic
French.*

- -

**Restaurant
Wiesental**
Zürichstrasse 25
Winkel
41 1 860 15 00
•*All areas. Humidor.
Cuisine: Italian.*

**Gourmet Hôtel
Zürich**
Neumuhlequai 42
Zürich
41 1 363 63 63
•*Smoking section.
Humidor. Cuisine:
French, Italian and
Thai.*

Taverna Catalana
Glockengasse 8
Zürich
41 1 221 12 62
•*All areas. Humidor.
Cuisine: Mediter-
ranean and Spanish.*

Turks and Caicos Islands

**Banana Boat
Caribbean Grill**
Turtle Cove Marina
Providenciales
(809) 941-5706
•*All areas. Humidor.
Cuisine: Caribbean,
with Yucatan and
Jamaican influences.*

**Tiki Hut Cabana
Bar and Grill at
the Turtle Grove
Inn**
Turtle Cove Marina
Providenciales
(809) 941-5341
•*All areas. Humidor.
Cuisine: Caribbean.*

United Kingdom

**Terrace at the
Waldos**
Cliveden Taplow
Berkshire
44 1628 668 561
•*Bar/lounge, private
room and patio. Hu-
midor. Cuisine: Eng-
lish and French.*

**The New Mill
Restaurant and
Grill**
New Mill Rd.,
Eversley
Hampshire
44 173 473 2105
•*Bar. Humidor.
Cuisine: British.*

LONDON

**Albero & Grana at
the Chelsea
Cloisters**
89 Sloane Ave.
London
44 171 225 1048
•*All areas. Humidor.
Cuisine: Spanish.*

Annabel's
44 Berkeley Square
London
44 171 629 1096
•*All areas. Humidor.
Cuisine: French, Ital-
ian and English.*
Private nightclub.

**Bentleys Seafood
Restaurant**
11-15 Swallow St.
London
44 171 734 4756
•*All areas. Humidor.
Cuisine: seafood.*

**The Berkley
Restaurant**
Wilton Place
London
44 171 235 6000
•*Dining room, bar,
lounge and private
rooms. Humidor.
Cuisine: French.*

**Bibendum at the
Michelin House**
81 Fulham Rd.
London
44 171 581 5817
•*All areas. Humidor.
Cuisine: modern
British.*

**Blue Print Cafe at
the The Deskin
Museum**
Butlers Wharf
London
44 171 378 7031
•*All areas. Humidor.
Cuisine: modern
British.* **Cafe.**

Bombay Brasserie
Courtfield Rd.
London
44 171 370 4040
•*Smoking section.
Humidor. Cuisine:
Indian.*

**The Butlers Wharf
Chop-House**
The Butlers Wharf
Building, 36-E
Shad Thames
London
44 171 403 3403
•*All areas. Humidor.
Cuisine: British and
French.*

**Cafe Nico at the
Grosvenor House**
Grosvenor Park Lane
London
44 171 499 6363
•*Smoking section.
Humidor. Cuisine:
English bistro.*

Cantina del Ponte
The Butlers Wharf
   Building, 36-C
   Shad Thames
London
44 171 403 5403
•*Back area of dining
room. Humidor. Cuisine: Mediterranean.*

Caviar House
161 Piccadilly
London
44 171 409 0445
•*Main dining room.
Humidor. Cuisine:
caviar, smoked salmon
and other seafood.*

Cecconi Restaurant
5-A Burlington
   Gardens
London
44 171 434 1509
•*All areas. Humidor.
Cuisine: international.*

**Christopher's/The
   American Grill**
28 Wellington St.
London
44 171 240 4222
•*All areas. Humidor.
Cuisine: American.*

City Circle
10 Basinghall St.
London
44 171 600 8479
•*All areas. Humidor.
Cuisine: Continental.*

Corney & Barrow
44 Cannon St.
London
44 171 248 1700
•*All areas. Humidor.*
Wine bar.

Cornucopia
6 Garrick St.,
   Covent Garden
London
44 171 240 4866
•*Smoking dining
room, bar and patio.
Humidor. Cuisine:
Continental, International and Mediterranean, with an emphasis on seafood.*

**Elephant on the
   River**
129 Grosvenor Rd.
London
44 171 834 1621
•*All areas. Humidor.
Cuisine: International.*

**The English
   Garden
   Restaurant**
10 Lincoln St.,
   Chelsea
London
44 171 584 7272
•*Smoking areas.
Humidor. Cuisine:
English.*

**The English House
   Restaurant**
3 Milner St.,
   Chelsea
London
44 171 584 3002
•*Smoking areas.
Humidor. Cuisine:
English.* **Private
club.**

**Fifth Floor
   Restaurant Bar
   Cafe at the
   Harvey Nichols**
109 Knightsbridge

London
44 171 235 5250
•*Café, bar and dining
room (with consideration to other diners).
Humidor. Cuisine:
modern British, featuring lobster.*

Finos Wine Cellar
123 Mount St.
London
44 171 491 1640
•*All areas. Humidor.
Cuisine: English/
Continental.*

Four Seasons Hotel
Hamilton Place,
   Park Lane
London
44 171 499 0888
•*All areas. Humidor.
Cuisine: French with
an international
influence.*

Gattis Restaurant
1 Finsbury Ave.
London
44 171 247 1051
•*Small area only.
Humidor. Cuisine:
Italian.*

**Green's Restaurant
   & Oyster Bar**
36 Duke St., St.
   James's
London
44 171 930 4566
•*All areas. Humidor.
Cuisine: traditional
English.*

**Greenhouse
   Restaurant**
27-A Hays Mews
London
44 171 499 3331
•*All areas. Humidor.
Cuisine: English.*

**The Grill Room -
   Dorchester**
53 Park Lane
London
44 171 629 8888
•*All areas. Humidor.
Cuisine: English.*

Grill St. Quinten
3 Yeomans Row
London
44 171 581 8377
•*Most areas. Humidor. Cuisine: French.*

**Halcyon Hotel &
   Restaurant**
81 Holland Park
London
44 171 727 7288
•*Bar/lounge, private
room and patio. Humidor. Cuisine: British
and French.*

Harry's Bar
26 S. Audley St.
London
44 171 408 0844
•*All areas. Humidor.
Cuisine: Italian.*
**Private luncheon &
dining club.**

Howard Hotel
Temple Place
London
44 171 836 3555
•*All areas. Humidor.
Cuisine: French and
English.*

La Tante Claire
Restaurant
68 Royal Hospital Rd.
London
44 171 352 6045
•*All areas. Humidor.*
Cuisine: French.

The Lanesborough
1 Lanesborough Place
London
44 171 259 5599
•*All areas (but not at*
breakfast). Humidor.
Cuisine: international.
Bar.

Le Pont de la Tour
The Butlers Wharf
  Building, 36-D
  Shad Thames
London
44 171 403 8403
•*All areas. Humidor.*
Cuisine: British, mod-
ern European and
French.

Les Saveurs
37-A Curzon St.,
  Mayfair
London
44 171 491 8919
•*Bar. Humidor.*
Cuisine: French.

Lindsay House
Restaurant
21 Romilly St.
London
44 171 439 0450
•*Private rooms.*
Humidor. Cuisine:
English.

Mark's Club
46 Charles St.
London
44 171 499 2936
•*All areas. Humidor.*
Cuisine: English.
Private club.

Mezzo
100 Wardour St.
London
44 171 314 4000
•*All areas. Humidor.*
Cuisine: British,
French and Asian.

Monte's
164 Sloane St.
London
44 171 245 0892
•*All areas. Humidor.*
Cuisine: Mediter-
ranean. ***Private club***
(temporary member-
ship available).

Mosimann's
Belgrave Square/
  11-B W. Halkin St.
London
44 171 235 9625
•*All areas. Humidor.*
Cuisine: Continental
and French.
Private club.

Motcombs Club
5 Halkin Arcade, W.
  Halkin St.
London
44 171 235 5532
•*All areas. Humidor.*
Cuisine: Continental.

Overtons
Restaurant
5 St. James's St.
London
44 171 839 3774
•*Smoking dining*
room, bar and private
rooms. Humidor.
Cuisine: French.

Pine Bar at the
Britannia
Intercontinental
Grosvenor Square
London
44 171 629 9400
•*Bar area. Humidor.*
Cuisine: light snacks.
Bar.

Poissonnerie de
l'Avenue
82 Sloane Ave.
London
44 171 589 2457
•*All areas. Humidor.*
Cuisine: French
seafood.

Quaglino's
16 Bury St.
London
44 171 930 6767
•*All areas. Humidor.*
Cuisine: British.

Rules Restaurant
35 Maiden Lane
London
44 171 836 5314
•*All areas. Humidor.*
Cuisine: British,
specializing in game
animals.

Sale e Pepe
Restaurant
9 Pavilion Rd.
London
44 171 235 0098
•*All areas. Cuisine:*
Italian.

Savoy Grill at the
Savoy
1 Savoy Hill
London
44 171 836 4343
•*All areas. Humidor.*
Cuisine: English/
French.

Scalini Restaurant
1-2-3 Walton St.
London
44 171 225 2301
•*All areas. Humidor.*
Cuisine: Italian.

Scott's Restaurant
20 Mount St.
London
44 171 629 5248
•*Bar. Humidor. Cui-*
sine: modern British.

Sheekey's
Restaurant
28/32 St. Martins
  Court, London
44 171 240 2565
•*All areas. Humidor.*
Cuisine: seafood.

Signor Sassi
14 Knightsbridge
  Gardens
London
44 171 584 2277
•*All areas. Cuisine:*
Italian.

Simpsons-in-the-Strand
100 Strand
London
44 171 836 9112
•*All areas. Humidor. Cuisine: traditional British.*

The Square
6-10 Breuton St., Mayfair, London
44 171 495 7100
•*All areas after dinner only. Cuisine: modern British.*

Toto Restaurant at the Walton House
Walton St.
London SW1
44 171 589 2062
•*All areas. Humidor. Cuisine: Italian.*

Trader Vic Restaurant at The London Hilton
Park Lane, London
44 171 208 4113
•*All areas. Humidor. Cuisine: Island-style.*

Tramp
40 Jermyn St.
London
44 171 734 0565
•*All areas. Humidor. Cuisine: modern English.* **Exclusive club.**

Walsh's Seafood & Shellfish Restaurant
5 Charlotte St.
London
44 171 637 0222
•*All areas and private room. Humidor. Cuisine: French.*

Waltons Restaurant
121 Walton St.
London
44 171 584 0204
•*All areas. Humidor. Cuisine: English.*

Wig & Pen Club
229 Strand
London
44 171 583 7255
•*All areas. Humidor. Cuisine: traditional English.* **Gentleman's dining club.**

Wiltons Restaurant
55 Jermyn St.
London
44 171 629 9955
•*All areas (with consideration to other diners). Humidor. Cuisine: features deluxe fish & game.*

Hambleton Hall
Hambleton, Oakham
Rutland
44 1572 768 145
•*Bar/lounge. Humidor. Cuisine: English.*

The Whitehorse at Chilgrove
Chichester
West Sussex
44 1243 535 219
•*Bar/lounge. Humidor. Cuisine: English and French.*

U.S. Virgin Islands

ST. CROIX

The Galleon
5000 Estate Southgate
Christiansted
(809) 773-9949
•*Bar. Cuisine: Continental, Northern Italian and French cuisines.*

The Great House at Villa Madeleine
Box 3109,
Christiansted
(809) 778-7377
•*All areas. Humidor. Cuisine: Caribbean, Mediterranean and Continental.*

Lizards
1111 Strand St.
Christiansted
(809) 773-4485
•*All areas. Cuisine: Caribbean.*

Personal Tasting Log

(paste your cigar bands here)

Name _____

Size _____

Price _____

Notes _____

_____

_____

Name _____

Size _____

Price _____

Notes _____

_____

_____

Name _____

Size _____

Price _____

Notes _____

_____

_____

Name _____

Size _____

Price _____

Notes _____

_____

_____

	Name _____
	Size _____
	Price _____
	Notes _____
	_____
	_____

	Name _____
	Size _____
	Price _____
	Notes _____
	_____
	_____

	Name _____
	Size _____
	Price _____
	Notes _____
	_____
	_____

	Name _____
	Size _____
	Price _____
	Notes _____
	_____
	_____

	Name _____
	Size _____
	Price _____
	Notes _____
	_____
	_____

	Name _____
	Size _____
	Price _____
	Notes _____
	_____
	_____

	Name _____
	Size _____
	Price _____
	Notes _____
	_____
	_____

	Name _____
	Size _____
	Price _____
	Notes _____
	_____
	_____

	Name _____
	Size _____
	Price _____
	Notes _____
	_____
	_____

	Name _____
	Size _____
	Price _____
	Notes _____
	_____
	_____

PERSONAL TASTING LOG

Name _____
Size _____
Price _____
Notes _____
_____
_____

Name _____
Size _____
Price _____
Notes _____
_____
_____

Name _____
Size _____
Price _____
Notes _____
_____
_____

Name _____
Size _____
Price _____
Notes _____
_____
_____

Name _____
Size _____
Price _____
Notes _____
_____
_____

Name _____

Size _____

Price _____

Notes _____

_____

_____

Name _____

Size _____

Price _____

Notes _____

_____

_____

Name _____

Size _____

Price _____

Notes _____

_____

_____

Name _____

Size _____

Price _____

Notes _____

_____

_____

Name _____

Size _____

Price _____

Notes _____

_____

_____

	Name _____
	Size _____
	Price _____
	Notes _____
	_____
	_____

	Name _____
	Size _____
	Price _____
	Notes _____
	_____
	_____

	Name _____
	Size _____
	Price _____
	Notes _____
	_____
	_____

	Name _____
	Size _____
	Price _____
	Notes _____
	_____
	_____

	Name _____
	Size _____
	Price _____
	Notes _____
	_____
	_____

Name _____

Size _____

Price _____

Notes _____

_____

_____

Name _____

Size _____

Price _____

Notes _____

_____

_____

Name _____

Size _____

Price _____

Notes _____

_____

_____

Name _____

Size _____

Price _____

Notes _____

_____

_____

Name _____

Size _____

Price _____

Notes _____

_____

_____

Name _____

Size _____

Price _____

Notes _____

_____

_____

Name _____

Size _____

Price _____

Notes _____

_____

_____

Name _____

Size _____

Price _____

Notes _____

_____

_____

Name _____

Size _____

Price _____

Notes _____

_____

_____

Name _____

Size _____

Price _____

Notes _____

_____

_____

Name _____

Size _____

Price _____

Notes _____

_____

_____

Name _____

Size _____

Price _____

Notes _____

_____

_____

Name _____

Size _____

Price _____

Notes _____

_____

_____

Name _____

Size _____

Price _____

Notes _____

_____

_____

Name _____

Size _____

Price _____

Notes _____

_____

_____

COVER PHOTO BY JEFF HARRIS